SOMETHING is KILLING the CHILDREN

™

BOOK ONE

Published by

BOOM!™
STUDIOS

COLLECTED EDITION DESIGNER
MARIE KRUPINA

COLLECTED EDITION ASSISTANT EDITOR
RAMIRO PORTNOY

COLLECTED EDITION ASSOCIATE EDITOR
JONATHAN MANNING

ORIGINAL SERIES DESIGNER
MICHELLE ANKLEY

ORIGINAL SERIES ASSISTANT EDITOR
GWEN WALLER

EDITOR
ERIC HARBURN

ROSS RICHIE Chairman & Founder
JEN HARNED CFO
MATT GAGNON Editor-in-Chief
FILIP SABLIK President, Publishing & Marketing
STEPHEN CHRISTY President, Development
LANCE KREITER Vice President, Licensing & Merchandising
BRYCE CARLSON Vice President, Editorial & Creative Strategy
HUNTER GORINSON Vice President, Business Development
JOSH HAYES Vice President, Sales
RYAN MATSUNAGA Director, Marketing
STEPHANIE LAZARSKI Director, Operations
ELYSE STRANDBERG Manager, Finance
MICHELLE ANKLEY Manager, Production Design
CHERYL PARKER Manager, Human Resources
SIERRA HAHN Executive Editor
ERIC HARBURN Executive Editor
DAFNA PLEBAN Senior Editor
ELIZABETH BREI Editor
KATHLEEN WISNESKI Editor
SOPHIE PHILIPS-ROBERTS Editor
ALLYSON GRONOWITZ Associate Editor
GAVIN GRONENTHAL Assistant Editor
GWEN WALLER Assistant Editor
RAMIRO PORTNOY Assistant Editor
KENZIE RZONCA Assistant Editor
REY NETSCHKE Editorial Assistant
MARIE KRUPINA Design Lead
CRYSTAL WHITE Design Lead
GRACE PARK Design Coordinator
MADISON GOYETTE Production Designer
VERONICA GUTIERREZ Production Designer
JESSY GOULD Production Designer
NANCY MOJICA Production Designer
SAMANTHA KNAPP Production Design Assistant
ESTHER KIM Marketing Lead
BREANNA SARPY Marketing Lead, Digital
AMANDA LAWSON Marketing Coordinator
ALEX LORENZEN Marketing Coordinator, Copywriter
GRECIA MARTINEZ Marketing Assistant, Digital
JOSÉ MEZA Consumer Sales Lead
ASHLEY TROUB Consumer Sales Coordinator
MORGAN PERRY Retail Sales Lead
HARLEY SALBACKA Sales Coordinator
MEGAN CHRISTOPHER Operations Lead
RODRIGO HERNANDEZ Operations Coordinator
JASON LEE Senior Accountant
SABRINA LESIN Accounting Assistant

SOMETHING IS KILLING THE CHILDREN DELUXE EDITION BOOK ONE, JULY 2022. Published by BOOM! Studios, a division of Boom Entertainment, Inc. Something is Killing the Children is ™ & © 2022 James Tynion IV & Werther Dell'Edera. Originally published in single magazine form as SOMETHING IS KILLING THE CHILDREN No. 1-15. ™ & © 2019, 2020, 2021 James Tynion IV & Werther Dell'Edera. All rights reserved. BOOM! Studios™ and the BOOM! Studios logo are trademarks of Boom Entertainment, Inc., registered in various countries and categories. All characters, events, and institutions depicted herein are fictional. Any similarity between any of the names, characters, persons, events, and/or institutions in this publication to actual names, characters, and persons, whether living or dead, events, and/or institutions is unintended and purely coincidental. BOOM! Studios does not read or accept unsolicited submissions of ideas, stories, or artwork.

BOOM! Studios, 5670 Wilshire Boulevard, Suite 400, Los Angeles, CA, 90036-5679. Printed in China. Second Printing.

ISBN: 978-1-68415-764-8, eISBN: 978-1-64668-399-4

Sanctum Sanctorum Comics & Oddities Exclusive ISBN: 978-1-68415-822-5

Anti-Hero Gallery Exclusive ISBN: 978-1-68415-823-2

Nocturnal Rabbit Exclusive ISBN: 978-1-68415-824-9

Hive Comics LLC & The Nerd Store Exclusive ISBN: 978-1-68415-825-6

Limited Slipcase Edition ISBN: 978-1-68415-826-3

WRITTEN BY

JAMES TYNION IV

ILLUSTRATED BY

WERTHER DELL'EDERA

COLORED BY

MIQUEL MUERTO

LETTERED BY

ANDWORLD DESIGN

COVER BY
WERTHER DELL'EDERA
WITH COLORS BY MIQUEL MUERTO

SANCTUM SANCTORUM COMICS & ODDITIES
EXCLUSIVE COVER BY
JENNY FRISON

ANTI-HERO GALLERY EXCLUSIVE COVER BY
WERTHER DELL'EDERA
WITH COLORS BY GIOVANNA NIRO

NOCTURNAL RABBIT EXCLUSIVE COVER BY
ADAM GORHAM

HIVE COMICS & THE NERD STORE
EXCLUSIVE COVER BY
NICK ROBLES

SOMETHING IS KILLING THE CHILDREN
CREATED BY JAMES TYNION IV
& WERTHER DELL'EDERA

CHAPTER ONE

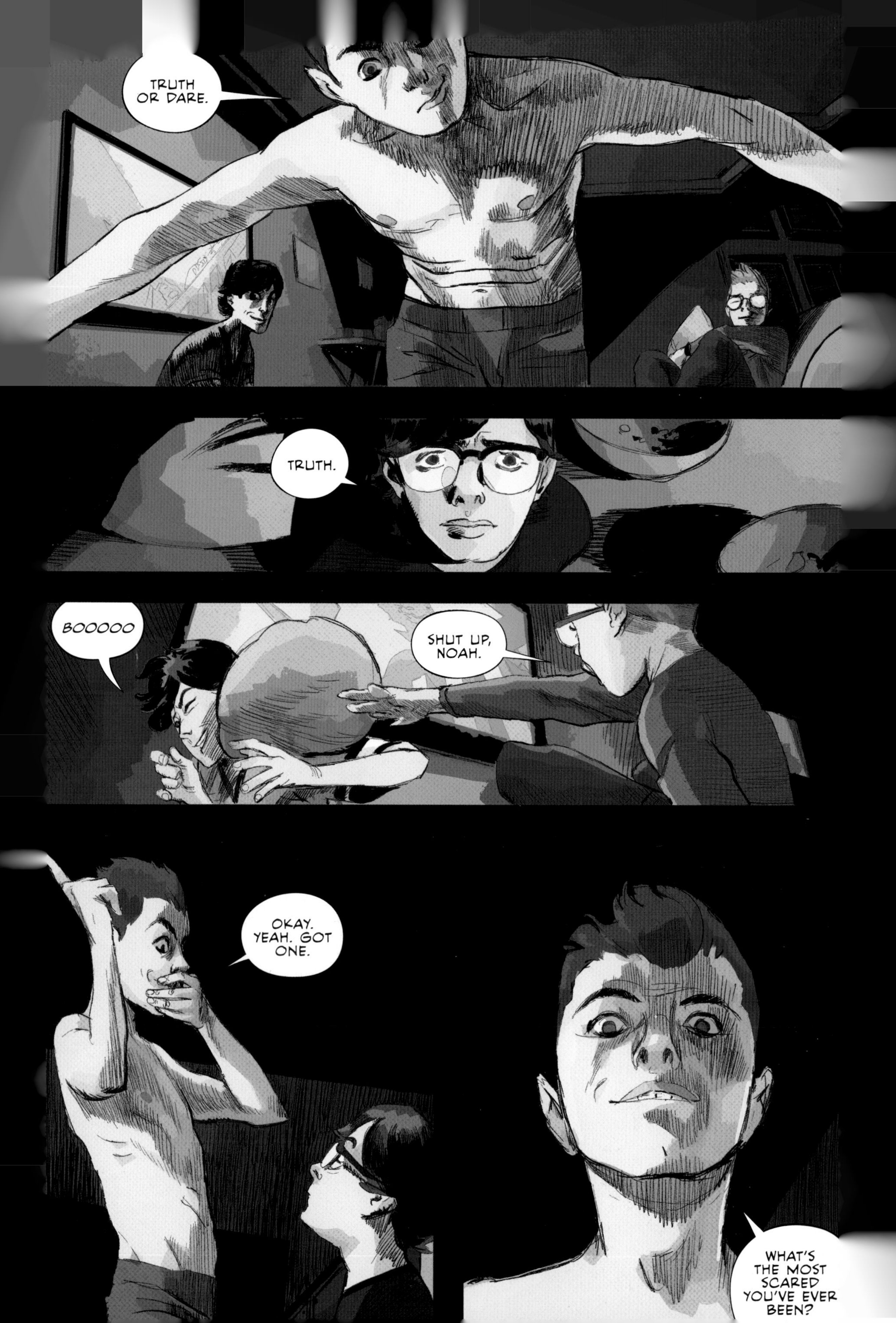
TRUTH OR DARE.
TRUTH.
BOOOOO
SHUT UP, NOAH.
OKAY. YEAH. GOT ONE.
WHAT'S THE MOST SCARED YOU'VE EVER BEEN?

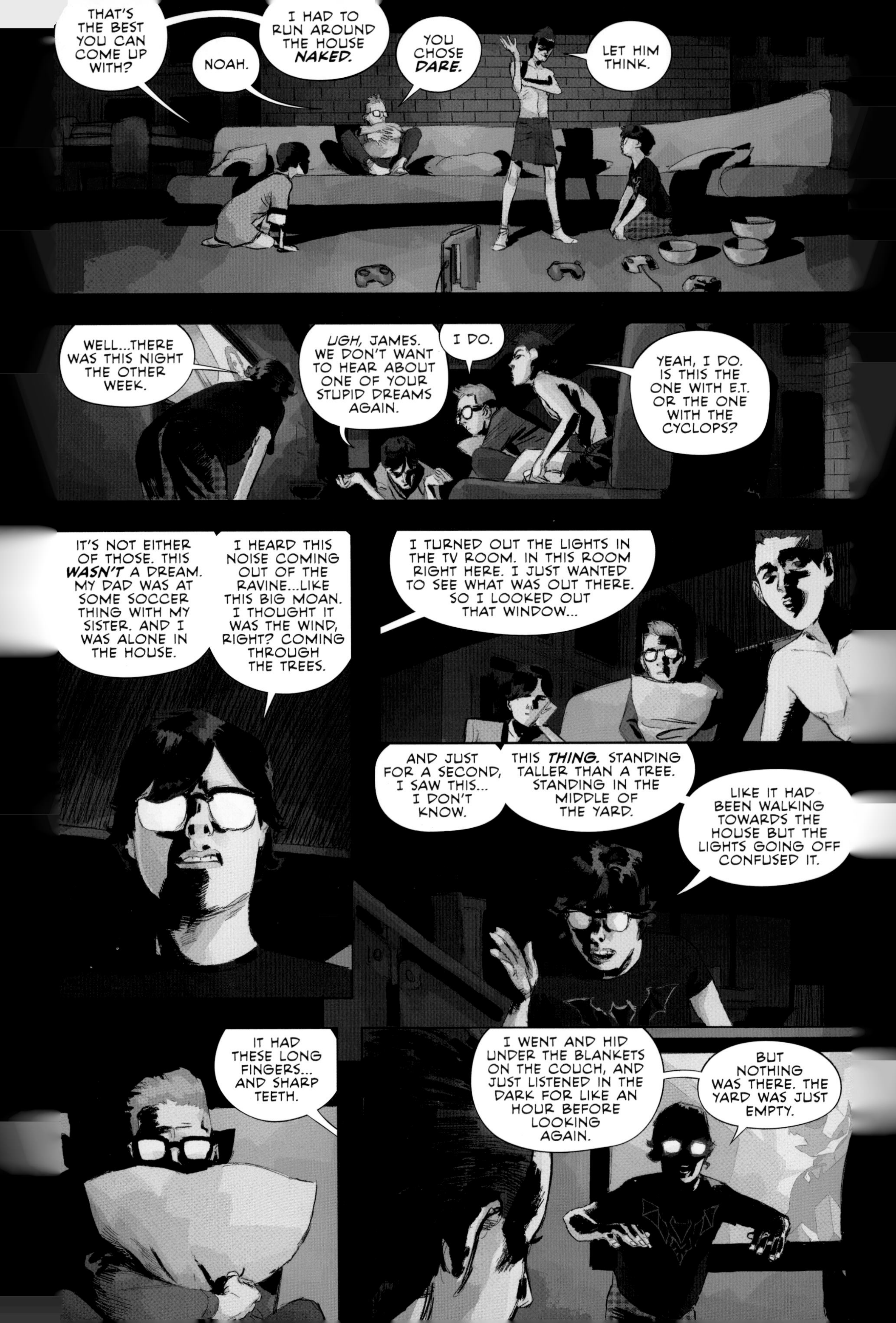
THAT'S THE BEST YOU CAN COME UP WITH?
NOAH.
I HAD TO RUN AROUND THE HOUSE **NAKED.**
YOU CHOSE **DARE.**
LET HIM THINK.
WELL...THERE WAS THIS NIGHT THE OTHER WEEK.
UGH, JAMES. WE DON'T WANT TO HEAR ABOUT ONE OF YOUR STUPID DREAMS AGAIN.
I DO.
YEAH, I DO. IS THIS THE ONE WITH E.T. OR THE ONE WITH THE CYCLOPS?
IT'S NOT EITHER OF THOSE. THIS **WASN'T** A DREAM. MY DAD WAS AT SOME SOCCER THING WITH MY SISTER. AND I WAS ALONE IN THE HOUSE.
I HEARD THIS NOISE COMING OUT OF THE RAVINE...LIKE THIS BIG MOAN. I THOUGHT IT WAS THE WIND, RIGHT? COMING THROUGH THE TREES.
I TURNED OUT THE LIGHTS IN THE TV ROOM. IN THIS ROOM RIGHT HERE. I JUST WANTED TO SEE WHAT WAS OUT THERE. SO I LOOKED OUT THAT WINDOW...
AND JUST FOR A SECOND, I SAW THIS... I DON'T KNOW.
THIS **THING.** STANDING TALLER THAN A TREE. STANDING IN THE MIDDLE OF THE YARD.
LIKE IT HAD BEEN WALKING TOWARDS THE HOUSE BUT THE LIGHTS GOING OFF CONFUSED IT.
IT HAD THESE LONG FINGERS... AND SHARP TEETH.
I WENT AND HID UNDER THE BLANKETS ON THE COUCH, AND JUST LISTENED IN THE DARK FOR LIKE AN HOUR BEFORE LOOKING AGAIN.
BUT NOTHING WAS THERE. THE YARD WAS JUST EMPTY.

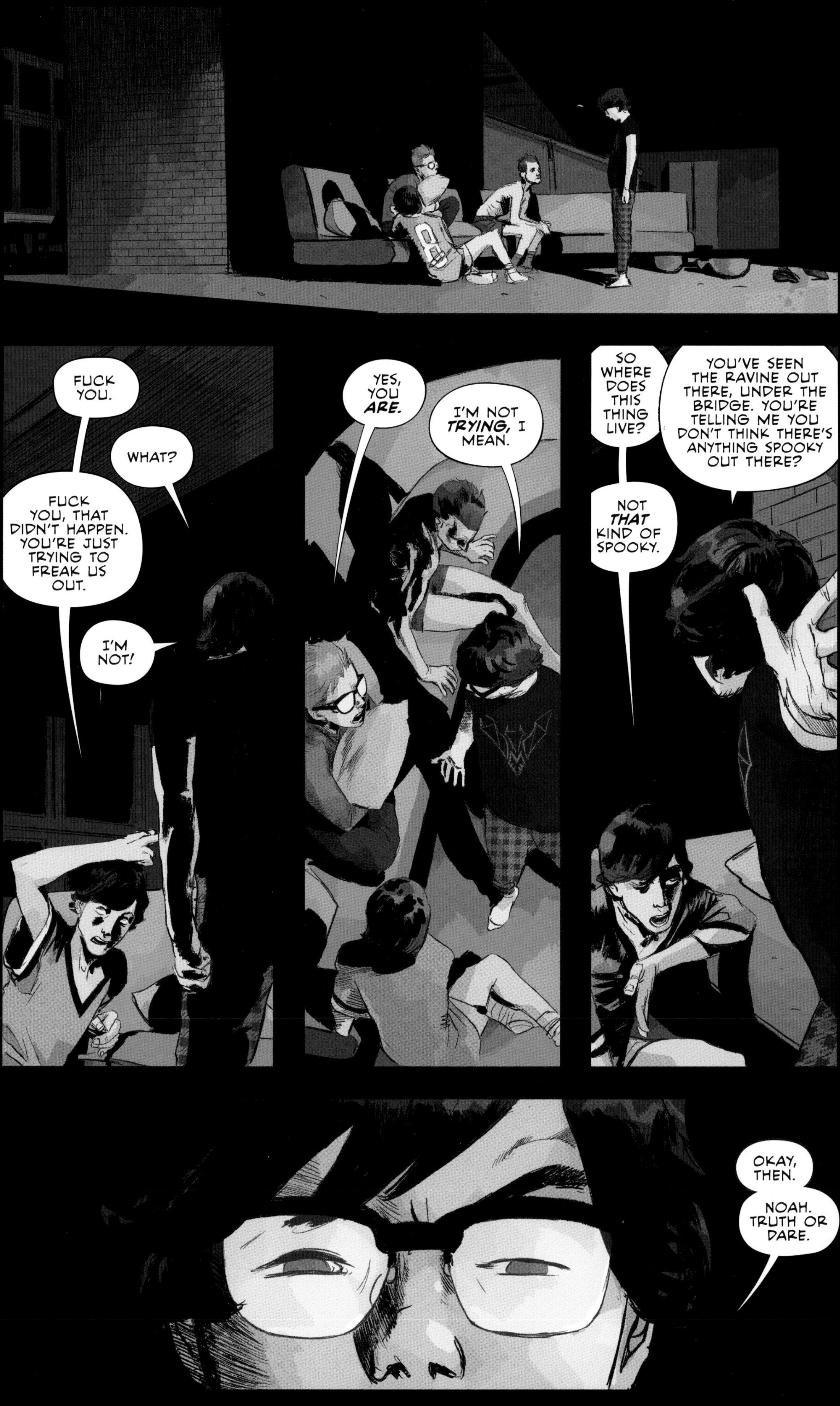
FUCK YOU.
WHAT?
FUCK YOU, THAT DIDN'T HAPPEN. YOU'RE JUST TRYING TO FREAK US OUT.
I'M NOT!
YES, YOU *ARE.*
I'M NOT *TRYING,* I MEAN.
SO WHERE DOES THIS THING LIVE?
YOU'VE SEEN THE RAVINE OUT THERE, UNDER THE BRIDGE. YOU'RE TELLING ME YOU DON'T THINK THERE'S ANYTHING SPOOKY OUT THERE?
NOT *THAT* KIND OF SPOOKY.
OKAY, THEN.
NOAH. TRUTH OR DARE.

IT WASN'T REAL. I DIDN'T SEE A THING IN THE YARD...MY SISTER DOESN'T EVEN *HAVE* SOCCER THIS TIME OF YEAR.

THEY LIKED WHEN I TOLD THEM MY NIGHT-MARES. I *LIKED* THAT THEY LIKED THEM. I HADN'T HAD, Y'KNOW... SLEEPOVER FRIENDS BEFORE.

AND I'D BEEN DOWN IN THE RAVINE. WE'D EVEN SNUCK OUT BEFORE DURING TRUTH OR DARE. ON OTHER SLEEPOVERS.

SO, WHAT WAS DIFFERENT THIS TIME...?

I...I...I SLIPPED ON A ROOT...THEY GET WET AT NIGHT WITH DEW AND I FELL LIKE A HUNDRED FEET. OR, I DON'T KNOW, I FELL DOWN FAR ENOUGH SO THEY COULDN'T SEE ME.

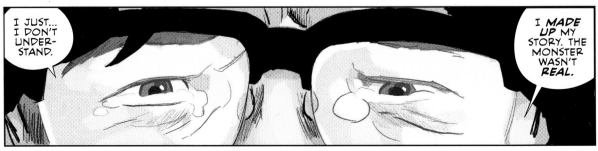

I JUST... I DON'T UNDER-STAND.

I *MADE UP* MY STORY. THE MONSTER WASN'T *REAL.*

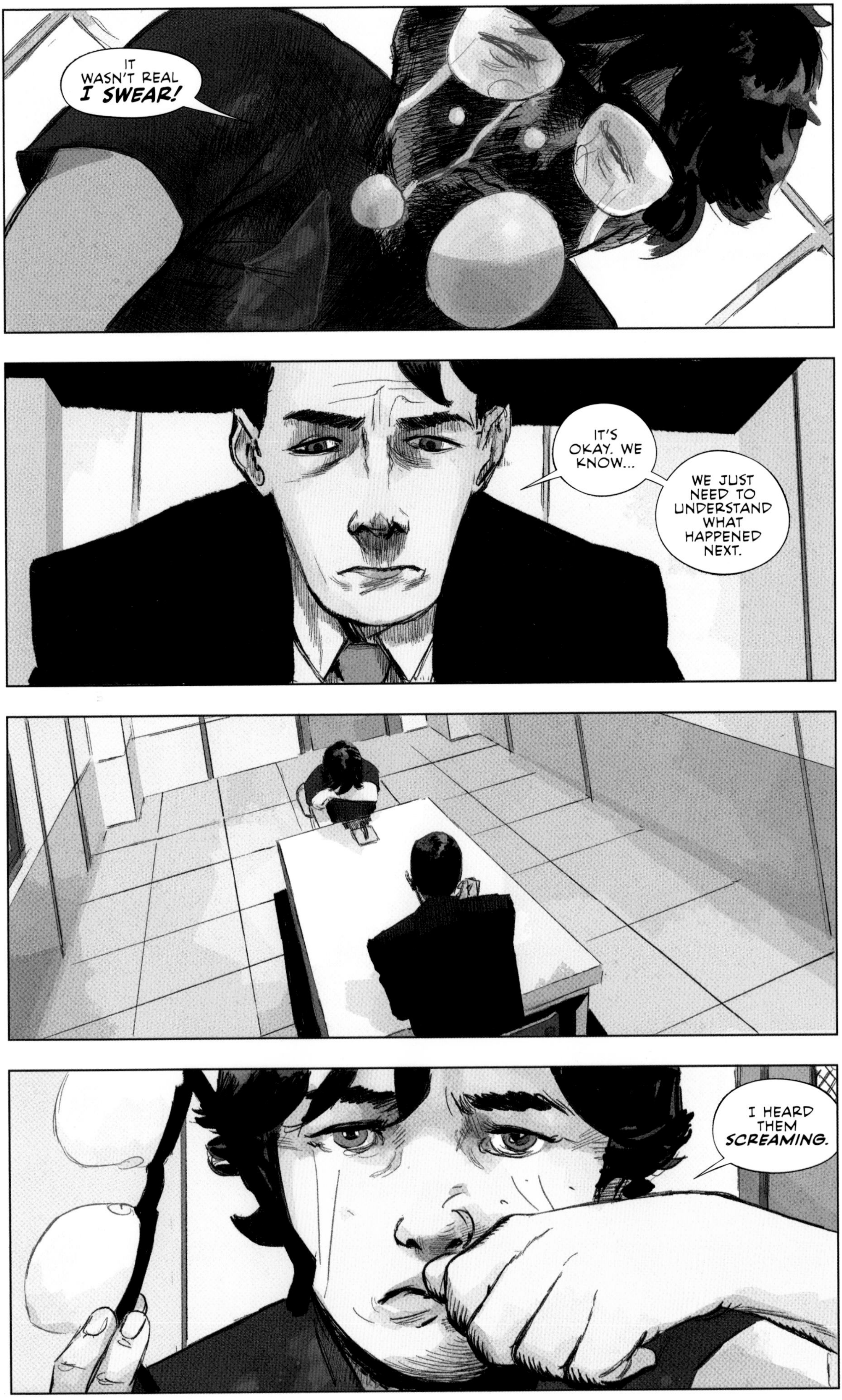
IT WASN'T REAL I SWEAR!
IT'S OKAY. WE KNOW...
WE JUST NEED TO UNDERSTAND WHAT HAPPENED NEXT.
I HEARD THEM SCREAMING.

SOME

is

KILL

CHILD

THING

LING

the

DREN

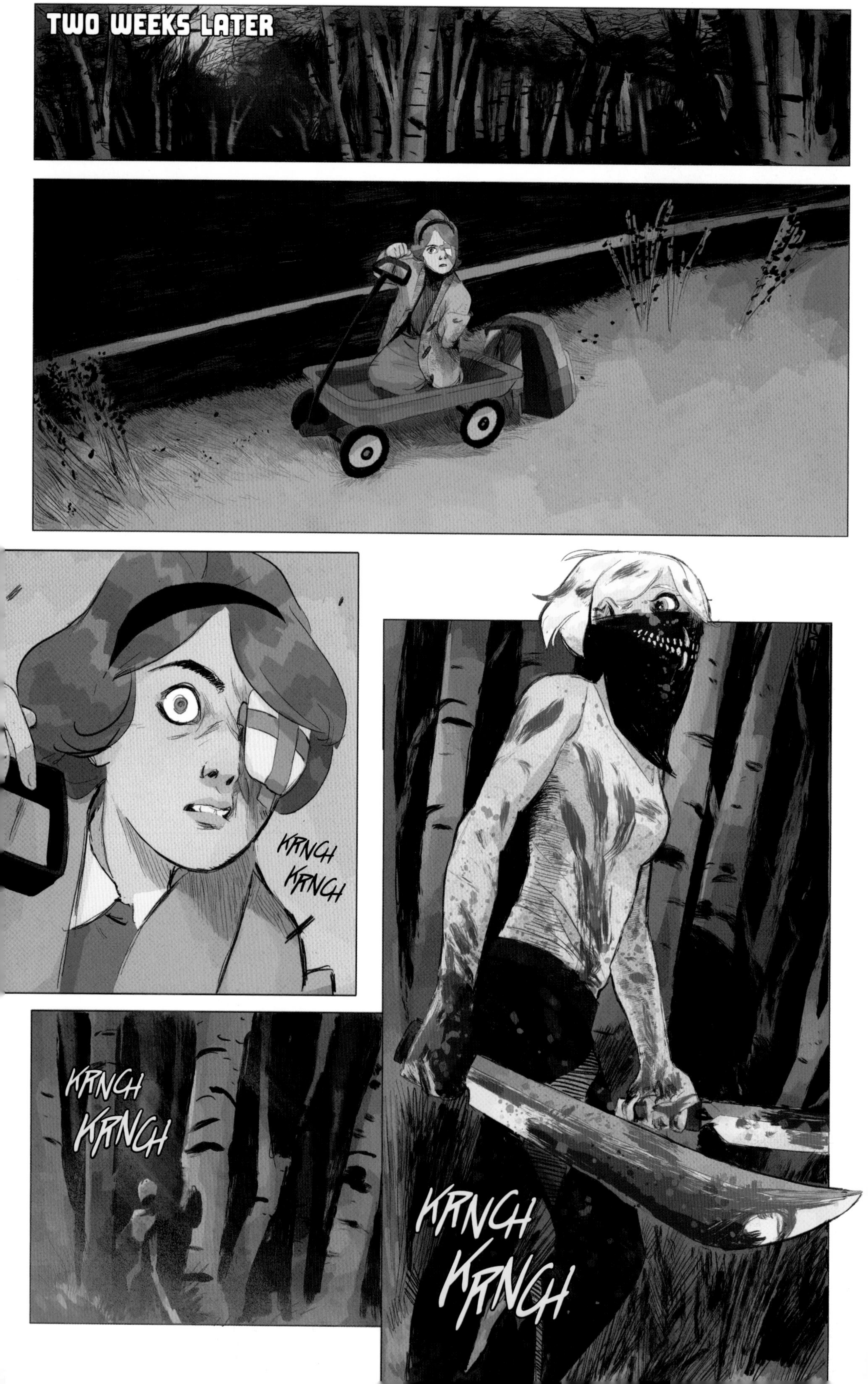
TWO WEEKS LATER
KRNCH
KRNCH
KRNCH
KRNCH
KRNCH
KRNCH

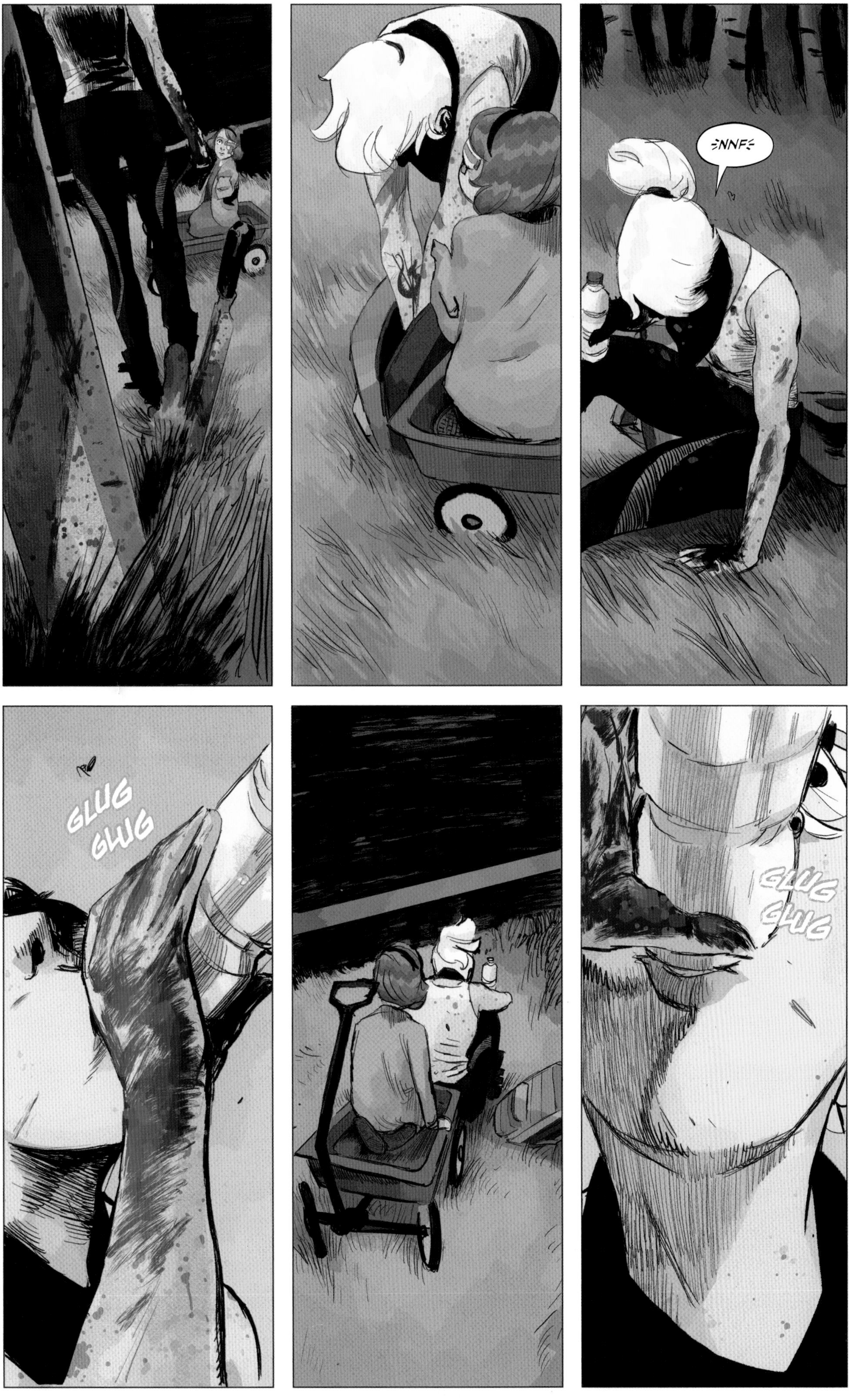
NNF
GLUG GLUG
GLUG GLUG

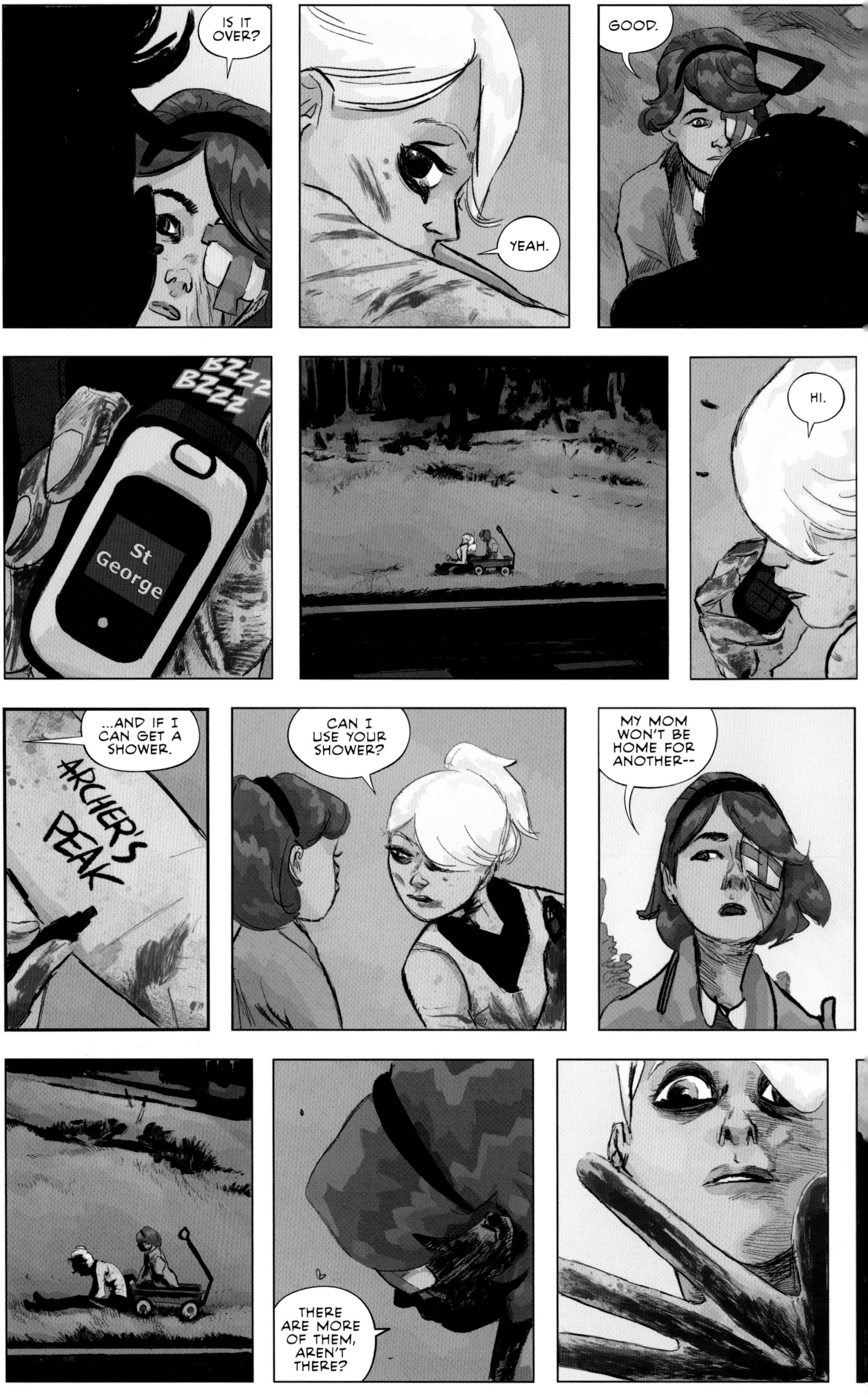
IS IT OVER?
YEAH.
GOOD.
BZZZ BZZZ
St George
HI.
...AND IF I CAN GET A SHOWER.
ARCHER'S PEAK
CAN I USE YOUR SHOWER?
MY MOM WON'T BE HOME FOR ANOTHER--
THERE ARE MORE OF THEM, AREN'T THERE?

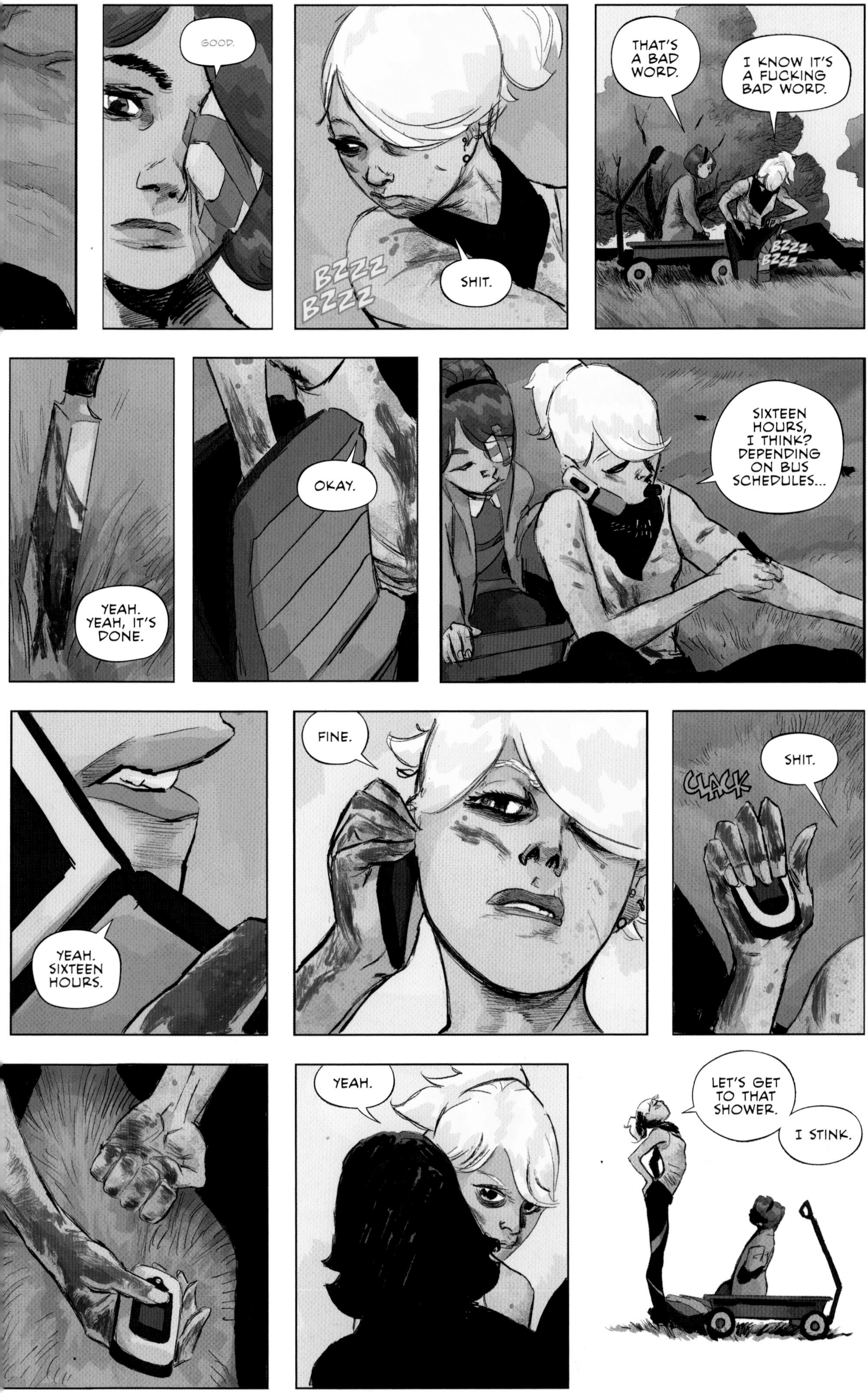
GOOD.
BZZZ BZZZ
SHIT.
THAT'S A BAD WORD.
I KNOW IT'S A FUCKING BAD WORD.
BZZZ BZZZ
YEAH. YEAH, IT'S DONE.
OKAY.
SIXTEEN HOURS, I THINK? DEPENDING ON BUS SCHEDULES...
YEAH. SIXTEEN HOURS.
FINE.
CLACK
SHIT.
YEAH.
LET'S GET TO THAT SHOWER.
I STINK.

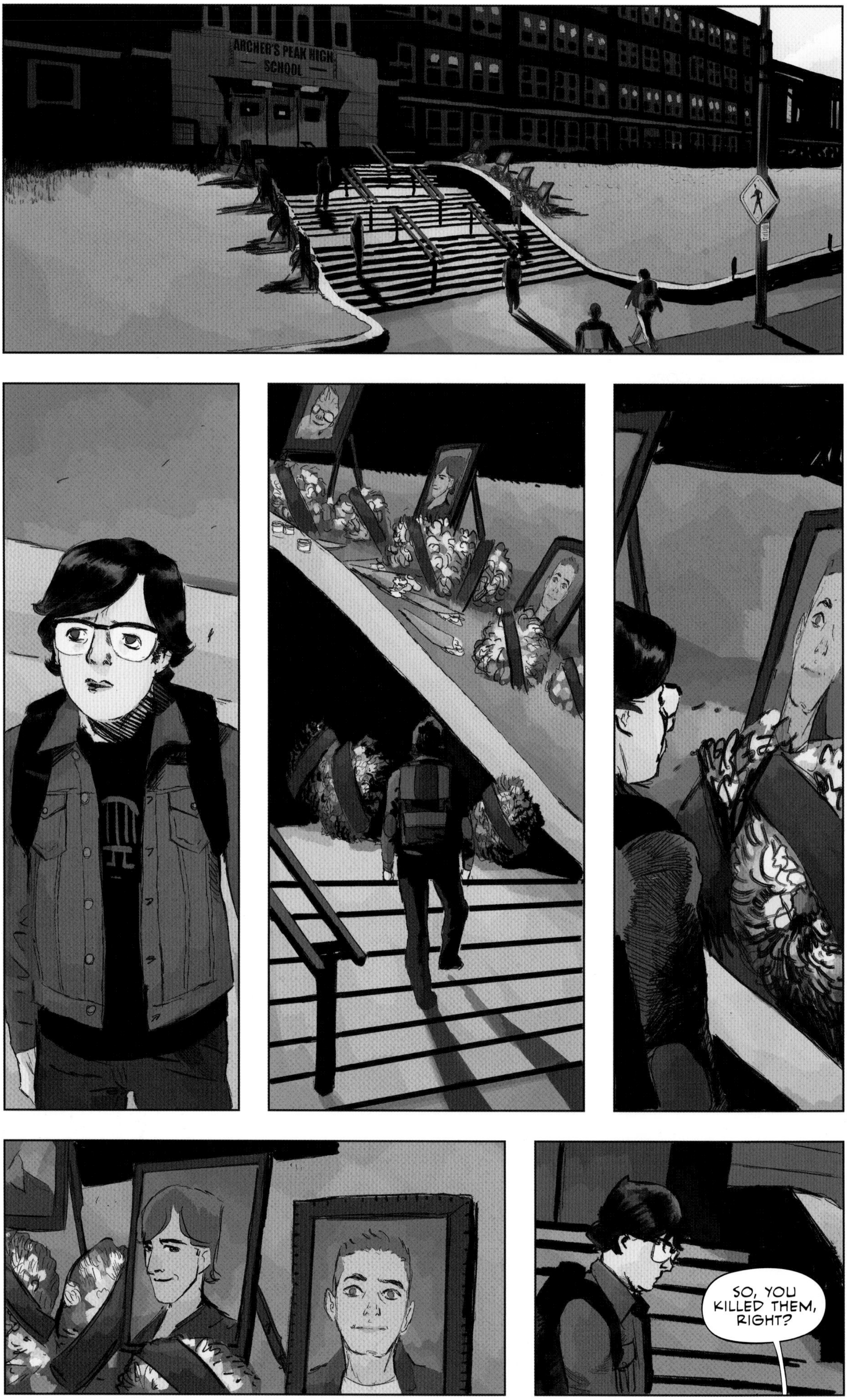
ARCHER'S PEAK HIGH SCHOOL
SO, YOU KILLED THEM, RIGHT?

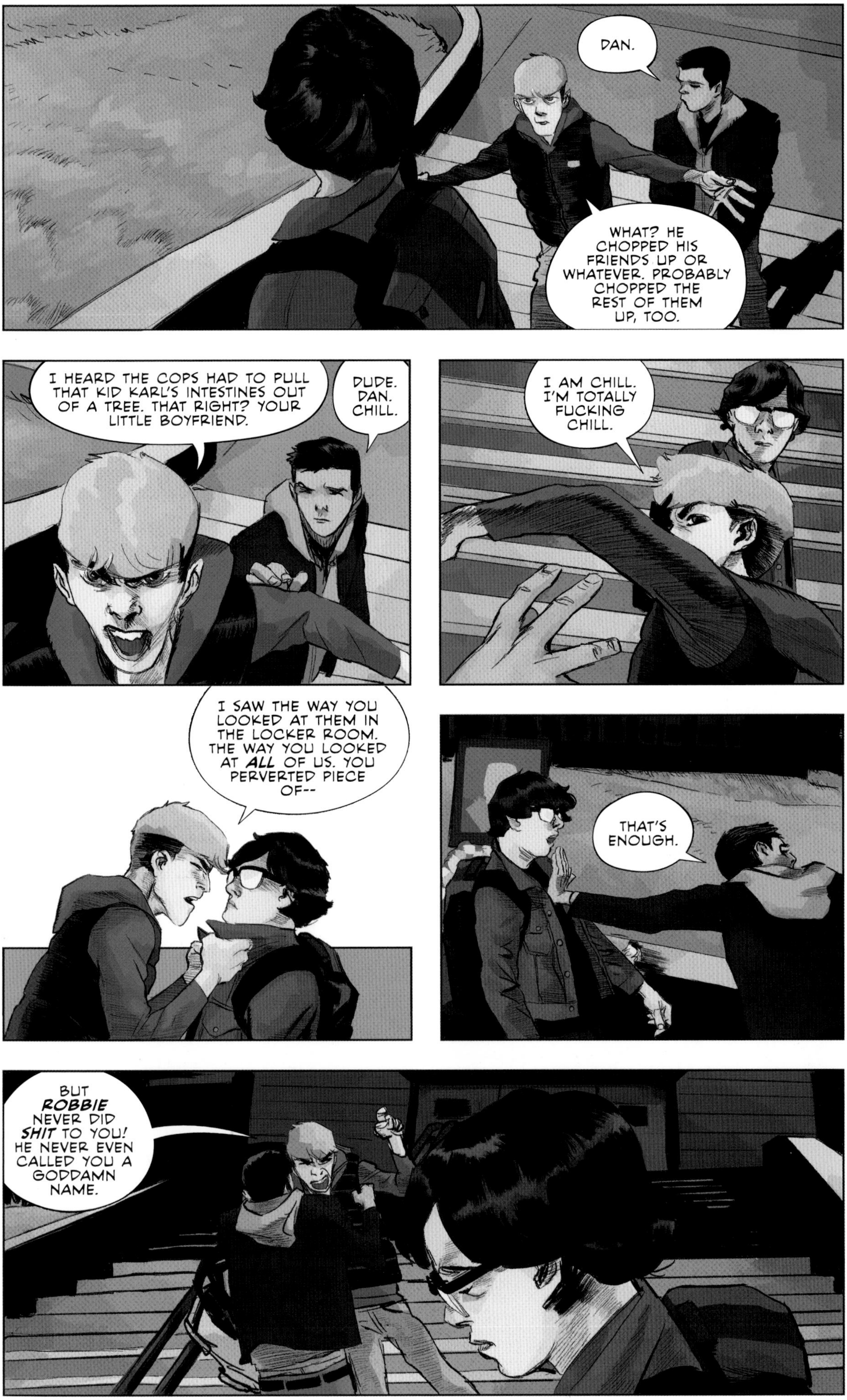
DAN.
WHAT? HE CHOPPED HIS FRIENDS UP OR WHATEVER. PROBABLY CHOPPED THE REST OF THEM UP, TOO.
I HEARD THE COPS HAD TO PULL THAT KID KARL'S INTESTINES OUT OF A TREE. THAT RIGHT? YOUR LITTLE BOYFRIEND.
DUDE. DAN. CHILL.
I AM CHILL. I'M TOTALLY FUCKING CHILL.
I SAW THE WAY YOU LOOKED AT THEM IN THE LOCKER ROOM. THE WAY YOU LOOKED AT ALL OF US. YOU PERVERTED PIECE OF--
THAT'S ENOUGH.
BUT ROBBIE NEVER DID SHIT TO YOU! HE NEVER EVEN CALLED YOU A GODDAMN NAME.

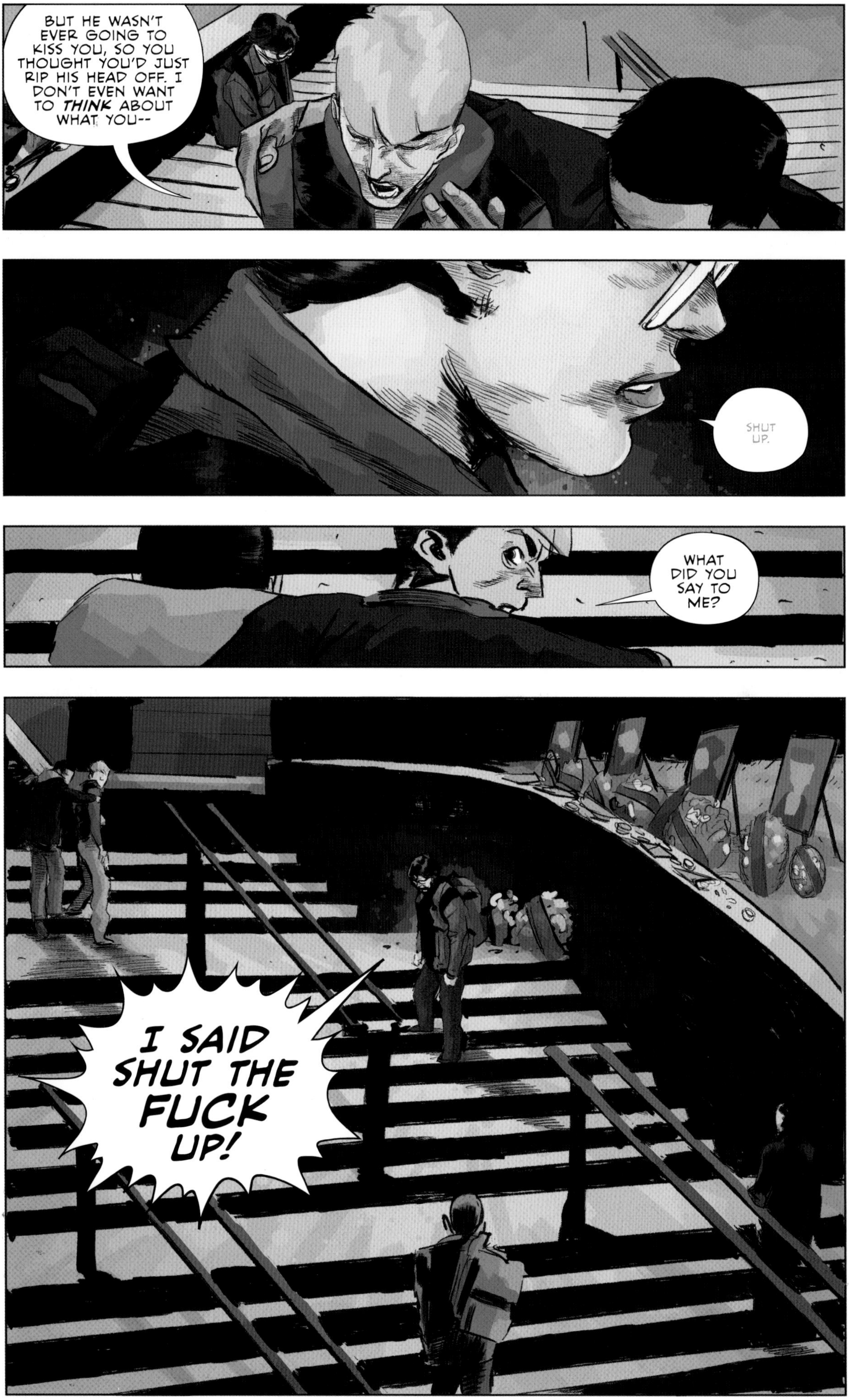
BUT HE WASN'T EVER GOING TO KISS YOU, SO YOU THOUGHT YOU'D JUST RIP HIS HEAD OFF. I DON'T EVEN WANT TO *THINK* ABOUT WHAT YOU--
SHUT UP.
WHAT DID YOU SAY TO ME?
I SAID SHUT THE FUCK UP!

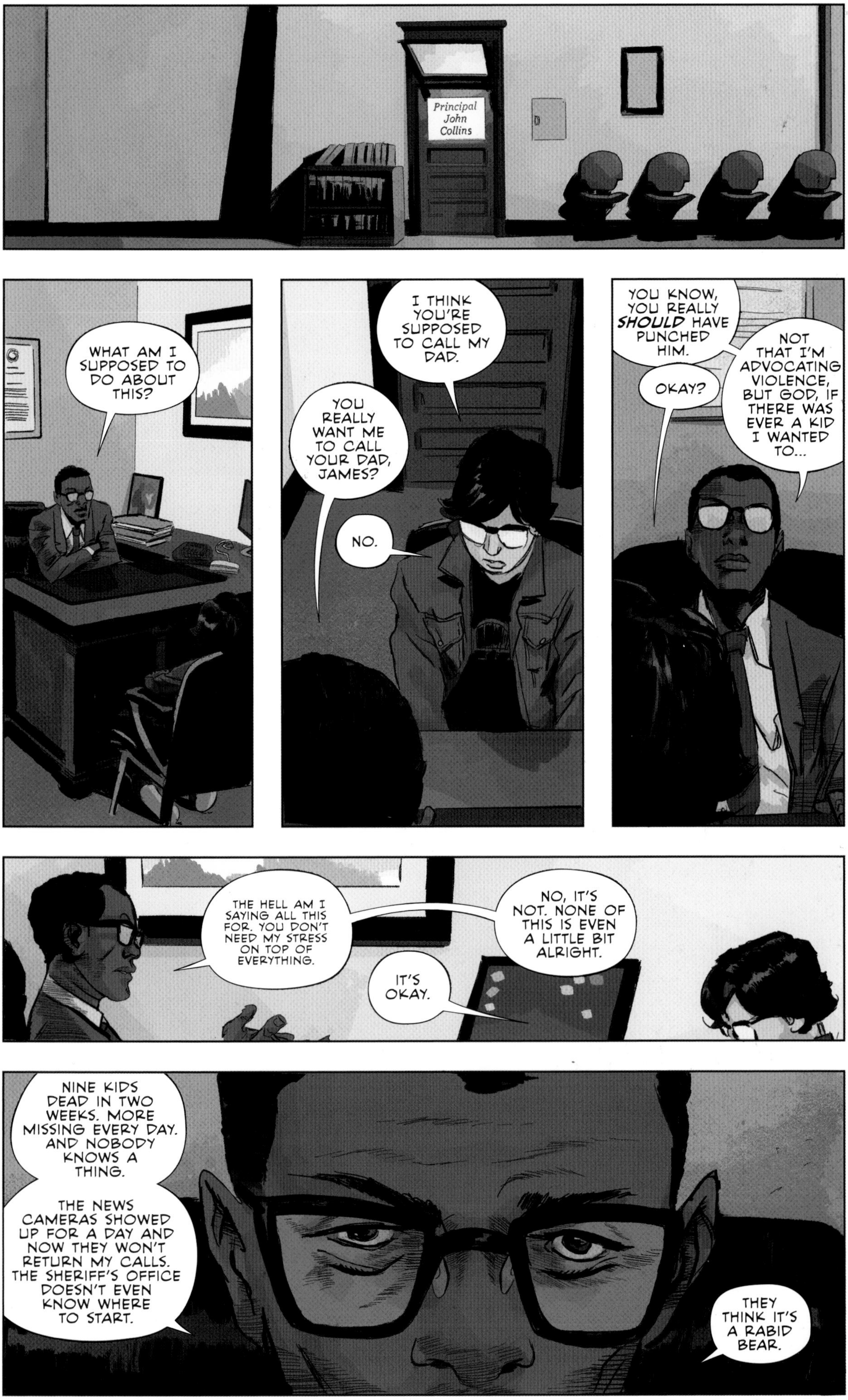
Principal John Collins
WHAT AM I SUPPOSED TO DO ABOUT THIS?
I THINK YOU'RE SUPPOSED TO CALL MY DAD.
YOU REALLY WANT ME TO CALL YOUR DAD, JAMES?
NO.
YOU KNOW, YOU REALLY SHOULD HAVE PUNCHED HIM.
OKAY?
NOT THAT I'M ADVOCATING VIOLENCE, BUT GOD, IF THERE WAS EVER A KID I WANTED TO...
THE HELL AM I SAYING ALL THIS FOR. YOU DON'T NEED MY STRESS ON TOP OF EVERYTHING.
IT'S OKAY.
NO, IT'S NOT. NONE OF THIS IS EVEN A LITTLE BIT ALRIGHT.
NINE KIDS DEAD IN TWO WEEKS. MORE MISSING EVERY DAY. AND NOBODY KNOWS A THING.
THE NEWS CAMERAS SHOWED UP FOR A DAY AND NOW THEY WON'T RETURN MY CALLS. THE SHERIFF'S OFFICE DOESN'T EVEN KNOW WHERE TO START.
THEY THINK IT'S A RABID BEAR.

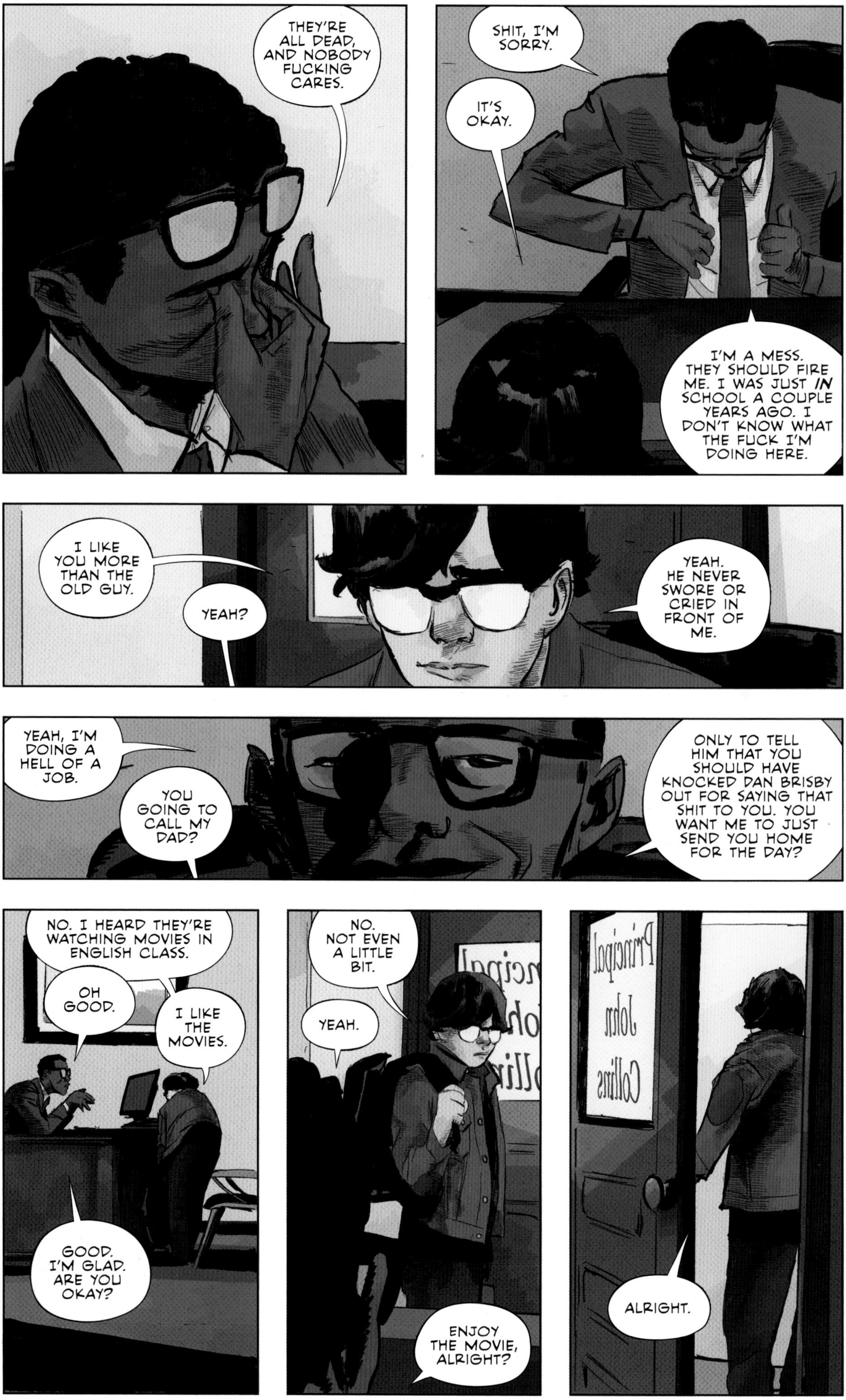
THEY'RE ALL DEAD, AND NOBODY FUCKING CARES.
SHIT, I'M SORRY.
IT'S OKAY.
I'M A MESS. THEY SHOULD FIRE ME. I WAS JUST *IN* SCHOOL A COUPLE YEARS AGO. I DON'T KNOW WHAT THE FUCK I'M DOING HERE.
I LIKE YOU MORE THAN THE OLD GUY.
YEAH?
YEAH. HE NEVER SWORE OR CRIED IN FRONT OF ME.
YEAH, I'M DOING A HELL OF A JOB.
YOU GOING TO CALL MY DAD?
ONLY TO TELL HIM THAT YOU SHOULD HAVE KNOCKED DAN BRISBY OUT FOR SAYING THAT SHIT TO YOU. YOU WANT ME TO JUST SEND YOU HOME FOR THE DAY?
NO. I HEARD THEY'RE WATCHING MOVIES IN ENGLISH CLASS.
OH GOOD.
I LIKE THE MOVIES.
GOOD. I'M GLAD. ARE YOU OKAY?
NO. NOT EVEN A LITTLE BIT.
YEAH.
ENJOY THE MOVIE, ALRIGHT?
Principal John Collins
ALRIGHT.

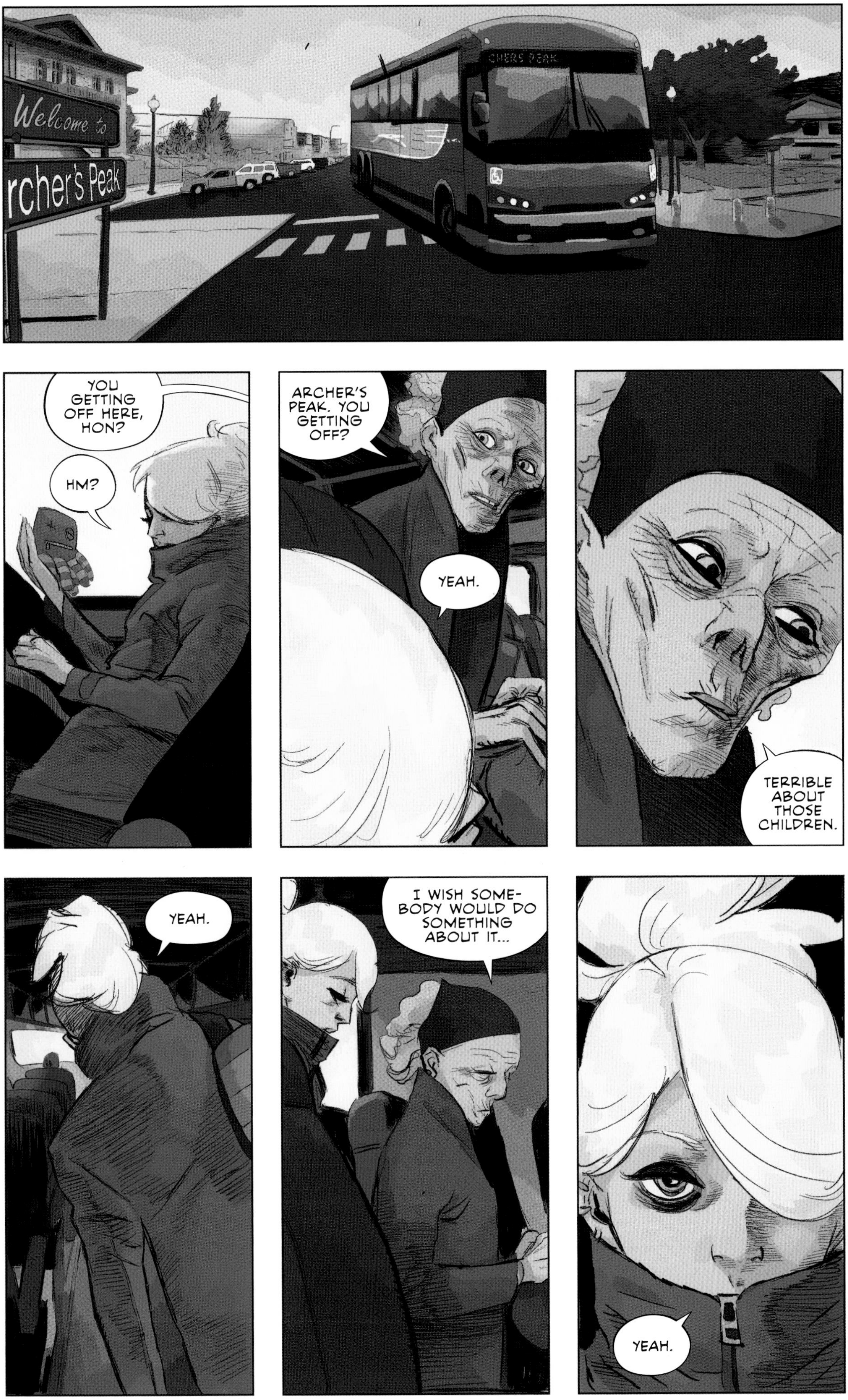
Welcome to
rcher's Peak
CHERS PEAK
YOU GETTING OFF HERE, HON?
HM?
ARCHER'S PEAK. YOU GETTING OFF?
YEAH.
TERRIBLE ABOUT THOSE CHILDREN.
YEAH.
I WISH SOME-BODY WOULD DO SOMETHING ABOUT IT...
YEAH.

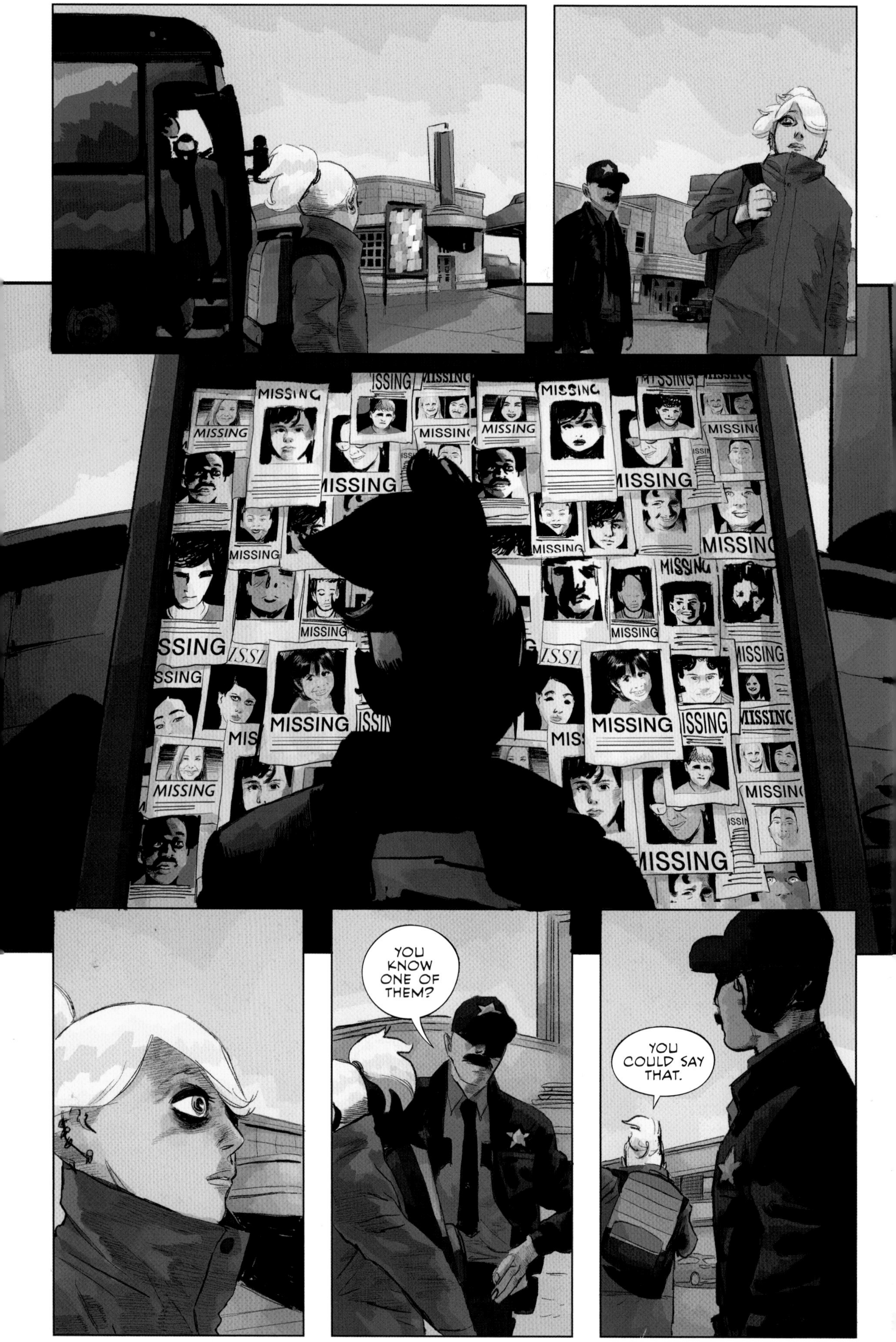
YOU KNOW ONE OF THEM?
YOU COULD SAY THAT.

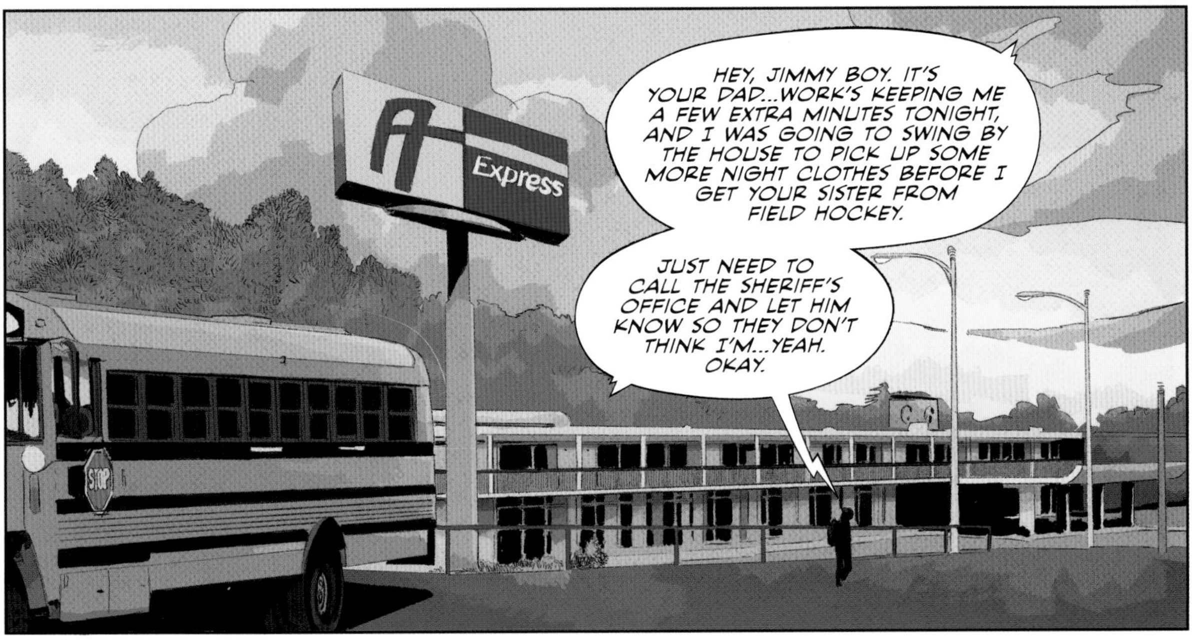
Express
HEY, JIMMY BOY. IT'S YOUR DAD...WORK'S KEEPING ME A FEW EXTRA MINUTES TONIGHT, AND I WAS GOING TO SWING BY THE HOUSE TO PICK UP SOME MORE NIGHT CLOTHES BEFORE I GET YOUR SISTER FROM FIELD HOCKEY.
JUST NEED TO CALL THE SHERIFF'S OFFICE AND LET HIM KNOW SO THEY DON'T THINK I'M...YEAH. OKAY.

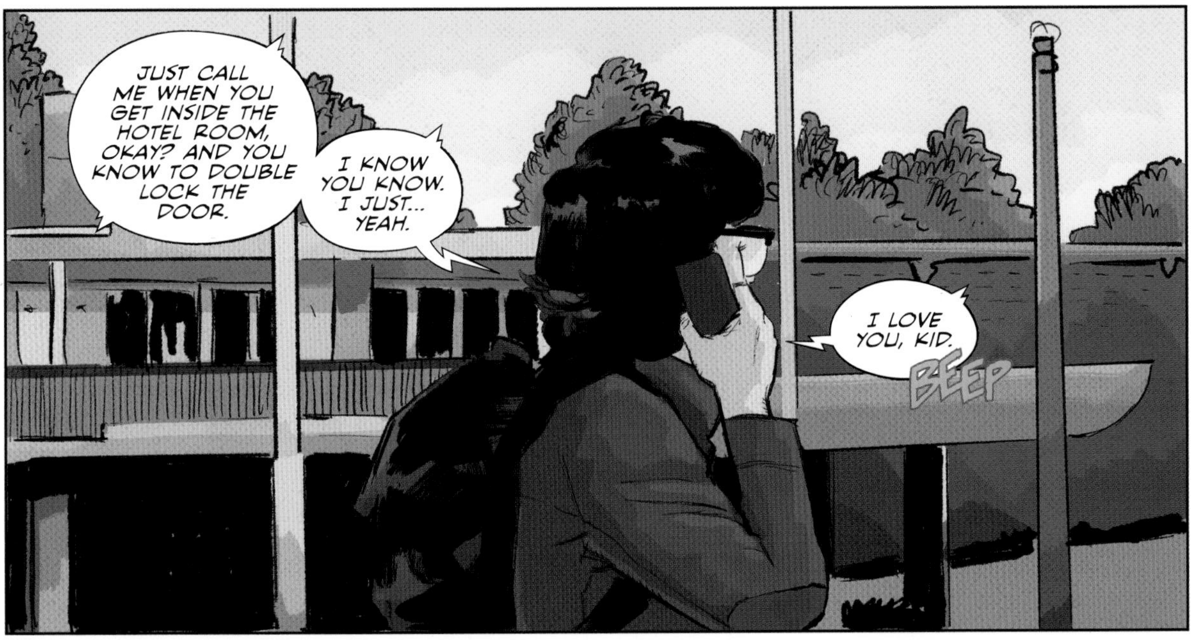
JUST CALL ME WHEN YOU GET INSIDE THE HOTEL ROOM, OKAY? AND YOU KNOW TO DOUBLE LOCK THE DOOR.
I KNOW YOU KNOW. I JUST... YEAH.
I LOVE YOU, KID.
BEEP

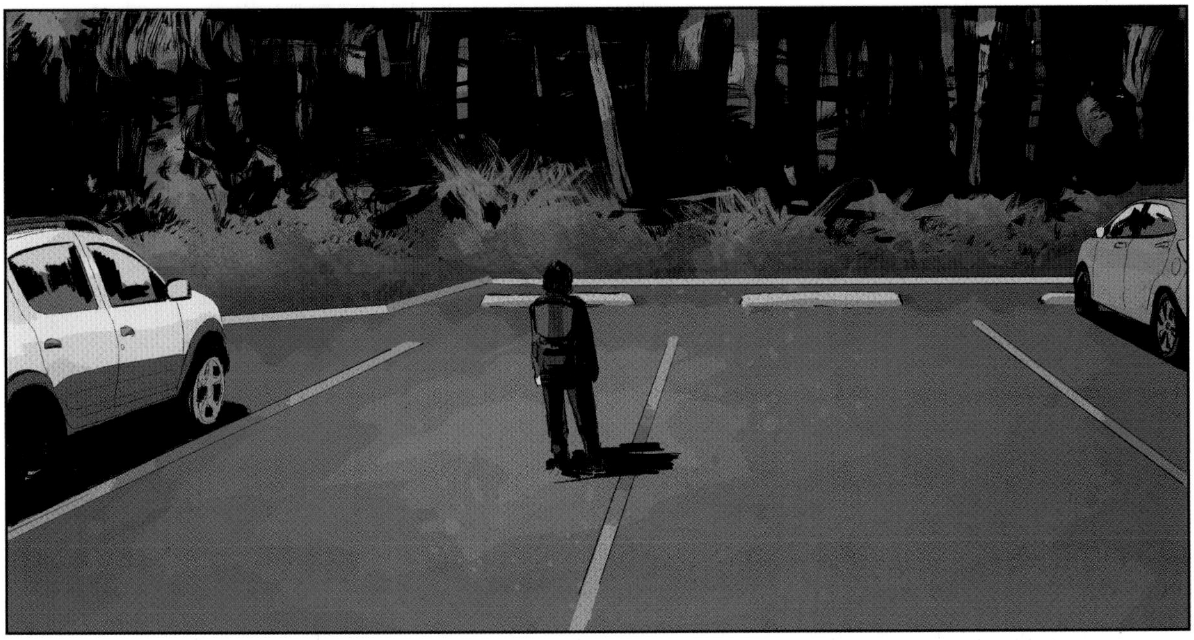

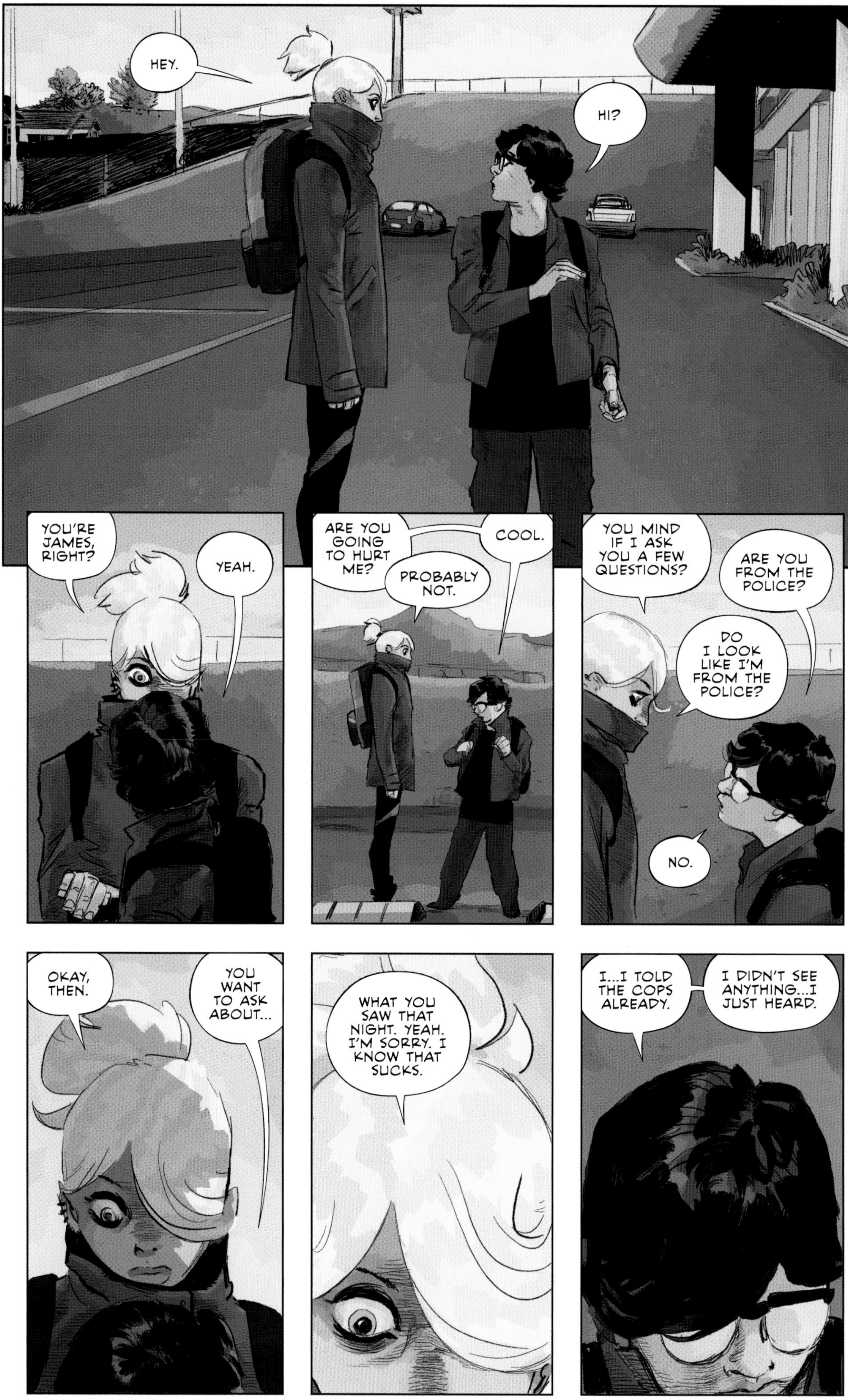
HEY.
HI?
YOU'RE JAMES, RIGHT?
YEAH.
ARE YOU GOING TO HURT ME?
PROBABLY NOT.
COOL.
YOU MIND IF I ASK YOU A FEW QUESTIONS?
ARE YOU FROM THE POLICE?
DO I LOOK LIKE I'M FROM THE POLICE?
NO.
OKAY, THEN.
YOU WANT TO ASK ABOUT...
WHAT YOU SAW THAT NIGHT. YEAH. I'M SORRY. I KNOW THAT SUCKS.
I...I TOLD THE COPS ALREADY.
I DIDN'T SEE ANYTHING...I JUST HEARD.

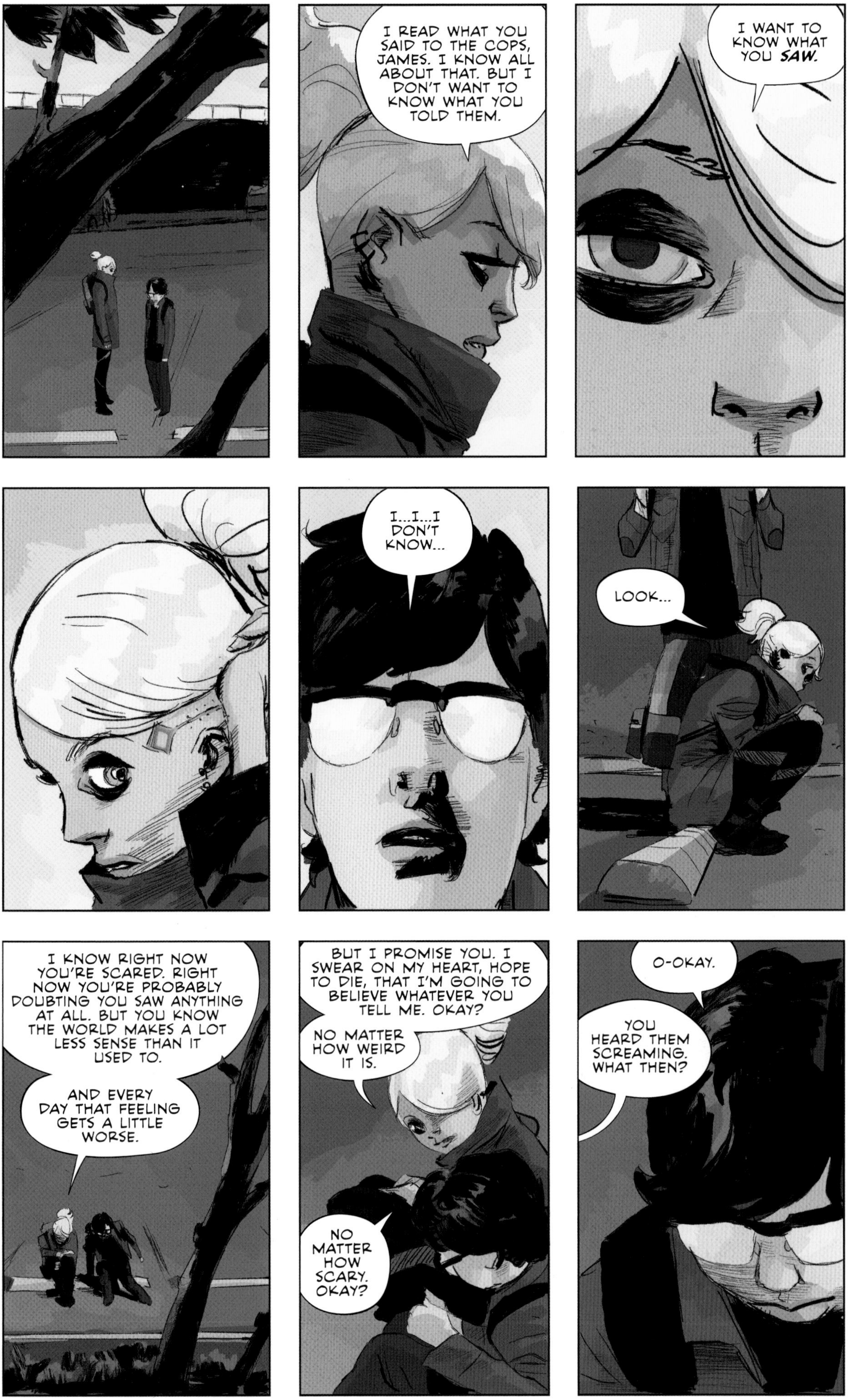
I READ WHAT YOU SAID TO THE COPS, JAMES. I KNOW ALL ABOUT THAT. BUT I DON'T WANT TO KNOW WHAT YOU TOLD THEM.
I WANT TO KNOW WHAT YOU SAW.
I...I...I DON'T KNOW...
LOOK...
I KNOW RIGHT NOW YOU'RE SCARED. RIGHT NOW YOU'RE PROBABLY DOUBTING YOU SAW ANYTHING AT ALL. BUT YOU KNOW THE WORLD MAKES A LOT LESS SENSE THAN IT USED TO.
AND EVERY DAY THAT FEELING GETS A LITTLE WORSE.
BUT I PROMISE YOU. I SWEAR ON MY HEART, HOPE TO DIE, THAT I'M GOING TO BELIEVE WHATEVER YOU TELL ME. OKAY?
NO MATTER HOW WEIRD IT IS.
NO MATTER HOW SCARY. OKAY?
O-OKAY.
YOU HEARD THEM SCREAMING. WHAT THEN?

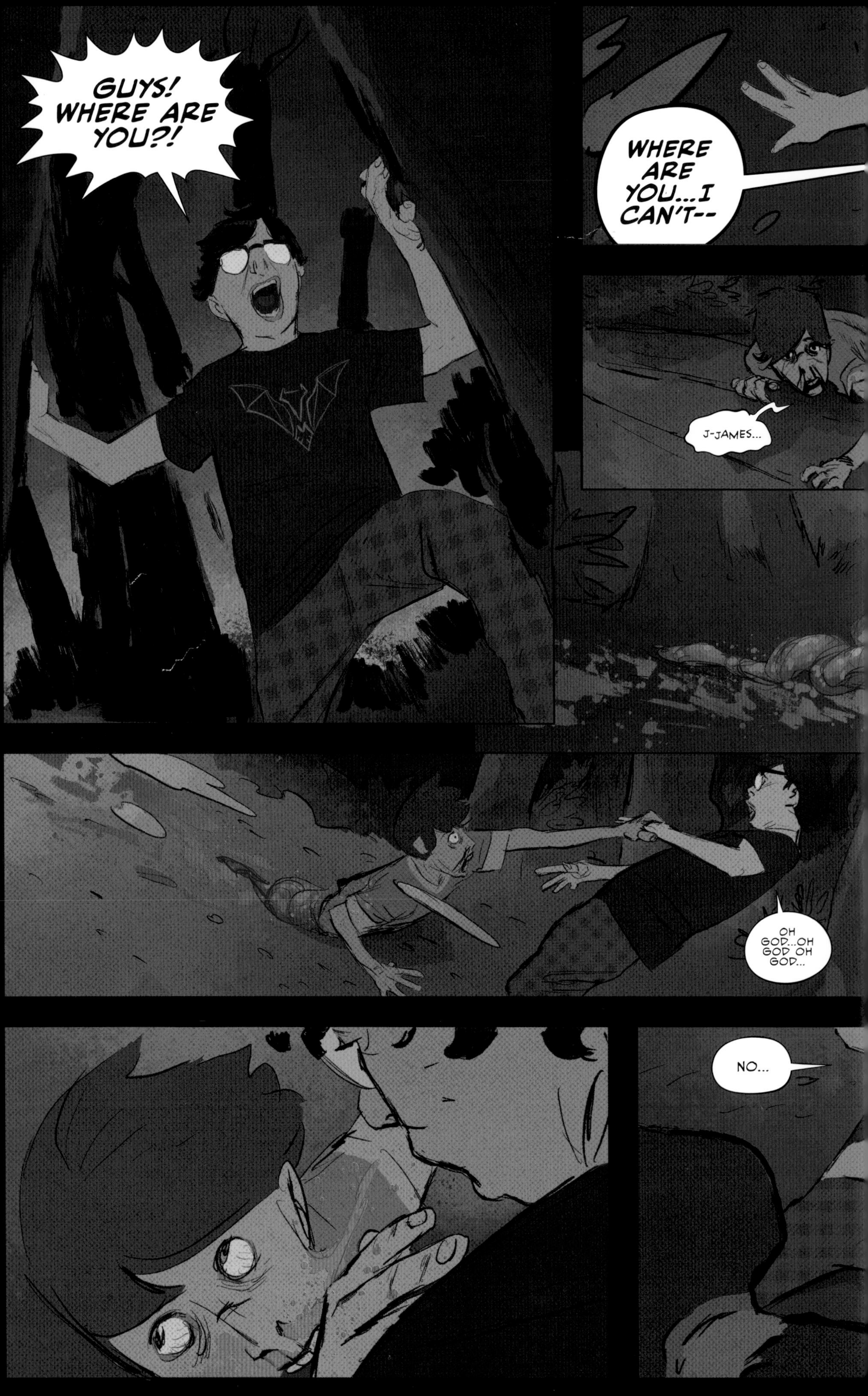
GUYS! WHERE ARE YOU?!
WHERE ARE YOU...I CAN'T--
J-JAMES...
OH GOD...OH GOD OH GOD...
NO...

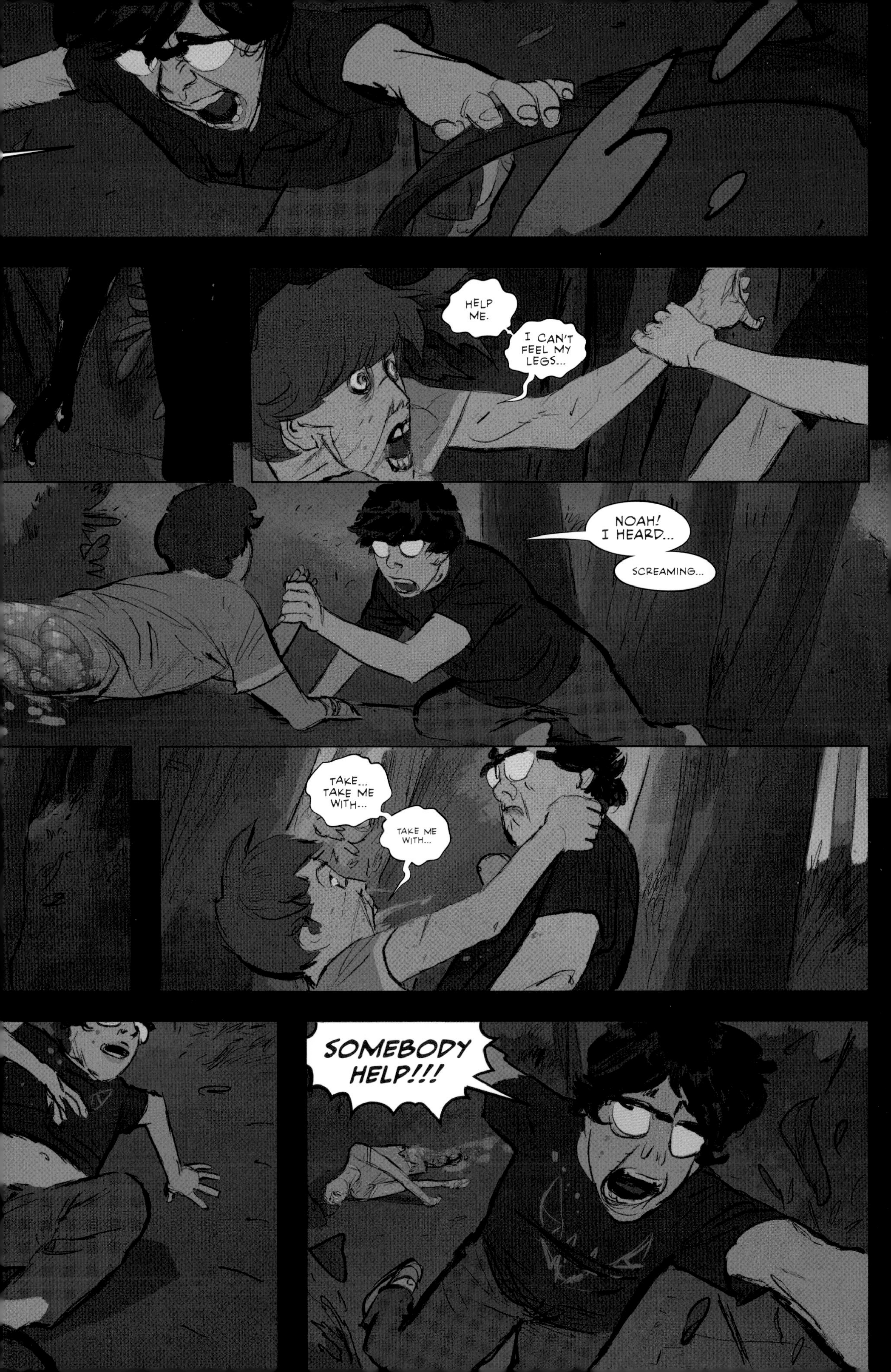
HELP ME.
I CAN'T FEEL MY LEGS...
NOAH! I HEARD...
SCREAMING...
TAKE... TAKE ME WITH...
TAKE ME WITH...
SOMEBODY HELP!!!

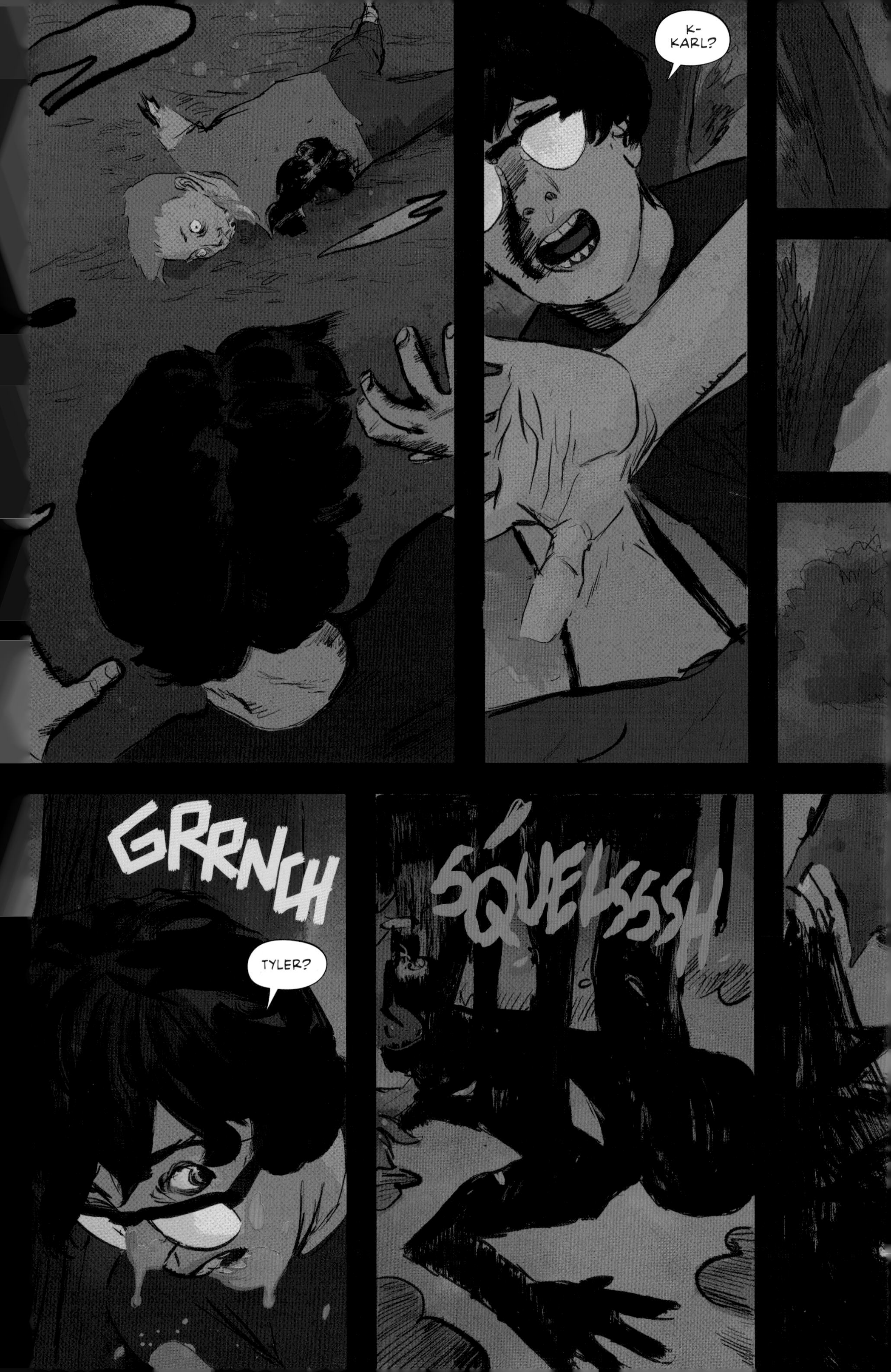
K-
KARL?
GRRNCH
TYLER?
SQUELSSSH

THIS ISN'T REAL...THIS CAN'T BE REAL.

NO...NO NO NO...

Heb...

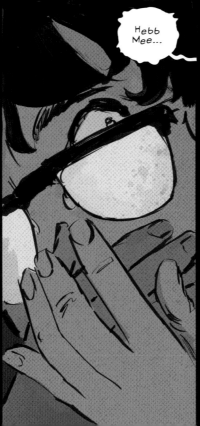

Hebb Mee...

Jmms

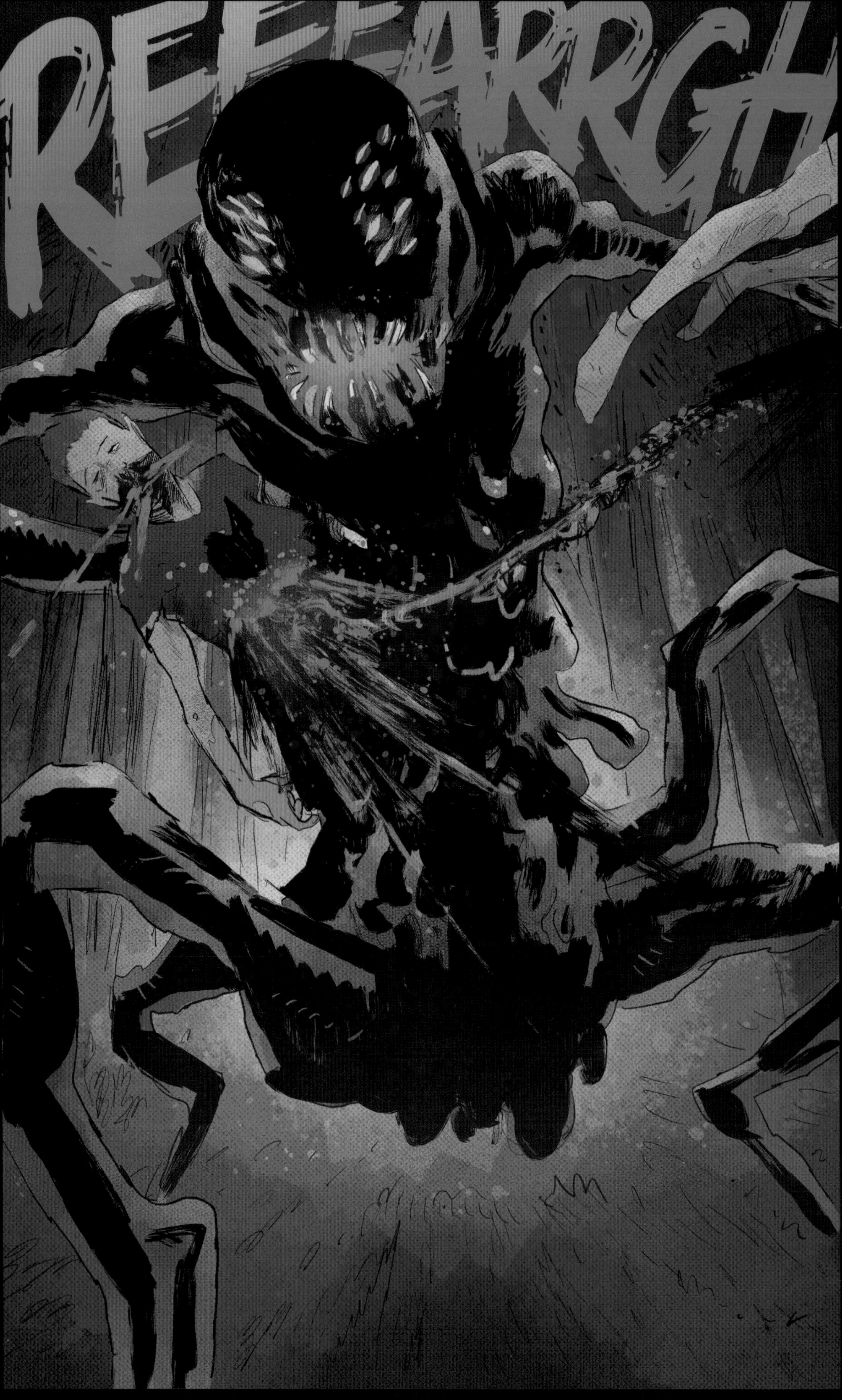
REEEARRGH

THANK YOU.

THIS FUCKING THING.

BZZZ BZZZ

WHAT--

YEAH.

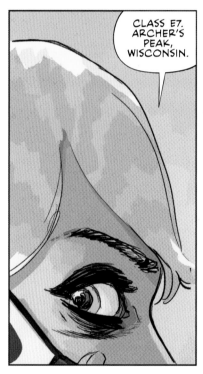

CLASS E7. ARCHER'S PEAK, WISCONSIN.

YEAH. I'VE GOT IT HANDLED.

YOU'VE GOT IT HANDLED?

WHAT DO YOU MEAN YOU'VE GOT IT HANDLED?

CLACK

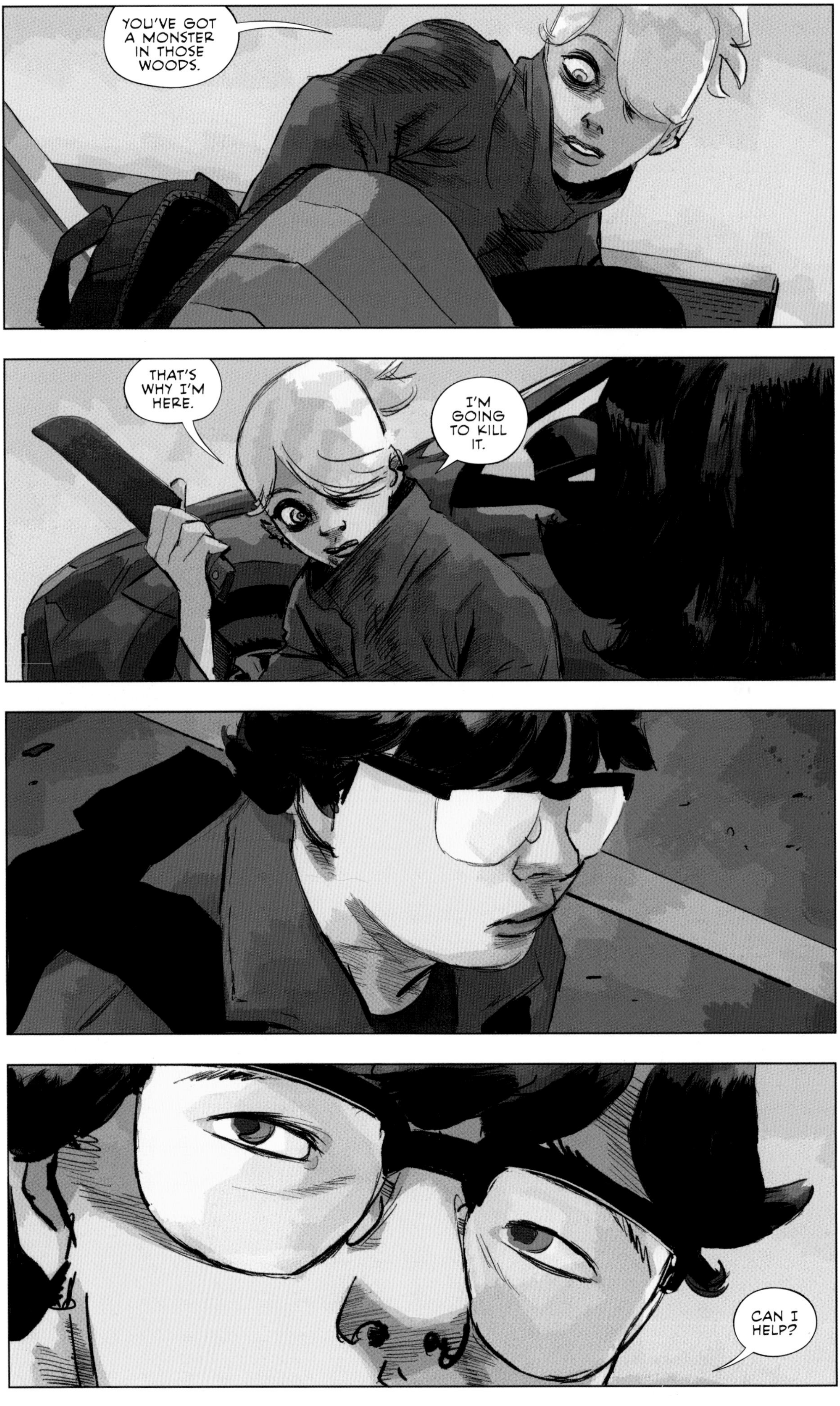
YOU'VE GOT A MONSTER IN THOSE WOODS.
THAT'S WHY I'M HERE.
I'M GOING TO KILL IT.
CAN I HELP?

CHAPTER TWO

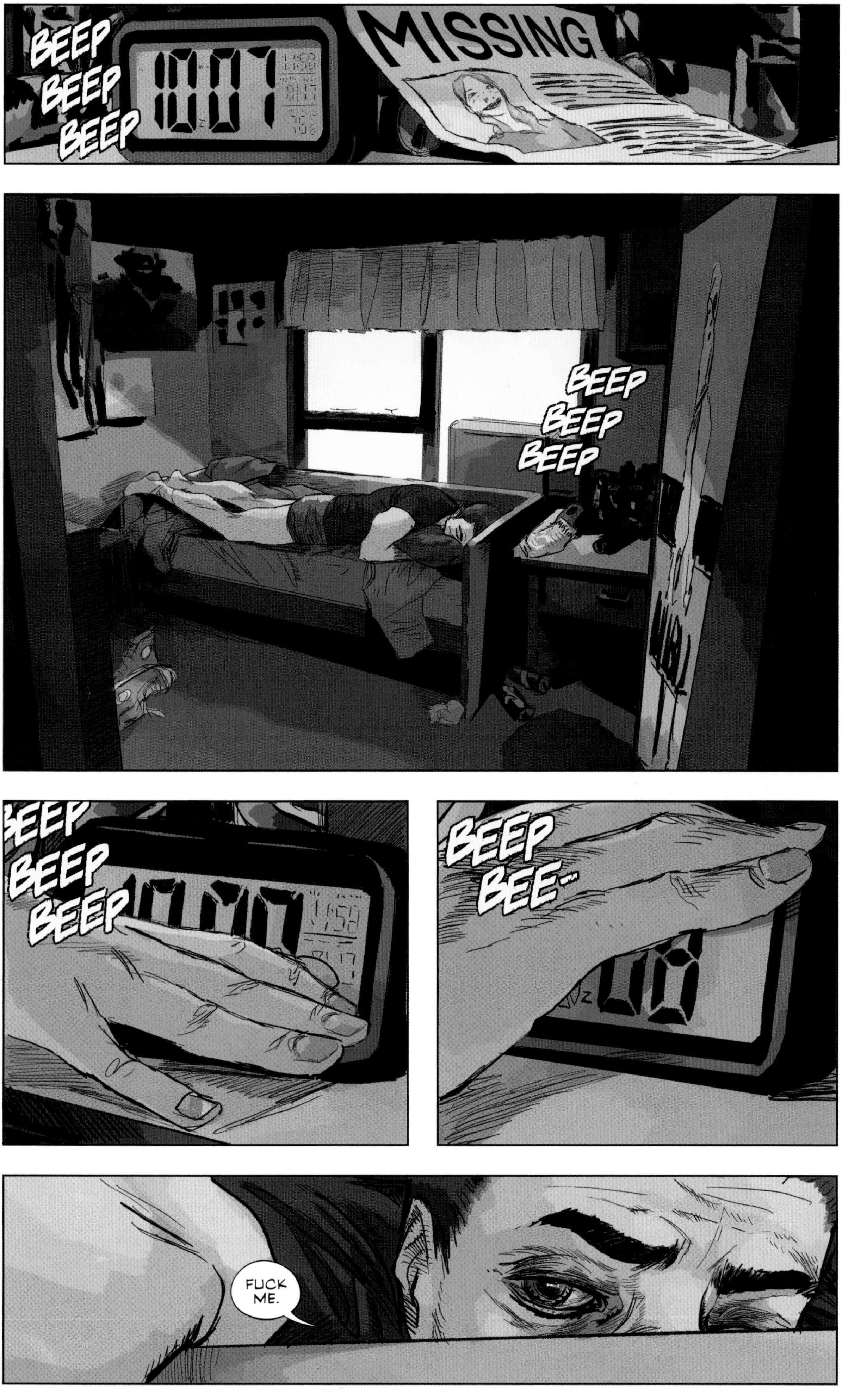
BEEP
BEEP
BEEP
MISSING
BEEP
BEEP
BEEP
BEEP
BEEP
BEEP
BEEP
BEE--
FUCK ME.

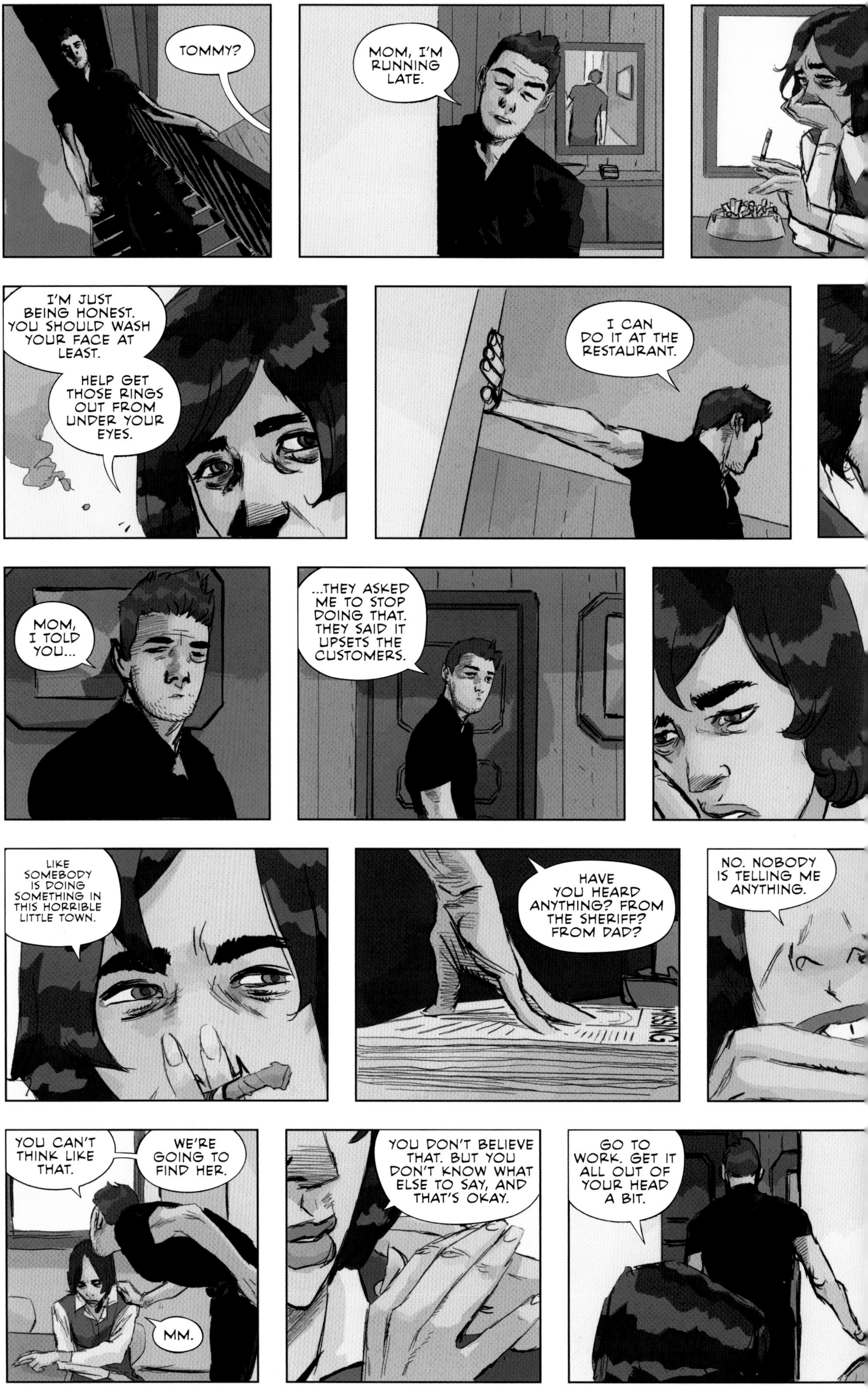
TOMMY?
MOM, I'M RUNNING LATE.
I'M JUST BEING HONEST. YOU SHOULD WASH YOUR FACE AT LEAST.
HELP GET THOSE RINGS OUT FROM UNDER YOUR EYES.
I CAN DO IT AT THE RESTAURANT.
MOM, I TOLD YOU...
...THEY ASKED ME TO STOP DOING THAT. THEY SAID IT UPSETS THE CUSTOMERS.
LIKE SOMEBODY IS DOING SOMETHING IN THIS HORRIBLE LITTLE TOWN.
HAVE YOU HEARD ANYTHING? FROM THE SHERIFF? FROM DAD?
MISSING
NO. NOBODY IS TELLING ME ANYTHING.
YOU CAN'T THINK LIKE THAT.
WE'RE GOING TO FIND HER.
MM.
YOU DON'T BELIEVE THAT. BUT YOU DON'T KNOW WHAT ELSE TO SAY, AND THAT'S OKAY.
GO TO WORK. GET IT ALL OUT OF YOUR HEAD A BIT.

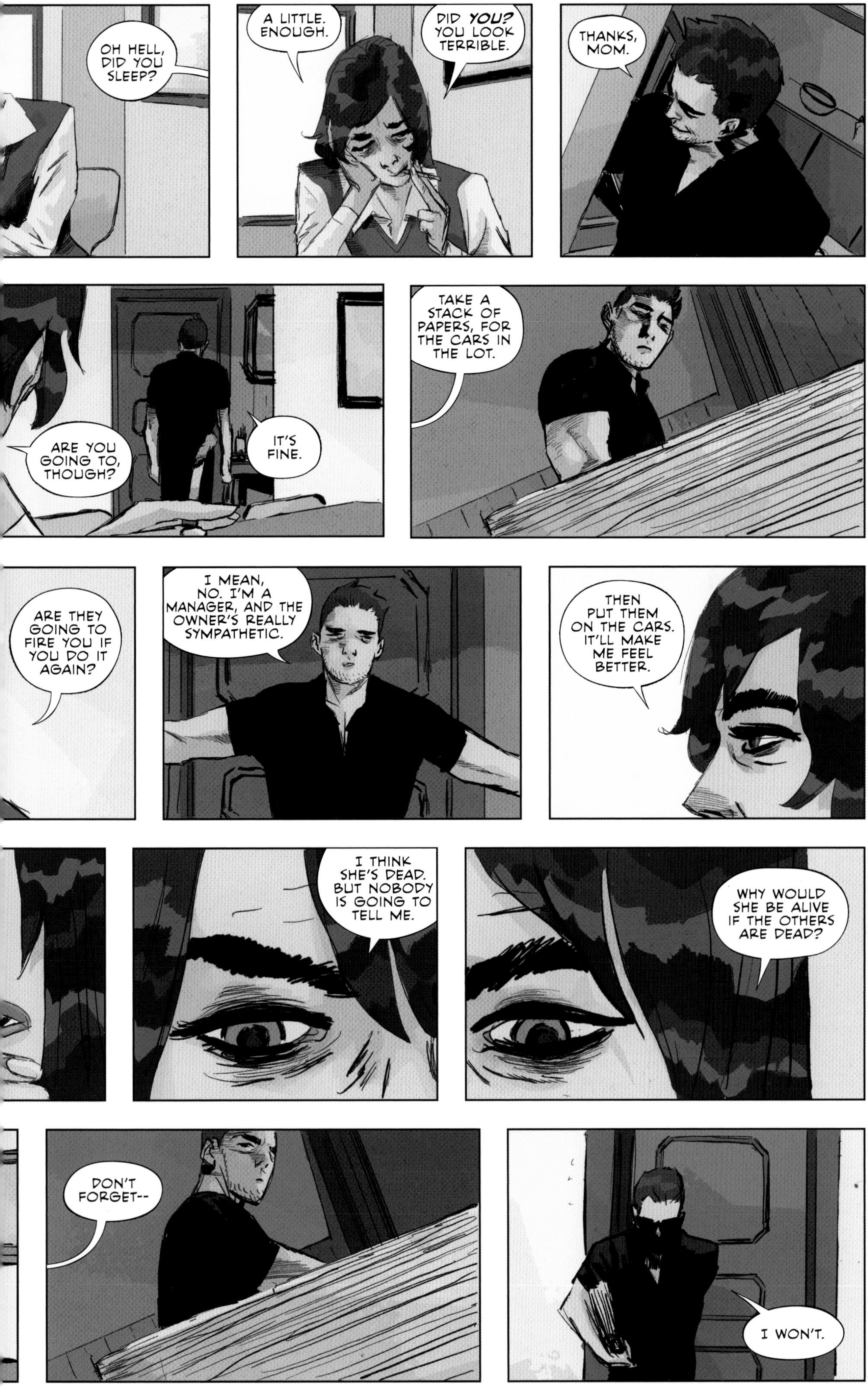
OH HELL, DID YOU SLEEP?
A LITTLE. ENOUGH.
DID *YOU?* YOU LOOK TERRIBLE.
THANKS, MOM.
ARE YOU GOING TO, THOUGH?
IT'S FINE.
TAKE A STACK OF PAPERS, FOR THE CARS IN THE LOT.
ARE THEY GOING TO FIRE YOU IF YOU DO IT AGAIN?
I MEAN, NO. I'M A MANAGER, AND THE OWNER'S REALLY SYMPATHETIC.
THEN PUT THEM ON THE CARS. IT'LL MAKE ME FEEL BETTER.
I THINK SHE'S DEAD. BUT NOBODY IS GOING TO TELL ME.
WHY WOULD SHE BE ALIVE IF THE OTHERS ARE DEAD?
DON'T FORGET--
I WON'T.

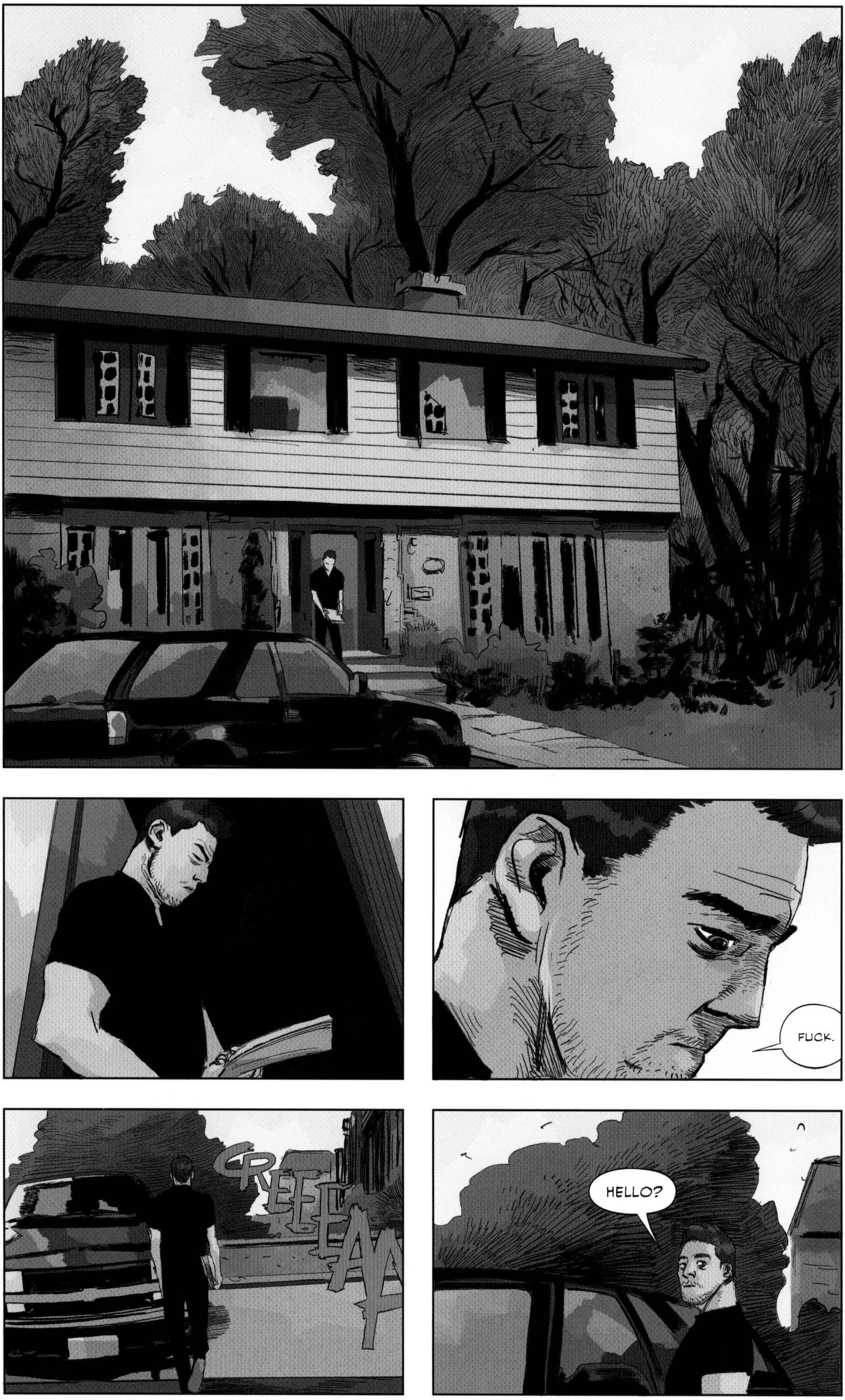
FUCK.
CREEEEAAA
HELLO?

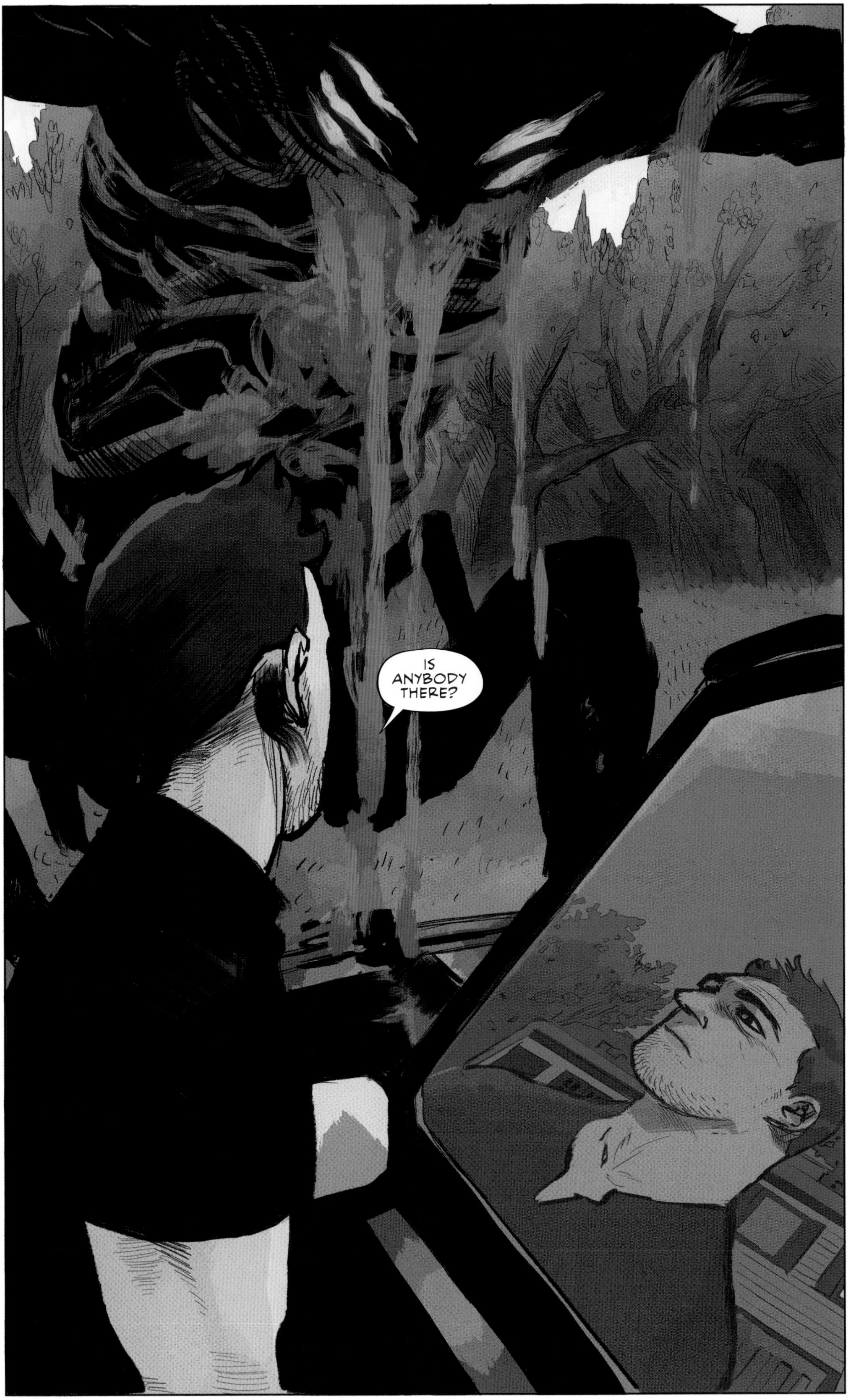
IS ANYBODY THERE?

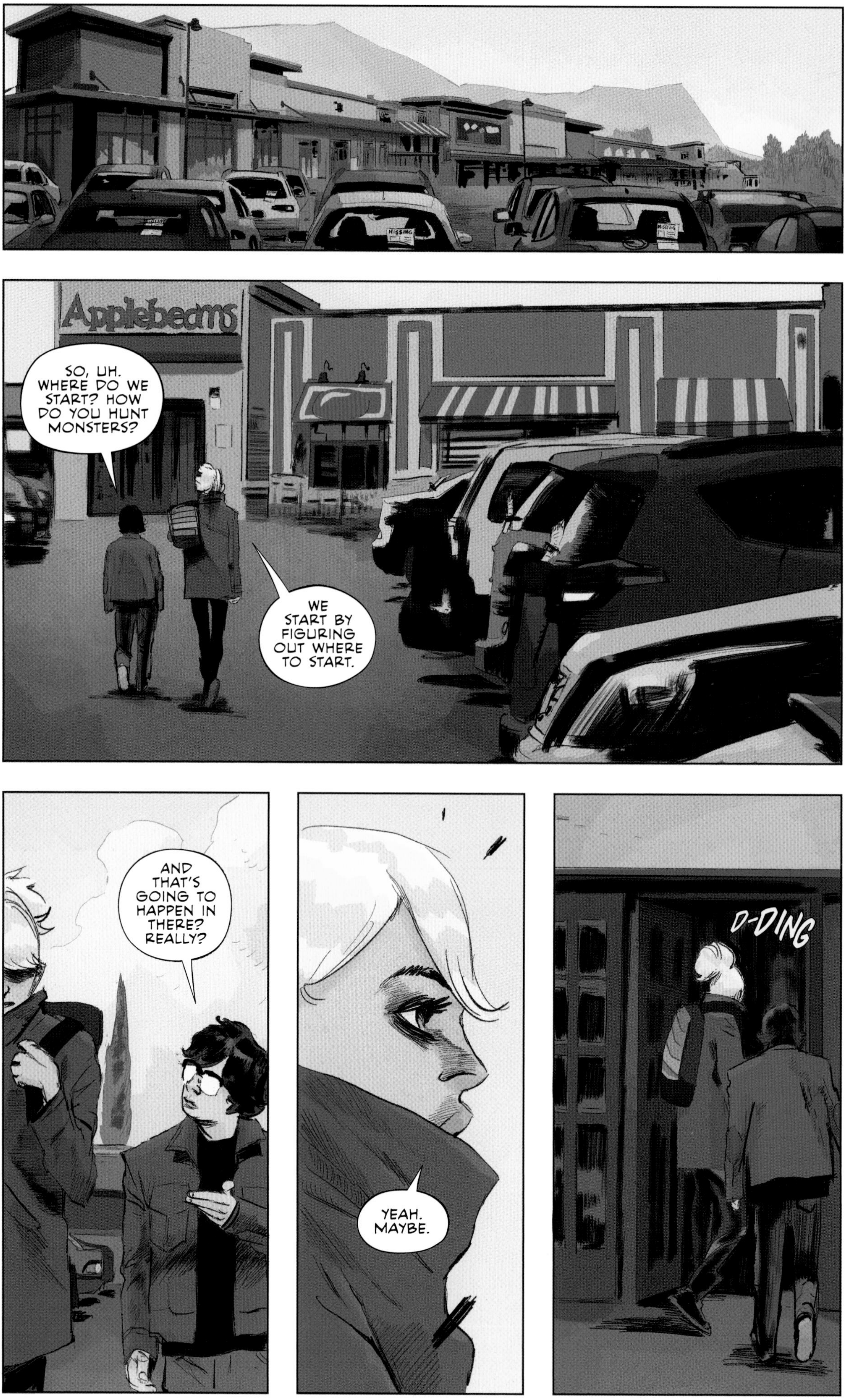
MISSING
MISSING
Applebeams
SO, UH. WHERE DO WE START? HOW DO YOU HUNT MONSTERS?
WE START BY FIGURING OUT WHERE TO START.
AND THAT'S GOING TO HAPPEN IN THERE? REALLY?
YEAH. MAYBE.
D-DING

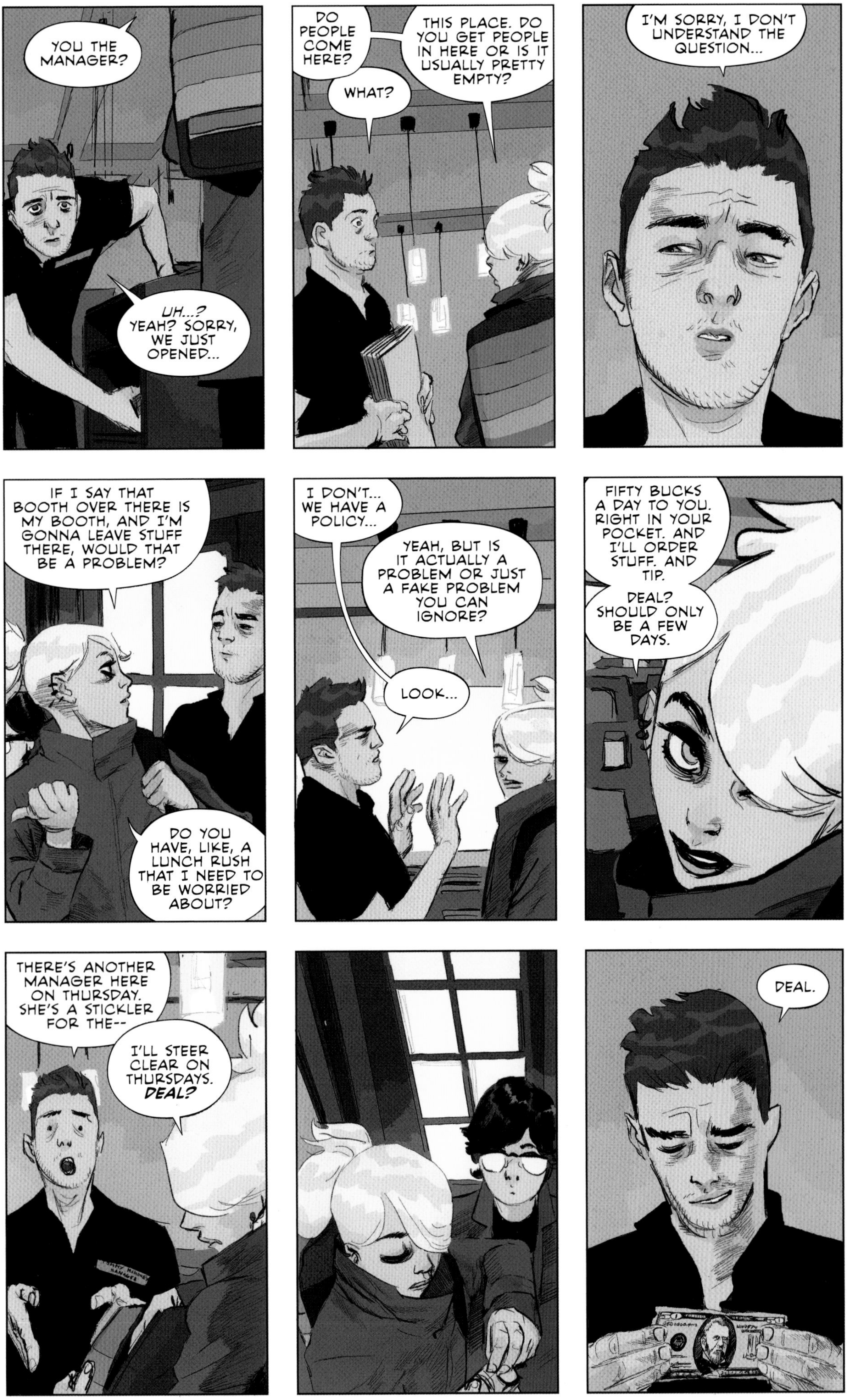
YOU THE MANAGER?
UH...? YEAH? SORRY, WE JUST OPENED...
DO PEOPLE COME HERE?
WHAT?
THIS PLACE. DO YOU GET PEOPLE IN HERE OR IS IT USUALLY PRETTY EMPTY?
I'M SORRY, I DON'T UNDERSTAND THE QUESTION...
IF I SAY THAT BOOTH OVER THERE IS MY BOOTH, AND I'M GONNA LEAVE STUFF THERE, WOULD THAT BE A PROBLEM?
DO YOU HAVE, LIKE, A LUNCH RUSH THAT I NEED TO BE WORRIED ABOUT?
I DON'T... WE HAVE A POLICY...
YEAH, BUT IS IT ACTUALLY A PROBLEM OR JUST A FAKE PROBLEM YOU CAN IGNORE?
LOOK...
FIFTY BUCKS A DAY TO YOU. RIGHT IN YOUR POCKET. AND I'LL ORDER STUFF. AND TIP.
DEAL? SHOULD ONLY BE A FEW DAYS.
THERE'S ANOTHER MANAGER HERE ON THURSDAY. SHE'S A STICKLER FOR THE--
I'LL STEER CLEAR ON THURSDAYS. DEAL?
DEAL.

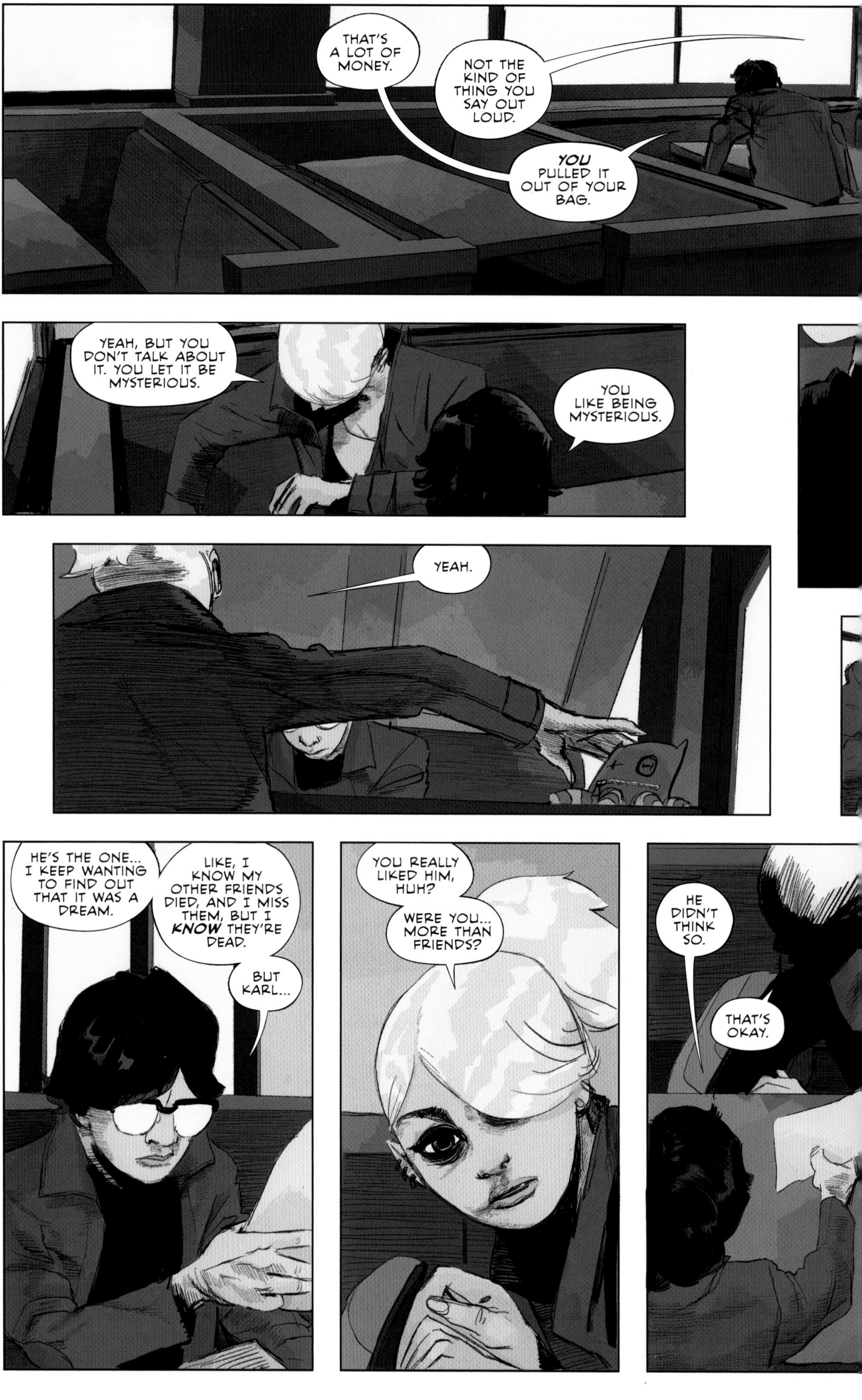
THAT'S A LOT OF MONEY.
NOT THE KIND OF THING YOU SAY OUT LOUD.
YOU PULLED IT OUT OF YOUR BAG.
YEAH, BUT YOU DON'T TALK ABOUT IT. YOU LET IT BE MYSTERIOUS.
YOU LIKE BEING MYSTERIOUS.
YEAH.
HE'S THE ONE... I KEEP WANTING TO FIND OUT THAT IT WAS A DREAM.
LIKE, I KNOW MY OTHER FRIENDS DIED, AND I MISS THEM, BUT I KNOW THEY'RE DEAD.
BUT KARL...
YOU REALLY LIKED HIM, HUH?
WERE YOU... MORE THAN FRIENDS?
HE DIDN'T THINK SO.
THAT'S OKAY.

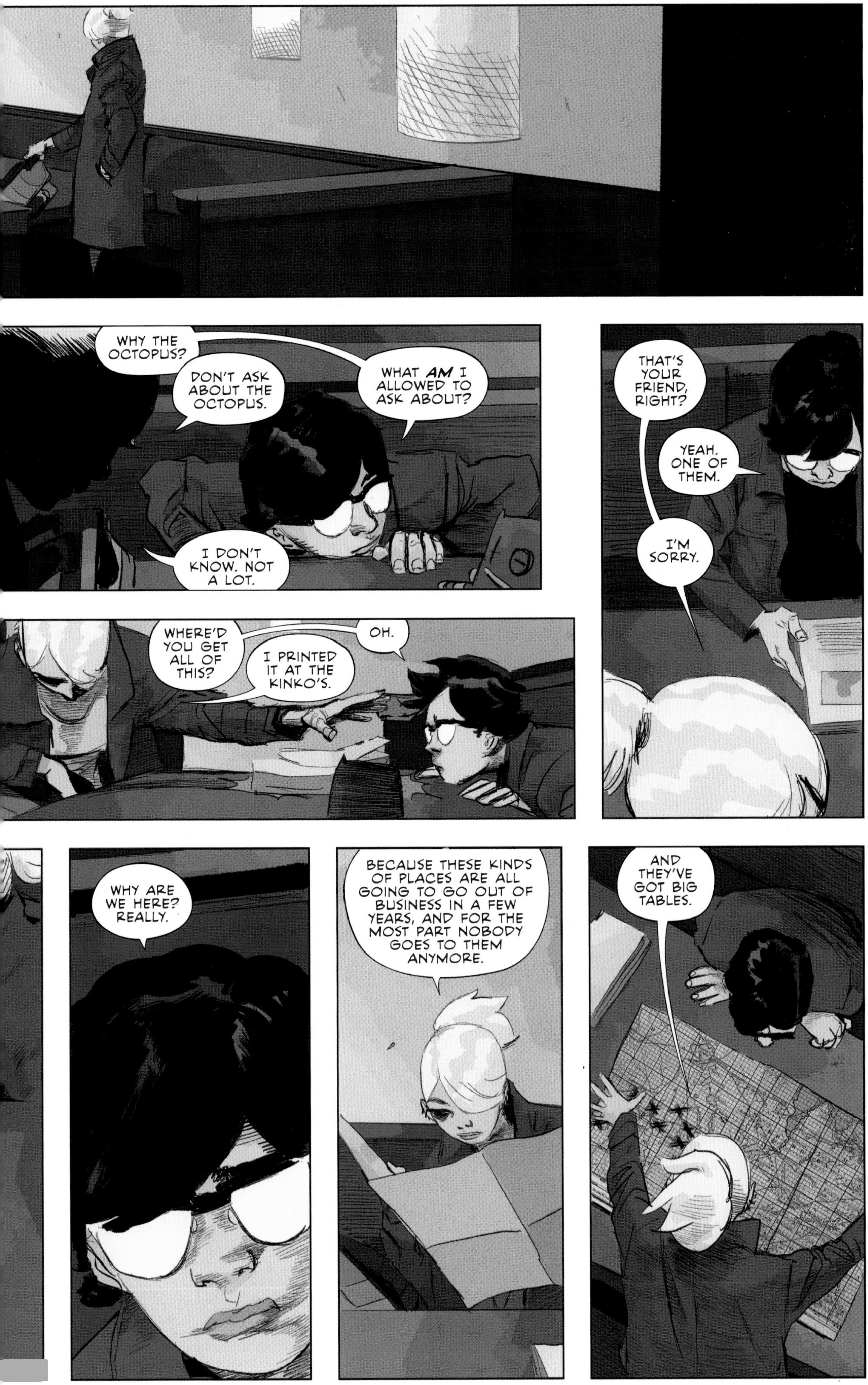
WHY THE OCTOPUS?
DON'T ASK ABOUT THE OCTOPUS.
WHAT AM I ALLOWED TO ASK ABOUT?
I DON'T KNOW. NOT A LOT.
THAT'S YOUR FRIEND, RIGHT?
YEAH. ONE OF THEM.
I'M SORRY.
WHERE'D YOU GET ALL OF THIS?
I PRINTED IT AT THE KINKO'S.
OH.
WHY ARE WE HERE? REALLY.
BECAUSE THESE KINDS OF PLACES ARE ALL GOING TO GO OUT OF BUSINESS IN A FEW YEARS, AND FOR THE MOST PART NOBODY GOES TO THEM ANYMORE.
AND THEY'VE GOT BIG TABLES.

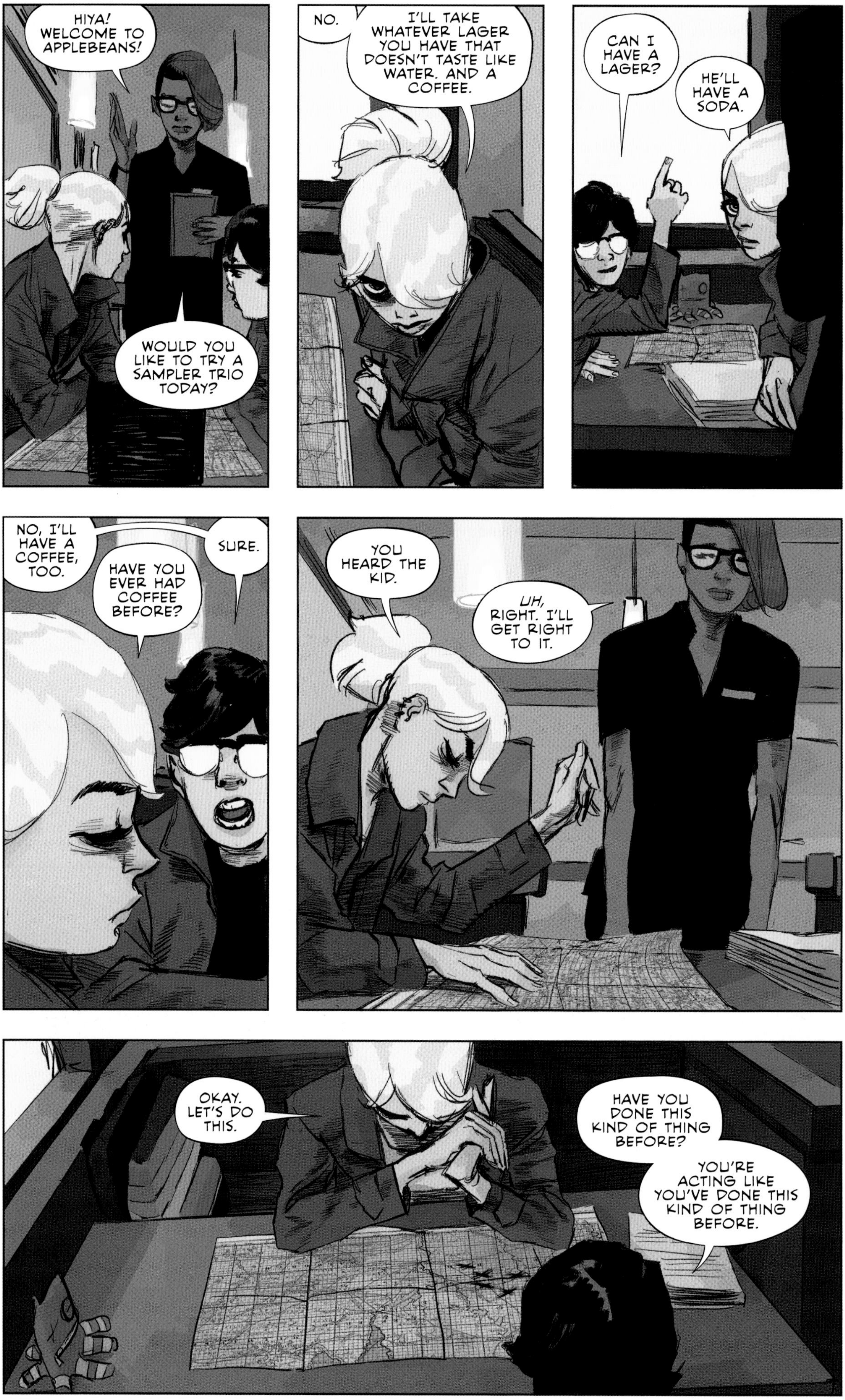
HIYA! WELCOME TO APPLEBEANS!
WOULD YOU LIKE TO TRY A SAMPLER TRIO TODAY?
NO.
I'LL TAKE WHATEVER LAGER YOU HAVE THAT DOESN'T TASTE LIKE WATER. AND A COFFEE.
CAN I HAVE A LAGER?
HE'LL HAVE A SODA.
NO, I'LL HAVE A COFFEE, TOO.
SURE.
HAVE YOU EVER HAD COFFEE BEFORE?
YOU HEARD THE KID.
UH, RIGHT. I'LL GET RIGHT TO IT.
OKAY. LET'S DO THIS.
HAVE YOU DONE THIS KIND OF THING BEFORE?
YOU'RE ACTING LIKE YOU'VE DONE THIS KIND OF THING BEFORE.

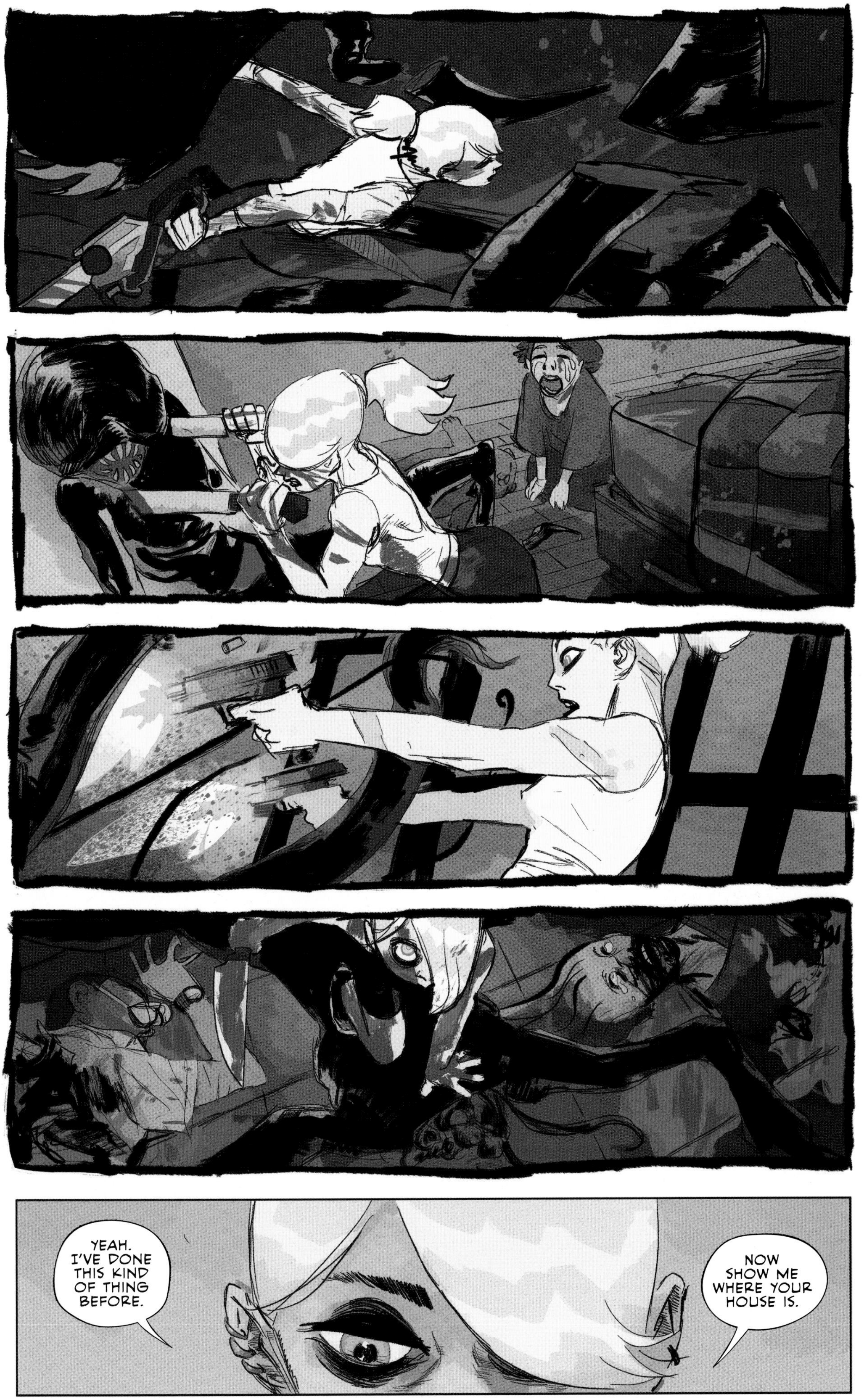
YEAH. I'VE DONE THIS KIND OF THING BEFORE.
NOW SHOW ME WHERE YOUR HOUSE IS.

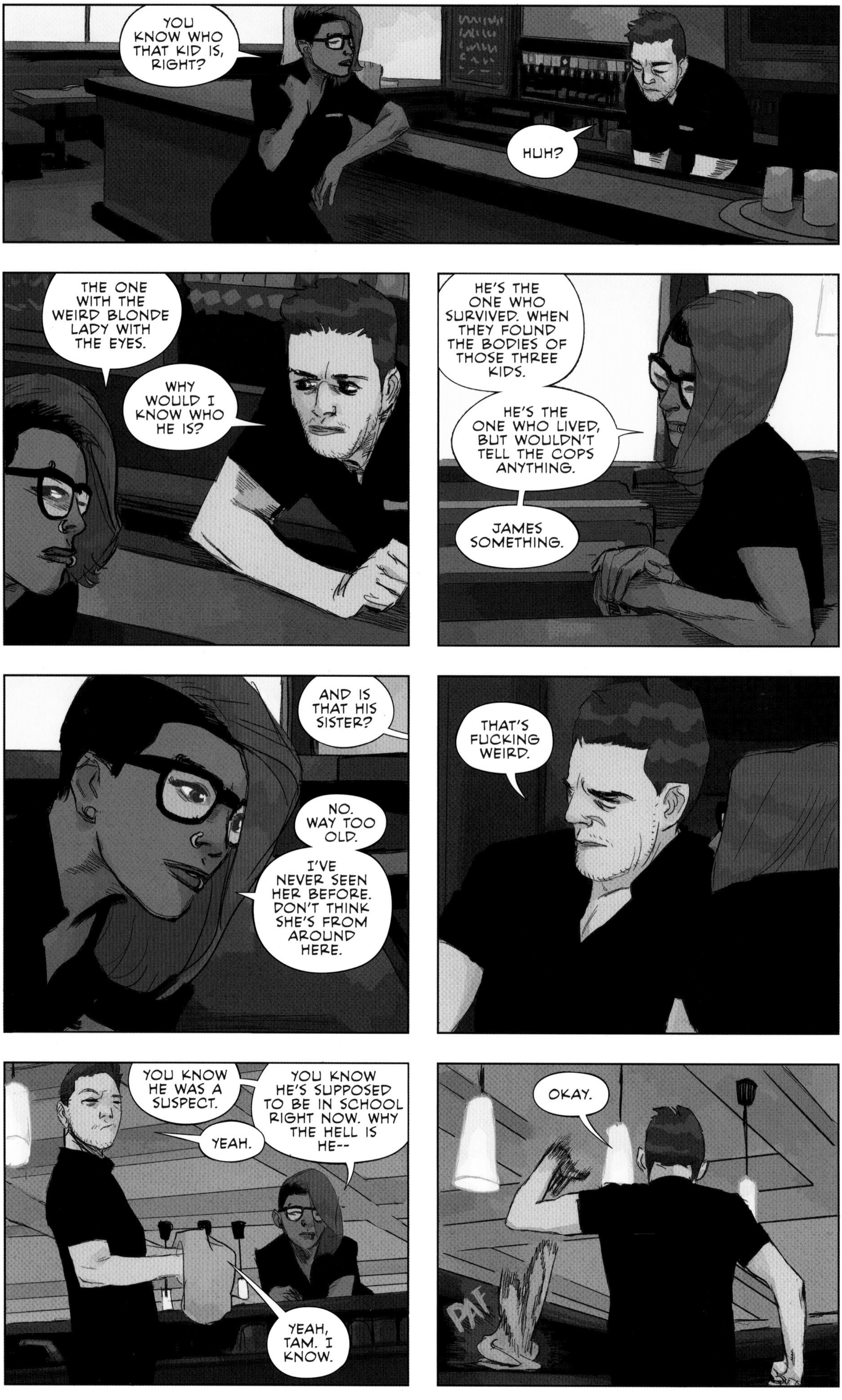
YOU KNOW WHO THAT KID IS, RIGHT?
HUH?
THE ONE WITH THE WEIRD BLONDE LADY WITH THE EYES.
WHY WOULD I KNOW WHO HE IS?
HE'S THE ONE WHO SURVIVED. WHEN THEY FOUND THE BODIES OF THOSE THREE KIDS.
HE'S THE ONE WHO LIVED, BUT WOULDN'T TELL THE COPS ANYTHING.
JAMES SOMETHING.
AND IS THAT HIS SISTER?
NO. WAY TOO OLD.
I'VE NEVER SEEN HER BEFORE. DON'T THINK SHE'S FROM AROUND HERE.
THAT'S FUCKING WEIRD.
YOU KNOW HE WAS A SUSPECT.
YEAH.
YOU KNOW HE'S SUPPOSED TO BE IN SCHOOL RIGHT NOW. WHY THE HELL IS HE--
YEAH, TAM. I KNOW.
OKAY.
PAF

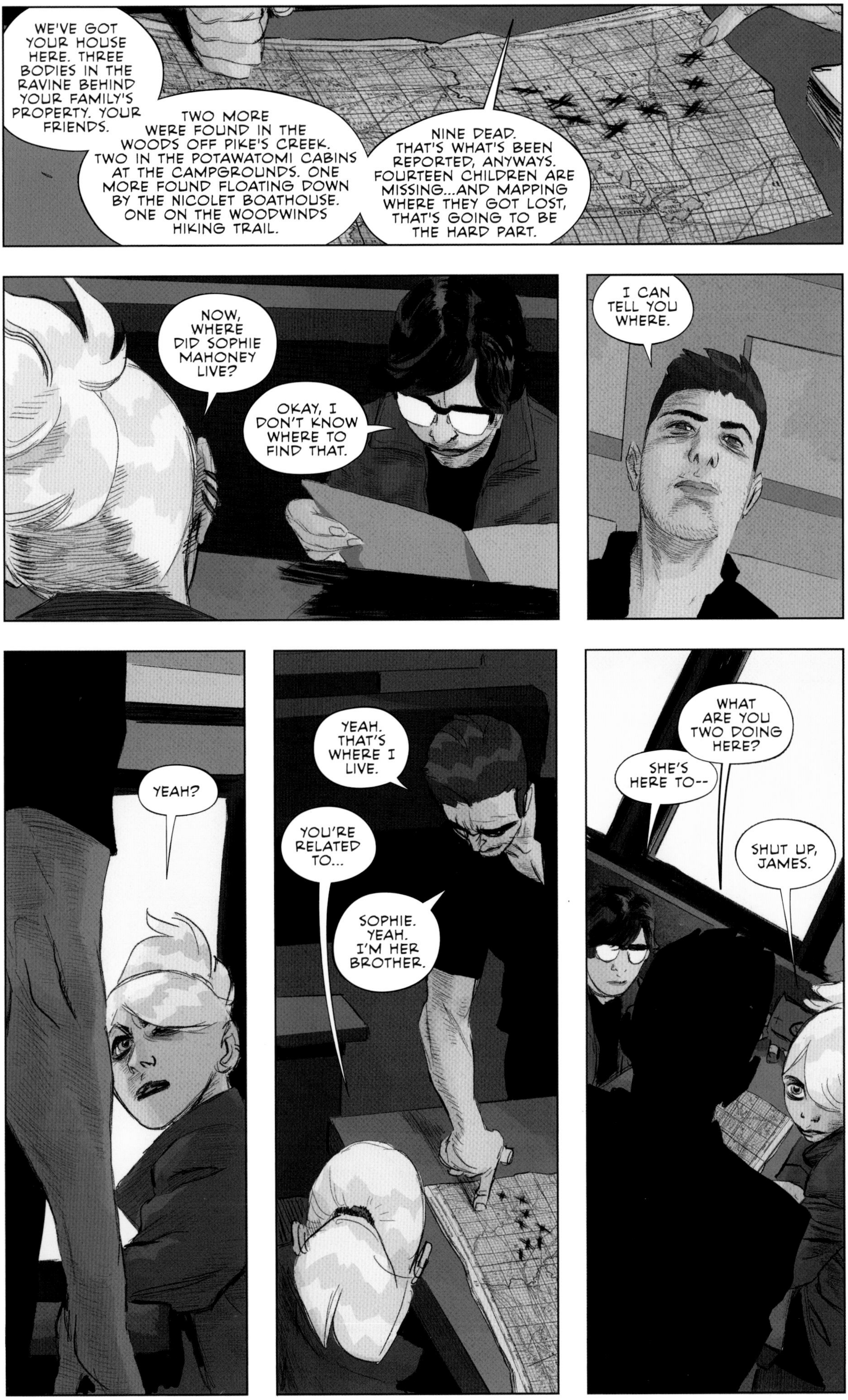
WE'VE GOT YOUR HOUSE HERE. THREE BODIES IN THE RAVINE BEHIND YOUR FAMILY'S PROPERTY. YOUR FRIENDS.
TWO MORE WERE FOUND IN THE WOODS OFF PIKE'S CREEK. TWO IN THE POTAWATOMI CABINS AT THE CAMPGROUNDS. ONE MORE FOUND FLOATING DOWN BY THE NICOLET BOATHOUSE. ONE ON THE WOODWINDS HIKING TRAIL.
NINE DEAD. THAT'S WHAT'S BEEN REPORTED, ANYWAYS. FOURTEEN CHILDREN ARE MISSING...AND MAPPING WHERE THEY GOT LOST, THAT'S GOING TO BE THE HARD PART.
NOW, WHERE DID SOPHIE MAHONEY LIVE?
OKAY, I DON'T KNOW WHERE TO FIND THAT.
I CAN TELL YOU WHERE.
YEAH?
YEAH. THAT'S WHERE I LIVE.
YOU'RE RELATED TO...
SOPHIE. YEAH. I'M HER BROTHER.
WHAT ARE YOU TWO DOING HERE?
SHE'S HERE TO--
SHUT UP, JAMES.

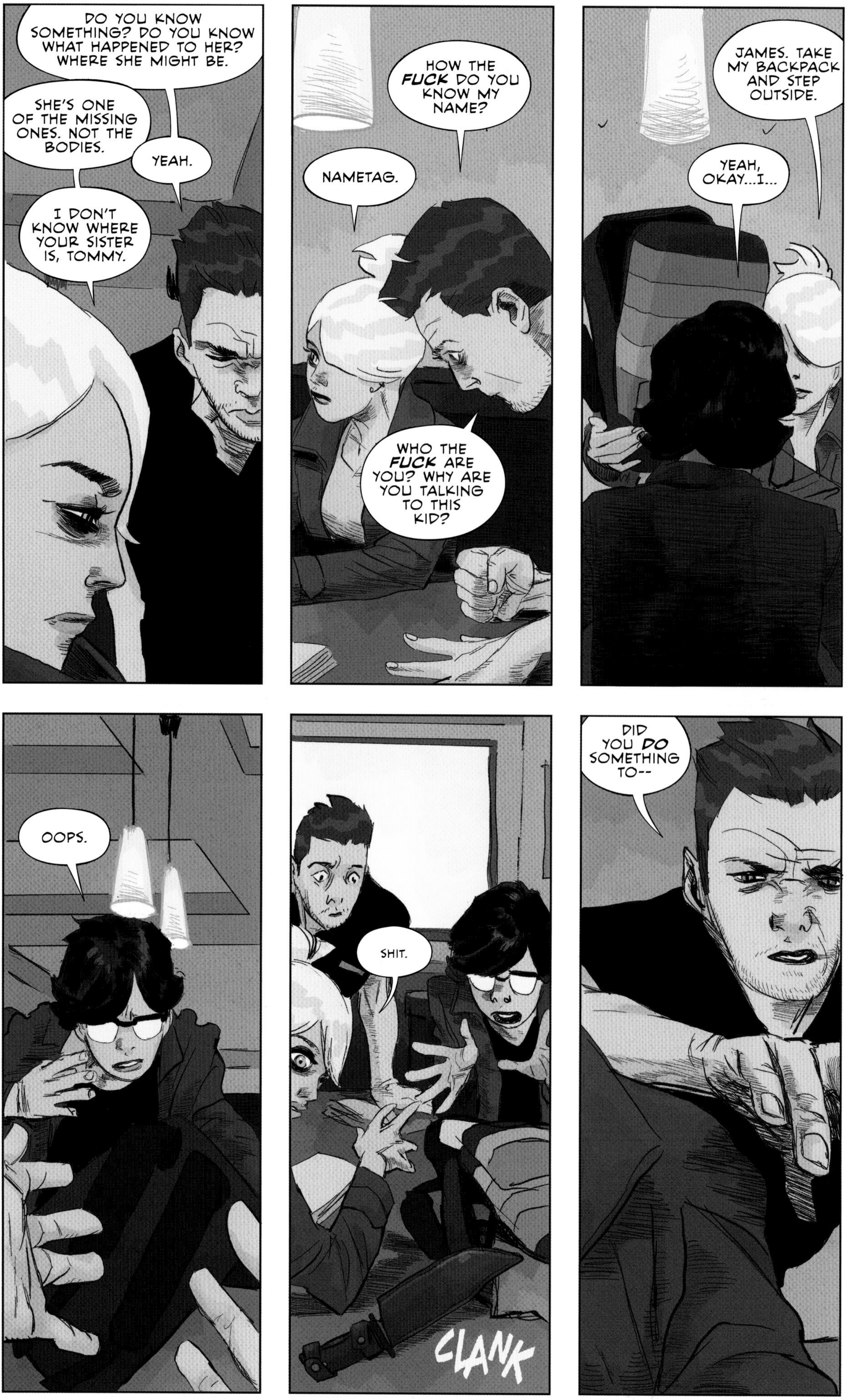
DO YOU KNOW SOMETHING? DO YOU KNOW WHAT HAPPENED TO HER? WHERE SHE MIGHT BE.
SHE'S ONE OF THE MISSING ONES. NOT THE BODIES.
YEAH.
I DON'T KNOW WHERE YOUR SISTER IS, TOMMY.
HOW THE FUCK DO YOU KNOW MY NAME?
NAMETAG.
WHO THE FUCK ARE YOU? WHY ARE YOU TALKING TO THIS KID?
JAMES. TAKE MY BACKPACK AND STEP OUTSIDE.
YEAH, OKAY...I...
OOPS.
SHIT.
CLANK
DID YOU DO SOMETHING TO--

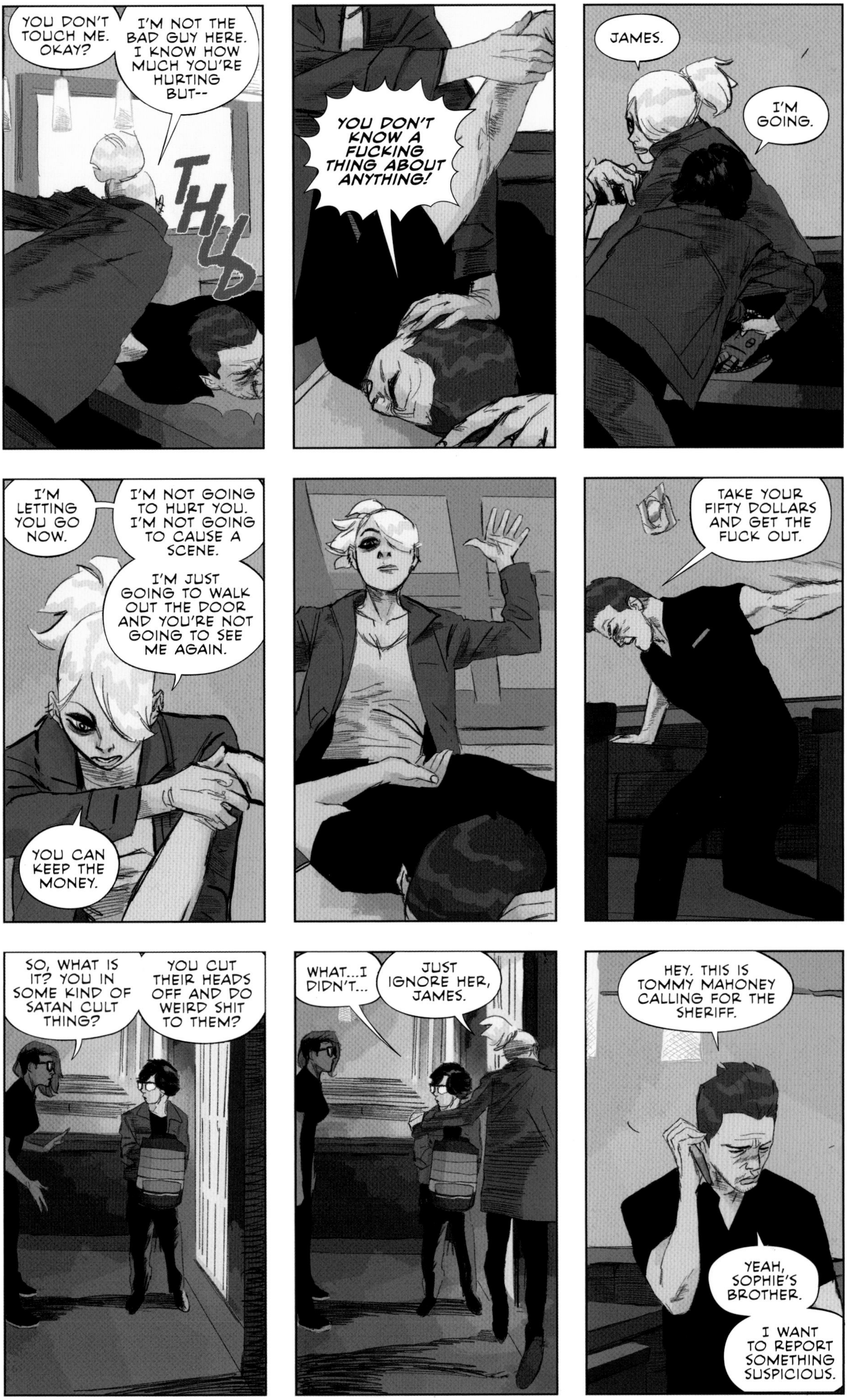
YOU DON'T TOUCH ME. OKAY?
I'M NOT THE BAD GUY HERE. I KNOW HOW MUCH YOU'RE HURTING BUT--
THUD
YOU DON'T KNOW A FUCKING THING ABOUT ANYTHING!
JAMES.
I'M GOING.
I'M LETTING YOU GO NOW.
I'M NOT GOING TO HURT YOU. I'M NOT GOING TO CAUSE A SCENE.
I'M JUST GOING TO WALK OUT THE DOOR AND YOU'RE NOT GOING TO SEE ME AGAIN.
YOU CAN KEEP THE MONEY.
TAKE YOUR FIFTY DOLLARS AND GET THE FUCK OUT.
SO, WHAT IS IT? YOU IN SOME KIND OF SATAN CULT THING?
YOU CUT THEIR HEADS OFF AND DO WEIRD SHIT TO THEM?
WHAT...I DIDN'T...
JUST IGNORE HER, JAMES.
HEY. THIS IS TOMMY MAHONEY CALLING FOR THE SHERIFF.
YEAH, SOPHIE'S BROTHER.
I WANT TO REPORT SOMETHING SUSPICIOUS.

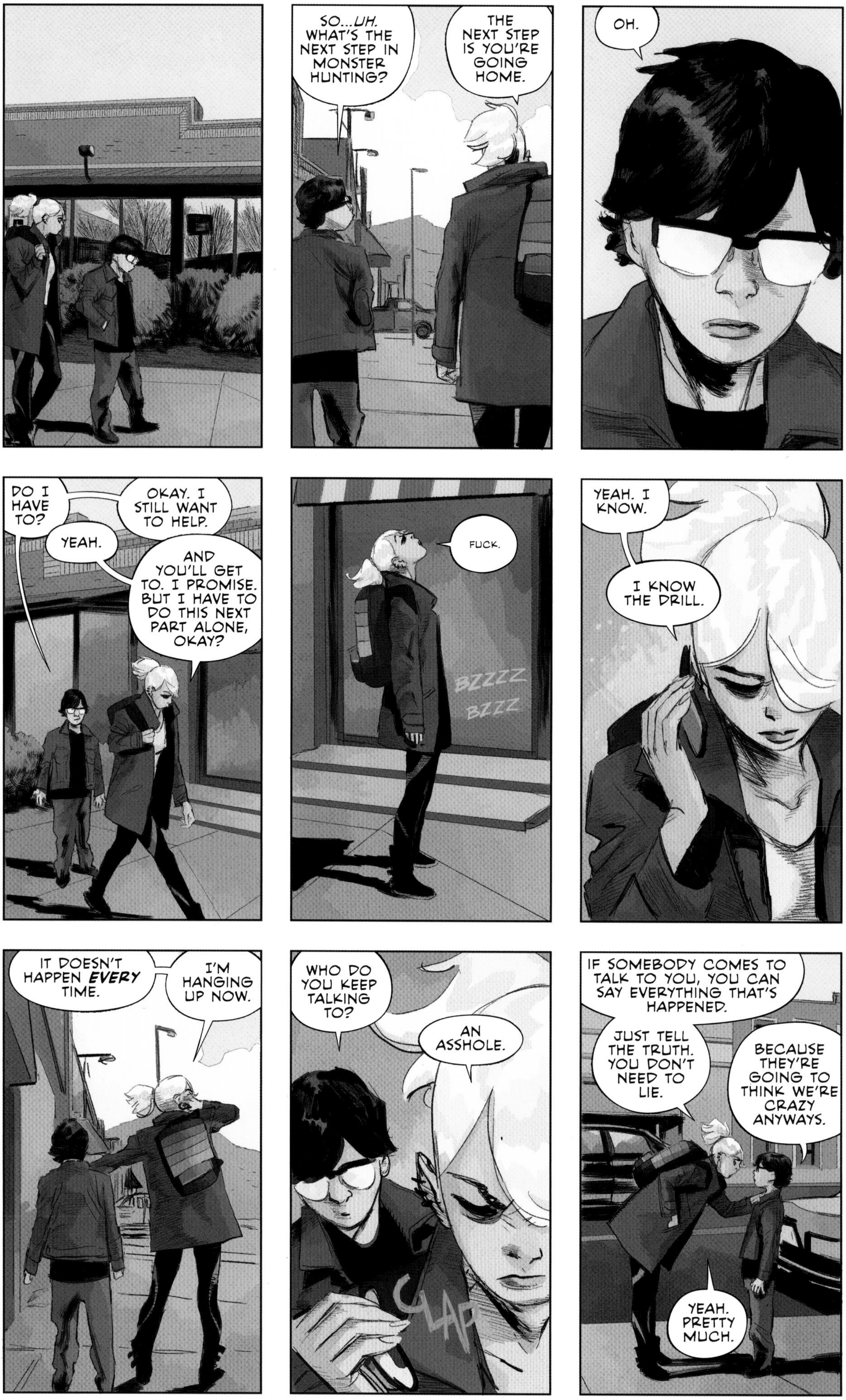
SO...UH. WHAT'S THE NEXT STEP IN MONSTER HUNTING?
THE NEXT STEP IS YOU'RE GOING HOME.
OH.
DO I HAVE TO?
YEAH.
OKAY. I STILL WANT TO HELP.
AND YOU'LL GET TO. I PROMISE. BUT I HAVE TO DO THIS NEXT PART ALONE, OKAY?
FUCK.
BZZZZ
BZZZ
YEAH. I KNOW.
I KNOW THE DRILL.
IT DOESN'T HAPPEN EVERY TIME.
I'M HANGING UP NOW.
WHO DO YOU KEEP TALKING TO?
AN ASSHOLE.
CLAP
IF SOMEBODY COMES TO TALK TO YOU, YOU CAN SAY EVERYTHING THAT'S HAPPENED.
JUST TELL THE TRUTH. YOU DON'T NEED TO LIE.
BECAUSE THEY'RE GOING TO THINK WE'RE CRAZY ANYWAYS.
YEAH. PRETTY MUCH.

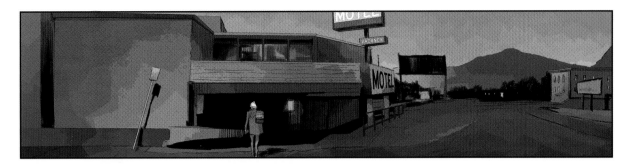

YOU HAD A CALL.

YEAH?

YEAH.

TOO BAD THEY MISSED ME.

HEY, I DON'T WANT TROUBLE.

ME NEITHER.

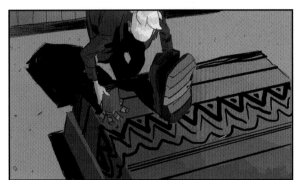

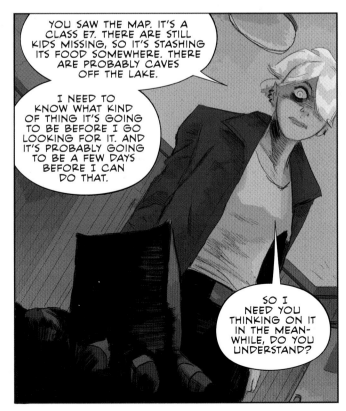

YOU SAW THE MAP. IT'S A CLASS E7. THERE ARE STILL KIDS MISSING, SO IT'S STASHING ITS FOOD SOMEWHERE. THERE ARE PROBABLY CAVES OFF THE LAKE.

I NEED TO KNOW WHAT KIND OF THING IT'S GOING TO BE BEFORE I GO LOOKING FOR IT. AND IT'S PROBABLY GOING TO BE A FEW DAYS BEFORE I CAN DO THAT.

SO I NEED YOU THINKING ON IT IN THE MEAN-WHILE, DO YOU UNDERSTAND?

YES.

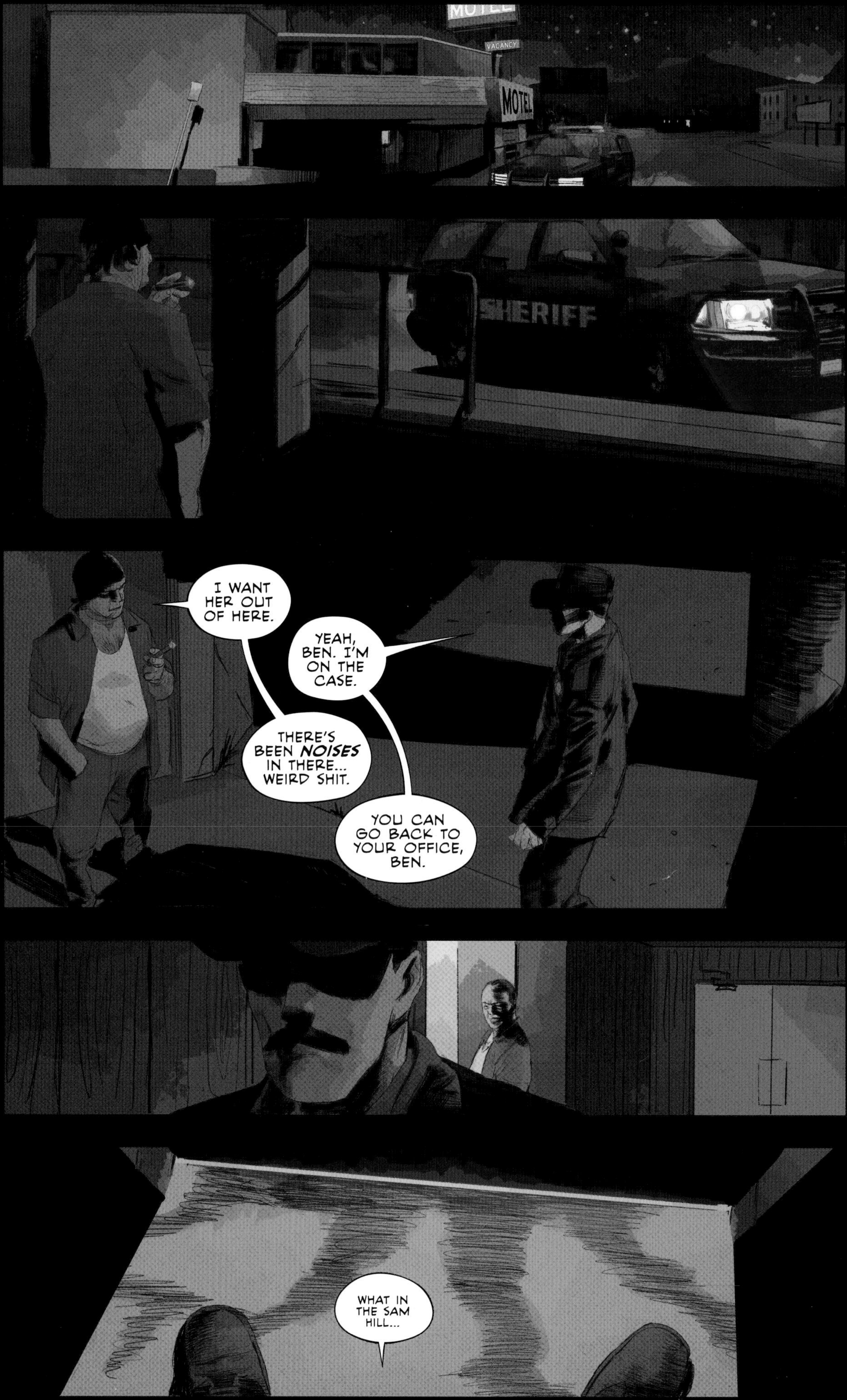
MOTEL
VACANCY
MOTEL
SHERIFF
I WANT HER OUT OF HERE.
YEAH, BEN. I'M ON THE CASE.
THERE'S BEEN *NOISES* IN THERE... WEIRD SHIT.
YOU CAN GO BACK TO YOUR OFFICE, BEN.
WHAT IN THE SAM HILL...

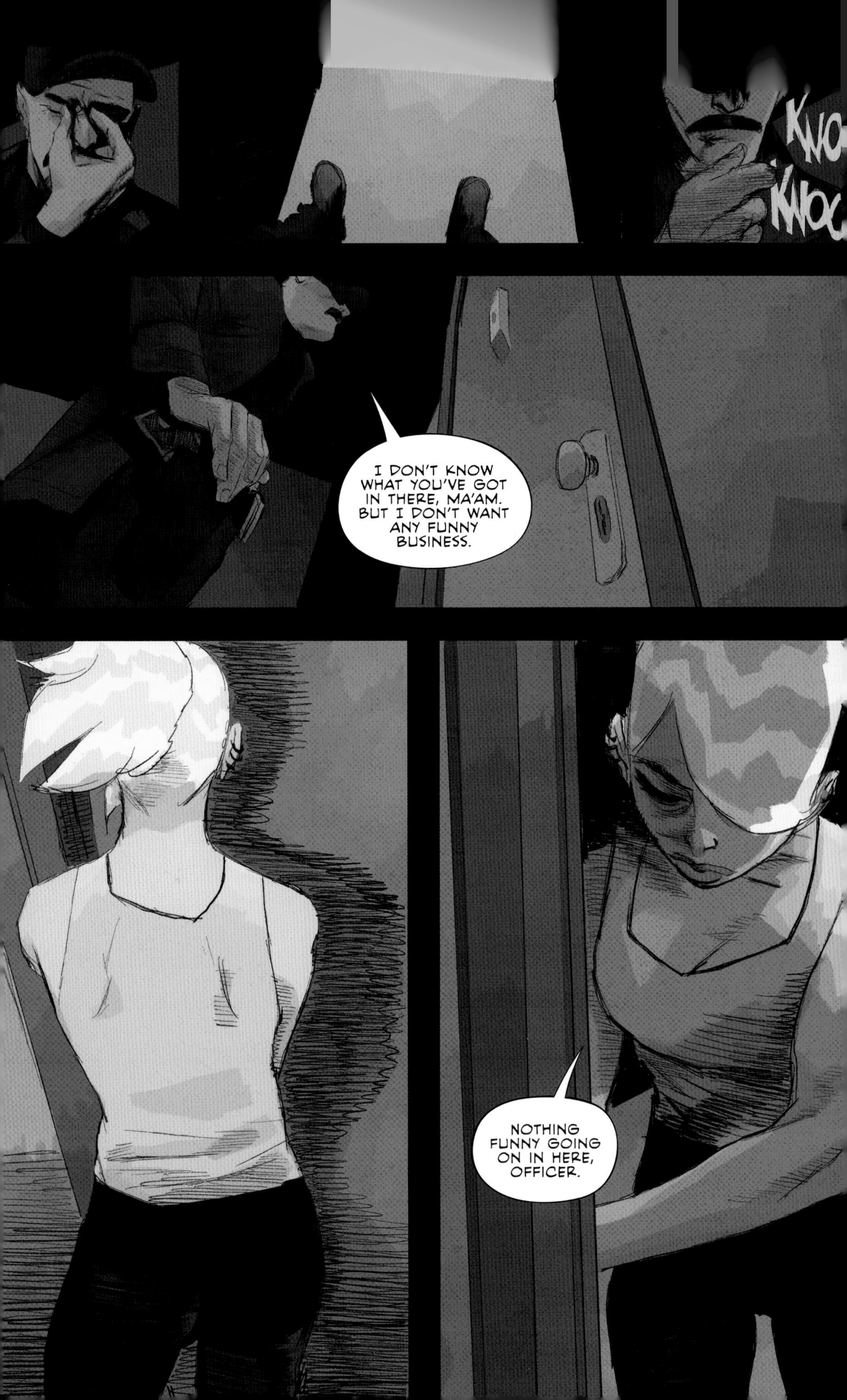
KNOC KNOC
I DON'T KNOW WHAT YOU'VE GOT IN THERE, MA'AM. BUT I DON'T WANT ANY FUNNY BUSINESS.
NOTHING FUNNY GOING ON IN HERE, OFFICER.

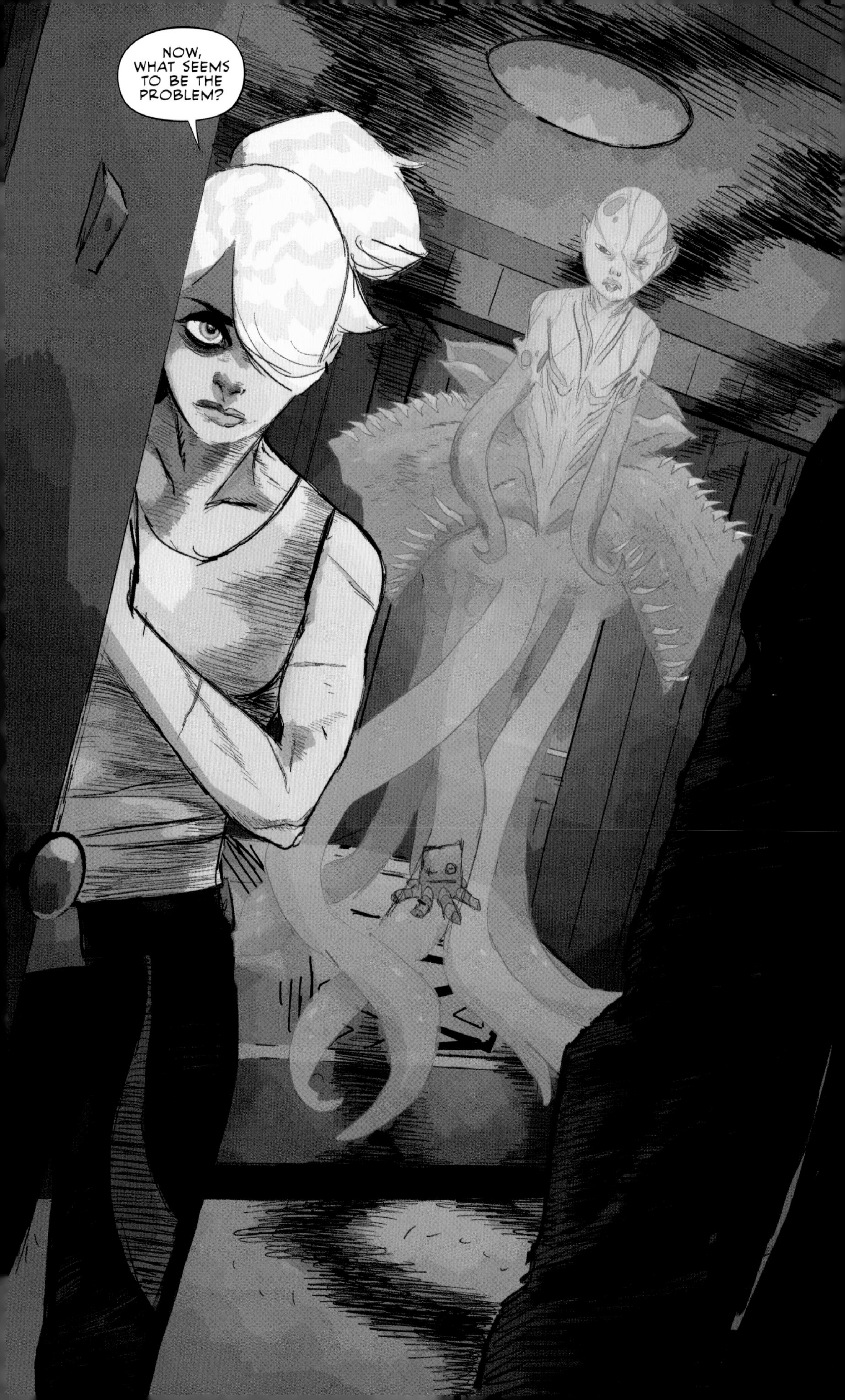
NOW, WHAT SEEMS TO BE THE PROBLEM?

CHAPTER THREE

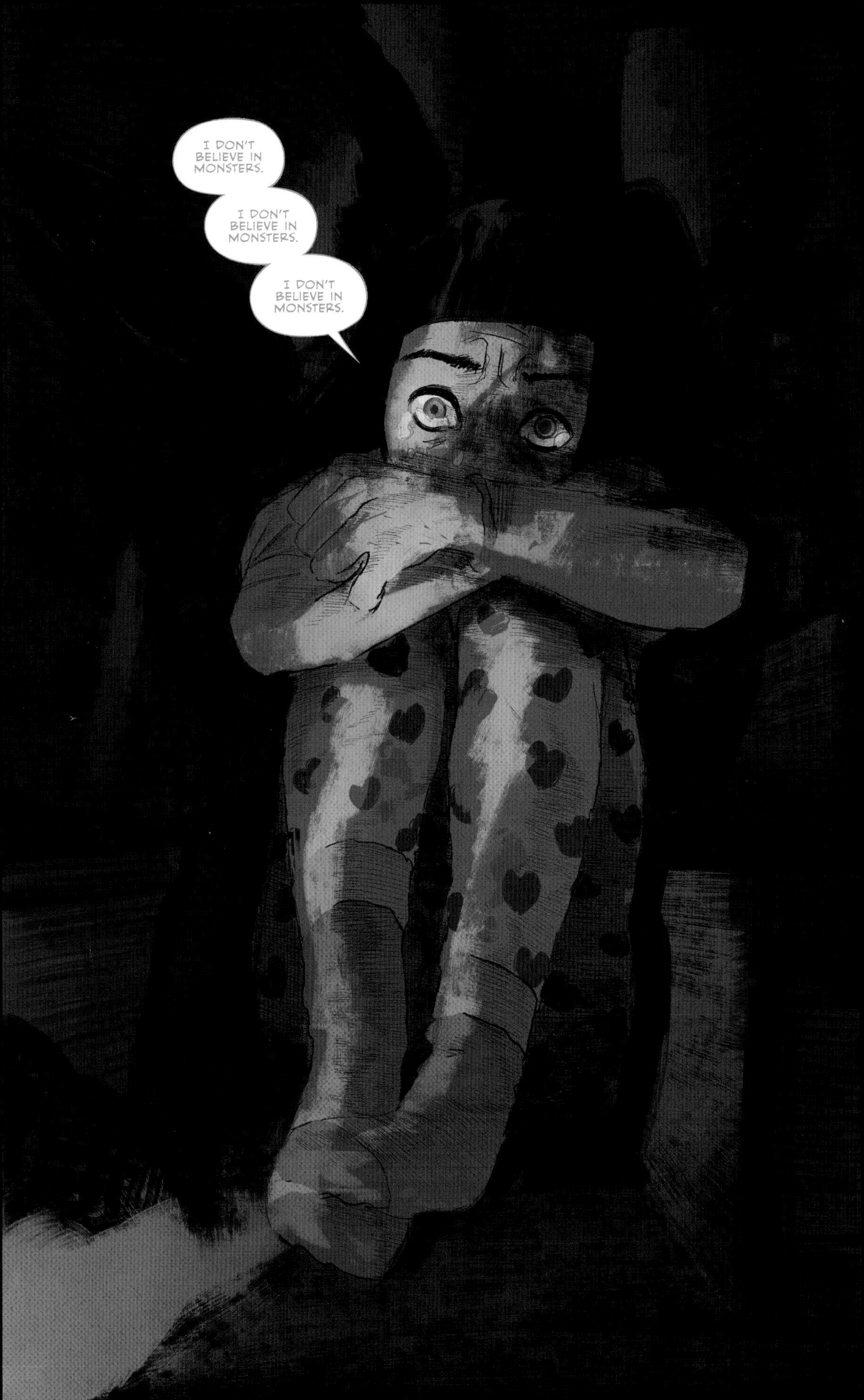
I DON'T BELIEVE IN MONSTERS.
I DON'T BELIEVE IN MONSTERS.
I DON'T BELIEVE IN MONSTERS.

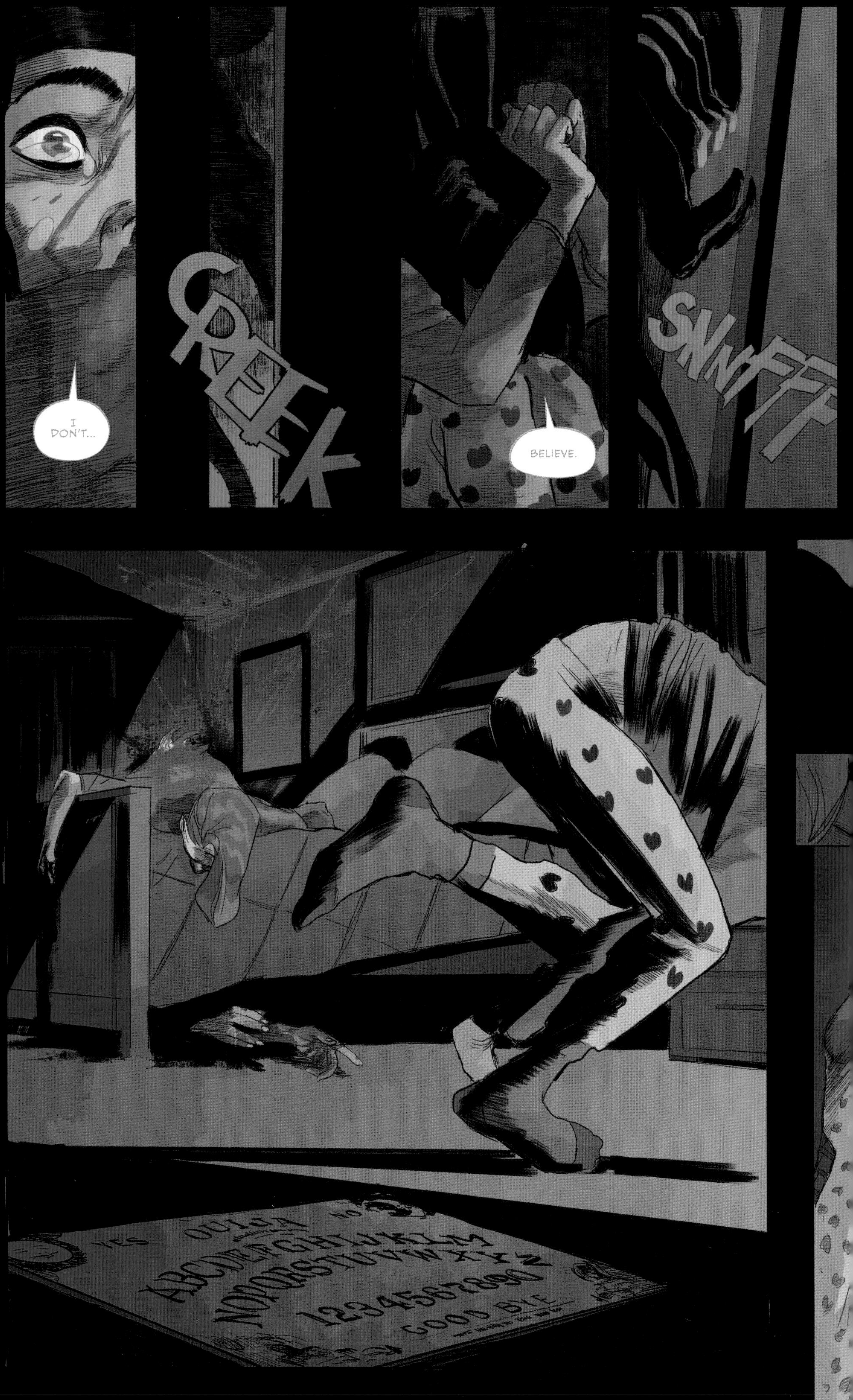
I DON'T...
CREEEK
BELIEVE.
SNNIFFF
YES
OUIJA
NO
ABCDEFGHIJKLM
NOPQRSTUVWXYZ
1234567890
GOOD BYE

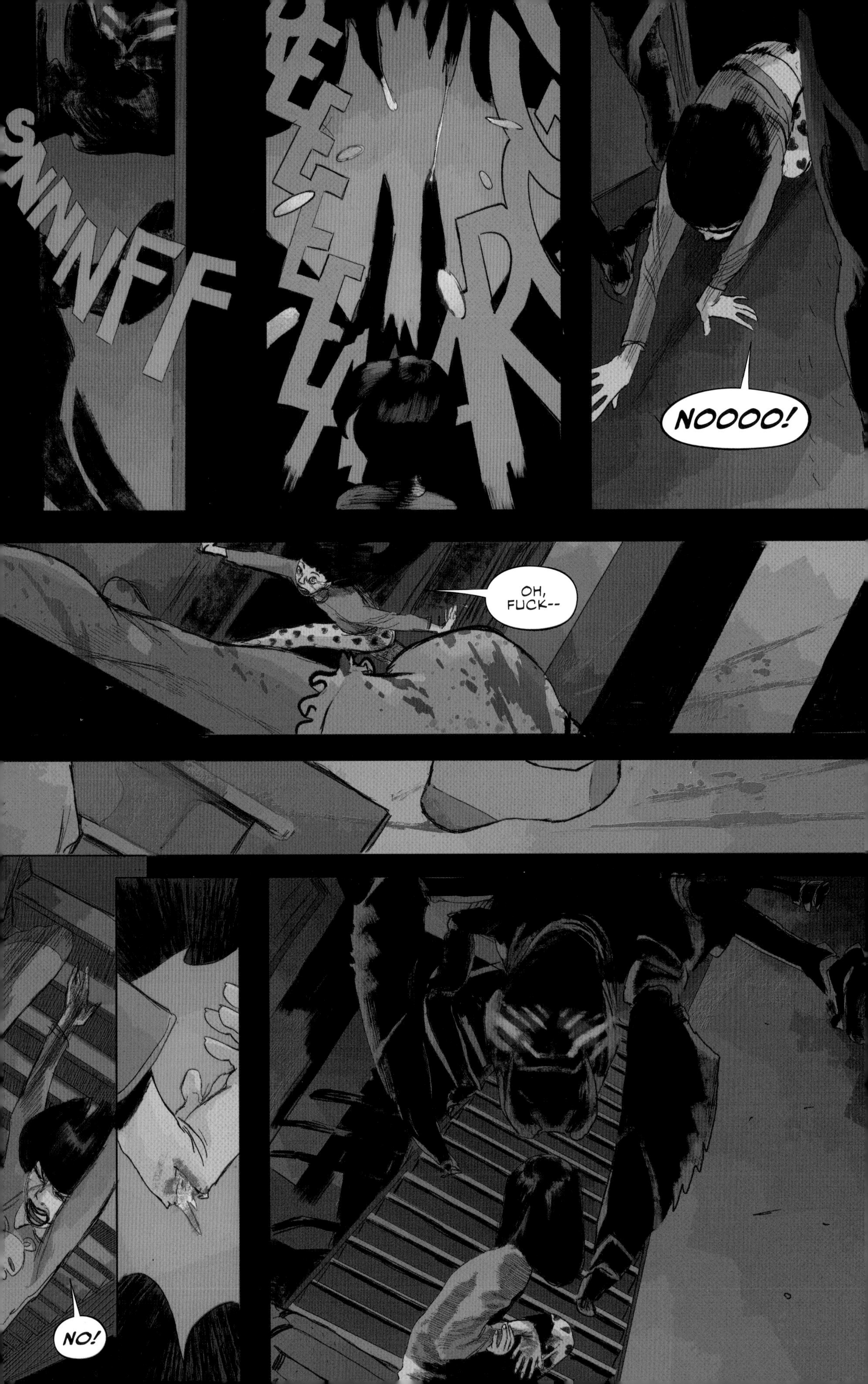
SNNNFF
NOOOO!
OH, FUCK--
NO!

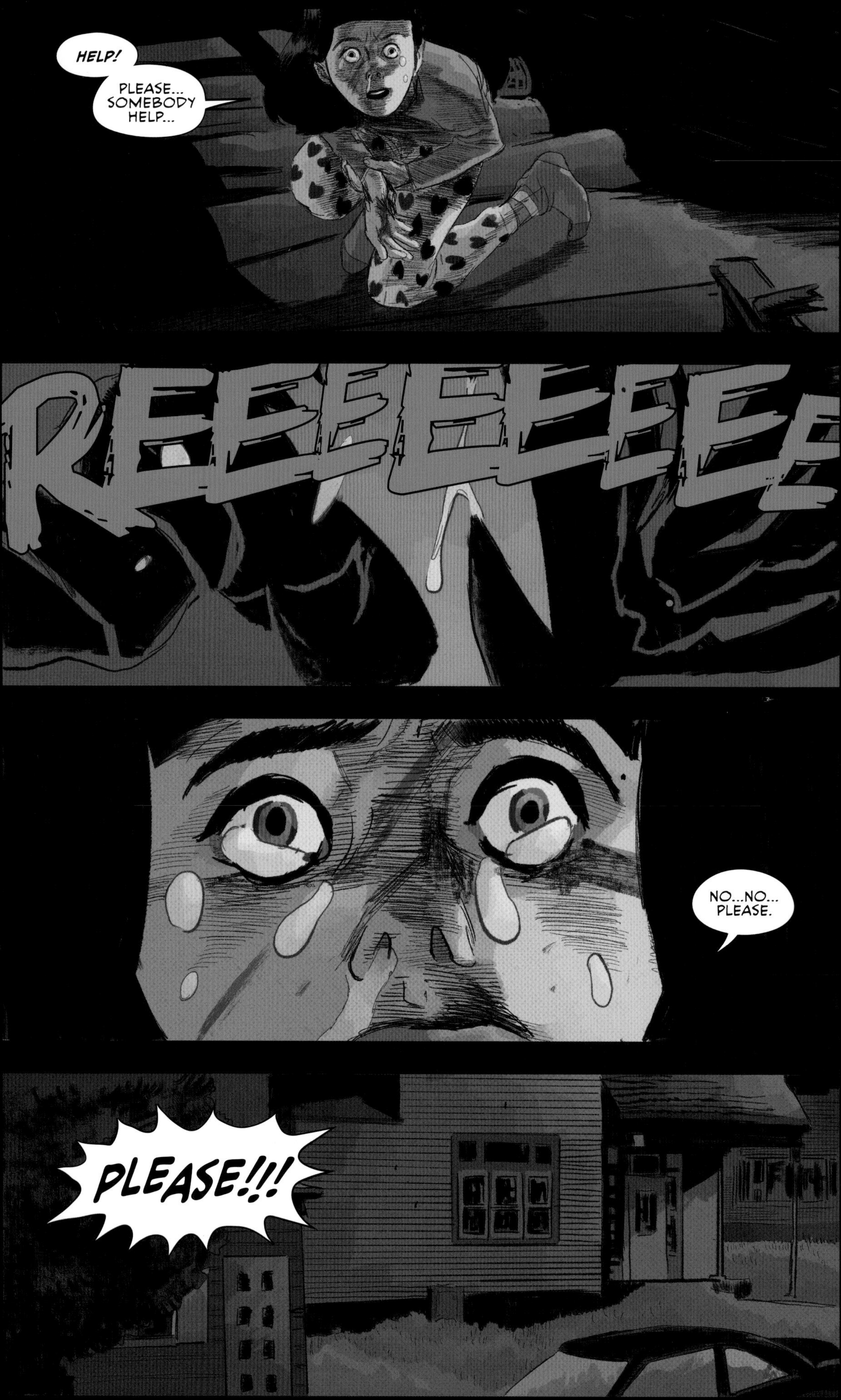
HELP!
PLEASE... SOMEBODY HELP...
REEEEEEEEEE
NO...NO... PLEASE.
PLEASE!!!

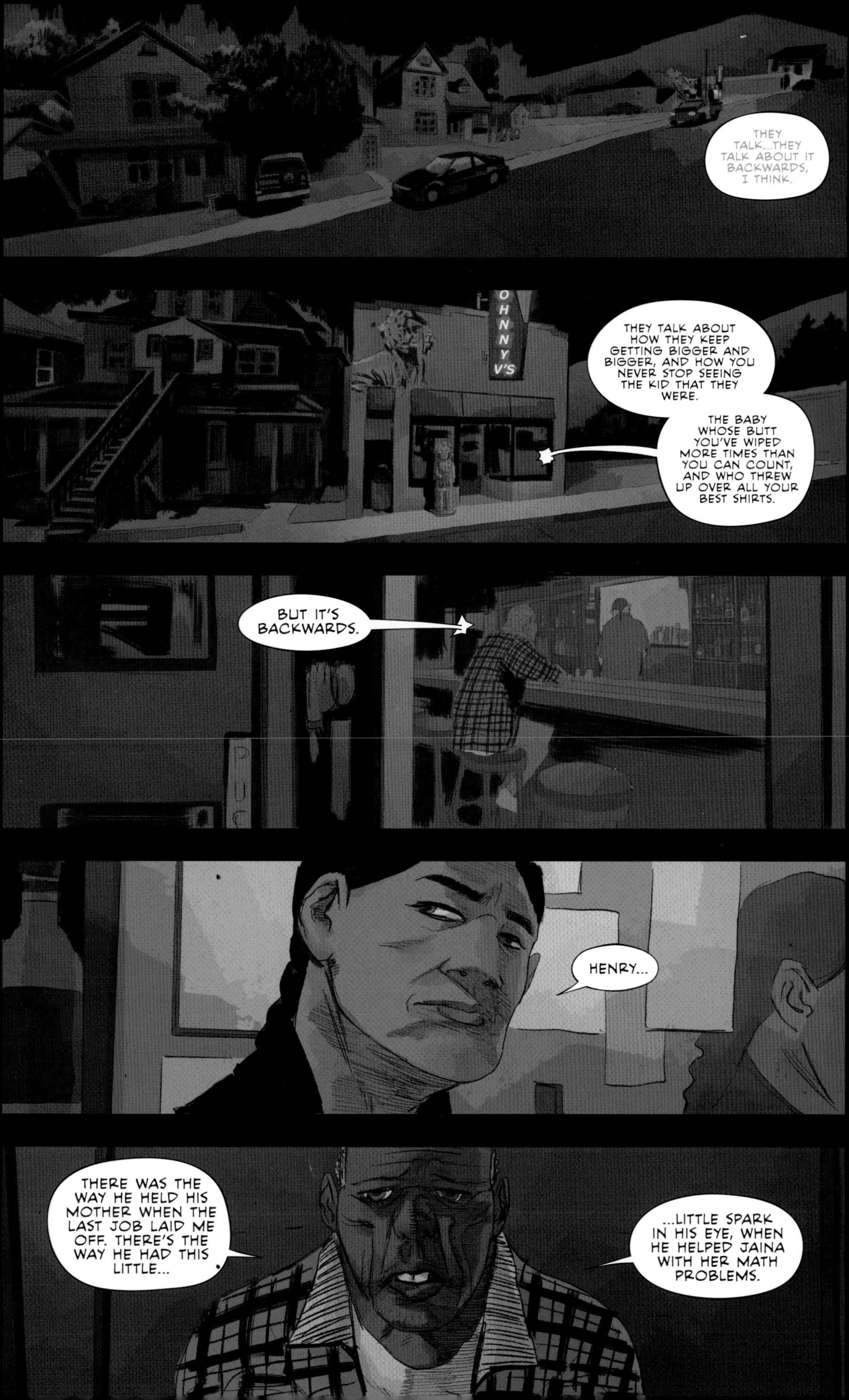

THEY TALK...THEY TALK ABOUT IT BACKWARDS, I THINK.
OHNNY V'S
THEY TALK ABOUT HOW THEY KEEP GETTING BIGGER AND BIGGER, AND HOW YOU NEVER STOP SEEING THE KID THAT THEY WERE.
THE BABY WHOSE BUTT YOU'VE WIPED MORE TIMES THAN YOU CAN COUNT, AND WHO THREW UP OVER ALL YOUR BEST SHIRTS.
BUT IT'S BACKWARDS.
HENRY...
THERE WAS THE WAY HE HELD HIS MOTHER WHEN THE LAST JOB LAID ME OFF. THERE'S THE WAY HE HAD THIS LITTLE...
...LITTLE SPARK IN HIS EYE, WHEN HE HELPED JAINA WITH HER MATH PROBLEMS.

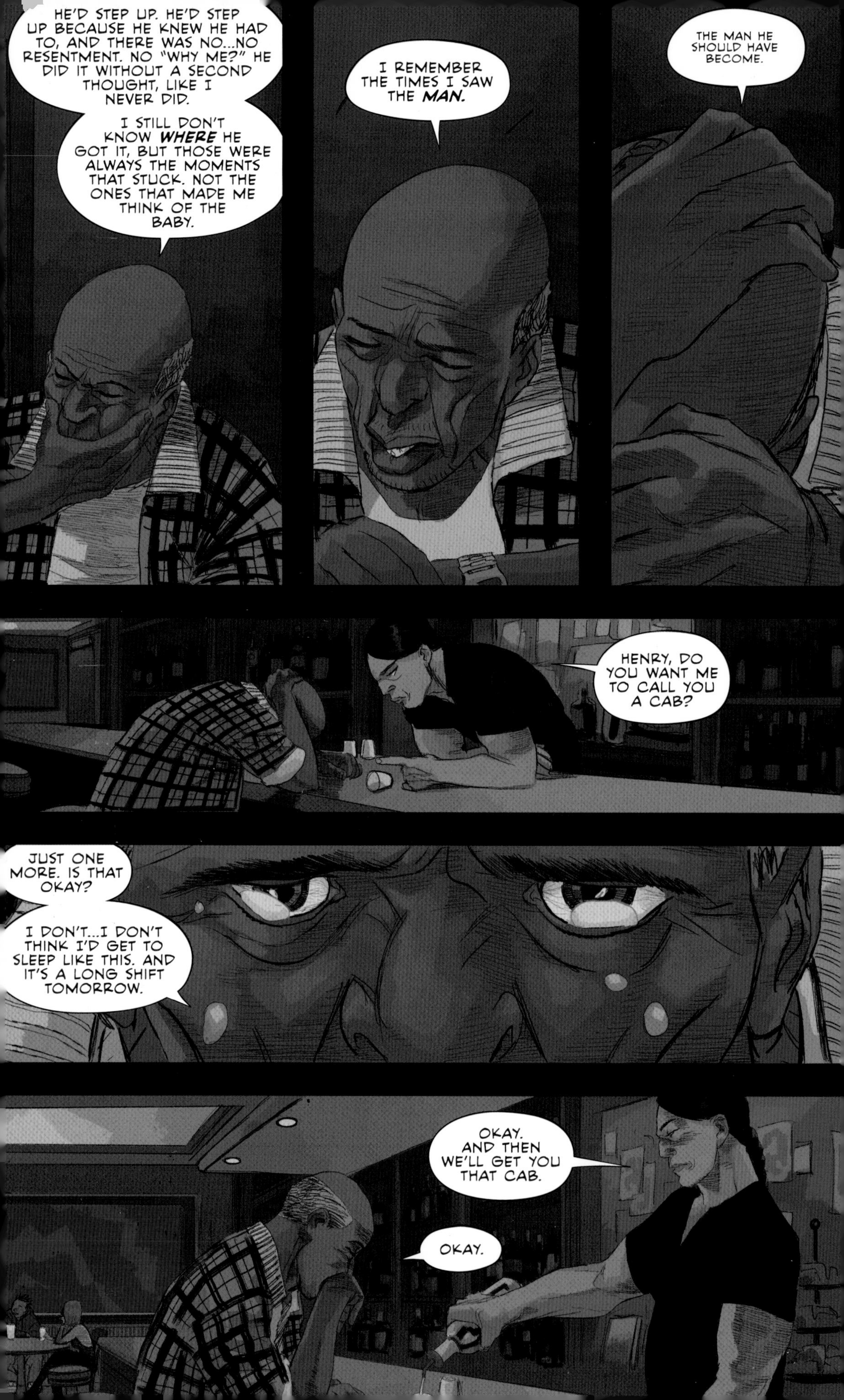
HE'D STEP UP. HE'D STEP UP BECAUSE HE KNEW HE HAD TO, AND THERE WAS NO...NO RESENTMENT. NO "WHY ME?" HE DID IT WITHOUT A SECOND THOUGHT, LIKE I NEVER DID.
I STILL DON'T KNOW WHERE HE GOT IT, BUT THOSE WERE ALWAYS THE MOMENTS THAT STUCK. NOT THE ONES THAT MADE ME THINK OF THE BABY.
I REMEMBER THE TIMES I SAW THE MAN.
THE MAN HE SHOULD HAVE BECOME.
HENRY, DO YOU WANT ME TO CALL YOU A CAB?
JUST ONE MORE. IS THAT OKAY?
I DON'T...I DON'T THINK I'D GET TO SLEEP LIKE THIS. AND IT'S A LONG SHIFT TOMORROW.
OKAY. AND THEN WE'LL GET YOU THAT CAB.
OKAY.

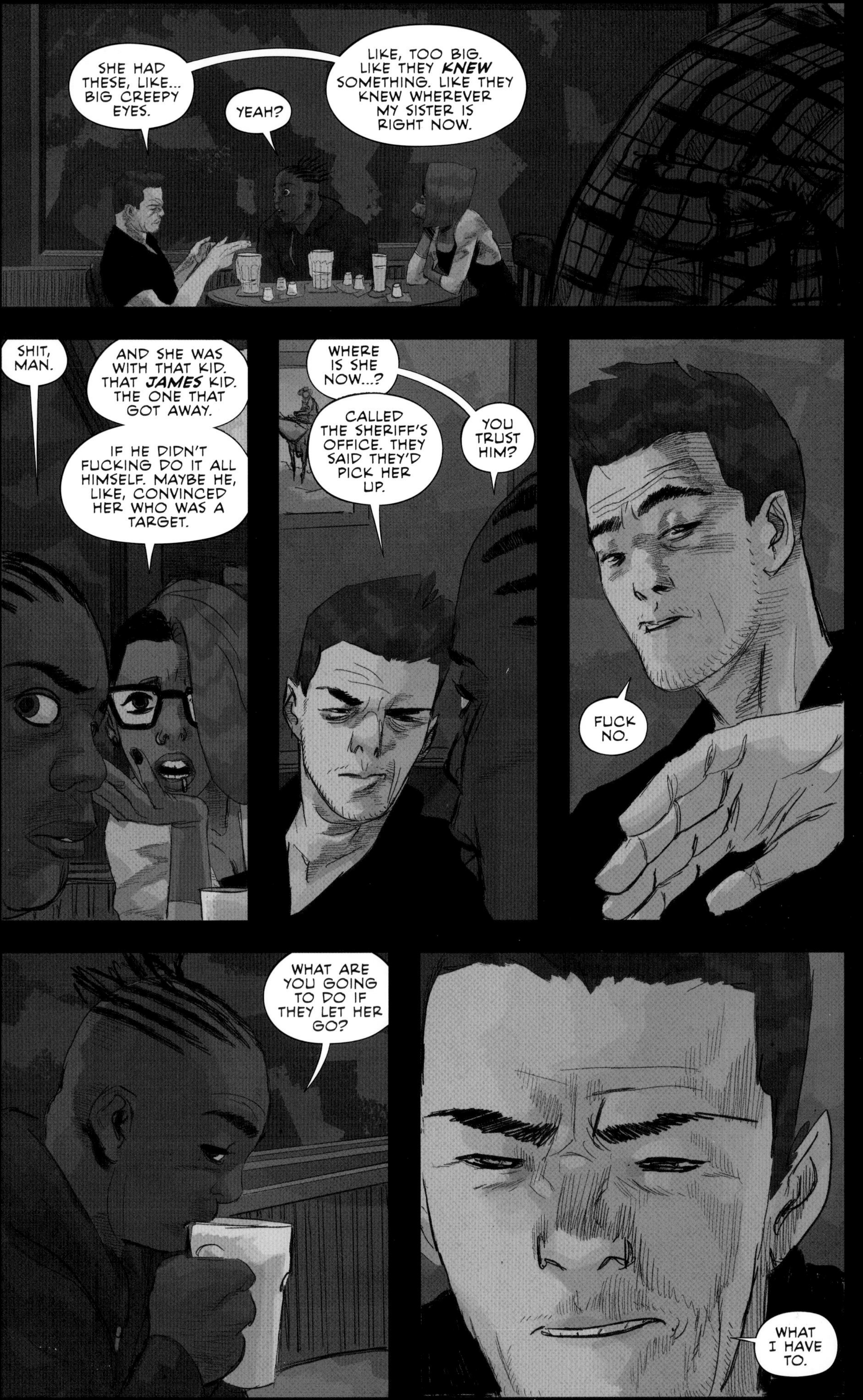
SHE HAD THESE, LIKE... BIG CREEPY EYES.
YEAH?
LIKE, TOO BIG. LIKE THEY *KNEW* SOMETHING. LIKE THEY KNEW WHEREVER MY SISTER IS RIGHT NOW.
SHIT, MAN.
AND SHE WAS WITH THAT KID. THAT *JAMES* KID. THE ONE THAT GOT AWAY.
IF HE DIDN'T FUCKING DO IT ALL HIMSELF. MAYBE HE, LIKE, CONVINCED HER WHO WAS A TARGET.
WHERE IS SHE NOW...?
CALLED THE SHERIFF'S OFFICE. THEY SAID THEY'D PICK HER UP.
YOU TRUST HIM?
FUCK NO.
WHAT ARE YOU GOING TO DO IF THEY LET HER GO?
WHAT I HAVE TO.

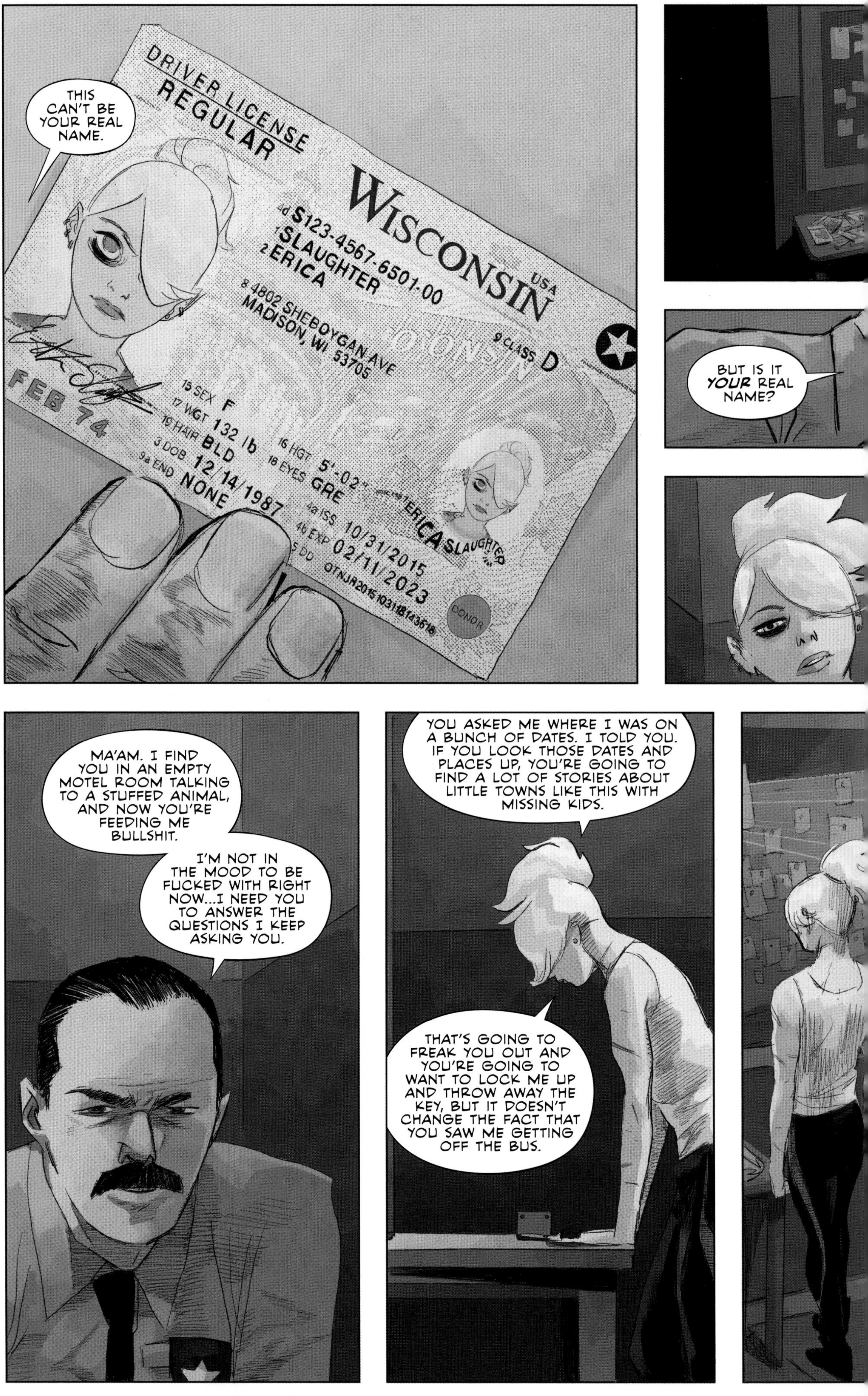
THIS CAN'T BE YOUR REAL NAME.
DRIVER LICENSE
REGULAR
WISCONSIN
USA
S123-4567-6501-00
SLAUGHTER
ERICA
4802 SHEBOYGAN AVE
MADISON, WI 53705
CLASS D
SEX F
WGT 132 lb
HAIR BLD
DOB 12/14/1987
END NONE
HGT 5'-02"
EYES GRE
ISS 10/31/2015
EXP 02/11/2023
FEB 74
ERICA SLAUGHTER
DONOR
BUT IS IT *YOUR* REAL NAME?
MA'AM. I FIND YOU IN AN EMPTY MOTEL ROOM TALKING TO A STUFFED ANIMAL, AND NOW YOU'RE FEEDING ME BULLSHIT.
I'M NOT IN THE MOOD TO BE FUCKED WITH RIGHT NOW...I NEED YOU TO ANSWER THE QUESTIONS I KEEP ASKING YOU.
YOU ASKED ME WHERE I WAS ON A BUNCH OF DATES. I TOLD YOU. IF YOU LOOK THOSE DATES AND PLACES UP, YOU'RE GOING TO FIND A LOT OF STORIES ABOUT LITTLE TOWNS LIKE THIS WITH MISSING KIDS.
THAT'S GOING TO FREAK YOU OUT AND YOU'RE GOING TO WANT TO LOCK ME UP AND THROW AWAY THE KEY, BUT IT DOESN'T CHANGE THE FACT THAT YOU SAW ME GETTING OFF THE BUS.

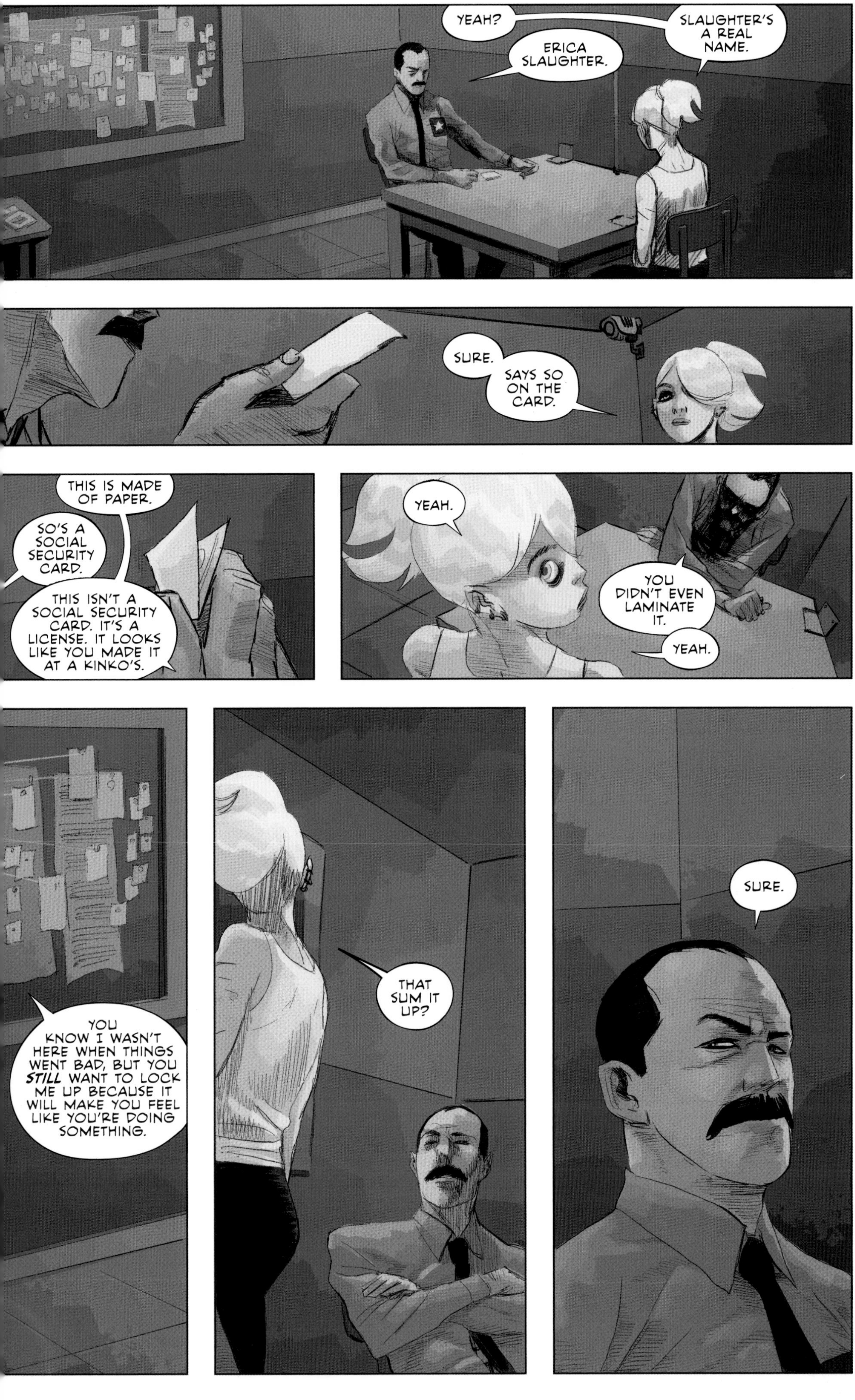
YEAH?
SLAUGHTER'S A REAL NAME.
ERICA SLAUGHTER.
SURE.
SAYS SO ON THE CARD.
THIS IS MADE OF PAPER.
SO'S A SOCIAL SECURITY CARD.
THIS ISN'T A SOCIAL SECURITY CARD. IT'S A LICENSE. IT LOOKS LIKE YOU MADE IT AT A KINKO'S.
YEAH.
YOU DIDN'T EVEN LAMINATE IT.
YEAH.
YOU KNOW I WASN'T HERE WHEN THINGS WENT BAD, BUT YOU *STILL* WANT TO LOCK ME UP BECAUSE IT WILL MAKE YOU FEEL LIKE YOU'RE DOING SOMETHING.
THAT SUM IT UP?
SURE.

WHO WENT MISSING FIRST?

EXCUSE ME?

THERE WERE PROBABLY A FEW CASES OF DISAPPEARANCES YOU WROTE OFF. BEFORE THERE WERE BODIES. BEFORE YOU KNEW THERE WAS SOMETHING KILLING THE CHILDREN.

THERE ARE KIDS MISSING THAT AREN'T ON THIS LIST BECAUSE YOU DON'T WANT THEM TO BE. BECAUSE YOU DON'T WANT TO GET CALLED OUT.

BUT YOU SEE...*YOU'RE* THE ONE WE'VE GOT LOCKED UP HERE.

YEAH, OKAY.

WHO WENT MISSING FIRST?

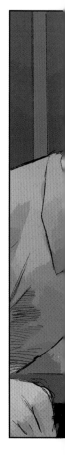

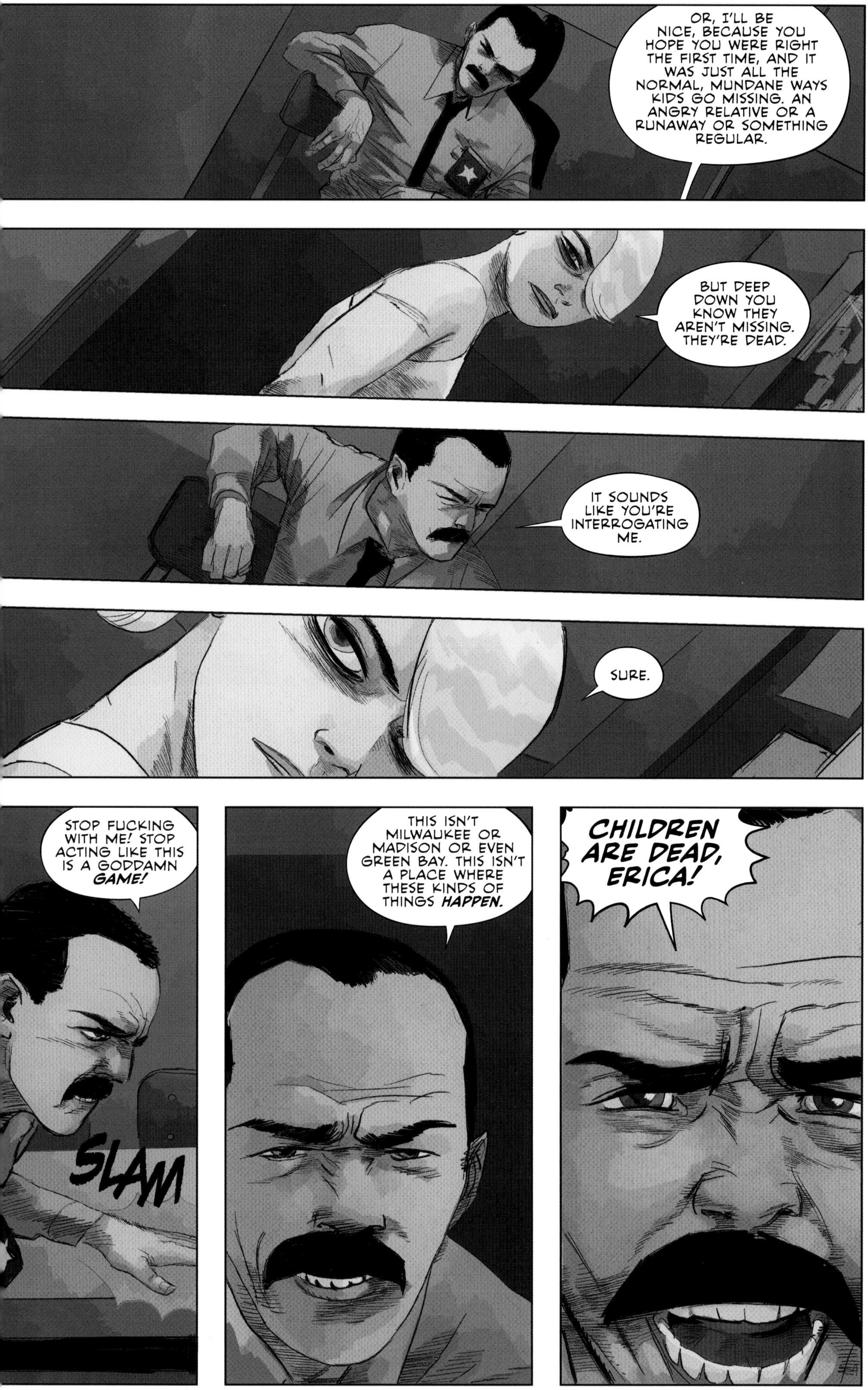
OR, I'LL BE NICE, BECAUSE YOU HOPE YOU WERE RIGHT THE FIRST TIME, AND IT WAS JUST ALL THE NORMAL, MUNDANE WAYS KIDS GO MISSING. AN ANGRY RELATIVE OR A RUNAWAY OR SOMETHING REGULAR.
BUT DEEP DOWN YOU KNOW THEY AREN'T MISSING. THEY'RE DEAD.
IT SOUNDS LIKE YOU'RE INTERROGATING ME.
SURE.
STOP FUCKING WITH ME! STOP ACTING LIKE THIS IS A GODDAMN *GAME!*
SLAM
THIS ISN'T MILWAUKEE OR MADISON OR EVEN GREEN BAY. THIS ISN'T A PLACE WHERE THESE KINDS OF THINGS *HAPPEN.*
CHILDREN ARE DEAD, ERICA!

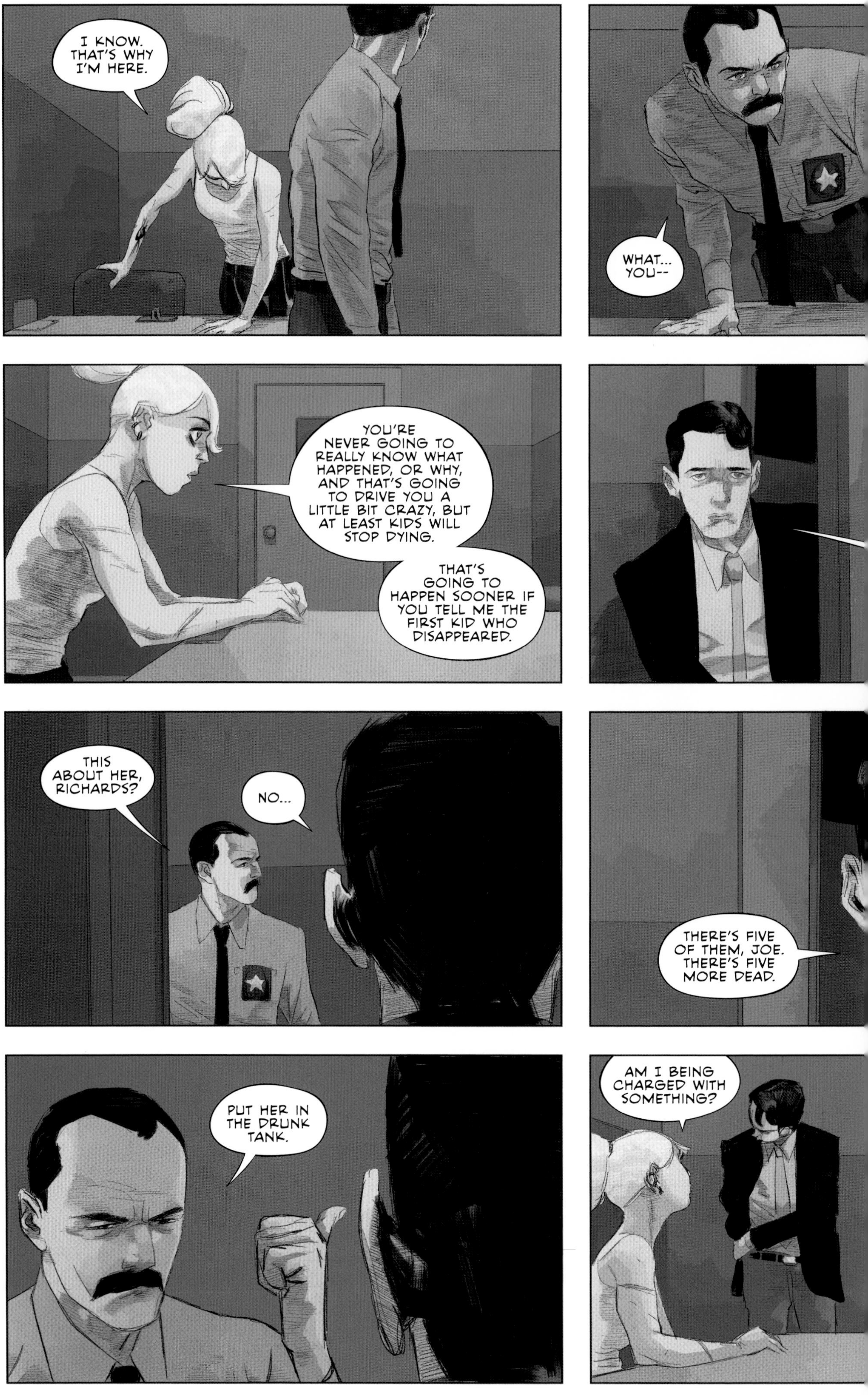
I KNOW. THAT'S WHY I'M HERE.
WHAT... YOU--
YOU'RE NEVER GOING TO REALLY KNOW WHAT HAPPENED, OR WHY, AND THAT'S GOING TO DRIVE YOU A LITTLE BIT CRAZY, BUT AT LEAST KIDS WILL STOP DYING.
THAT'S GOING TO HAPPEN SOONER IF YOU TELL ME THE FIRST KID WHO DISAPPEARED.
THIS ABOUT HER, RICHARDS?
NO...
THERE'S FIVE OF THEM, JOE. THERE'S FIVE MORE DEAD.
PUT HER IN THE DRUNK TANK.
AM I BEING CHARGED WITH SOMETHING?

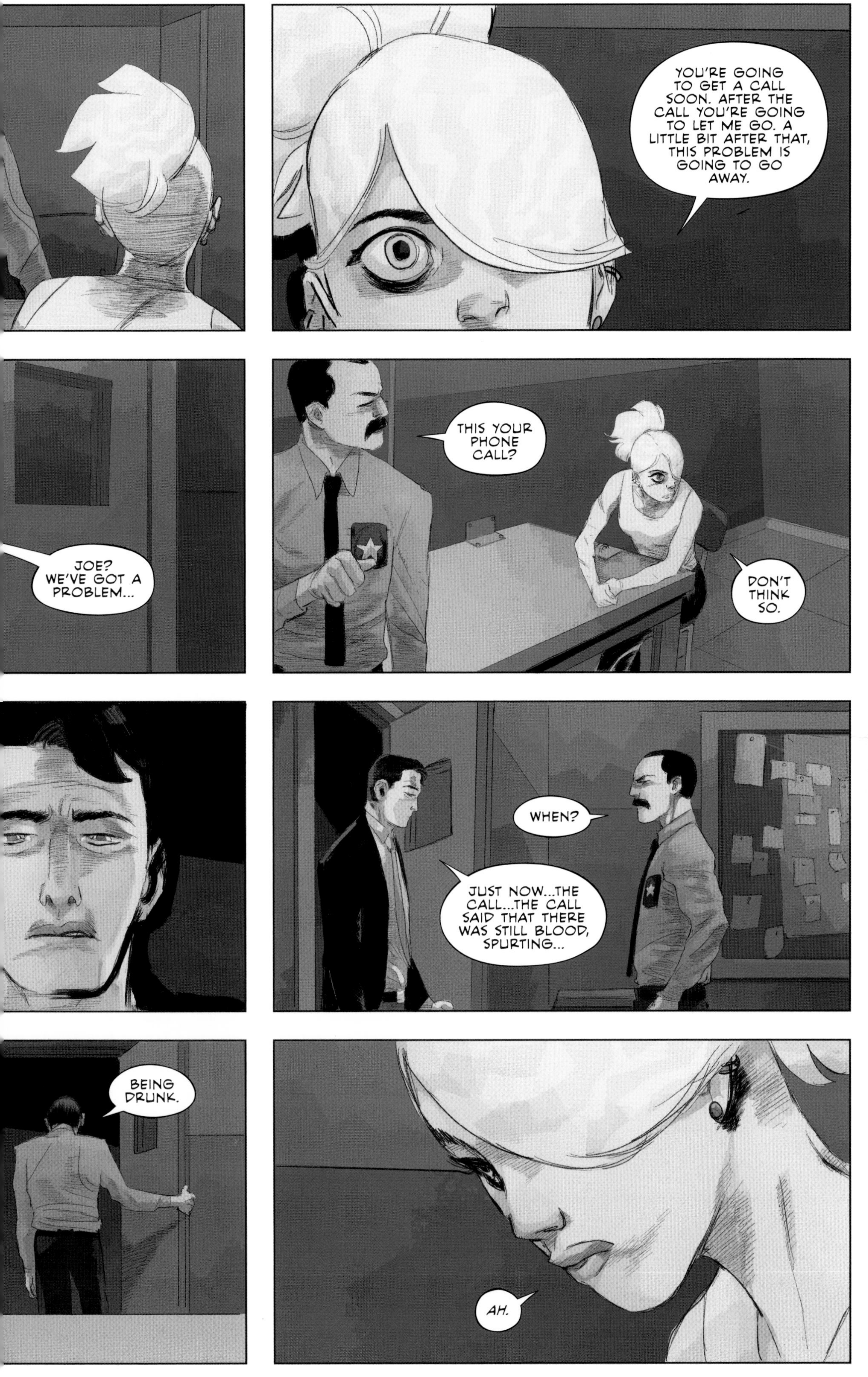
YOU'RE GOING TO GET A CALL SOON. AFTER THE CALL YOU'RE GOING TO LET ME GO. A LITTLE BIT AFTER THAT, THIS PROBLEM IS GOING TO GO AWAY.
JOE? WE'VE GOT A PROBLEM...
THIS YOUR PHONE CALL?
DON'T THINK SO.
WHEN?
JUST NOW...THE CALL...THE CALL SAID THAT THERE WAS STILL BLOOD, SPURTING...
BEING DRUNK.
AH.

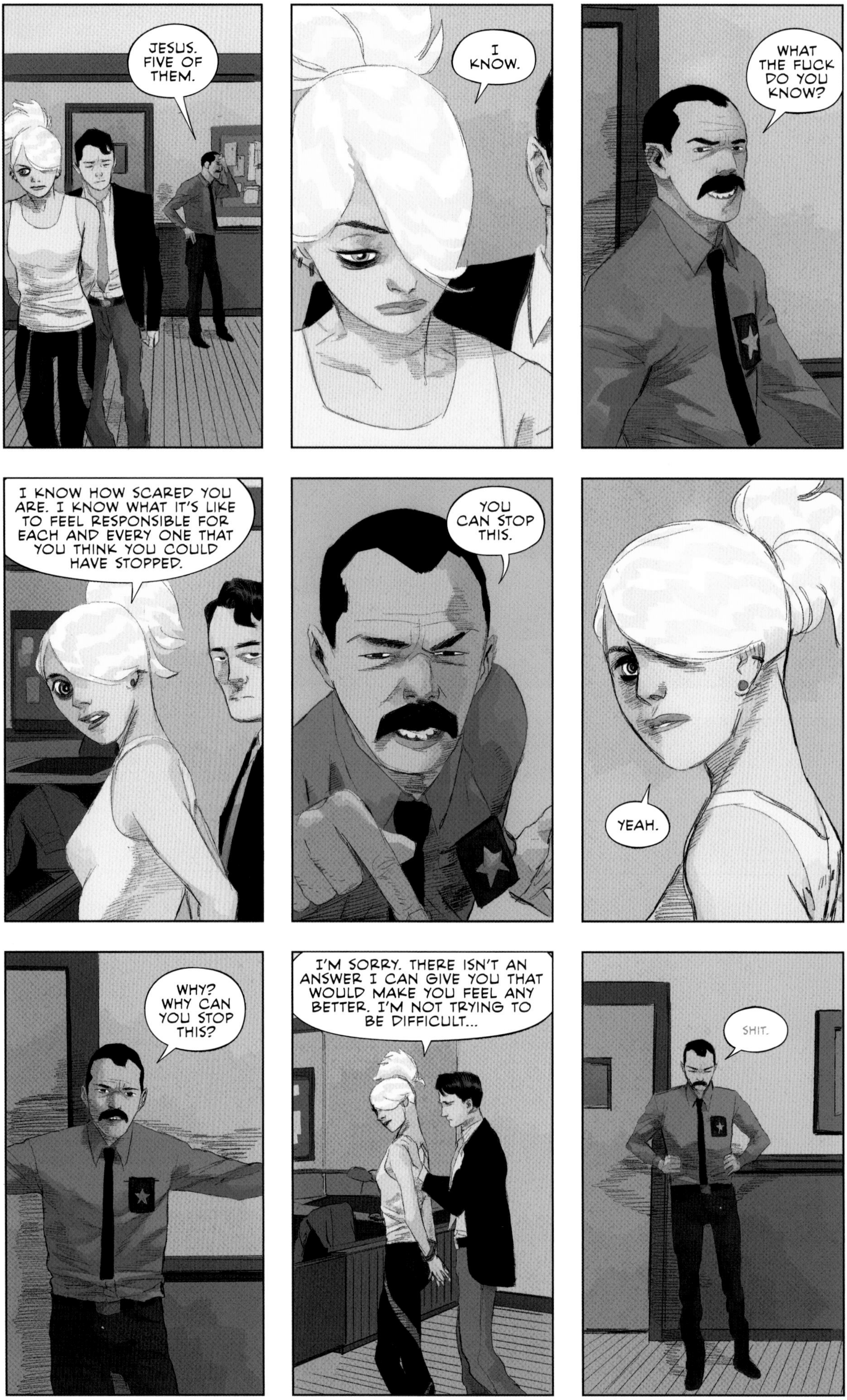
JESUS. FIVE OF THEM.
I KNOW.
WHAT THE FUCK DO YOU KNOW?
I KNOW HOW SCARED YOU ARE. I KNOW WHAT IT'S LIKE TO FEEL RESPONSIBLE FOR EACH AND EVERY ONE THAT YOU THINK YOU COULD HAVE STOPPED.
YOU CAN STOP THIS.
YEAH.
WHY? WHY CAN YOU STOP THIS?
I'M SORRY. THERE ISN'T AN ANSWER I CAN GIVE YOU THAT WOULD MAKE YOU FEEL ANY BETTER. I'M NOT TRYING TO BE DIFFICULT...
SHIT.

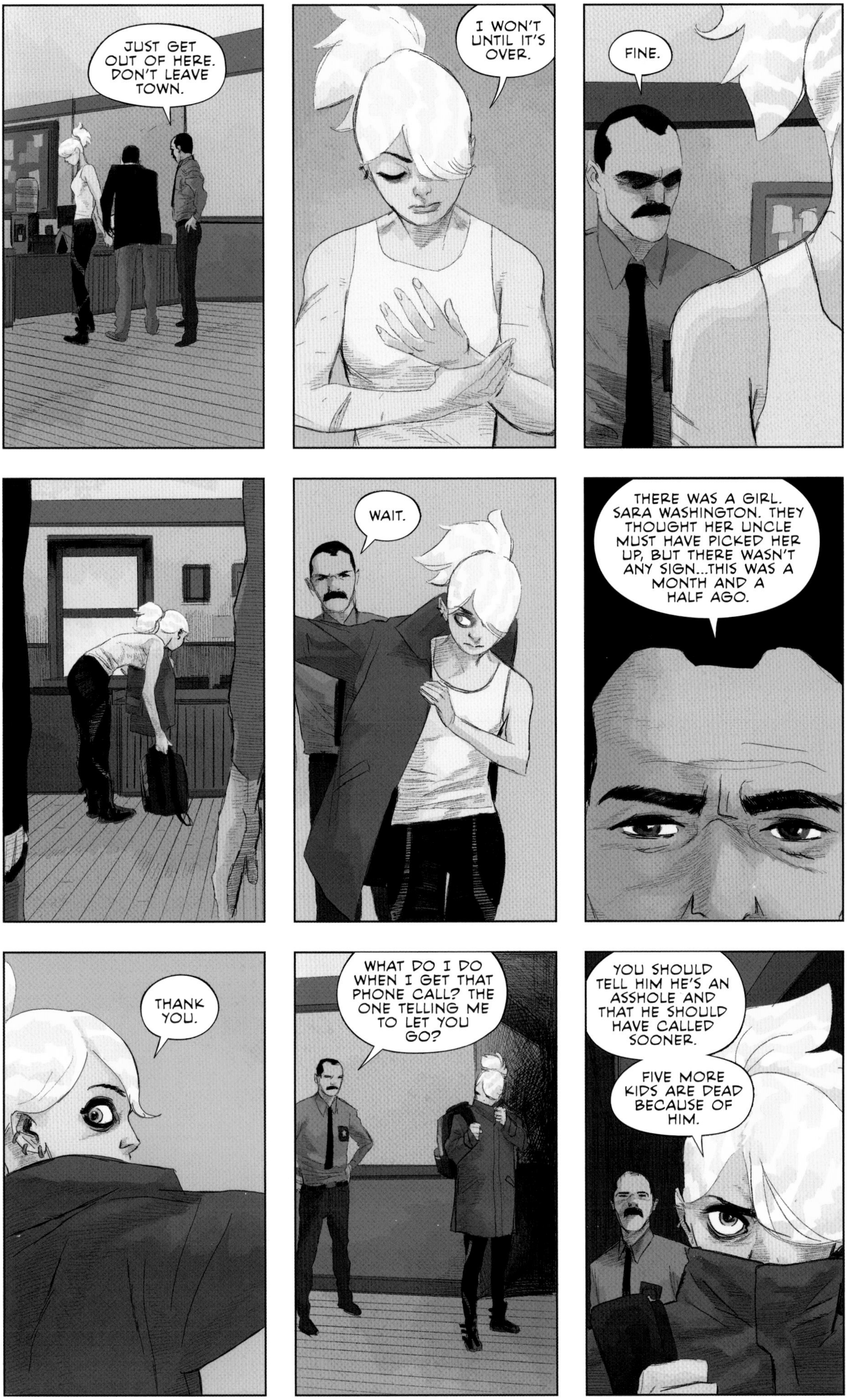
JUST GET OUT OF HERE. DON'T LEAVE TOWN.
I WON'T UNTIL IT'S OVER.
FINE.
WAIT.
THERE WAS A GIRL. SARA WASHINGTON. THEY THOUGHT HER UNCLE MUST HAVE PICKED HER UP, BUT THERE WASN'T ANY SIGN...THIS WAS A MONTH AND A HALF AGO.
THANK YOU.
WHAT DO I DO WHEN I GET THAT PHONE CALL? THE ONE TELLING ME TO LET YOU GO?
YOU SHOULD TELL HIM HE'S AN ASSHOLE AND THAT HE SHOULD HAVE CALLED SOONER.
FIVE MORE KIDS ARE DEAD BECAUSE OF HIM.

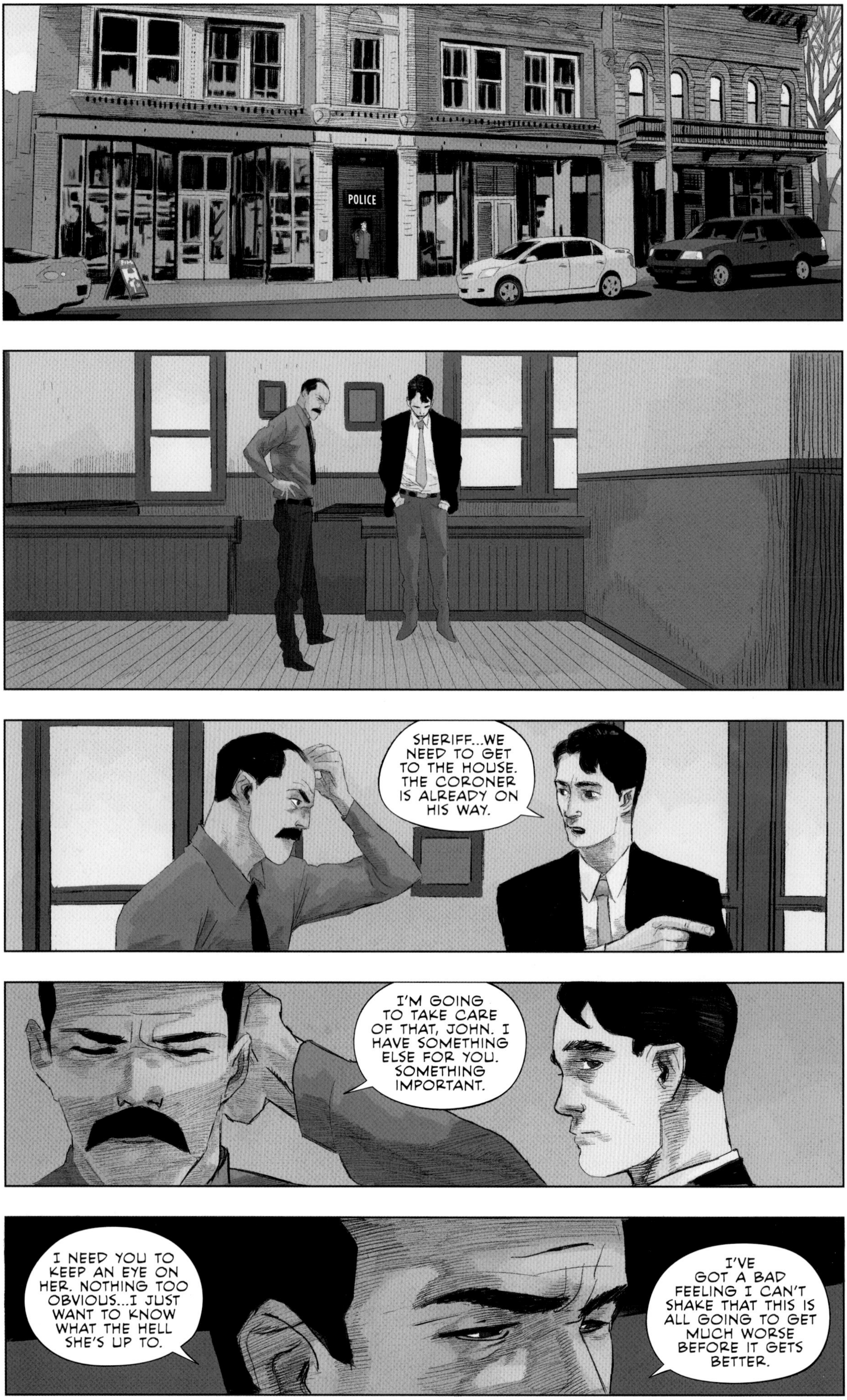
POLICE
SHERIFF...WE NEED TO GET TO THE HOUSE. THE CORONER IS ALREADY ON HIS WAY.
I'M GOING TO TAKE CARE OF THAT, JOHN. I HAVE SOMETHING ELSE FOR YOU. SOMETHING IMPORTANT.
I NEED YOU TO KEEP AN EYE ON HER. NOTHING TOO OBVIOUS...I JUST WANT TO KNOW WHAT THE HELL SHE'S UP TO.
I'VE GOT A BAD FEELING I CAN'T SHAKE THAT THIS IS ALL GOING TO GET MUCH WORSE BEFORE IT GETS BETTER.

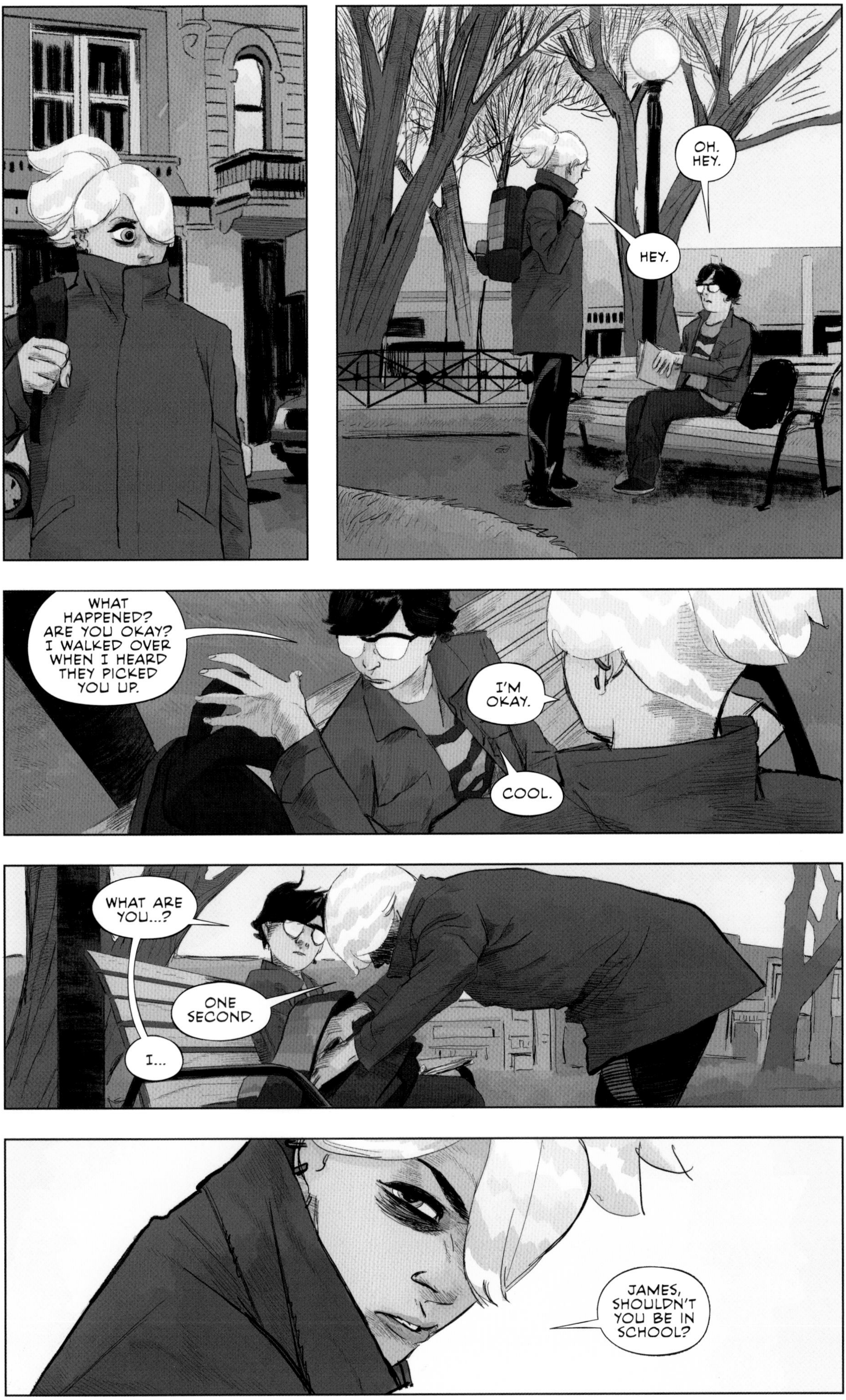
OH. HEY.
HEY.
WHAT HAPPENED? ARE YOU OKAY? I WALKED OVER WHEN I HEARD THEY PICKED YOU UP.
I'M OKAY.
COOL.
WHAT ARE YOU...?
ONE SECOND.
I...
JAMES, SHOULDN'T YOU BE IN SCHOOL?

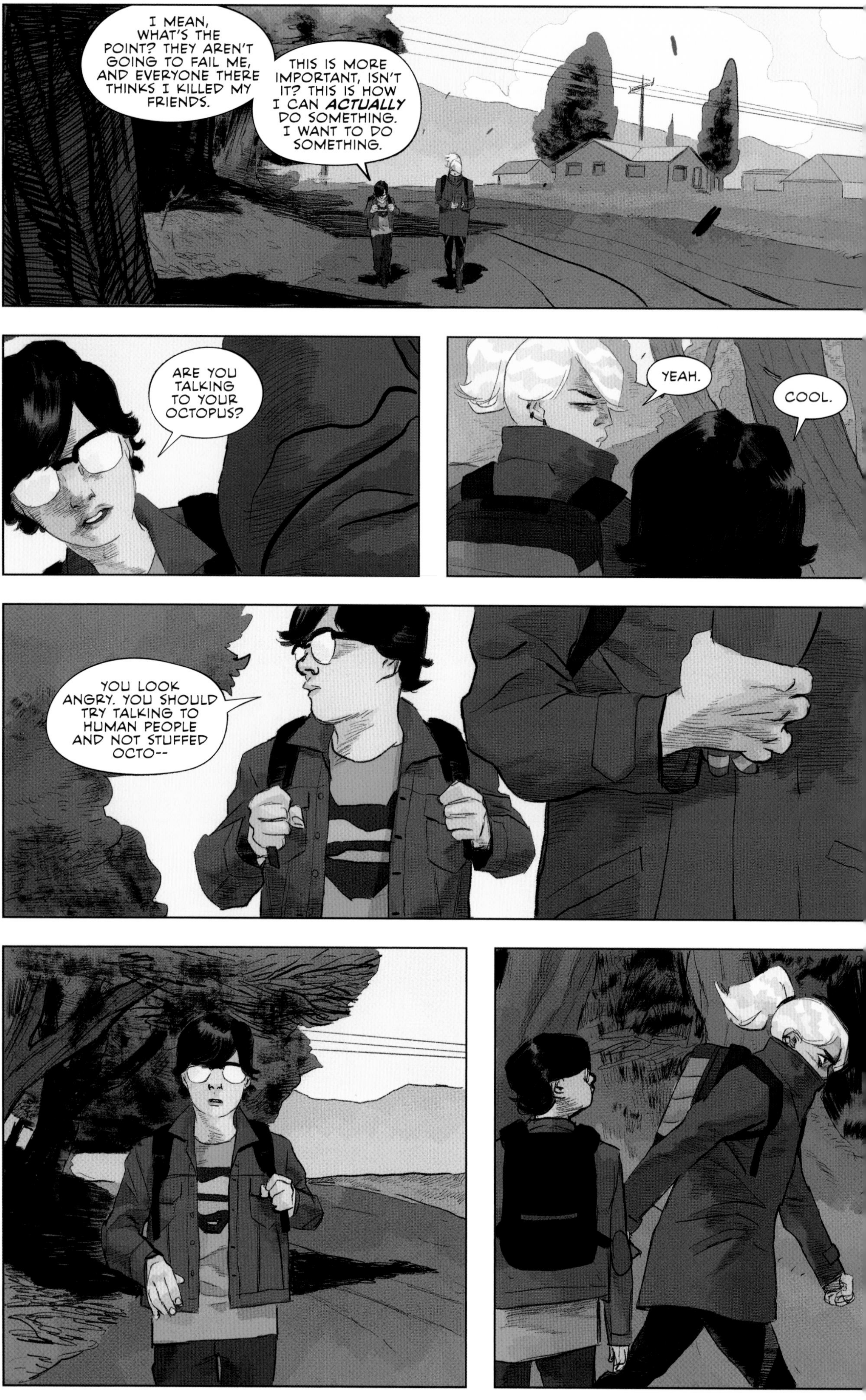
I MEAN, WHAT'S THE POINT? THEY AREN'T GOING TO FAIL ME, AND EVERYONE THERE THINKS I KILLED MY FRIENDS.
THIS IS MORE IMPORTANT, ISN'T IT? THIS IS HOW I CAN ACTUALLY DO SOMETHING. I WANT TO DO SOMETHING.
ARE YOU TALKING TO YOUR OCTOPUS?
YEAH.
COOL.
YOU LOOK ANGRY. YOU SHOULD TRY TALKING TO HUMAN PEOPLE AND NOT STUFFED OCTO--

DOING SOMETHING DOESN'T ALWAYS MAKE YOU FEEL BETTER, JAMES. FIVE MORE CHILDREN ARE DEAD. KILLED INSIDE A HOUSE.

YOU *KNOW* AN E7 WOULDN'T BE ABLE TO DO THAT. WHAT THE FUCK AM I UP AGAINST HERE?

THE KILL PATTERN IS NOW MORE CONSISTENT WITH A CLASS B OSCURATYPE THAN A CLASS E.

WE'LL FINISH THIS LATER.

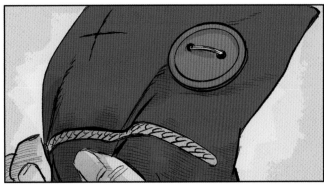

JAMES. JUST SHUT THE FUCK UP.

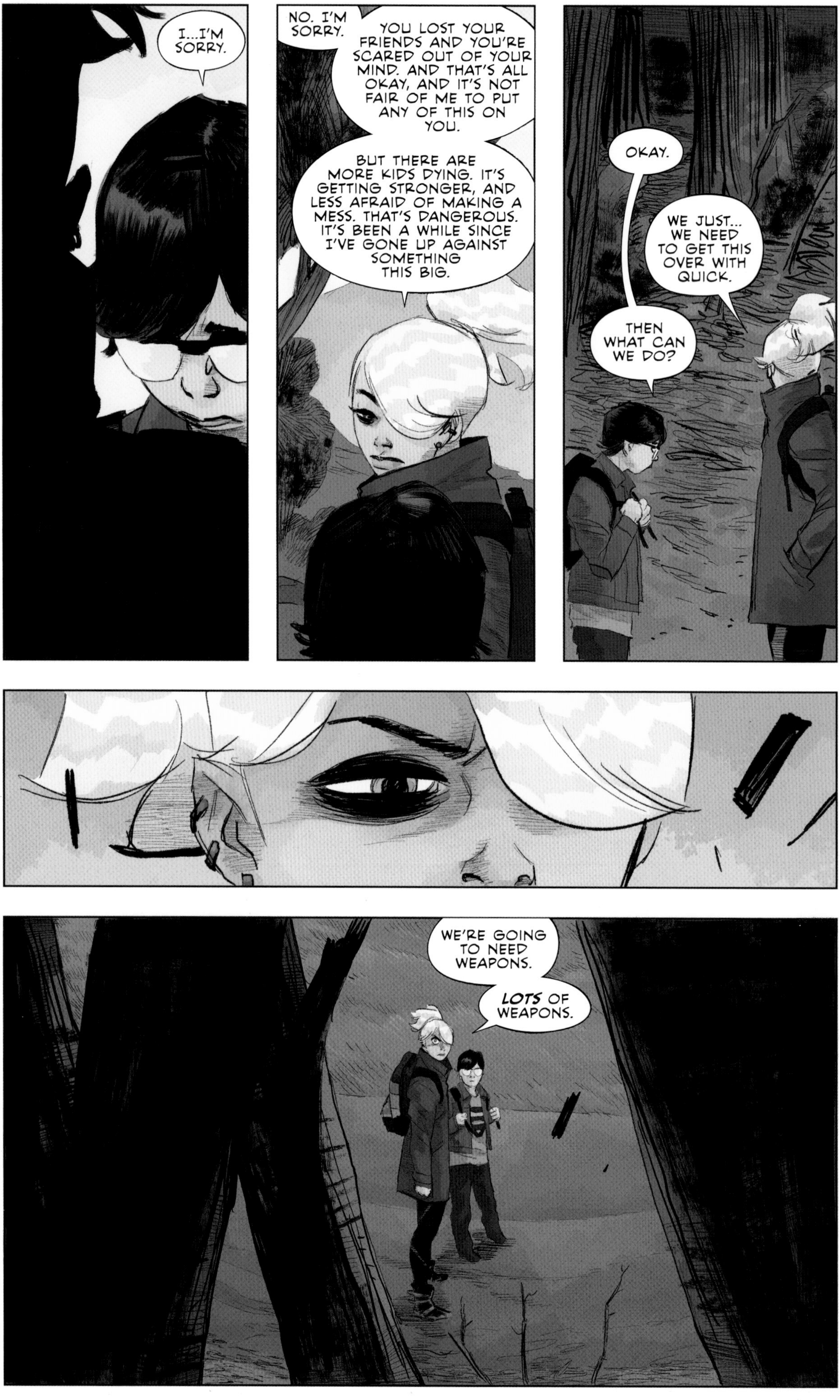
I...I'M SORRY.
NO. I'M SORRY.
YOU LOST YOUR FRIENDS AND YOU'RE SCARED OUT OF YOUR MIND. AND THAT'S ALL OKAY, AND IT'S NOT FAIR OF ME TO PUT ANY OF THIS ON YOU.
BUT THERE ARE MORE KIDS DYING. IT'S GETTING STRONGER, AND LESS AFRAID OF MAKING A MESS. THAT'S DANGEROUS. IT'S BEEN A WHILE SINCE I'VE GONE UP AGAINST SOMETHING THIS BIG.
OKAY.
WE JUST... WE NEED TO GET THIS OVER WITH QUICK.
THEN WHAT CAN WE DO?
WE'RE GOING TO NEED WEAPONS.
LOTS OF WEAPONS.

CHAPTER
FOUR

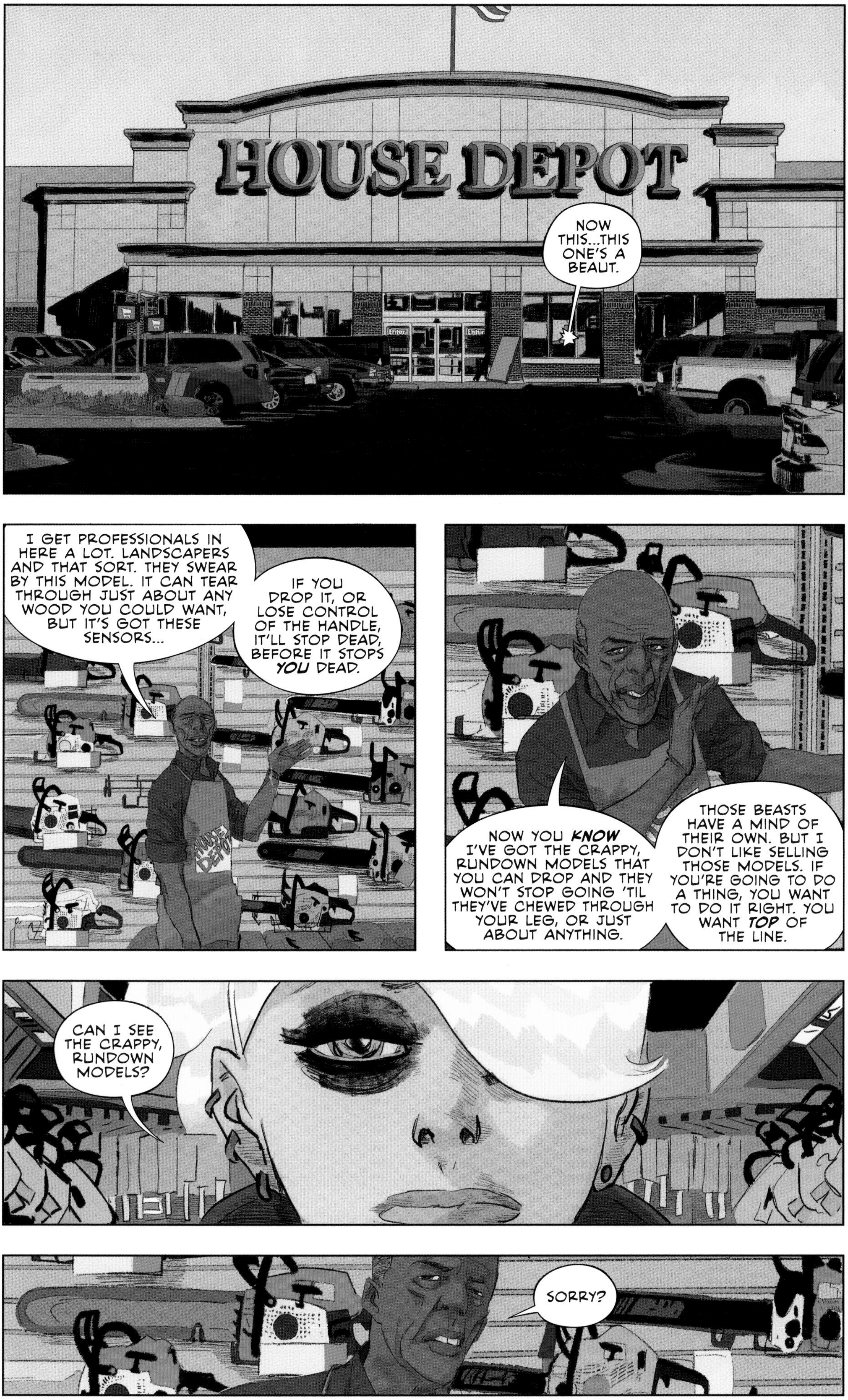
HOUSE DEPOT
NOW THIS...THIS ONE'S A BEAUT.
I GET PROFESSIONALS IN HERE A LOT. LANDSCAPERS AND THAT SORT. THEY SWEAR BY THIS MODEL. IT CAN TEAR THROUGH JUST ABOUT ANY WOOD YOU COULD WANT, BUT IT'S GOT THESE SENSORS...
IF YOU DROP IT, OR LOSE CONTROL OF THE HANDLE, IT'LL STOP DEAD, BEFORE IT STOPS *YOU* DEAD.
HOUSE DEPOT
NOW YOU *KNOW* I'VE GOT THE CRAPPY, RUNDOWN MODELS THAT YOU CAN DROP AND THEY WON'T STOP GOING 'TIL THEY'VE CHEWED THROUGH YOUR LEG, OR JUST ABOUT ANYTHING.
THOSE BEASTS HAVE A MIND OF THEIR OWN. BUT I DON'T LIKE SELLING THOSE MODELS. IF YOU'RE GOING TO DO A THING, YOU WANT TO DO IT RIGHT. YOU WANT *TOP* OF THE LINE.
CAN I SEE THE CRAPPY, RUNDOWN MODELS?
SORRY?

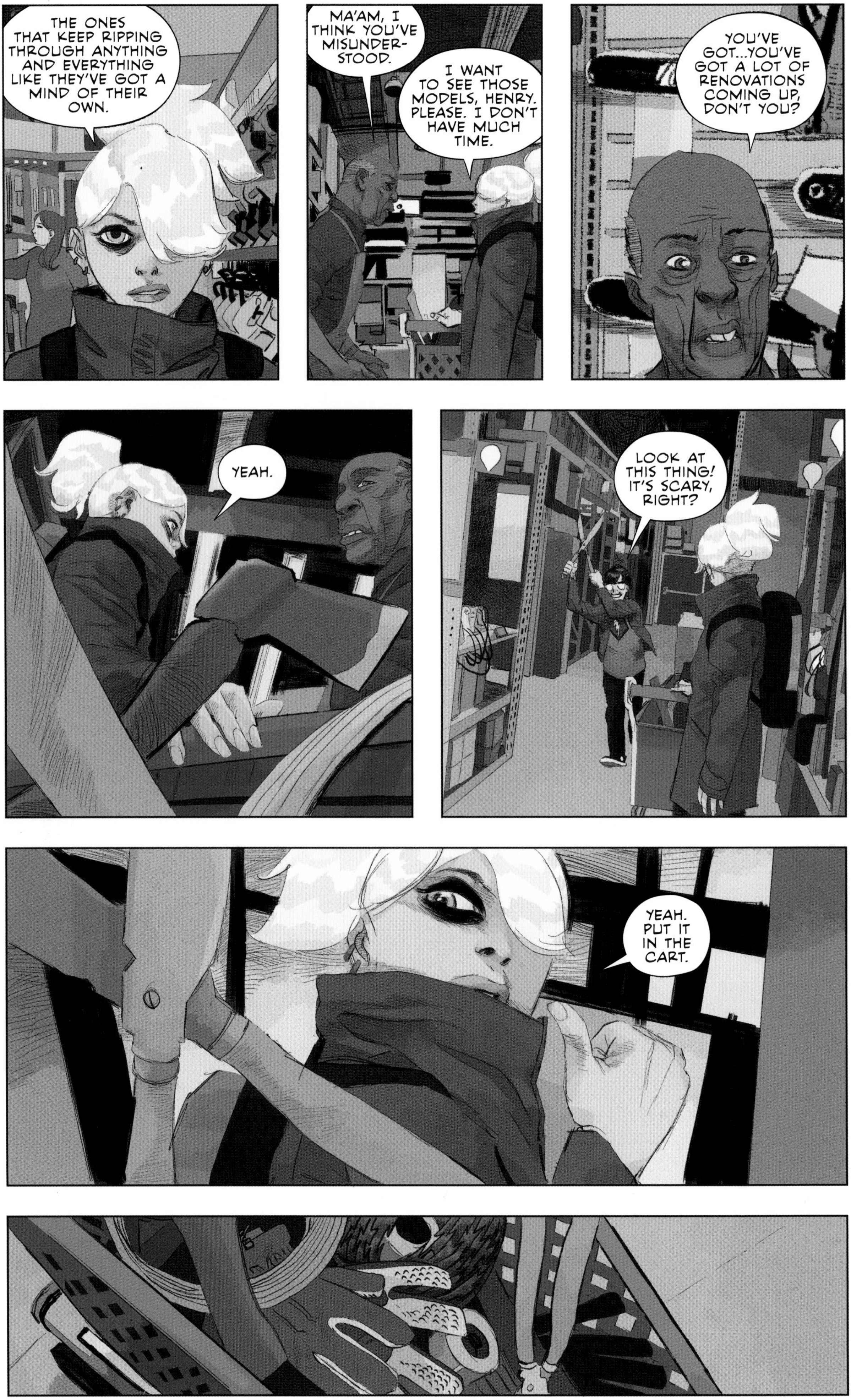
THE ONES THAT KEEP RIPPING THROUGH ANYTHING AND EVERYTHING LIKE THEY'VE GOT A MIND OF THEIR OWN.
MA'AM, I THINK YOU'VE MISUNDER-STOOD.
I WANT TO SEE THOSE MODELS, HENRY. PLEASE. I DON'T HAVE MUCH TIME.
YOU'VE GOT...YOU'VE GOT A LOT OF RENOVATIONS COMING UP, DON'T YOU?
YEAH.
LOOK AT THIS THING! IT'S SCARY, RIGHT?
YEAH. PUT IT IN THE CART.

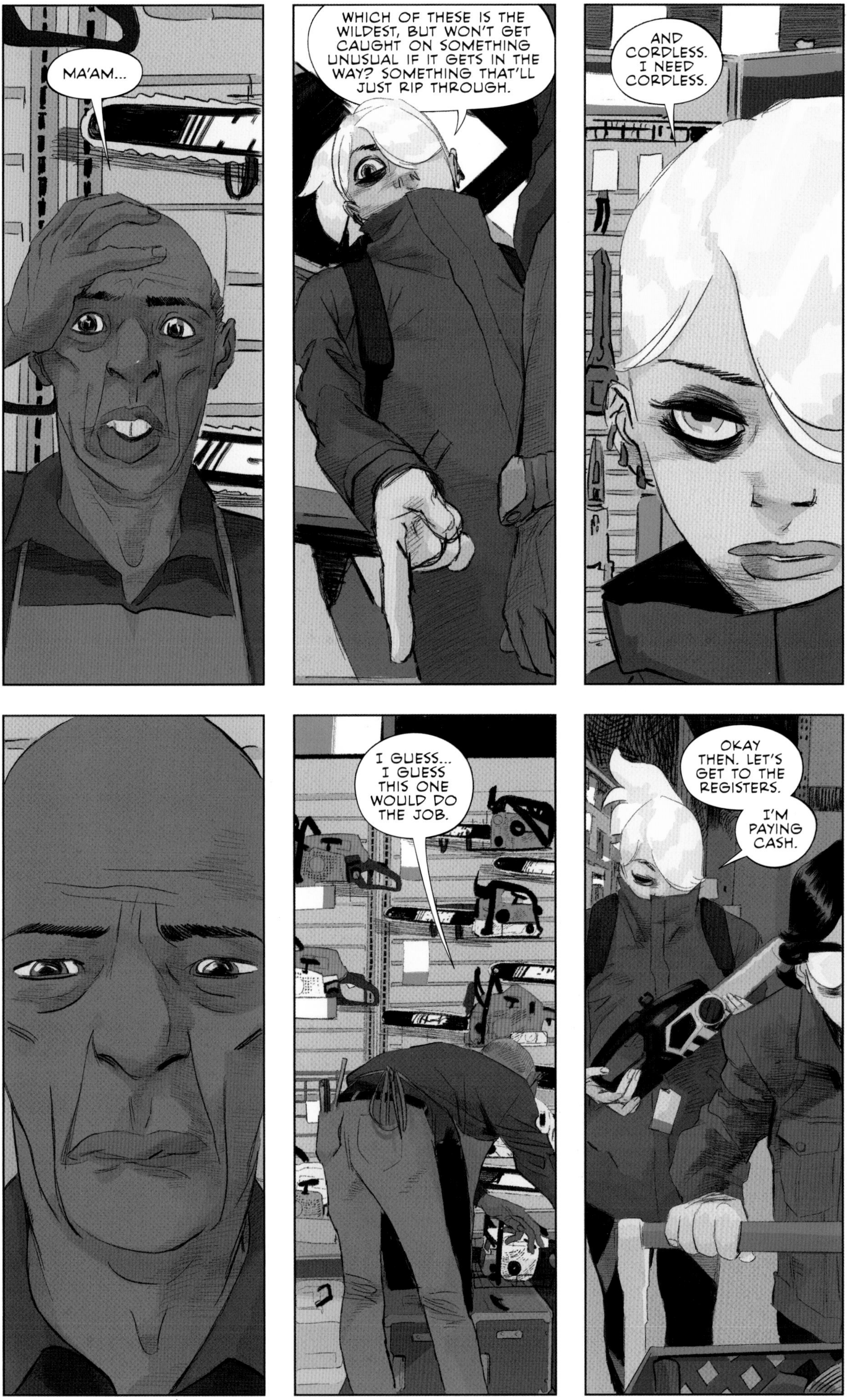
MA'AM...
WHICH OF THESE IS THE WILDEST, BUT WON'T GET CAUGHT ON SOMETHING UNUSUAL IF IT GETS IN THE WAY? SOMETHING THAT'LL JUST RIP THROUGH.
AND CORDLESS. I NEED CORDLESS.
I GUESS... I GUESS... THIS ONE WOULD DO THE JOB.
OKAY THEN. LET'S GET TO THE REGISTERS.
I'M PAYING CASH.

DAD, YOU IN HERE?

DAD. IT'S TOMMY.

OH.

HOW'S YOUR MOTHER?

CALL HER IF YOU REALLY WANT TO KNOW.

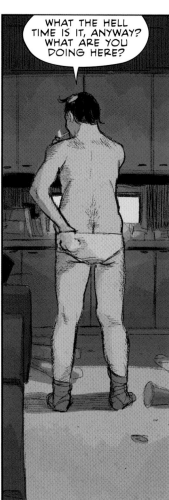

WHAT THE HELL TIME IS IT, ANYWAY? WHAT ARE YOU DOING HERE?

IS THERE... IS THERE NEWS...?

IS SOPHIE...

DID THEY FIND HER BODY?

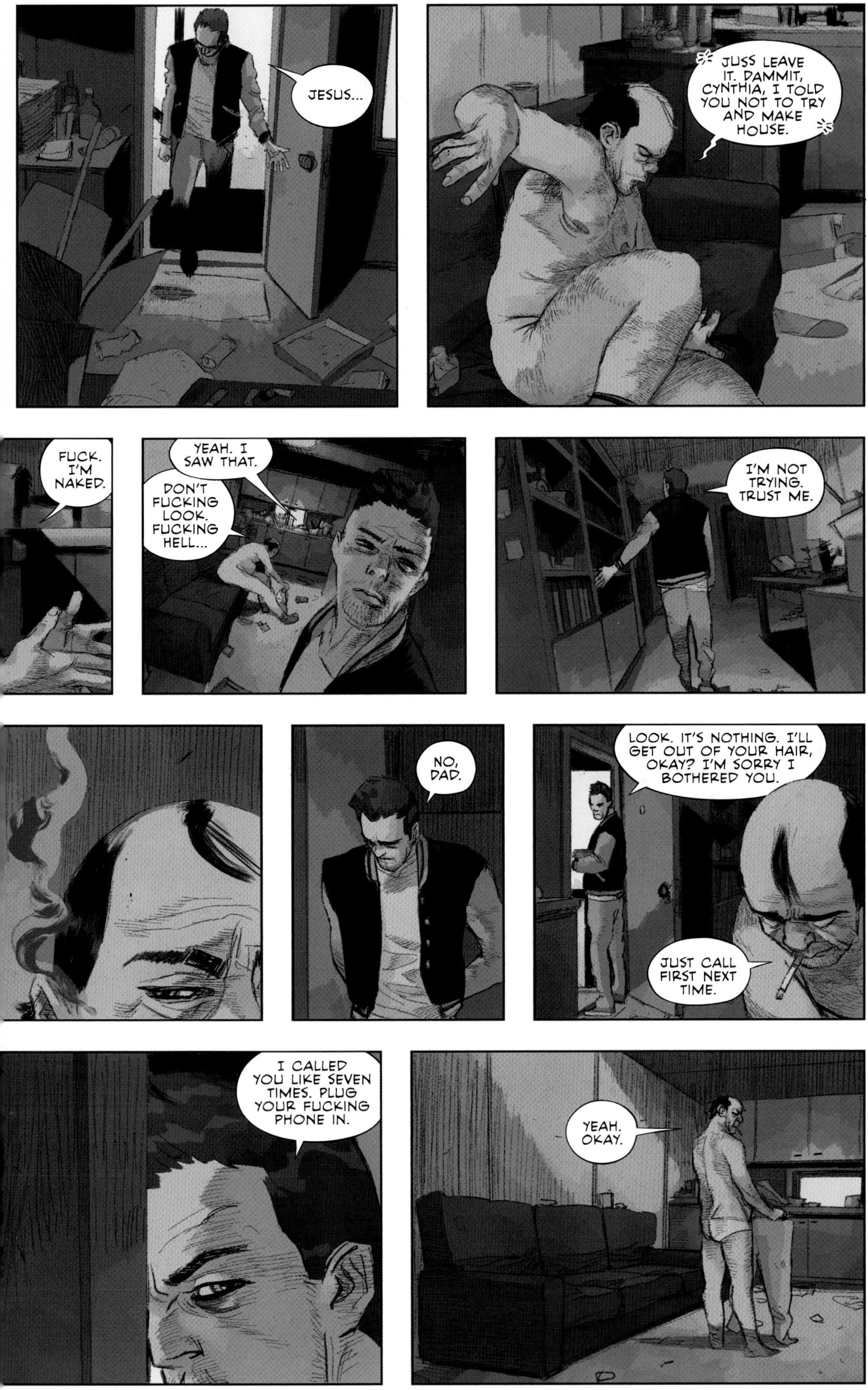
JESUS...
JUSS LEAVE IT. DAMMIT, CYNTHIA, I TOLD YOU NOT TO TRY AND MAKE HOUSE.
FUCK. I'M NAKED.
YEAH. I SAW THAT.
DON'T FUCKING LOOK. FUCKING HELL...
I'M NOT TRYING. TRUST ME.
NO, DAD.
LOOK. IT'S NOTHING. I'LL GET OUT OF YOUR HAIR, OKAY? I'M SORRY I BOTHERED YOU.
JUST CALL FIRST NEXT TIME.
I CALLED YOU LIKE SEVEN TIMES. PLUG YOUR FUCKING PHONE IN.
YEAH. OKAY.

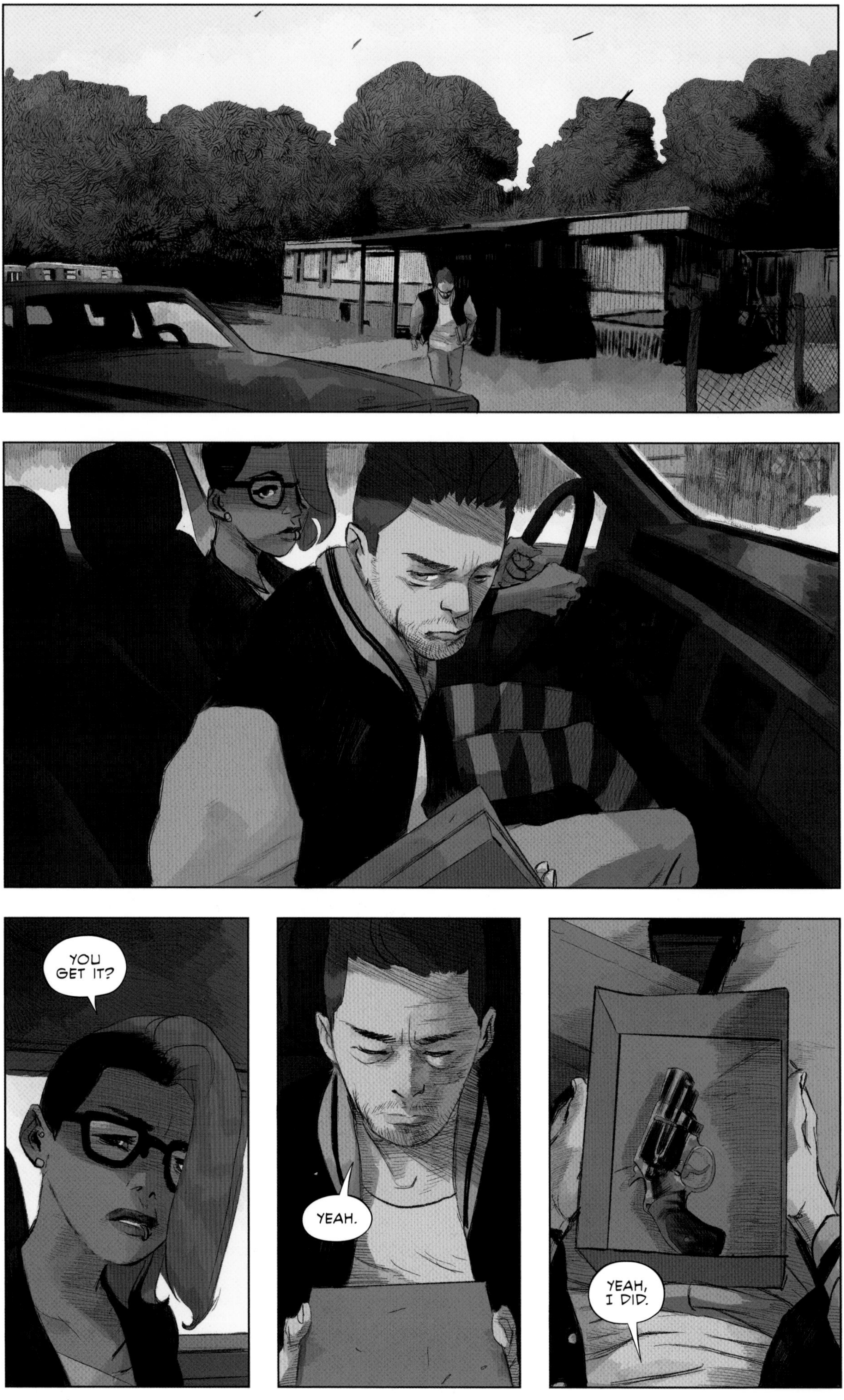
YOU GET IT?
YEAH.
YEAH, I DID.

I DON'T LIKE THIS.

I MEAN... I DON'T BLAME YOU. IT'S PRETTY GROSS.

POP

TIM...

HEY, BABY BROTHER. I LOOK AT BODIES ALL DAY. IF I'M SAYING IT'S GROSS, THAT MEANS I'M TAKING IT SERIOUS.

YOU KNOW WHAT'S THE WEIRDEST PART OF ALL OF THIS...?

PREDATORS GO FOR THE KILL. IF THEY WANT TO STOP YOU, THEY GO FOR THE SOFT TISSUE.

FASTER THEY GET THE KILL, LESS LIKELY YOU ARE TO DO IT SOME DAMAGE. THEN THEY CAN GET THE **MEAT** EASY.

BUT THIS THING DIDN'T **WANT** MEAT. NOT REALLY. IT RIPS INTO THEM, BUT THEN LEAVES THEM WHOLE.

PEOPLE, ON THE OTHER HAND, IF THEY'RE IN A KILLING MOOD AND THEY'RE ANGRY...THEY KNOW WHAT HURTS **THEM**, AND THAT'S WHERE THEY WANT TO HURT **YOU**. THEY WANT TO DRAW IT OUT.

THESE KILLINGS. THERE'S INTENT HERE...THERE'S... I DON'T KNOW HOW TO PUT IT.

THERE'S SOME SCARY SHIT AT WORK.

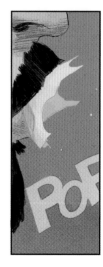

POP

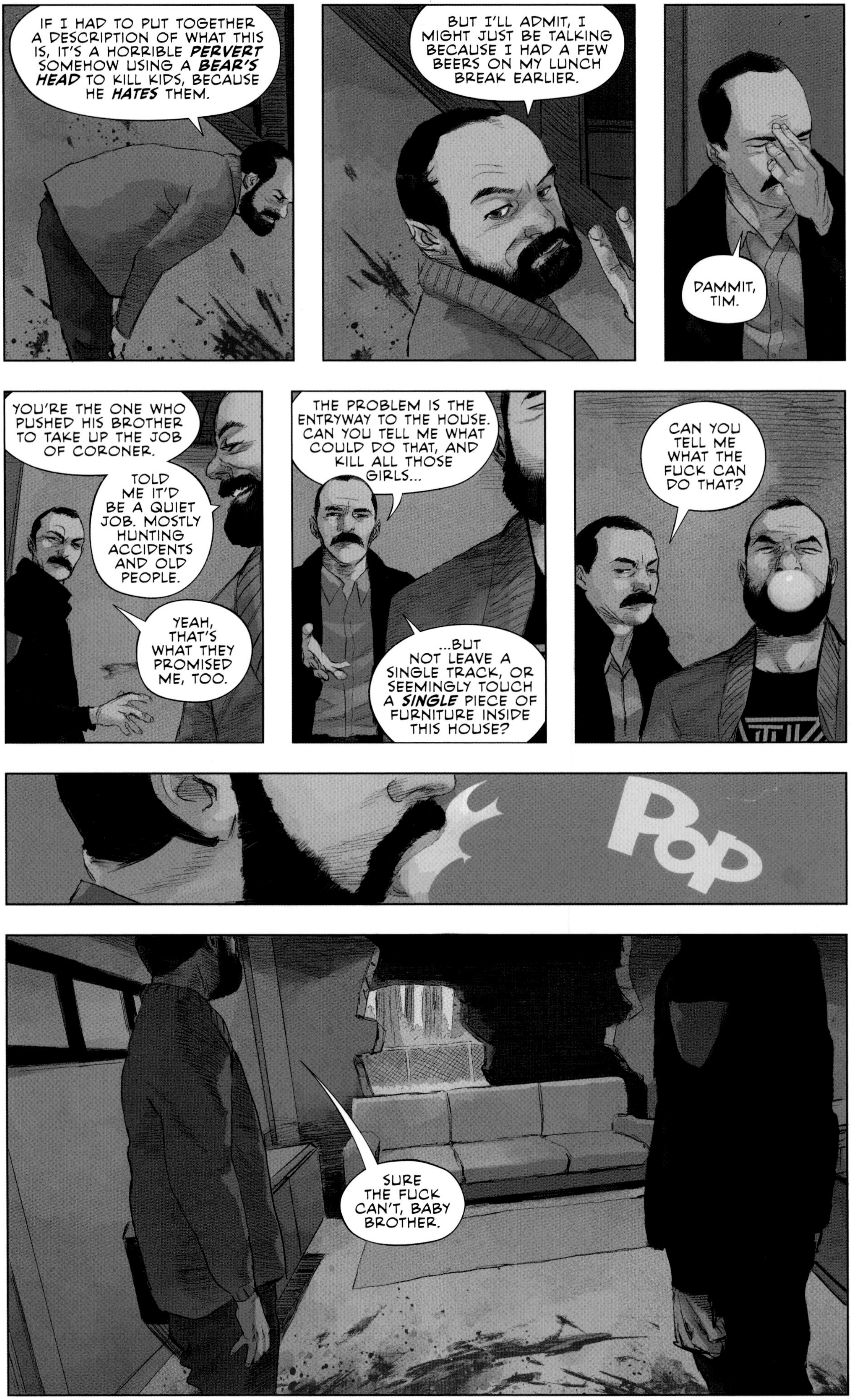
IF I HAD TO PUT TOGETHER A DESCRIPTION OF WHAT THIS IS, IT'S A HORRIBLE PERVERT SOMEHOW USING A BEAR'S HEAD TO KILL KIDS, BECAUSE HE HATES THEM.
BUT I'LL ADMIT, I MIGHT JUST BE TALKING BECAUSE I HAD A FEW BEERS ON MY LUNCH BREAK EARLIER.
DAMMIT, TIM.
YOU'RE THE ONE WHO PUSHED HIS BROTHER TO TAKE UP THE JOB OF CORONER.
TOLD ME IT'D BE A QUIET JOB. MOSTLY HUNTING ACCIDENTS AND OLD PEOPLE.
YEAH, THAT'S WHAT THEY PROMISED ME, TOO.
THE PROBLEM IS THE ENTRYWAY TO THE HOUSE. CAN YOU TELL ME WHAT COULD DO THAT, AND KILL ALL THOSE GIRLS...
...BUT NOT LEAVE A SINGLE TRACK, OR SEEMINGLY TOUCH A SINGLE PIECE OF FURNITURE INSIDE THIS HOUSE?
CAN YOU TELL ME WHAT THE FUCK CAN DO THAT?
POP
SURE THE FUCK CAN'T, BABY BROTHER.

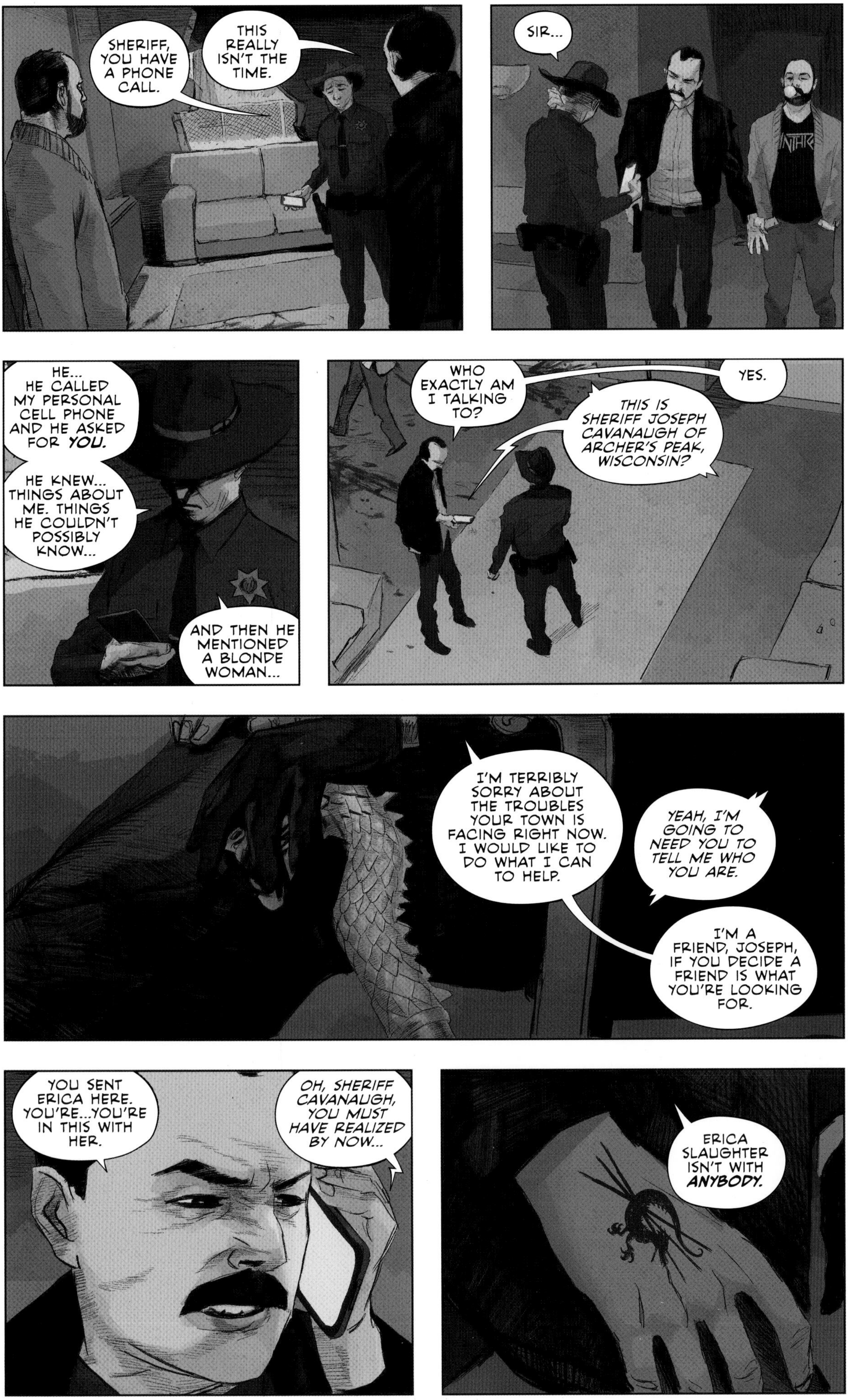
SHERIFF, YOU HAVE A PHONE CALL.
THIS REALLY ISN'T THE TIME.
SIR...
HE... HE CALLED MY PERSONAL CELL PHONE AND HE ASKED FOR *YOU.*
HE KNEW... THINGS ABOUT ME. THINGS HE COULDN'T POSSIBLY KNOW...
AND THEN HE MENTIONED A BLONDE WOMAN...
WHO EXACTLY AM I TALKING TO?
THIS IS SHERIFF JOSEPH CAVANAUGH OF ARCHER'S PEAK, WISCONSIN?
YES.
I'M TERRIBLY SORRY ABOUT THE TROUBLES YOUR TOWN IS FACING RIGHT NOW. I WOULD LIKE TO DO WHAT I CAN TO HELP.
YEAH, I'M GOING TO NEED YOU TO TELL ME WHO YOU ARE.
I'M A FRIEND, JOSEPH, IF YOU DECIDE A FRIEND IS WHAT YOU'RE LOOKING FOR.
YOU SENT ERICA HERE. YOU'RE...YOU'RE IN THIS WITH HER.
OH, SHERIFF CAVANAUGH, YOU MUST HAVE REALIZED BY NOW...
ERICA SLAUGHTER ISN'T WITH ***ANYBODY.***

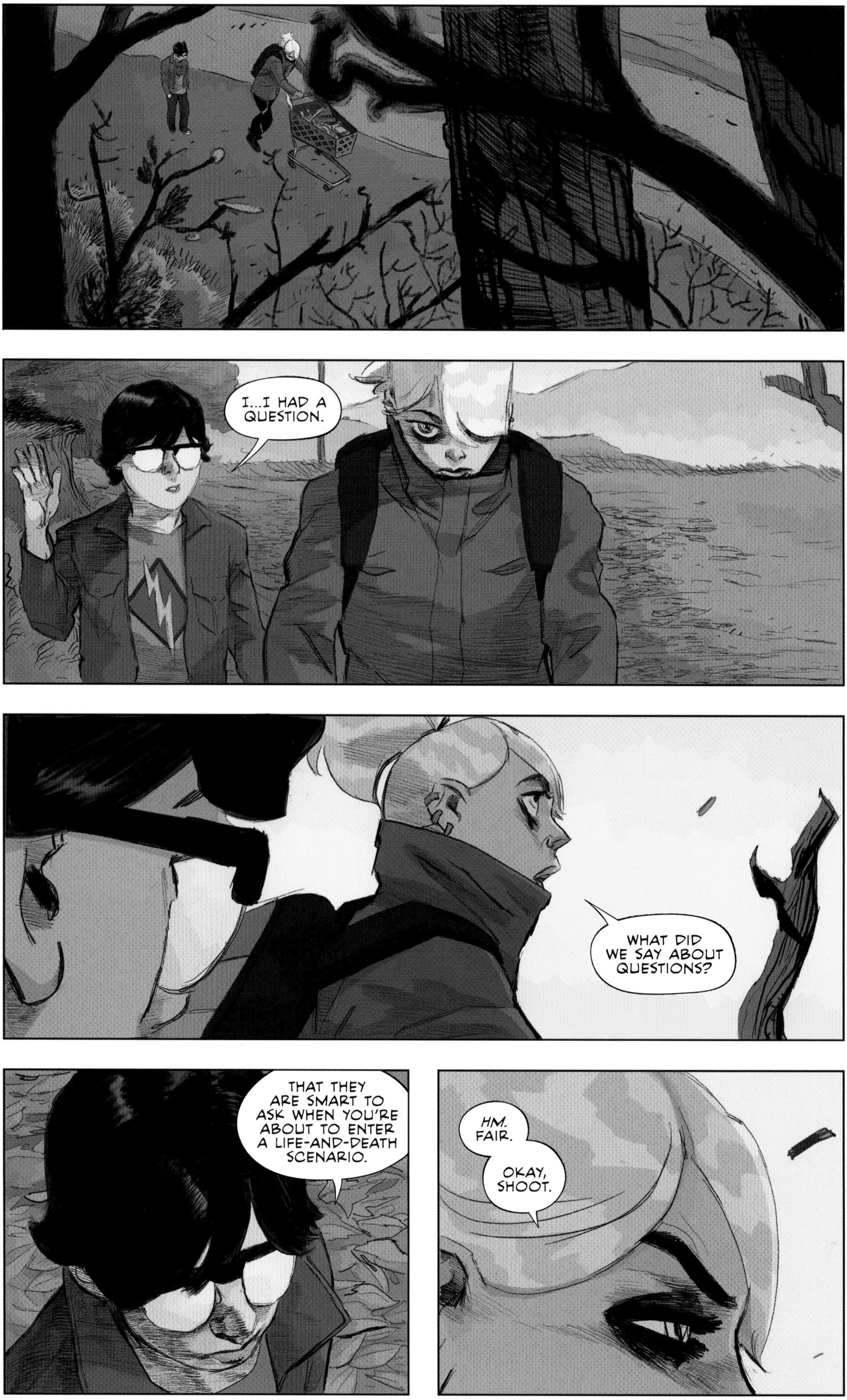
I...I HAD A QUESTION.
WHAT DID WE SAY ABOUT QUESTIONS?
THAT THEY ARE SMART TO ASK WHEN YOU'RE ABOUT TO ENTER A LIFE-AND-DEATH SCENARIO.
HM. FAIR.
OKAY, SHOOT.

WHAT ARE MONSTERS?

THEY'RE BIG SCARY THINGS THAT EAT CHILDREN.

OKAY.

WHAT, DID YOU THINK THERE WAS A BIGGER ANSWER THAN THAT?

I MEAN, YEAH. OF COURSE. THERE *HAS* TO BE A BIGGER ANSWER THAN THAT.

MONSTERS AREN'T *REAL.*

OF COURSE THEY ARE. YOU'VE SEEN ONE OF THEM. IT ATE YOUR FRIENDS.

BUT WHY...*WHY* DID IT EAT MY FRIENDS?

BECAUSE THEY COULD SEE IT. BECAUSE THEY BELIEVED IN IT.

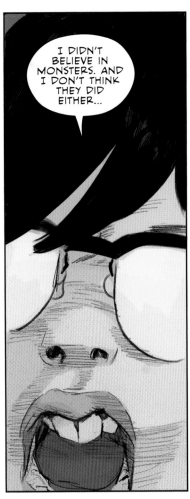

I DIDN'T BELIEVE IN MONSTERS. AND I DON'T THINK THEY DID EITHER...

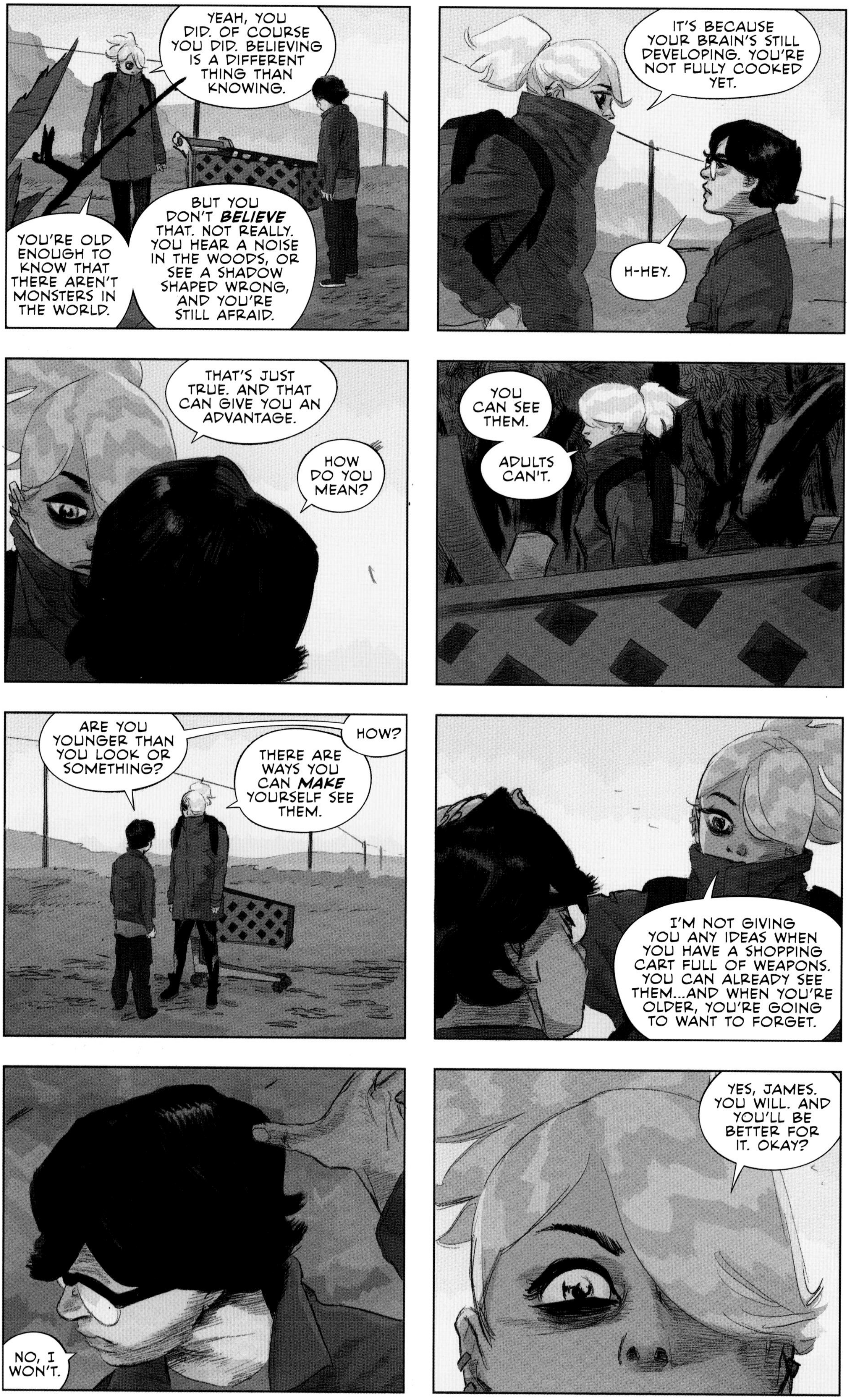
YEAH, YOU DID. OF COURSE YOU DID. BELIEVING IS A DIFFERENT THING THAN KNOWING.
YOU'RE OLD ENOUGH TO KNOW THAT THERE AREN'T MONSTERS IN THE WORLD.
BUT YOU DON'T *BELIEVE* THAT. NOT REALLY. YOU HEAR A NOISE IN THE WOODS, OR SEE A SHADOW SHAPED WRONG, AND YOU'RE STILL AFRAID.
IT'S BECAUSE YOUR BRAIN'S STILL DEVELOPING. YOU'RE NOT FULLY COOKED YET.
H-HEY.
THAT'S JUST TRUE. AND THAT CAN GIVE YOU AN ADVANTAGE.
HOW DO YOU MEAN?
YOU CAN SEE THEM.
ADULTS CAN'T.
ARE YOU YOUNGER THAN YOU LOOK OR SOMETHING?
HOW?
THERE ARE WAYS YOU CAN *MAKE* YOURSELF SEE THEM.
I'M NOT GIVING YOU ANY IDEAS WHEN YOU HAVE A SHOPPING CART FULL OF WEAPONS. YOU CAN ALREADY SEE THEM...AND WHEN YOU'RE OLDER, YOU'RE GOING TO WANT TO FORGET.
NO, I WON'T.
YES, JAMES. YOU WILL. AND YOU'LL BE BETTER FOR IT. OKAY?

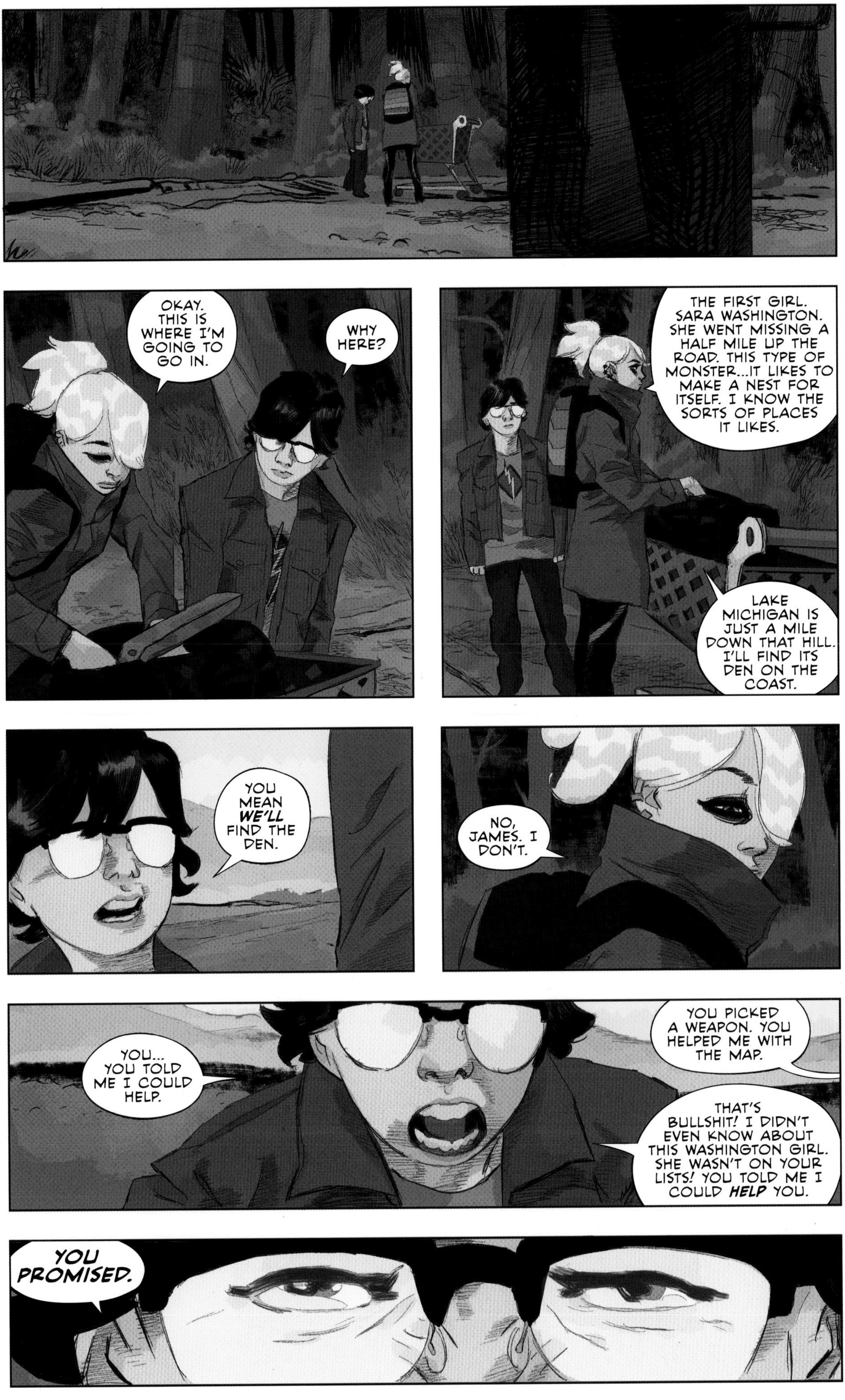
OKAY. THIS IS WHERE I'M GOING TO GO IN.
WHY HERE?
THE FIRST GIRL. SARA WASHINGTON. SHE WENT MISSING A HALF MILE UP THE ROAD. THIS TYPE OF MONSTER...IT LIKES TO MAKE A NEST FOR ITSELF. I KNOW THE SORTS OF PLACES IT LIKES.
LAKE MICHIGAN IS JUST A MILE DOWN THAT HILL. I'LL FIND ITS DEN ON THE COAST.
YOU MEAN WE'LL FIND THE DEN.
NO, JAMES. I DON'T.
YOU... YOU TOLD ME I COULD HELP.
YOU PICKED A WEAPON. YOU HELPED ME WITH THE MAP.
THAT'S BULLSHIT! I DIDN'T EVEN KNOW ABOUT THIS WASHINGTON GIRL. SHE WASN'T ON YOUR LISTS! YOU TOLD ME I COULD HELP YOU.
YOU PROMISED.

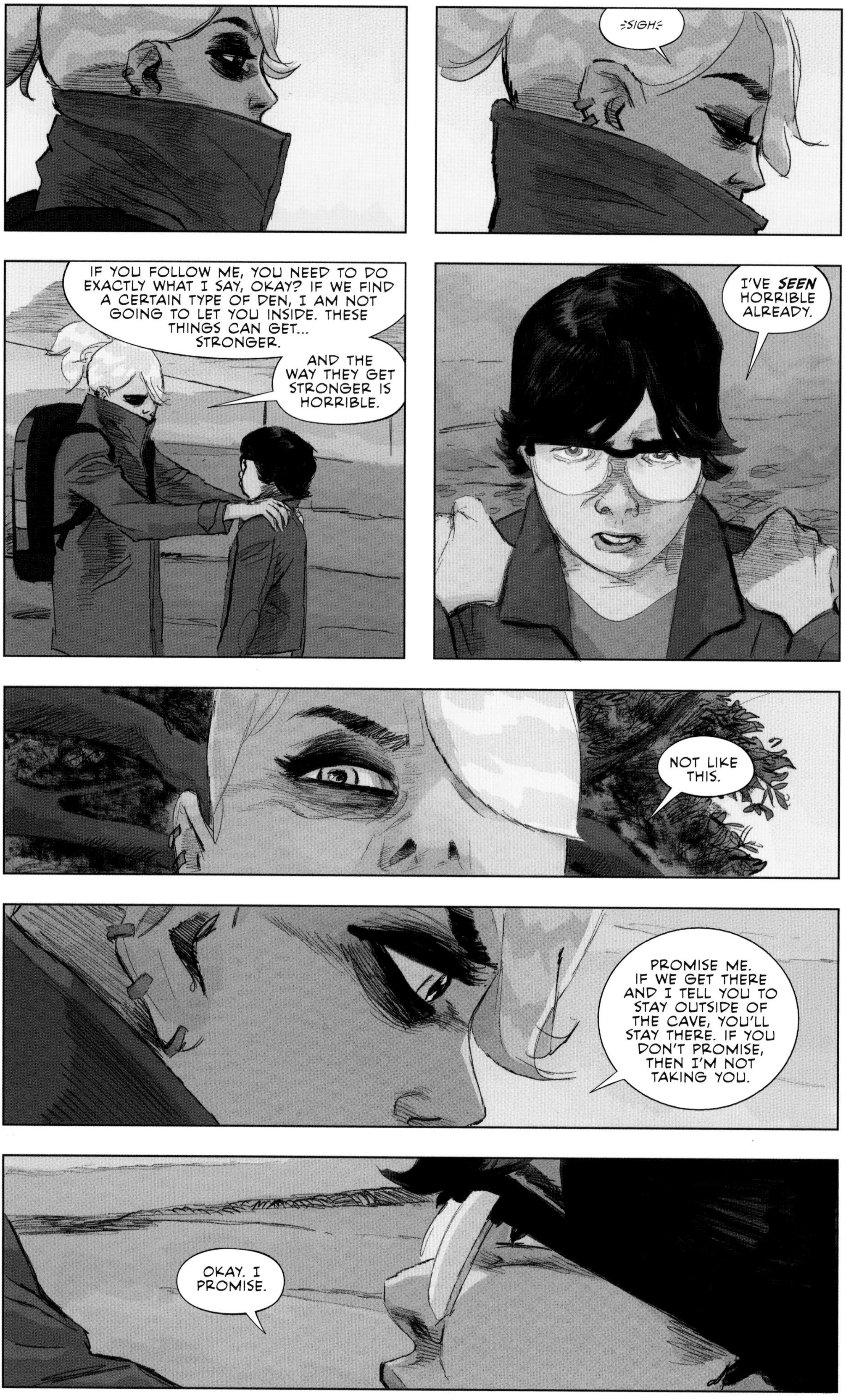

⇒SIGH⇐
IF YOU FOLLOW ME, YOU NEED TO DO EXACTLY WHAT I SAY, OKAY? IF WE FIND A CERTAIN TYPE OF DEN, I AM NOT GOING TO LET YOU INSIDE. THESE THINGS CAN GET... STRONGER.
AND THE WAY THEY GET STRONGER IS HORRIBLE.
I'VE *SEEN* HORRIBLE ALREADY.
NOT LIKE THIS.
PROMISE ME. IF WE GET THERE AND I TELL YOU TO STAY OUTSIDE OF THE CAVE, YOU'LL STAY THERE. IF YOU DON'T PROMISE, THEN I'M NOT TAKING YOU.
OKAY. I PROMISE.

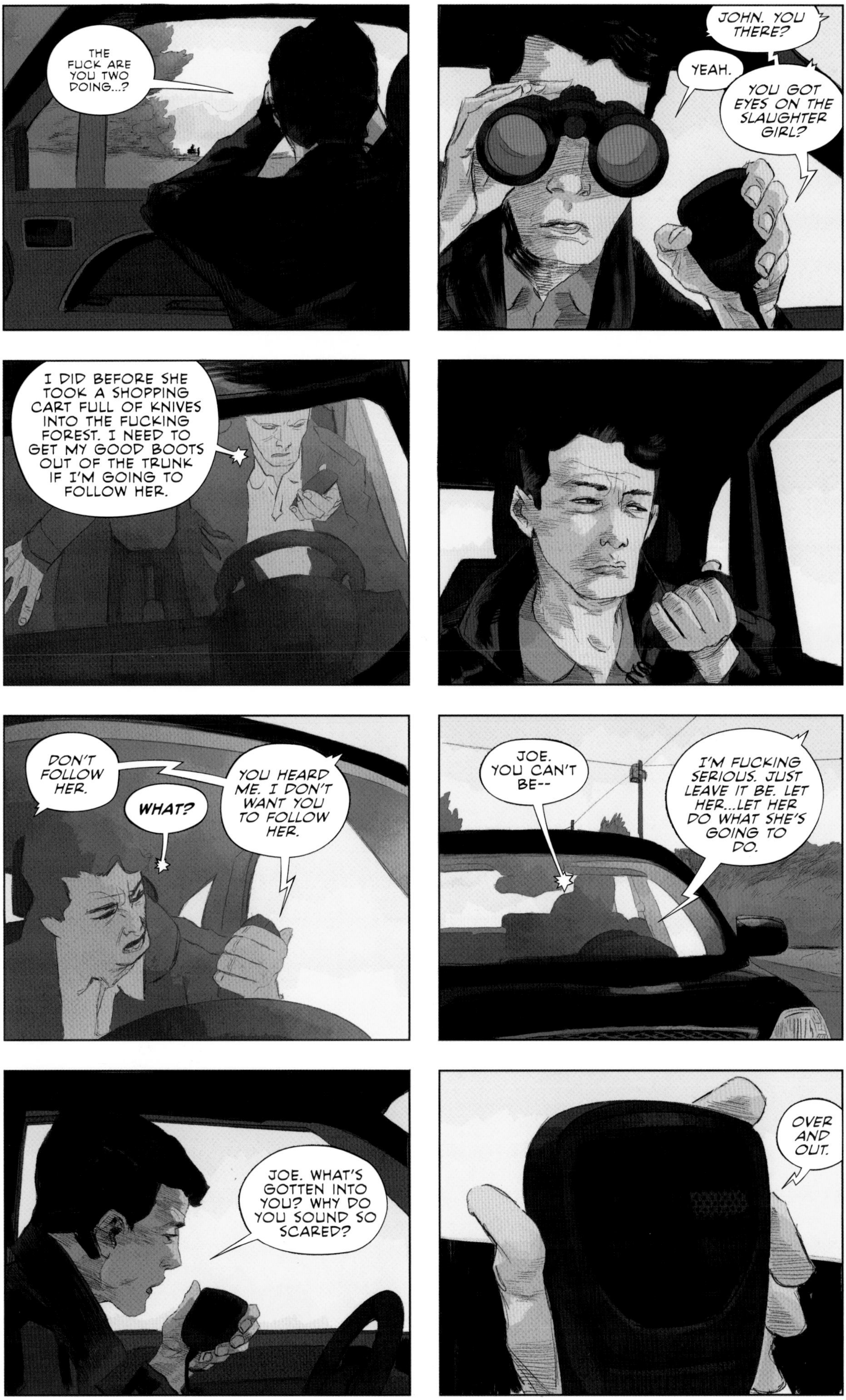
THE FUCK ARE YOU TWO DOING...?
JOHN. YOU THERE?
YEAH.
YOU GOT EYES ON THE SLAUGHTER GIRL?
I DID BEFORE SHE TOOK A SHOPPING CART FULL OF KNIVES INTO THE FUCKING FOREST. I NEED TO GET MY GOOD BOOTS OUT OF THE TRUNK IF I'M GOING TO FOLLOW HER.
DON'T FOLLOW HER.
WHAT?
YOU HEARD ME. I DON'T WANT YOU TO FOLLOW HER.
JOE. YOU CAN'T BE--
I'M FUCKING SERIOUS. JUST LEAVE IT BE. LET HER...LET HER DO WHAT SHE'S GOING TO DO.
JOE. WHAT'S GOTTEN INTO YOU? WHY DO YOU SOUND SO SCARED?
OVER AND OUT.

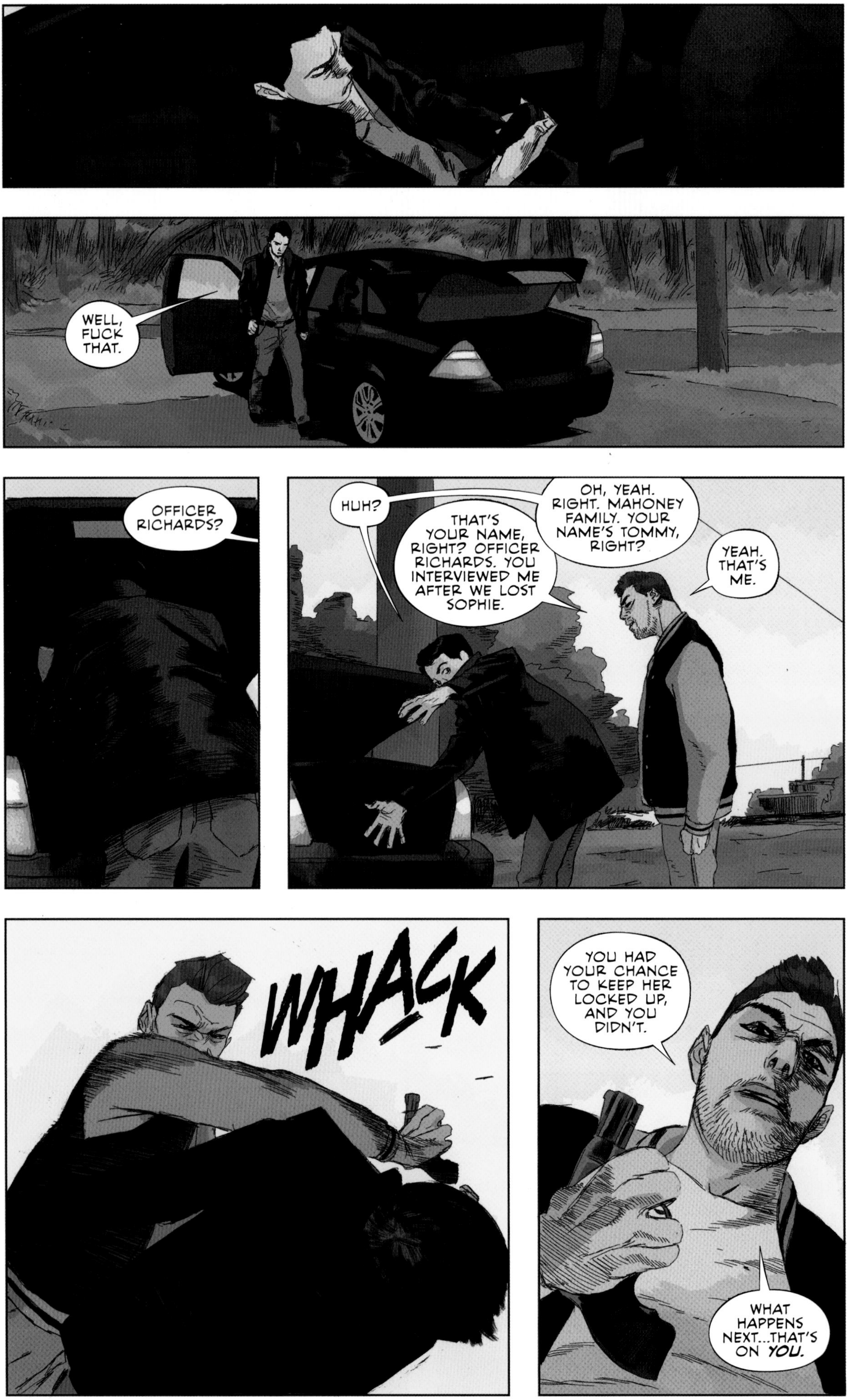
WELL, FUCK THAT.
OFFICER RICHARDS?
HUH?
THAT'S YOUR NAME, RIGHT? OFFICER RICHARDS. YOU INTERVIEWED ME AFTER WE LOST SOPHIE.
OH, YEAH. RIGHT. MAHONEY FAMILY. YOUR NAME'S TOMMY, RIGHT?
YEAH. THAT'S ME.
WHACK
YOU HAD YOUR CHANCE TO KEEP HER LOCKED UP, AND YOU DIDN'T.
WHAT HAPPENS NEXT...THAT'S ON *YOU.*

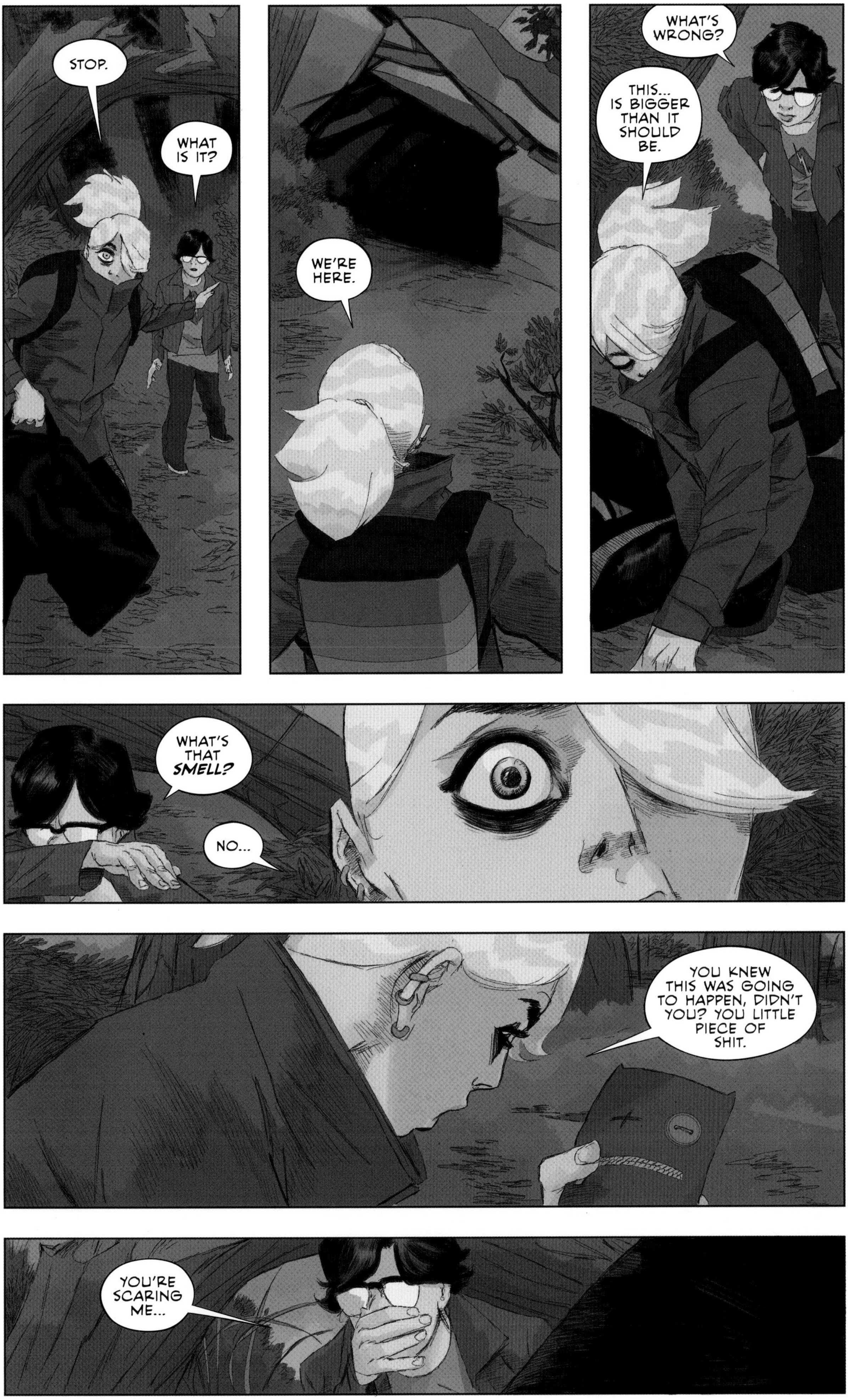
STOP.
WHAT IS IT?
WE'RE HERE.
WHAT'S WRONG?
THIS... IS BIGGER THAN IT SHOULD BE.
WHAT'S THAT *SMELL?*
NO...
YOU KNEW THIS WAS GOING TO HAPPEN, DIDN'T YOU? YOU LITTLE PIECE OF SHIT.
YOU'RE SCARING ME...

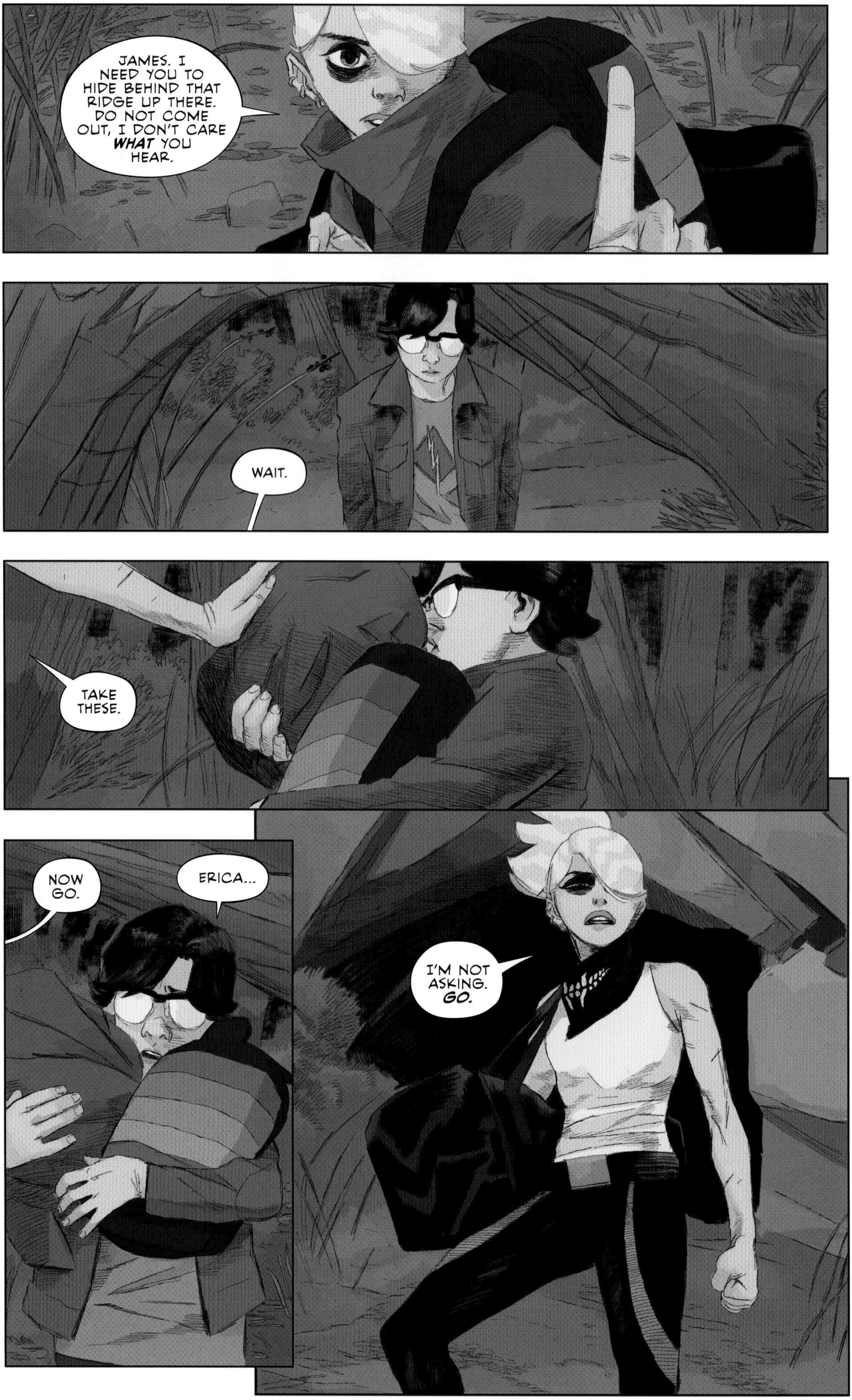
JAMES. I NEED YOU TO HIDE BEHIND THAT RIDGE UP THERE. DO NOT COME OUT, I DON'T CARE **WHAT** YOU HEAR.
WAIT.
TAKE THESE.
NOW GO.
ERICA...
I'M NOT ASKING. **GO.**

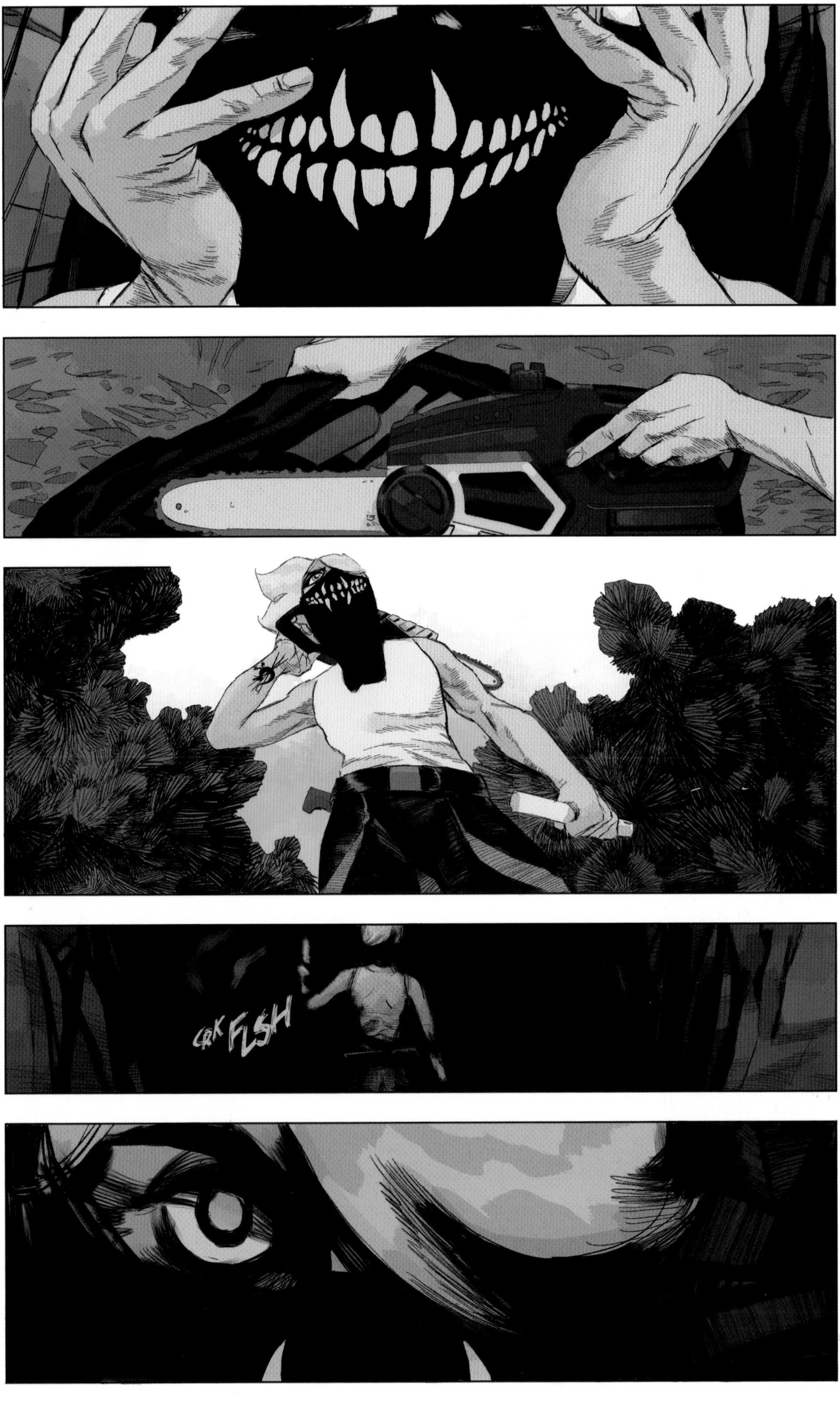
CRK FLSH

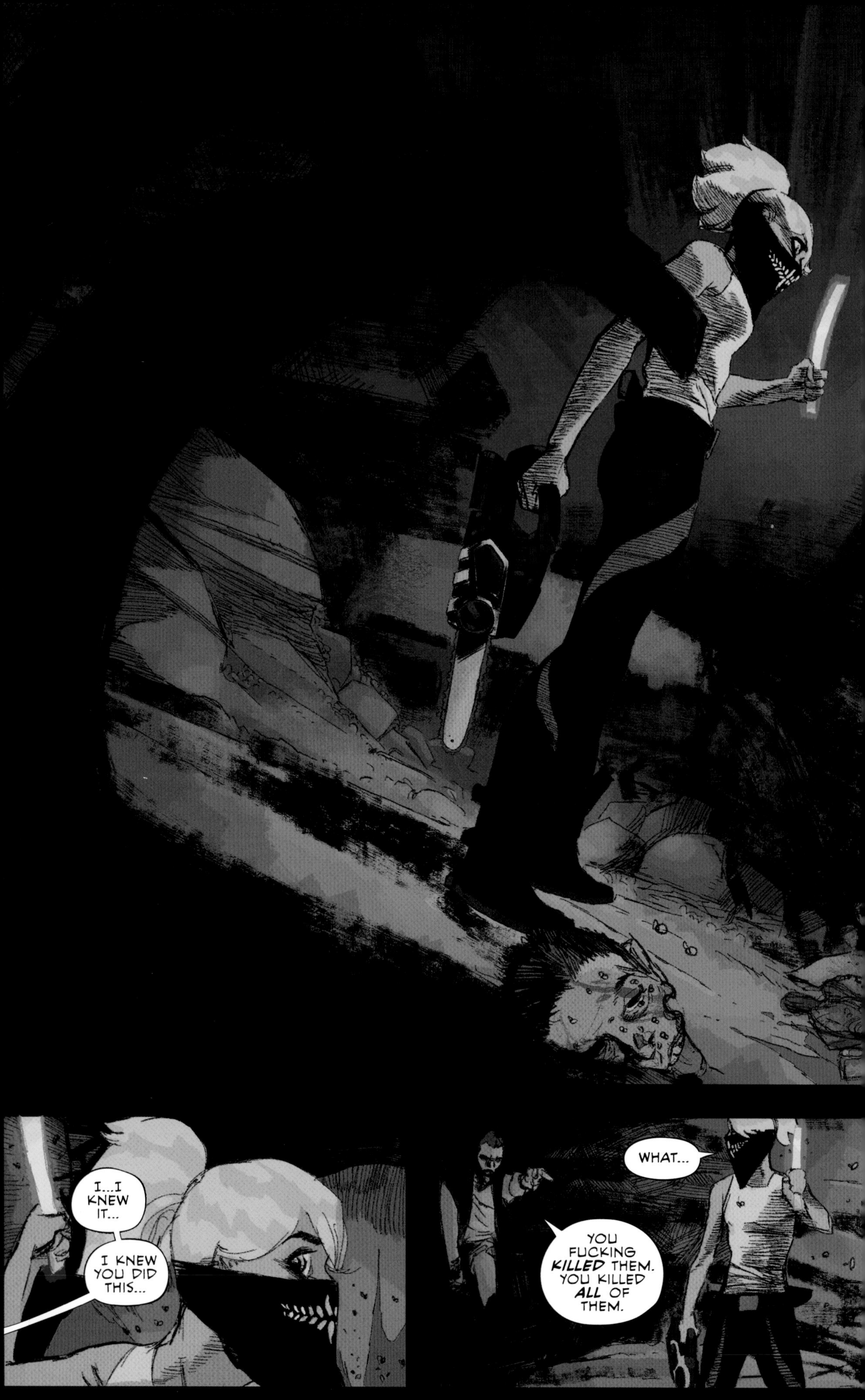
I...I KNEW IT...
I KNEW YOU DID THIS...
WHAT...
YOU FUCKING *KILLED* THEM. YOU KILLED *ALL* OF THEM.

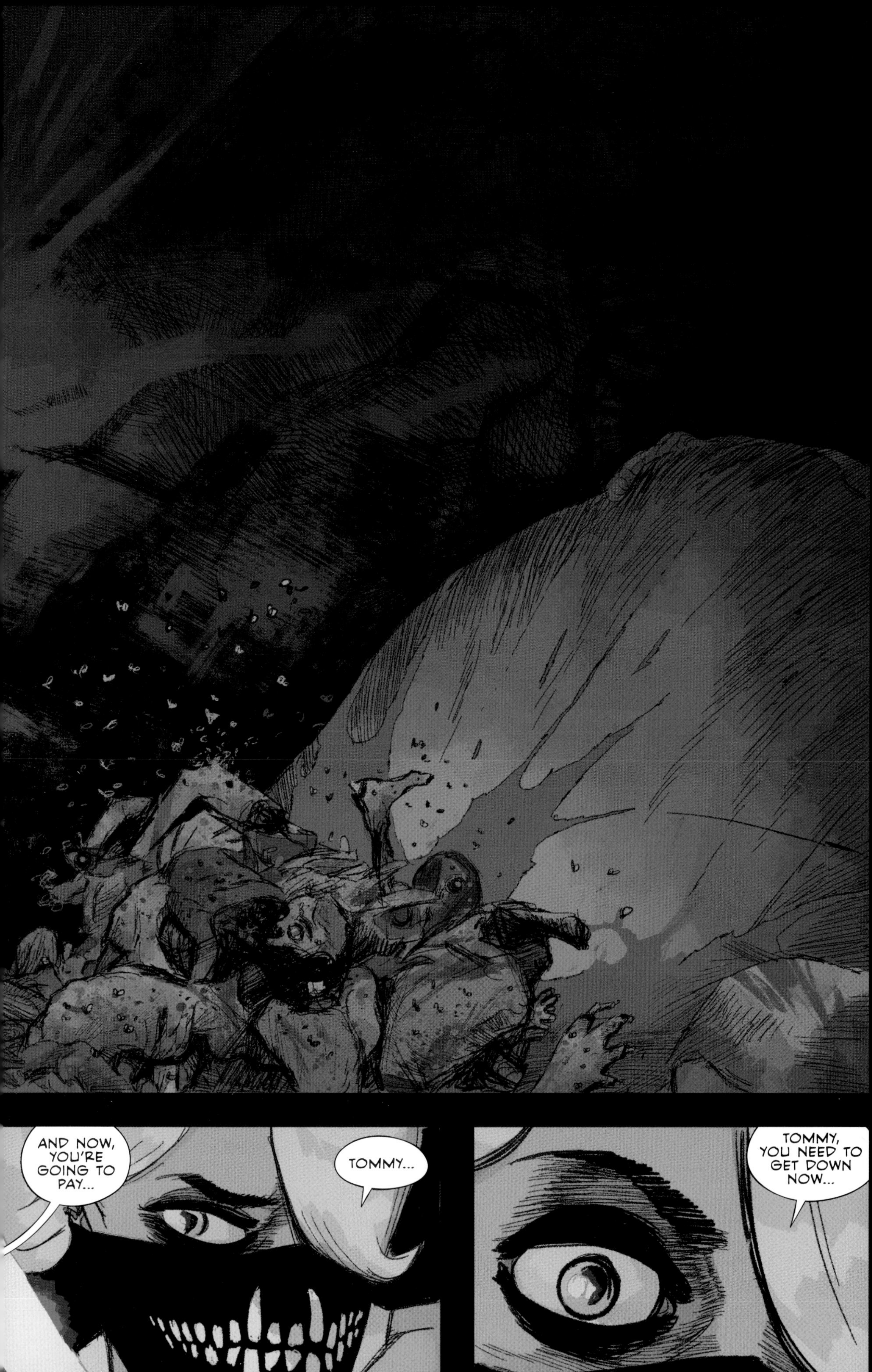
AND NOW, YOU'RE GOING TO PAY...
TOMMY...
TOMMY, YOU NEED TO GET DOWN NOW...

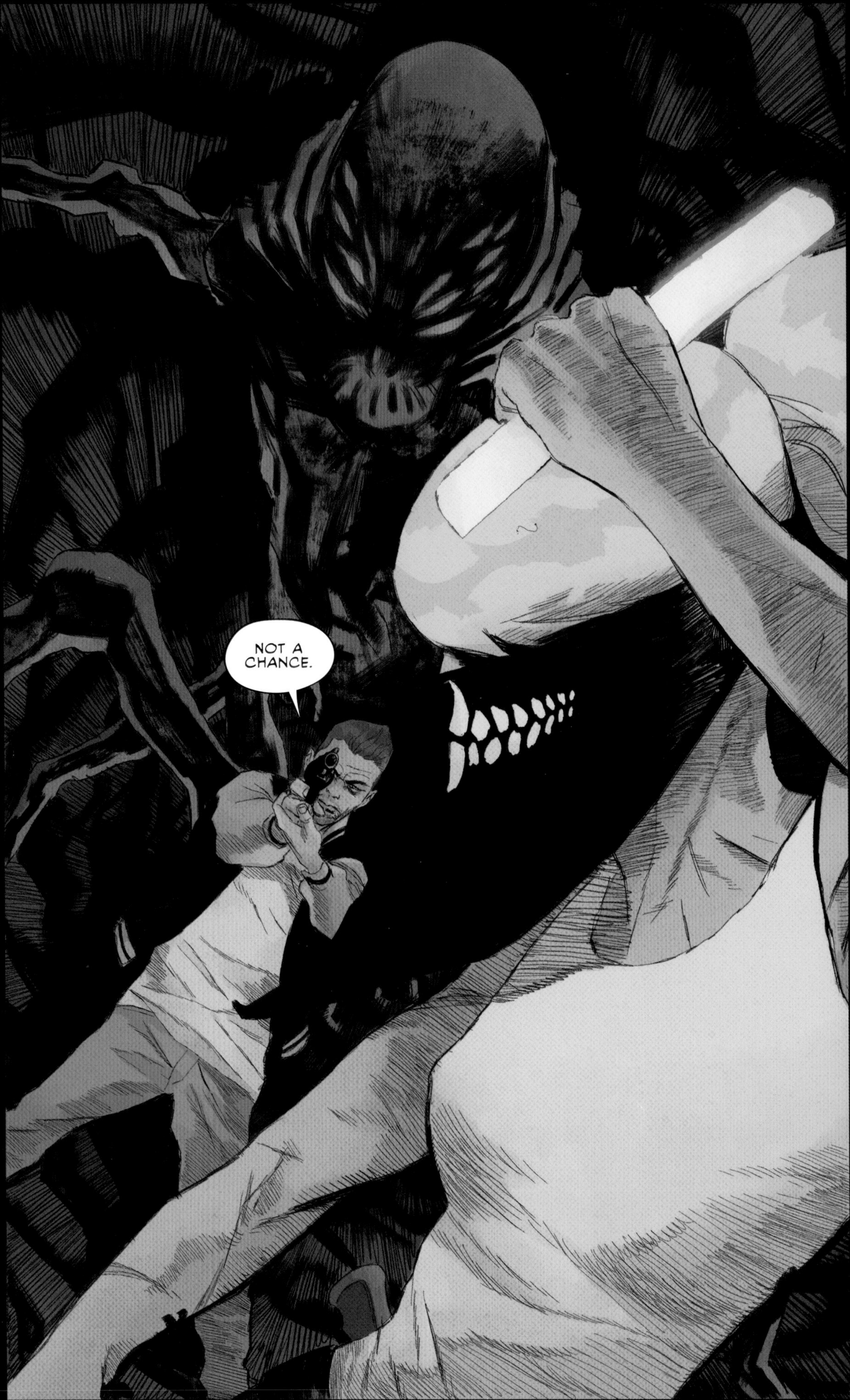
NOT A CHANCE.

CHAPTER FIVE

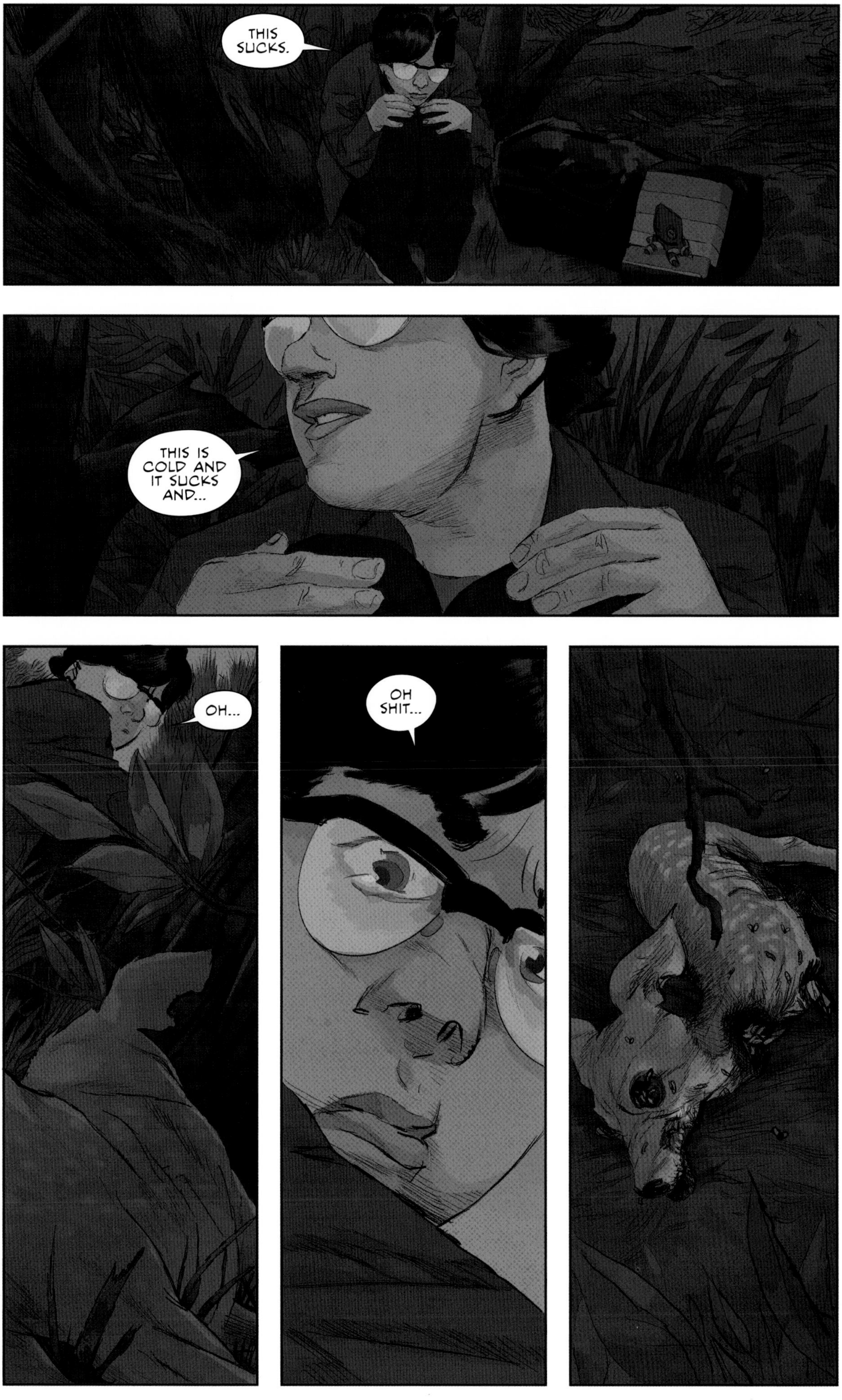
THIS SUCKS.
THIS IS COLD AND IT SUCKS AND...
OH...
OH SHIT...

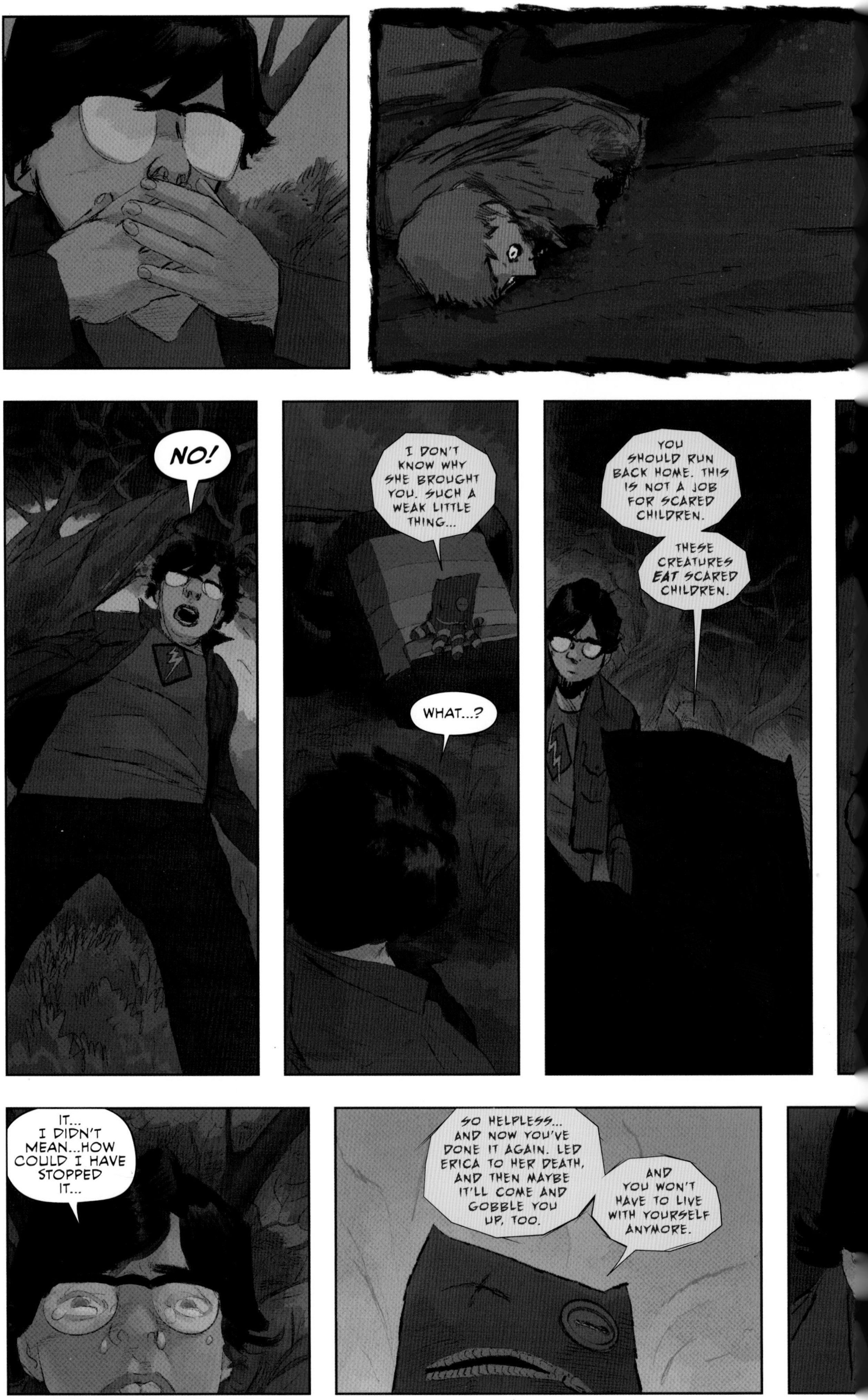
NO!
I DON'T KNOW WHY SHE BROUGHT YOU. SUCH A WEAK LITTLE THING...
WHAT...?
YOU SHOULD RUN BACK HOME. THIS IS NOT A JOB FOR SCARED CHILDREN.
THESE CREATURES EAT SCARED CHILDREN.
IT... I DIDN'T MEAN...HOW COULD I HAVE STOPPED IT...
SO HELPLESS... AND NOW YOU'VE DONE IT AGAIN. LED ERICA TO HER DEATH, AND THEN MAYBE IT'LL COME AND GOBBLE YOU UP, TOO.
AND YOU WON'T HAVE TO LIVE WITH YOURSELF ANYMORE.

NO.

I'M...I'M NOT AFRAID! AND YOU'RE... YOU'RE NOT REAL.

YES, THAT'S RIGHT. I'M NOT REAL. THIS IS ALL A NIGHTMARE. A NIGHTMARE THAT GUTTED YOUR FRIENDS. IT'S EASIER TO THINK THAT WAY, YES?

SO YOU DON'T HAVE TO FACE THAT YOU LED THEM DOWN INTO THE DARK WOODS LATE AT NIGHT, TO THEIR DEATHS.

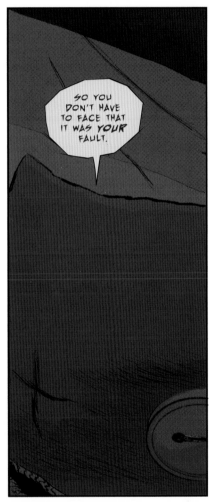

SO YOU DON'T HAVE TO FACE THAT IT WAS YOUR FAULT.

THAT'S NOT WHAT I WANT!

THEN DO SOMETHING ABOUT IT.

YOU HAVE THE WEAPONS SHE DOESN'T. YOU HAVE THE MEANS TO HELP.

IF YOU DON'T WANT ERICA TO DIE, NOW IS THE TIME TO ACT.

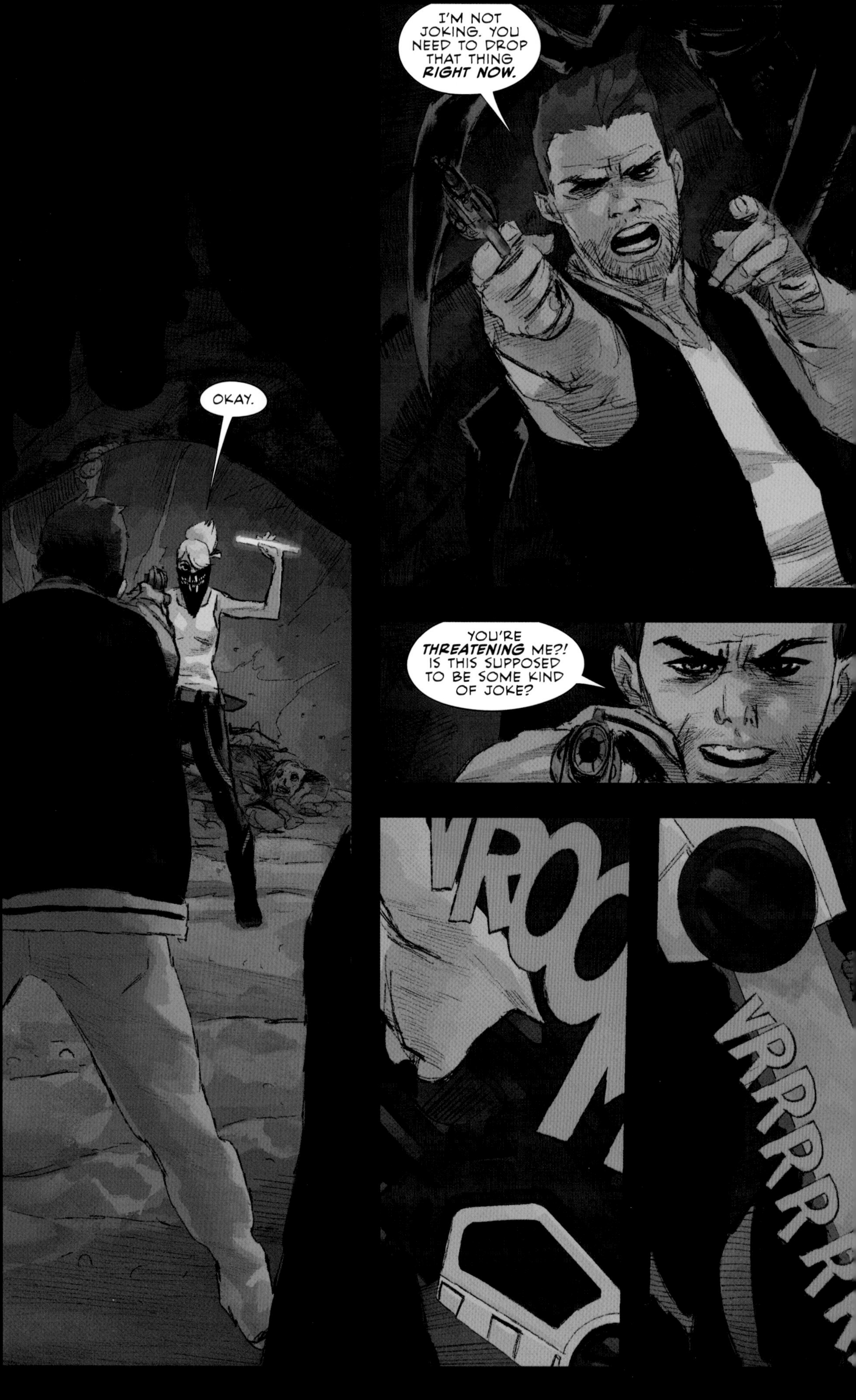
I'M NOT JOKING. YOU NEED TO DROP THAT THING RIGHT NOW.
OKAY.
YOU'RE THREATENING ME?! IS THIS SUPPOSED TO BE SOME KIND OF JOKE?
VROOO
VRRRRR

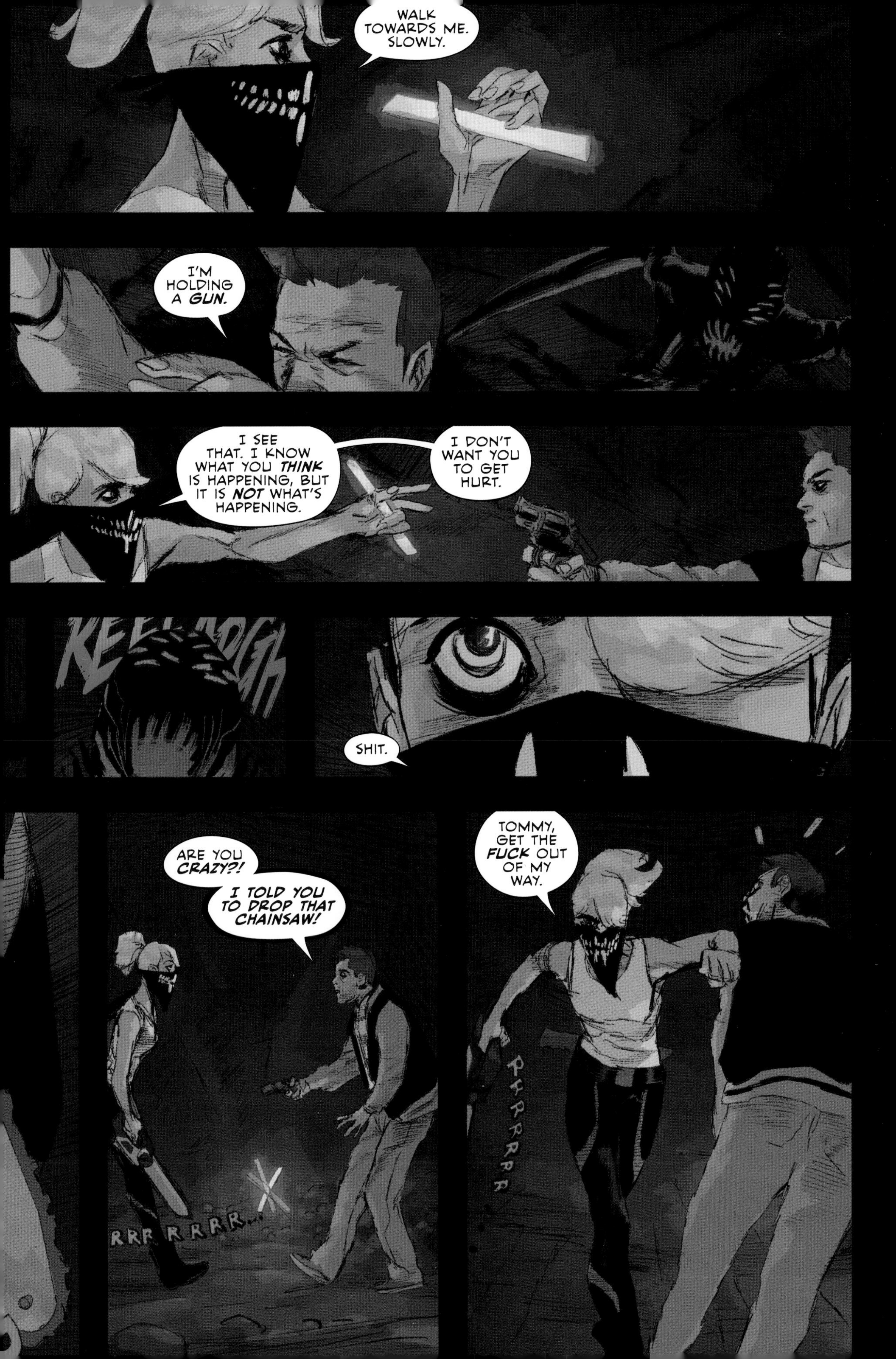
WALK TOWARDS ME. SLOWLY.
I'M HOLDING A *GUN.*
I SEE THAT. I KNOW WHAT YOU *THINK* IS HAPPENING, BUT IT IS *NOT* WHAT'S HAPPENING.
I DON'T WANT YOU TO GET HURT.
SHIT.
ARE YOU *CRAZY?!*
I TOLD YOU TO DROP THAT CHAINSAW!
TOMMY, GET THE *FUCK* OUT OF MY WAY.

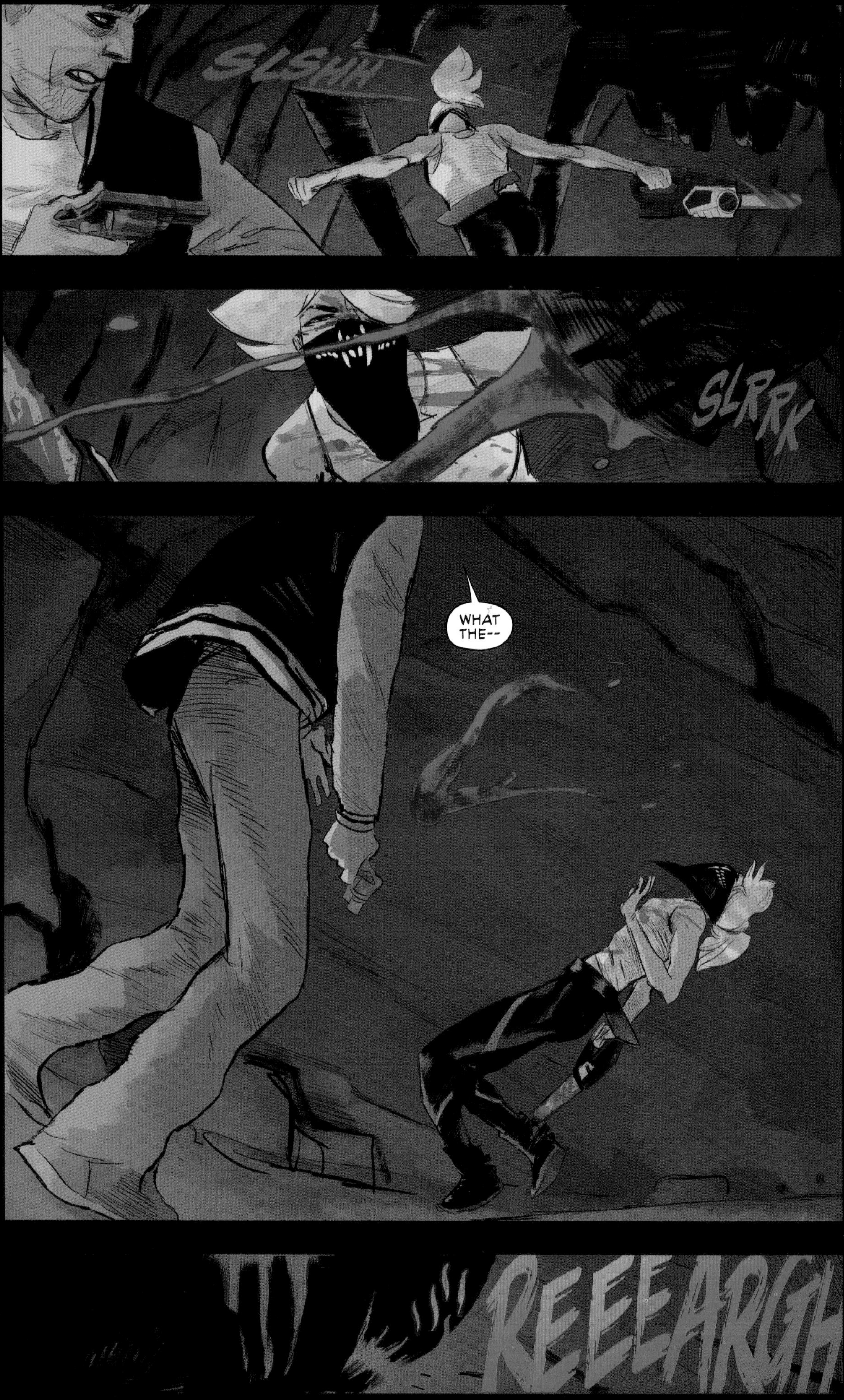
SLSHH
SLRRK
WHAT THE--
REEEARGH

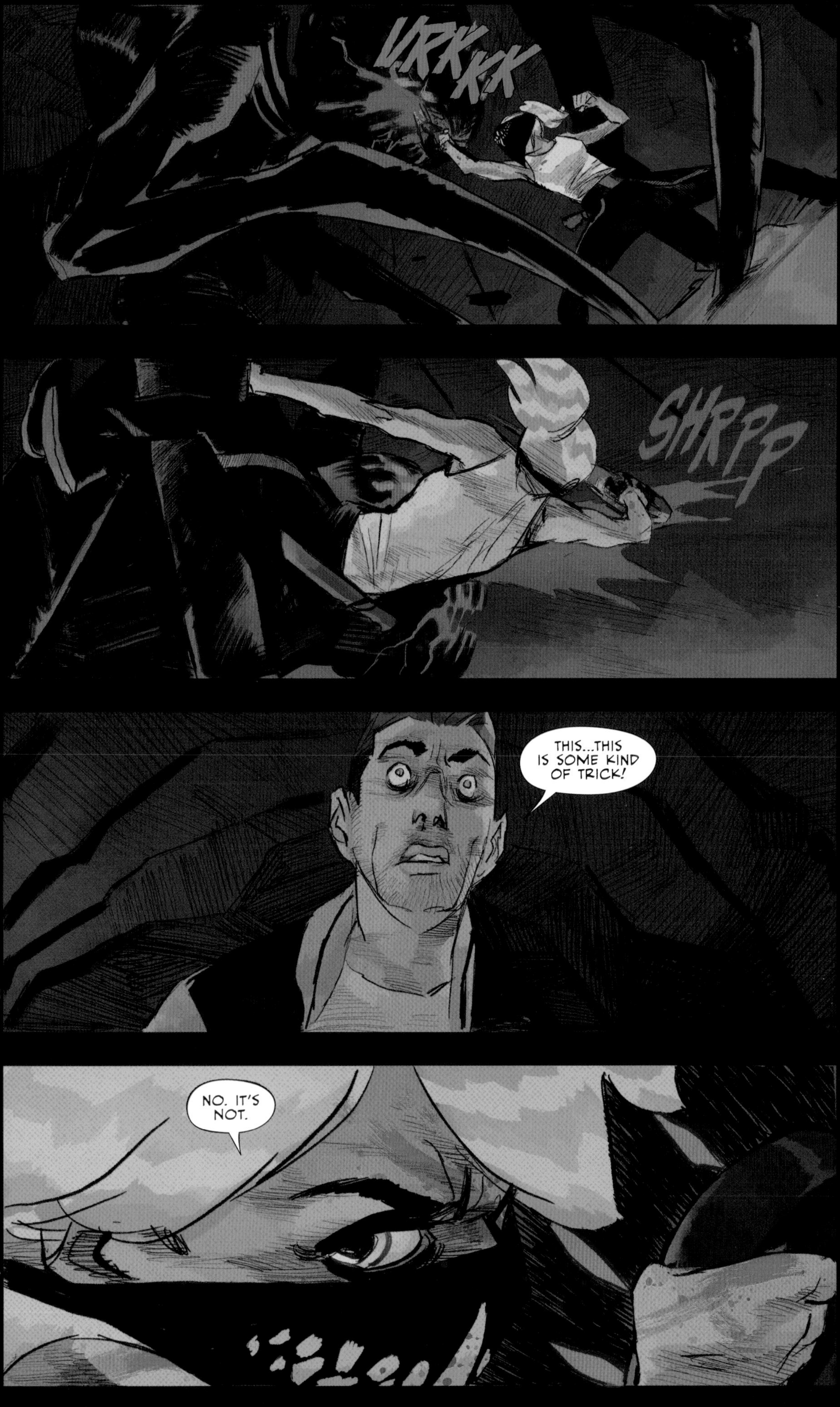
URKKK
SHRPP
THIS...THIS IS SOME KIND OF TRICK!
NO. IT'S NOT.

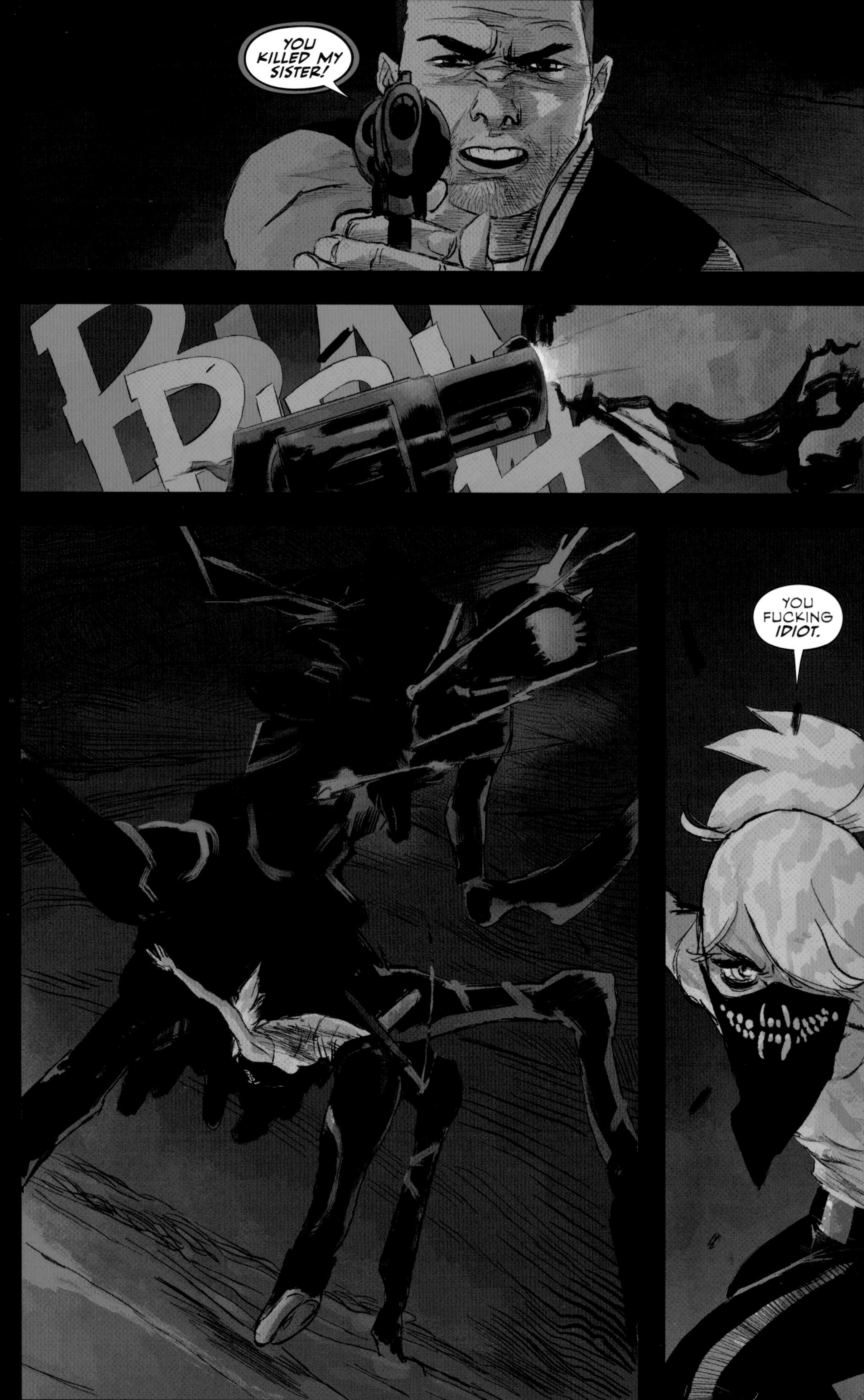
YOU KILLED MY SISTER!
YOU FUCKING IDIOT.

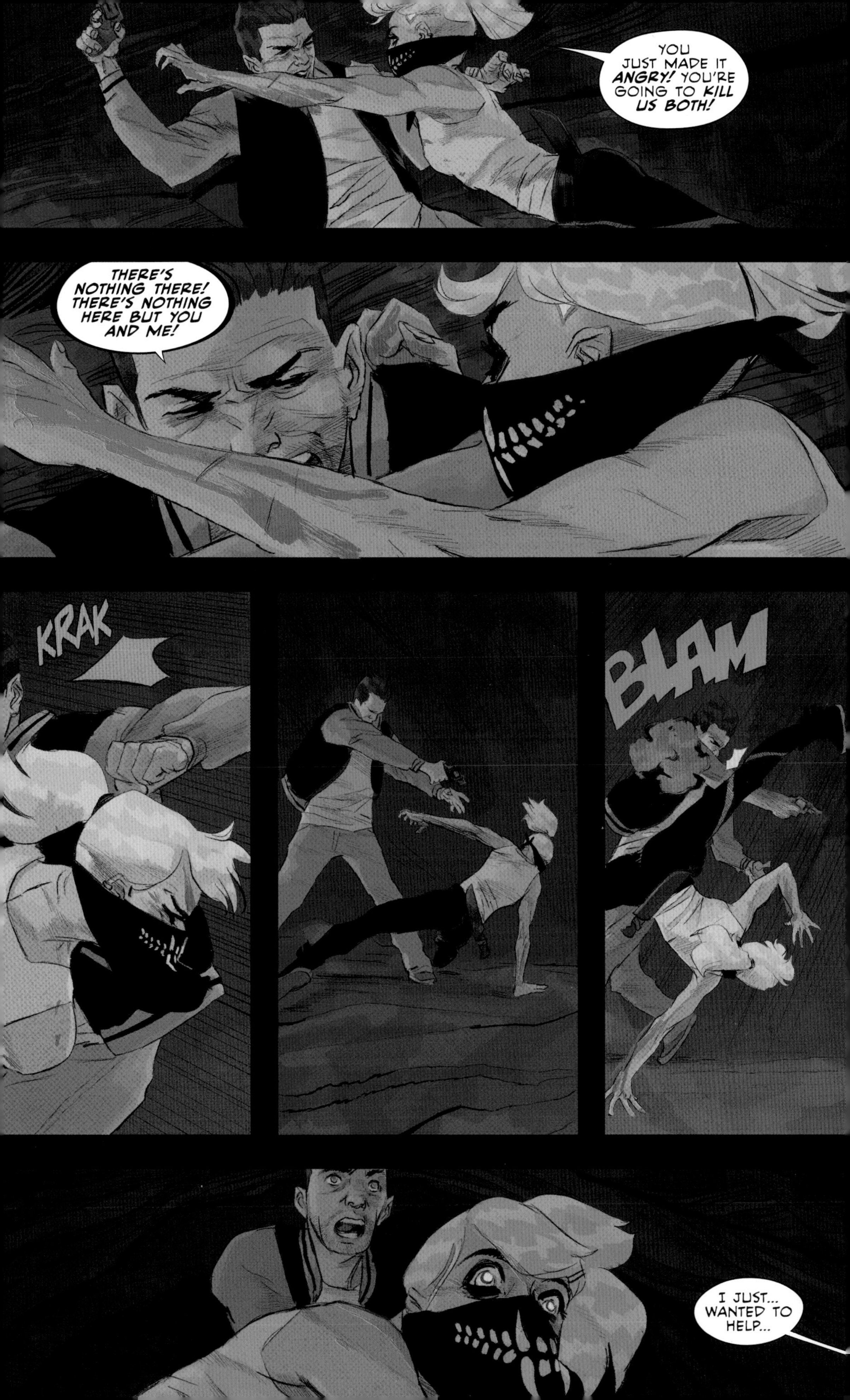

YOU JUST MADE IT ANGRY! YOU'RE GOING TO KILL US BOTH!
THERE'S NOTHING THERE! THERE'S NOTHING HERE BUT YOU AND ME!
KRAK
BLAM
I JUST... WANTED TO HELP...

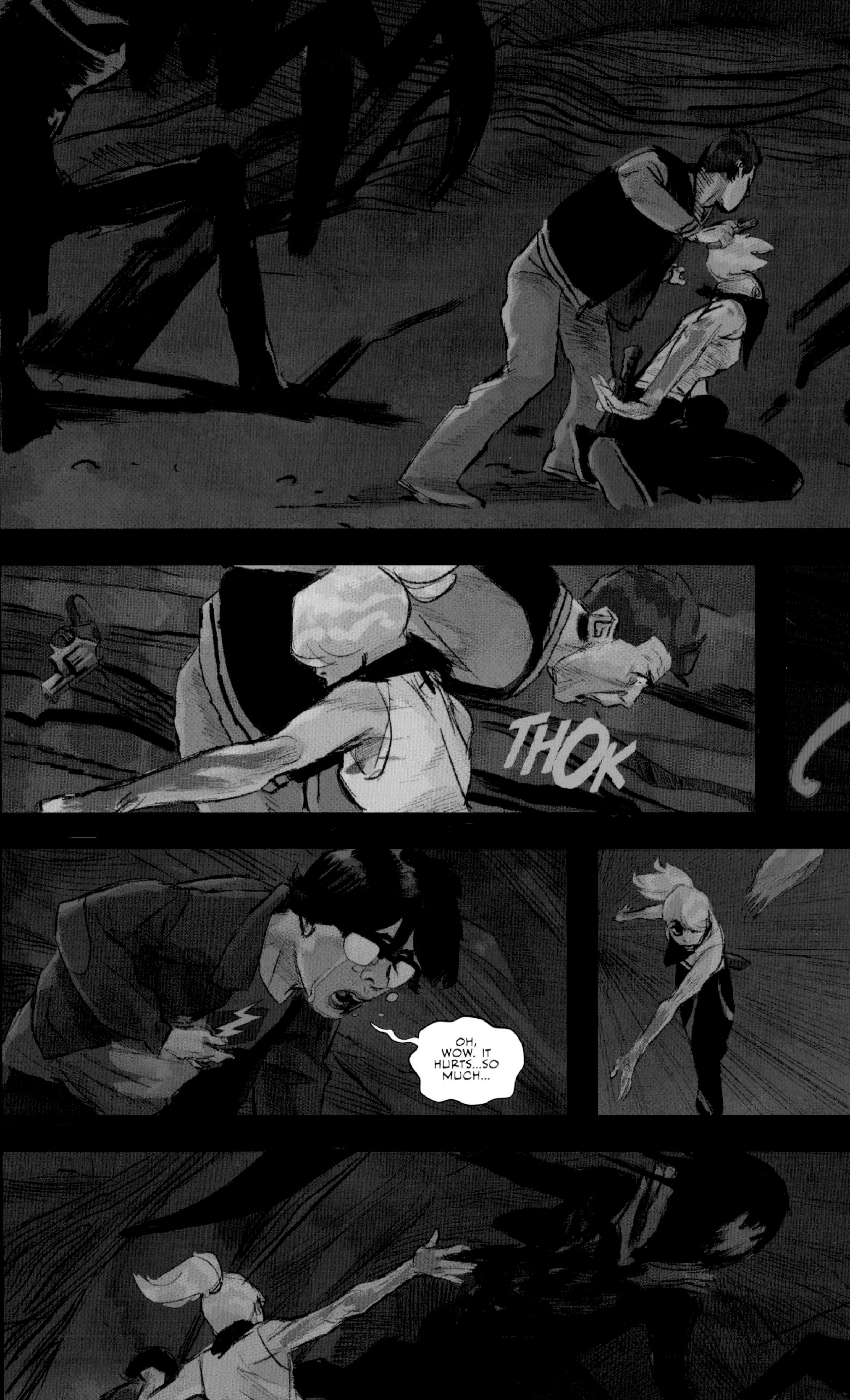
THOK
OH, WOW. IT HURTS...SO MUCH...

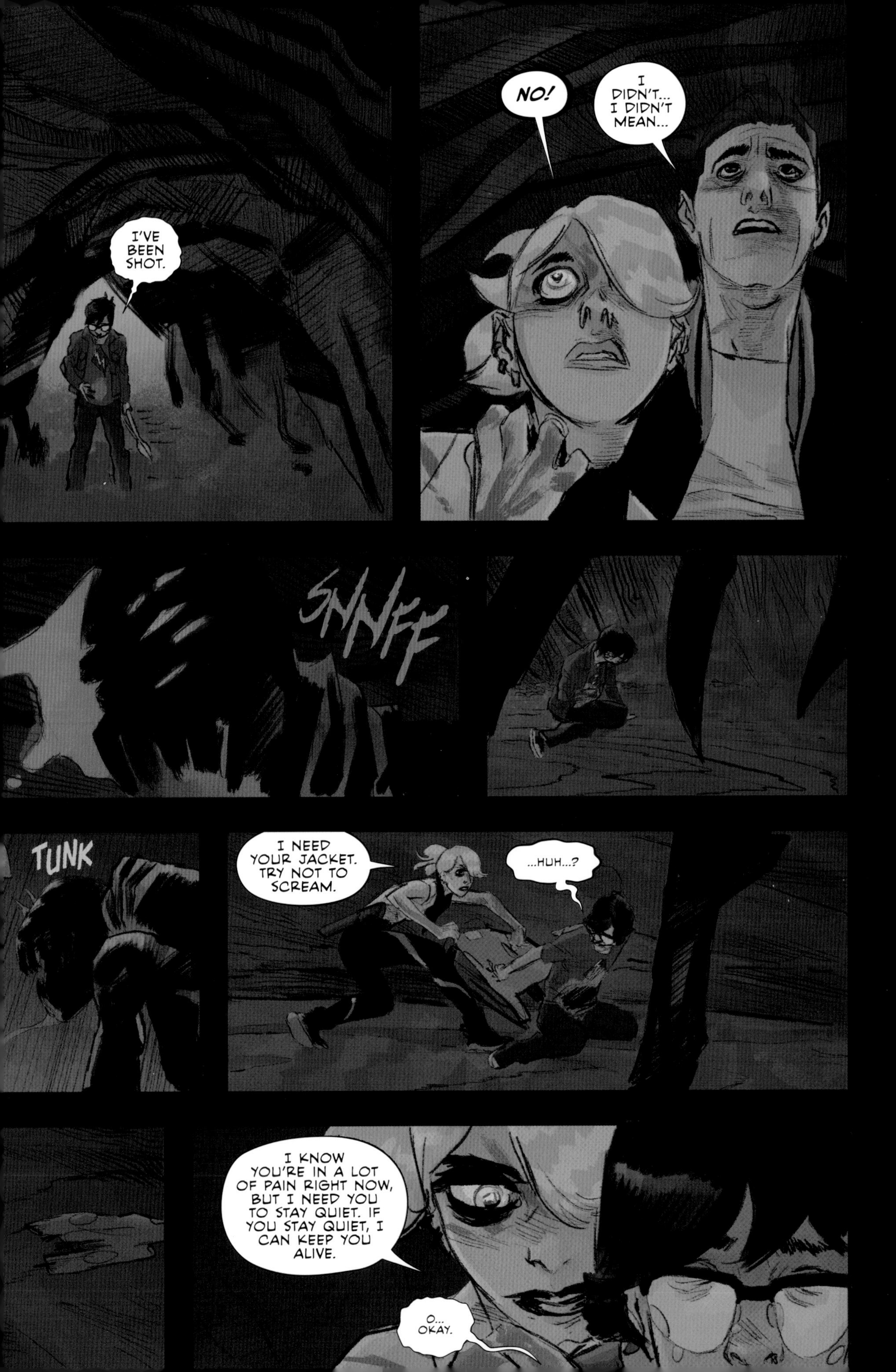
I'VE BEEN SHOT.
NO!
I DIDN'T... I DIDN'T MEAN...
SNNFF
TUNK
I NEED YOUR JACKET. TRY NOT TO SCREAM.
...HUH...?
I KNOW YOU'RE IN A LOT OF PAIN RIGHT NOW, BUT I NEED YOU TO STAY QUIET. IF YOU STAY QUIET, I CAN KEEP YOU ALIVE.
O... OKAY.

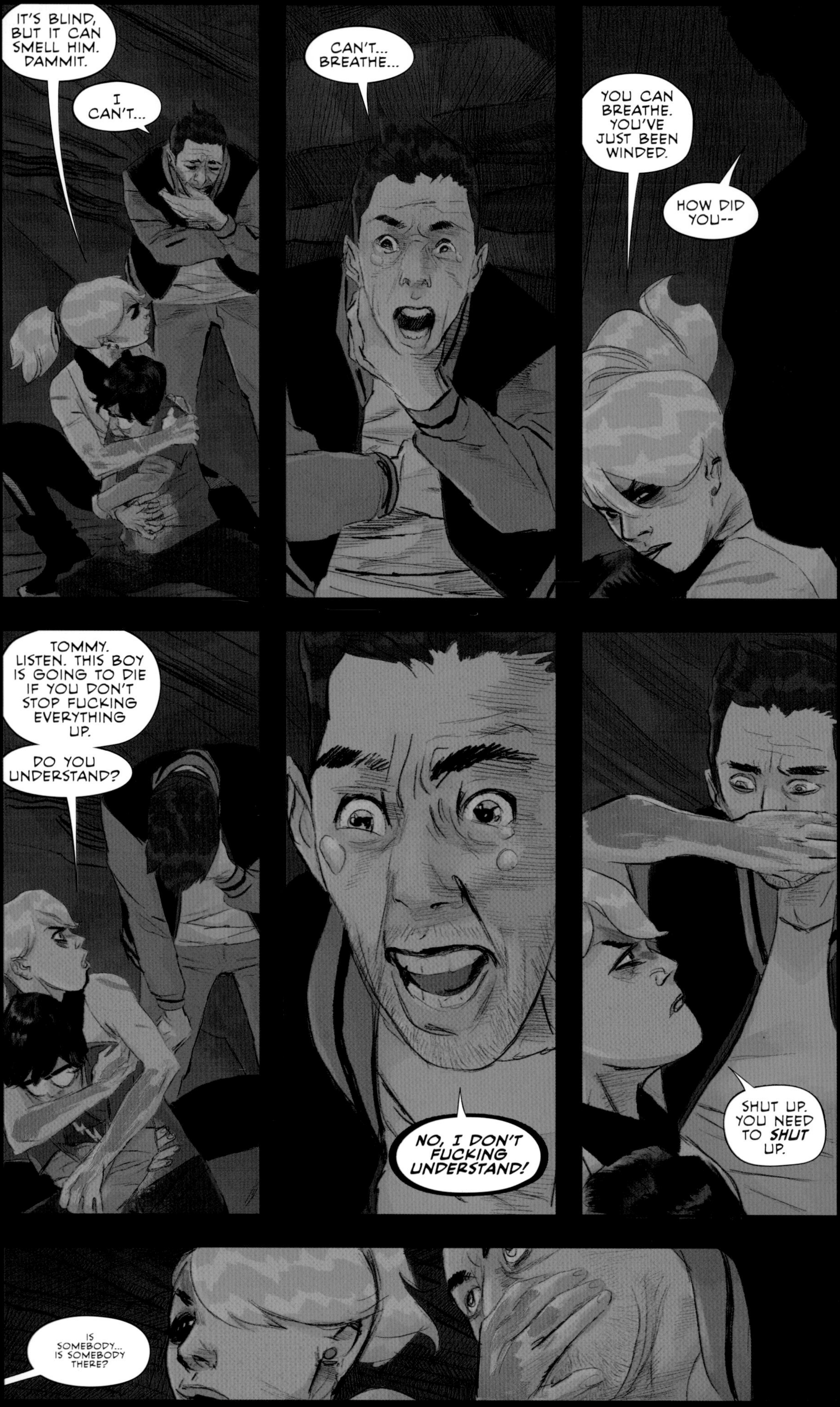
IT'S BLIND, BUT IT CAN SMELL HIM. DAMMIT.
I CAN'T...
CAN'T... BREATHE...
YOU CAN BREATHE. YOU'VE JUST BEEN WINDED.
HOW DID YOU--
TOMMY. LISTEN. THIS BOY IS GOING TO DIE IF YOU DON'T STOP FUCKING EVERYTHING UP.
DO YOU UNDERSTAND?
NO, I DON'T FUCKING UNDERSTAND!
SHUT UP. YOU NEED TO SHUT UP.
IS SOMEBODY... IS SOMEBODY THERE?

IT TOOK ME...

IT ATE MY SISTER. IT ATE SO MANY OF THEM...

WHAT'S YOUR NAME?

I'M...I'M BIAN.

BIAN? THERE WASN'T A BIAN ON MY LIST...

I'M...I'M SORRY.

NO, DON'T BE SORRY. ARE YOU OKAY? HOW LONG HAVE YOU BEEN IN HERE?

A LONG TIME...A LONG, LONG TIME.

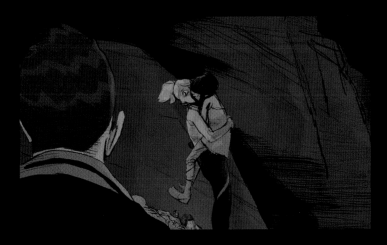

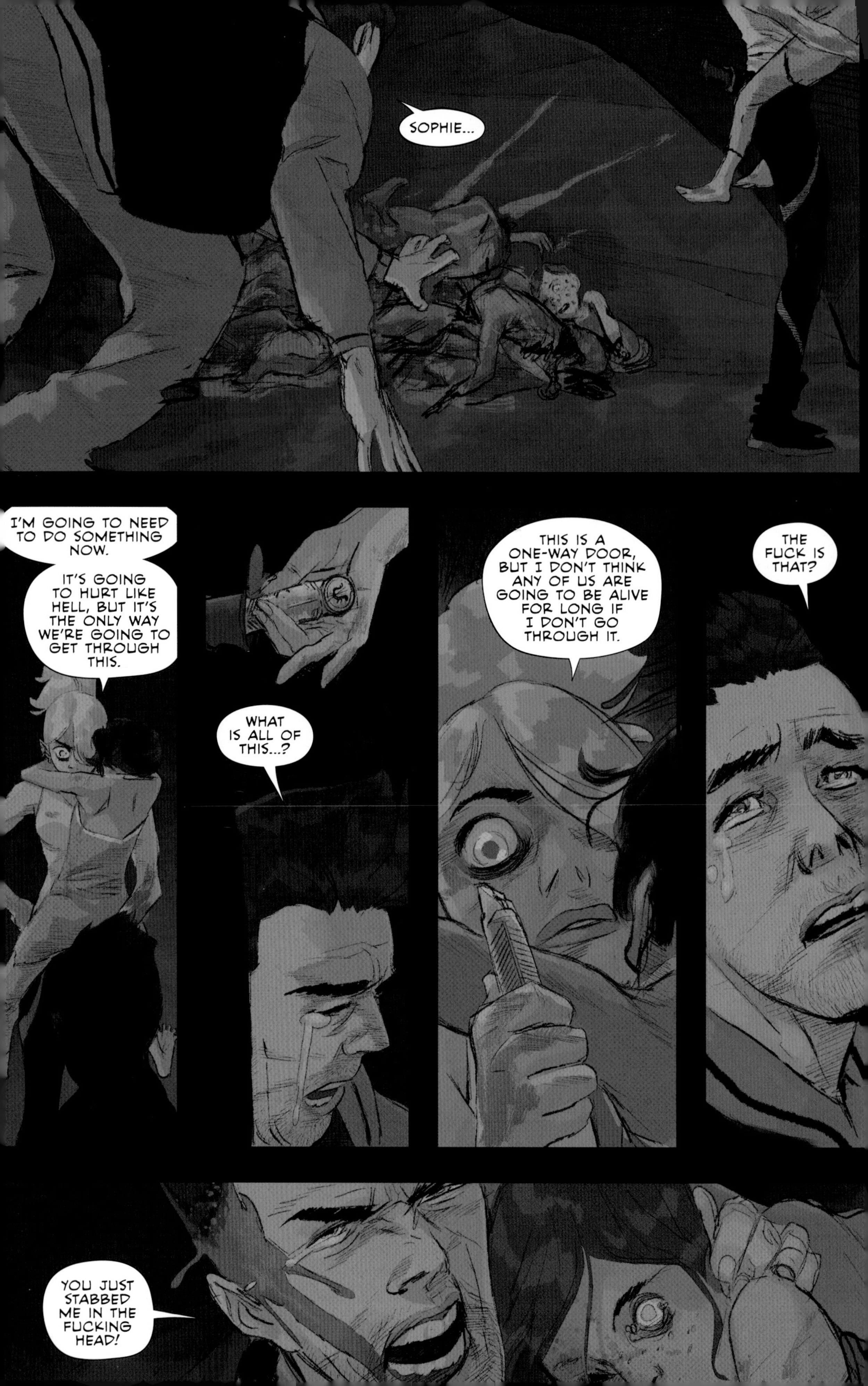
SOPHIE...
I'M GOING TO NEED TO DO SOMETHING NOW.
IT'S GOING TO HURT LIKE HELL, BUT IT'S THE ONLY WAY WE'RE GOING TO GET THROUGH THIS.
WHAT IS ALL OF THIS...?
THIS IS A ONE-WAY DOOR, BUT I DON'T THINK ANY OF US ARE GOING TO BE ALIVE FOR LONG IF I DON'T GO THROUGH IT.
THE FUCK IS THAT?
YOU JUST STABBED ME IN THE FUCKING HEAD!

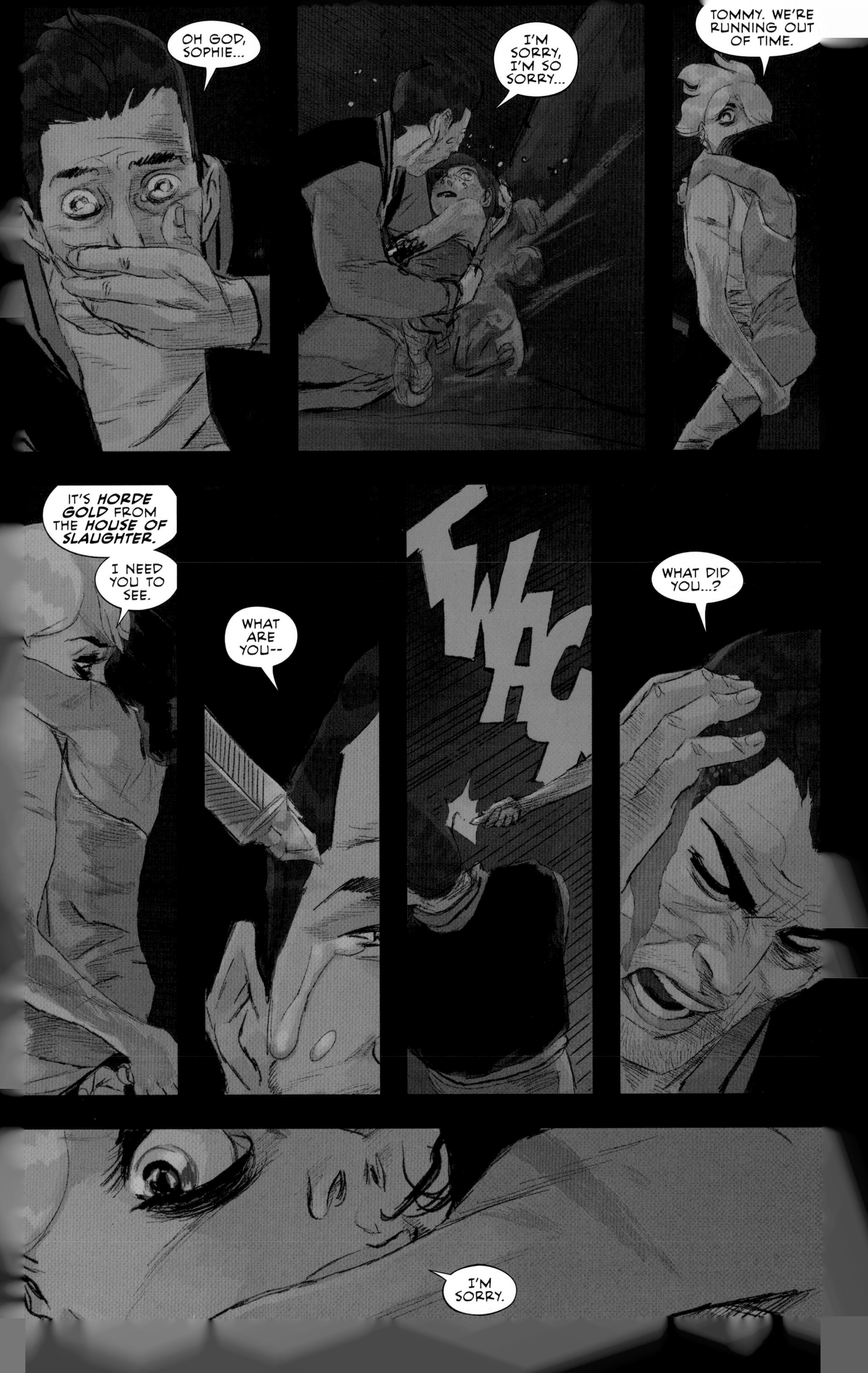
OH GOD, SOPHIE...
I'M SORRY, I'M SO SORRY...
TOMMY. WE'RE RUNNING OUT OF TIME.
IT'S **HORDE GOLD** FROM THE **HOUSE OF SLAUGHTER.**
I NEED YOU TO SEE.
WHAT ARE YOU--
WHAC
WHAT DID YOU...?
I'M SORRY.

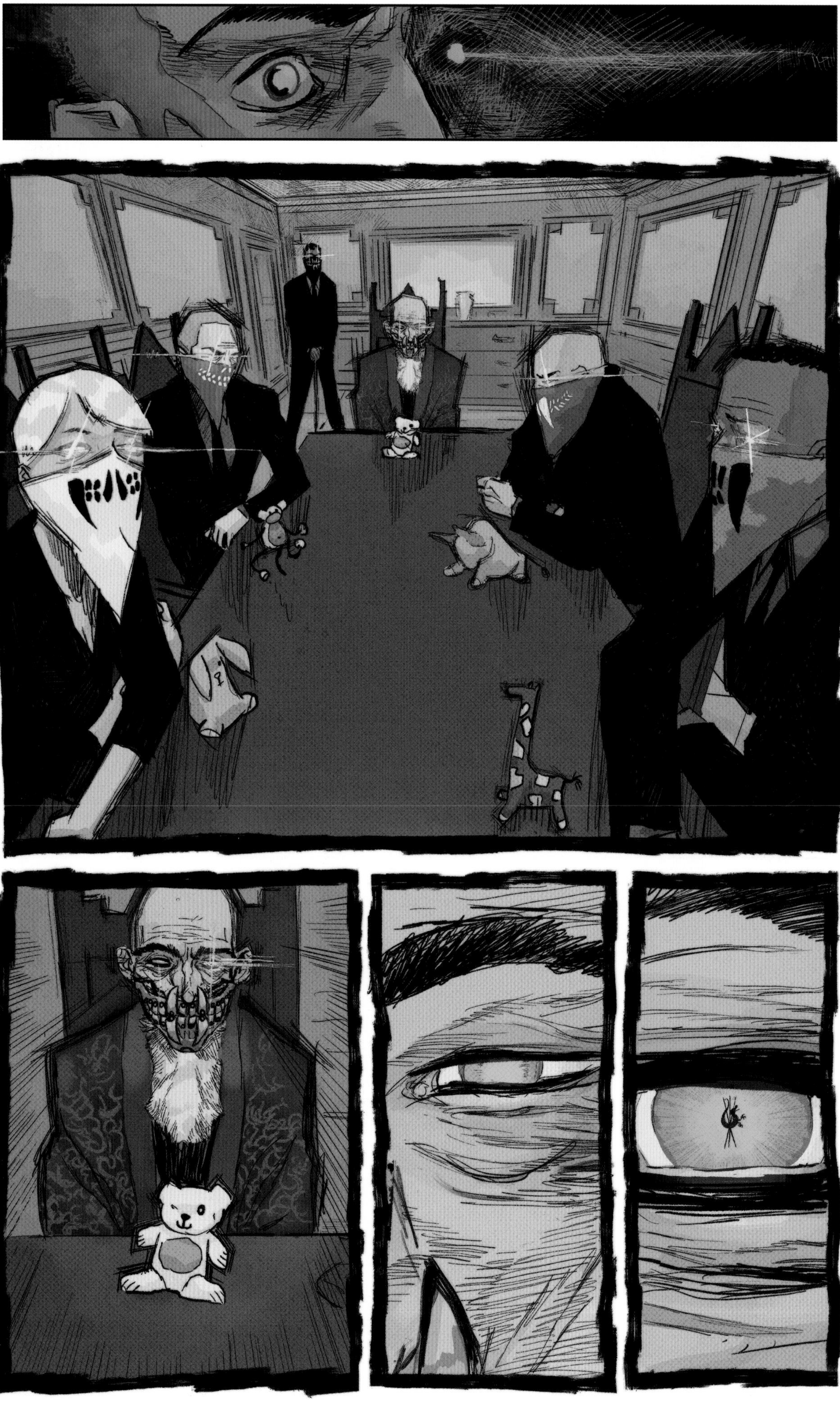

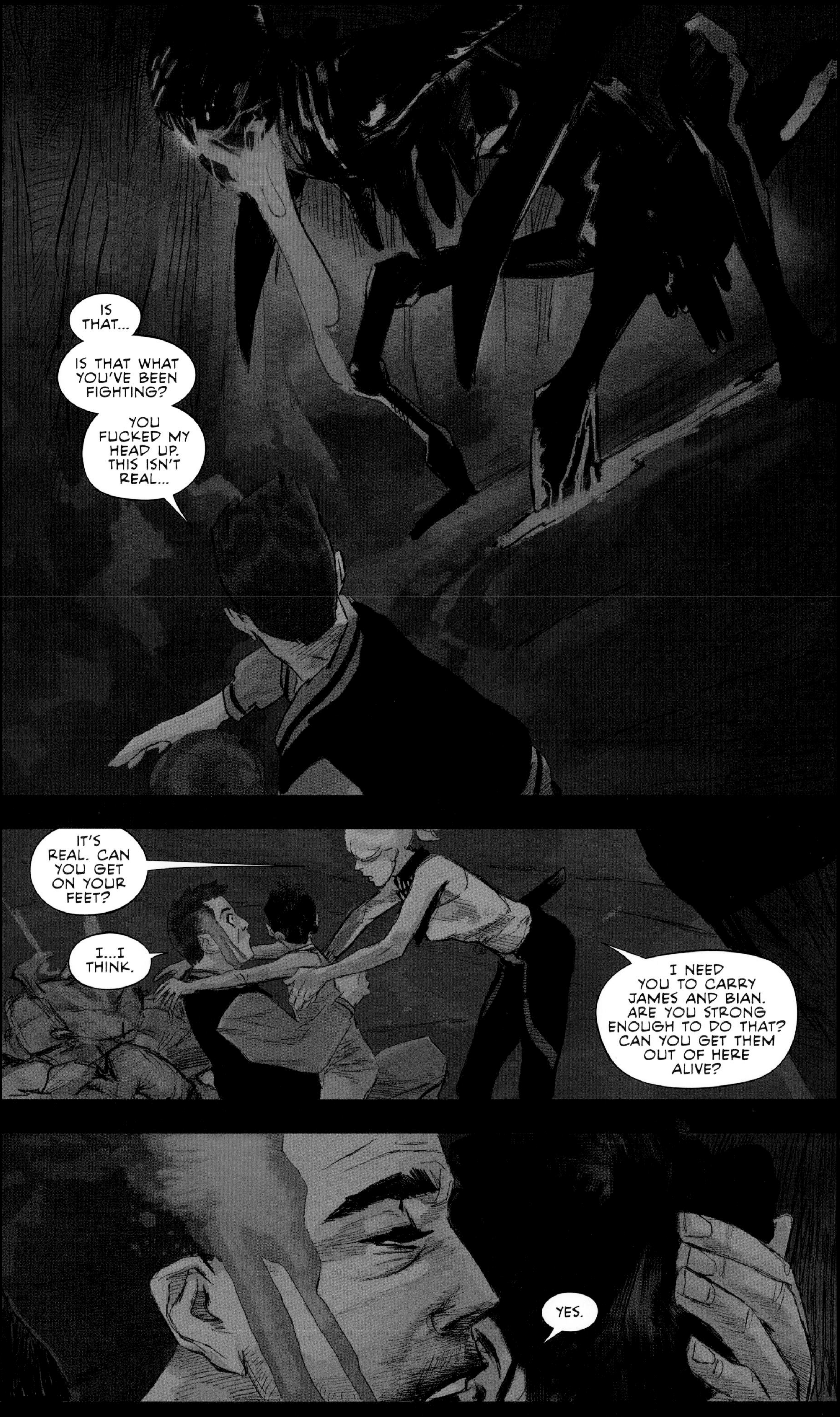
IS THAT...
IS THAT WHAT YOU'VE BEEN FIGHTING?
YOU FUCKED MY HEAD UP. THIS ISN'T REAL...
IT'S REAL. CAN YOU GET ON YOUR FEET?
I...I THINK.
I NEED YOU TO CARRY JAMES AND BIAN. ARE YOU STRONG ENOUGH TO DO THAT? CAN YOU GET THEM OUT OF HERE ALIVE?
YES.

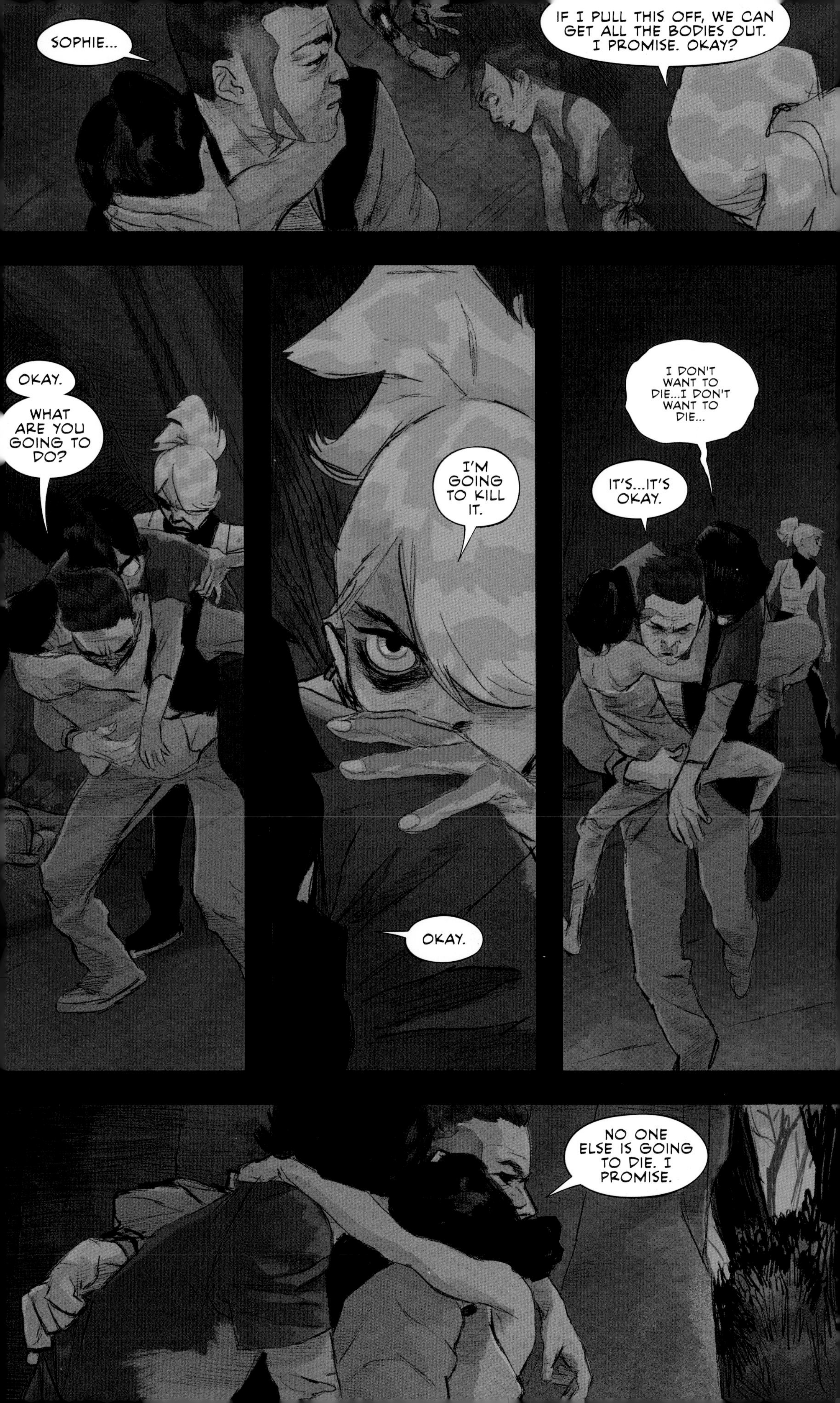
SOPHIE...
IF I PULL THIS OFF, WE CAN GET ALL THE BODIES OUT. I PROMISE. OKAY?
OKAY.
WHAT ARE YOU GOING TO DO?
I'M GOING TO KILL IT.
OKAY.
I DON'T WANT TO DIE...I DON'T WANT TO DIE...
IT'S...IT'S OKAY.
NO ONE ELSE IS GOING TO DIE. I PROMISE.

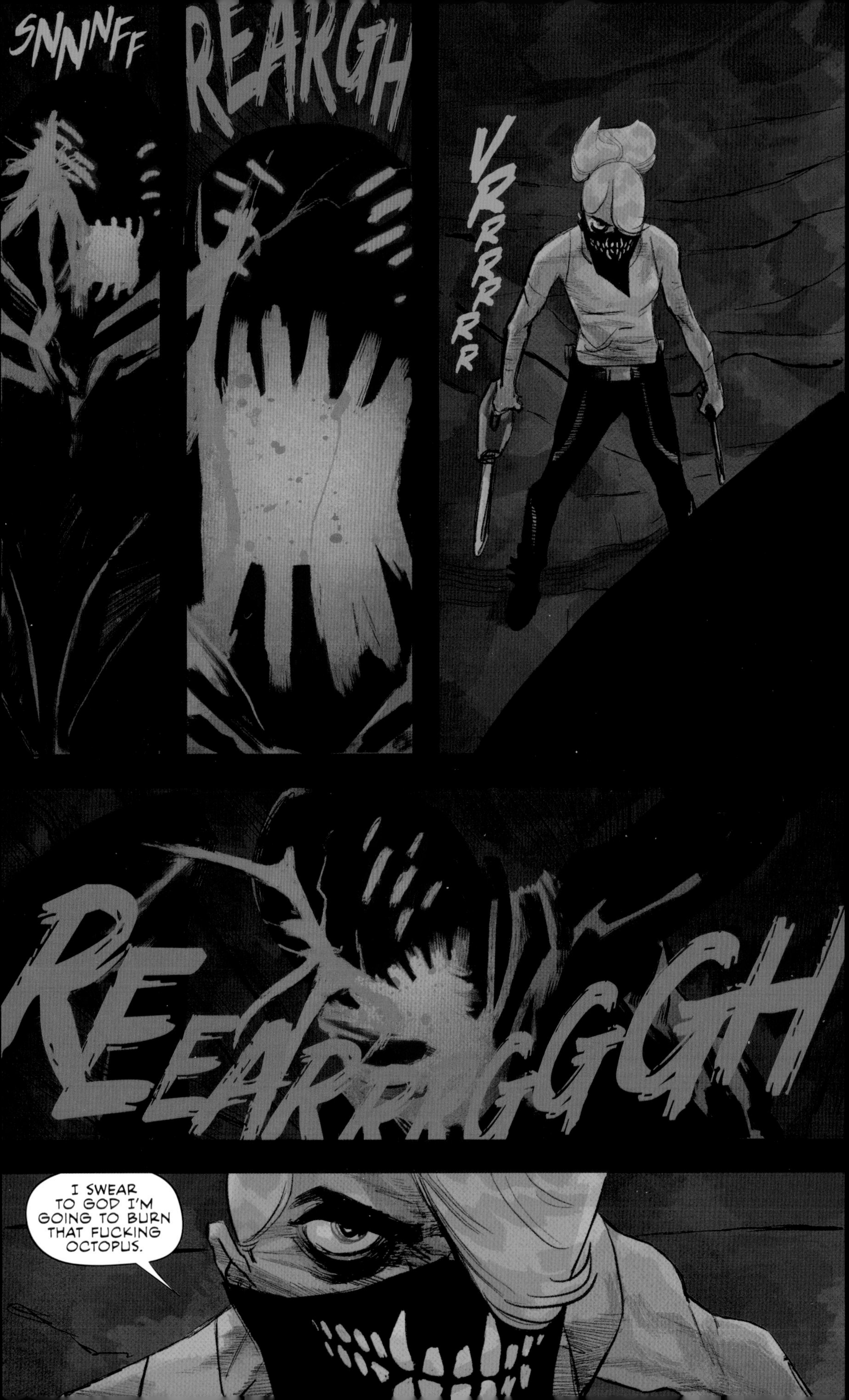
SNNNFF
REARGH
VRRRRRRR
REEARRRGGGH
I SWEAR TO GOD I'M GOING TO BURN THAT FUCKING OCTOPUS.

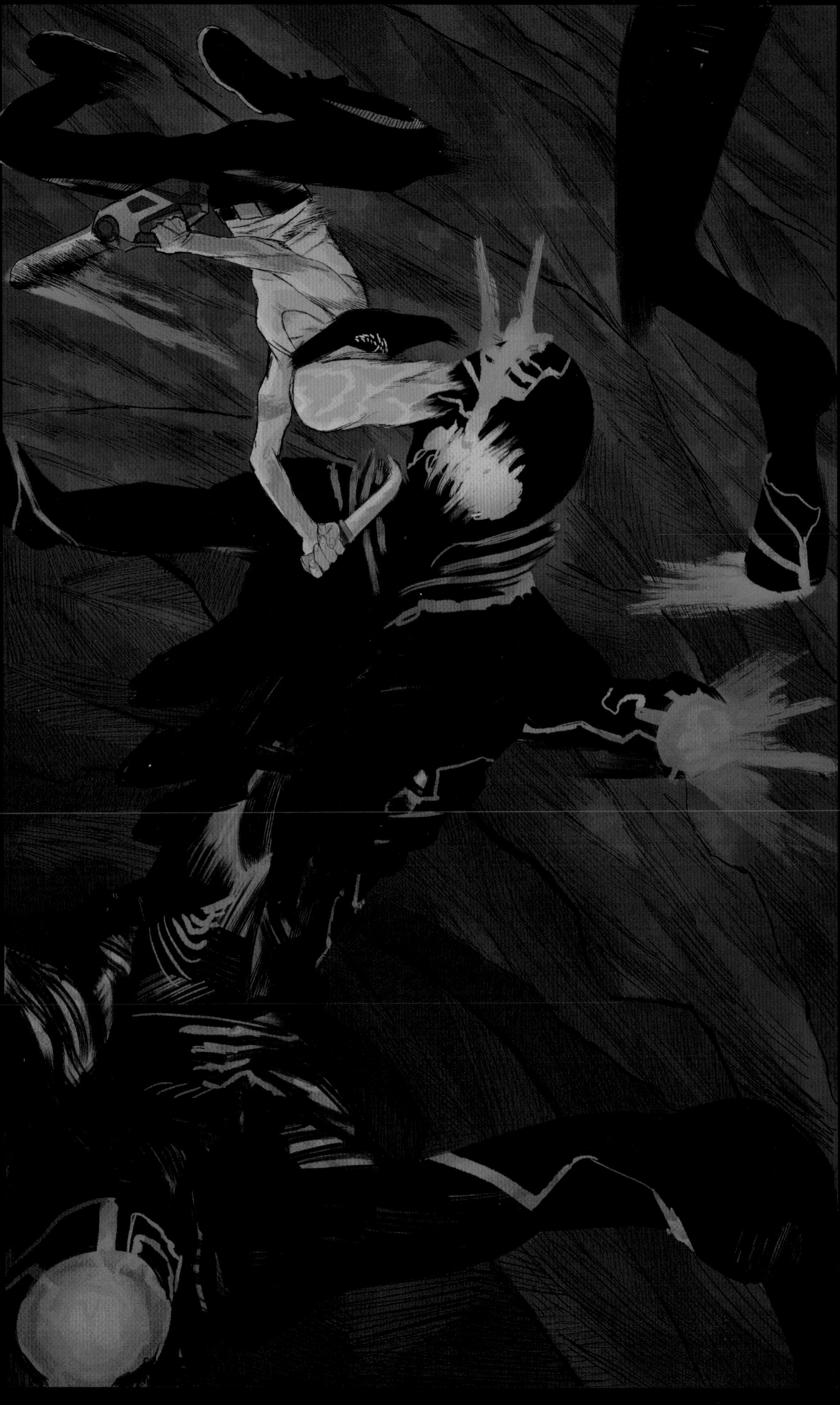

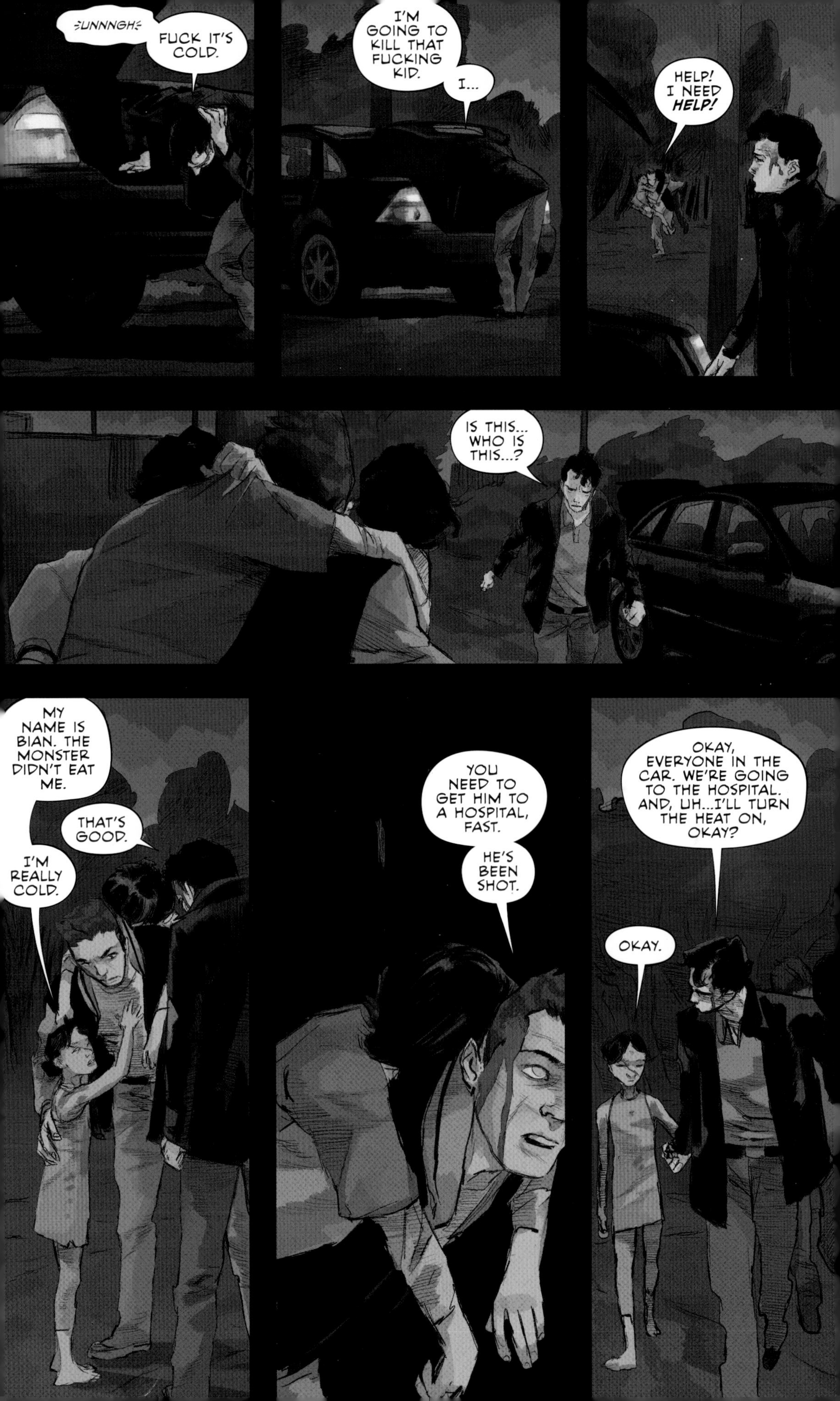

=UNNNGH=
FUCK IT'S COLD.
I'M GOING TO KILL THAT FUCKING KID.
I...
HELP! I NEED *HELP!*
IS THIS... WHO IS THIS...?
MY NAME IS BIAN. THE MONSTER DIDN'T EAT ME.
THAT'S GOOD.
I'M REALLY COLD.
YOU NEED TO GET HIM TO A HOSPITAL, FAST.
HE'S BEEN SHOT.
OKAY, EVERYONE IN THE CAR. WE'RE GOING TO THE HOSPITAL. AND, UH...I'LL TURN THE HEAT ON, OKAY?
OKAY.

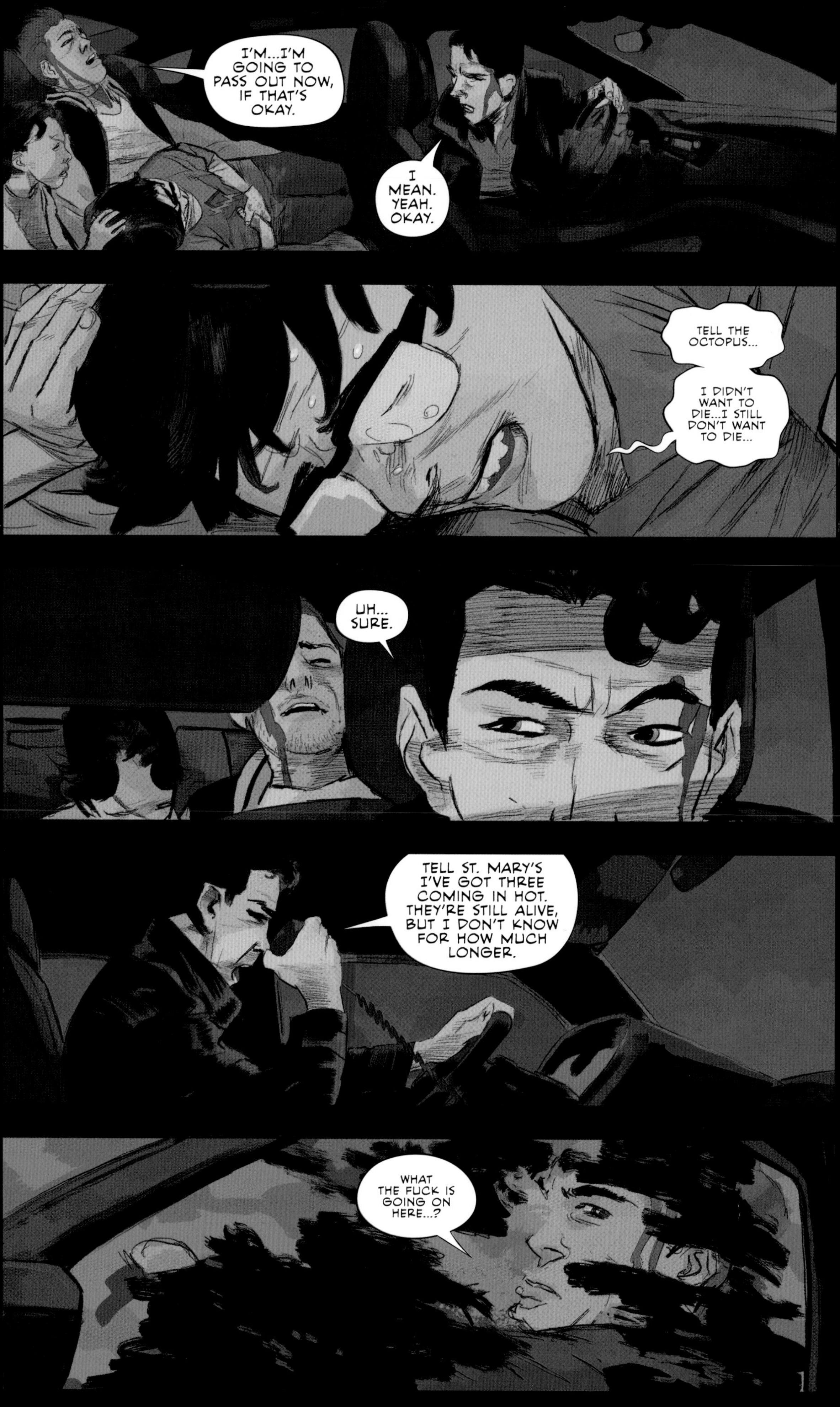
I'M...I'M GOING TO PASS OUT NOW, IF THAT'S OKAY.
I MEAN. YEAH. OKAY.
TELL THE OCTOPUS...
I DIDN'T WANT TO DIE...I STILL DON'T WANT TO DIE...
UH... SURE.
TELL ST. MARY'S I'VE GOT THREE COMING IN HOT. THEY'RE STILL ALIVE, BUT I DON'T KNOW FOR HOW MUCH LONGER.
WHAT THE FUCK IS GOING ON HERE...?

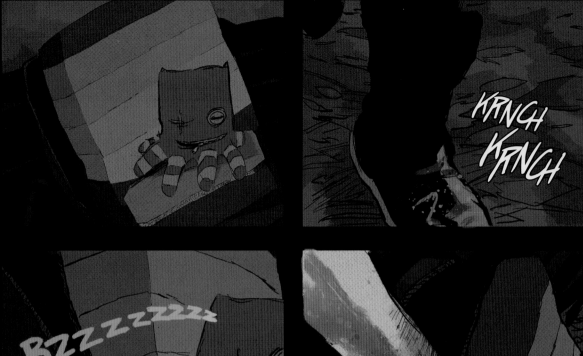

KRNCH
KRNCH

BZZZZZZZ

BZZZZZZ

YEAH.

I DID WHAT I HAD TO DO TO SAVE TWO LIVES. I'LL DEAL WITH THE CONSEQUENCES.

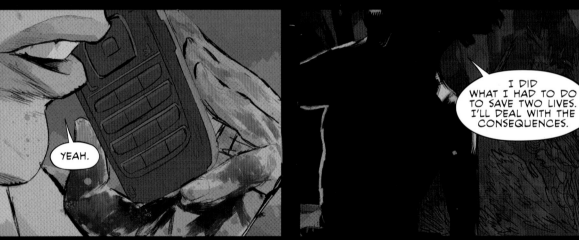

NO, LISTEN TO ME. YOU DIDN'T CLASSIFY THIS CORRECTLY. THIS WASN'T A FOOD STASH, IT WAS A *NEST*.

NO. FUCKING *LISTEN.*

IT WAS A MOTHER, AARON.

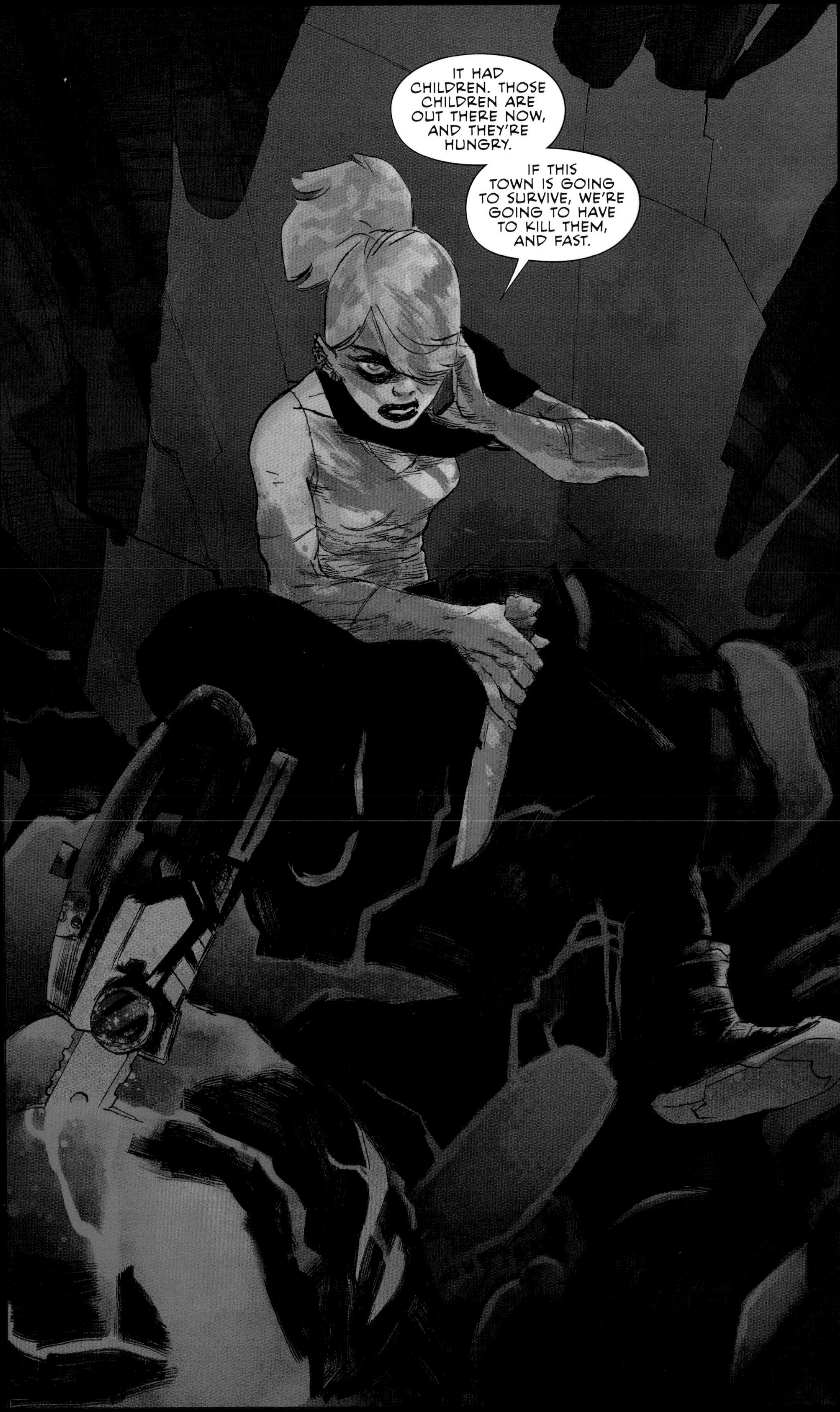
IT HAD CHILDREN. THOSE CHILDREN ARE OUT THERE NOW, AND THEY'RE HUNGRY.
IF THIS TOWN IS GOING TO SURVIVE, WE'RE GOING TO HAVE TO KILL THEM, AND FAST.

CHAPTER
SIX

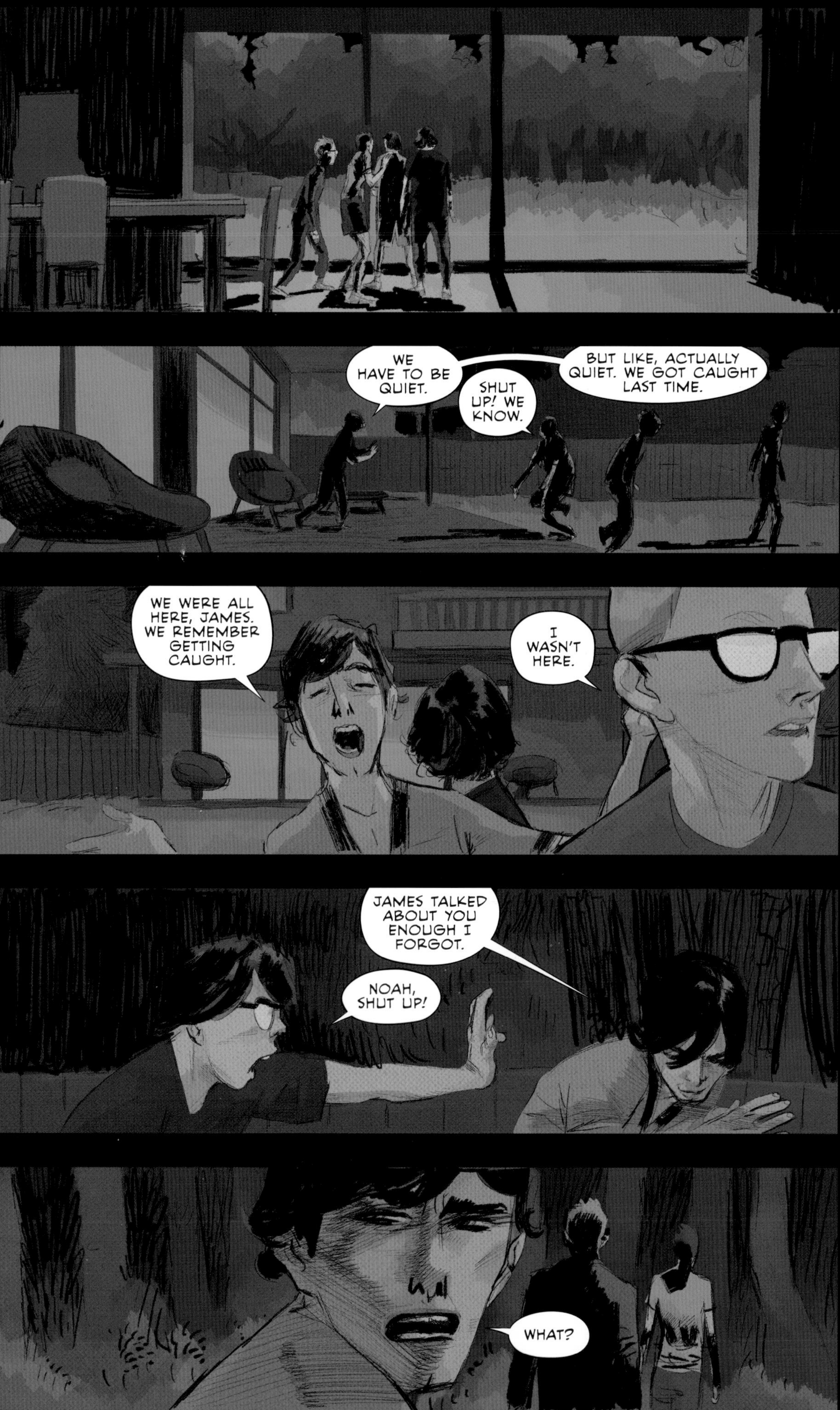
WE HAVE TO BE QUIET.
BUT LIKE, ACTUALLY QUIET. WE GOT CAUGHT LAST TIME.
SHUT UP! WE KNOW.
WE WERE ALL HERE, JAMES. WE REMEMBER GETTING CAUGHT.
I WASN'T HERE.
JAMES TALKED ABOUT YOU ENOUGH I FORGOT.
NOAH, SHUT UP!
WHAT?

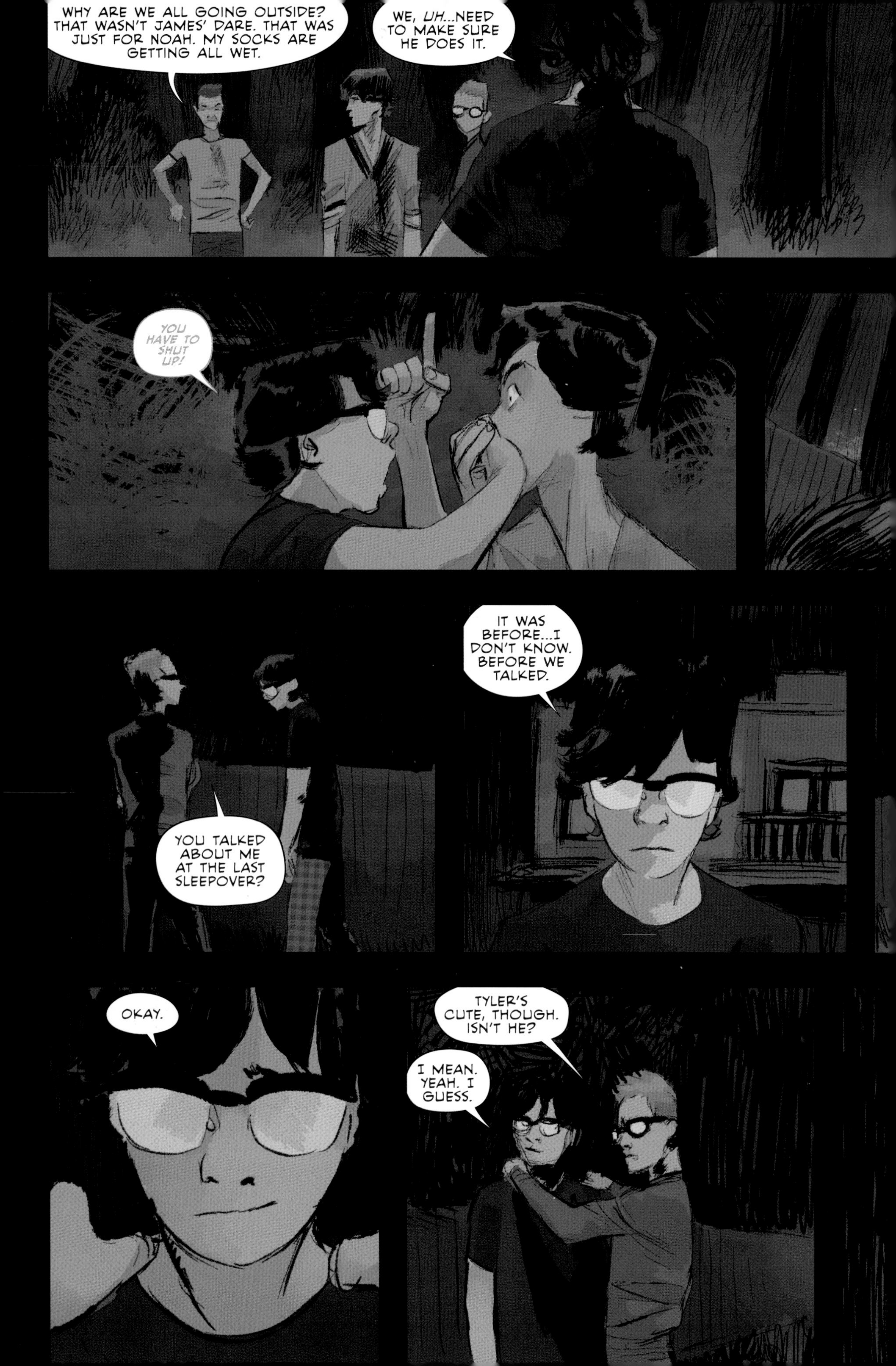
WHY ARE WE ALL GOING OUTSIDE? THAT WASN'T JAMES' DARE. THAT WAS JUST FOR NOAH. MY SOCKS ARE GETTING ALL WET.
WE, *UH*...NEED TO MAKE SURE HE DOES IT.
YOU HAVE TO SHUT UP!
YOU TALKED ABOUT ME AT THE LAST SLEEPOVER?
IT WAS BEFORE...I DON'T KNOW. BEFORE WE TALKED.
OKAY.
TYLER'S CUTE, THOUGH. ISN'T HE?
I MEAN. YEAH. I GUESS.

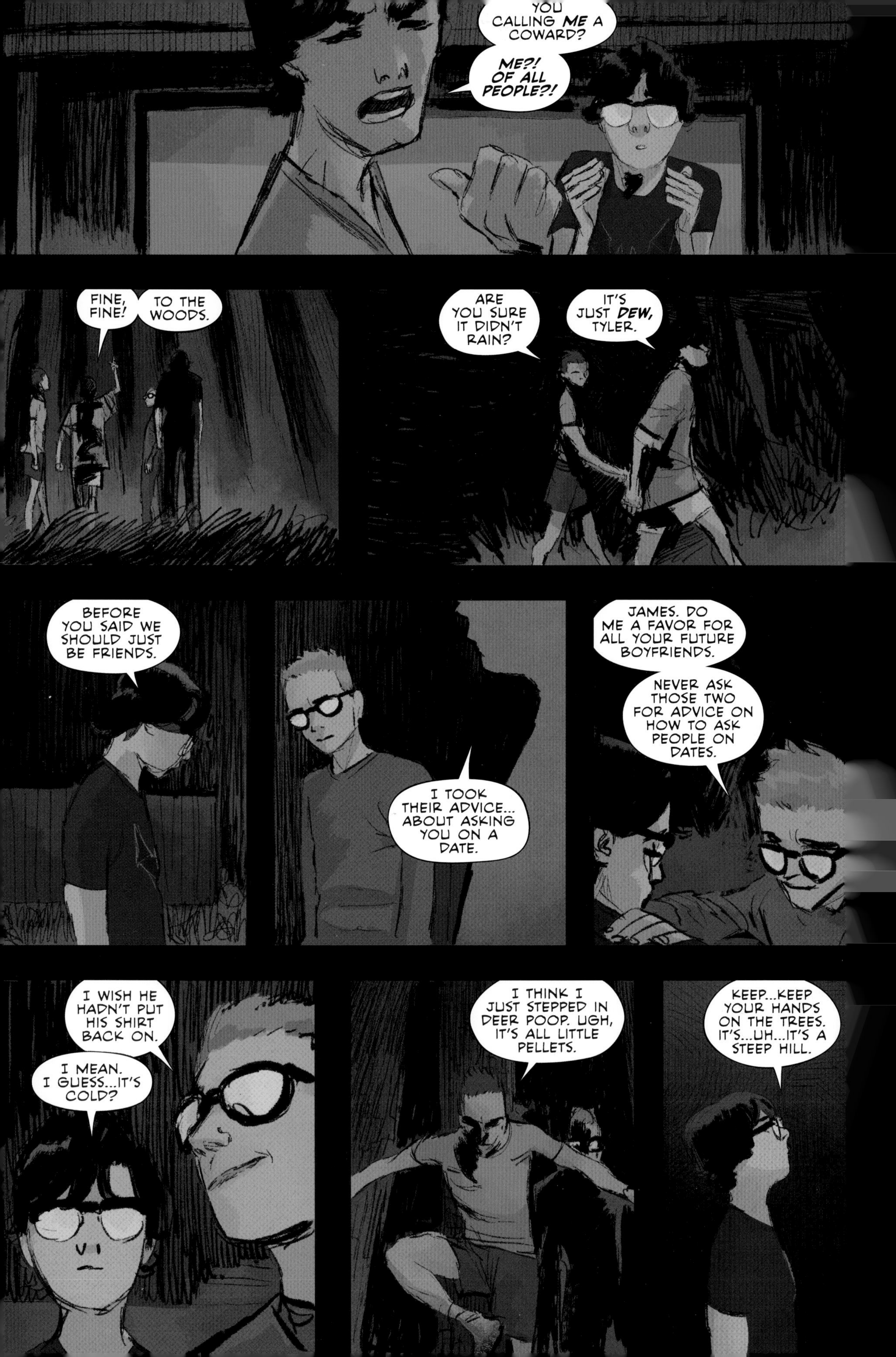
YOU CALLING *ME* A COWARD?
ME?! OF ALL PEOPLE?!
FINE, FINE!
TO THE WOODS.
ARE YOU SURE IT DIDN'T RAIN?
IT'S JUST *DEW,* TYLER.
BEFORE YOU SAID WE SHOULD JUST BE FRIENDS.
I TOOK THEIR ADVICE... ABOUT ASKING YOU ON A DATE.
JAMES. DO ME A FAVOR FOR ALL YOUR FUTURE BOYFRIENDS.
NEVER ASK THOSE TWO FOR ADVICE ON HOW TO ASK PEOPLE ON DATES.
I WISH HE HADN'T PUT HIS SHIRT BACK ON.
I MEAN. I GUESS...IT'S COLD?
I THINK I JUST STEPPED IN DEER POOP. UGH, IT'S ALL LITTLE PELLETS.
KEEP...KEEP YOUR HANDS ON THE TREES. IT'S...UH...IT'S A STEEP HILL.

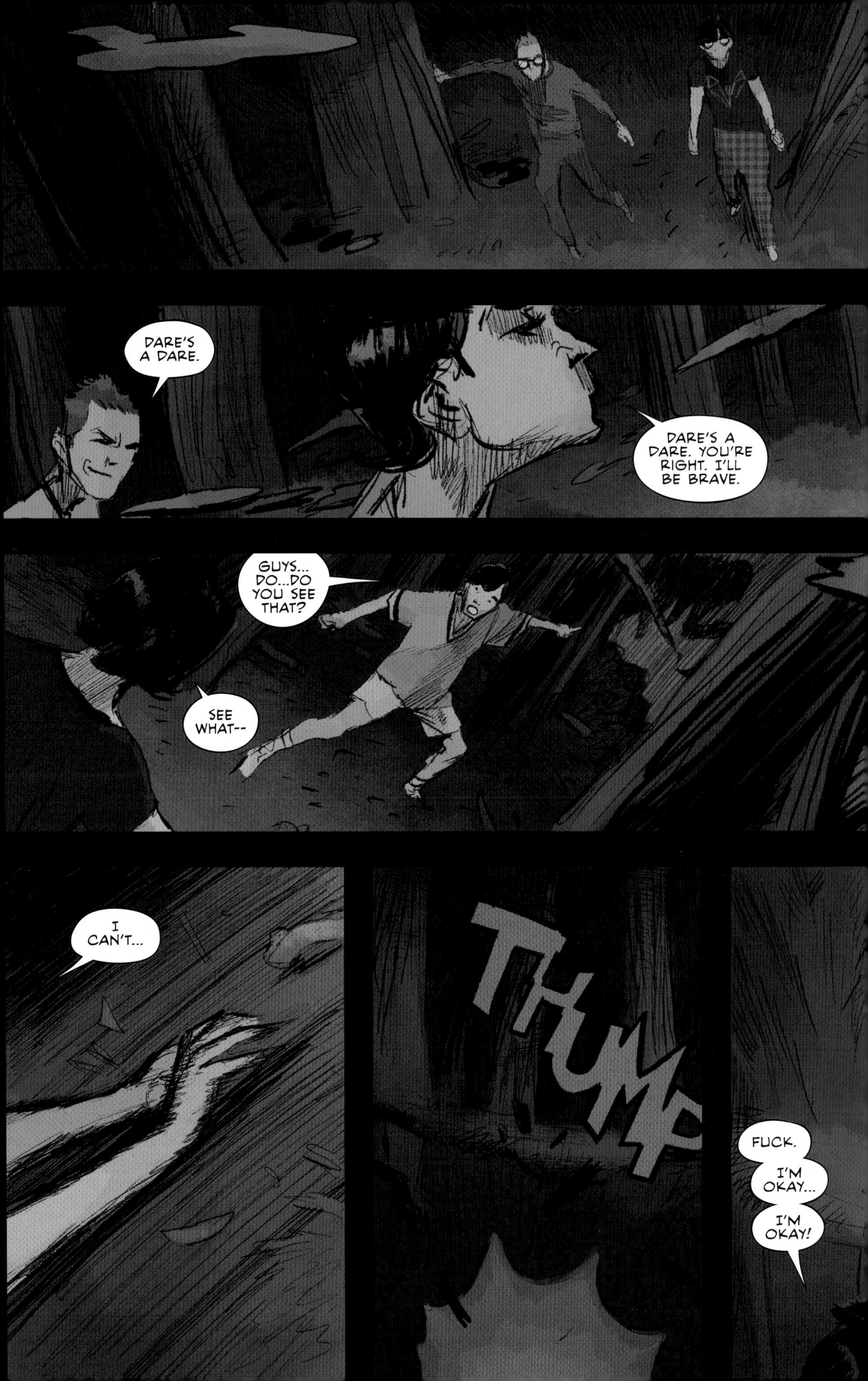
DARE'S A DARE.
DARE'S A DARE. YOU'RE RIGHT. I'LL BE BRAVE.
GUYS... DO...DO YOU SEE THAT?
SEE WHAT--
I CAN'T...
THUMP
FUCK.
I'M OKAY...
I'M OKAY!

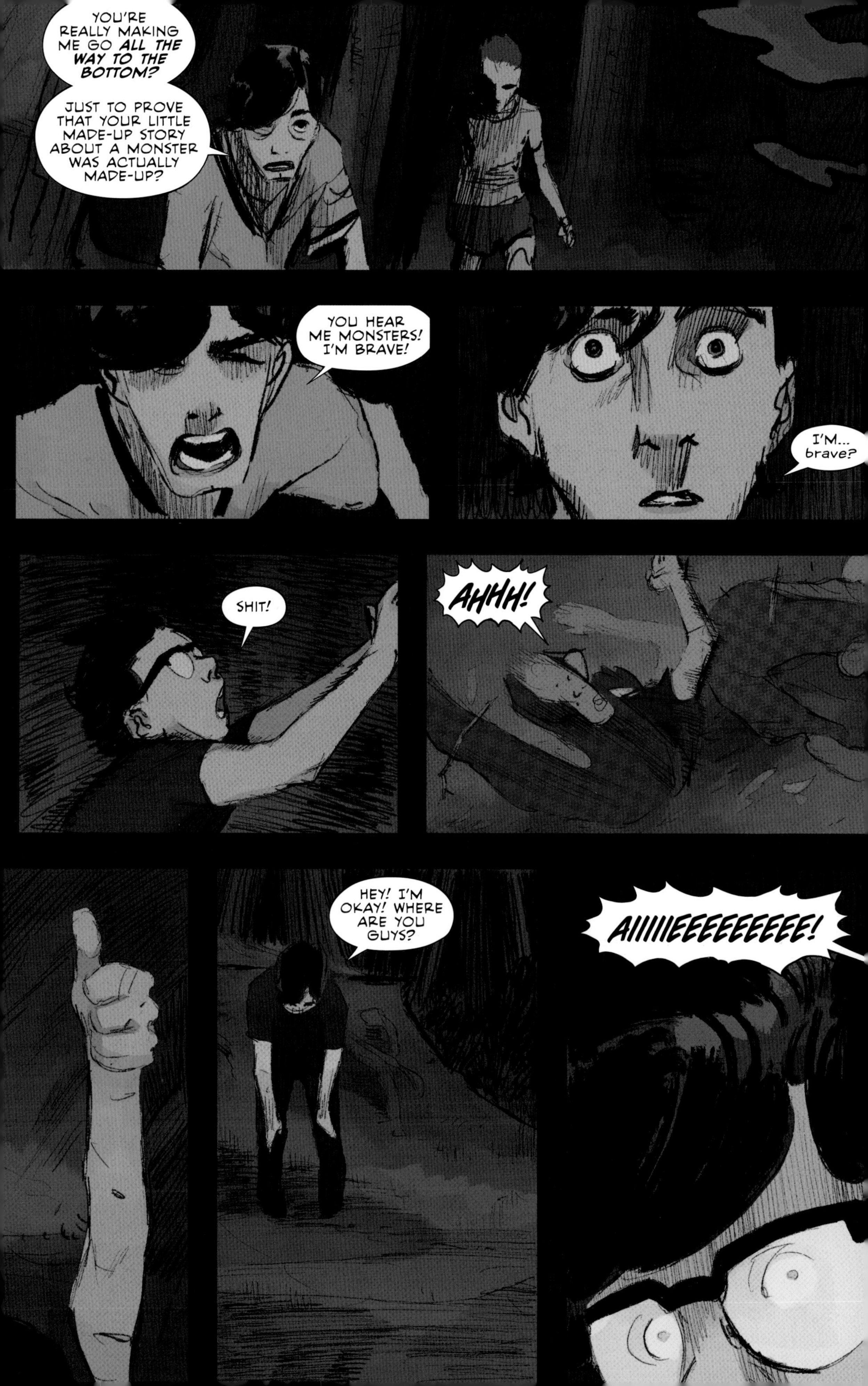
YOU'RE REALLY MAKING ME GO *ALL THE WAY TO THE BOTTOM?*
JUST TO PROVE THAT YOUR LITTLE MADE-UP STORY ABOUT A MONSTER WAS ACTUALLY MADE-UP?
YOU HEAR ME MONSTERS! I'M BRAVE!
I'M... brave?
SHIT!
AHHH!
HEY! I'M OKAY! WHERE ARE YOU GUYS?
AIIIIIEEEEEEEEEE!

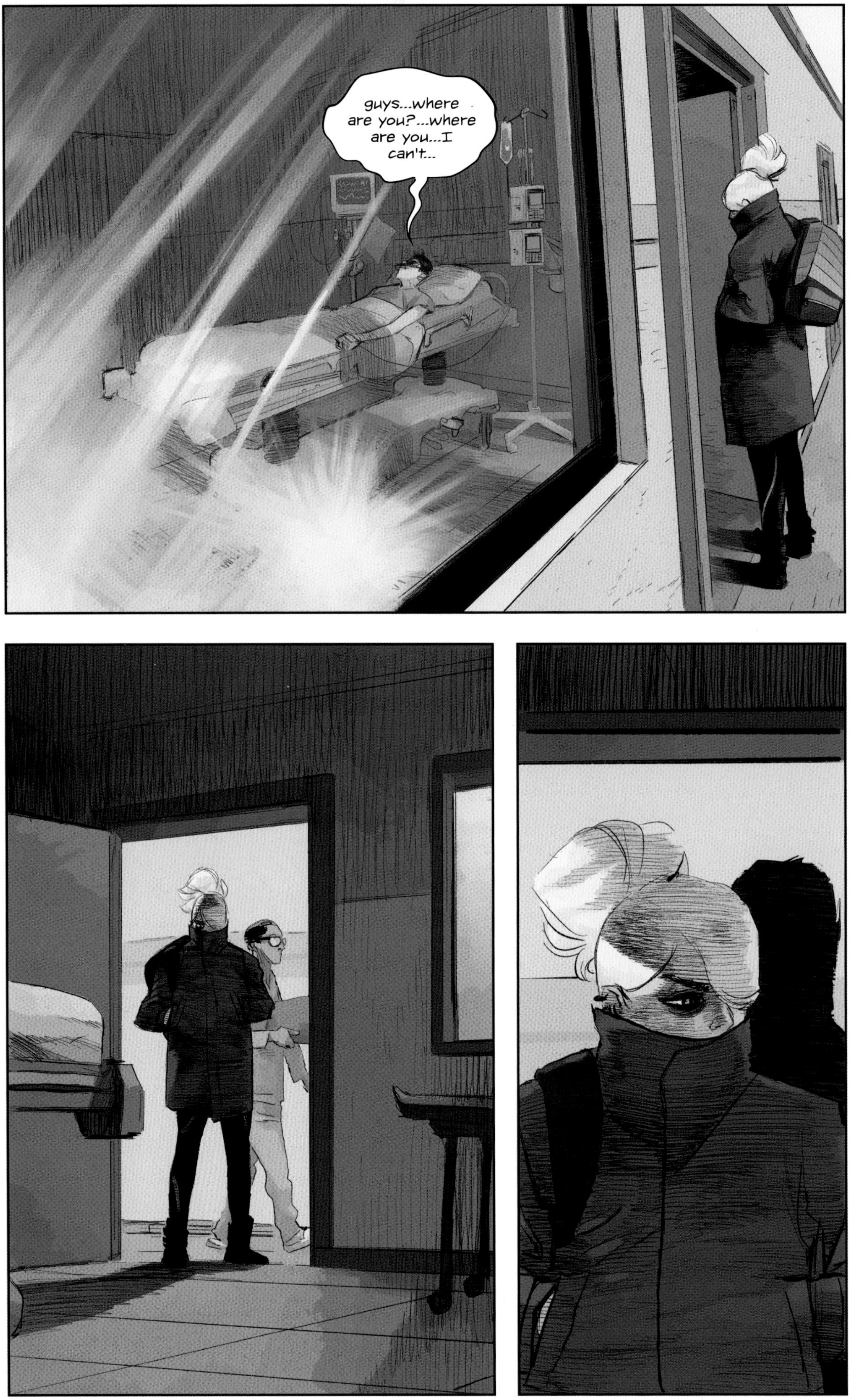
guys...where are you?...where are you...I can't...

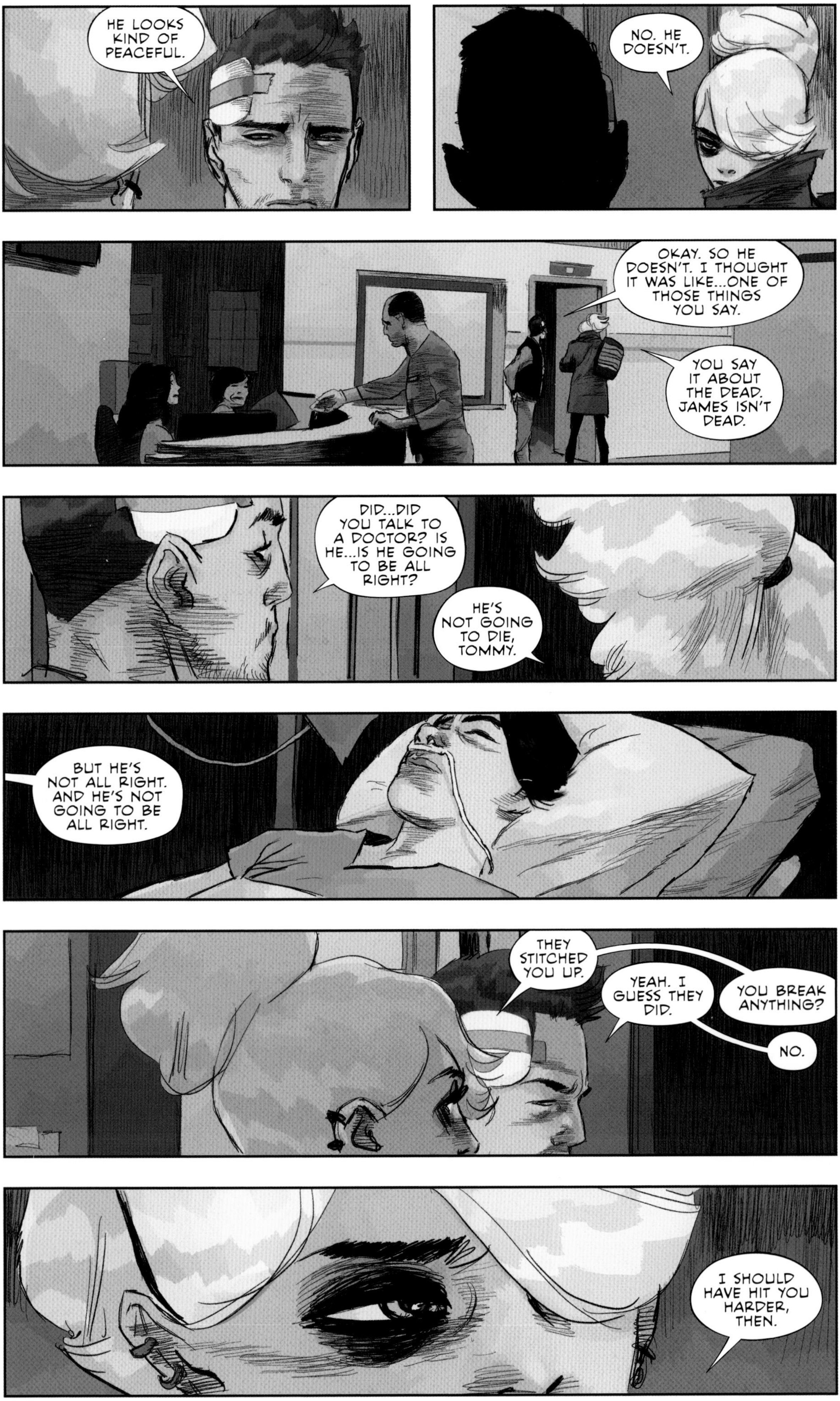
HE LOOKS KIND OF PEACEFUL.
NO. HE DOESN'T.
OKAY. SO HE DOESN'T. I THOUGHT IT WAS LIKE...ONE OF THOSE THINGS YOU SAY.
YOU SAY IT ABOUT THE DEAD. JAMES ISN'T DEAD.
DID...DID YOU TALK TO A DOCTOR? IS HE...IS HE GOING TO BE ALL RIGHT?
HE'S NOT GOING TO DIE, TOMMY.
BUT HE'S NOT ALL RIGHT. AND HE'S NOT GOING TO BE ALL RIGHT.
THEY STITCHED YOU UP.
YEAH. I GUESS THEY DID.
YOU BREAK ANYTHING?
NO.
I SHOULD HAVE HIT YOU HARDER, THEN.

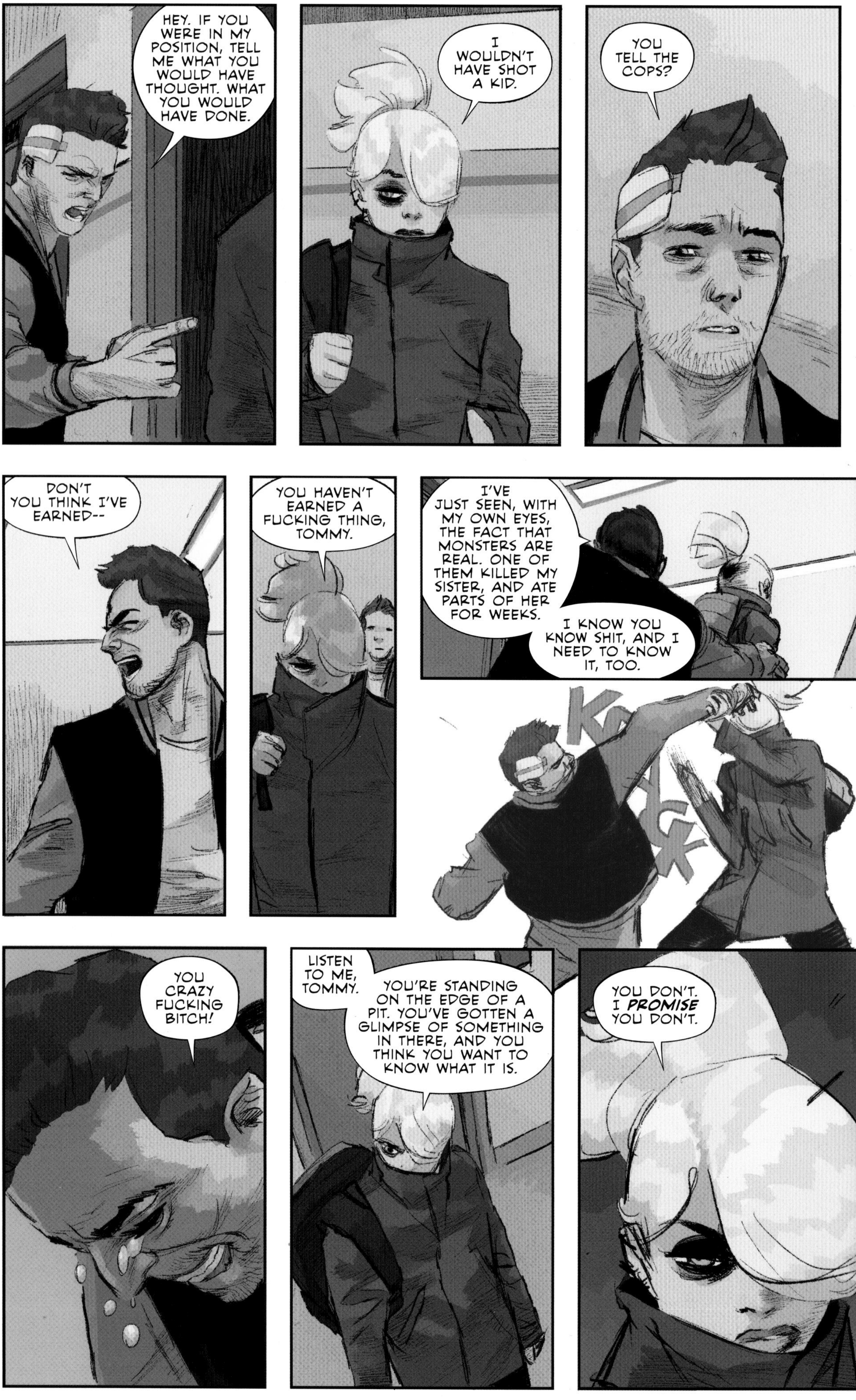
HEY. IF YOU WERE IN MY POSITION, TELL ME WHAT YOU WOULD HAVE THOUGHT. WHAT YOU WOULD HAVE DONE.
I WOULDN'T HAVE SHOT A KID.
YOU TELL THE COPS?
DON'T YOU THINK I'VE EARNED--
YOU HAVEN'T EARNED A FUCKING THING, TOMMY.
I'VE JUST SEEN, WITH MY OWN EYES, THE FACT THAT MONSTERS ARE REAL. ONE OF THEM KILLED MY SISTER, AND ATE PARTS OF HER FOR WEEKS.
I KNOW YOU KNOW SHIT, AND I NEED TO KNOW IT, TOO.
KRACK
YOU CRAZY FUCKING BITCH!
LISTEN TO ME, TOMMY.
YOU'RE STANDING ON THE EDGE OF A PIT. YOU'VE GOTTEN A GLIMPSE OF SOMETHING IN THERE, AND YOU THINK YOU WANT TO KNOW WHAT IT IS.
YOU DON'T. I ***PROMISE*** YOU DON'T.

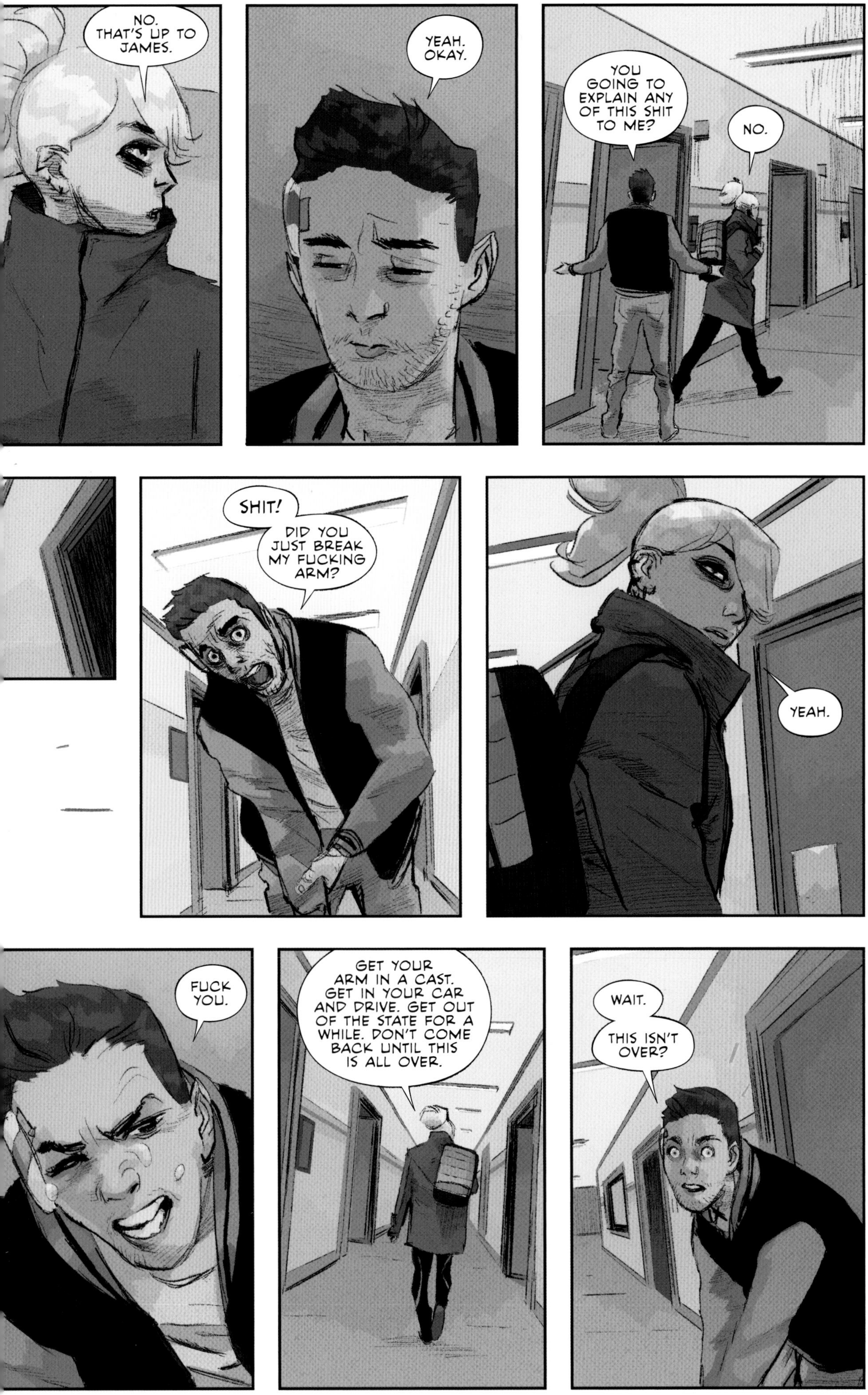
NO. THAT'S UP TO JAMES.
YEAH. OKAY.
YOU GOING TO EXPLAIN ANY OF THIS SHIT TO ME?
NO.
SHIT!
DID YOU JUST BREAK MY FUCKING ARM?
YEAH.
FUCK YOU.
GET YOUR ARM IN A CAST. GET IN YOUR CAR AND DRIVE. GET OUT OF THE STATE FOR A WHILE. DON'T COME BACK UNTIL THIS IS ALL OVER.
WAIT.
THIS ISN'T OVER?

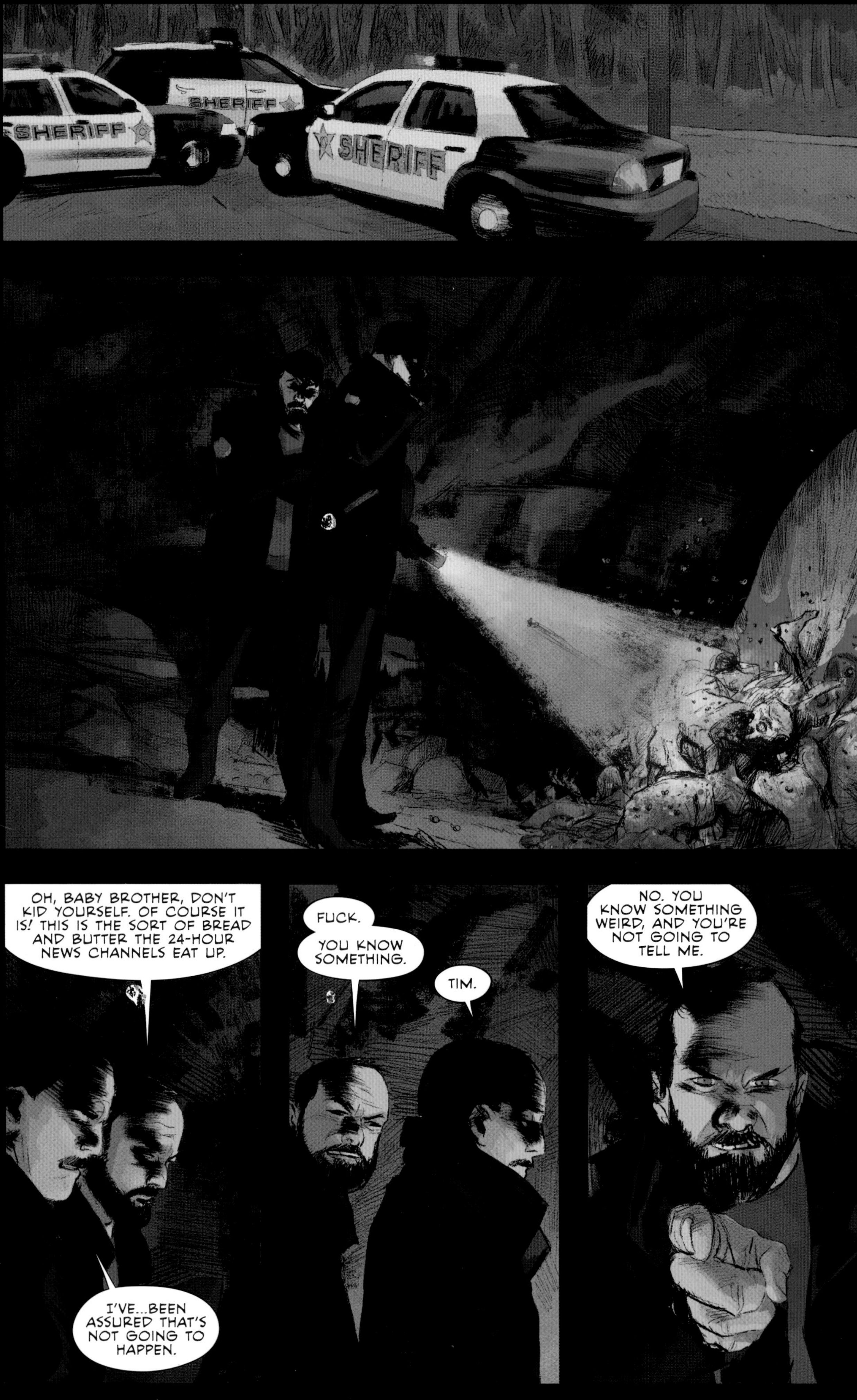
SHERIFF
SHERIFF
SHERIFF
OH, BABY BROTHER, DON'T KID YOURSELF. OF COURSE IT IS! THIS IS THE SORT OF BREAD AND BUTTER THE 24-HOUR NEWS CHANNELS EAT UP.
I'VE...BEEN ASSURED THAT'S NOT GOING TO HAPPEN.
FUCK.
YOU KNOW SOMETHING.
TIM.
NO. YOU KNOW SOMETHING WEIRD, AND YOU'RE NOT GOING TO TELL ME.

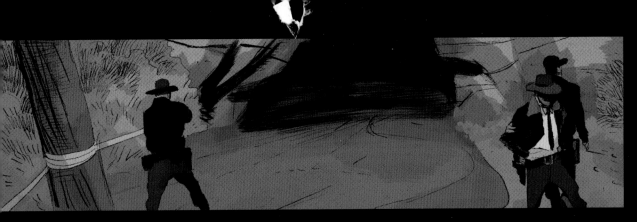

YOU KNOW WHAT, I QUIT.

NO, YOU DON'T, TIM.

I AM FULLY AND TOTALLY WITHIN MY RIGHTS TO QUIT. AND I QUIT.

I DON'T HAVE TIME TO PLAY A GAME WITH YOU, TIM.

WE'RE GOING TO NEED TO SPEND THE NEXT FEW DAYS IDENTIFYING EACH OF THESE KIDS AND INFORMING THEIR PARENTS.

I HAVEN'T SLEPT IN A GODDAMN WEEK AND I DON'T THINK THAT'S ABOUT TO CHANGE.

YOU'RE DAMN RIGHT. THIS IS GOING TO GET PRESS. WE'RE GOING TO HAVE NATIONAL MEDIA UP OUR ASS IN ABOUT FIVE MINUTES.

THAT'S NOT GOING TO HAPPEN.

NO. I'M NOT. NOW, I KNOW THE MORGUE ISN'T BIG ENOUGH FOR ALL OF THESE KIDS.

I HAD ONE OF THE GIRLS CALL THE SCHOOL. WE'RE COMMANDEERING THE GYMNASIUM. ONLY PLACE BIG ENOUGH I CAN THINK OF IN ARCHER'S PEAK.

IT'S GONNA FUCK THE KIDS UP PRETTY GOOD, THOUGH. THEIR BROTHERS AND SISTERS IN CHUNKS WHERE THEY PLAY DODGEBALL.

BUT HELL, I GUESS WE'RE PLENTY FUCKED UP ALREADY.

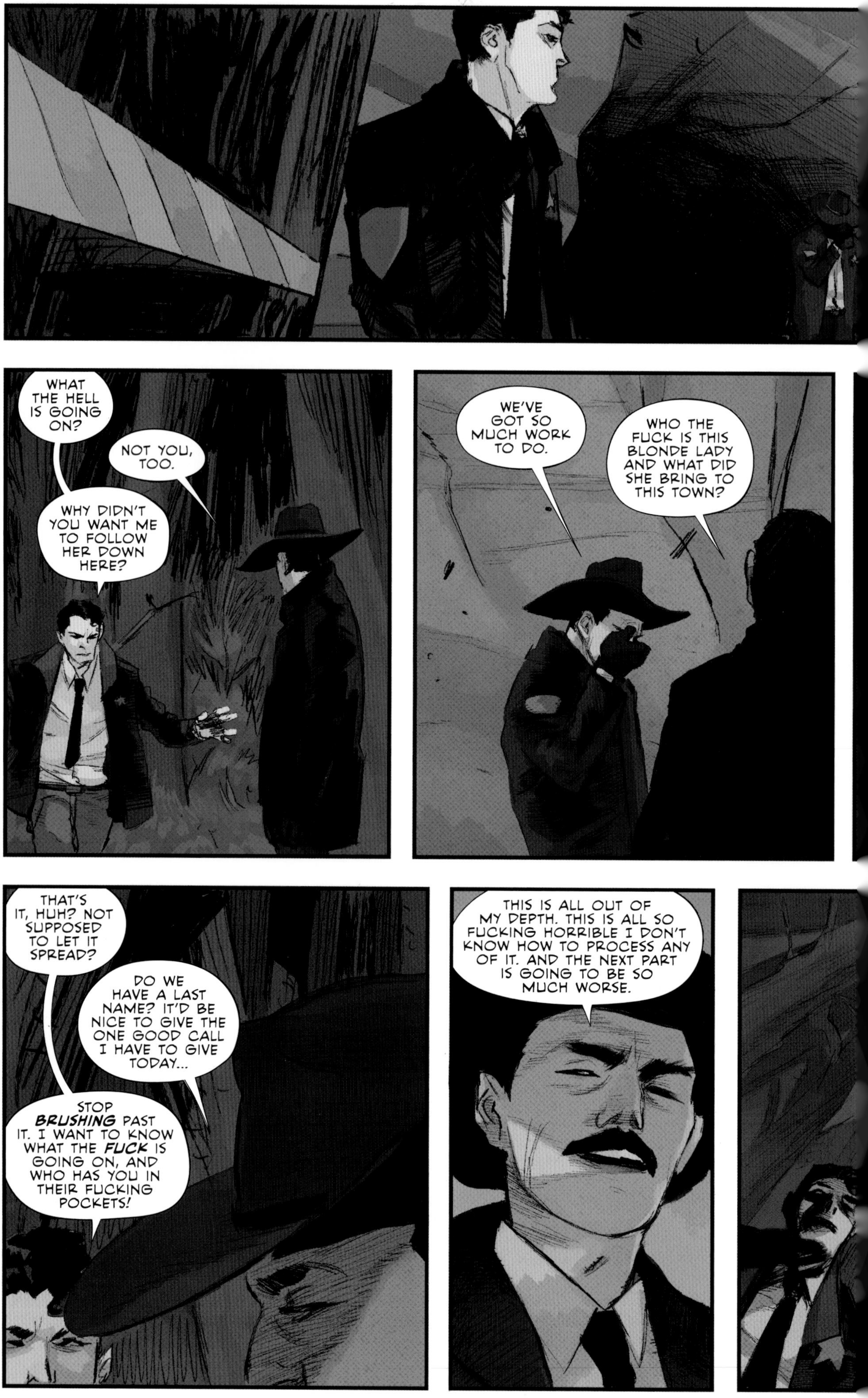
WHAT THE HELL IS GOING ON?
NOT YOU, TOO.
WHY DIDN'T YOU WANT ME TO FOLLOW HER DOWN HERE?
WE'VE GOT SO MUCH WORK TO DO.
WHO THE FUCK IS THIS BLONDE LADY AND WHAT DID SHE BRING TO THIS TOWN?
THAT'S IT, HUH? NOT SUPPOSED TO LET IT SPREAD?
DO WE HAVE A LAST NAME? IT'D BE NICE TO GIVE THE ONE GOOD CALL I HAVE TO GIVE TODAY...
STOP BRUSHING PAST IT. I WANT TO KNOW WHAT THE FUCK IS GOING ON, AND WHO HAS YOU IN THEIR FUCKING POCKETS!
THIS IS ALL OUT OF MY DEPTH. THIS IS ALL SO FUCKING HORRIBLE I DON'T KNOW HOW TO PROCESS ANY OF IT. AND THE NEXT PART IS GOING TO BE SO MUCH WORSE.

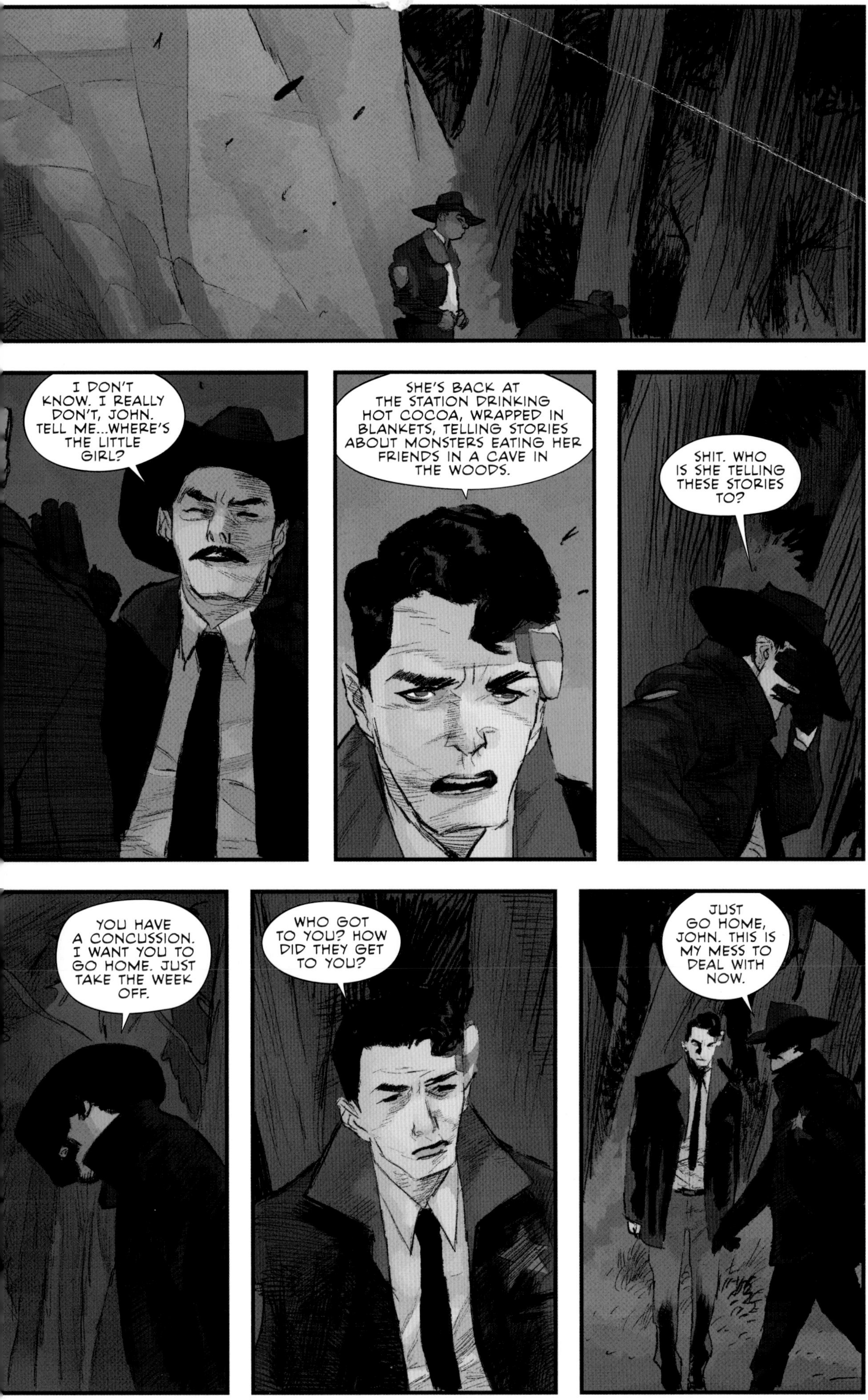
I DON'T KNOW. I REALLY DON'T, JOHN. TELL ME...WHERE'S THE LITTLE GIRL?
SHE'S BACK AT THE STATION DRINKING HOT COCOA, WRAPPED IN BLANKETS, TELLING STORIES ABOUT MONSTERS EATING HER FRIENDS IN A CAVE IN THE WOODS.
SHIT. WHO IS SHE TELLING THESE STORIES TO?
YOU HAVE A CONCUSSION. I WANT YOU TO GO HOME. JUST TAKE THE WEEK OFF.
WHO GOT TO YOU? HOW DID THEY GET TO YOU?
JUST GO HOME, JOHN. THIS IS MY MESS TO DEAL WITH NOW.

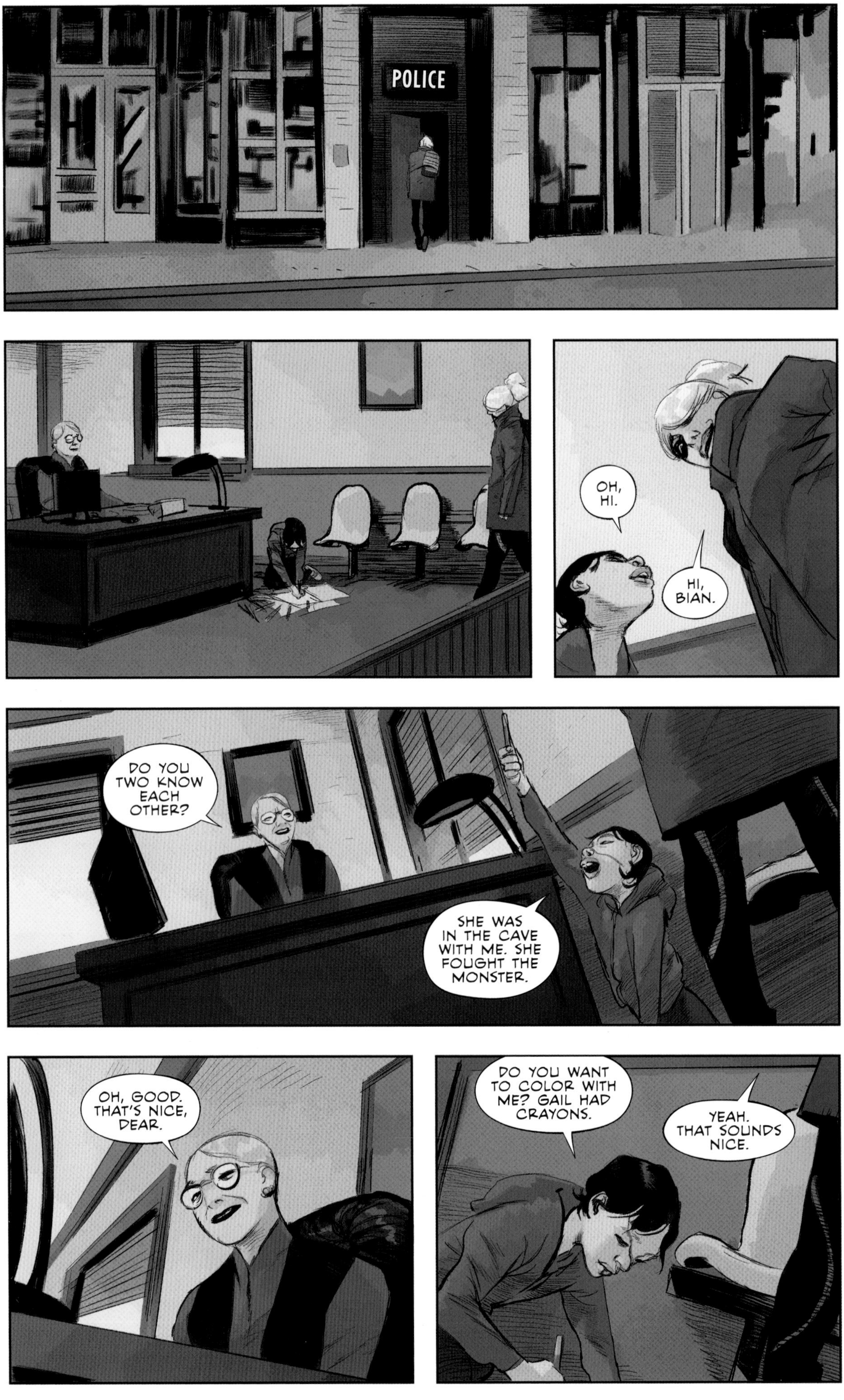
POLICE
OH, HI.
HI, BIAN.
DO YOU TWO KNOW EACH OTHER?
SHE WAS IN THE CAVE WITH ME. SHE FOUGHT THE MONSTER.
OH, GOOD. THAT'S NICE, DEAR.
DO YOU WANT TO COLOR WITH ME? GAIL HAD CRAYONS.
YEAH. THAT SOUNDS NICE.

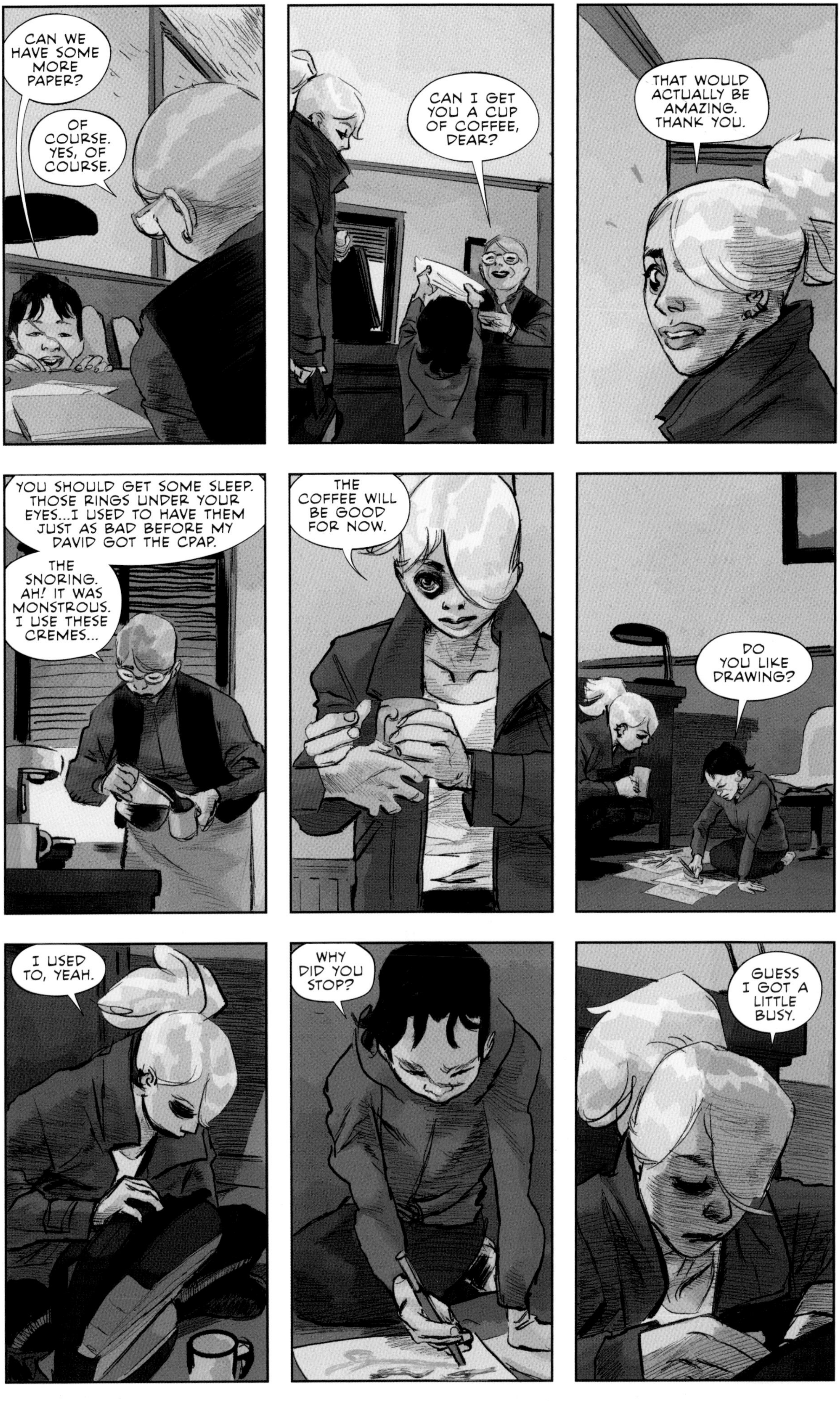
CAN WE HAVE SOME MORE PAPER?
OF COURSE. YES, OF COURSE.
CAN I GET YOU A CUP OF COFFEE, DEAR?
THAT WOULD ACTUALLY BE AMAZING. THANK YOU.
YOU SHOULD GET SOME SLEEP. THOSE RINGS UNDER YOUR EYES...I USED TO HAVE THEM JUST AS BAD BEFORE MY DAVID GOT THE CPAP.
THE SNORING. AH! IT WAS MONSTROUS. I USE THESE CREMES...
THE COFFEE WILL BE GOOD FOR NOW.
DO YOU LIKE DRAWING?
I USED TO, YEAH.
WHY DID YOU STOP?
GUESS I GOT A LITTLE BUSY.

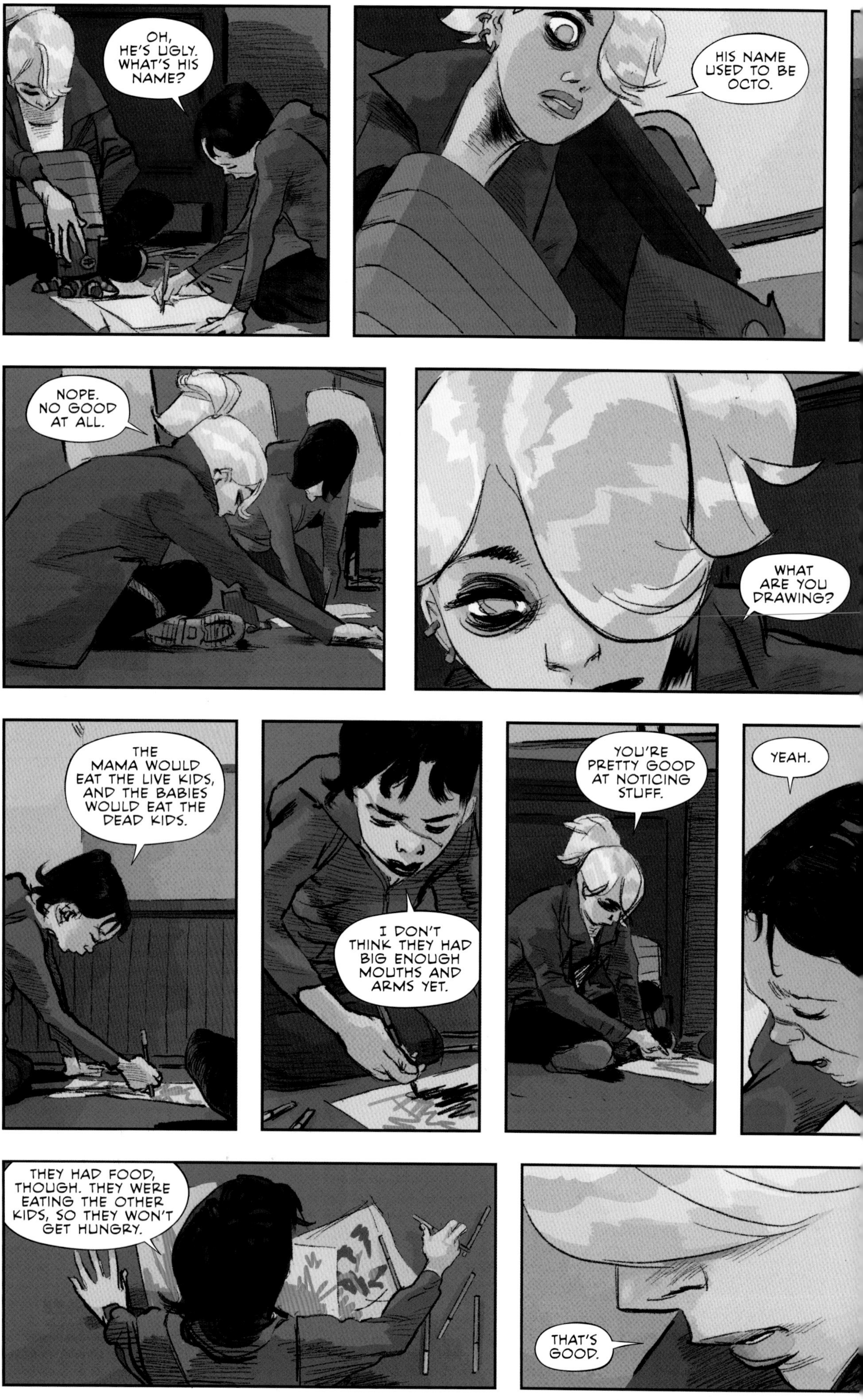
OH, HE'S UGLY. WHAT'S HIS NAME?
HIS NAME USED TO BE OCTO.
NOPE. NO GOOD AT ALL.
WHAT ARE YOU DRAWING?
THE MAMA WOULD EAT THE LIVE KIDS, AND THE BABIES WOULD EAT THE DEAD KIDS.
I DON'T THINK THEY HAD BIG ENOUGH MOUTHS AND ARMS YET.
YOU'RE PRETTY GOOD AT NOTICING STUFF.
YEAH.
THEY HAD FOOD, THOUGH. THEY WERE EATING THE OTHER KIDS, SO THEY WON'T GET HUNGRY.
THAT'S GOOD.

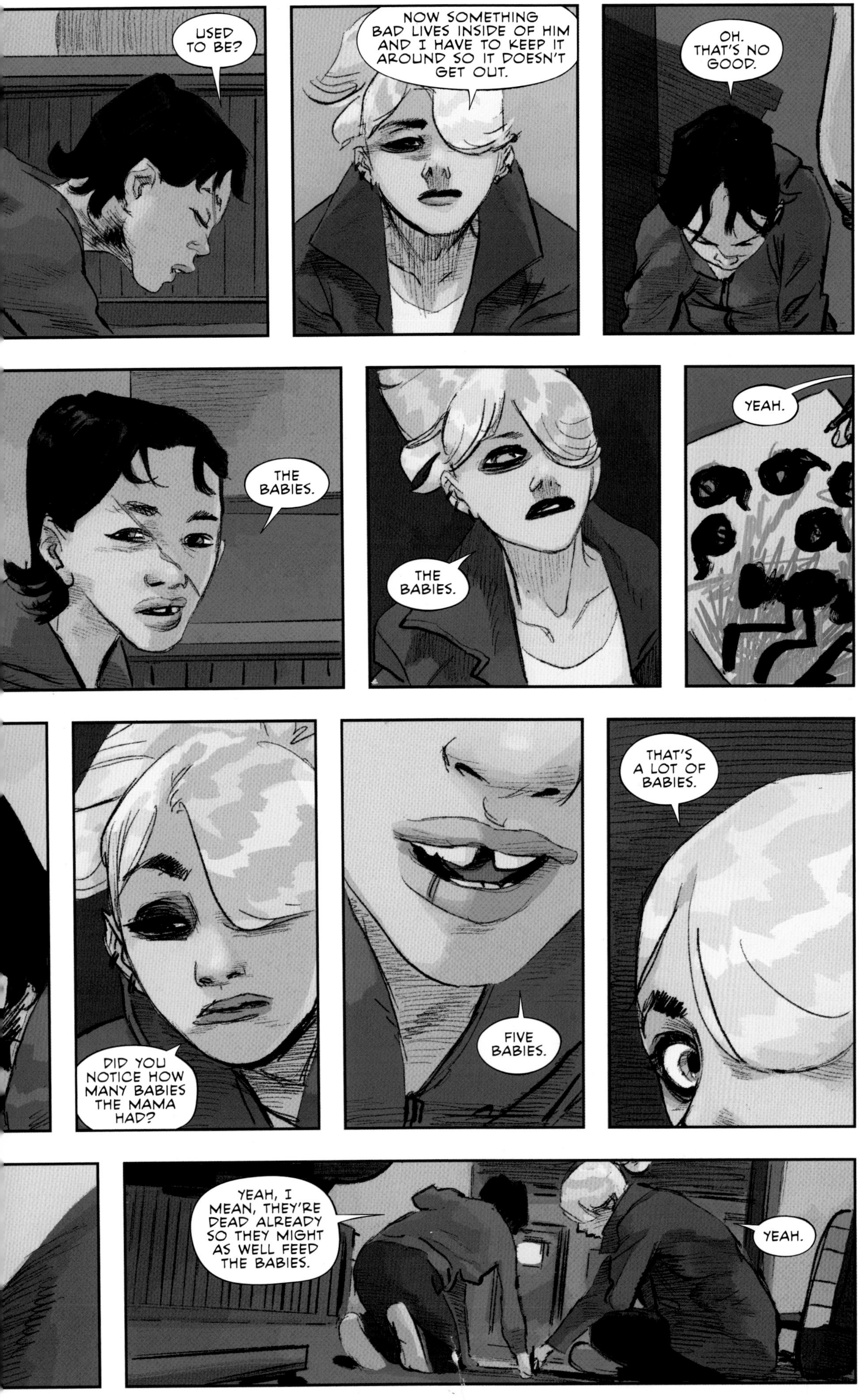
USED TO BE?
NOW SOMETHING BAD LIVES INSIDE OF HIM AND I HAVE TO KEEP IT AROUND SO IT DOESN'T GET OUT.
OH. THAT'S NO GOOD.
THE BABIES.
THE BABIES.
YEAH.
DID YOU NOTICE HOW MANY BABIES THE MAMA HAD?
FIVE BABIES.
THAT'S A LOT OF BABIES.
YEAH, I MEAN, THEY'RE DEAD ALREADY SO THEY MIGHT AS WELL FEED THE BABIES.
YEAH.

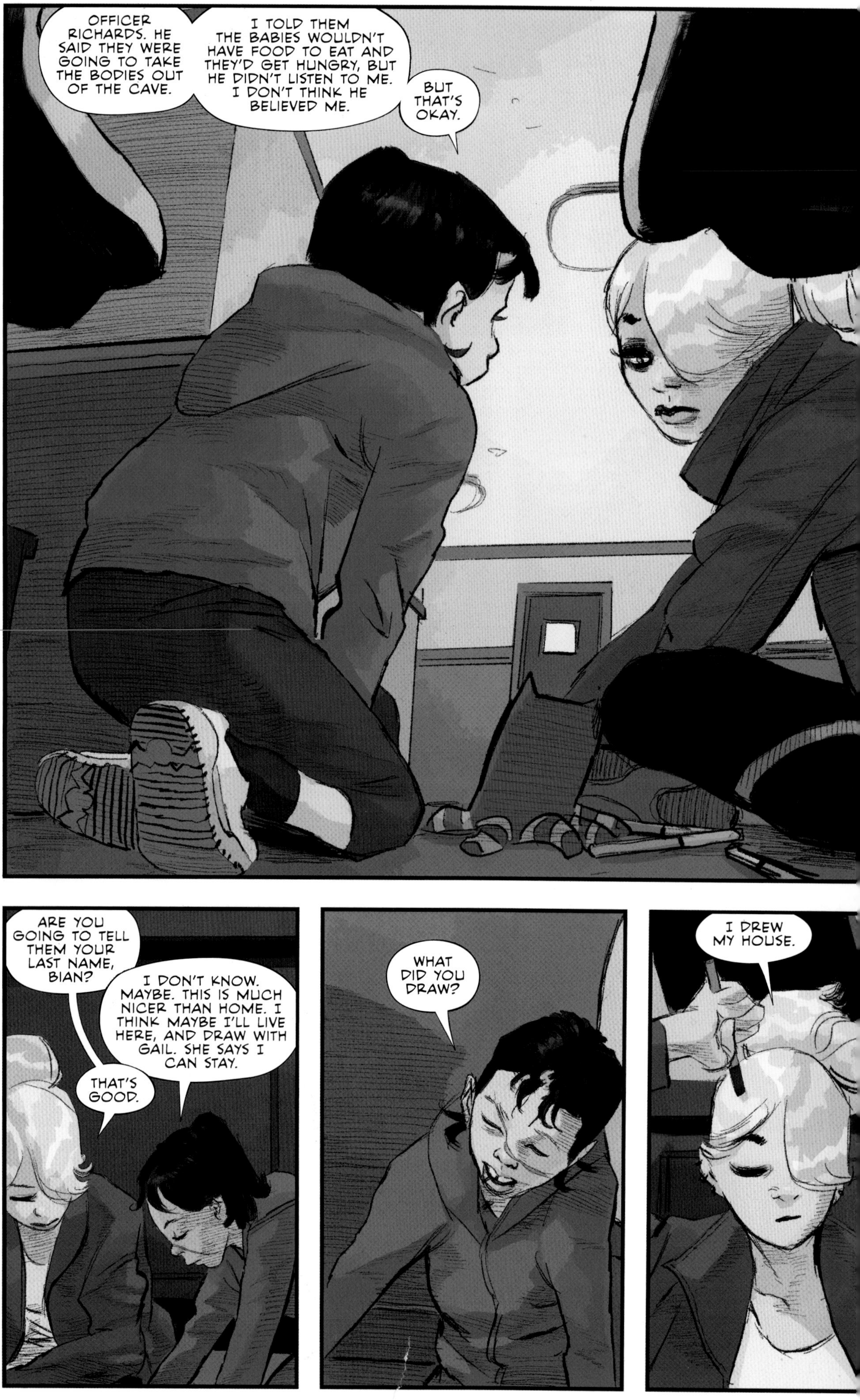
OFFICER RICHARDS. HE SAID THEY WERE GOING TO TAKE THE BODIES OUT OF THE CAVE.
I TOLD THEM THE BABIES WOULDN'T HAVE FOOD TO EAT AND THEY'D GET HUNGRY, BUT HE DIDN'T LISTEN TO ME. I DON'T THINK HE BELIEVED ME.
BUT THAT'S OKAY.
ARE YOU GOING TO TELL THEM YOUR LAST NAME, BIAN?
I DON'T KNOW. MAYBE. THIS IS MUCH NICER THAN HOME. I THINK MAYBE I'LL LIVE HERE, AND DRAW WITH GAIL. SHE SAYS I CAN STAY.
THAT'S GOOD.
WHAT DID YOU DRAW?
I DREW MY HOUSE.

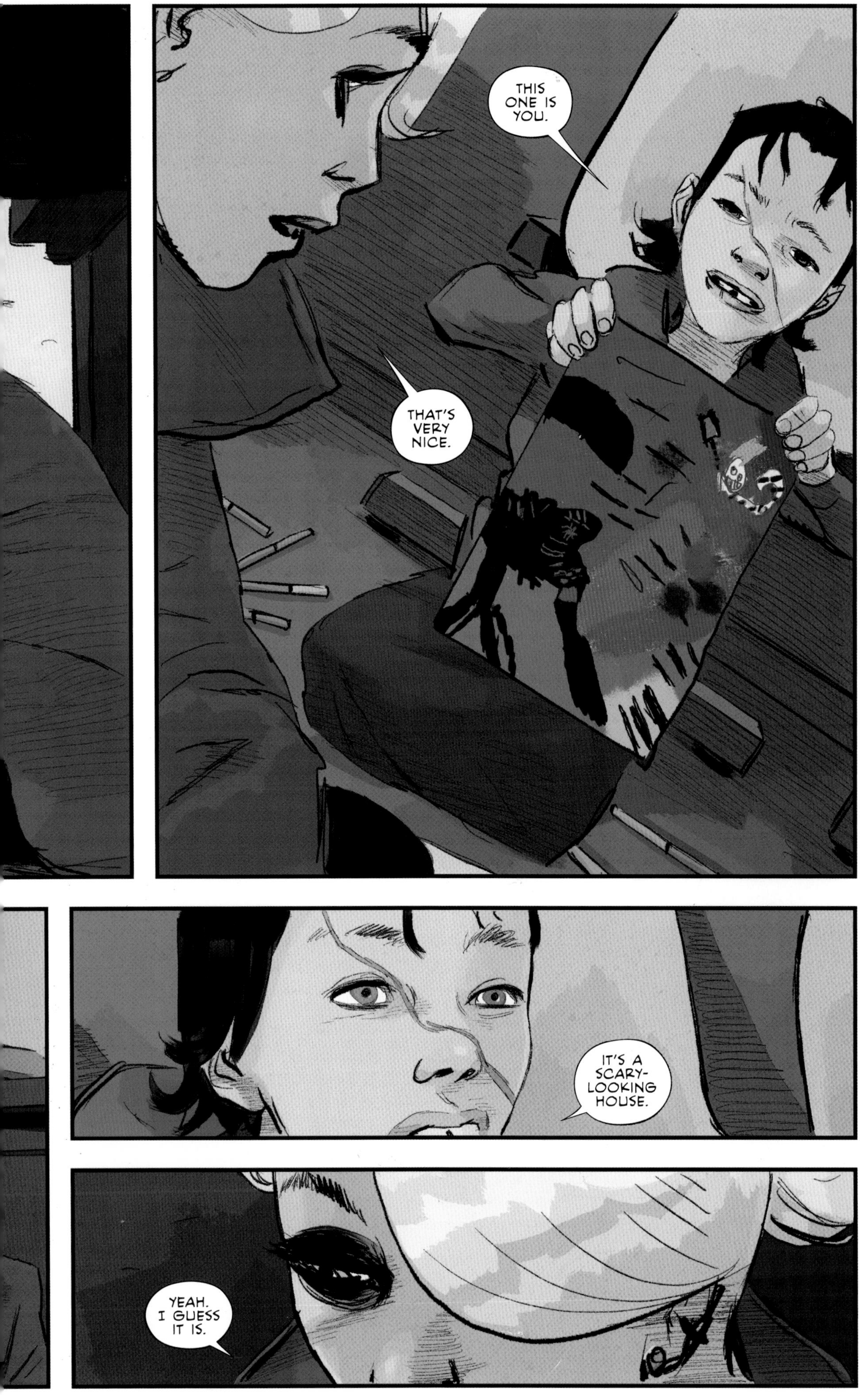
THIS ONE IS YOU.
THAT'S VERY NICE.
IT'S A SCARY-LOOKING HOUSE.
YEAH. I GUESS IT IS.

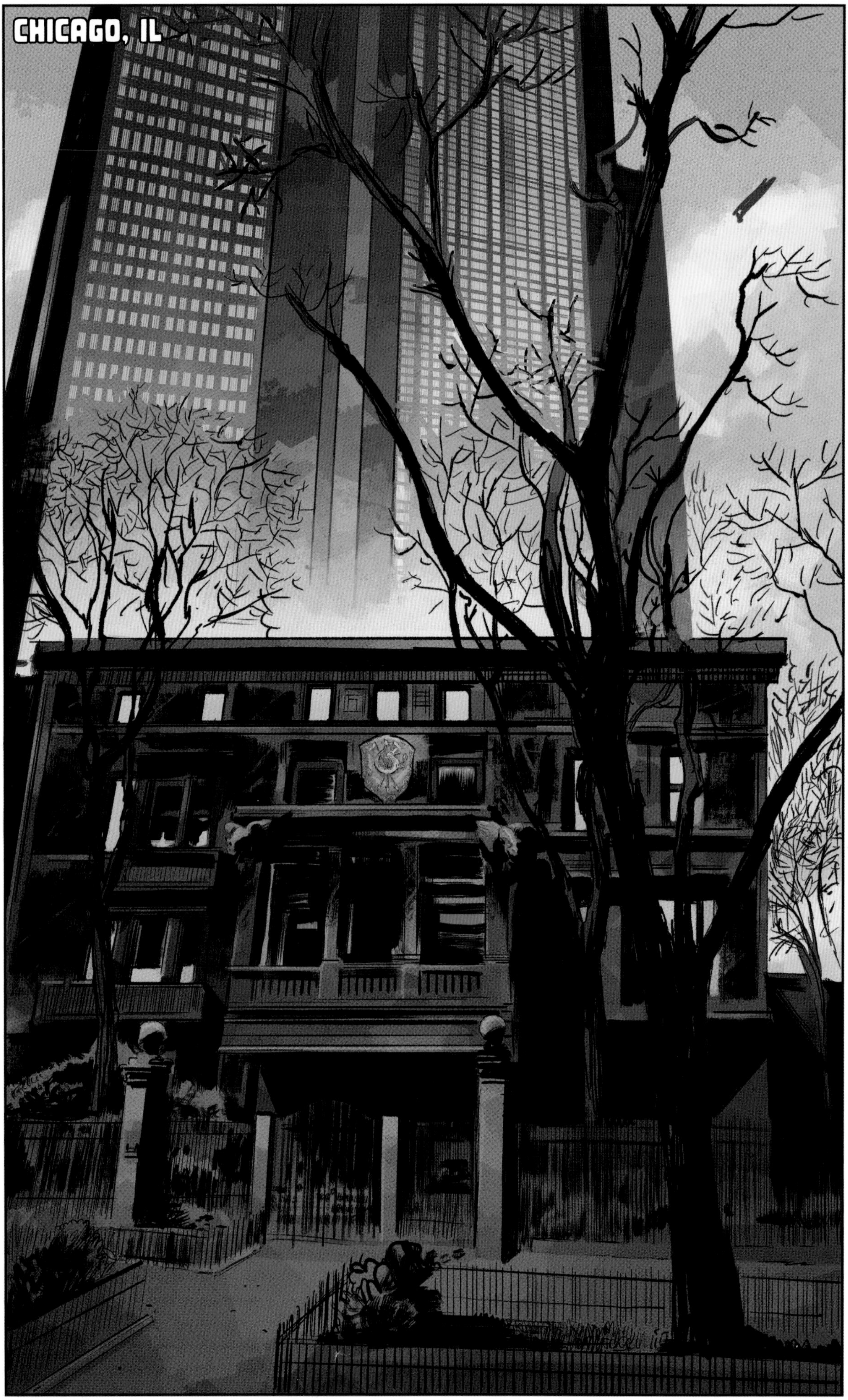
CHICAGO, IL

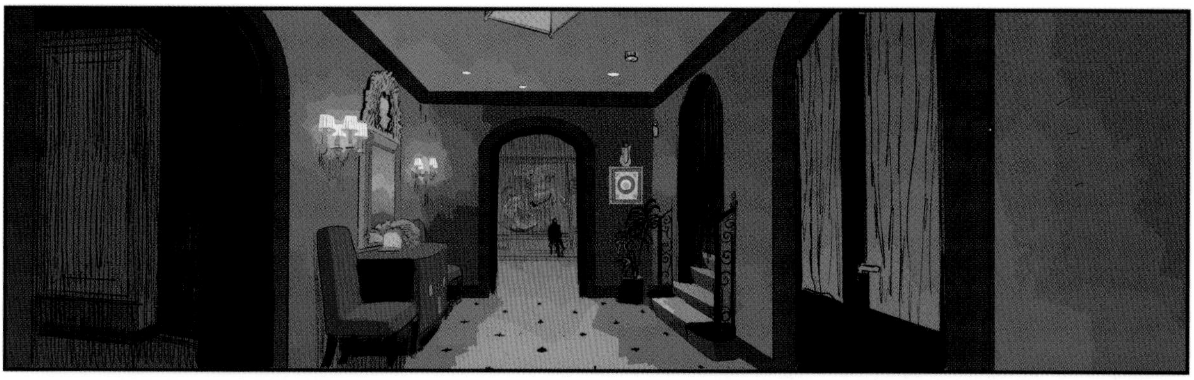

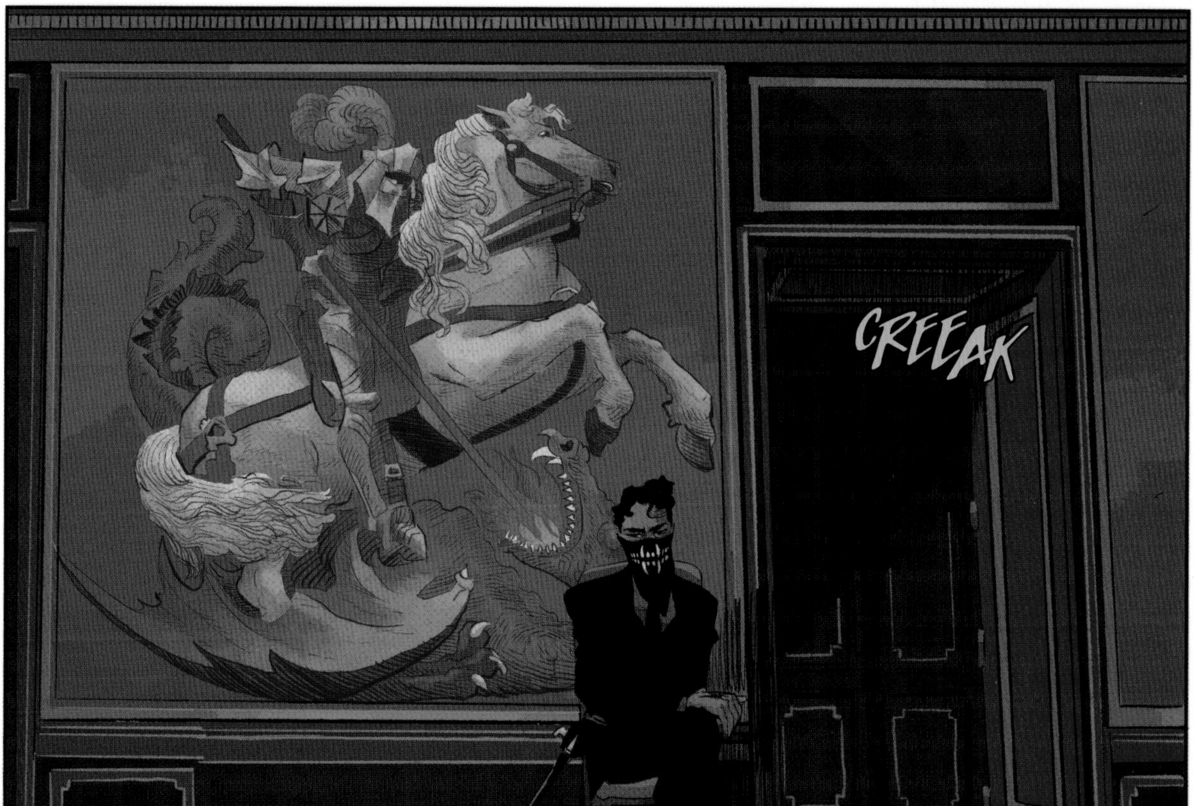
CREEAK

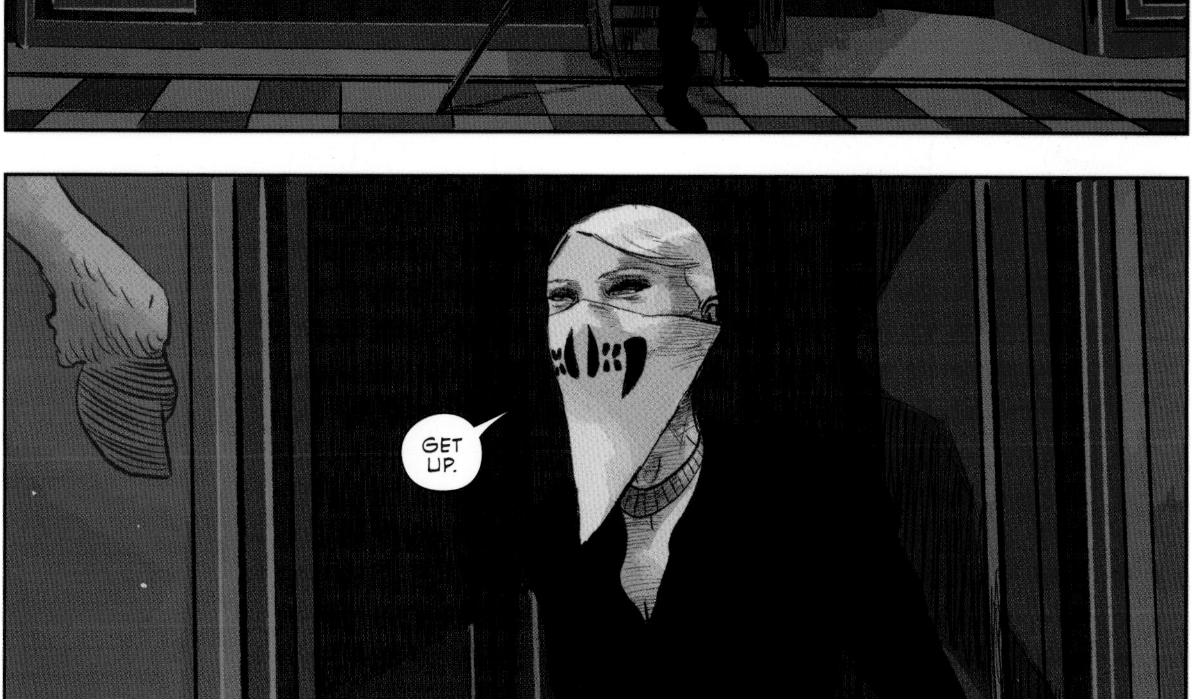
GET UP.

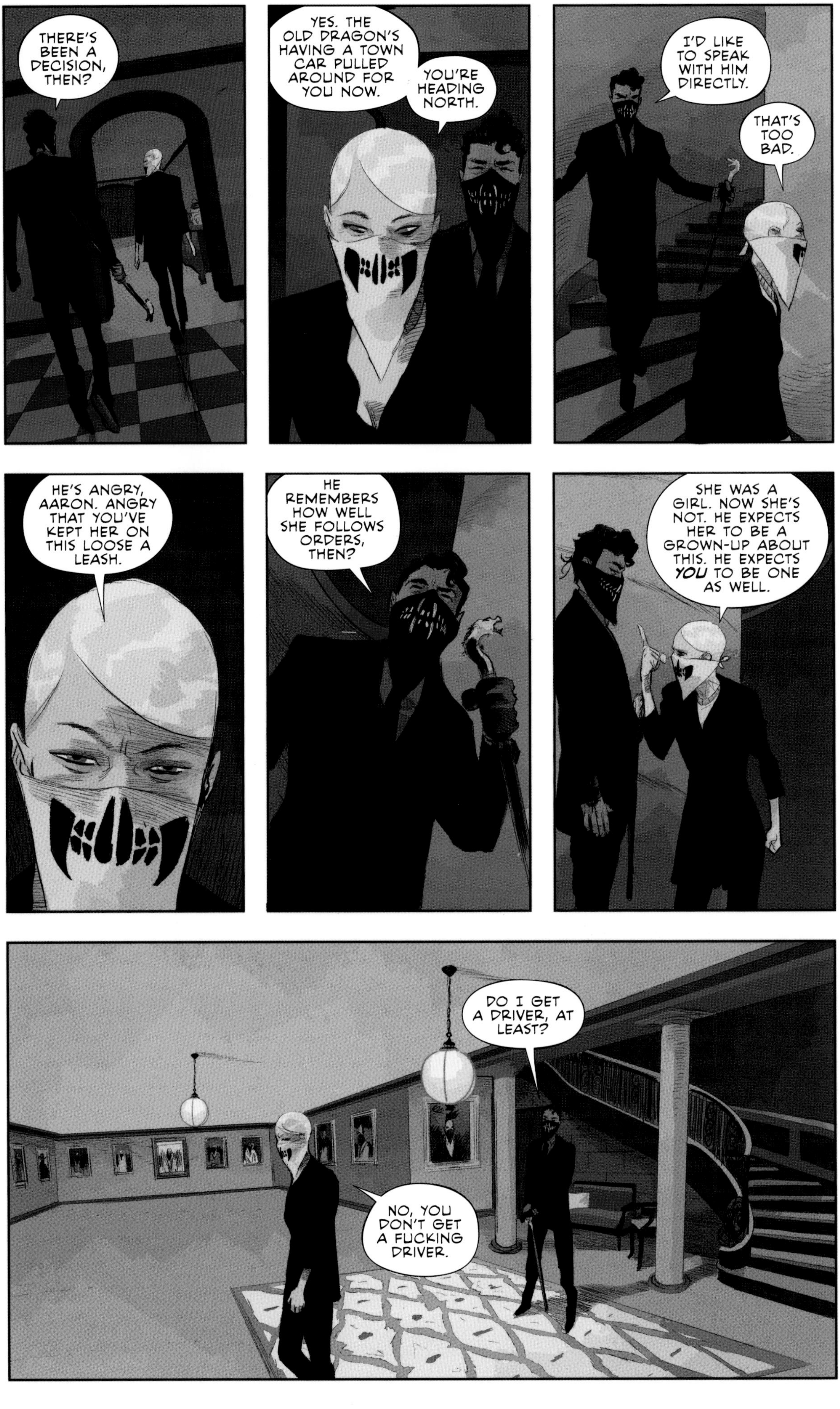
THERE'S BEEN A DECISION, THEN?
YES. THE OLD DRAGON'S HAVING A TOWN CAR PULLED AROUND FOR YOU NOW.
YOU'RE HEADING NORTH.
I'D LIKE TO SPEAK WITH HIM DIRECTLY.
THAT'S TOO BAD.
HE'S ANGRY, AARON. ANGRY THAT YOU'VE KEPT HER ON THIS LOOSE A LEASH.
HE REMEMBERS HOW WELL SHE FOLLOWS ORDERS, THEN?
SHE WAS A GIRL. NOW SHE'S NOT. HE EXPECTS HER TO BE A GROWN-UP ABOUT THIS. HE EXPECTS YOU TO BE ONE AS WELL.
DO I GET A DRIVER, AT LEAST?
NO, YOU DON'T GET A FUCKING DRIVER.

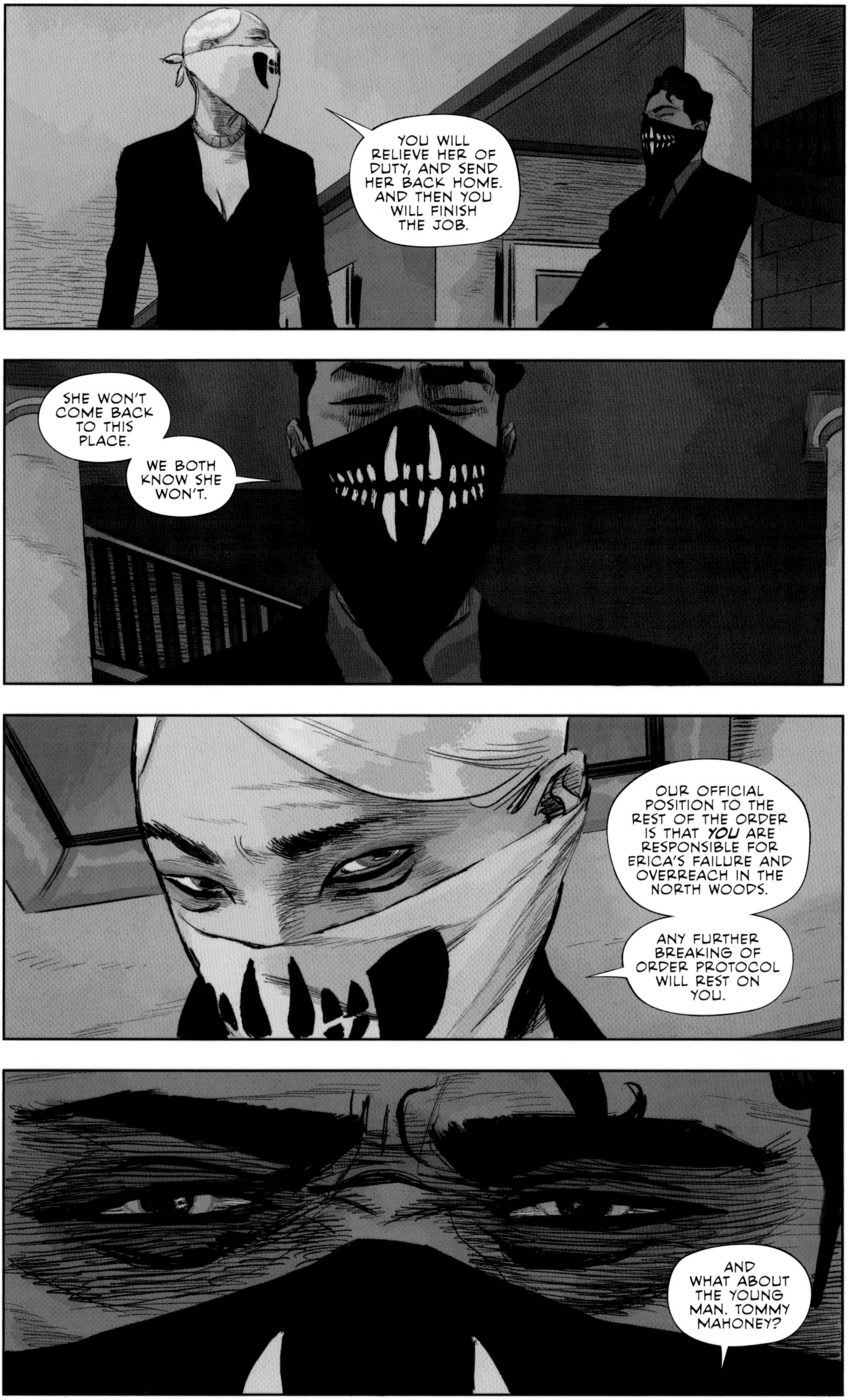
YOU WILL RELIEVE HER OF DUTY, AND SEND HER BACK HOME. AND THEN YOU WILL FINISH THE JOB.
SHE WON'T COME BACK TO THIS PLACE.
WE BOTH KNOW SHE WON'T.
OUR OFFICIAL POSITION TO THE REST OF THE ORDER IS THAT *YOU* ARE RESPONSIBLE FOR ERICA'S FAILURE AND OVERREACH IN THE NORTH WOODS.
ANY FURTHER BREAKING OF ORDER PROTOCOL WILL REST ON YOU.
AND WHAT ABOUT THE YOUNG MAN. TOMMY MAHONEY?

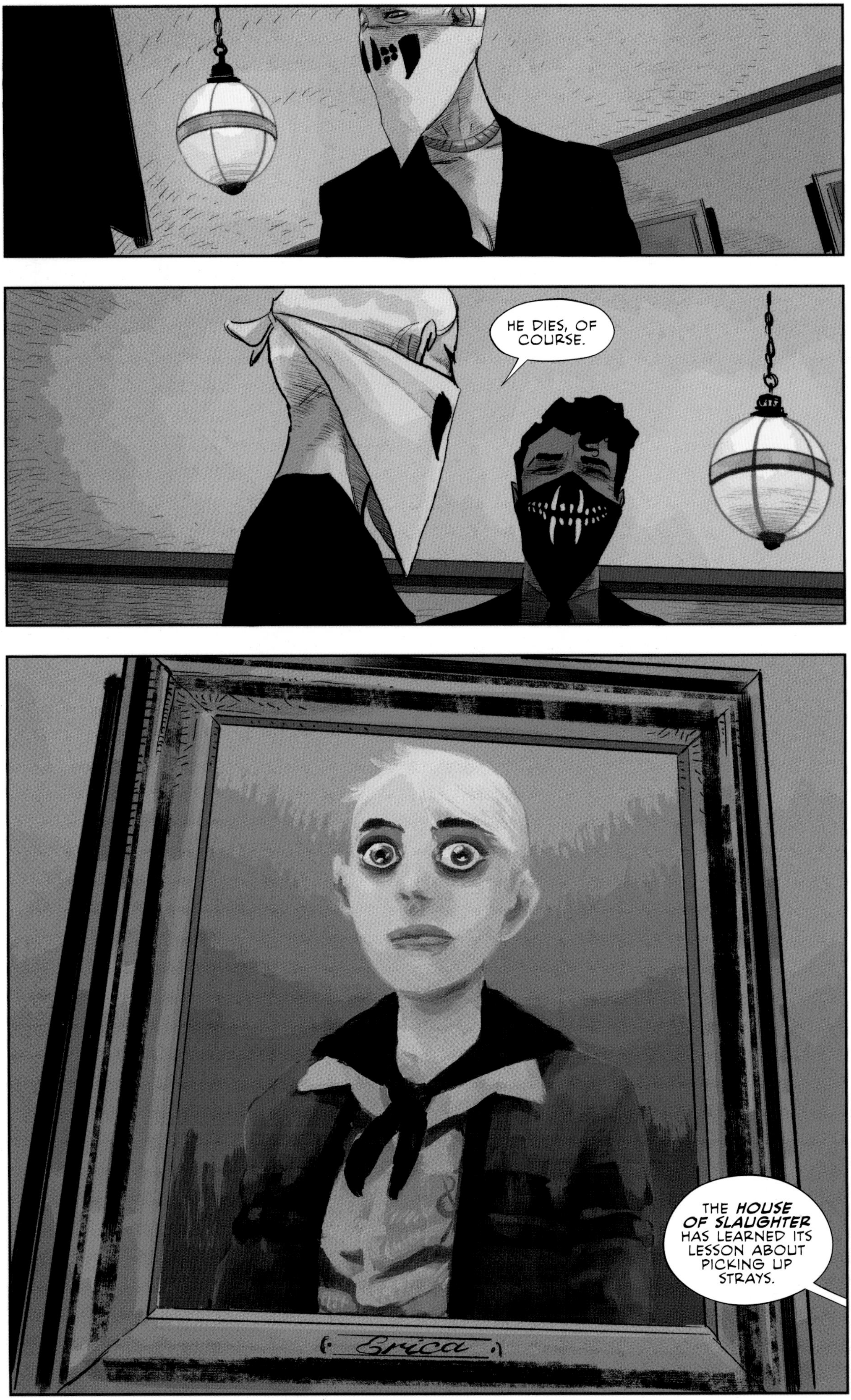
HE DIES, OF COURSE.
THE **HOUSE OF SLAUGHTER** HAS LEARNED ITS LESSON ABOUT PICKING UP STRAYS.
Erica

CHAPTER
SEVEN

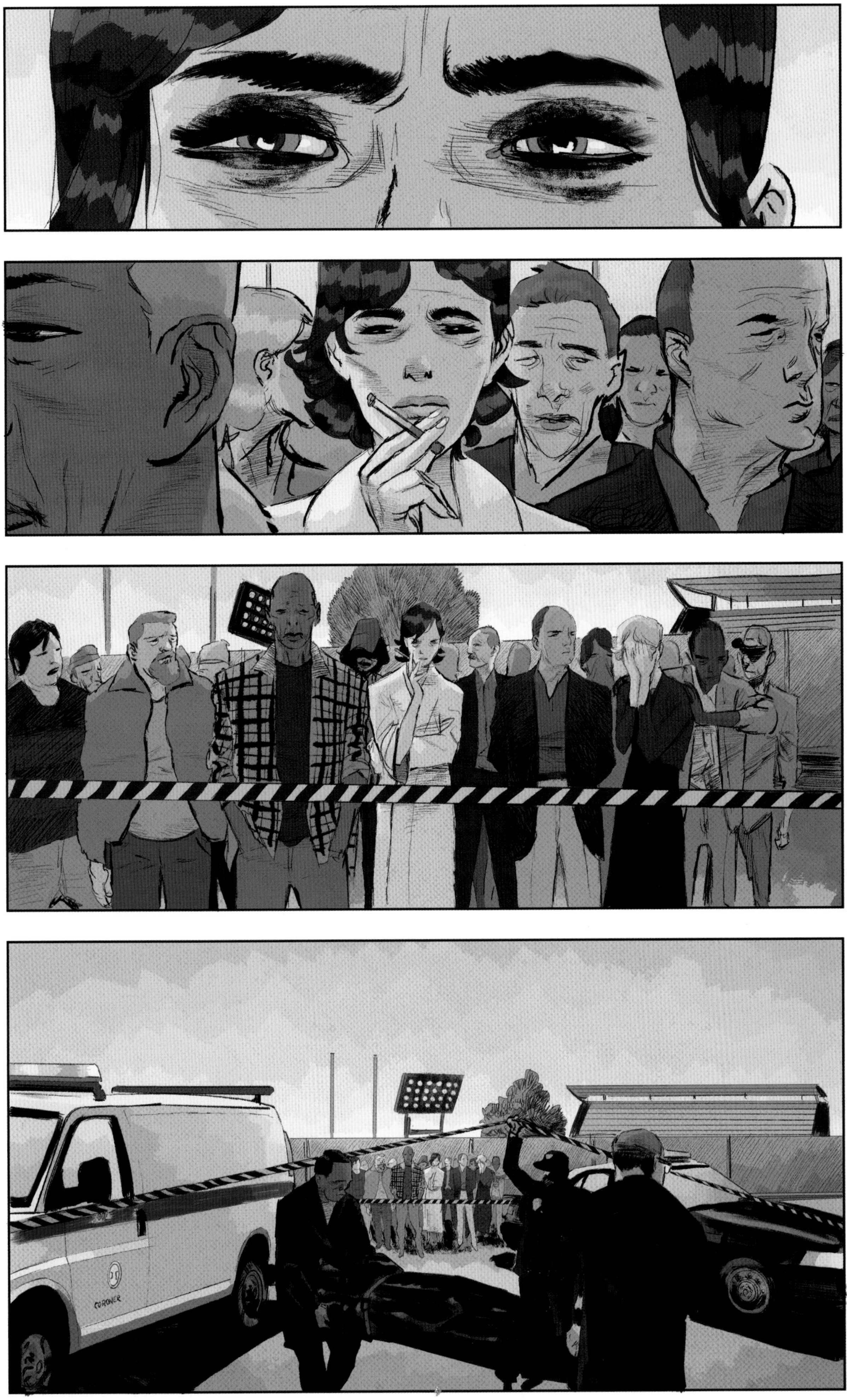
CORONER

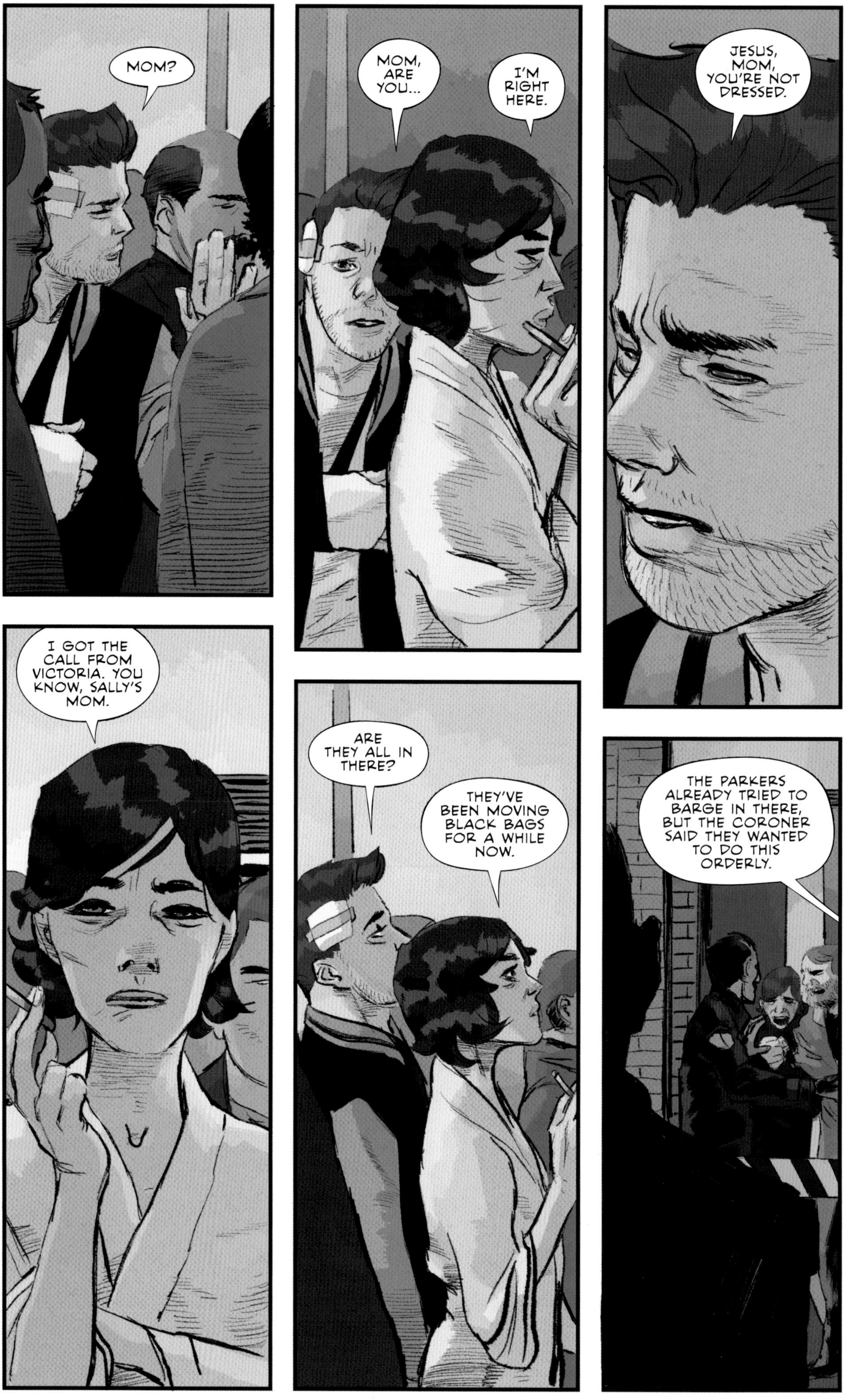
MOM?
MOM, ARE YOU...
I'M RIGHT HERE.
JESUS, MOM, YOU'RE NOT DRESSED.
I GOT THE CALL FROM VICTORIA. YOU KNOW, SALLY'S MOM.
ARE THEY ALL IN THERE?
THEY'VE BEEN MOVING BLACK BAGS FOR A WHILE NOW.
THE PARKERS ALREADY TRIED TO BARGE IN THERE, BUT THE CORONER SAID THEY WANTED TO DO THIS ORDERLY.

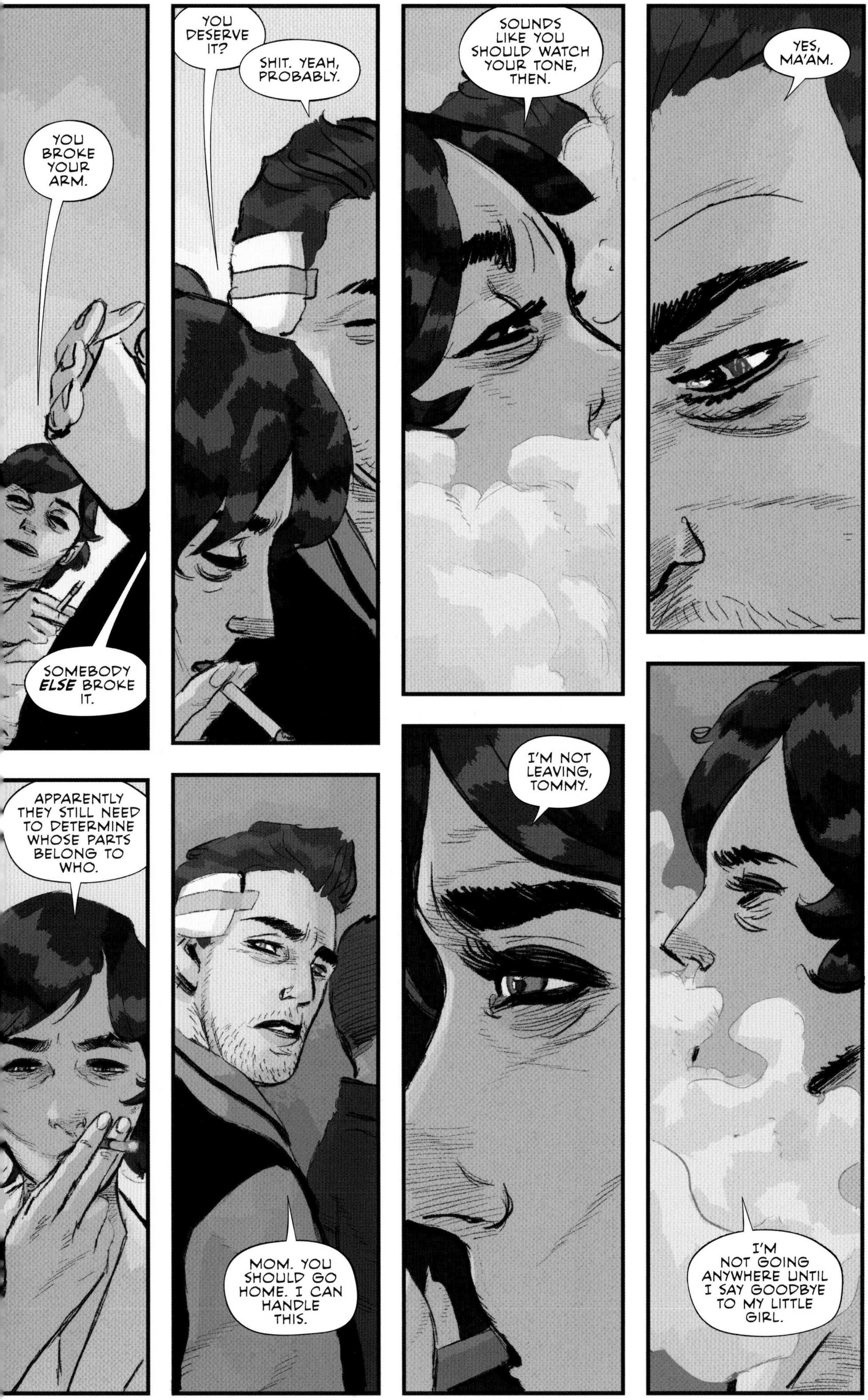
YOU BROKE YOUR ARM.
SOMEBODY ELSE BROKE IT.
YOU DESERVE IT?
SHIT. YEAH, PROBABLY.
SOUNDS LIKE YOU SHOULD WATCH YOUR TONE, THEN.
YES, MA'AM.
APPARENTLY THEY STILL NEED TO DETERMINE WHOSE PARTS BELONG TO WHO.
MOM. YOU SHOULD GO HOME. I CAN HANDLE THIS.
I'M NOT LEAVING, TOMMY.
I'M NOT GOING ANYWHERE UNTIL I SAY GOODBYE TO MY LITTLE GIRL.

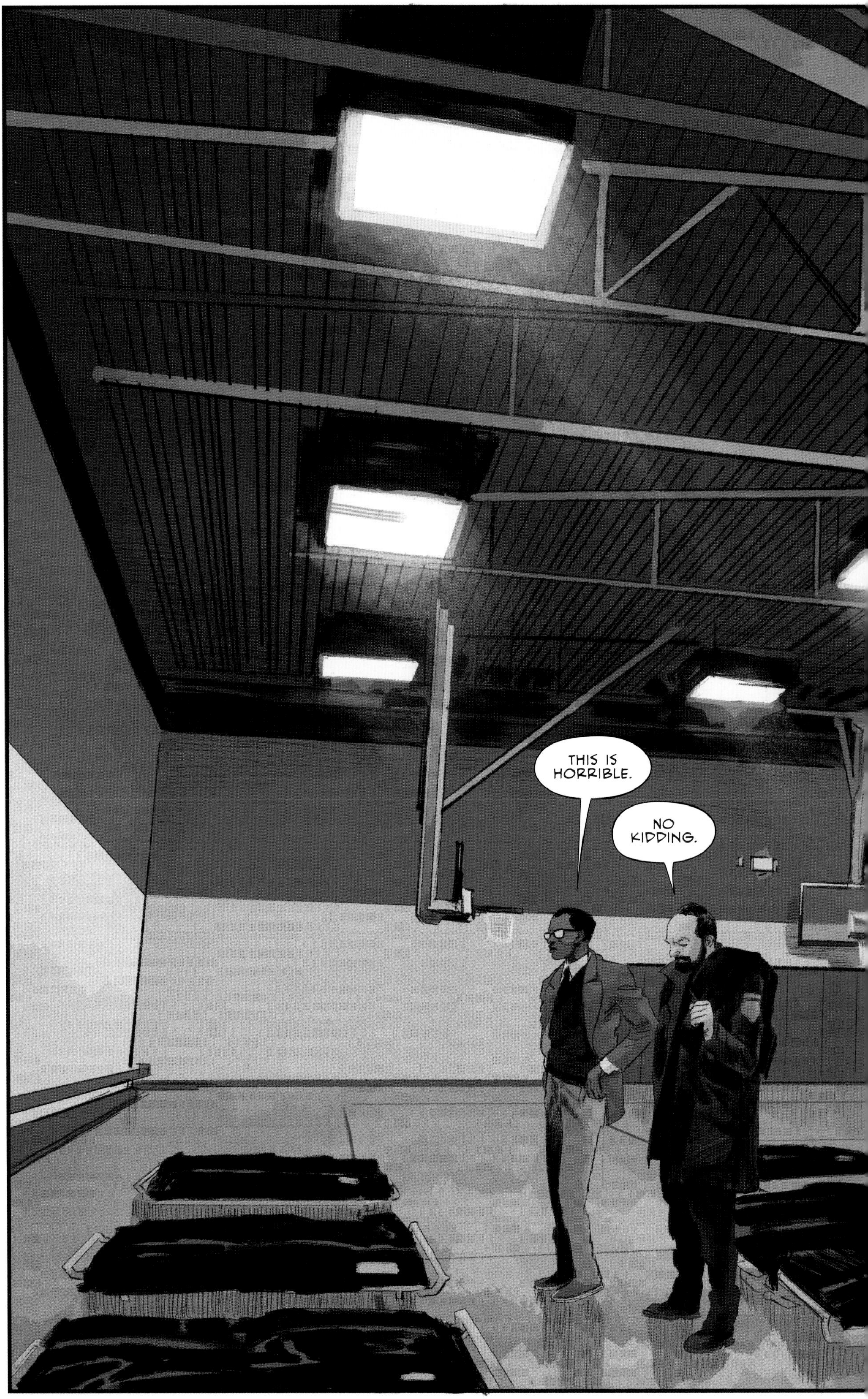
THIS IS HORRIBLE.
NO KIDDING.

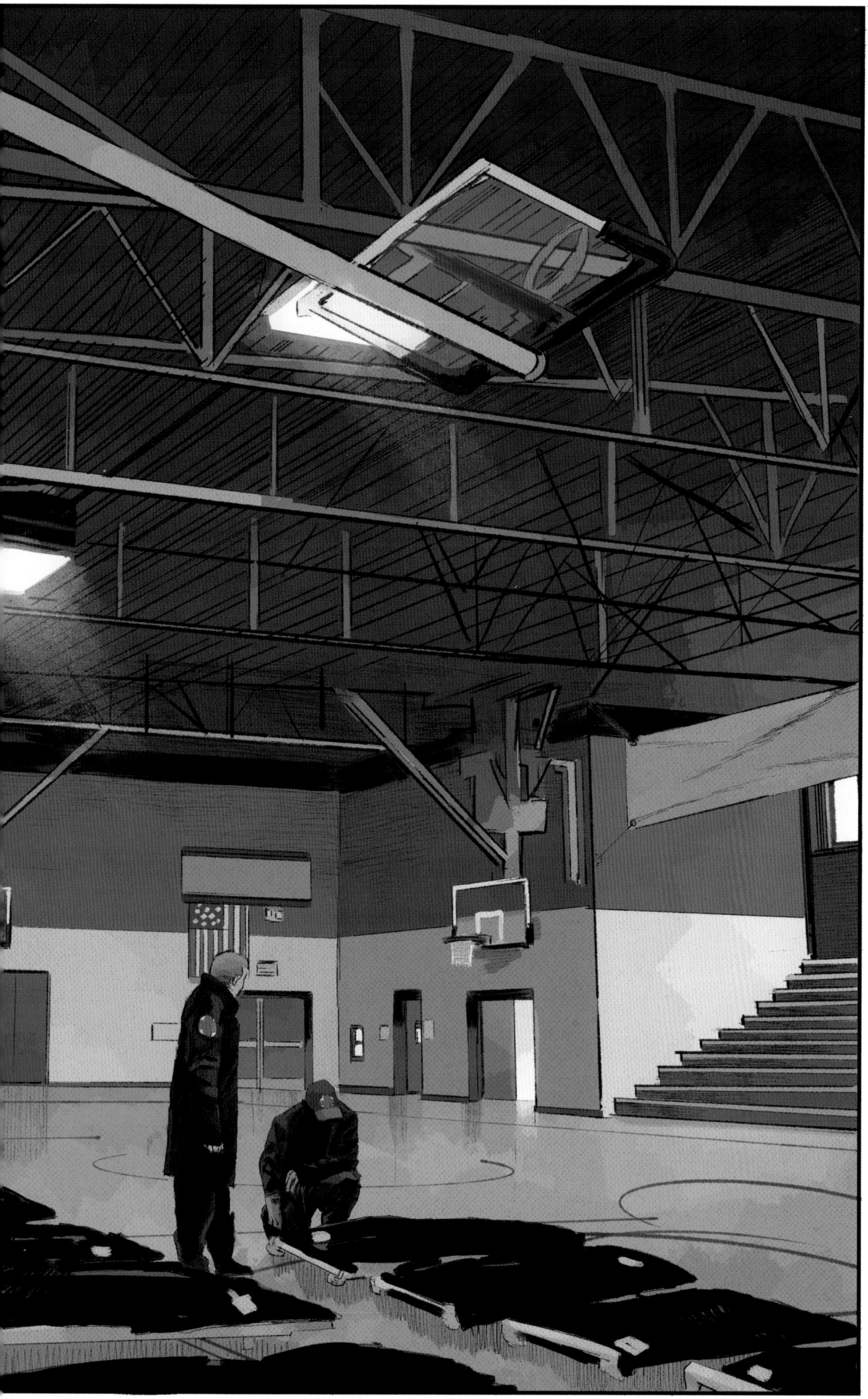

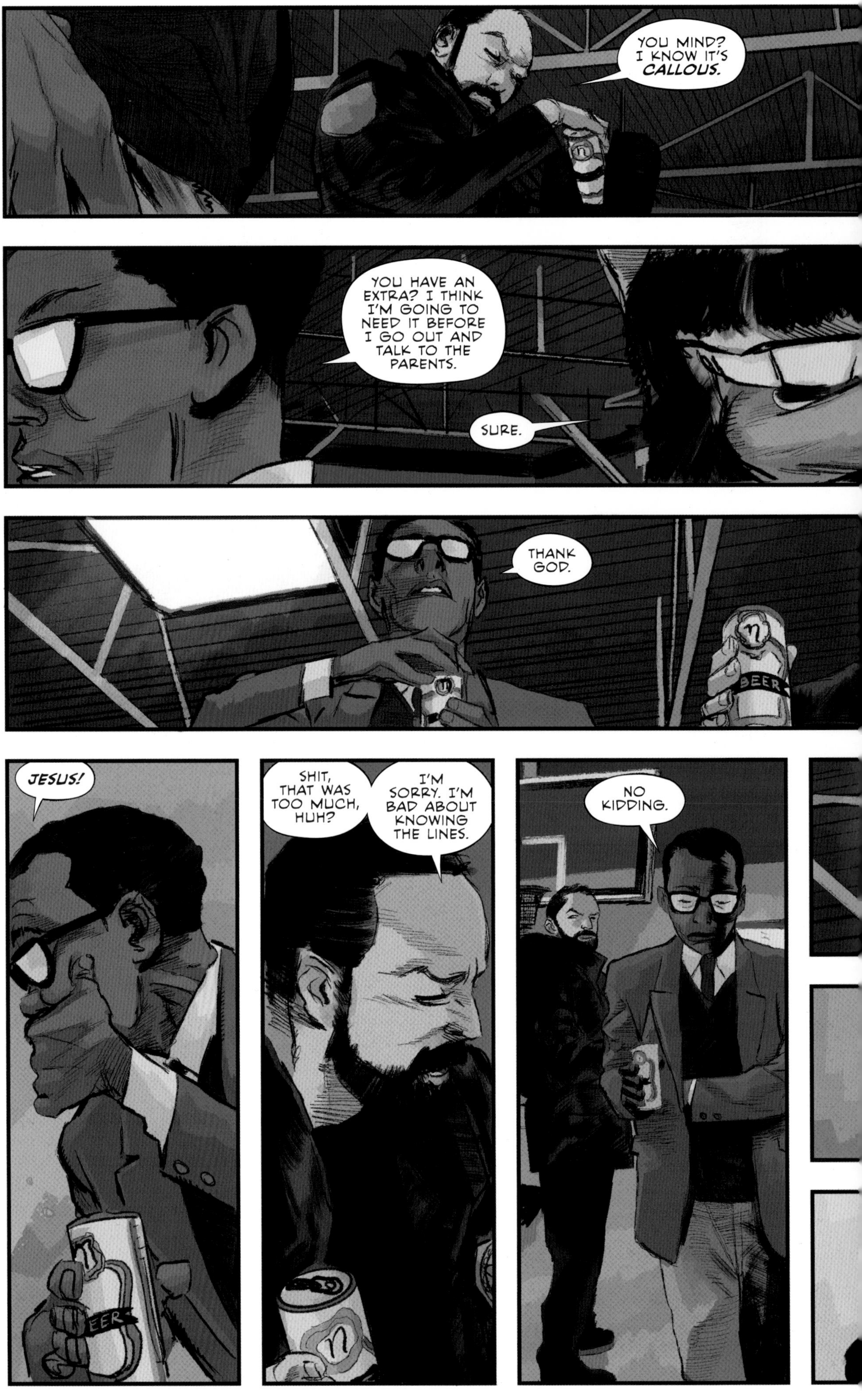
YOU MIND? I KNOW IT'S CALLOUS.
YOU HAVE AN EXTRA? I THINK I'M GOING TO NEED IT BEFORE I GO OUT AND TALK TO THE PARENTS.
SURE.
THANK GOD.
BEER
JESUS!
EER
SHIT, THAT WAS TOO MUCH, HUH?
I'M SORRY. I'M BAD ABOUT KNOWING THE LINES.
NO KIDDING.

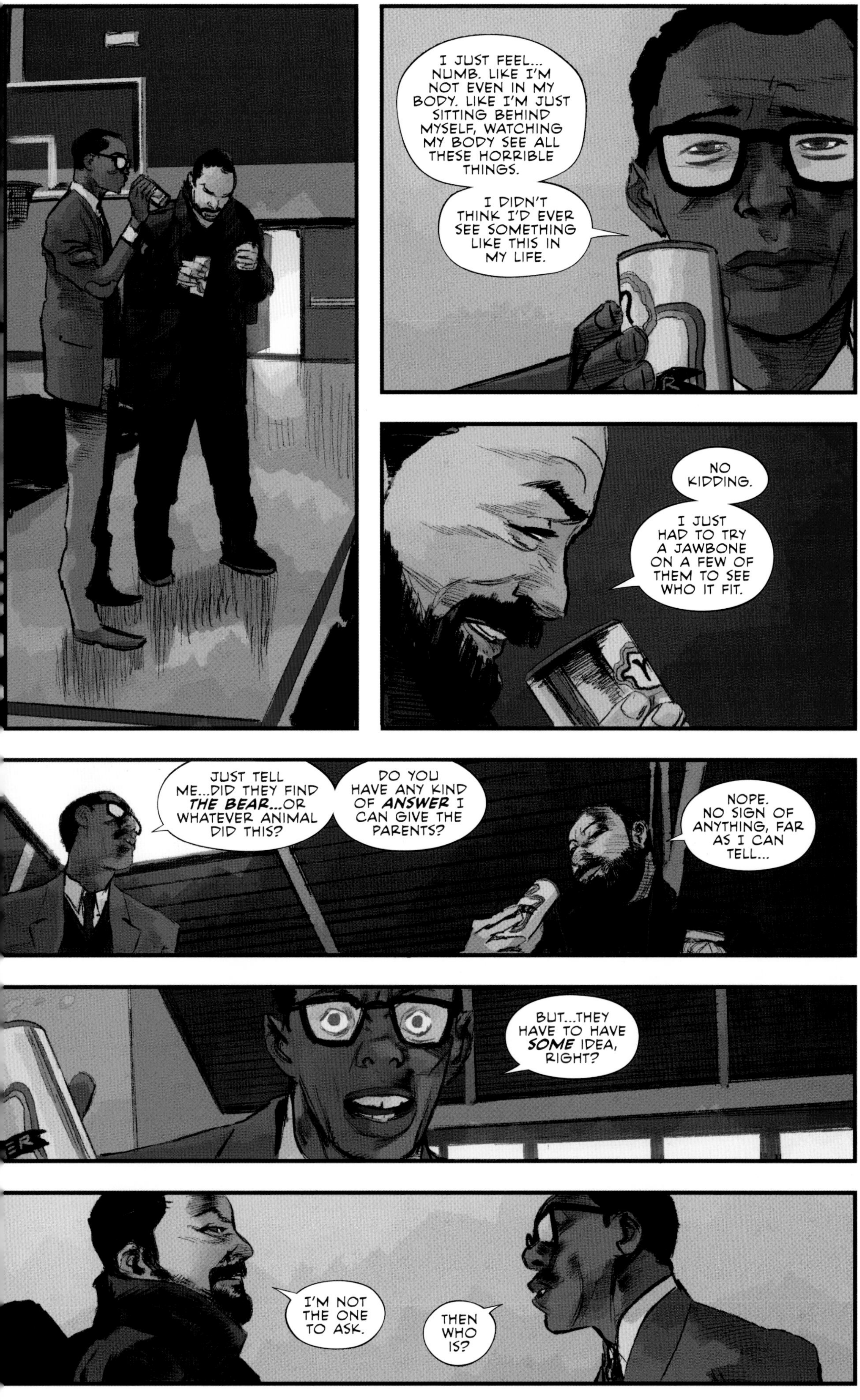

I JUST FEEL... NUMB. LIKE I'M NOT EVEN IN MY BODY. LIKE I'M JUST SITTING BEHIND MYSELF, WATCHING MY BODY SEE ALL THESE HORRIBLE THINGS.
I DIDN'T THINK I'D EVER SEE SOMETHING LIKE THIS IN MY LIFE.
NO KIDDING.
I JUST HAD TO TRY A JAWBONE ON A FEW OF THEM TO SEE WHO IT FIT.
JUST TELL ME...DID THEY FIND ***THE BEAR...***OR WHATEVER ANIMAL DID THIS?
DO YOU HAVE ANY KIND OF ***ANSWER*** I CAN GIVE THE PARENTS?
NOPE. NO SIGN OF ANYTHING, FAR AS I CAN TELL...
BUT...THEY HAVE TO HAVE ***SOME*** IDEA, RIGHT?
I'M NOT THE ONE TO ASK.
THEN WHO IS?

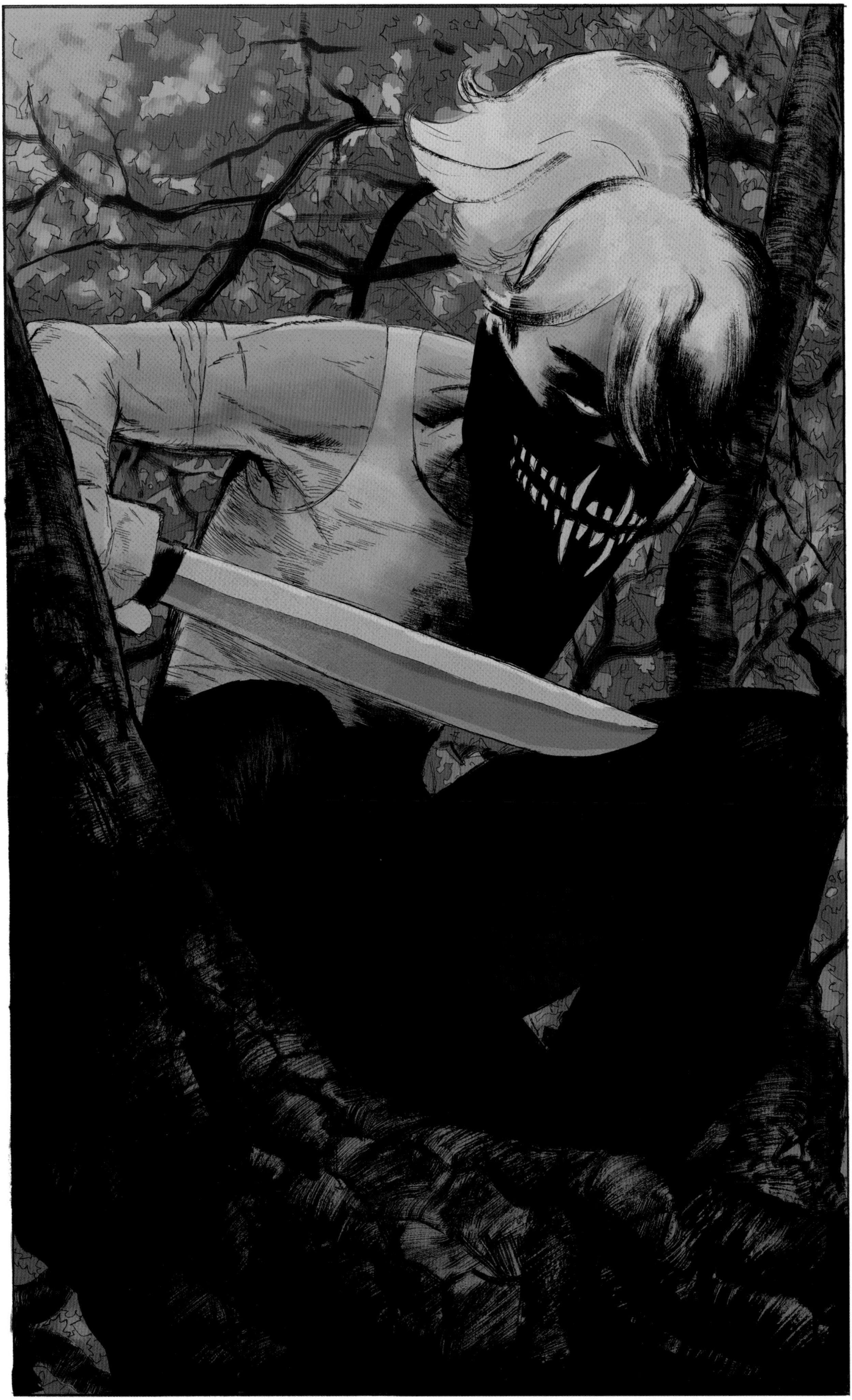

THIS WON'T WORK.
QUIET.
YOU KNOW THIS WON'T WORK.
I SAID BE QUIET. I HEAR SOMETHING.
RUSTLE

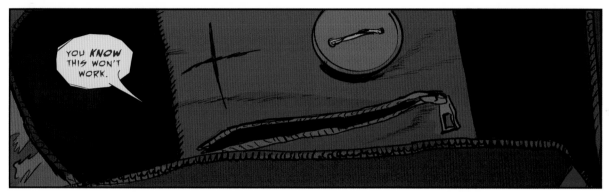

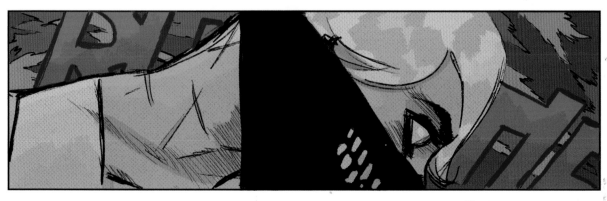

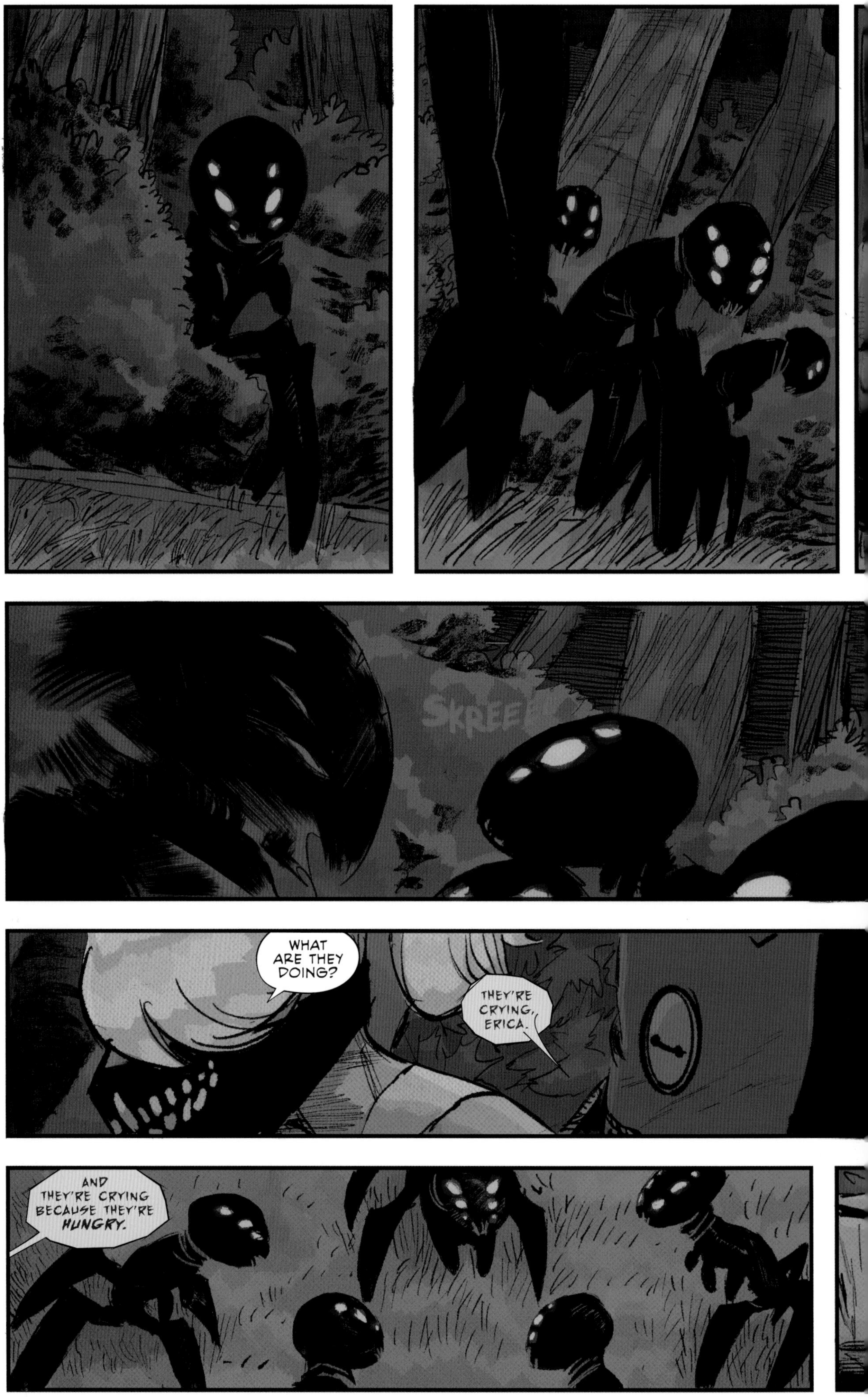
SKREE
WHAT ARE THEY DOING?
THEY'RE CRYING, ERICA.
AND THEY'RE CRYING BECAUSE THEY'RE ***HUNGRY.***

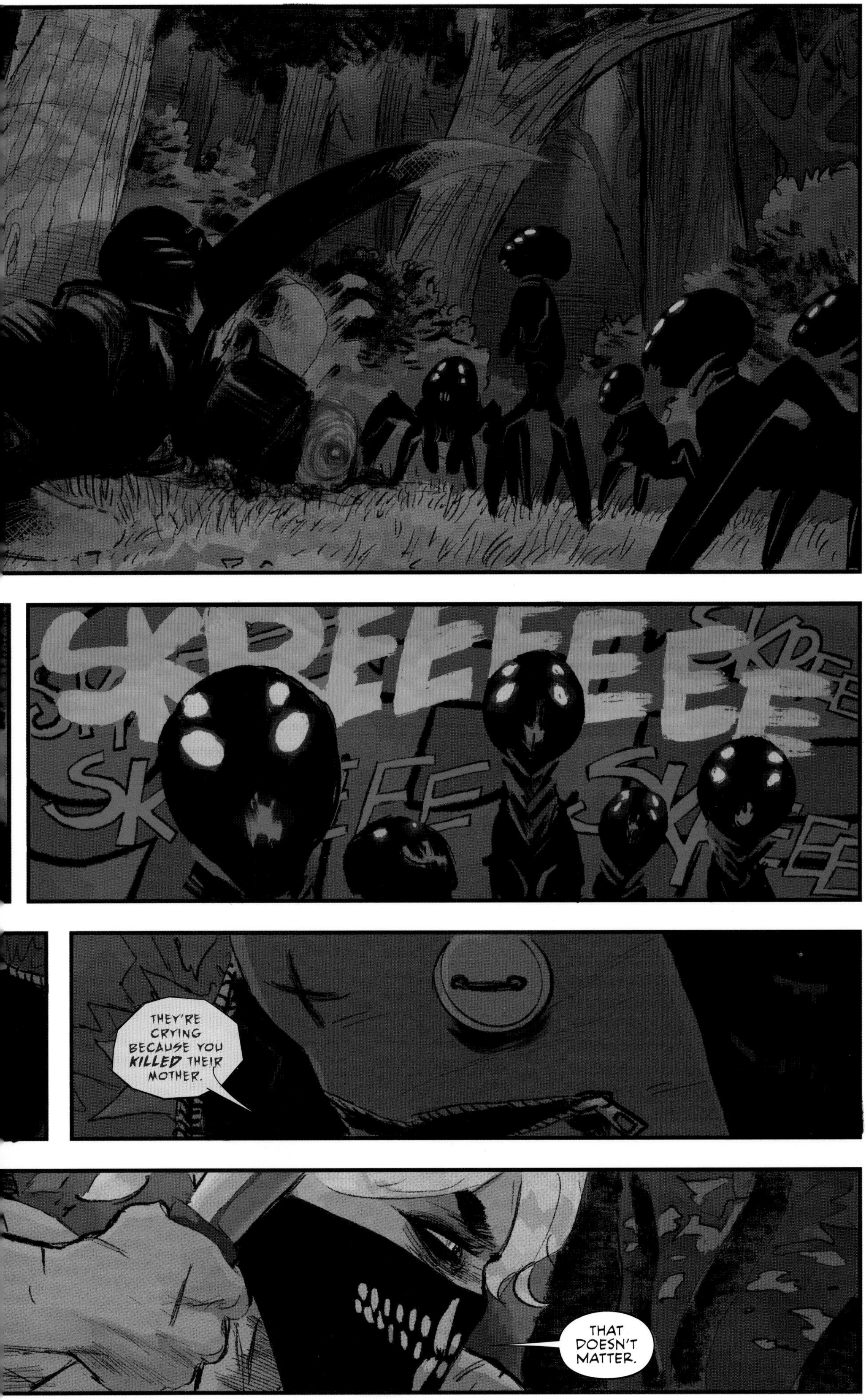
THEY'RE CRYING BECAUSE YOU *KILLED* THEIR MOTHER.
THAT DOESN'T MATTER.

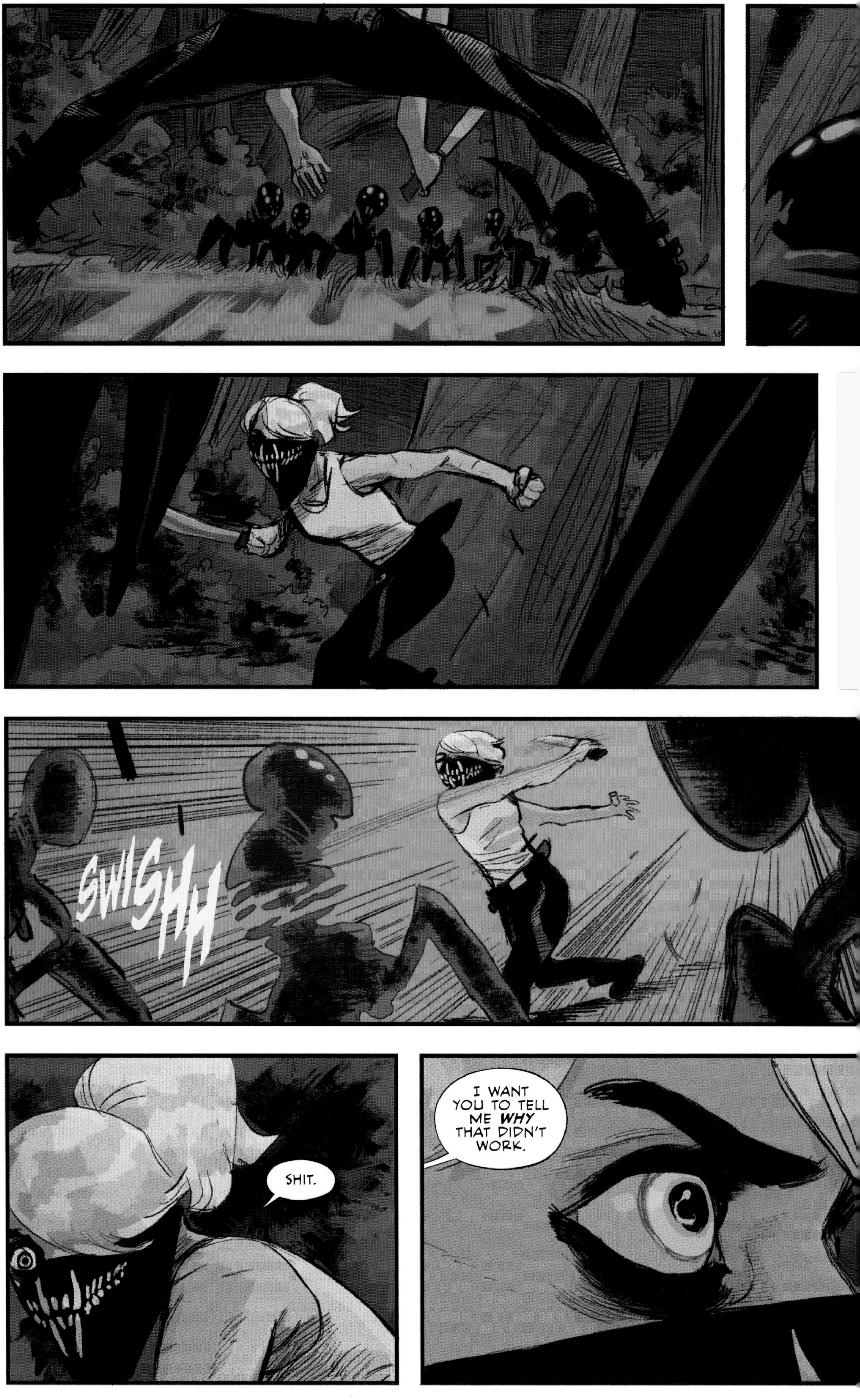
THUMP
SWISHH
SHIT.
I WANT YOU TO TELL ME *WHY* THAT DIDN'T WORK.

REeEARRRGh

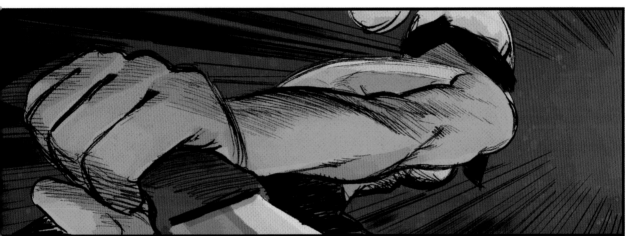

NO!

SHIT.

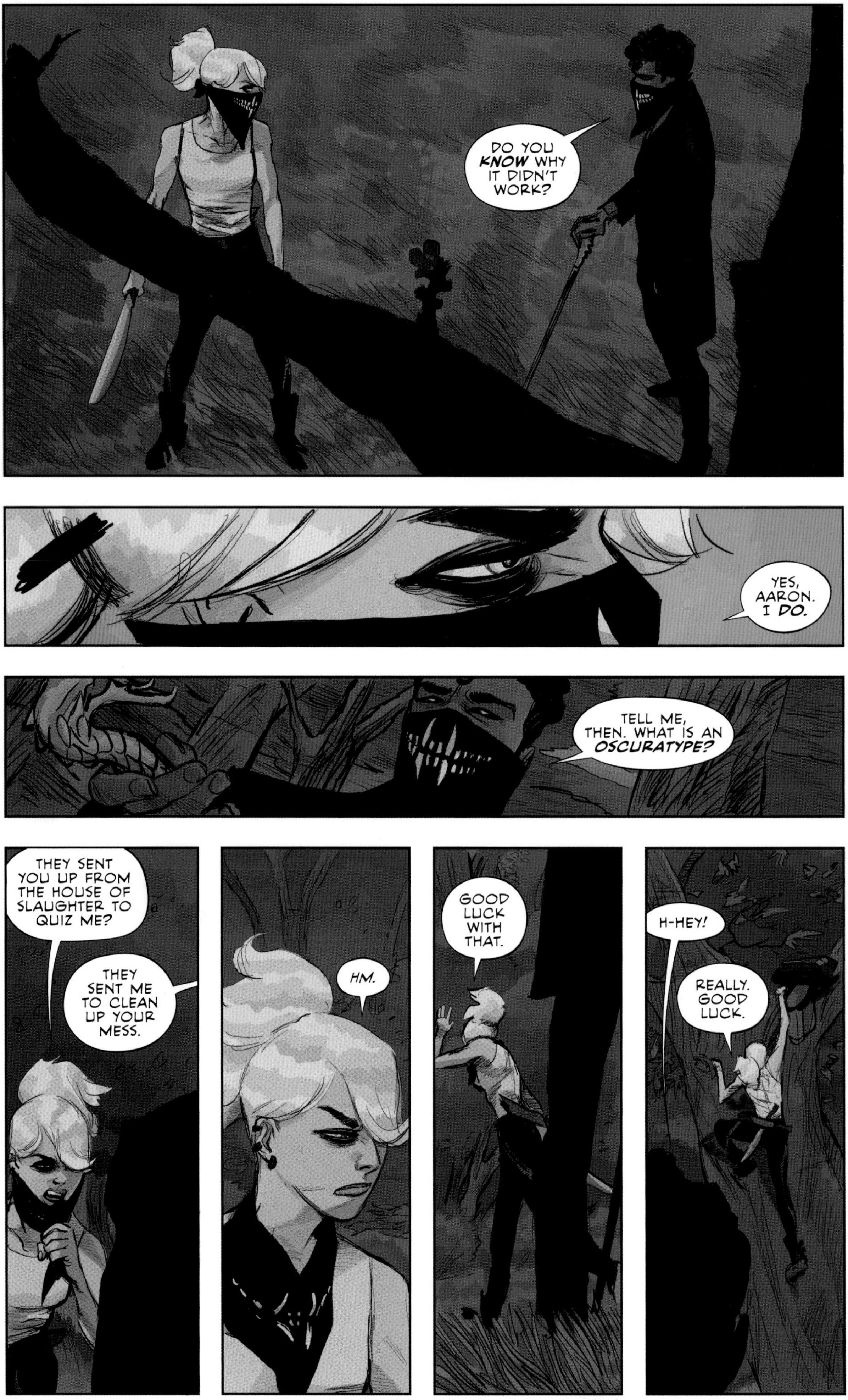
DO YOU KNOW WHY IT DIDN'T WORK?
YES, AARON. I DO.
TELL ME, THEN. WHAT IS AN OSCURATYPE?
THEY SENT YOU UP FROM THE HOUSE OF SLAUGHTER TO QUIZ ME?
THEY SENT ME TO CLEAN UP YOUR MESS.
HM.
GOOD LUCK WITH THAT.
H-HEY!
REALLY. GOOD LUCK.

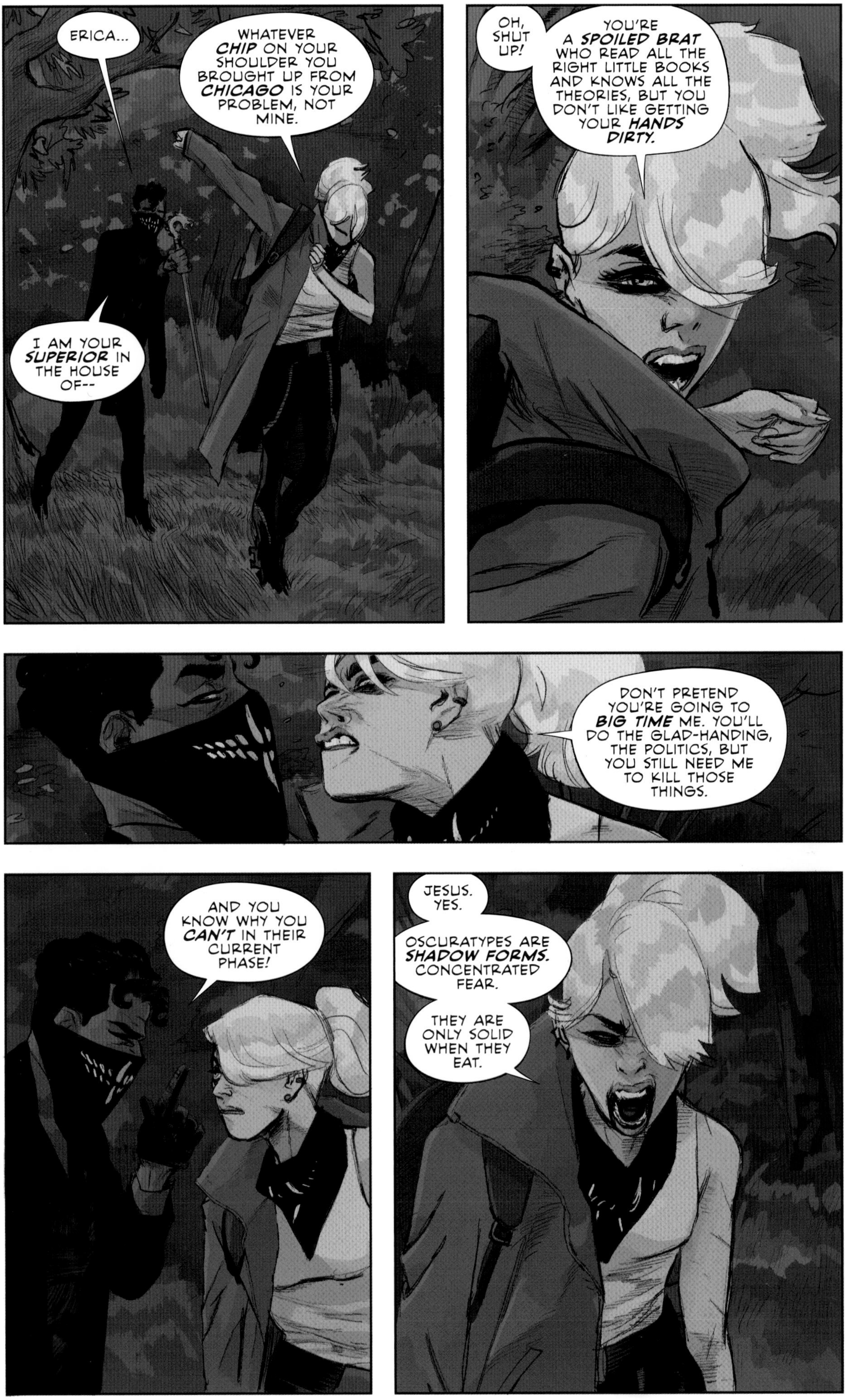
ERICA...
WHATEVER CHIP ON YOUR SHOULDER YOU BROUGHT UP FROM CHICAGO IS YOUR PROBLEM, NOT MINE.
I AM YOUR SUPERIOR IN THE HOUSE OF--
OH, SHUT UP!
YOU'RE A SPOILED BRAT WHO READ ALL THE RIGHT LITTLE BOOKS AND KNOWS ALL THE THEORIES, BUT YOU DON'T LIKE GETTING YOUR HANDS DIRTY.
DON'T PRETEND YOU'RE GOING TO BIG TIME ME. YOU'LL DO THE GLAD-HANDING, THE POLITICS, BUT YOU STILL NEED ME TO KILL THOSE THINGS.
AND YOU KNOW WHY YOU CAN'T IN THEIR CURRENT PHASE!
JESUS. YES.
OSCURATYPES ARE SHADOW FORMS. CONCENTRATED FEAR.
THEY ARE ONLY SOLID WHEN THEY EAT.

THEN IT SEEMS PRETTY *FUCKING POINTLESS* TO STAB ONE WHEN THERE'S NOTHING FOR IT TO SINK ITS TEETH INTO. NO?

THANKS FOR CLEARING THAT UP.

THEN WHY WASTE YOUR TIME--

BECAUSE THERE ARE DEAD CHILDREN, AARON, AND I DIDN'T WANT TO WAIT UNTIL THE NEXT ONE DIED BEFORE I COULD DO SOMETHING ABOUT IT!

I'M SORRY.

I KNOW THIS BREED IS MORE... PERSONAL.

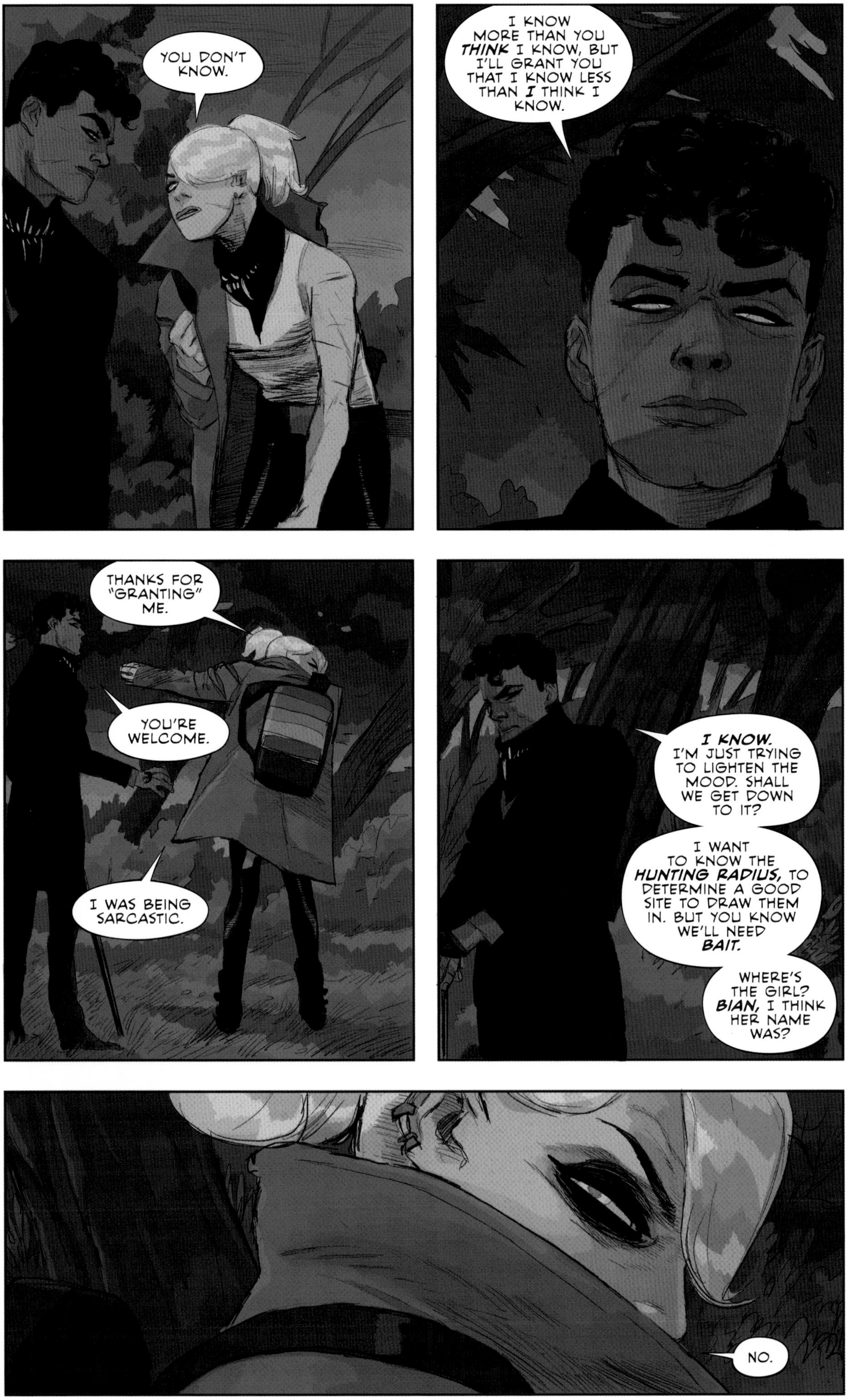
YOU DON'T KNOW.
I KNOW MORE THAN YOU *THINK* I KNOW, BUT I'LL GRANT YOU THAT I KNOW LESS THAN *I* THINK I KNOW.
THANKS FOR "GRANTING" ME.
YOU'RE WELCOME.
I WAS BEING SARCASTIC.
I KNOW. I'M JUST TRYING TO LIGHTEN THE MOOD. SHALL WE GET DOWN TO IT?
I WANT TO KNOW THE *HUNTING RADIUS,* TO DETERMINE A GOOD SITE TO DRAW THEM IN. BUT YOU KNOW WE'LL NEED *BAIT.*
WHERE'S THE GIRL? *BIAN,* I THINK HER NAME WAS?
NO.

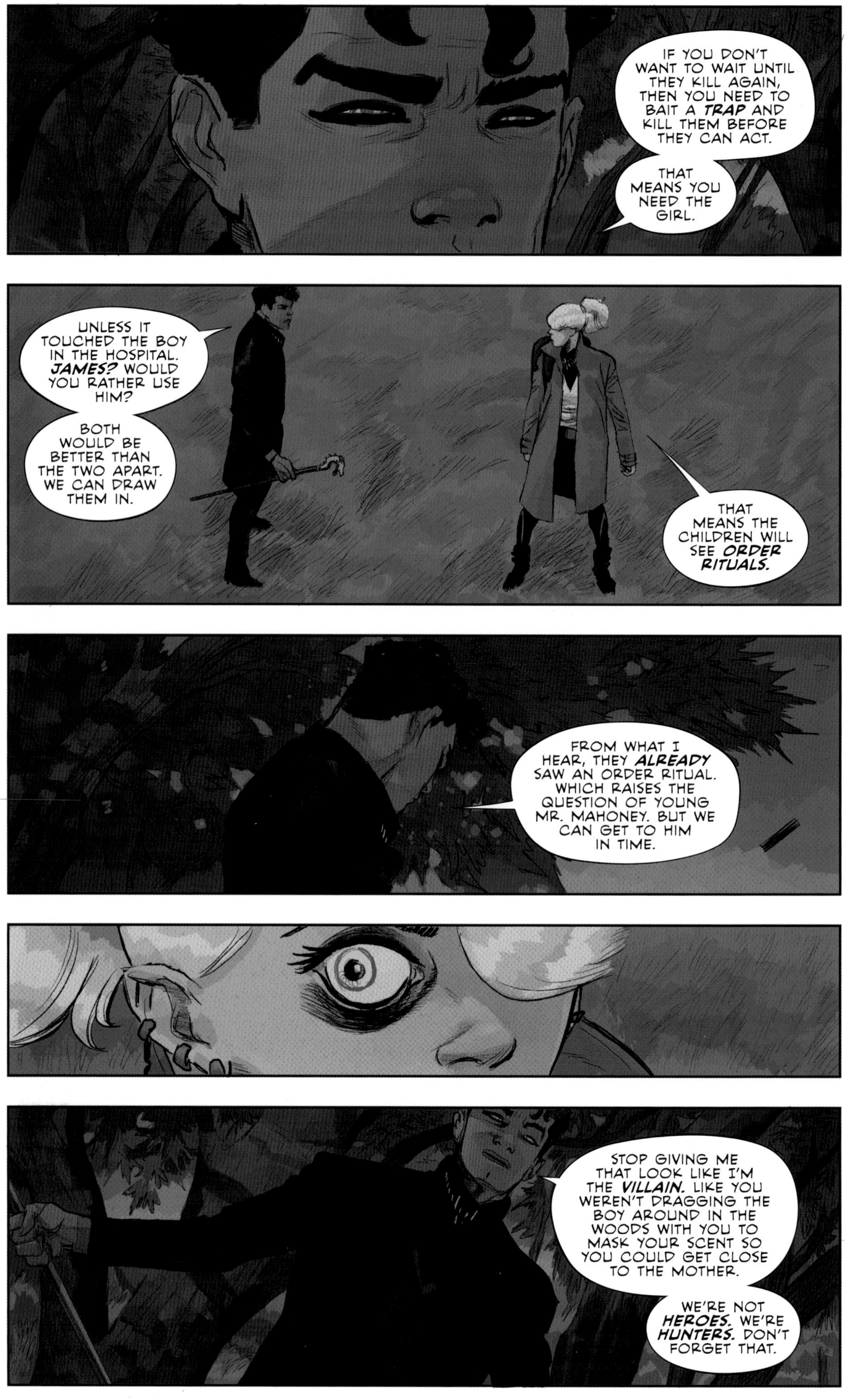

IF YOU DON'T WANT TO WAIT UNTIL THEY KILL AGAIN, THEN YOU NEED TO BAIT A TRAP AND KILL THEM BEFORE THEY CAN ACT.
THAT MEANS YOU NEED THE GIRL.
UNLESS IT TOUCHED THE BOY IN THE HOSPITAL. JAMES? WOULD YOU RATHER USE HIM?
BOTH WOULD BE BETTER THAN THE TWO APART. WE CAN DRAW THEM IN.
THAT MEANS THE CHILDREN WILL SEE ORDER RITUALS.
FROM WHAT I HEAR, THEY ALREADY SAW AN ORDER RITUAL. WHICH RAISES THE QUESTION OF YOUNG MR. MAHONEY. BUT WE CAN GET TO HIM IN TIME.
STOP GIVING ME THAT LOOK LIKE I'M THE VILLAIN. LIKE YOU WEREN'T DRAGGING THE BOY AROUND IN THE WOODS WITH YOU TO MASK YOUR SCENT SO YOU COULD GET CLOSE TO THE MOTHER.
WE'RE NOT HEROES. WE'RE HUNTERS. DON'T FORGET THAT.

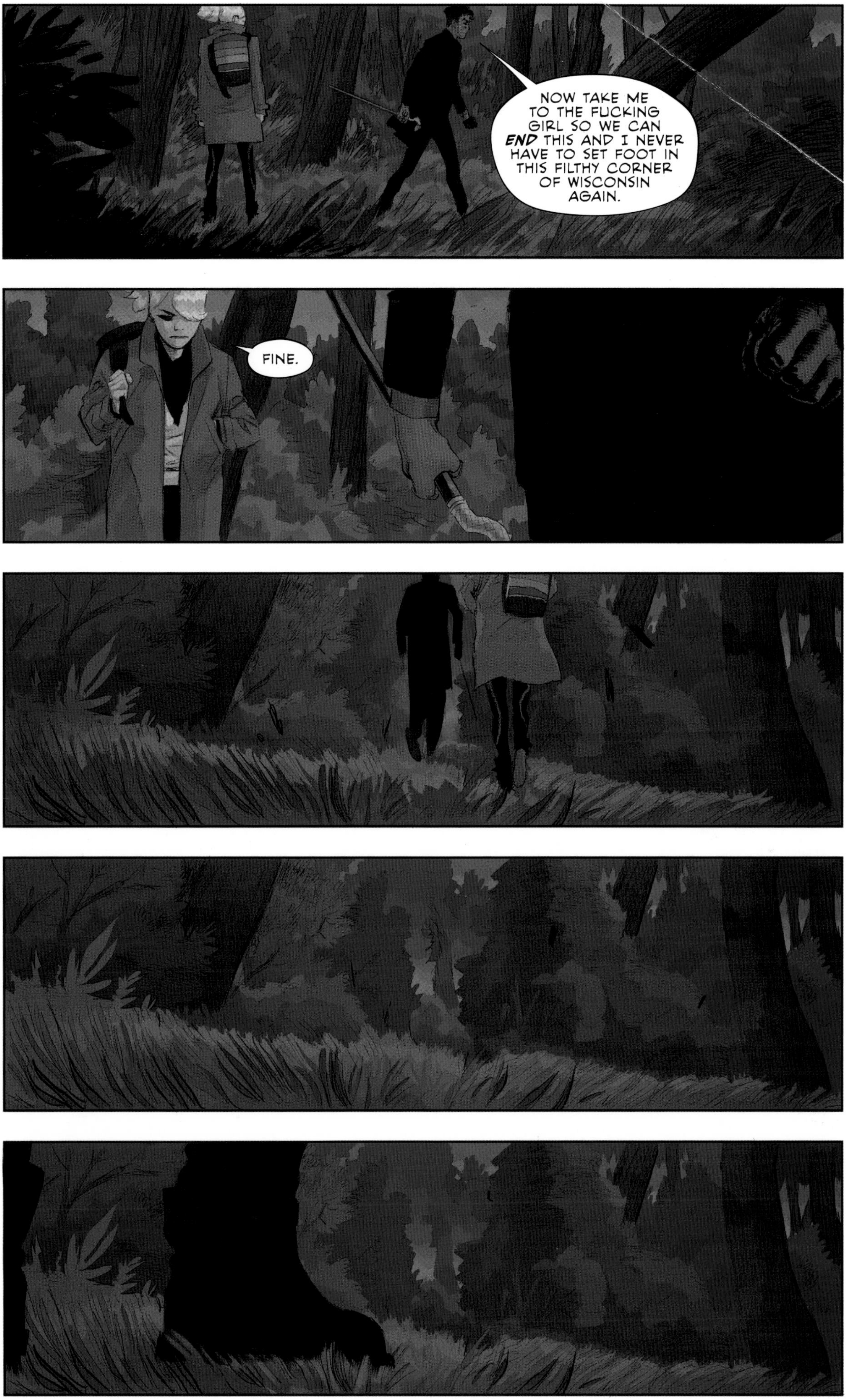
NOW TAKE ME TO THE FUCKING GIRL SO WE CAN **END** THIS AND I NEVER HAVE TO SET FOOT IN THIS FILTHY CORNER OF WISCONSIN AGAIN.
FINE.

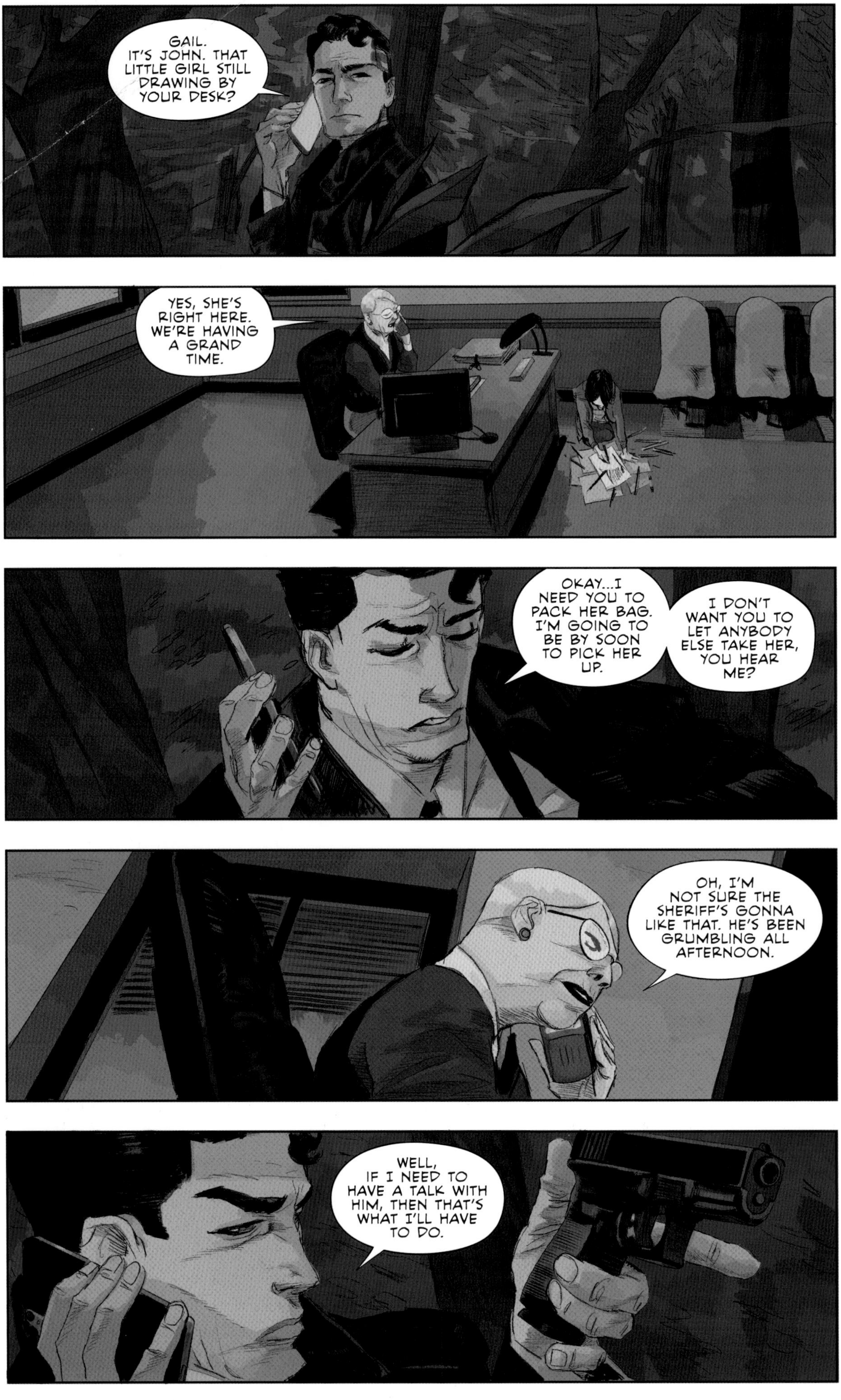
GAIL. IT'S JOHN. THAT LITTLE GIRL STILL DRAWING BY YOUR DESK?
YES, SHE'S RIGHT HERE. WE'RE HAVING A GRAND TIME.
OKAY...I NEED YOU TO PACK HER BAG. I'M GOING TO BE BY SOON TO PICK HER UP.
I DON'T WANT YOU TO LET ANYBODY ELSE TAKE HER, YOU HEAR ME?
OH, I'M NOT SURE THE SHERIFF'S GONNA LIKE THAT. HE'S BEEN GRUMBLING ALL AFTERNOON.
WELL, IF I NEED TO HAVE A TALK WITH HIM, THEN THAT'S WHAT I'LL HAVE TO DO.

CHAPTER EIGHT

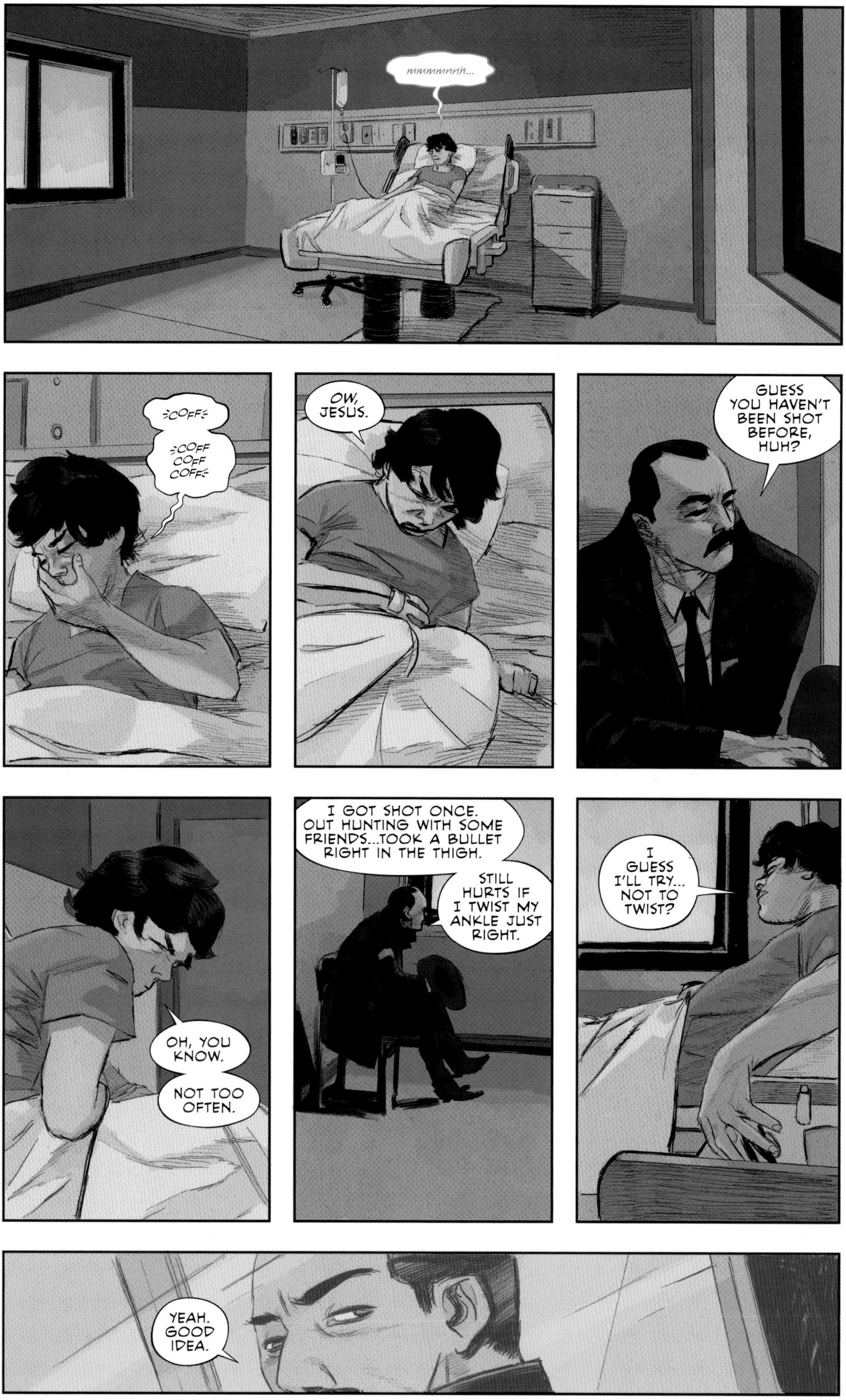
mmmmmnh...
COFF
COFF COFF COFF
OW, JESUS.
GUESS YOU HAVEN'T BEEN SHOT BEFORE, HUH?
OH, YOU KNOW.
NOT TOO OFTEN.
I GOT SHOT ONCE. OUT HUNTING WITH SOME FRIENDS...TOOK A BULLET RIGHT IN THE THIGH.
STILL HURTS IF I TWIST MY ANKLE JUST RIGHT.
I GUESS I'LL TRY... NOT TO TWIST?
YEAH. GOOD IDEA.

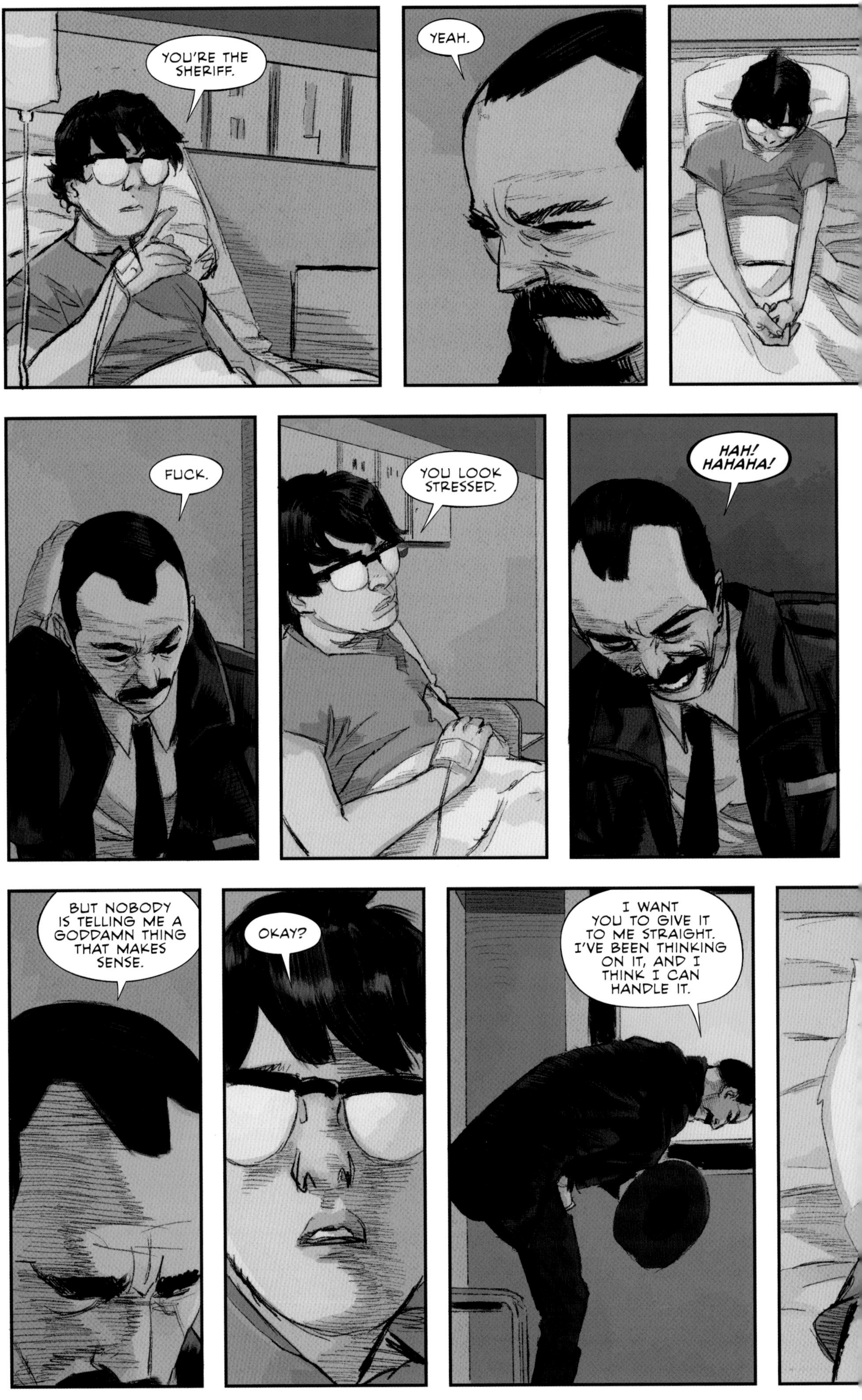
YOU'RE THE SHERIFF.
YEAH.
FUCK.
YOU LOOK STRESSED.
HAH! HAHAHA!
BUT NOBODY IS TELLING ME A GODDAMN THING THAT MAKES SENSE.
OKAY?
I WANT YOU TO GIVE IT TO ME STRAIGHT. I'VE BEEN THINKING ON IT, AND I THINK I CAN HANDLE IT.

ARE YOU HERE TO ARREST ME?

NO.

I JUST... I DON'T KNOW...

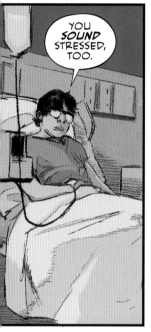

YOU *SOUND* STRESSED, TOO.

THEY'RE COMING AT ME FROM ALL ANGLES, KID.

WHAT ARE YOU TALKING ABOUT?

JAMES. I NEED YOU TO TELL ME ABOUT THE ALIENS.

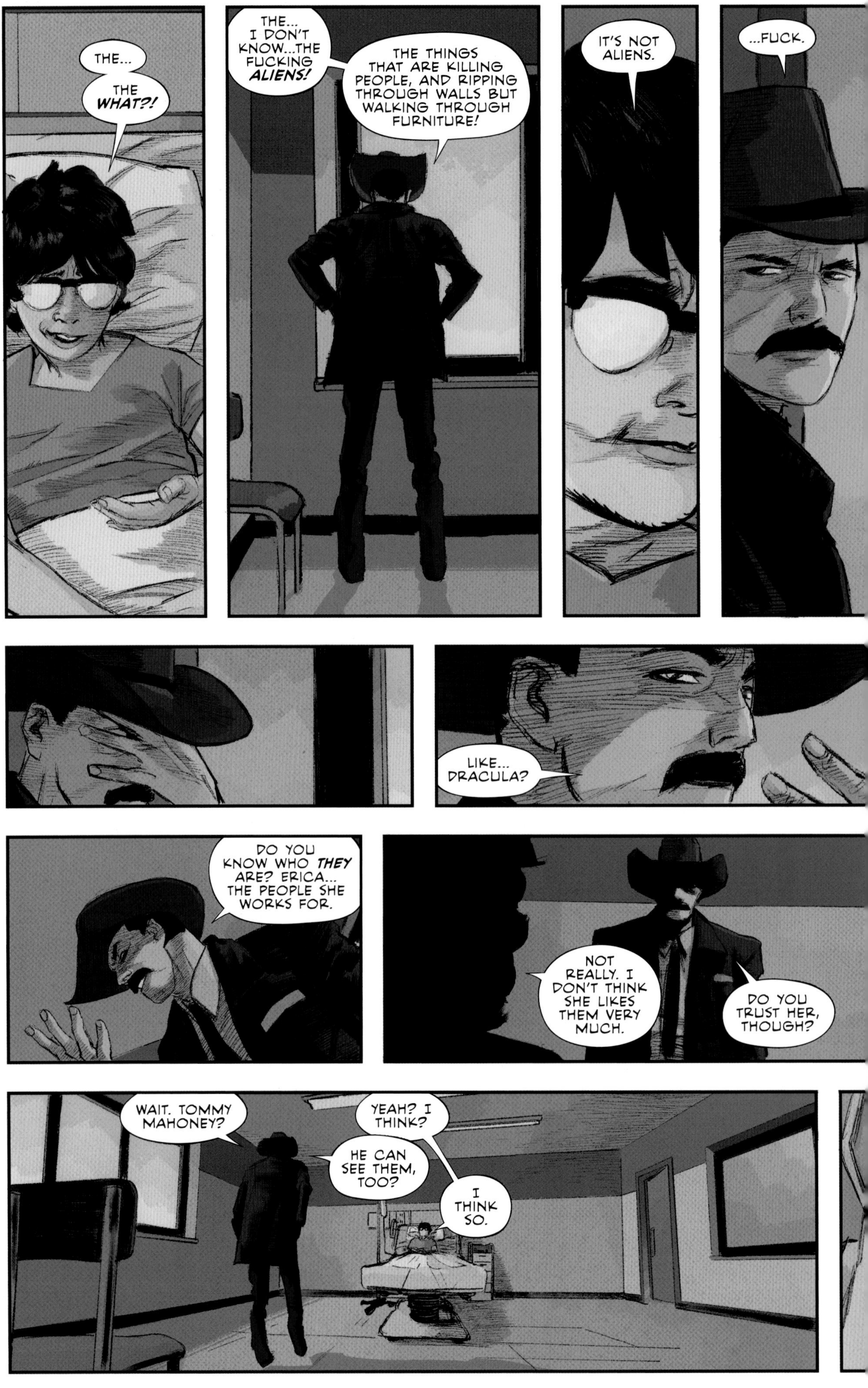
THE...
THE WHAT?!
THE... I DON'T KNOW...THE FUCKING ALIENS!
THE THINGS THAT ARE KILLING PEOPLE, AND RIPPING THROUGH WALLS BUT WALKING THROUGH FURNITURE!
IT'S NOT ALIENS.
...FUCK.
LIKE... DRACULA?
DO YOU KNOW WHO THEY ARE? ERICA... THE PEOPLE SHE WORKS FOR.
NOT REALLY. I DON'T THINK SHE LIKES THEM VERY MUCH.
DO YOU TRUST HER, THOUGH?
WAIT. TOMMY MAHONEY?
YEAH? I THINK?
HE CAN SEE THEM, TOO?
I THINK SO.

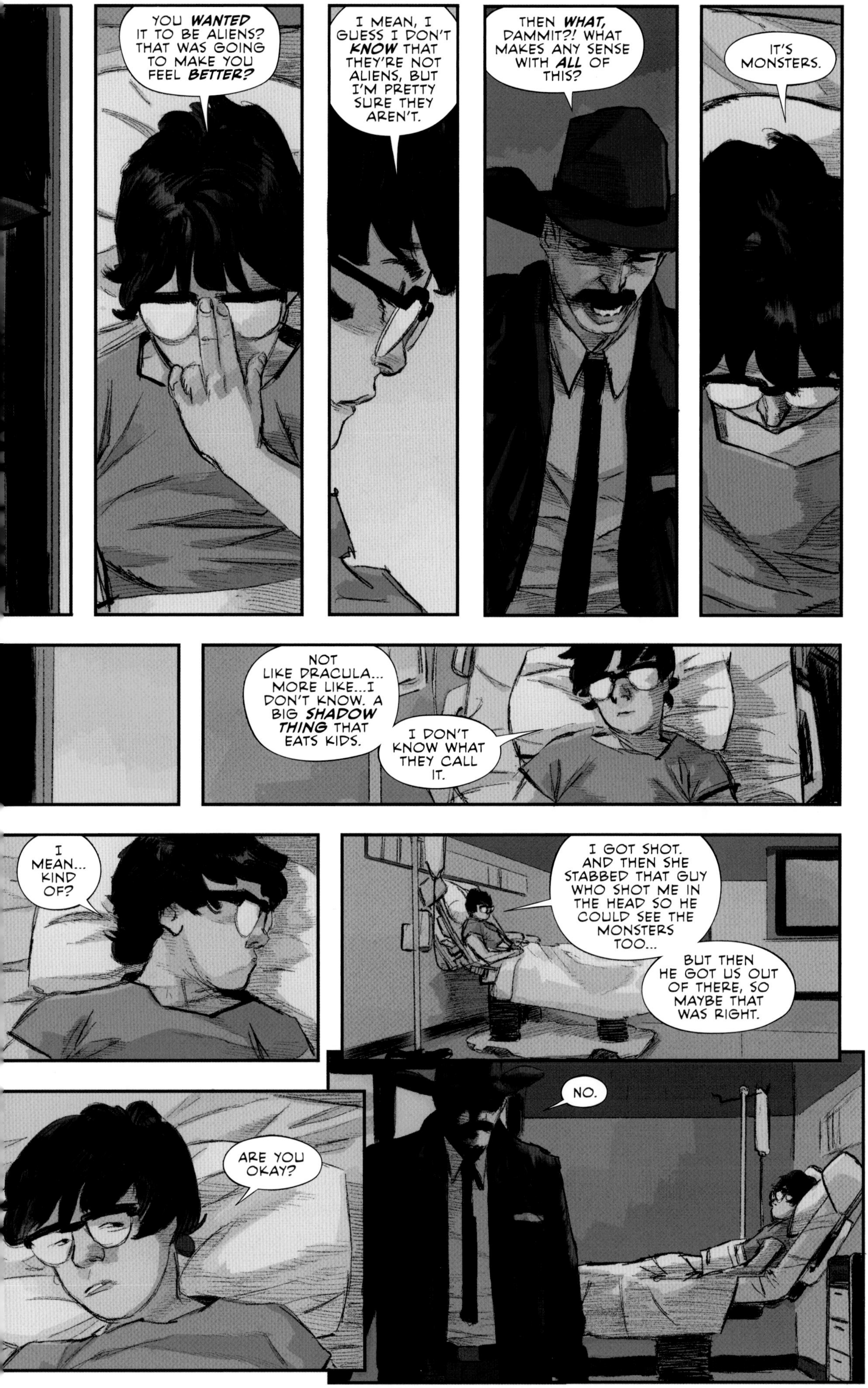
YOU WANTED IT TO BE ALIENS? THAT WAS GOING TO MAKE YOU FEEL BETTER?
I MEAN, I GUESS I DON'T KNOW THAT THEY'RE NOT ALIENS, BUT I'M PRETTY SURE THEY AREN'T.
THEN WHAT, DAMMIT?! WHAT MAKES ANY SENSE WITH ALL OF THIS?
IT'S MONSTERS.
NOT LIKE DRACULA... MORE LIKE...I DON'T KNOW. A BIG SHADOW THING THAT EATS KIDS.
I DON'T KNOW WHAT THEY CALL IT.
I MEAN... KIND OF?
I GOT SHOT. AND THEN SHE STABBED THAT GUY WHO SHOT ME IN THE HEAD SO HE COULD SEE THE MONSTERS TOO...
BUT THEN HE GOT US OUT OF THERE, SO MAYBE THAT WAS RIGHT.
ARE YOU OKAY?
NO.

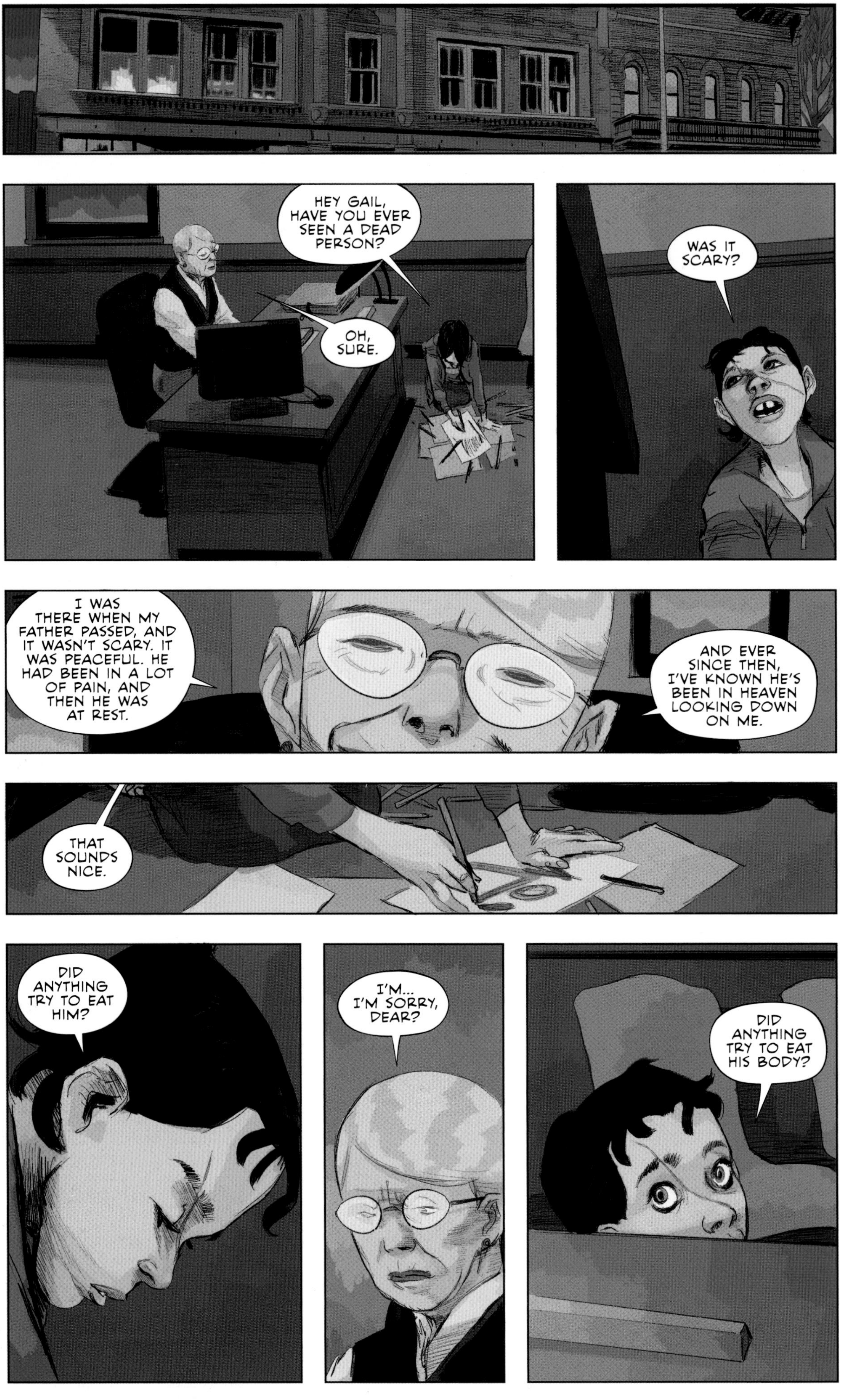
HEY GAIL, HAVE YOU EVER SEEN A DEAD PERSON?
OH, SURE.
WAS IT SCARY?
I WAS THERE WHEN MY FATHER PASSED, AND IT WASN'T SCARY. IT WAS PEACEFUL. HE HAD BEEN IN A LOT OF PAIN, AND THEN HE WAS AT REST.
AND EVER SINCE THEN, I'VE KNOWN HE'S BEEN IN HEAVEN LOOKING DOWN ON ME.
THAT SOUNDS NICE.
DID ANYTHING TRY TO EAT HIM?
I'M... I'M SORRY, DEAR?
DID ANYTHING TRY TO EAT HIS BODY?

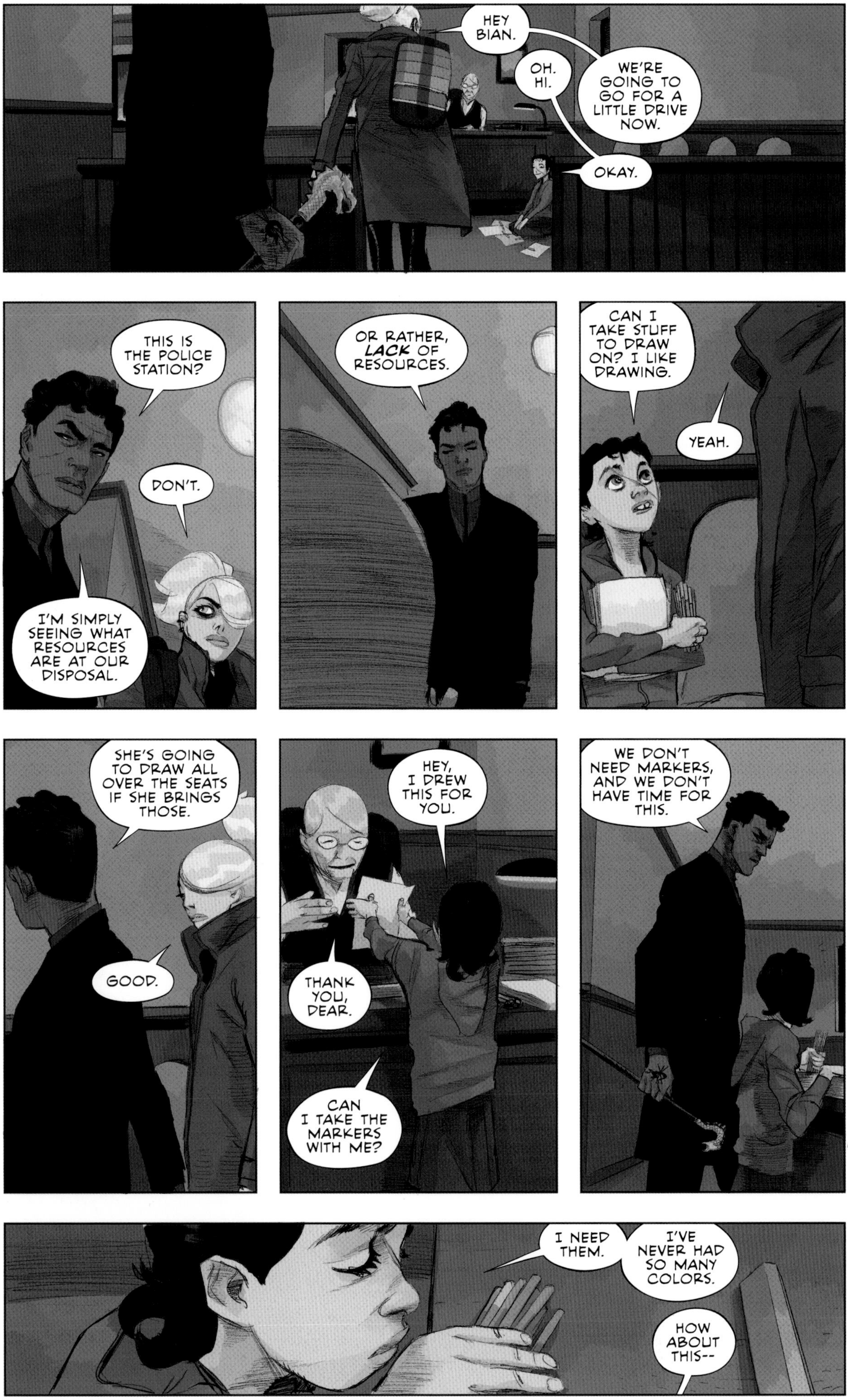
HEY BIAN.
OH. HI.
WE'RE GOING TO GO FOR A LITTLE DRIVE NOW.
OKAY.
THIS IS THE POLICE STATION?
DON'T.
I'M SIMPLY SEEING WHAT RESOURCES ARE AT OUR DISPOSAL.
OR RATHER, *LACK* OF RESOURCES.
CAN I TAKE STUFF TO DRAW ON? I LIKE DRAWING.
YEAH.
SHE'S GOING TO DRAW ALL OVER THE SEATS IF SHE BRINGS THOSE.
GOOD.
HEY, I DREW THIS FOR YOU.
THANK YOU, DEAR.
CAN I TAKE THE MARKERS WITH ME?
WE DON'T NEED MARKERS, AND WE DON'T HAVE TIME FOR THIS.
I NEED THEM.
I'VE NEVER HAD SO MANY COLORS.
HOW ABOUT THIS--

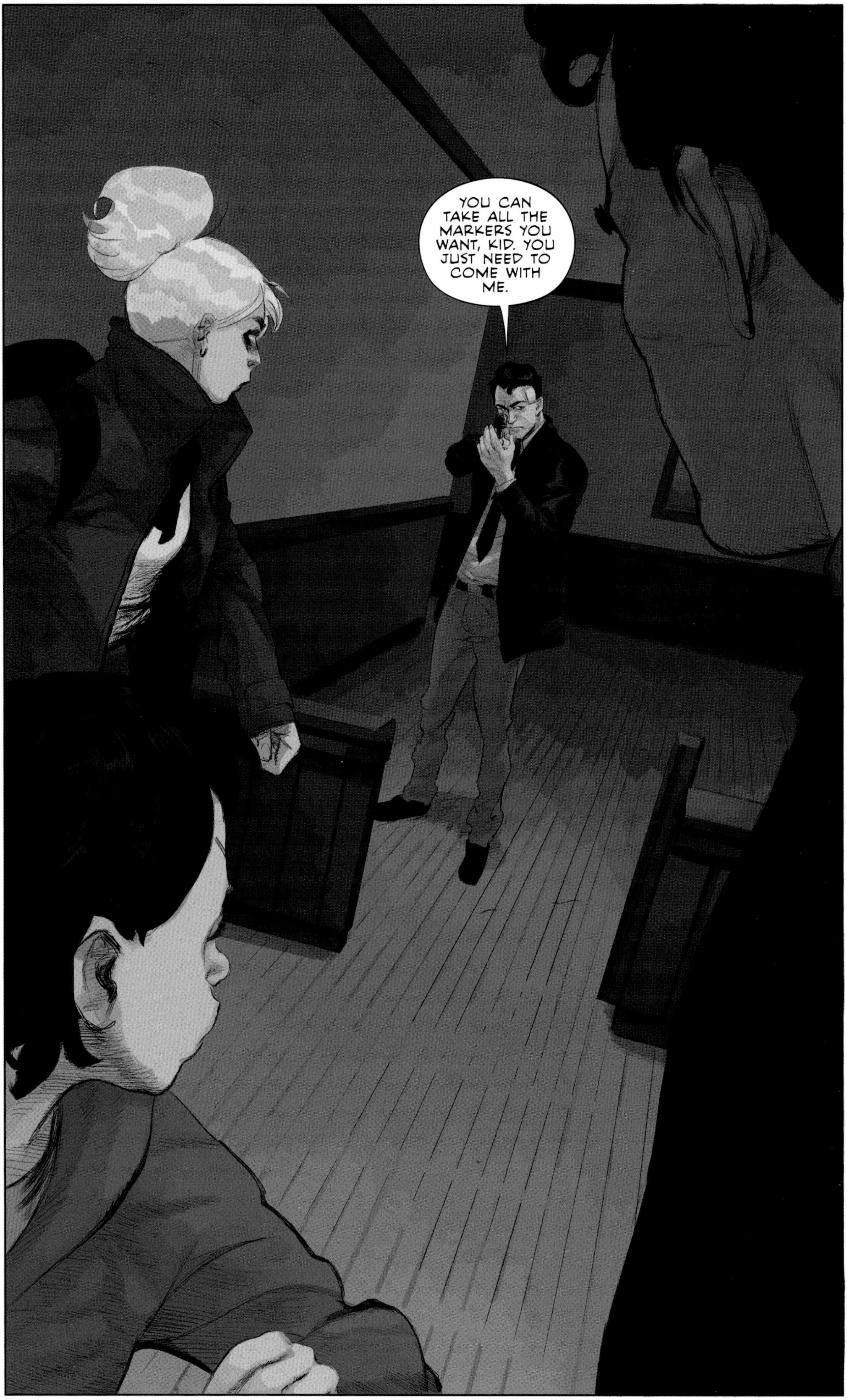
YOU CAN TAKE ALL THE MARKERS YOU WANT, KID. YOU JUST NEED TO COME WITH ME.

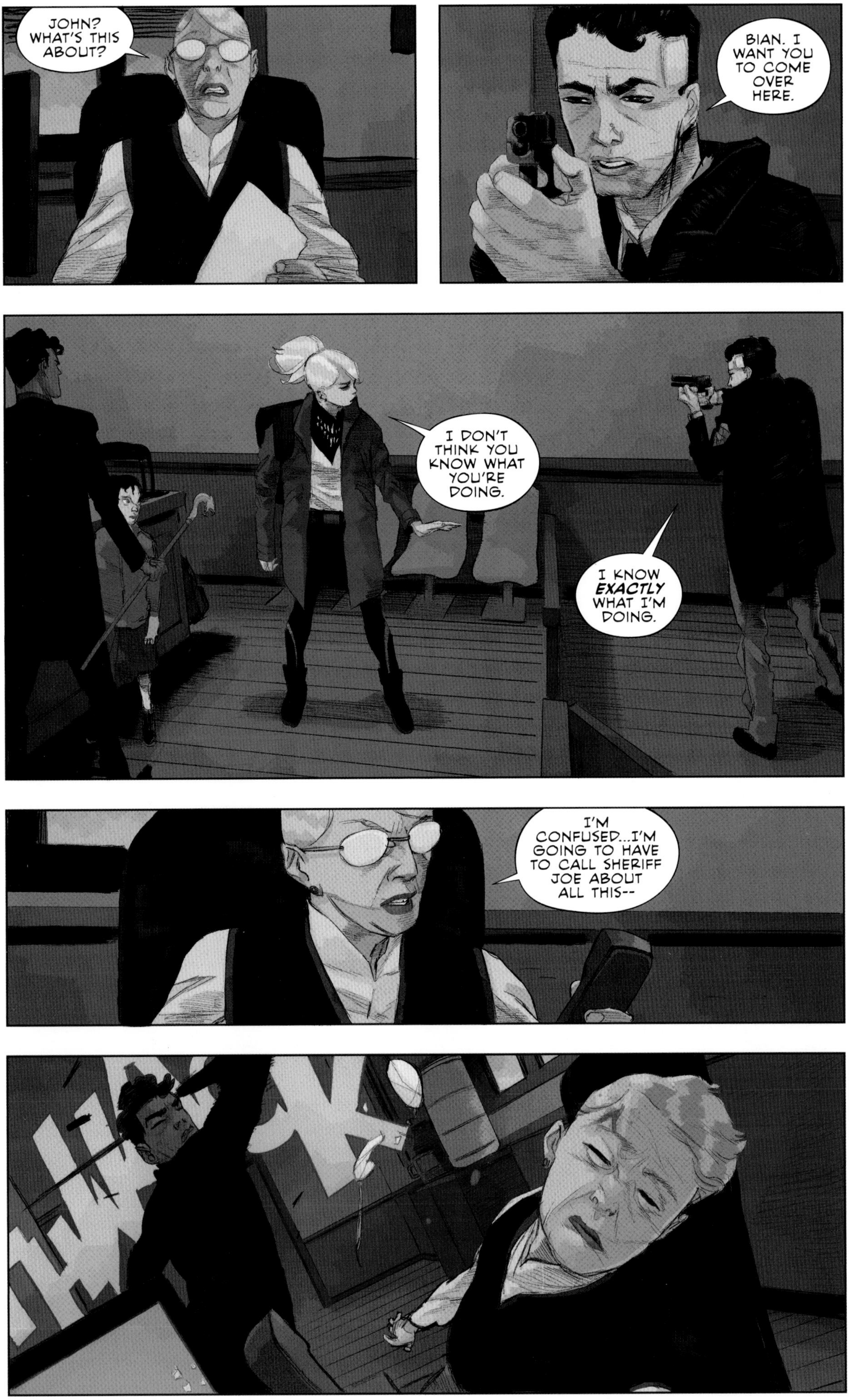

JOHN? WHAT'S THIS ABOUT?
BIAN. I WANT YOU TO COME OVER HERE.
I DON'T THINK YOU KNOW WHAT YOU'RE DOING.
I KNOW *EXACTLY* WHAT I'M DOING.
I'M CONFUSED...I'M GOING TO HAVE TO CALL SHERIFF JOE ABOUT ALL THIS--

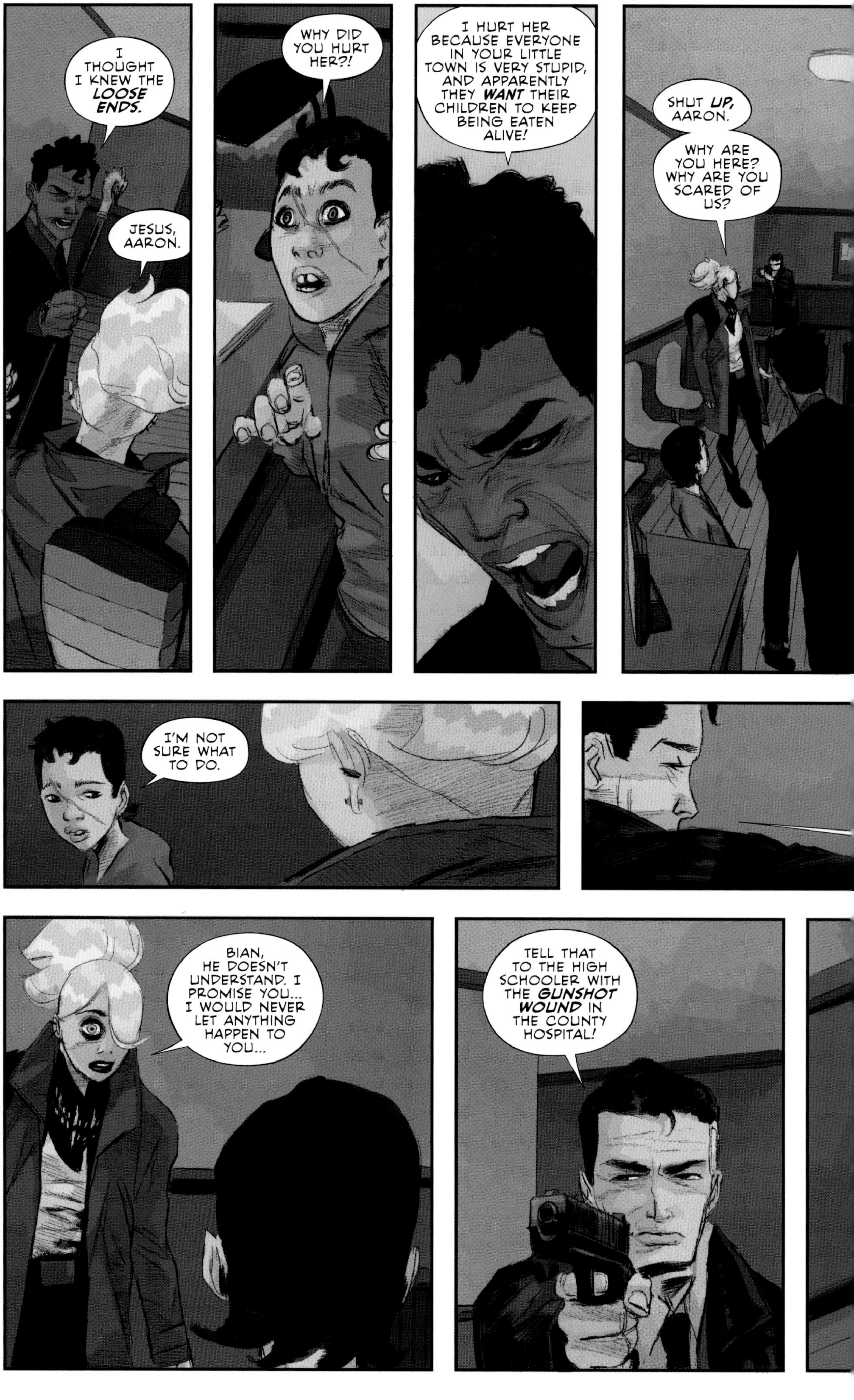

I THOUGHT I KNEW THE LOOSE ENDS.
JESUS, AARON.
WHY DID YOU HURT HER?!
I HURT HER BECAUSE EVERYONE IN YOUR LITTLE TOWN IS VERY STUPID, AND APPARENTLY THEY WANT THEIR CHILDREN TO KEEP BEING EATEN ALIVE!
SHUT UP, AARON.
WHY ARE YOU HERE? WHY ARE YOU SCARED OF US?
I'M NOT SURE WHAT TO DO.
BIAN, HE DOESN'T UNDERSTAND. I PROMISE YOU... I WOULD NEVER LET ANYTHING HAPPEN TO YOU...
TELL THAT TO THE HIGH SCHOOLER WITH THE GUNSHOT WOUND IN THE COUNTY HOSPITAL!

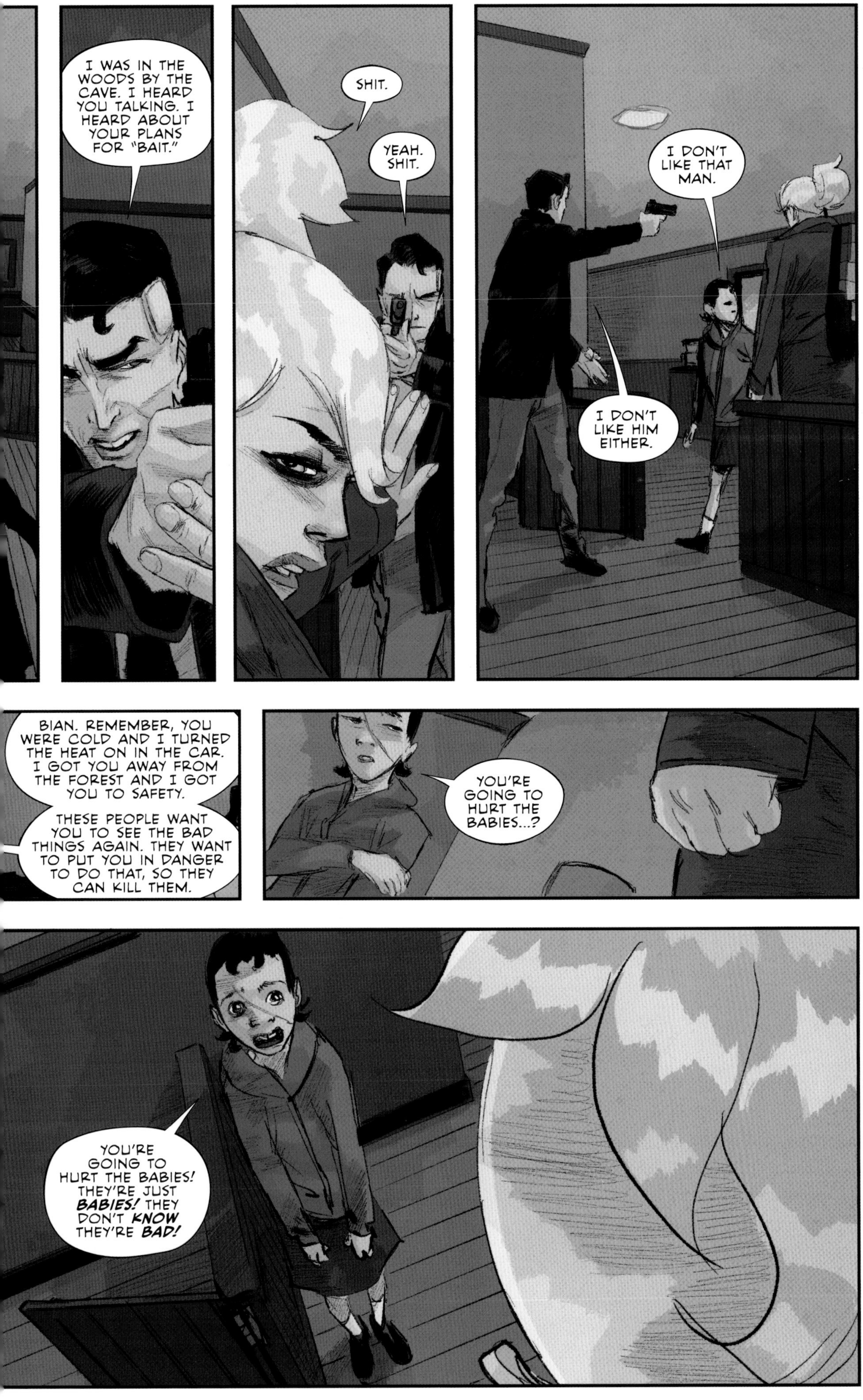
I WAS IN THE WOODS BY THE CAVE. I HEARD YOU TALKING. I HEARD ABOUT YOUR PLANS FOR "BAIT."
SHIT.
YEAH. SHIT.
I DON'T LIKE THAT MAN.
I DON'T LIKE HIM EITHER.
BIAN. REMEMBER, YOU WERE COLD AND I TURNED THE HEAT ON IN THE CAR. I GOT YOU AWAY FROM THE FOREST AND I GOT YOU TO SAFETY.
THESE PEOPLE WANT YOU TO SEE THE BAD THINGS AGAIN. THEY WANT TO PUT YOU IN DANGER TO DO THAT, SO THEY CAN KILL THEM.
YOU'RE GOING TO HURT THE BABIES...?
YOU'RE GOING TO HURT THE BABIES! THEY'RE JUST *BABIES!* THEY DON'T *KNOW* THEY'RE *BAD!*

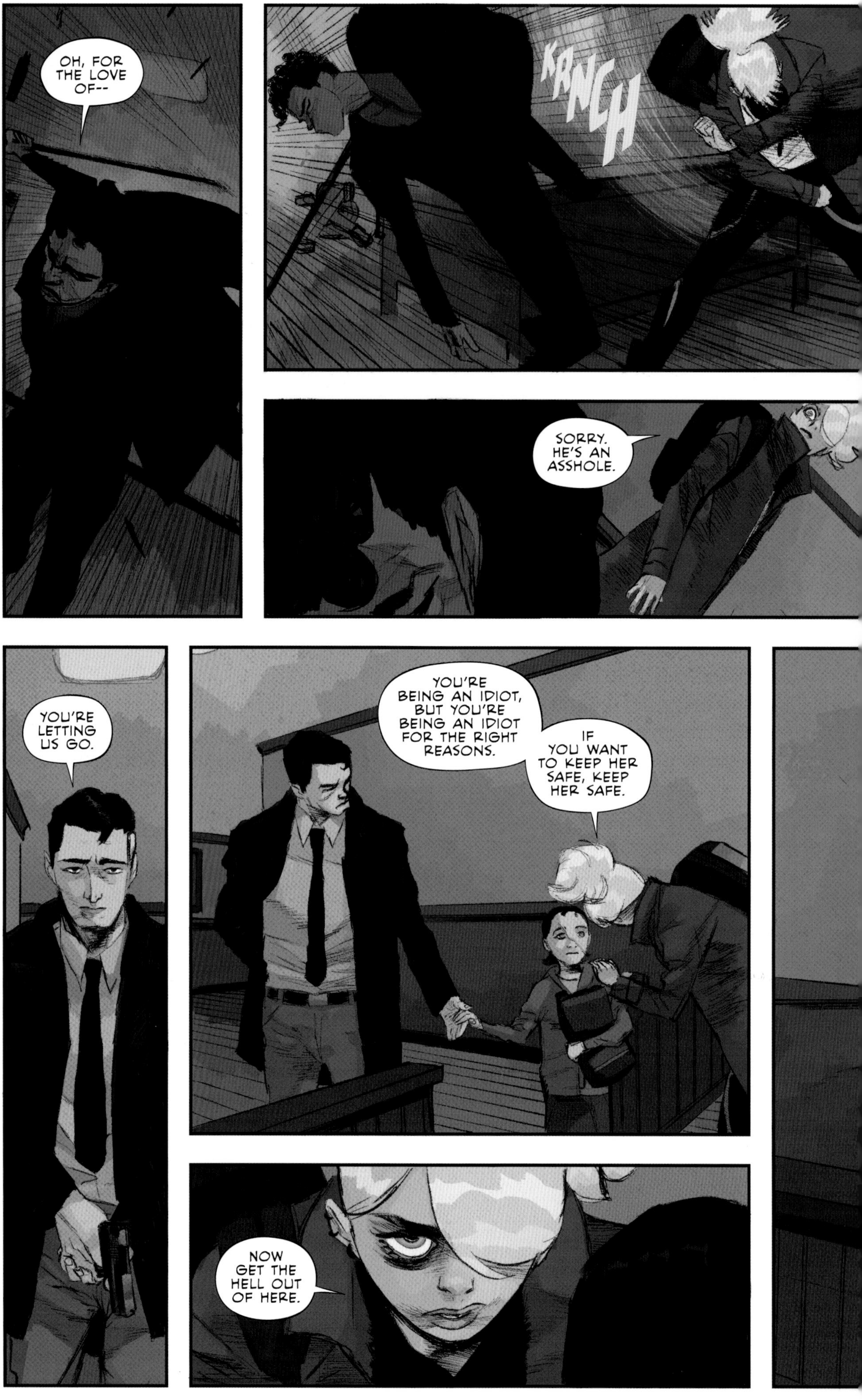
OH, FOR THE LOVE OF--
KRNCH
SORRY. HE'S AN ASSHOLE.
YOU'RE LETTING US GO.
YOU'RE BEING AN IDIOT, BUT YOU'RE BEING AN IDIOT FOR THE RIGHT REASONS.
IF YOU WANT TO KEEP HER SAFE, KEEP HER SAFE.
NOW GET THE HELL OUT OF HERE.

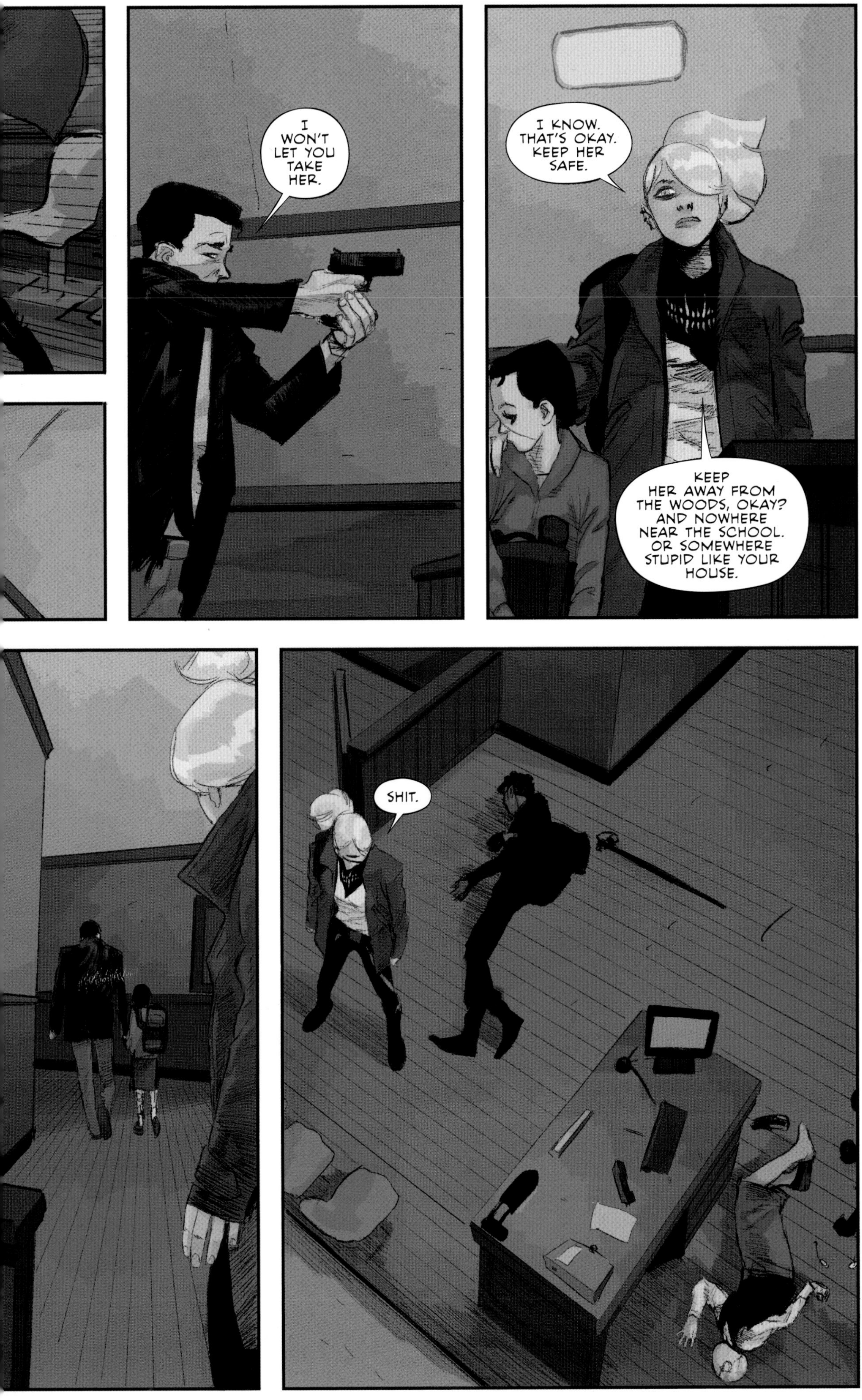
I WON'T LET YOU TAKE HER.
I KNOW. THAT'S OKAY. KEEP HER SAFE.
KEEP HER AWAY FROM THE WOODS, OKAY? AND NOWHERE NEAR THE SCHOOL. OR SOMEWHERE STUPID LIKE YOUR HOUSE.
SHIT.

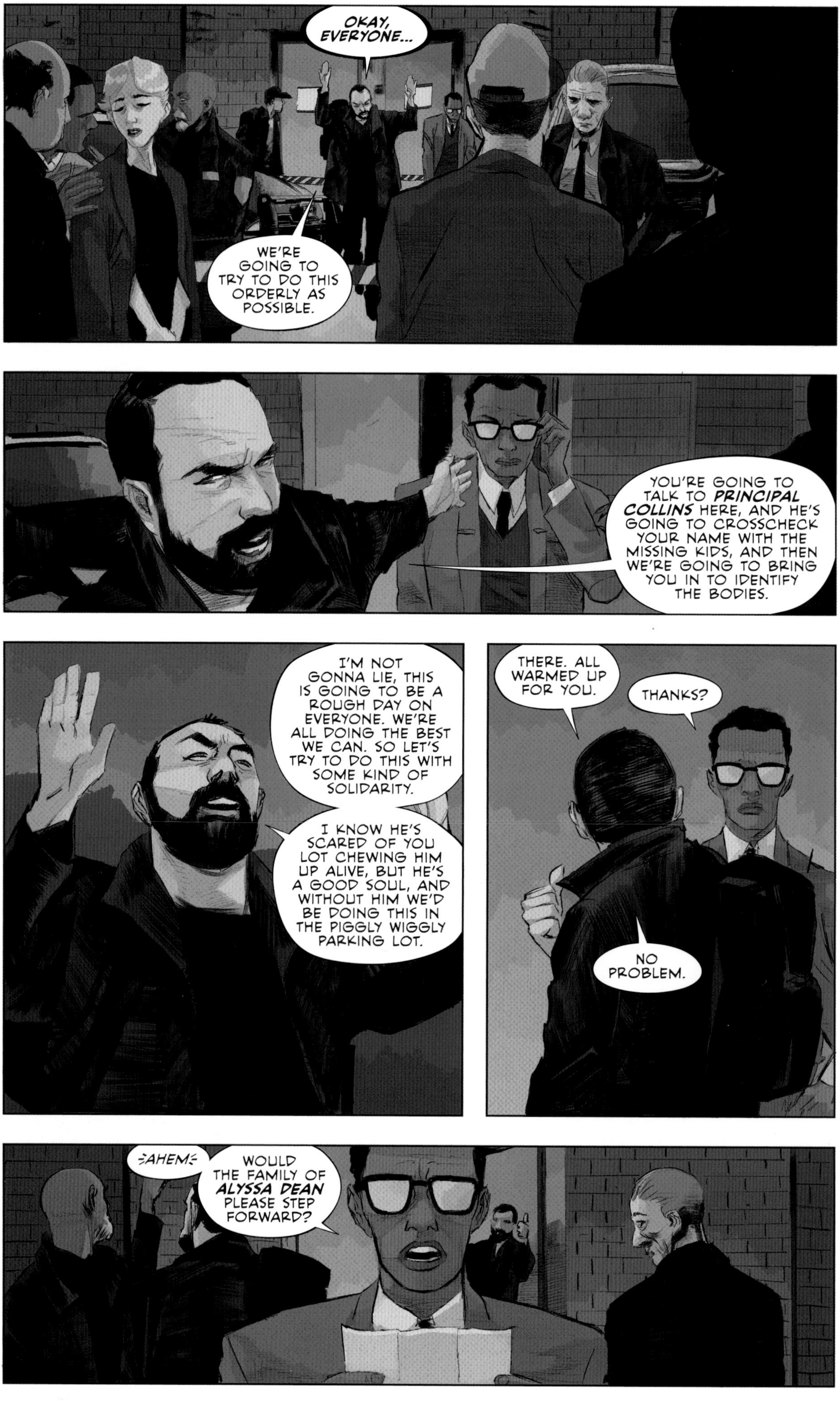

OKAY, EVERYONE...
WE'RE GOING TO TRY TO DO THIS ORDERLY AS POSSIBLE.
YOU'RE GOING TO TALK TO ***PRINCIPAL COLLINS*** HERE, AND HE'S GOING TO CROSSCHECK YOUR NAME WITH THE MISSING KIDS, AND THEN WE'RE GOING TO BRING YOU IN TO IDENTIFY THE BODIES.
I'M NOT GONNA LIE, THIS IS GOING TO BE A ROUGH DAY ON EVERYONE. WE'RE ALL DOING THE BEST WE CAN. SO LET'S TRY TO DO THIS WITH SOME KIND OF SOLIDARITY.
I KNOW HE'S SCARED OF YOU LOT CHEWING HIM UP ALIVE, BUT HE'S A GOOD SOUL, AND WITHOUT HIM WE'D BE DOING THIS IN THE PIGGLY WIGGLY PARKING LOT.
THERE. ALL WARMED UP FOR YOU.
THANKS?
NO PROBLEM.
=AHEM=
WOULD THE FAMILY OF ***ALYSSA DEAN*** PLEASE STEP FORWARD?

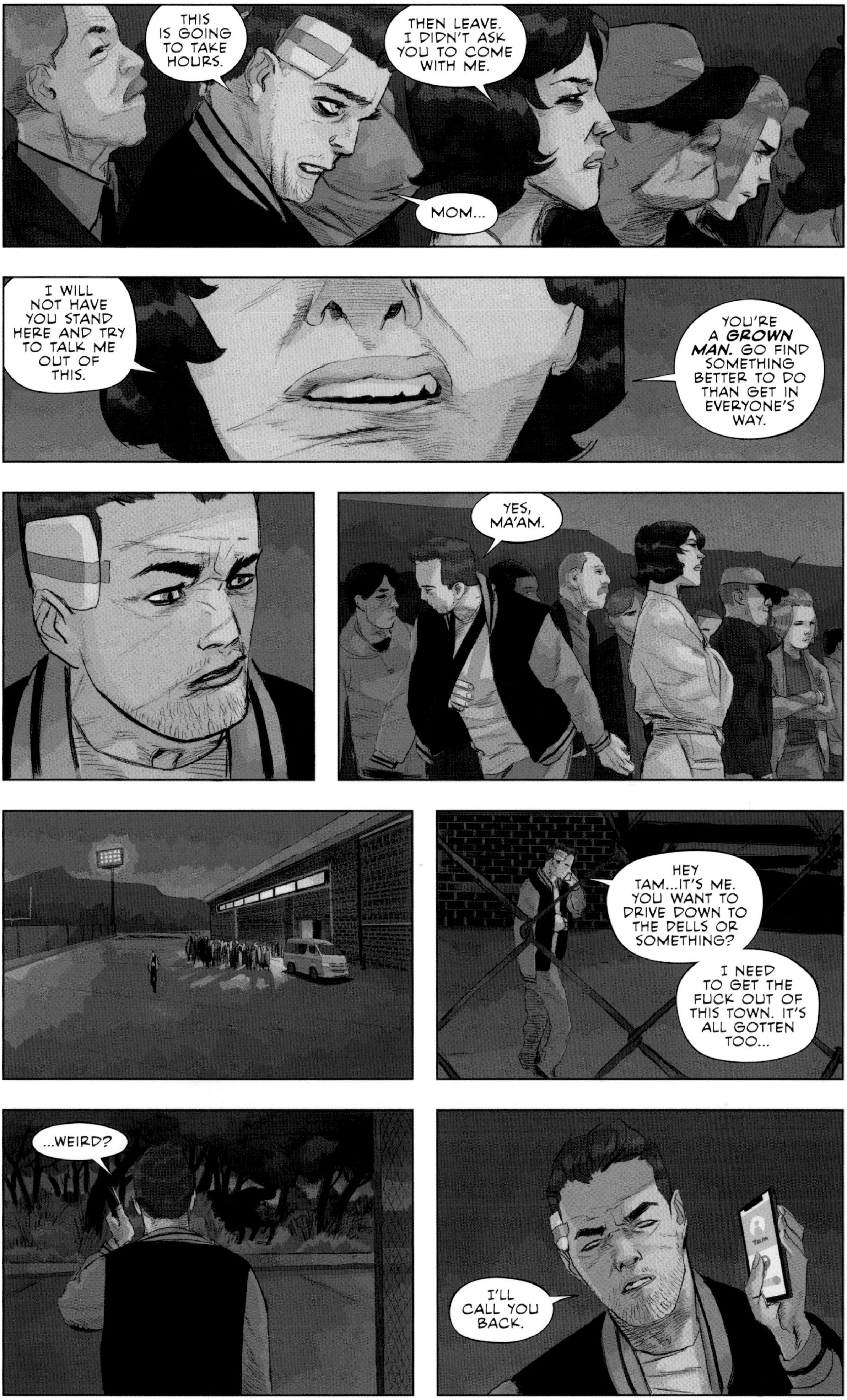
THIS IS GOING TO TAKE HOURS.
THEN LEAVE. I DIDN'T ASK YOU TO COME WITH ME.
MOM...
I WILL NOT HAVE YOU STAND HERE AND TRY TO TALK ME OUT OF THIS.
YOU'RE A GROWN MAN. GO FIND SOMETHING BETTER TO DO THAN GET IN EVERYONE'S WAY.
YES, MA'AM.
HEY TAM...IT'S ME. YOU WANT TO DRIVE DOWN TO THE DELLS OR SOMETHING?
I NEED TO GET THE FUCK OUT OF THIS TOWN. IT'S ALL GOTTEN TOO...
...WEIRD?
I'LL CALL YOU BACK.

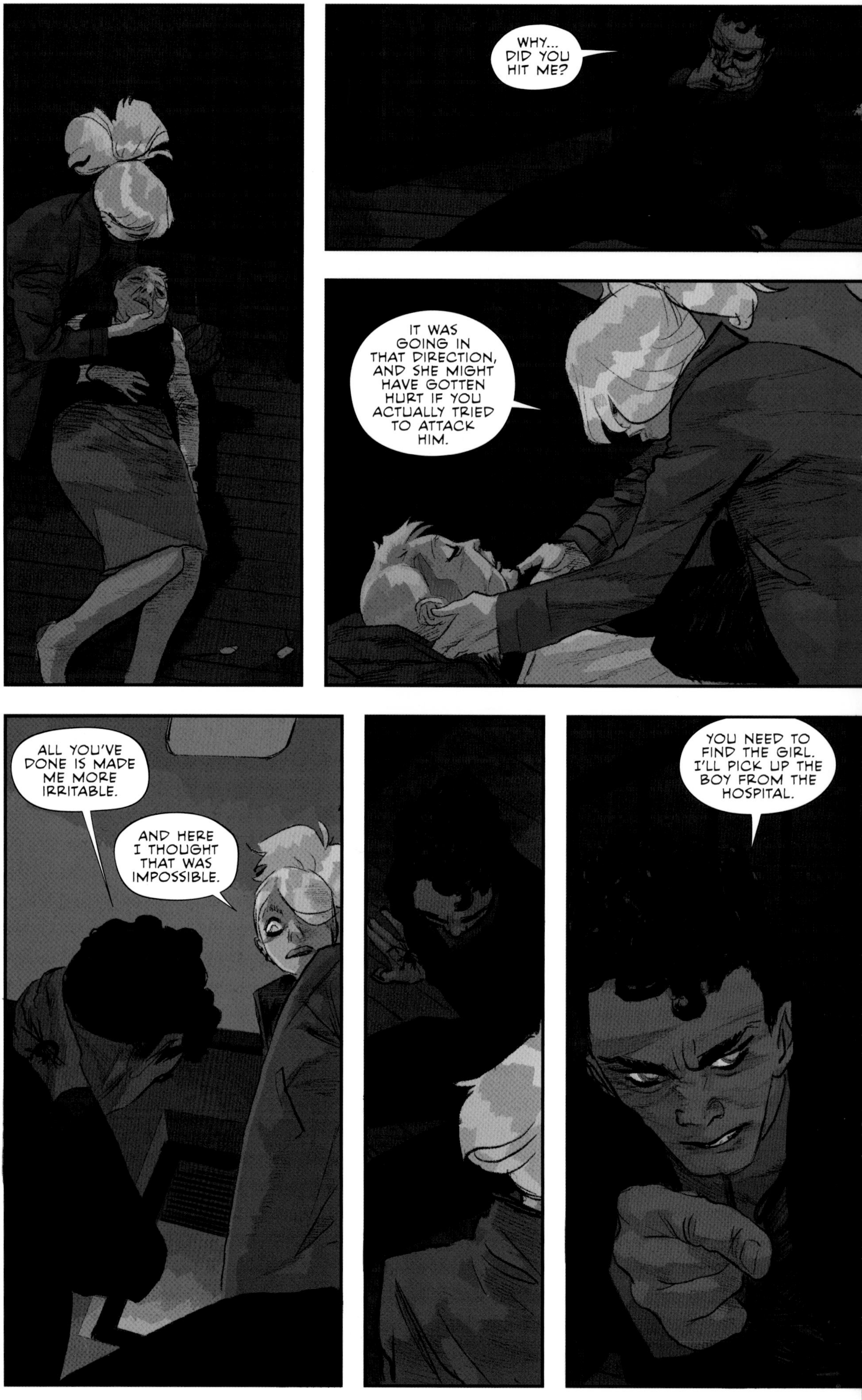
WHY... DID YOU HIT ME?
IT WAS GOING IN THAT DIRECTION, AND SHE MIGHT HAVE GOTTEN HURT IF YOU ACTUALLY TRIED TO ATTACK HIM.
ALL YOU'VE DONE IS MADE ME MORE IRRITABLE.
AND HERE I THOUGHT THAT WAS IMPOSSIBLE.
YOU NEED TO FIND THE GIRL. I'LL PICK UP THE BOY FROM THE HOSPITAL.

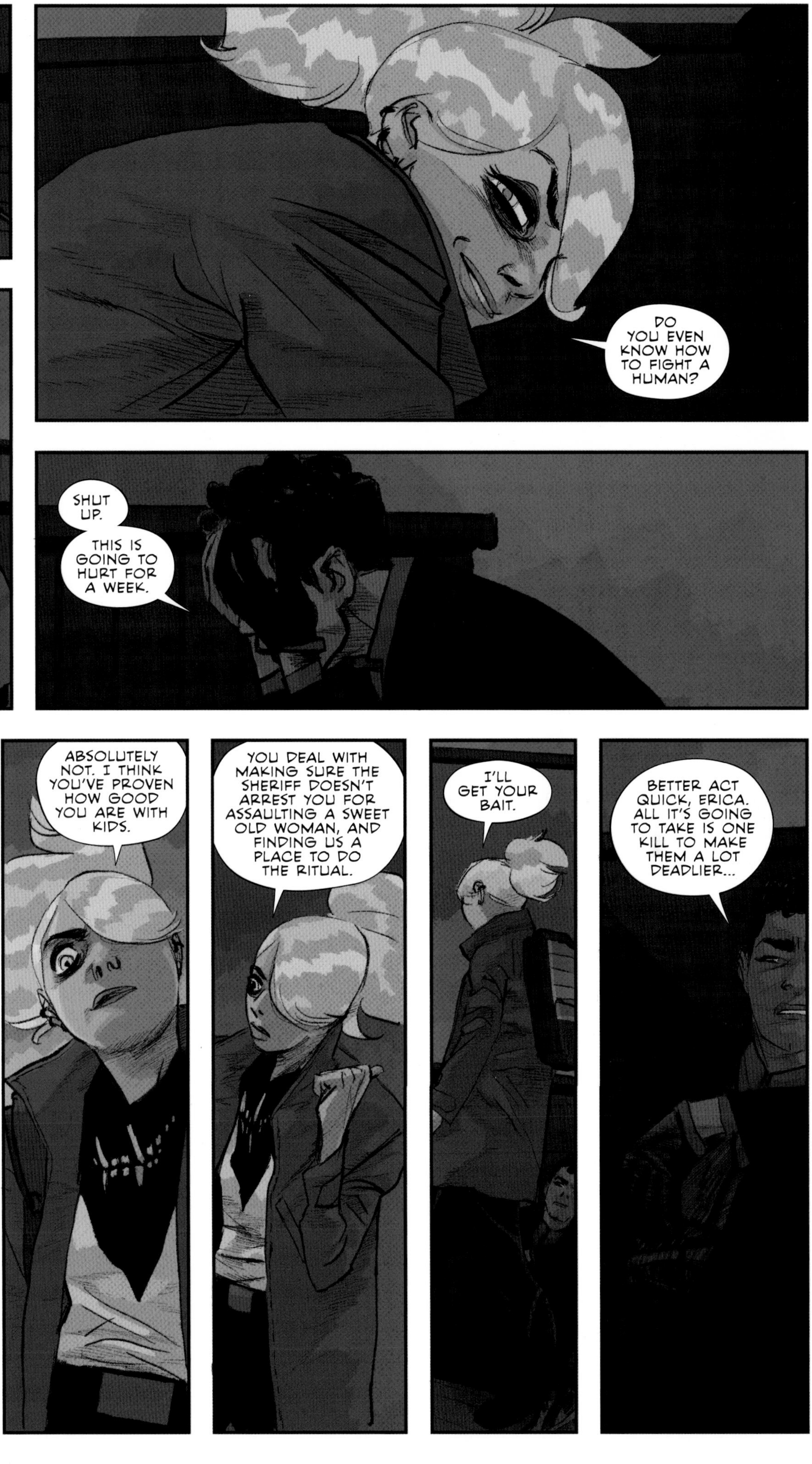
DO YOU EVEN KNOW HOW TO FIGHT A HUMAN?
SHUT UP.
THIS IS GOING TO HURT FOR A WEEK.
ABSOLUTELY NOT. I THINK YOU'VE PROVEN HOW GOOD YOU ARE WITH KIDS.
YOU DEAL WITH MAKING SURE THE SHERIFF DOESN'T ARREST YOU FOR ASSAULTING A SWEET OLD WOMAN, AND FINDING US A PLACE TO DO THE RITUAL.
I'LL GET YOUR BAIT.
BETTER ACT QUICK, ERICA. ALL IT'S GOING TO TAKE IS ONE KILL TO MAKE THEM A LOT DEADLIER...

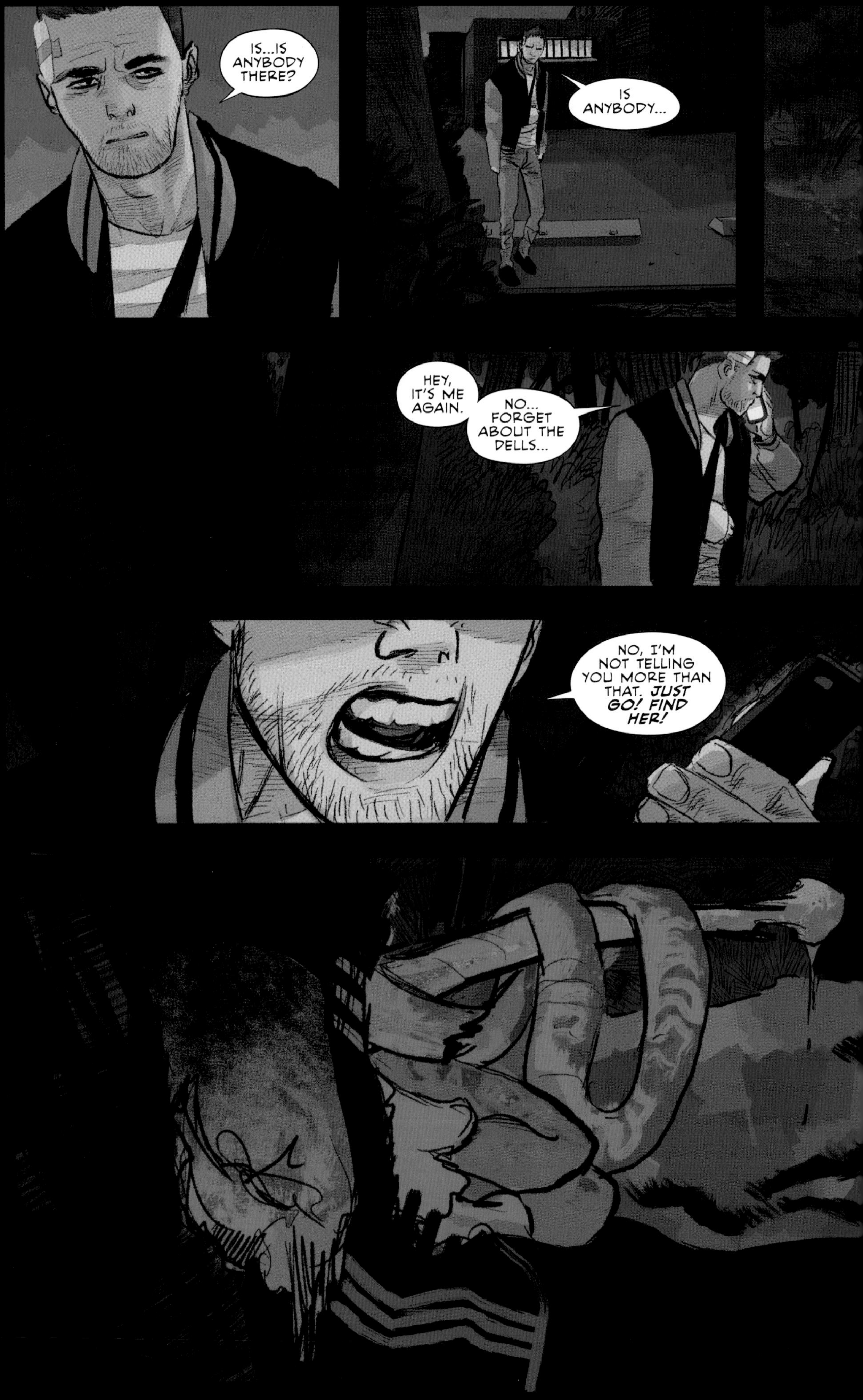
IS...IS ANYBODY THERE?
IS ANYBODY...
HEY, IT'S ME AGAIN.
NO... FORGET ABOUT THE DELLS...
NO, I'M NOT TELLING YOU MORE THAN THAT. *JUST GO! FIND HER!*

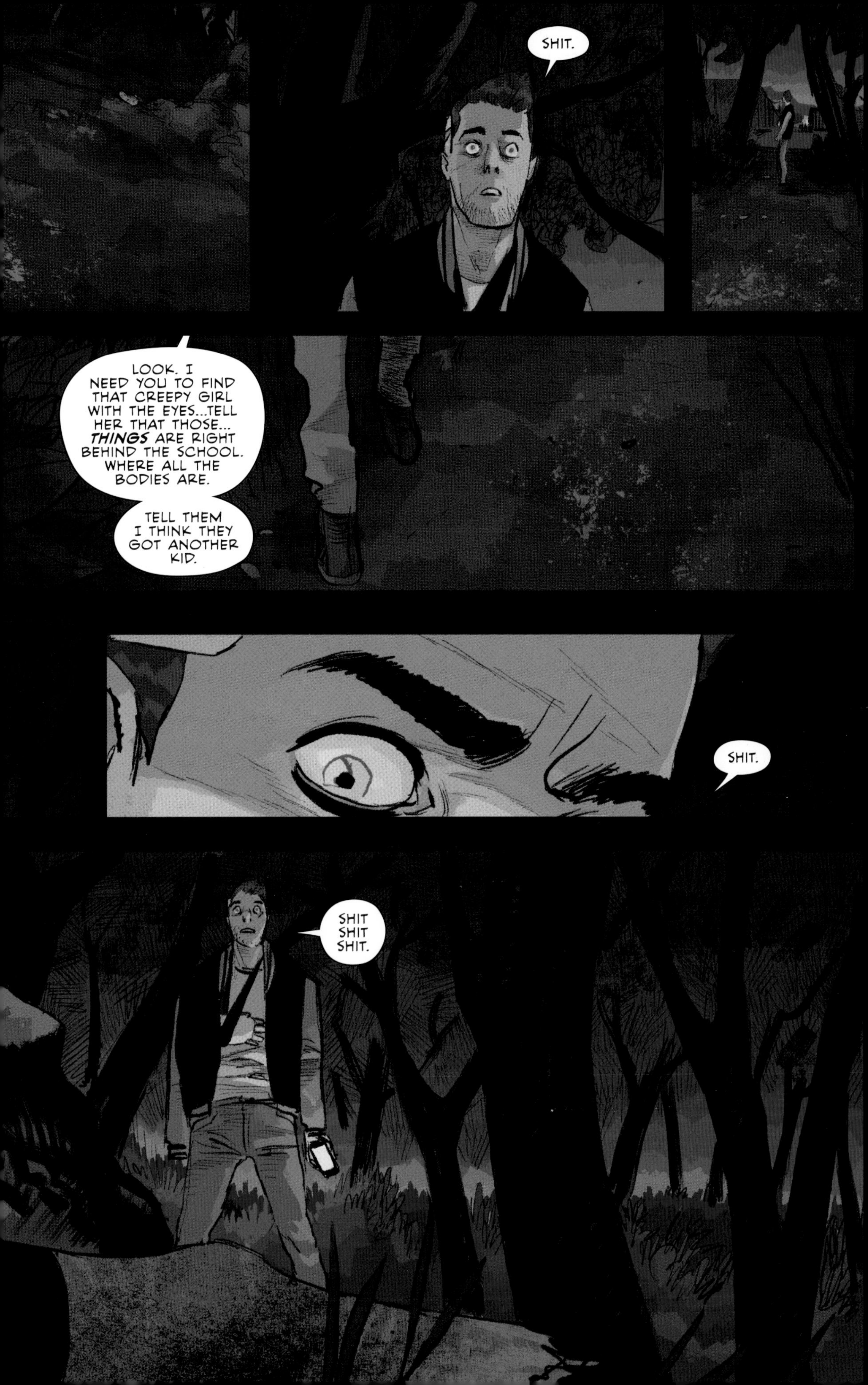
SHIT.
LOOK. I NEED YOU TO FIND THAT CREEPY GIRL WITH THE EYES...TELL HER THAT THOSE... *THINGS* ARE RIGHT BEHIND THE SCHOOL. WHERE ALL THE BODIES ARE.
TELL THEM I THINK THEY GOT ANOTHER KID.
SHIT.
SHIT SHIT SHIT.

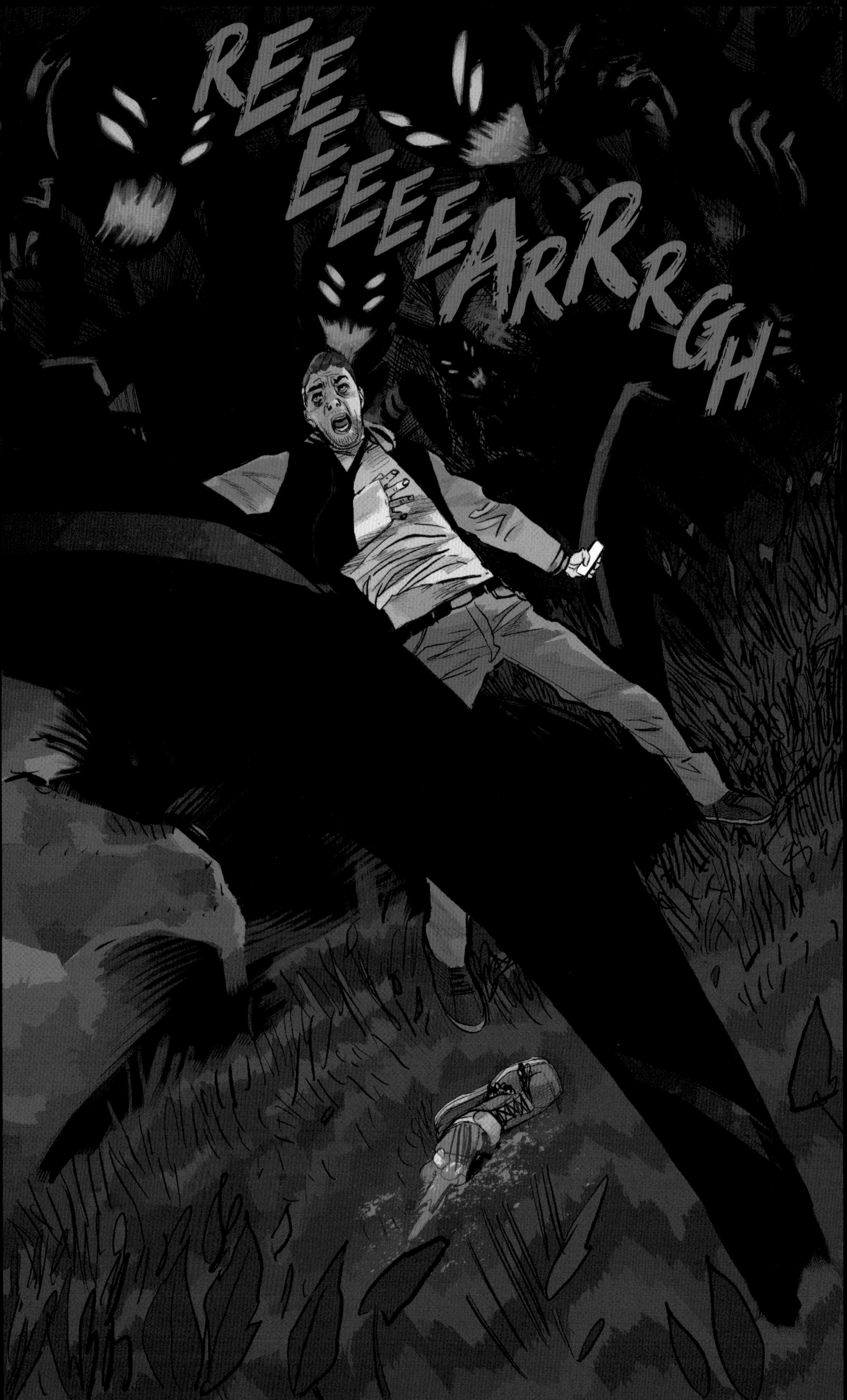
REEEEEEEARRRRGH

CHAPTER NINE

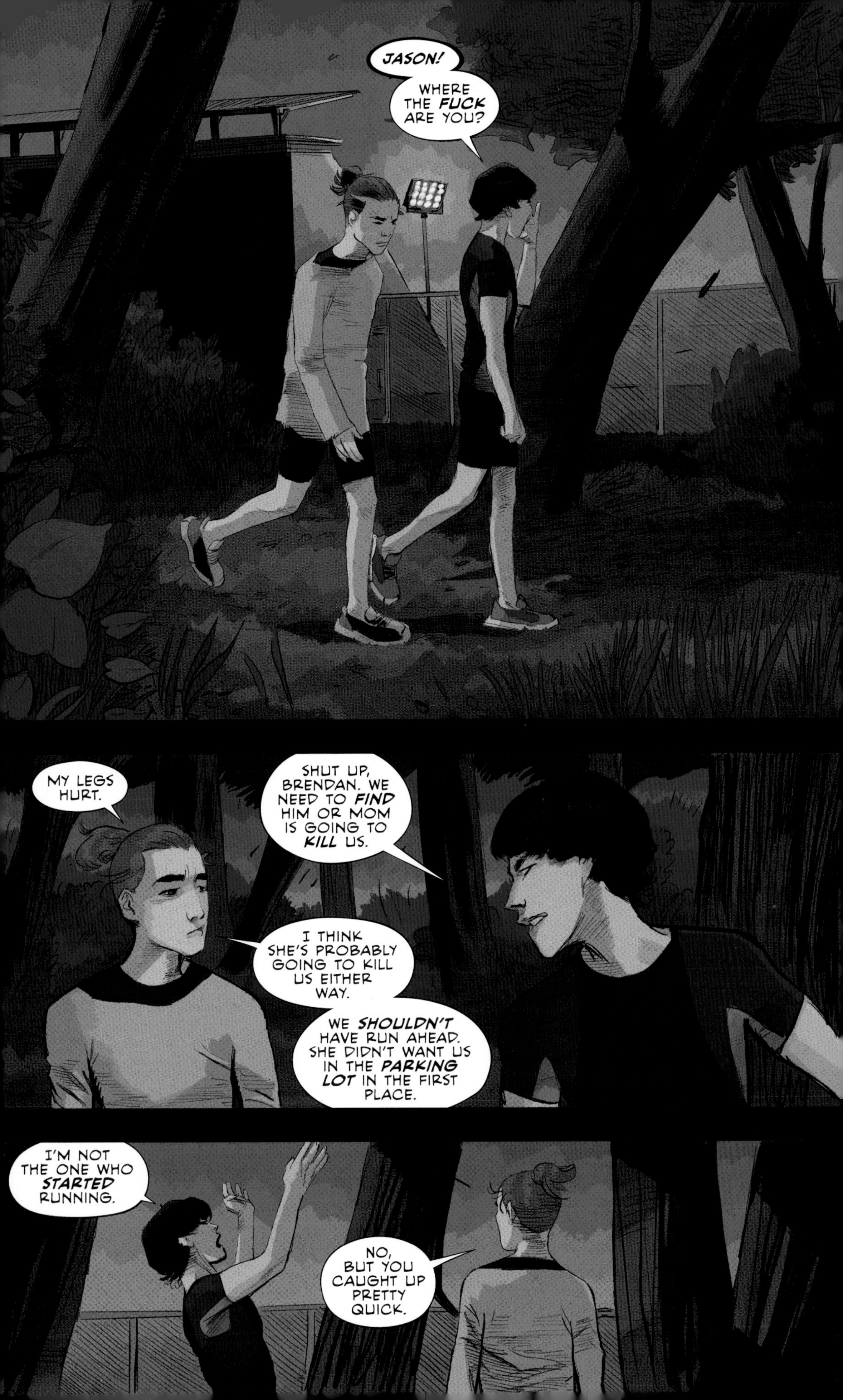
JASON!
WHERE THE FUCK ARE YOU?
MY LEGS HURT.
SHUT UP, BRENDAN. WE NEED TO FIND HIM OR MOM IS GOING TO KILL US.
I THINK SHE'S PROBABLY GOING TO KILL US EITHER WAY.
WE SHOULDN'T HAVE RUN AHEAD. SHE DIDN'T WANT US IN THE PARKING LOT IN THE FIRST PLACE.
I'M NOT THE ONE WHO STARTED RUNNING.
NO, BUT YOU CAUGHT UP PRETTY QUICK.

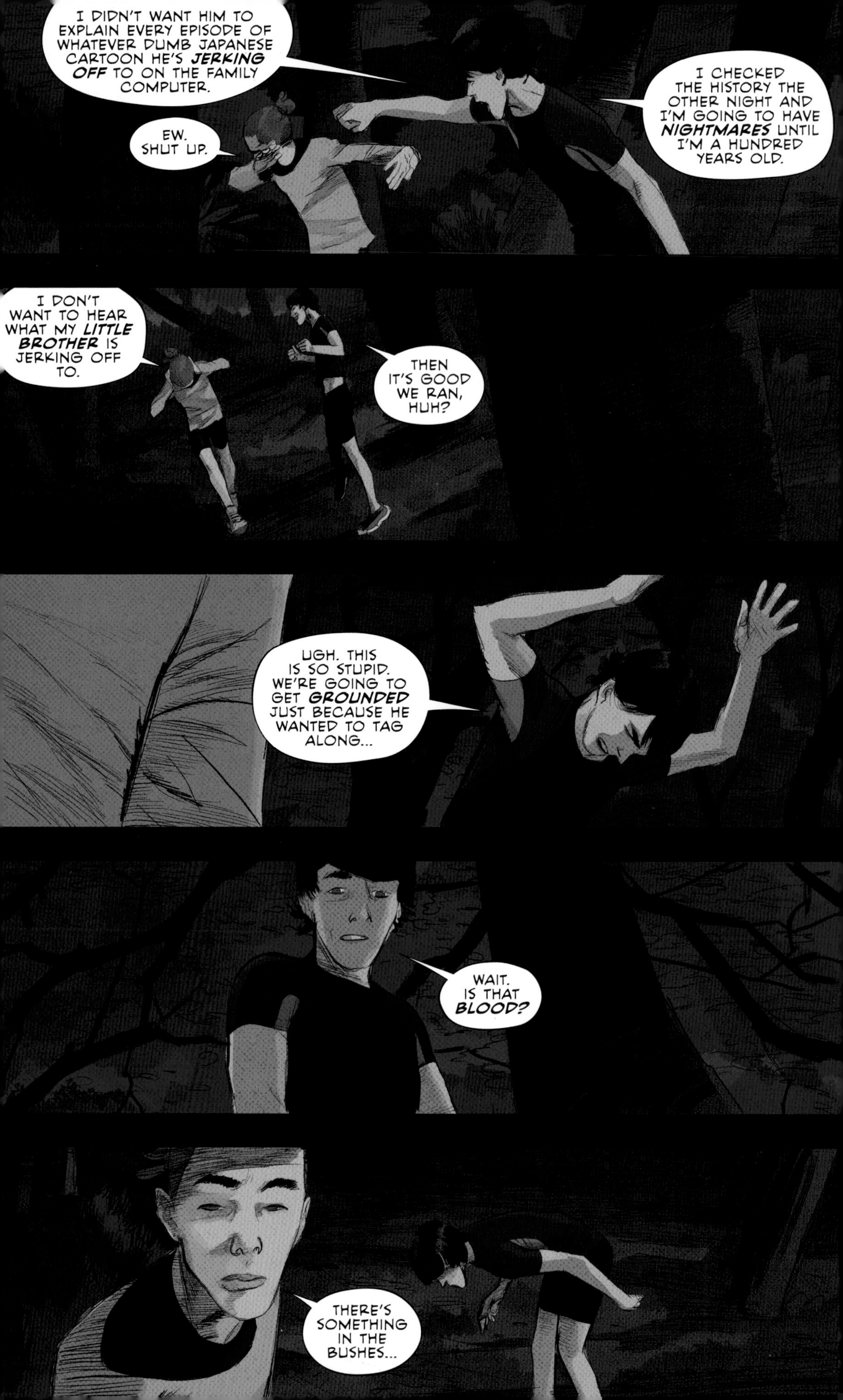
I DIDN'T WANT HIM TO EXPLAIN EVERY EPISODE OF WHATEVER DUMB JAPANESE CARTOON HE'S JERKING OFF TO ON THE FAMILY COMPUTER.
EW. SHUT UP.
I CHECKED THE HISTORY THE OTHER NIGHT AND I'M GOING TO HAVE NIGHTMARES UNTIL I'M A HUNDRED YEARS OLD.
I DON'T WANT TO HEAR WHAT MY LITTLE BROTHER IS JERKING OFF TO.
THEN IT'S GOOD WE RAN, HUH?
UGH. THIS IS SO STUPID. WE'RE GOING TO GET GROUNDED JUST BECAUSE HE WANTED TO TAG ALONG...
WAIT. IS THAT BLOOD?
THERE'S SOMETHING IN THE BUSHES...

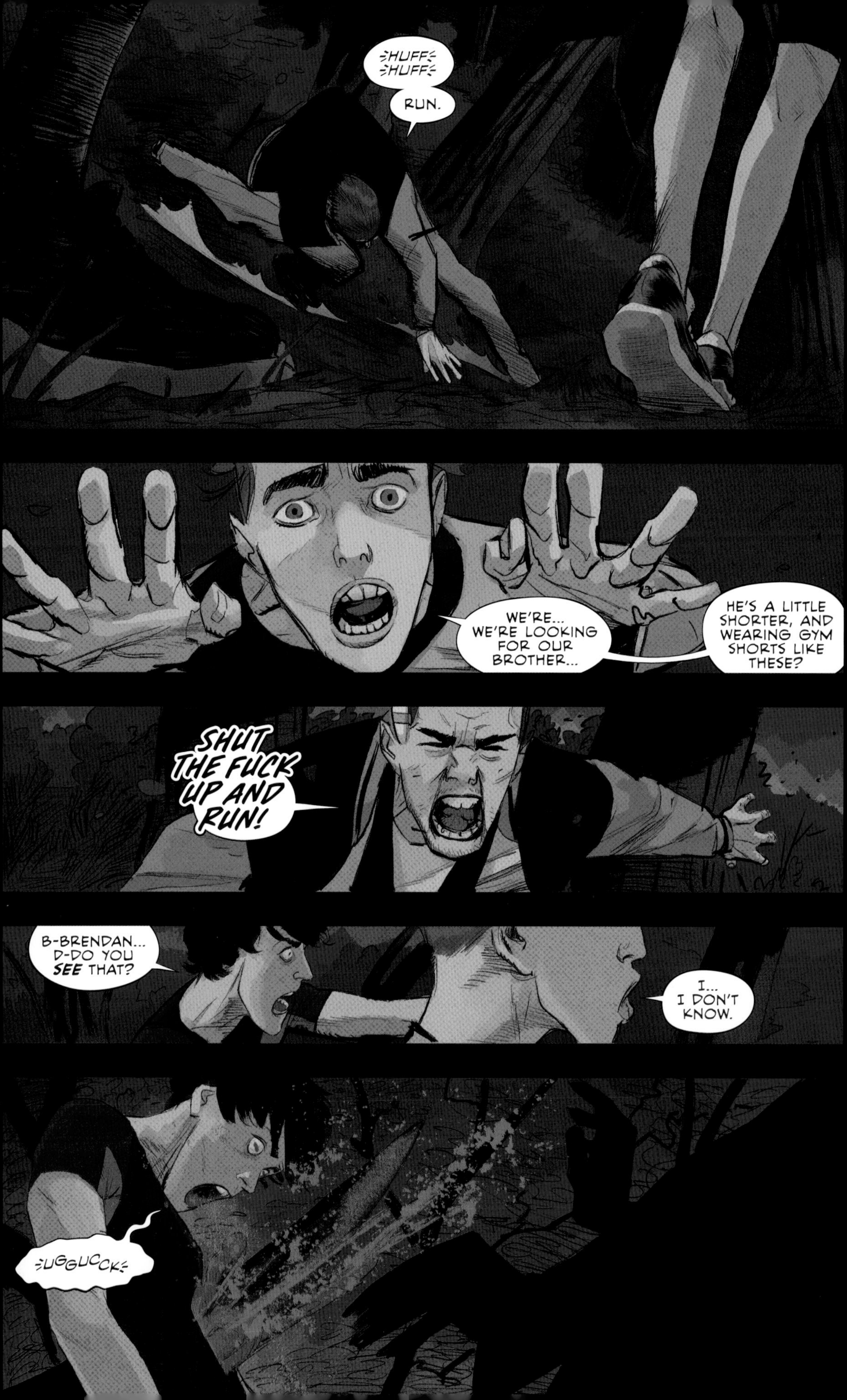
HUFF HUFF
RUN.
WE'RE... WE'RE LOOKING FOR OUR BROTHER...
HE'S A LITTLE SHORTER, AND WEARING GYM SHORTS LIKE THESE?
SHUT THE FUCK UP AND RUN!
B-BRENDAN... D-DO YOU SEE THAT?
I... I DON'T KNOW.
UGGUCCK

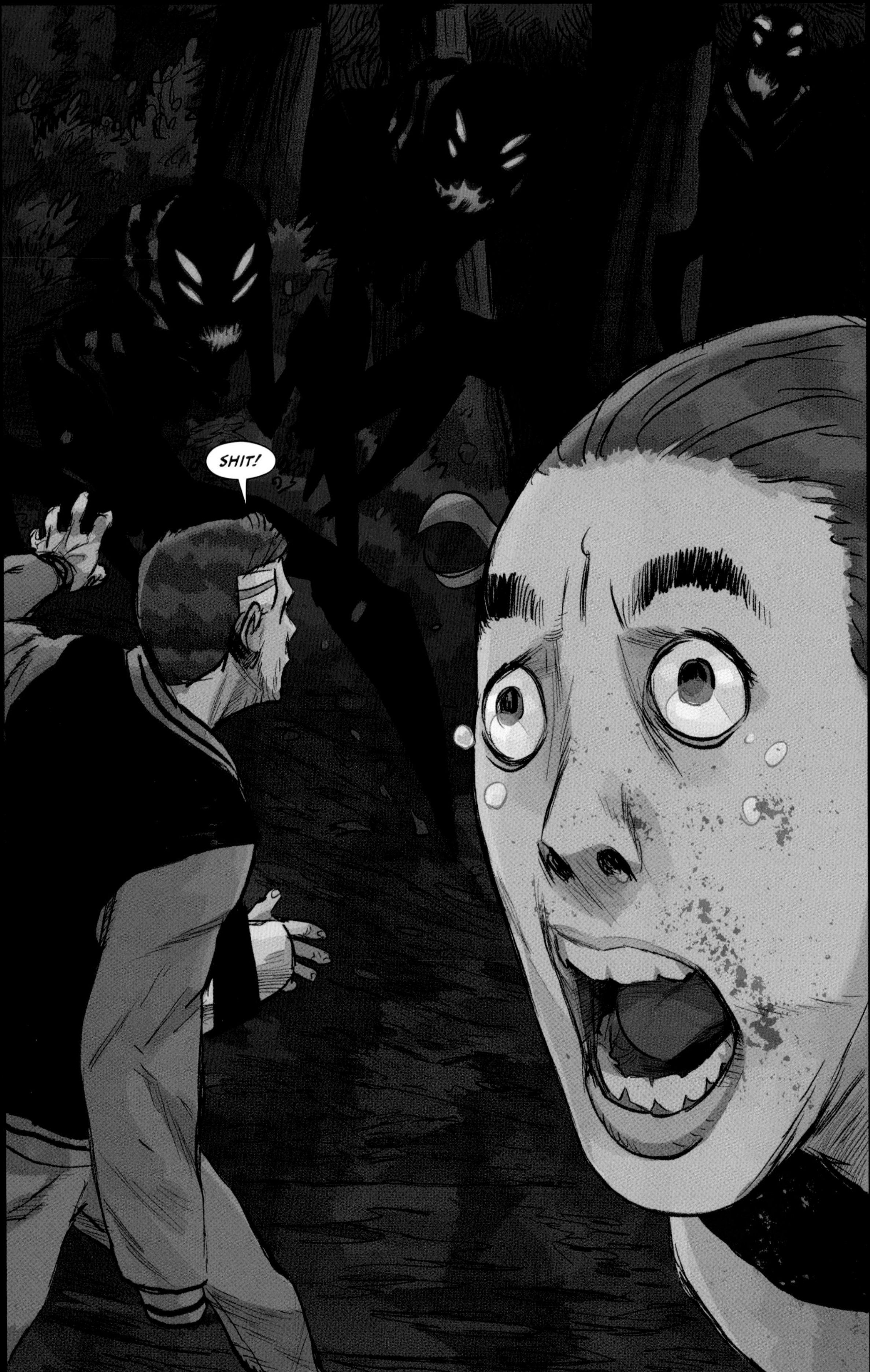
SHIT!

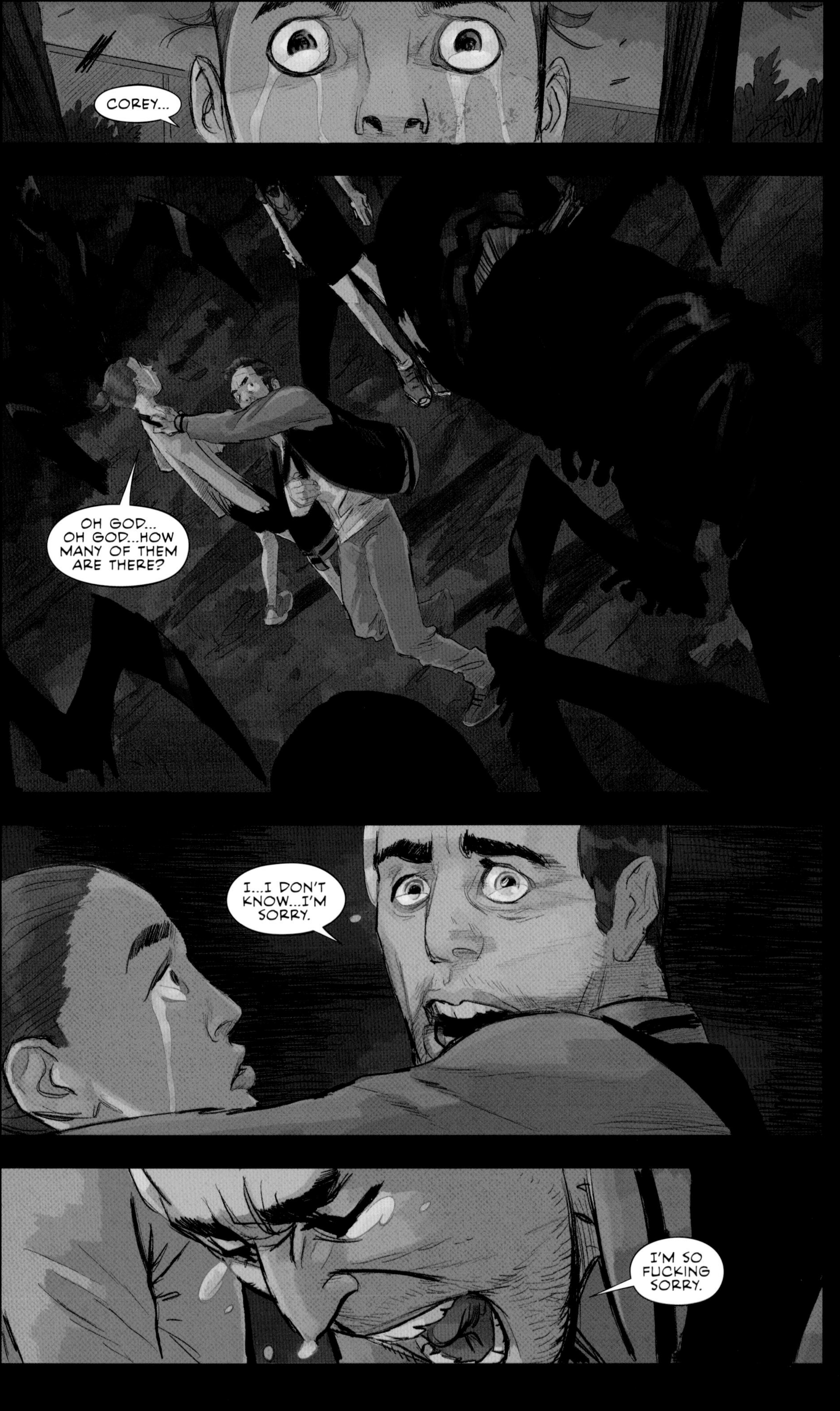
COREY...
OH GOD... OH GOD...HOW MANY OF THEM ARE THERE?
I...I DON'T KNOW...I'M SORRY.
I'M SO FUCKING SORRY.

HI.

CAN'T GET RID OF ME THAT EASY.

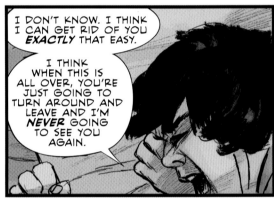

I DON'T KNOW. I THINK I CAN GET RID OF YOU *EXACTLY* THAT EASY.

I THINK WHEN THIS IS ALL OVER, YOU'RE JUST GOING TO TURN AROUND AND LEAVE AND I'M *NEVER* GOING TO SEE YOU AGAIN.

YOU'RE A SMART KID.

AND YOU'RE NOT HERE TO CHECK UP ON ME BECAUSE YOU CARE ABOUT ME.

YOU'RE HERE BECAUSE YOU NEED SOMETHING *HORRIBLE* FROM ME.

YOU NEED ME TO GET *SHOT,* OR TALK ABOUT THE MOMENT I WATCHED ALL OF MY FRIENDS GET *RIPPED APART* IN FRONT OF ME, OR PROBABLY SOMETHING *WORSE* THAN ALL OF THAT.

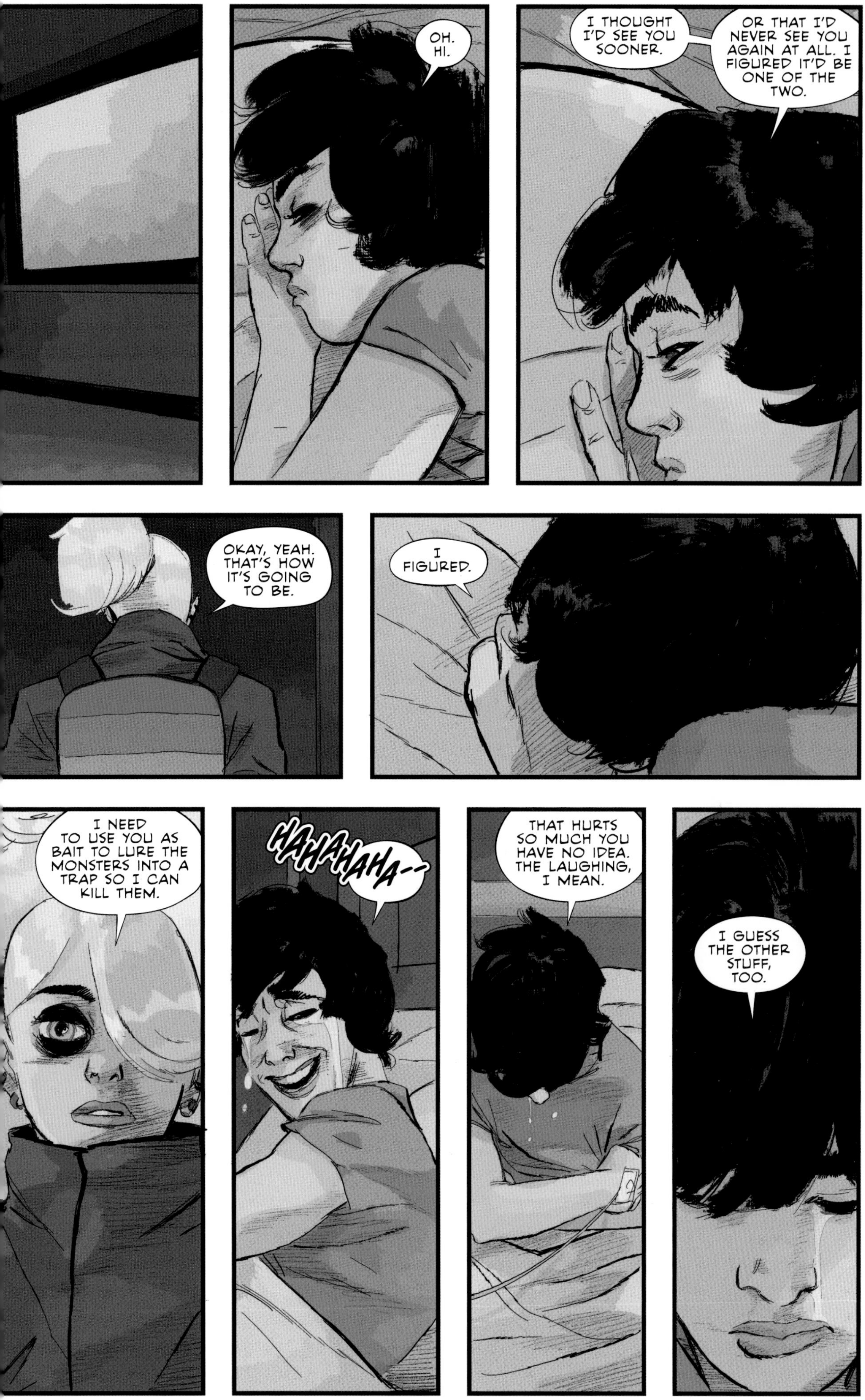
OH. HI.
I THOUGHT I'D SEE YOU SOONER.
OR THAT I'D NEVER SEE YOU AGAIN AT ALL. I FIGURED IT'D BE ONE OF THE TWO.
OKAY, YEAH. THAT'S HOW IT'S GOING TO BE.
I FIGURED.
I NEED TO USE YOU AS BAIT TO LURE THE MONSTERS INTO A TRAP SO I CAN KILL THEM.
HAHAHAHAHA--
THAT HURTS SO MUCH YOU HAVE NO IDEA. THE LAUGHING, I MEAN.
I GUESS THE OTHER STUFF, TOO.

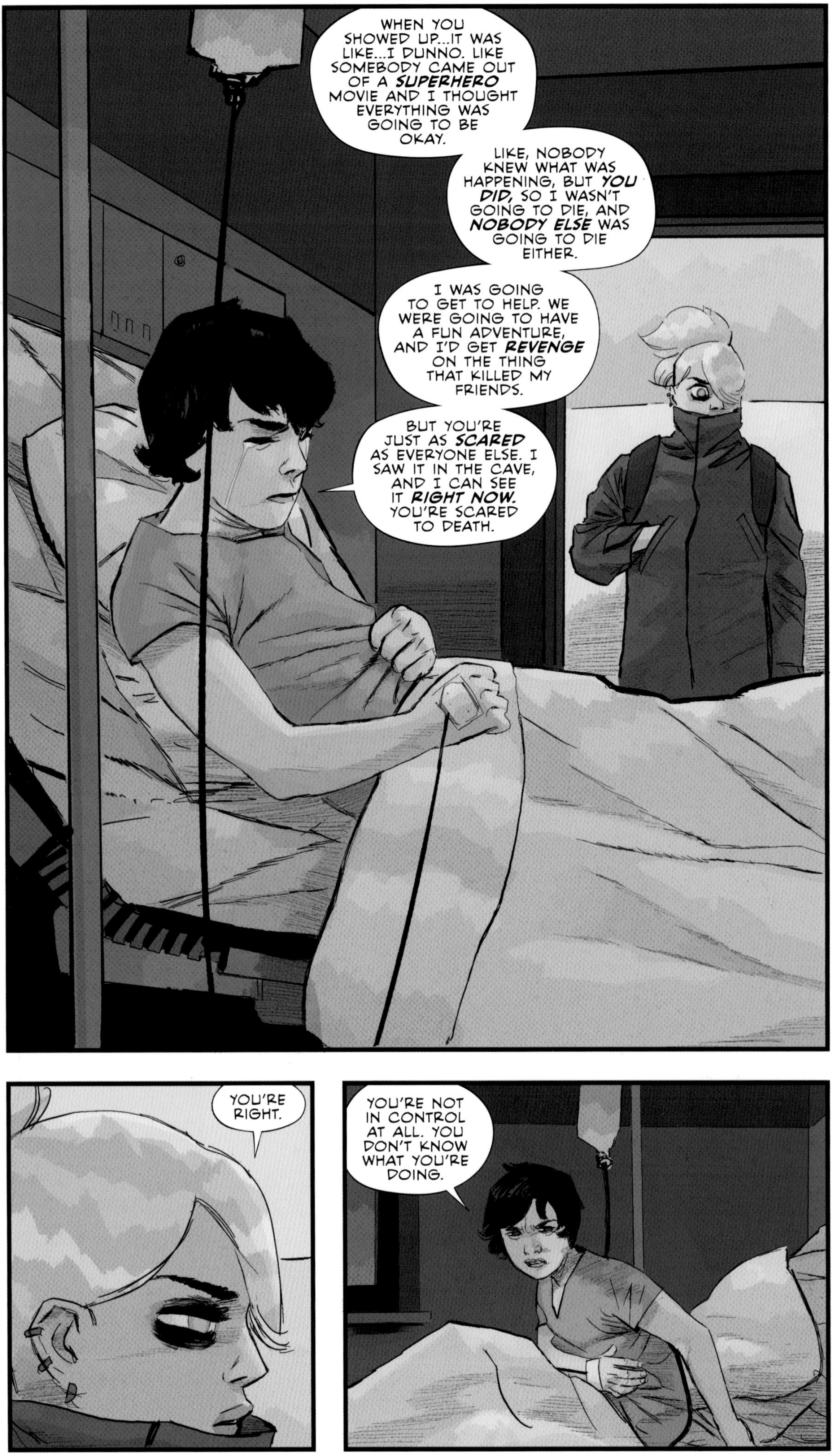
WHEN YOU SHOWED UP...IT WAS LIKE...I DUNNO. LIKE SOMEBODY CAME OUT OF A SUPERHERO MOVIE AND I THOUGHT EVERYTHING WAS GOING TO BE OKAY.
LIKE, NOBODY KNEW WHAT WAS HAPPENING, BUT YOU DID, SO I WASN'T GOING TO DIE, AND NOBODY ELSE WAS GOING TO DIE EITHER.
I WAS GOING TO GET TO HELP. WE WERE GOING TO HAVE A FUN ADVENTURE, AND I'D GET REVENGE ON THE THING THAT KILLED MY FRIENDS.
BUT YOU'RE JUST AS SCARED AS EVERYONE ELSE. I SAW IT IN THE CAVE, AND I CAN SEE IT RIGHT NOW. YOU'RE SCARED TO DEATH.
YOU'RE RIGHT.
YOU'RE NOT IN CONTROL AT ALL. YOU DON'T KNOW WHAT YOU'RE DOING.

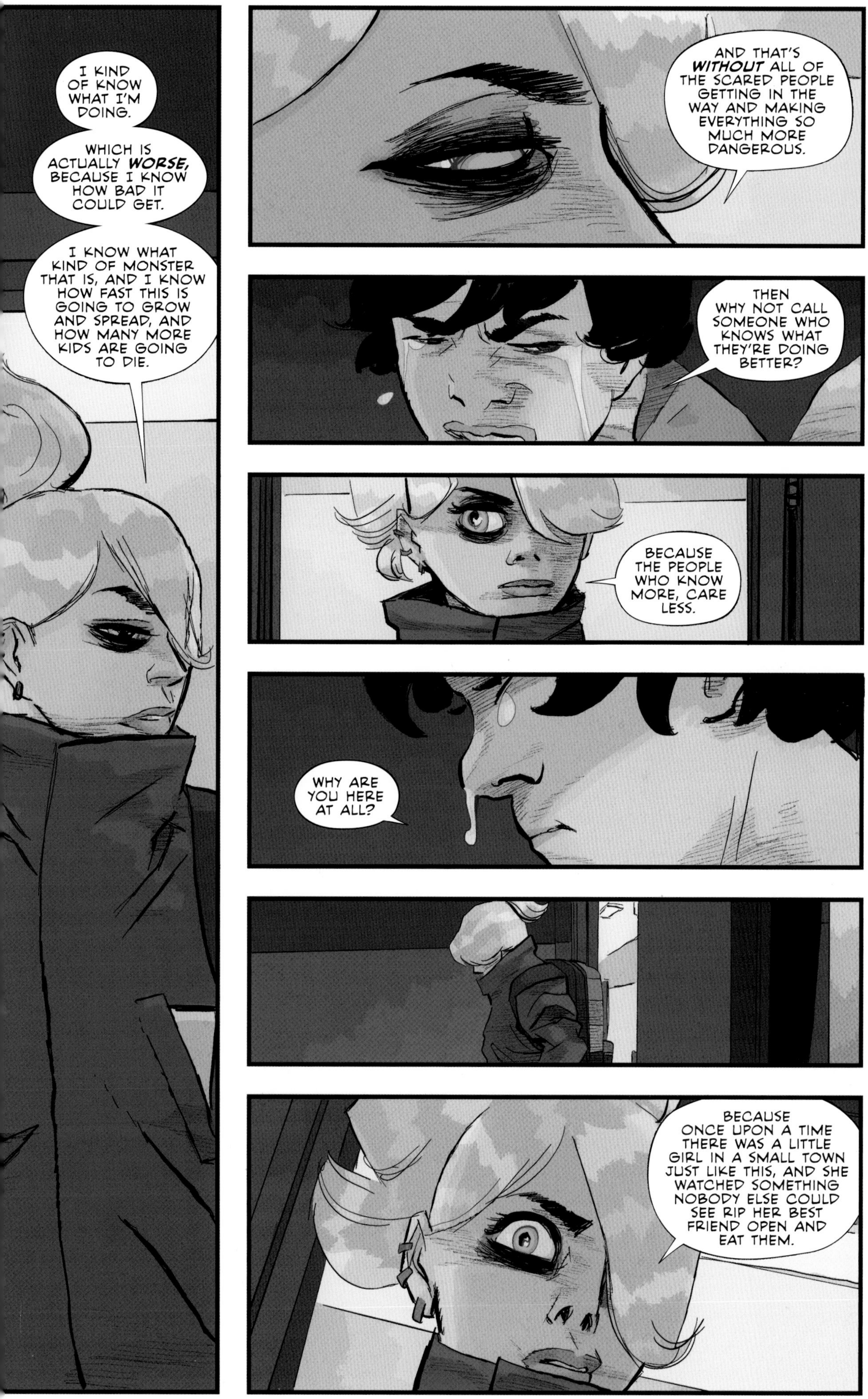

I KIND OF KNOW WHAT I'M DOING.
WHICH IS ACTUALLY **WORSE,** BECAUSE I KNOW HOW BAD IT COULD GET.
I KNOW WHAT KIND OF MONSTER THAT IS, AND I KNOW HOW FAST THIS IS GOING TO GROW AND SPREAD, AND HOW MANY MORE KIDS ARE GOING TO DIE.
AND THAT'S ***WITHOUT*** ALL OF THE SCARED PEOPLE GETTING IN THE WAY AND MAKING EVERYTHING SO MUCH MORE DANGEROUS.
THEN WHY NOT CALL SOMEONE WHO KNOWS WHAT THEY'RE DOING BETTER?
BECAUSE THE PEOPLE WHO KNOW MORE, CARE LESS.
WHY ARE YOU HERE AT ALL?
BECAUSE ONCE UPON A TIME THERE WAS A LITTLE GIRL IN A SMALL TOWN JUST LIKE THIS, AND SHE WATCHED SOMETHING NOBODY ELSE COULD SEE RIP HER BEST FRIEND OPEN AND EAT THEM.

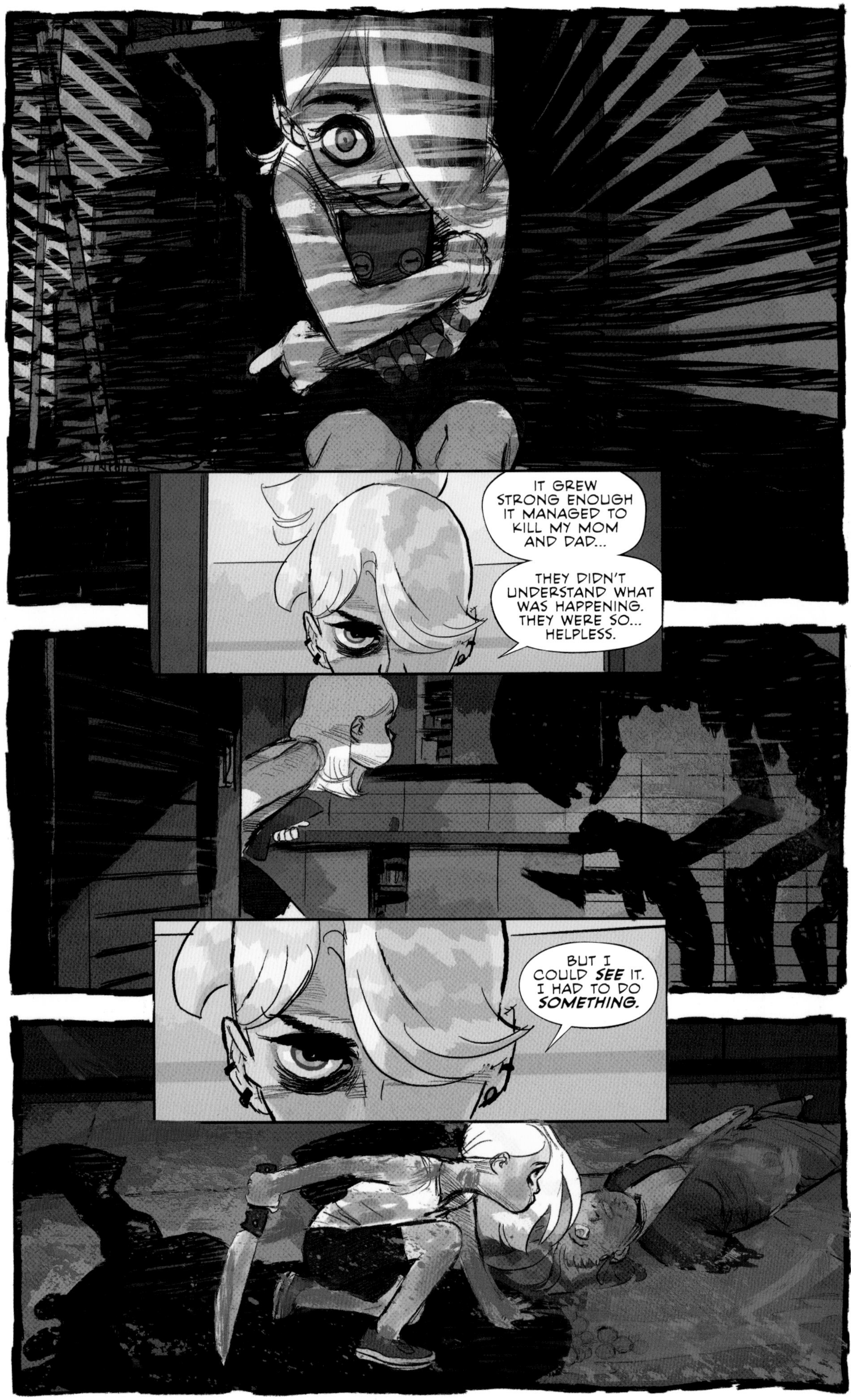
IT GREW STRONG ENOUGH IT MANAGED TO KILL MY MOM AND DAD...
THEY DIDN'T UNDERSTAND WHAT WAS HAPPENING. THEY WERE SO... HELPLESS.
BUT I COULD *SEE* IT. I HAD TO DO *SOMETHING.*

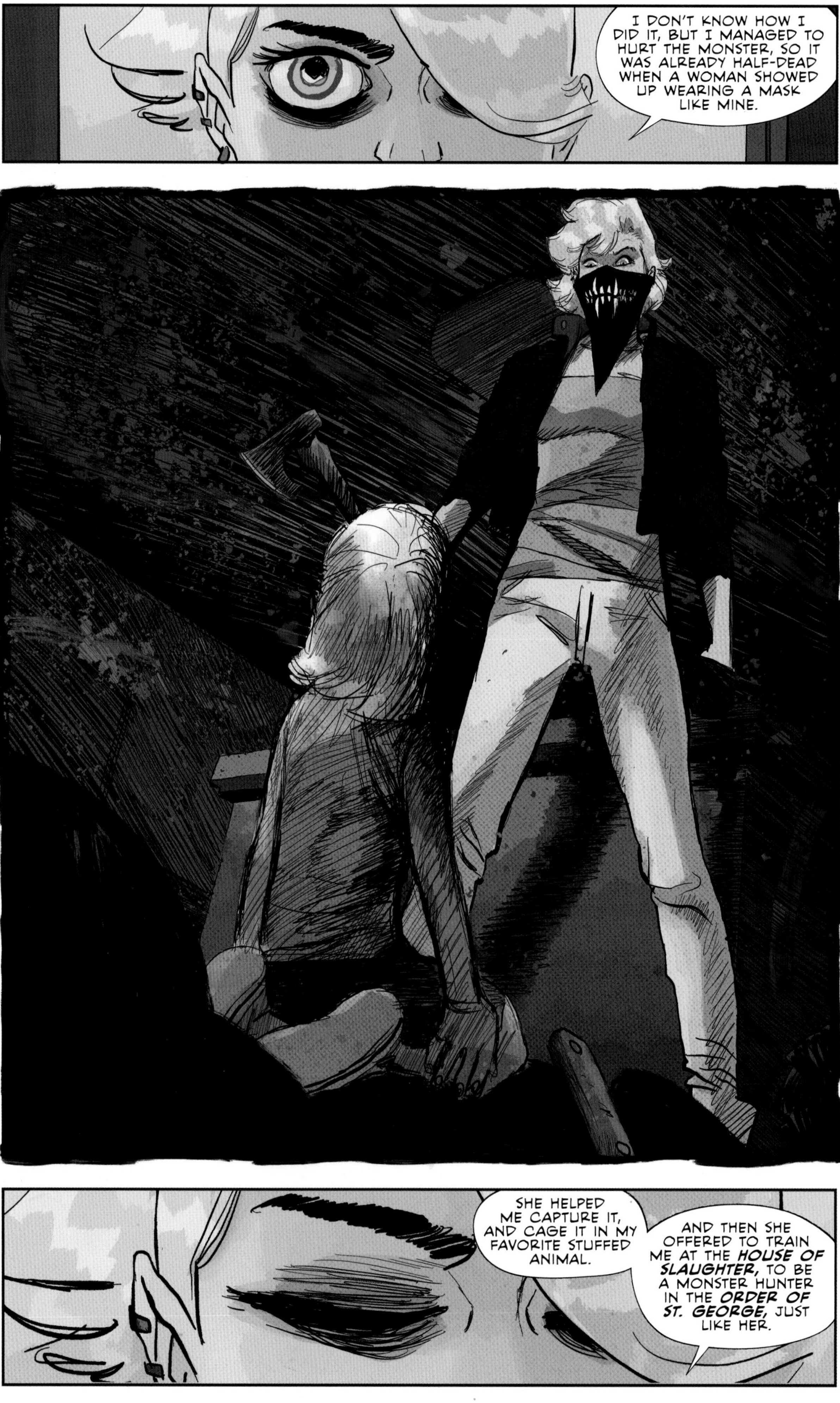
I DON'T KNOW HOW I DID IT, BUT I MANAGED TO HURT THE MONSTER, SO IT WAS ALREADY HALF-DEAD WHEN A WOMAN SHOWED UP WEARING A MASK LIKE MINE.
SHE HELPED ME CAPTURE IT, AND CAGE IT IN MY FAVORITE STUFFED ANIMAL.
AND THEN SHE OFFERED TO TRAIN ME AT THE HOUSE OF SLAUGHTER, TO BE A MONSTER HUNTER IN THE ORDER OF ST. GEORGE, JUST LIKE HER.

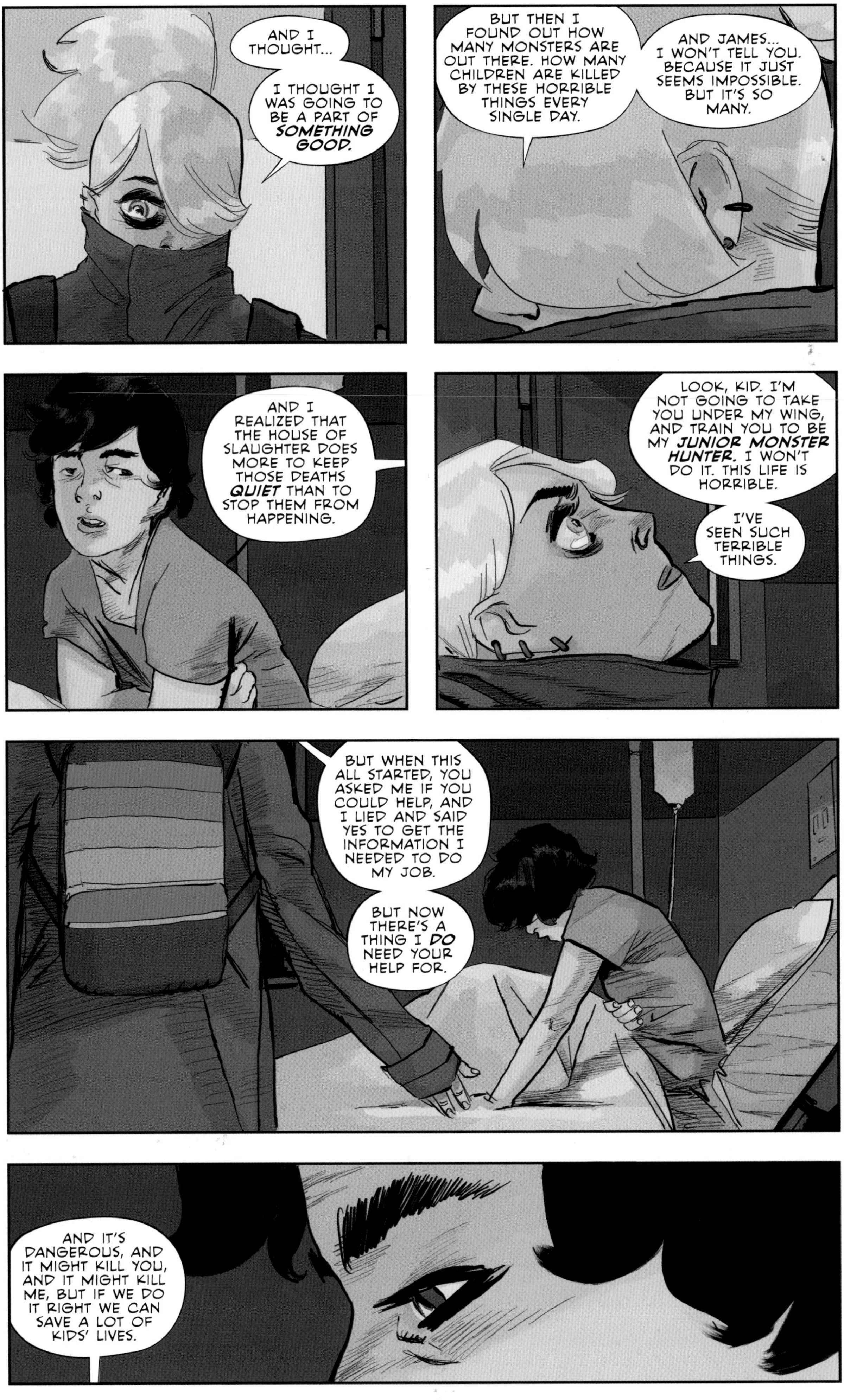
AND I THOUGHT...
I THOUGHT I WAS GOING TO BE A PART OF SOMETHING GOOD.
BUT THEN I FOUND OUT HOW MANY MONSTERS ARE OUT THERE. HOW MANY CHILDREN ARE KILLED BY THESE HORRIBLE THINGS EVERY SINGLE DAY.
AND JAMES... I WON'T TELL YOU. BECAUSE IT JUST SEEMS IMPOSSIBLE. BUT IT'S SO MANY.
AND I REALIZED THAT THE HOUSE OF SLAUGHTER DOES MORE TO KEEP THOSE DEATHS QUIET THAN TO STOP THEM FROM HAPPENING.
LOOK, KID. I'M NOT GOING TO TAKE YOU UNDER MY WING, AND TRAIN YOU TO BE MY JUNIOR MONSTER HUNTER. I WON'T DO IT. THIS LIFE IS HORRIBLE.
I'VE SEEN SUCH TERRIBLE THINGS.
BUT WHEN THIS ALL STARTED, YOU ASKED ME IF YOU COULD HELP, AND I LIED AND SAID YES TO GET THE INFORMATION I NEEDED TO DO MY JOB.
BUT NOW THERE'S A THING I DO NEED YOUR HELP FOR.
AND IT'S DANGEROUS, AND IT MIGHT KILL YOU, AND IT MIGHT KILL ME, BUT IF WE DO IT RIGHT WE CAN SAVE A LOT OF KIDS' LIVES.

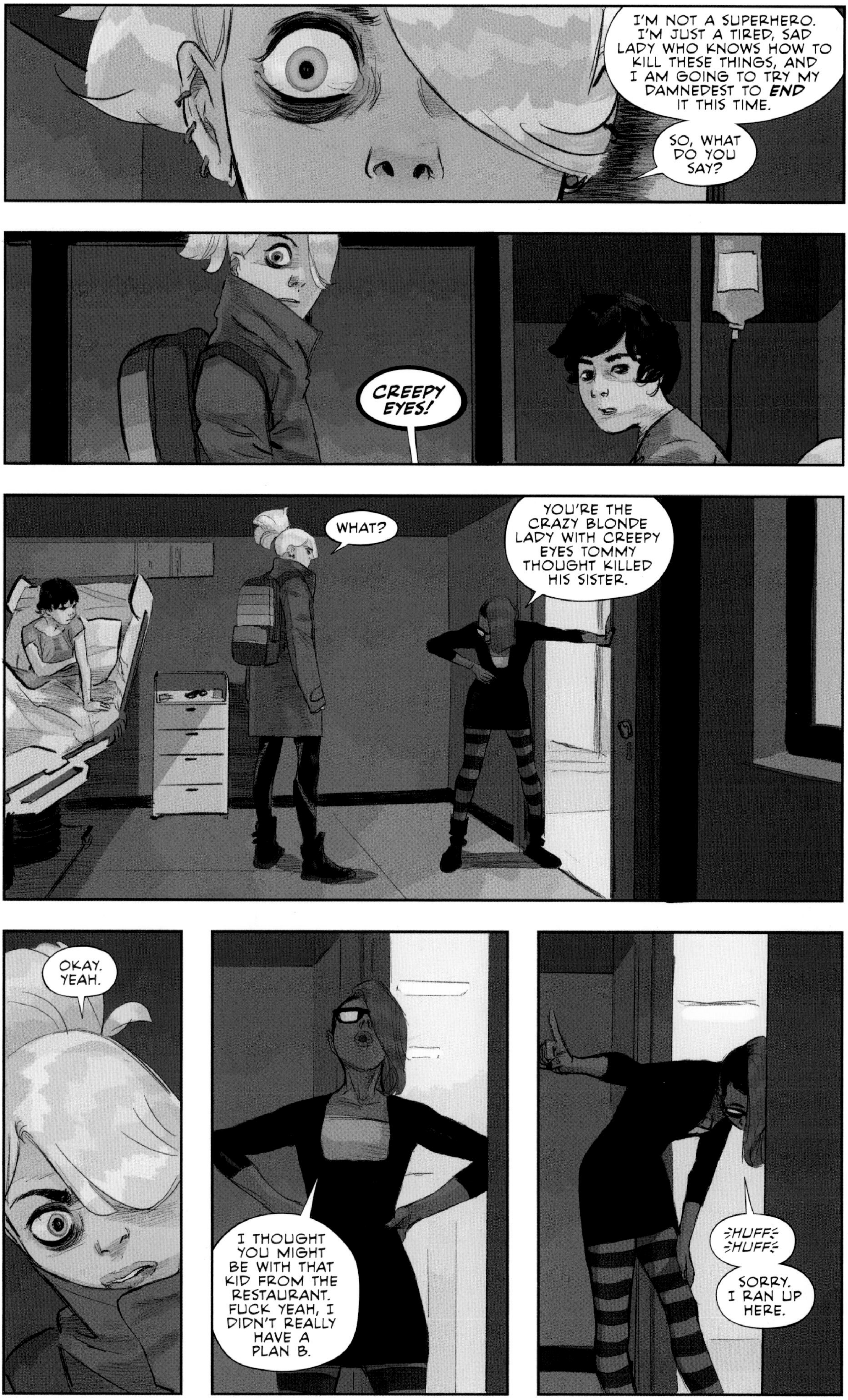
I'M NOT A SUPERHERO. I'M JUST A TIRED, SAD LADY WHO KNOWS HOW TO KILL THESE THINGS, AND I AM GOING TO TRY MY DAMNEDEST TO END IT THIS TIME.
SO, WHAT DO YOU SAY?
CREEPY EYES!
WHAT?
YOU'RE THE CRAZY BLONDE LADY WITH CREEPY EYES TOMMY THOUGHT KILLED HIS SISTER.
OKAY. YEAH.
I THOUGHT YOU MIGHT BE WITH THAT KID FROM THE RESTAURANT. FUCK YEAH, I DIDN'T REALLY HAVE A PLAN B.
HUFF HUFF
SORRY. I RAN UP HERE.

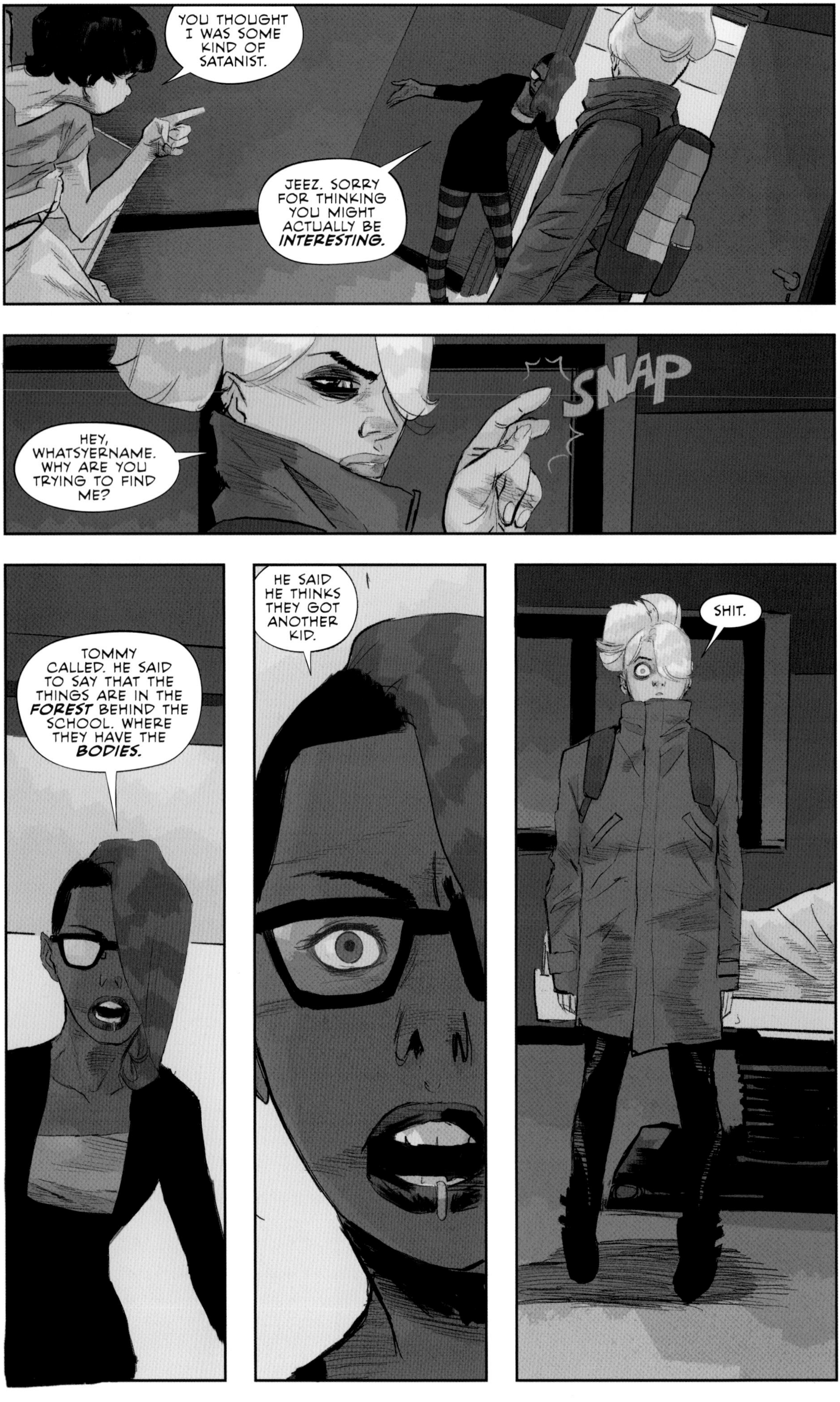
YOU THOUGHT I WAS SOME KIND OF SATANIST.
JEEZ. SORRY FOR THINKING YOU MIGHT ACTUALLY BE *INTERESTING.*
SNAP
HEY, WHATSYERNAME. WHY ARE YOU TRYING TO FIND ME?
TOMMY CALLED. HE SAID TO SAY THAT THE THINGS ARE IN THE *FOREST* BEHIND THE SCHOOL. WHERE THEY HAVE THE *BODIES.*
HE SAID HE THINKS THEY GOT ANOTHER KID.
SHIT.

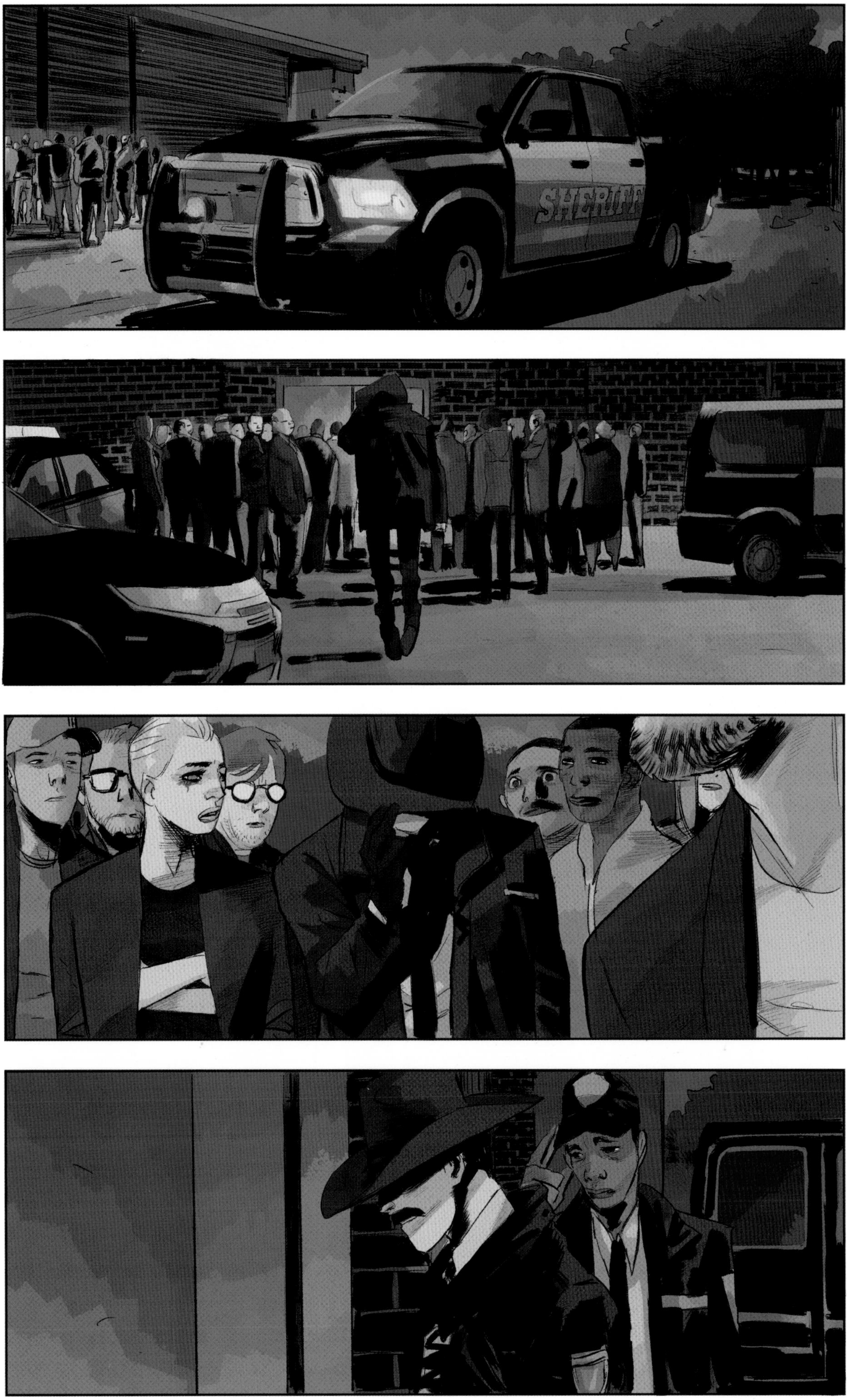

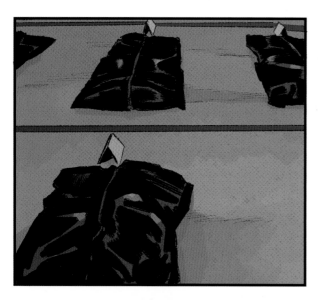

IF IT ISN'T OUR FEARLESS LEADER.

HAS SOPHIE MAHONEY'S FAMILY BEEN IN?

I WISH WE WERE AT THE Ms, BRO. WE'RE STILL IN THE Js, LAST I CHECKED.

THERE'S A SURPRISING NUMBER OF J NAMES IN ARCHER'S PEAK.

I'VE BEEN HANDING THEM OUT. NOTHING LIKE A BACKPACK BEER WHEN THERE'S SOME FUCKED-UP SHIT YOU NEED TO LOOK AT.

HERE, HAVE ONE. LOOSEN UP.

I DON'T WANT TO LOOSEN UP.

THEN HAVE TWO.

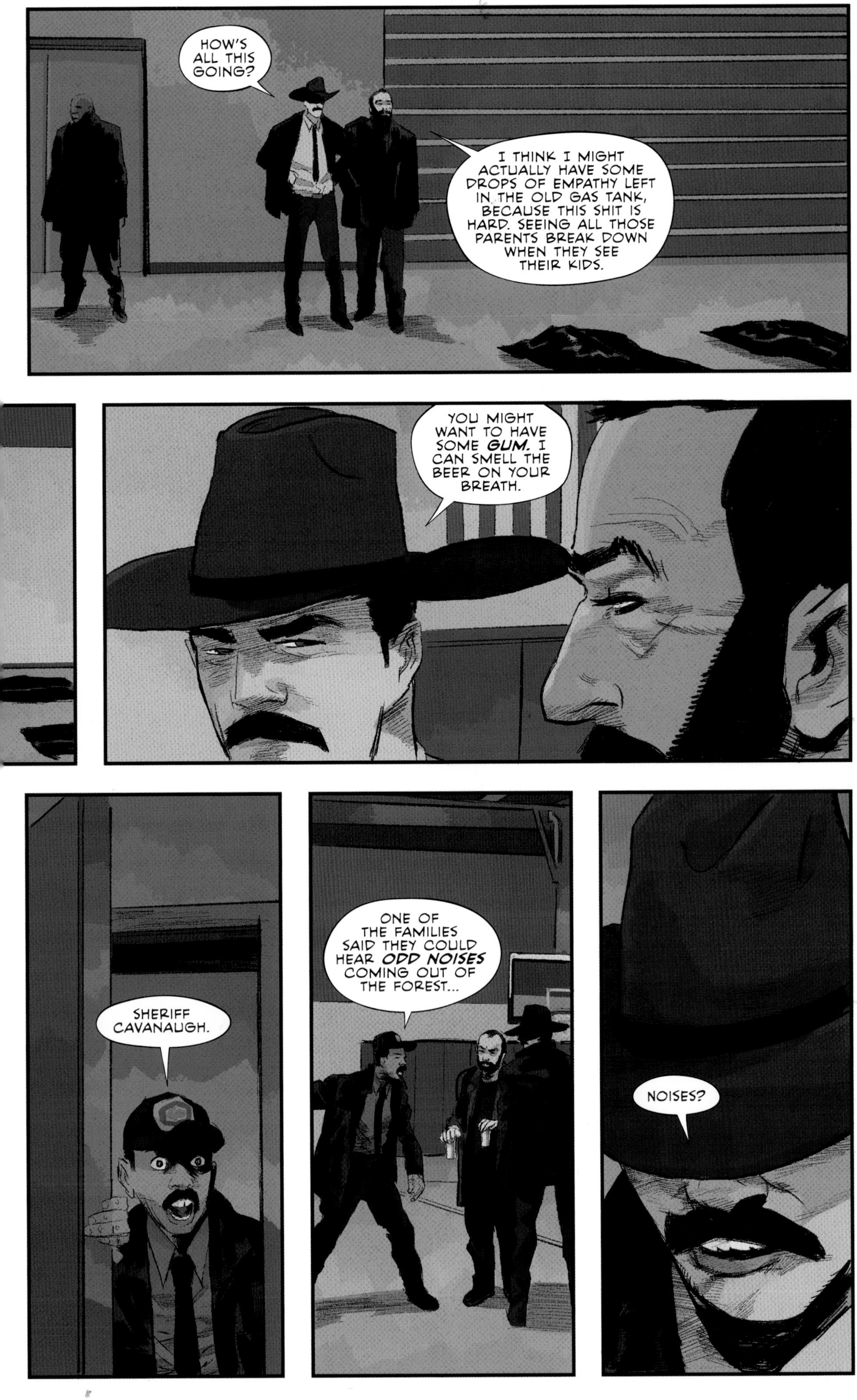
HOW'S ALL THIS GOING?
I THINK I MIGHT ACTUALLY HAVE SOME DROPS OF EMPATHY LEFT IN THE OLD GAS TANK, BECAUSE THIS SHIT IS HARD. SEEING ALL THOSE PARENTS BREAK DOWN WHEN THEY SEE THEIR KIDS.
YOU MIGHT WANT TO HAVE SOME **GUM.** I CAN SMELL THE BEER ON YOUR BREATH.
SHERIFF CAVANAUGH.
ONE OF THE FAMILIES SAID THEY COULD HEAR **ODD NOISES** COMING OUT OF THE FOREST...
NOISES?

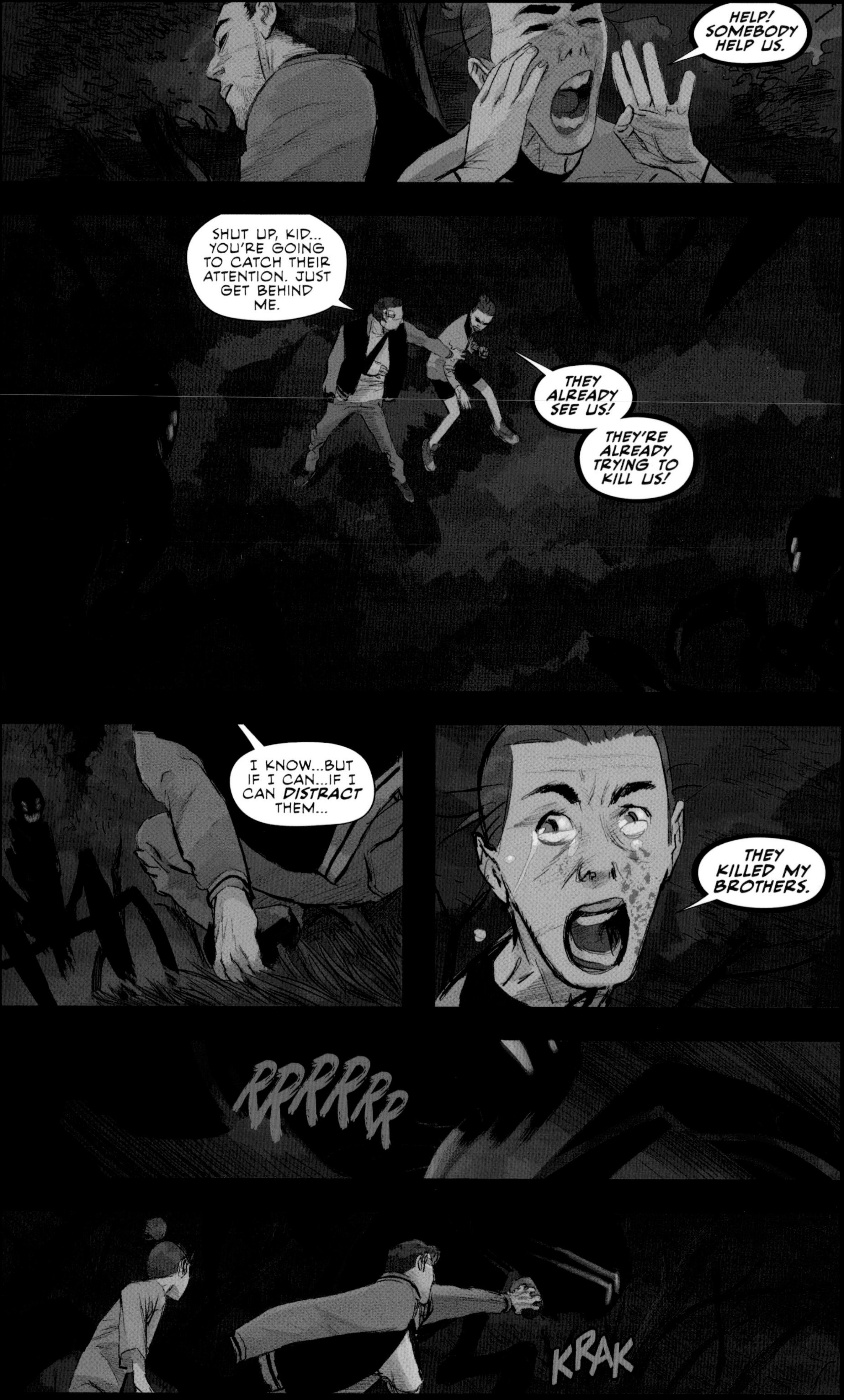
HELP! SOMEBODY HELP US.
SHUT UP, KID... YOU'RE GOING TO CATCH THEIR ATTENTION. JUST GET BEHIND ME.
THEY ALREADY SEE US!
THEY'RE ALREADY TRYING TO KILL US!
I KNOW...BUT IF I CAN...IF I CAN *DISTRACT* THEM...
THEY KILLED MY BROTHERS.
RRRRRR
KRAK

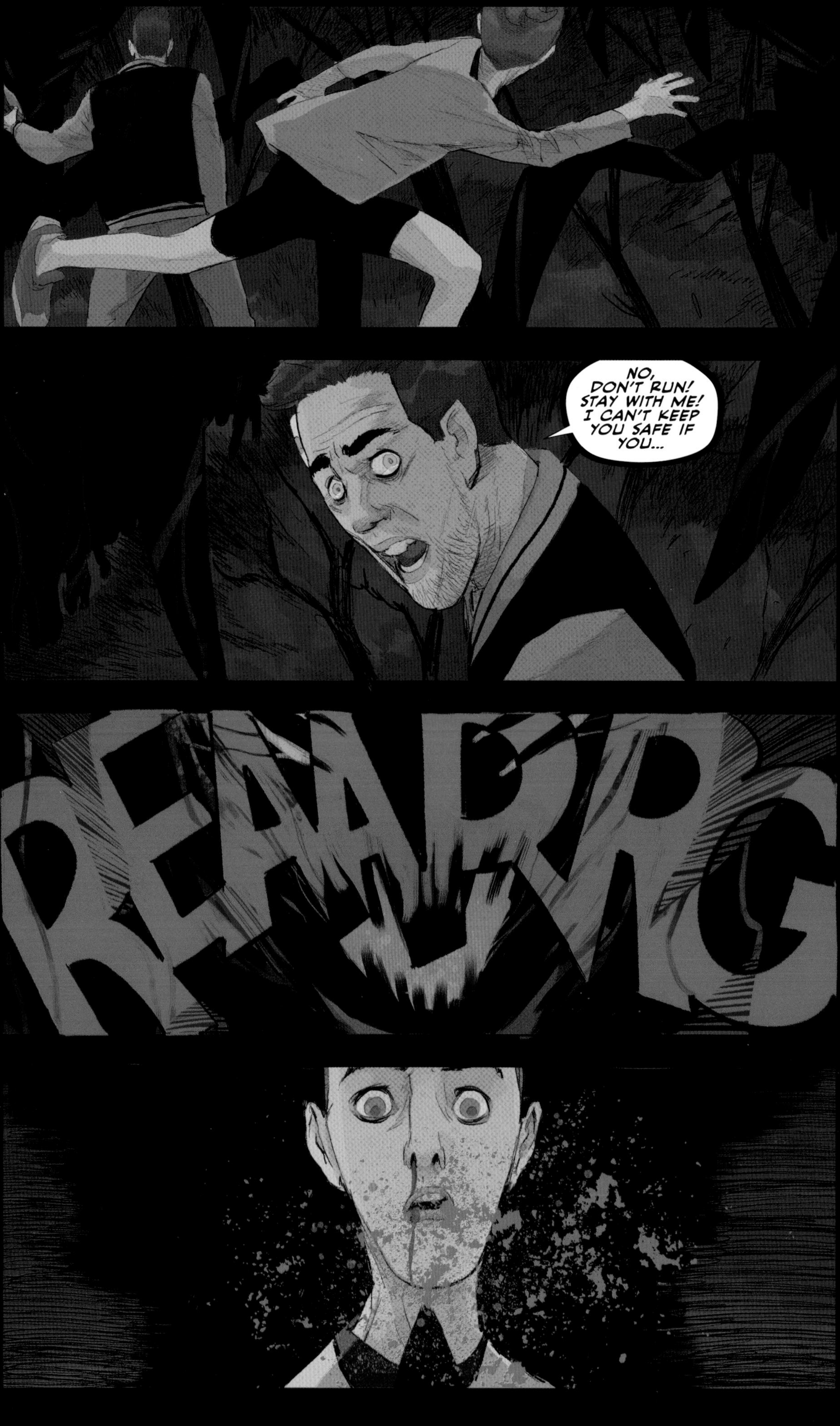
NO, DON'T RUN! STAY WITH ME! I CAN'T KEEP YOU SAFE IF YOU...

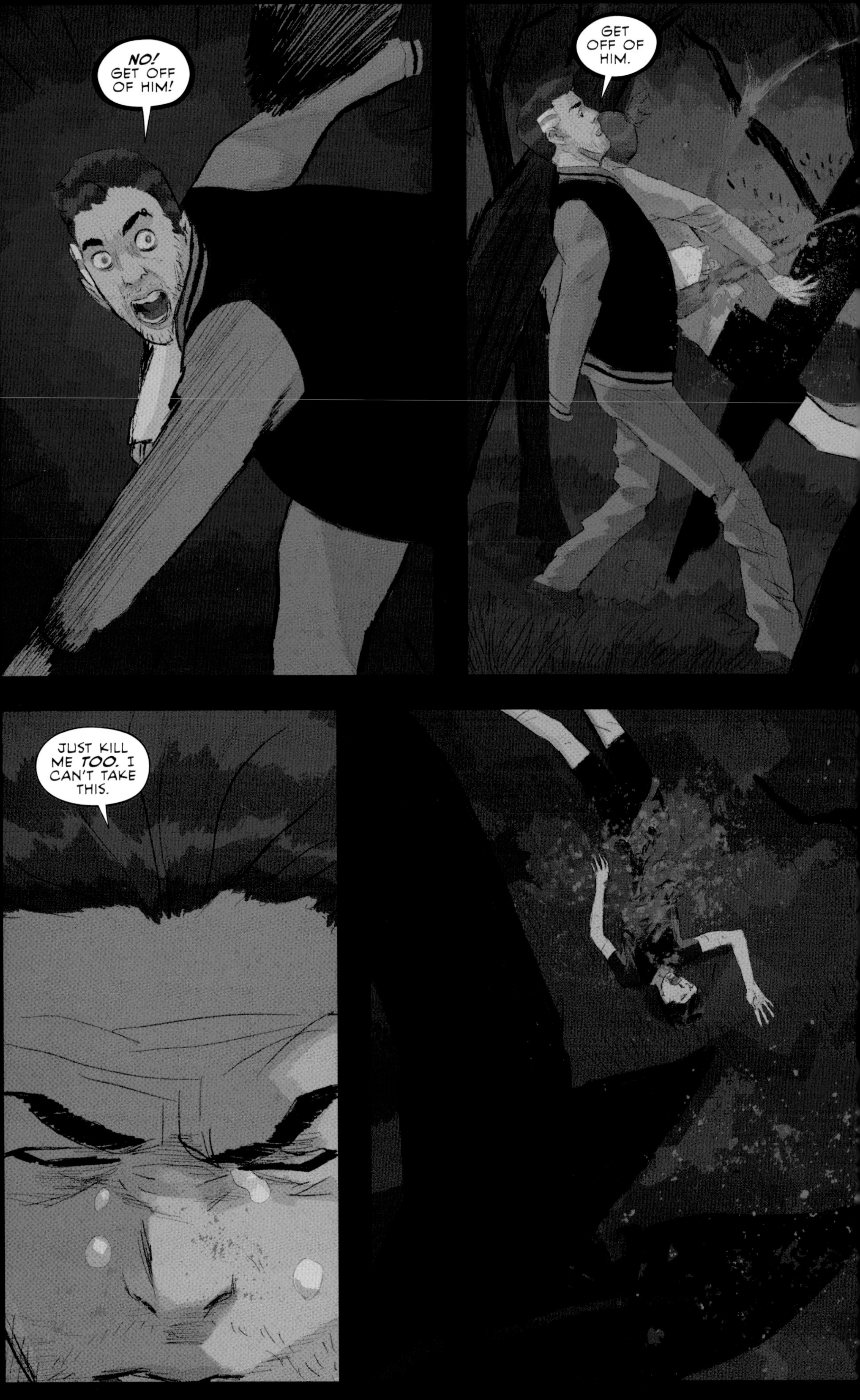
NO! GET OFF OF HIM!
GET OFF OF HIM.
JUST KILL ME *TOO.* I CAN'T TAKE THIS.

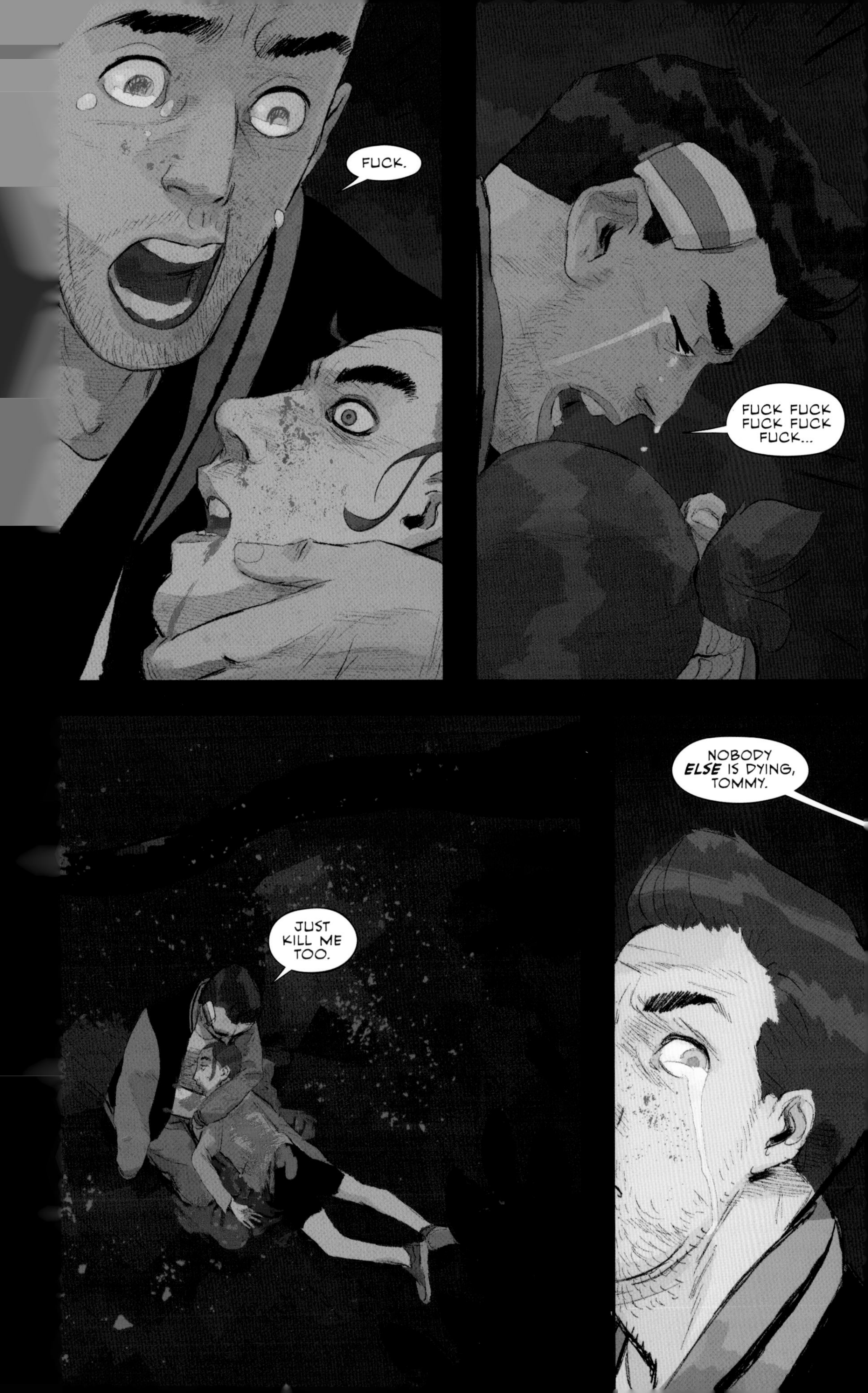
FUCK.
FUCK FUCK FUCK FUCK FUCK...
JUST KILL ME TOO.
NOBODY *ELSE* IS DYING, TOMMY.

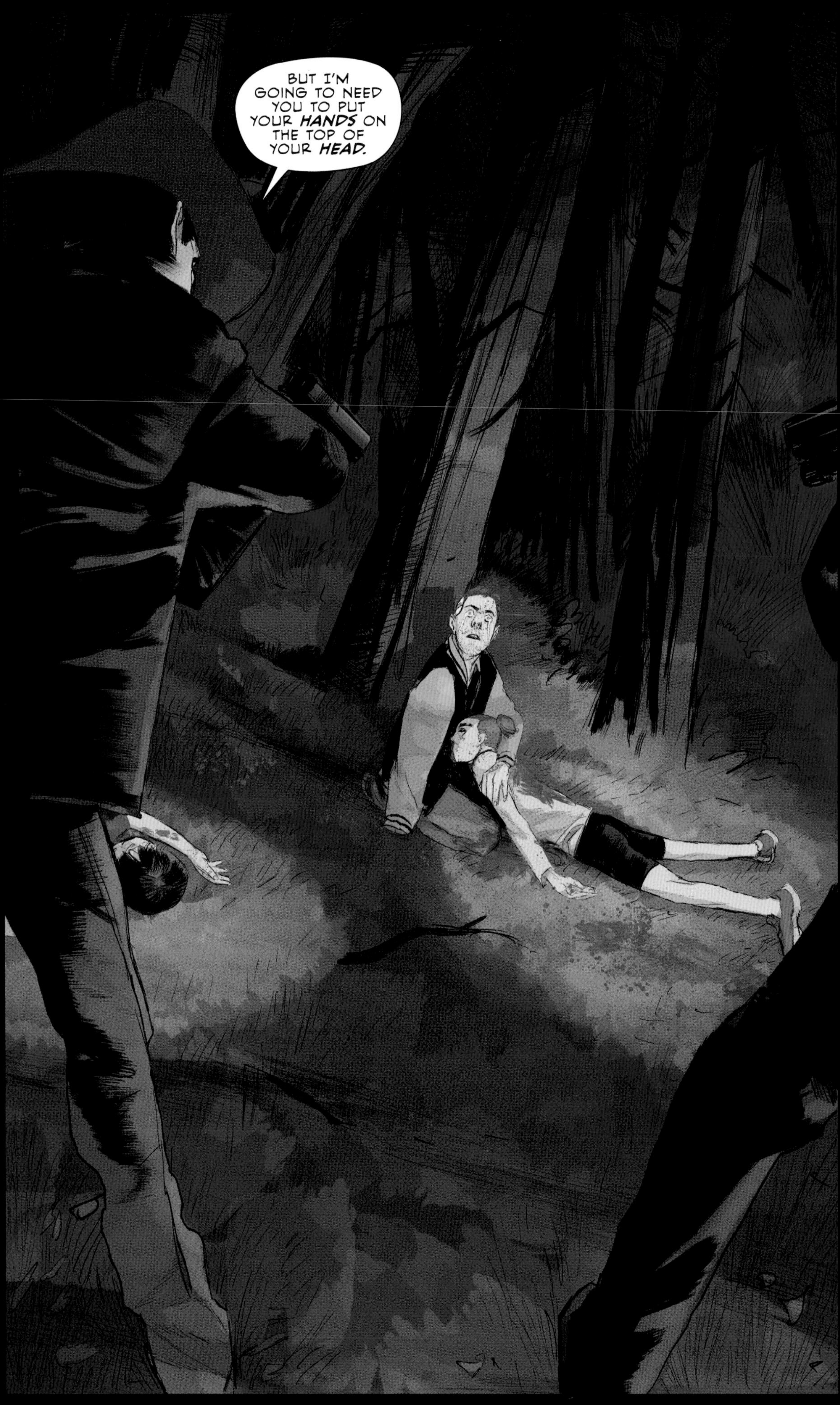
BUT I'M GOING TO NEED YOU TO PUT YOUR HANDS ON THE TOP OF YOUR HEAD.

CHAPTER TEN

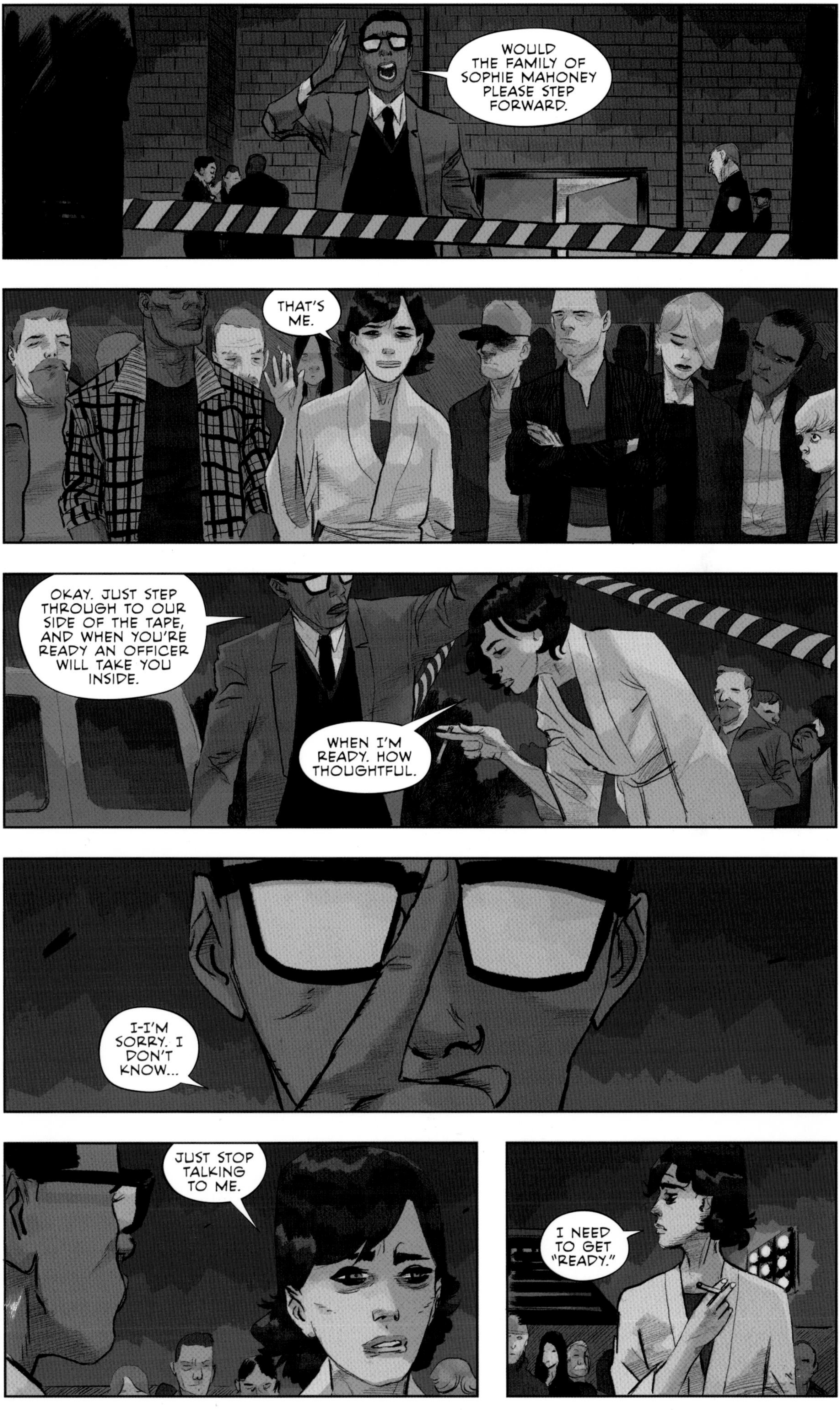
WOULD THE FAMILY OF SOPHIE MAHONEY PLEASE STEP FORWARD.
THAT'S ME.
OKAY. JUST STEP THROUGH TO OUR SIDE OF THE TAPE, AND WHEN YOU'RE READY AN OFFICER WILL TAKE YOU INSIDE.
WHEN I'M READY. HOW THOUGHTFUL.
I-I'M SORRY. I DON'T KNOW...
JUST STOP TALKING TO ME.
I NEED TO GET "READY."

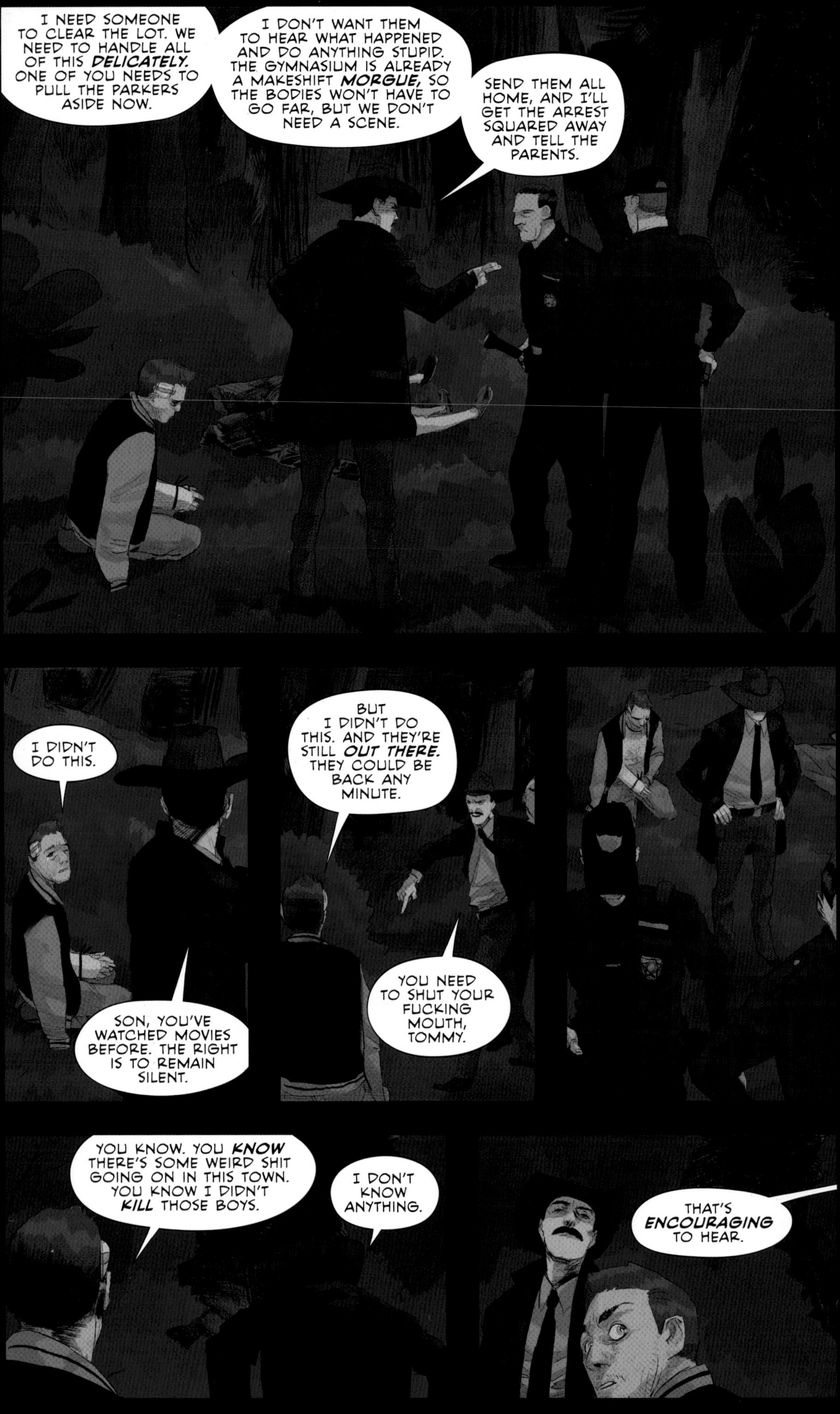
I NEED SOMEONE TO CLEAR THE LOT. WE NEED TO HANDLE ALL OF THIS DELICATELY. ONE OF YOU NEEDS TO PULL THE PARKERS ASIDE NOW.
I DON'T WANT THEM TO HEAR WHAT HAPPENED AND DO ANYTHING STUPID. THE GYMNASIUM IS ALREADY A MAKESHIFT MORGUE, SO THE BODIES WON'T HAVE TO GO FAR, BUT WE DON'T NEED A SCENE.
SEND THEM ALL HOME, AND I'LL GET THE ARREST SQUARED AWAY AND TELL THE PARENTS.
I DIDN'T DO THIS.
SON, YOU'VE WATCHED MOVIES BEFORE. THE RIGHT IS TO REMAIN SILENT.
BUT I DIDN'T DO THIS. AND THEY'RE STILL OUT THERE. THEY COULD BE BACK ANY MINUTE.
YOU NEED TO SHUT YOUR FUCKING MOUTH, TOMMY.
YOU KNOW. YOU KNOW THERE'S SOME WEIRD SHIT GOING ON IN THIS TOWN. YOU KNOW I DIDN'T KILL THOSE BOYS.
I DON'T KNOW ANYTHING.
THAT'S ENCOURAGING TO HEAR.

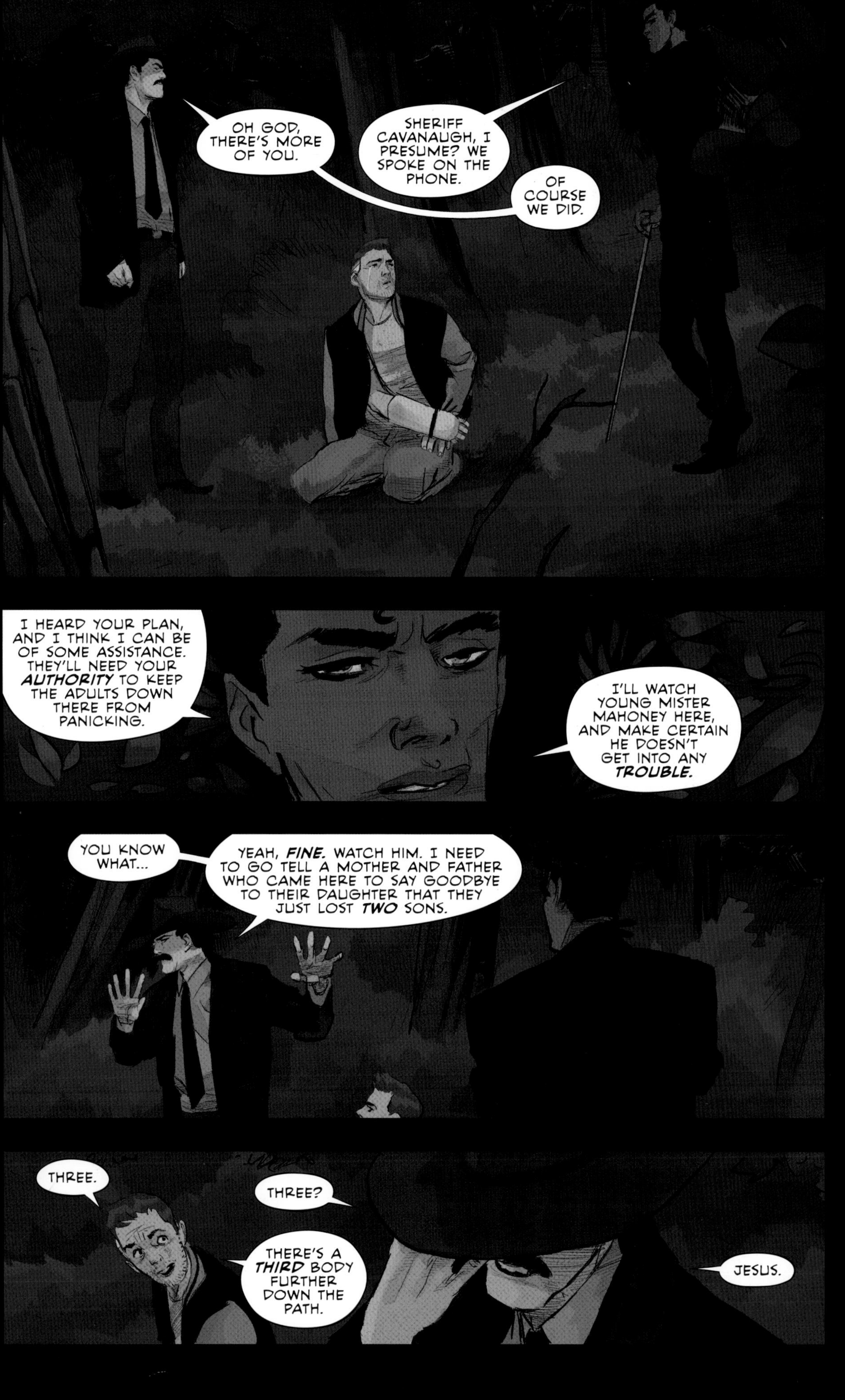
OH GOD, THERE'S MORE OF YOU.
SHERIFF CAVANAUGH, I PRESUME? WE SPOKE ON THE PHONE.
OF COURSE WE DID.
I HEARD YOUR PLAN, AND I THINK I CAN BE OF SOME ASSISTANCE. THEY'LL NEED YOUR AUTHORITY TO KEEP THE ADULTS DOWN THERE FROM PANICKING.
I'LL WATCH YOUNG MISTER MAHONEY HERE, AND MAKE CERTAIN HE DOESN'T GET INTO ANY TROUBLE.
YOU KNOW WHAT...
YEAH, FINE. WATCH HIM. I NEED TO GO TELL A MOTHER AND FATHER WHO CAME HERE TO SAY GOODBYE TO THEIR DAUGHTER THAT THEY JUST LOST TWO SONS.
THREE.
THREE?
THERE'S A THIRD BODY FURTHER DOWN THE PATH.
JESUS.

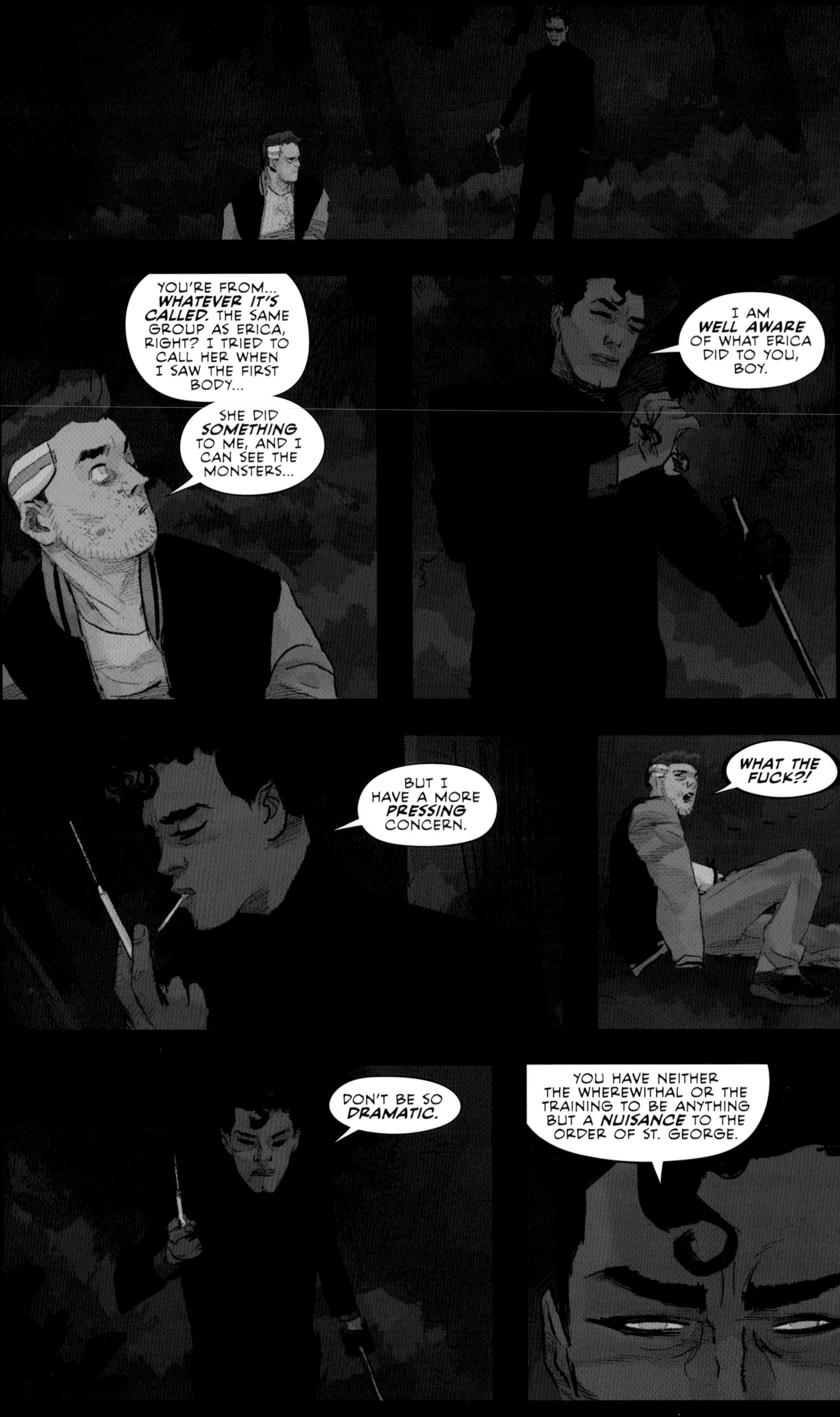
YOU'RE FROM... WHATEVER IT'S CALLED. THE SAME GROUP AS ERICA, RIGHT? I TRIED TO CALL HER WHEN I SAW THE FIRST BODY...
SHE DID SOMETHING TO ME, AND I CAN SEE THE MONSTERS...
I AM WELL AWARE OF WHAT ERICA DID TO YOU, BOY.
BUT I HAVE A MORE PRESSING CONCERN.
WHAT THE FUCK?!
DON'T BE SO DRAMATIC.
YOU HAVE NEITHER THE WHEREWITHAL OR THE TRAINING TO BE ANYTHING BUT A NUISANCE TO THE ORDER OF ST. GEORGE.

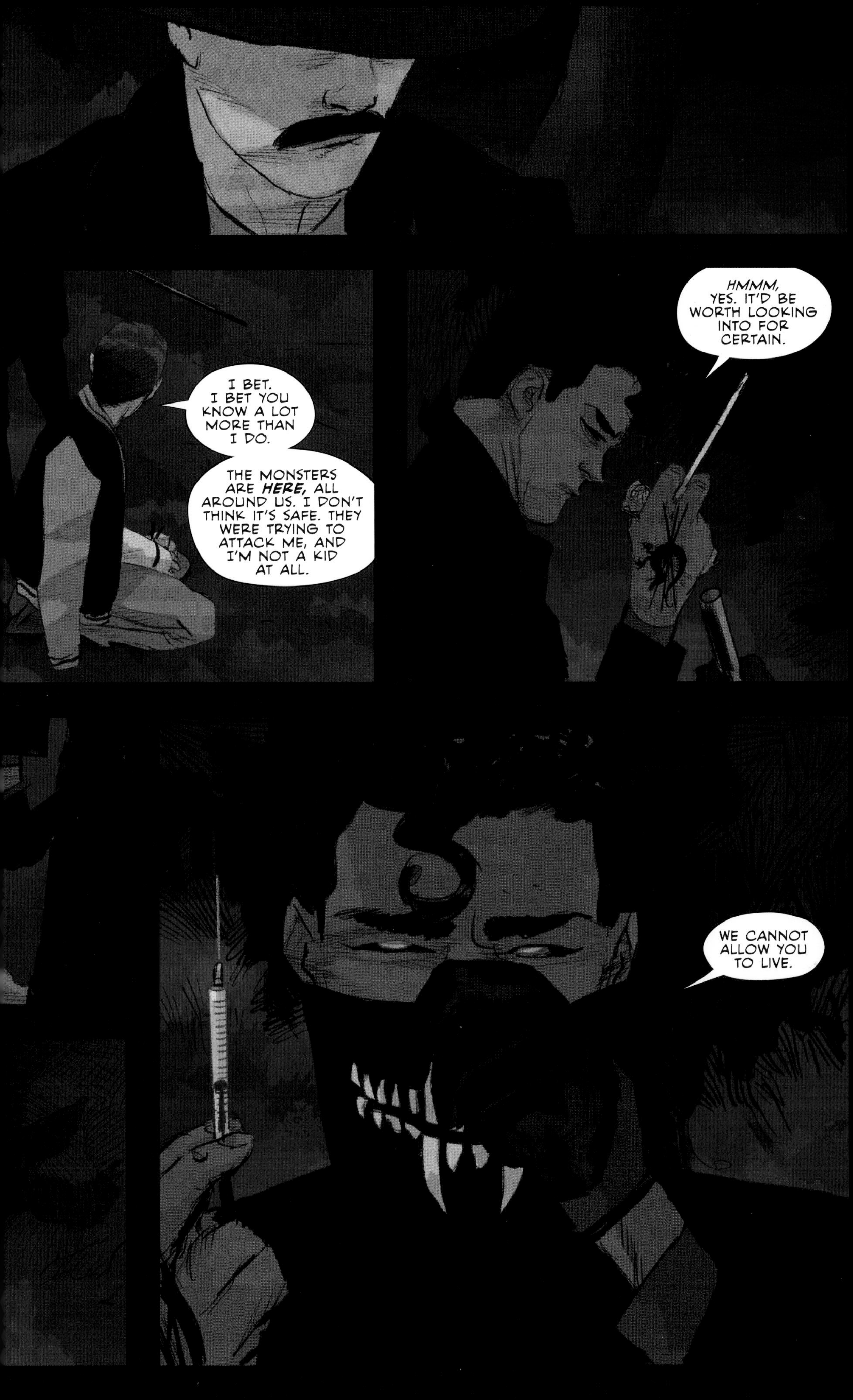
I BET. I BET YOU KNOW A LOT MORE THAN I DO.
THE MONSTERS ARE *HERE,* ALL AROUND US. I DON'T THINK IT'S SAFE. THEY WERE TRYING TO ATTACK ME, AND I'M NOT A KID AT ALL.
HMMM, YES. IT'D BE WORTH LOOKING INTO FOR CERTAIN.
WE CANNOT ALLOW YOU TO LIVE.

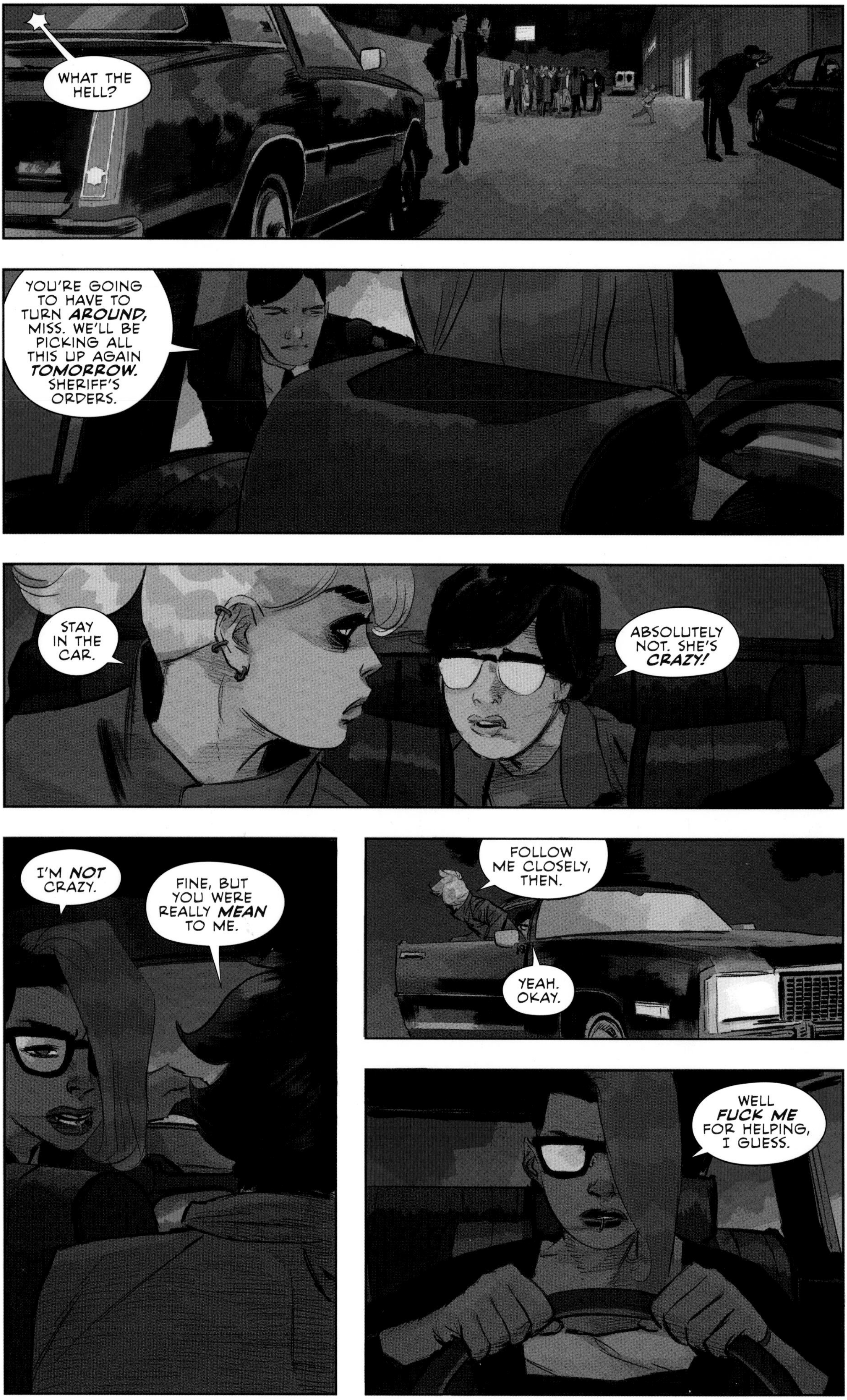
WHAT THE HELL?
YOU'RE GOING TO HAVE TO TURN AROUND, MISS. WE'LL BE PICKING ALL THIS UP AGAIN TOMORROW. SHERIFF'S ORDERS.
STAY IN THE CAR.
ABSOLUTELY NOT. SHE'S CRAZY!
I'M NOT CRAZY.
FINE, BUT YOU WERE REALLY MEAN TO ME.
FOLLOW ME CLOSELY, THEN.
YEAH. OKAY.
WELL FUCK ME FOR HELPING, I GUESS.

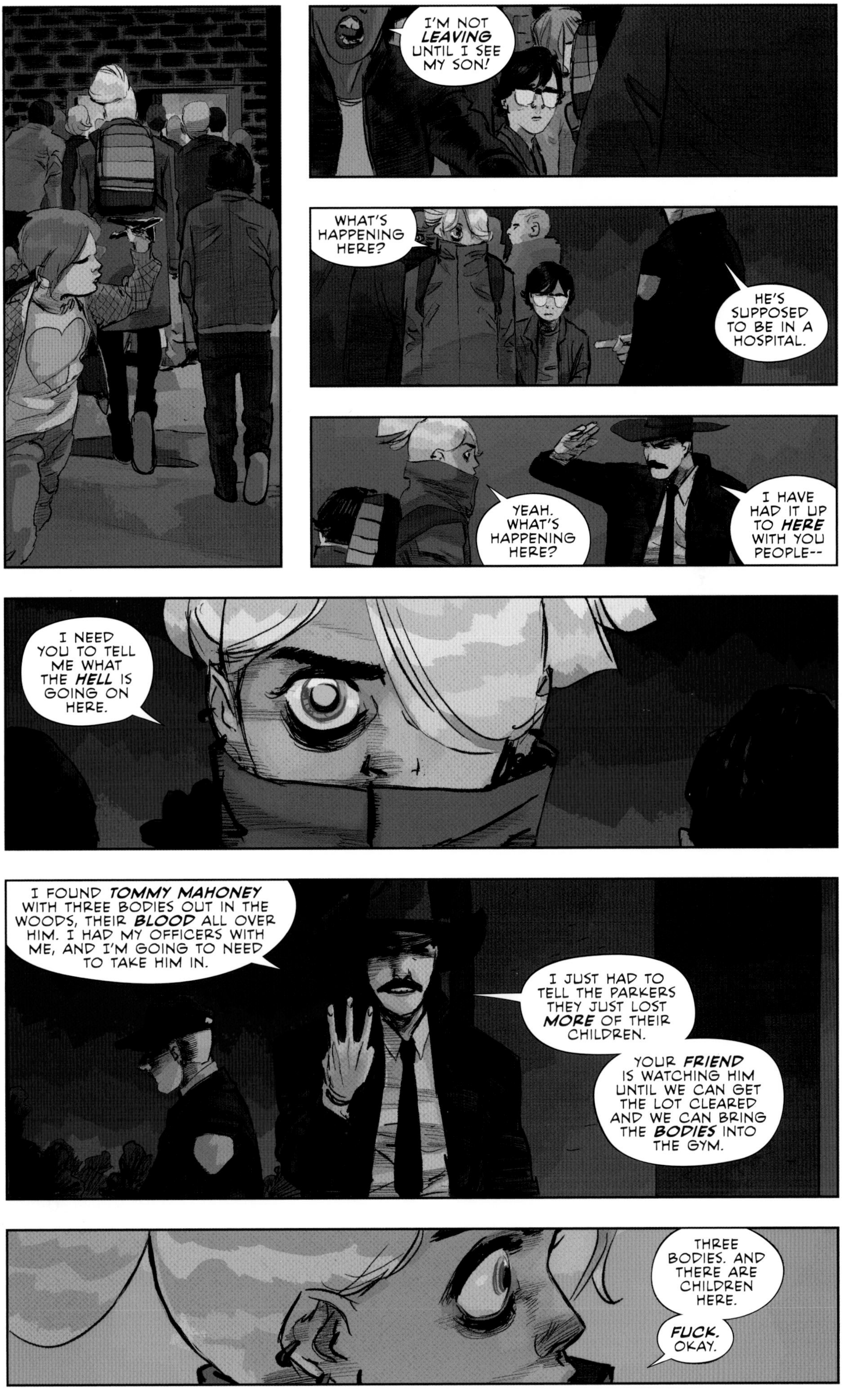
I'M NOT LEAVING UNTIL I SEE MY SON!
WHAT'S HAPPENING HERE?
HE'S SUPPOSED TO BE IN A HOSPITAL.
YEAH. WHAT'S HAPPENING HERE?
I HAVE HAD IT UP TO HERE WITH YOU PEOPLE--
I NEED YOU TO TELL ME WHAT THE HELL IS GOING ON HERE.
I FOUND TOMMY MAHONEY WITH THREE BODIES OUT IN THE WOODS, THEIR BLOOD ALL OVER HIM. I HAD MY OFFICERS WITH ME, AND I'M GOING TO NEED TO TAKE HIM IN.
I JUST HAD TO TELL THE PARKERS THEY JUST LOST MORE OF THEIR CHILDREN.
YOUR FRIEND IS WATCHING HIM UNTIL WE CAN GET THE LOT CLEARED AND WE CAN BRING THE BODIES INTO THE GYM.
THREE BODIES. AND THERE ARE CHILDREN HERE.
FUCK. OKAY.

I DON'T *APPRECIATE* THE WAY YOUR FRIEND TALKED TO ME...

SHUT UP.

NOW *WAIT* JUST A--

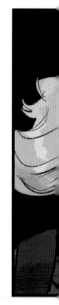

OKAY.

WHO CAN TAKE HIM?

=SIGH=

HOW LONG AGO DID THE CHILDREN DIE?

I DON'T...I DON'T KNOW. WHAT'S WRONG?

WHAT KILLED THEM IS ALMOST DEFINITELY STILL IN THOSE WOODS. AND THEY'RE STILL *HUNGRY.* GETTING HUNGRIER BY THE SECOND.

TAKE ME TO WHERE YOU LEFT MY "FRIEND."

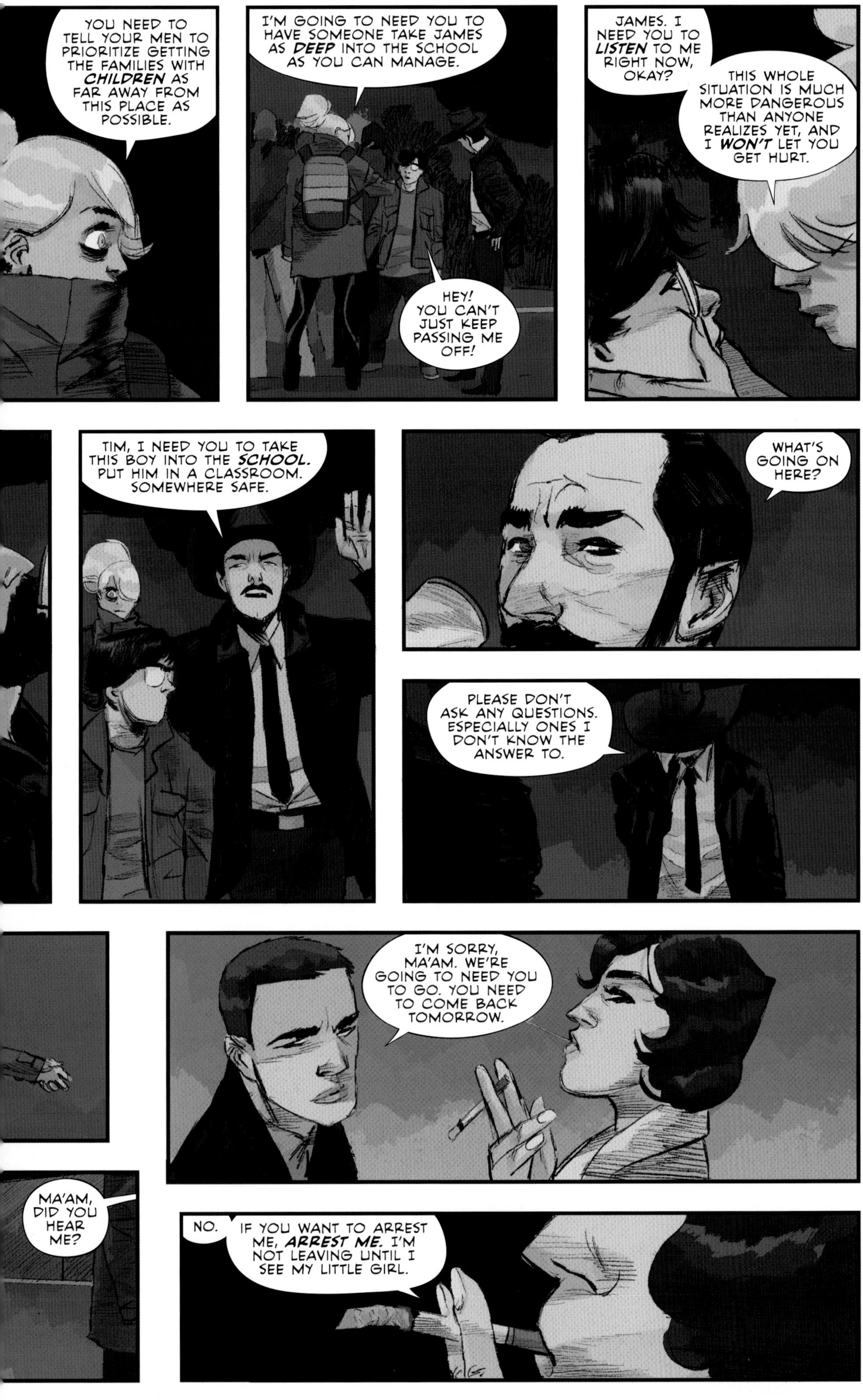
YOU NEED TO TELL YOUR MEN TO PRIORITIZE GETTING THE FAMILIES WITH *CHILDREN* AS FAR AWAY FROM THIS PLACE AS POSSIBLE.
I'M GOING TO NEED YOU TO HAVE SOMEONE TAKE JAMES AS *DEEP* INTO THE SCHOOL AS YOU CAN MANAGE.
HEY! YOU CAN'T JUST KEEP PASSING ME OFF!
JAMES. I NEED YOU TO *LISTEN* TO ME RIGHT NOW, OKAY?
THIS WHOLE SITUATION IS MUCH MORE DANGEROUS THAN ANYONE REALIZES YET, AND I *WON'T* LET YOU GET HURT.
TIM, I NEED YOU TO TAKE THIS BOY INTO THE *SCHOOL.* PUT HIM IN A CLASSROOM. SOMEWHERE SAFE.
WHAT'S GOING ON HERE?
PLEASE DON'T ASK ANY QUESTIONS. ESPECIALLY ONES I DON'T KNOW THE ANSWER TO.
I'M SORRY, MA'AM. WE'RE GOING TO NEED YOU TO GO. YOU NEED TO COME BACK TOMORROW.
MA'AM, DID YOU HEAR ME?
NO.
IF YOU WANT TO ARREST ME, *ARREST ME.* I'M NOT LEAVING UNTIL I SEE MY LITTLE GIRL.

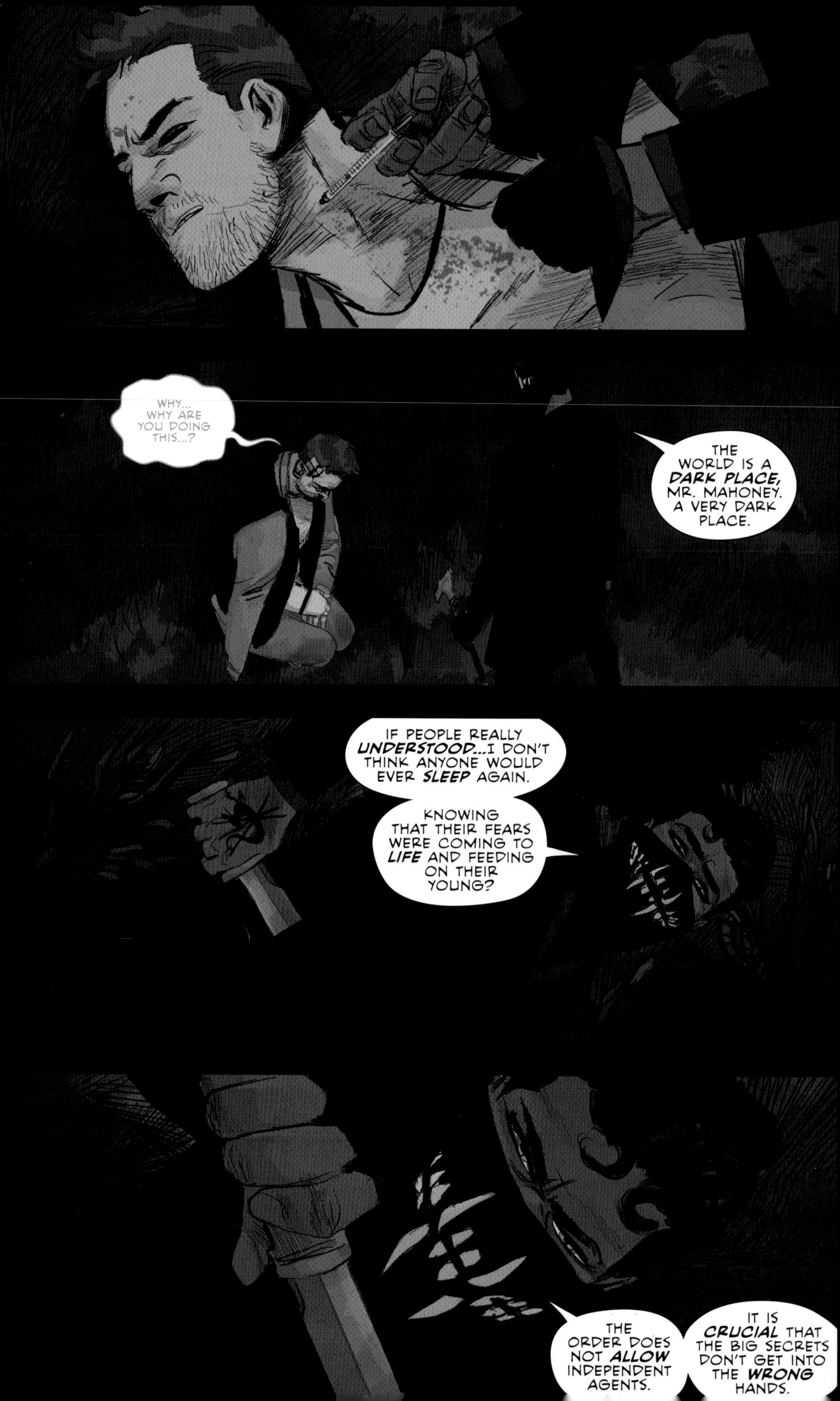
WHY... WHY ARE YOU DOING THIS...?
THE WORLD IS A DARK PLACE, MR. MAHONEY. A VERY DARK PLACE.
IF PEOPLE REALLY UNDERSTOOD...I DON'T THINK ANYONE WOULD EVER SLEEP AGAIN.
KNOWING THAT THEIR FEARS WERE COMING TO LIFE AND FEEDING ON THEIR YOUNG?
THE ORDER DOES NOT ALLOW INDEPENDENT AGENTS.
IT IS CRUCIAL THAT THE BIG SECRETS DON'T GET INTO THE WRONG HANDS.

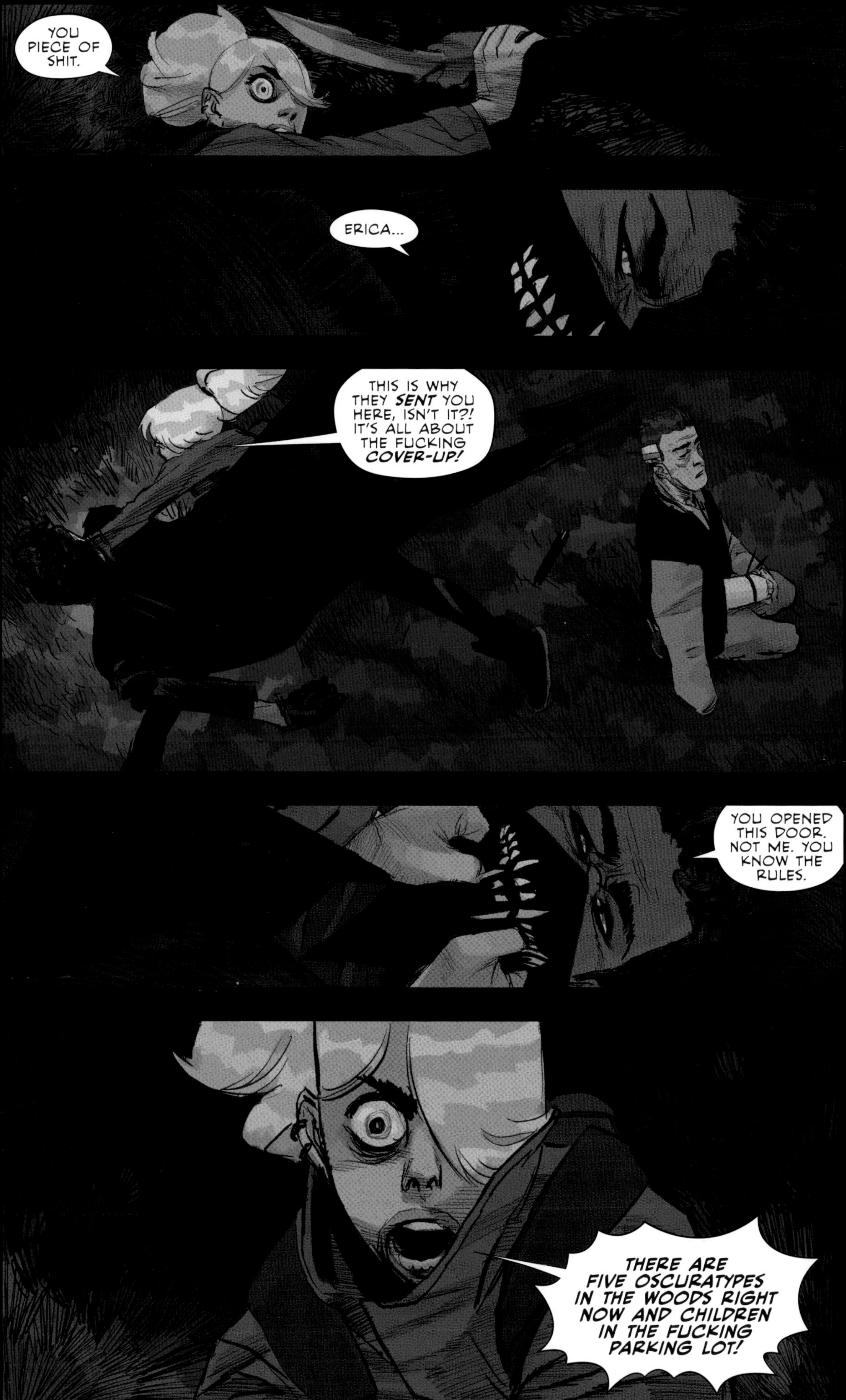
YOU PIECE OF SHIT.
ERICA...
THIS IS WHY THEY *SENT* YOU HERE, ISN'T IT?! IT'S ALL ABOUT THE FUCKING *COVER-UP!*
YOU OPENED THIS DOOR. NOT ME. YOU KNOW THE RULES.
THERE ARE FIVE OSCURATYPES IN THE WOODS RIGHT NOW AND CHILDREN IN THE FUCKING PARKING LOT!

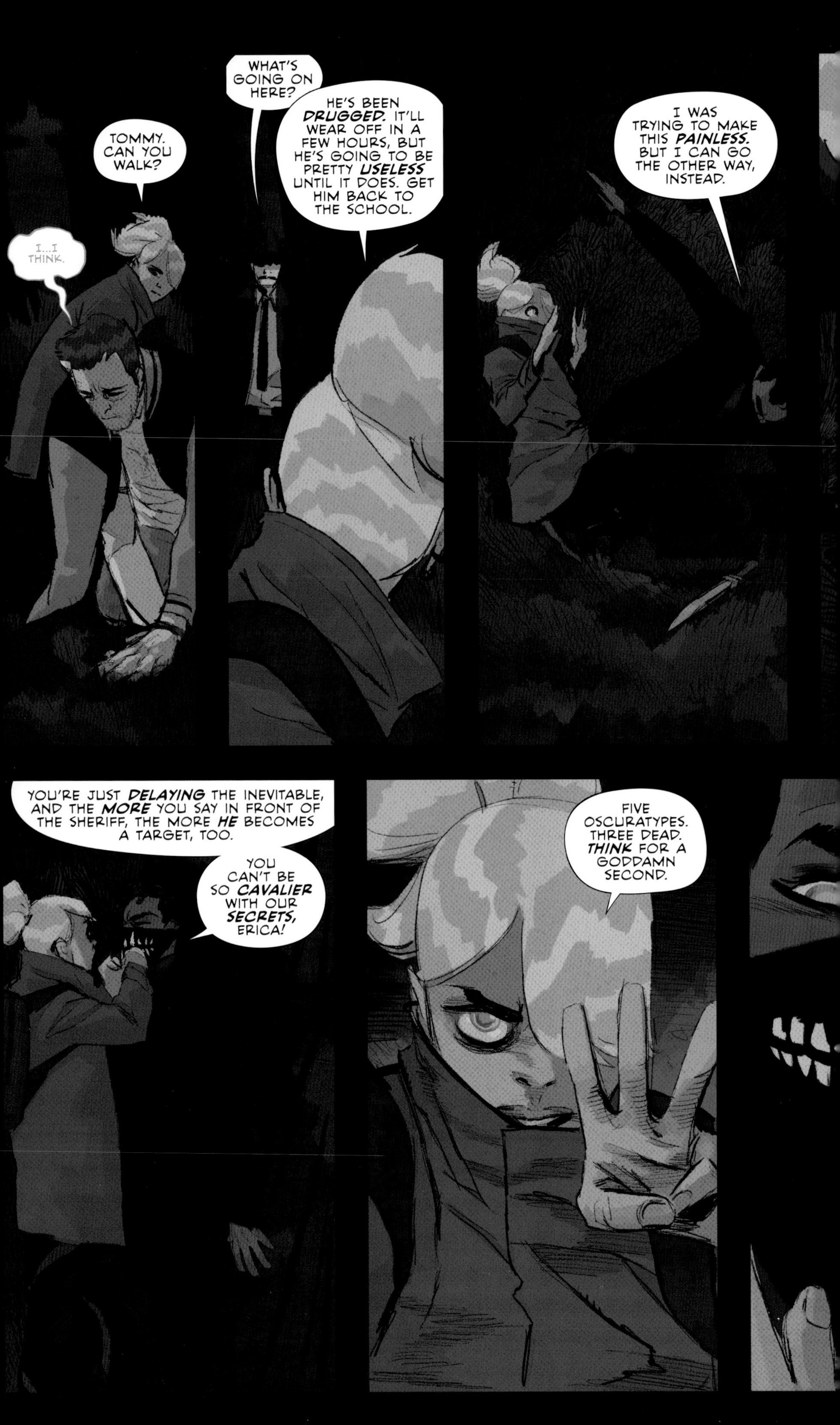
TOMMY. CAN YOU WALK?
I...I THINK.
WHAT'S GOING ON HERE?
HE'S BEEN DRUGGED. IT'LL WEAR OFF IN A FEW HOURS, BUT HE'S GOING TO BE PRETTY USELESS UNTIL IT DOES. GET HIM BACK TO THE SCHOOL.
I WAS TRYING TO MAKE THIS PAINLESS. BUT I CAN GO THE OTHER WAY, INSTEAD.
YOU'RE JUST DELAYING THE INEVITABLE, AND THE MORE YOU SAY IN FRONT OF THE SHERIFF, THE MORE HE BECOMES A TARGET, TOO.
YOU CAN'T BE SO CAVALIER WITH OUR SECRETS, ERICA!
FIVE OSCURATYPES. THREE DEAD. THINK FOR A GODDAMN SECOND.

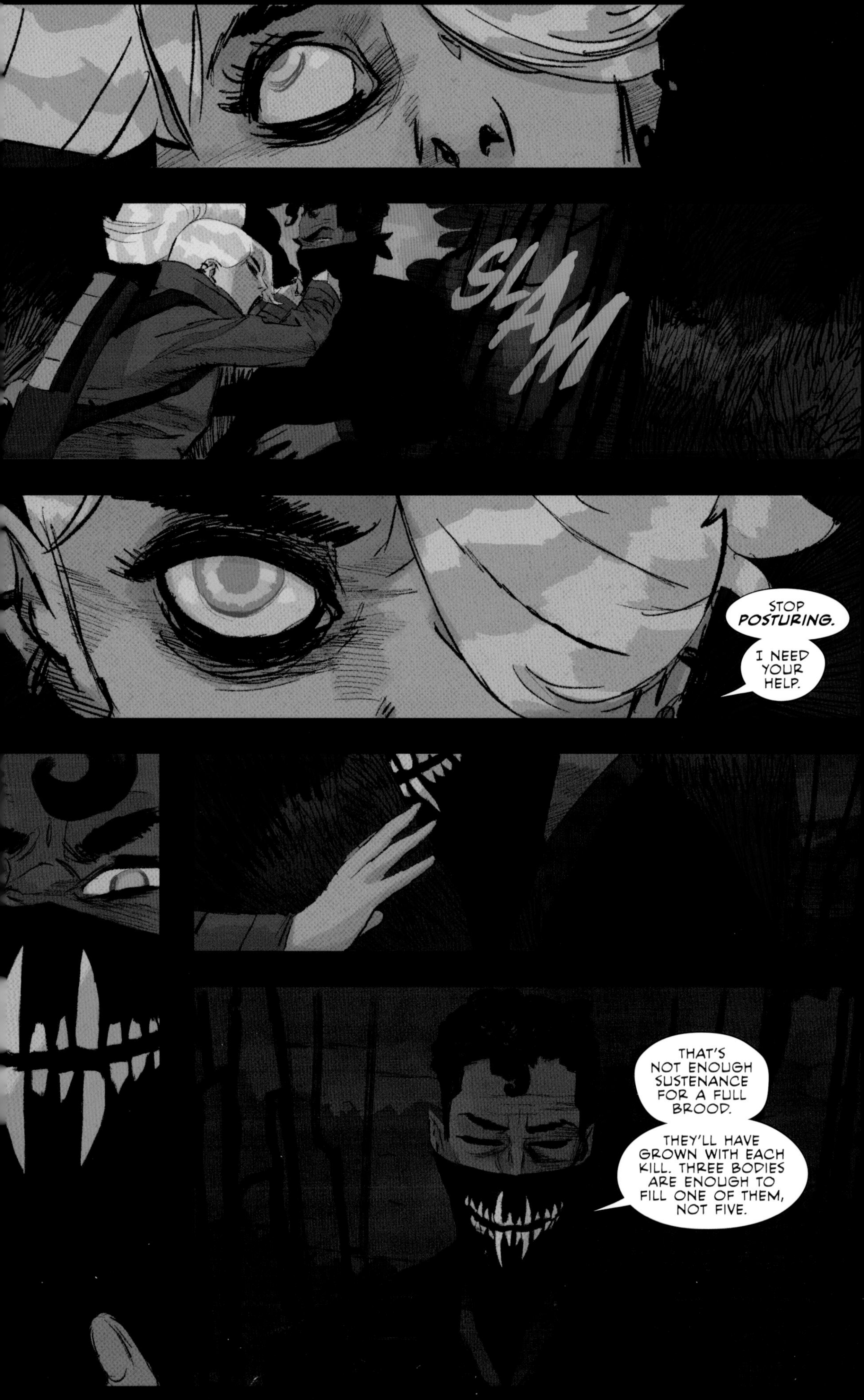
SLAM
STOP POSTURING.
I NEED YOUR HELP.
THAT'S NOT ENOUGH SUSTENANCE FOR A FULL BROOD.
THEY'LL HAVE GROWN WITH EACH KILL. THREE BODIES ARE ENOUGH TO FILL ONE OF THEM, NOT FIVE.

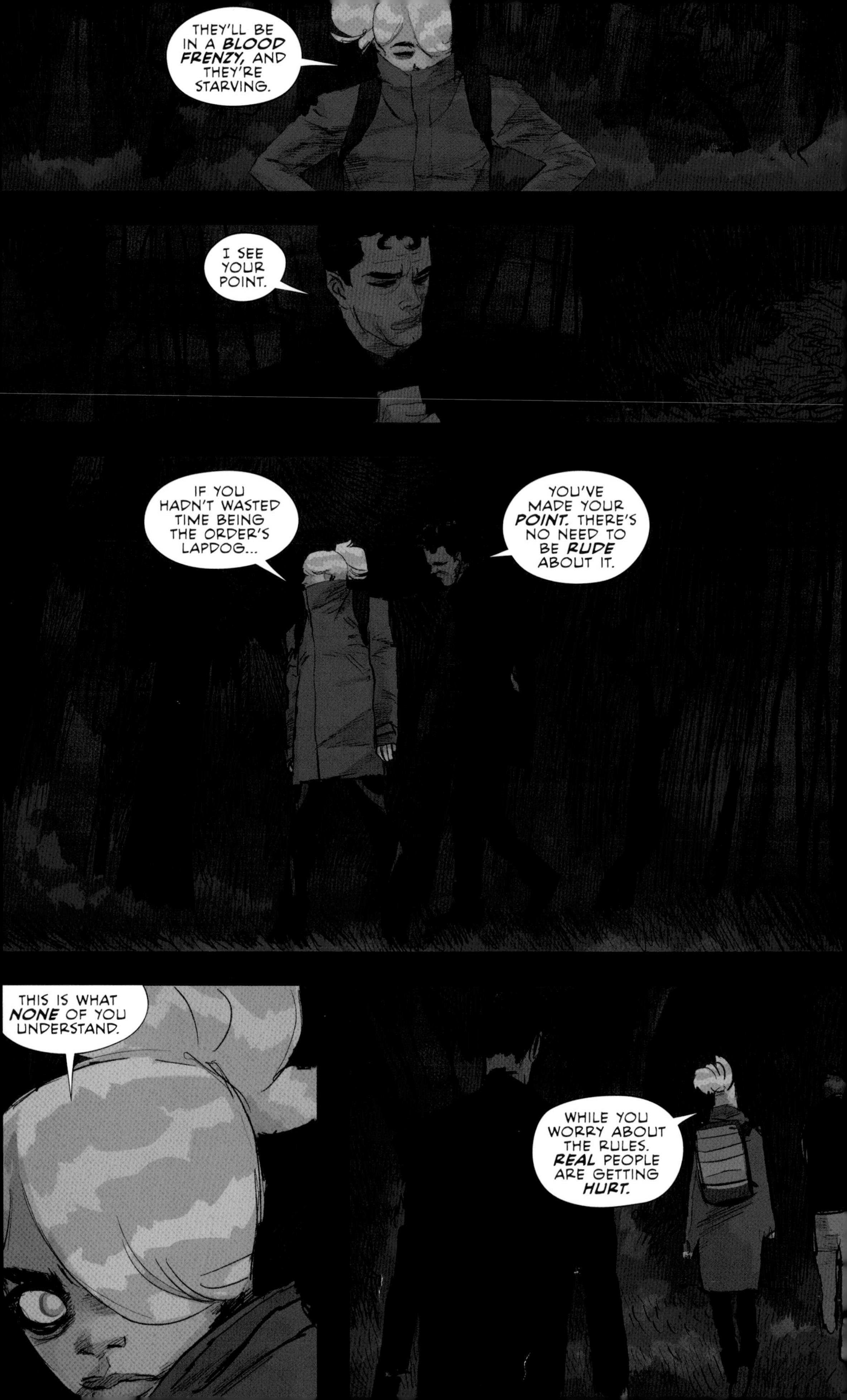
THEY'LL BE IN A BLOOD FRENZY, AND THEY'RE STARVING.
I SEE YOUR POINT.
IF YOU HADN'T WASTED TIME BEING THE ORDER'S LAPDOG...
YOU'VE MADE YOUR POINT. THERE'S NO NEED TO BE RUDE ABOUT IT.
THIS IS WHAT NONE OF YOU UNDERSTAND.
WHILE YOU WORRY ABOUT THE RULES. REAL PEOPLE ARE GETTING HURT.

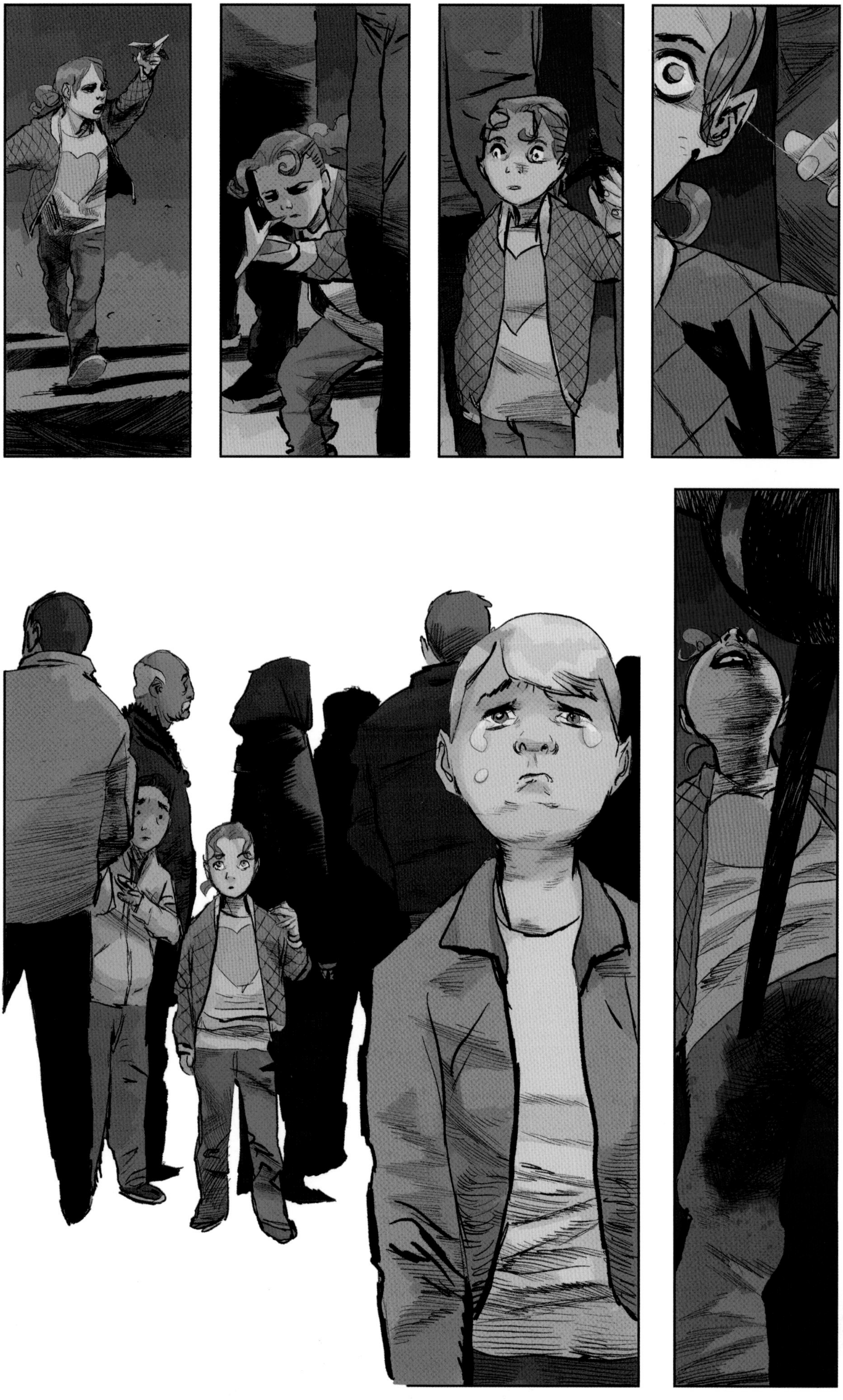

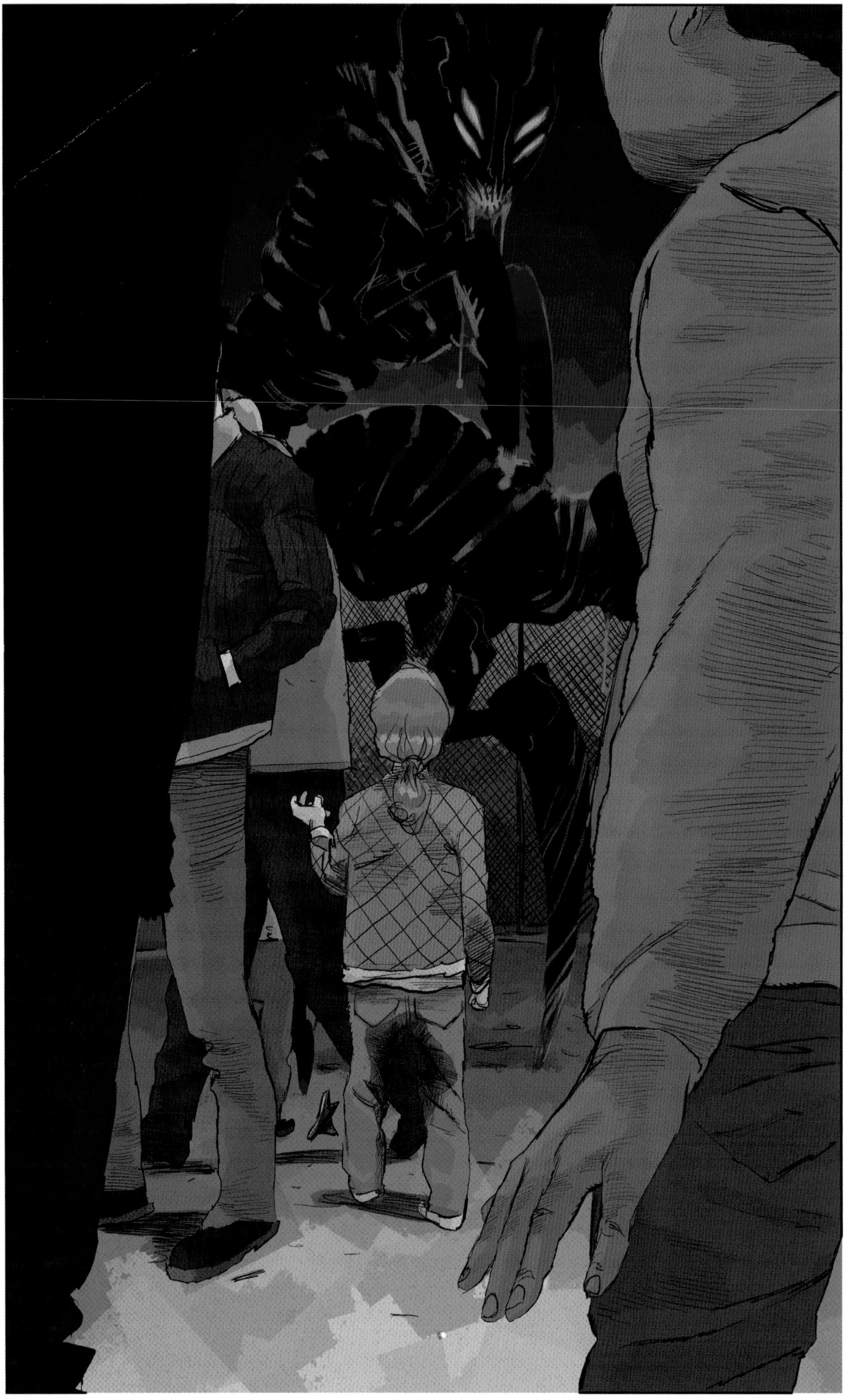

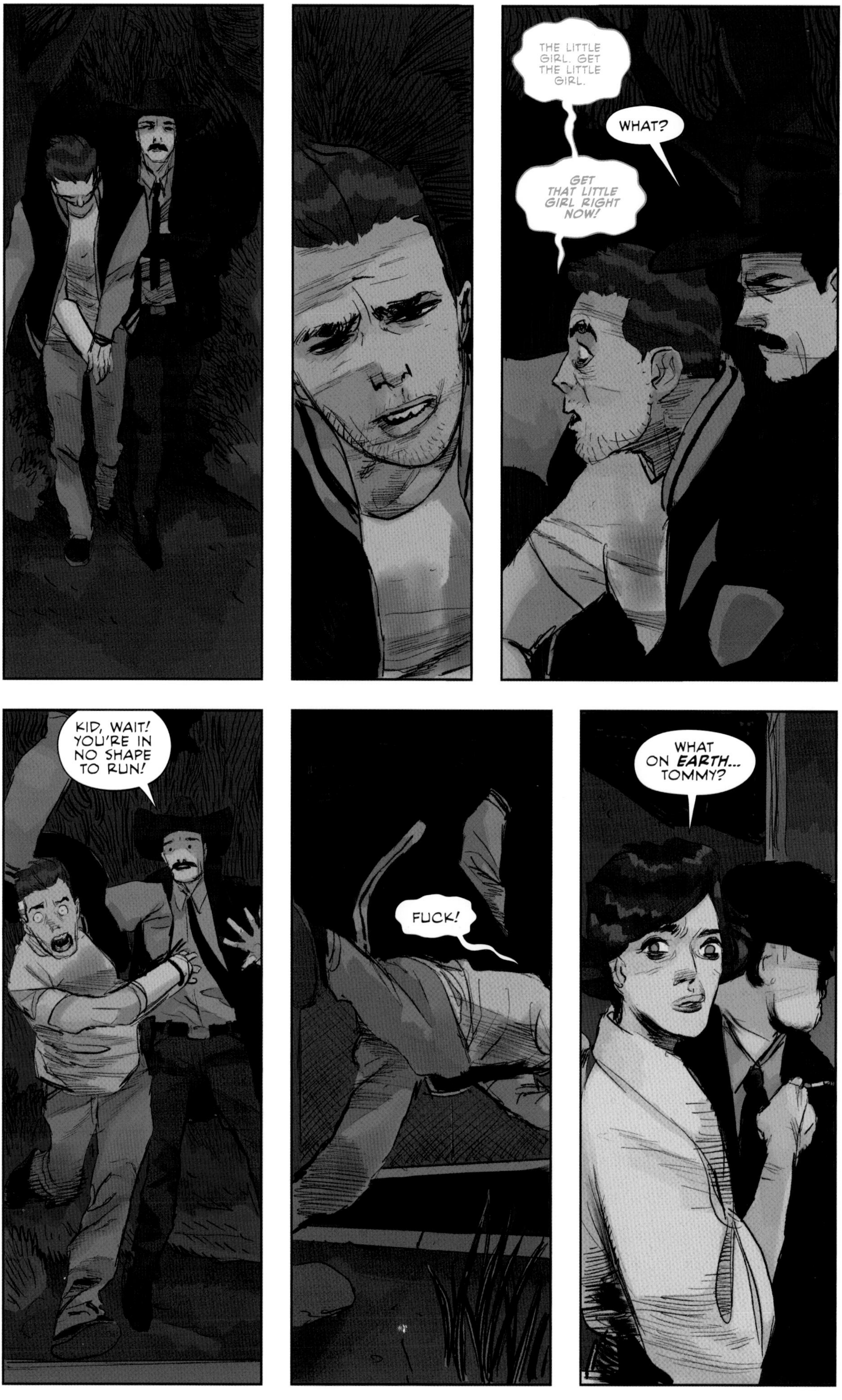
THE LITTLE GIRL. GET THE LITTLE GIRL.
WHAT?
GET THAT LITTLE GIRL RIGHT NOW!
KID, WAIT! YOU'RE IN NO SHAPE TO RUN!
FUCK!
WHAT ON EARTH... TOMMY?

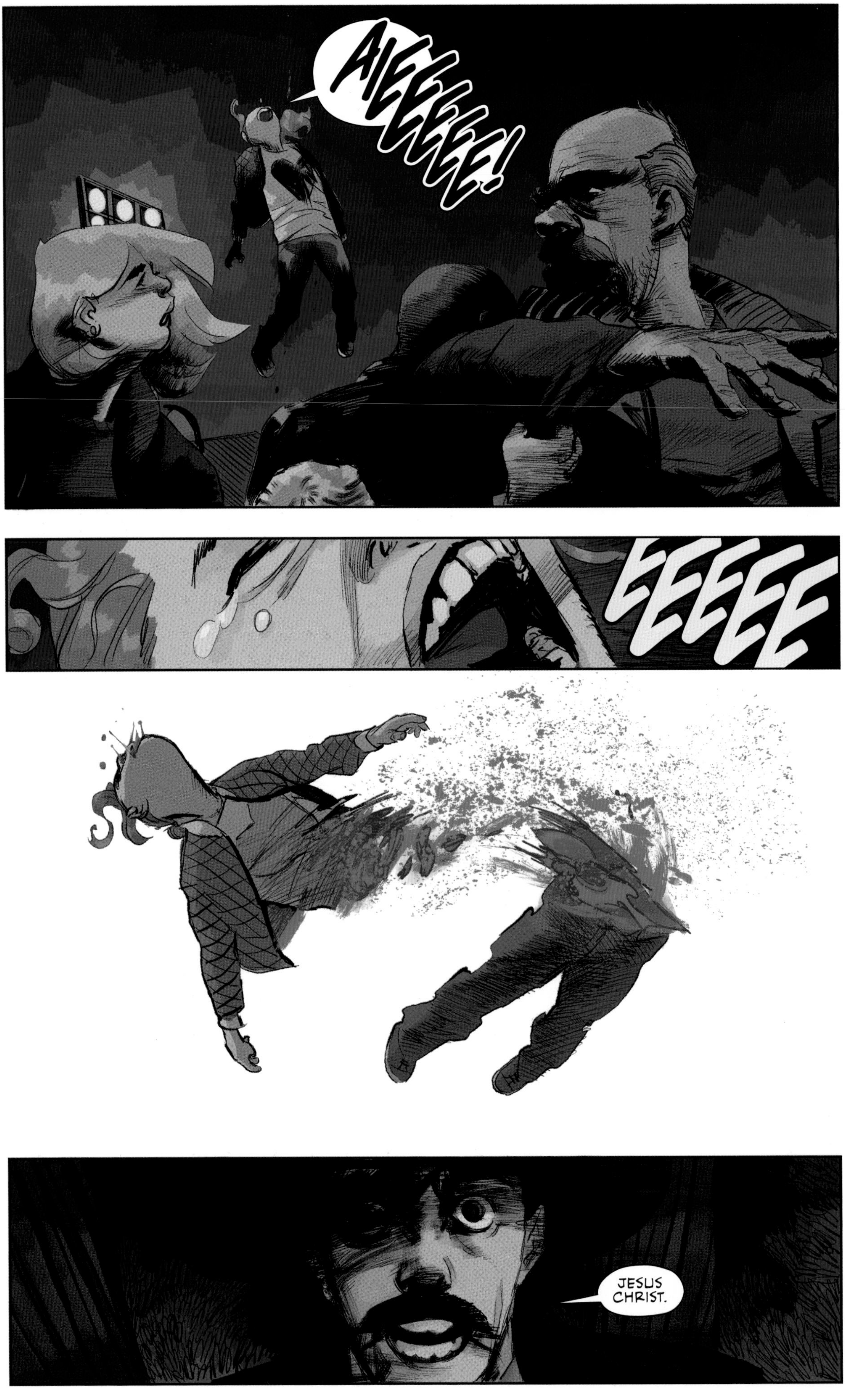
AIEEEEEE!
EEEEE
JESUS CHRIST.

I DON'T...

I DON'T UNDERSTAND.

MOM...

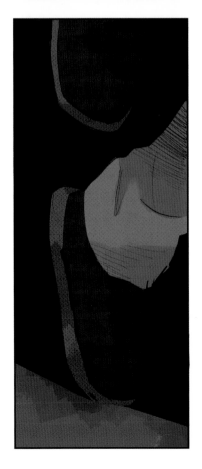

≶UNF≶

MOM, GET BACK!

THIS CAN'T BE REAL.

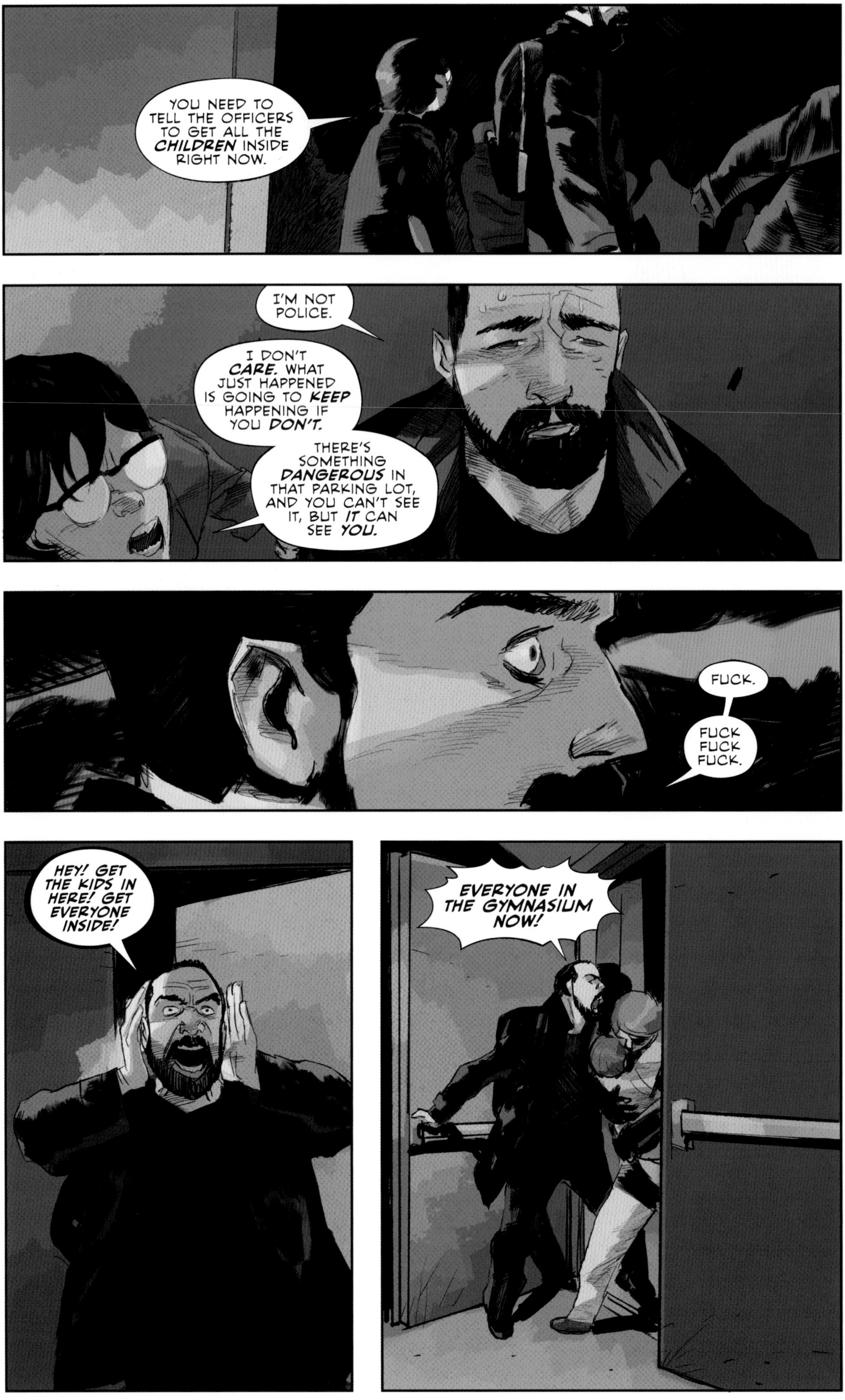
YOU NEED TO TELL THE OFFICERS TO GET ALL THE CHILDREN INSIDE RIGHT NOW.
I'M NOT POLICE.
I DON'T CARE. WHAT JUST HAPPENED IS GOING TO KEEP HAPPENING IF YOU DON'T.
THERE'S SOMETHING DANGEROUS IN THAT PARKING LOT, AND YOU CAN'T SEE IT, BUT IT CAN SEE YOU.
FUCK.
FUCK FUCK FUCK.
HEY! GET THE KIDS IN HERE! GET EVERYONE INSIDE!
EVERYONE IN THE GYMNASIUM NOW!

THIS IS BAD...THIS IS VERY BAD...

THEY'RE GOING TO START *MELEE KILLING*. EVERYONE'S SO AFRAID, IT DOESN'T MATTER THAT THEY CAN'T SEE THEM.

YOU BROUGHT THE BOY?

WHAT?

THE BOY FROM THE HOSPITAL?

YES.

YOU NEED TO GET HIM FAR *AWAY* FROM HERE. GET THE GIRL AS WELL. YOU'LL BE ABLE TO DRAW THEM INTO A *TRAP.*

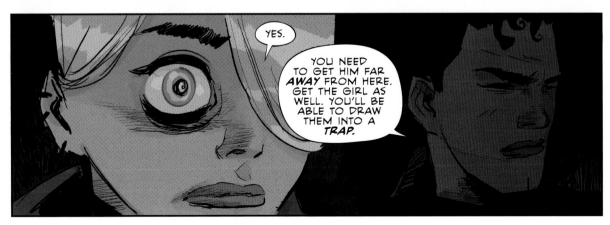

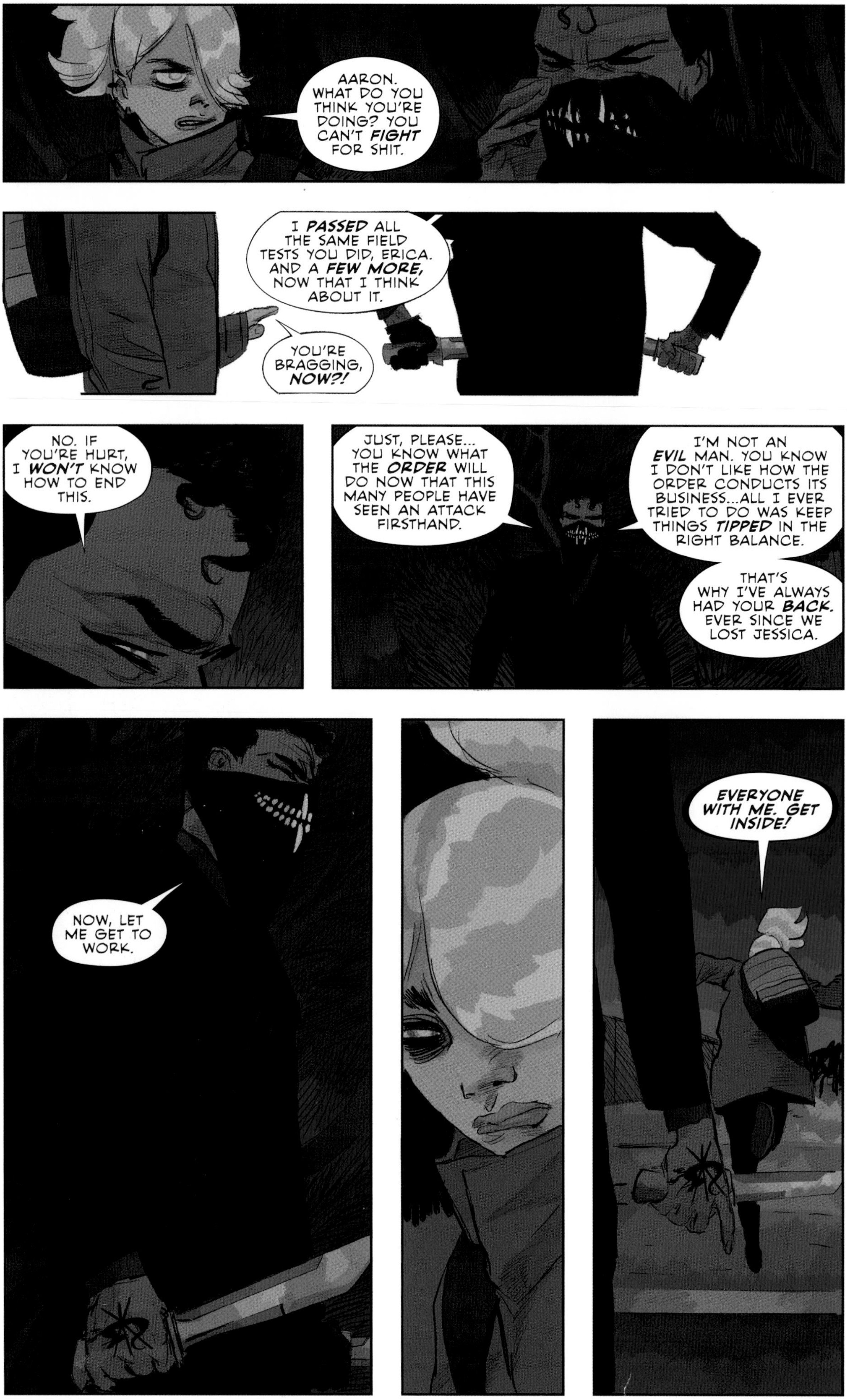
AARON. WHAT DO YOU THINK YOU'RE DOING? YOU CAN'T *FIGHT* FOR SHIT.
I *PASSED* ALL THE SAME FIELD TESTS YOU DID, ERICA. AND A *FEW MORE*, NOW THAT I THINK ABOUT IT.
YOU'RE BRAGGING, *NOW?!*
NO. IF YOU'RE HURT, I *WON'T* KNOW HOW TO END THIS.
JUST, PLEASE... YOU KNOW WHAT THE *ORDER* WILL DO NOW THAT THIS MANY PEOPLE HAVE SEEN AN ATTACK FIRSTHAND.
I'M NOT AN *EVIL* MAN. YOU KNOW I DON'T LIKE HOW THE ORDER CONDUCTS ITS BUSINESS...ALL I EVER TRIED TO DO WAS KEEP THINGS *TIPPED* IN THE RIGHT BALANCE.
THAT'S WHY I'VE ALWAYS HAD YOUR *BACK.* EVER SINCE WE LOST JESSICA.
NOW, LET ME GET TO WORK.
EVERYONE WITH ME. GET INSIDE!

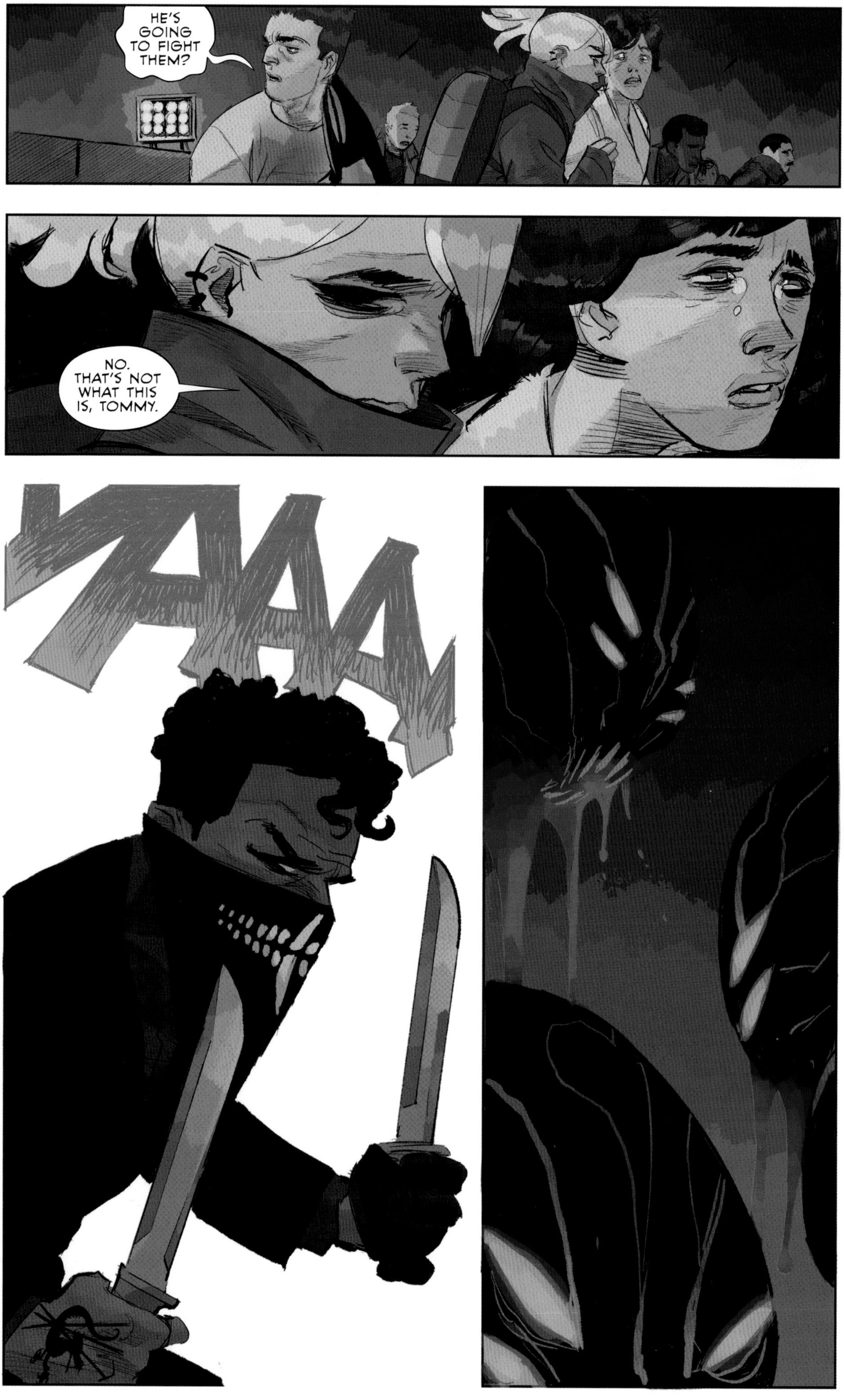
HE'S GOING TO FIGHT THEM?
NO. THAT'S NOT WHAT THIS IS, TOMMY.
YAAA

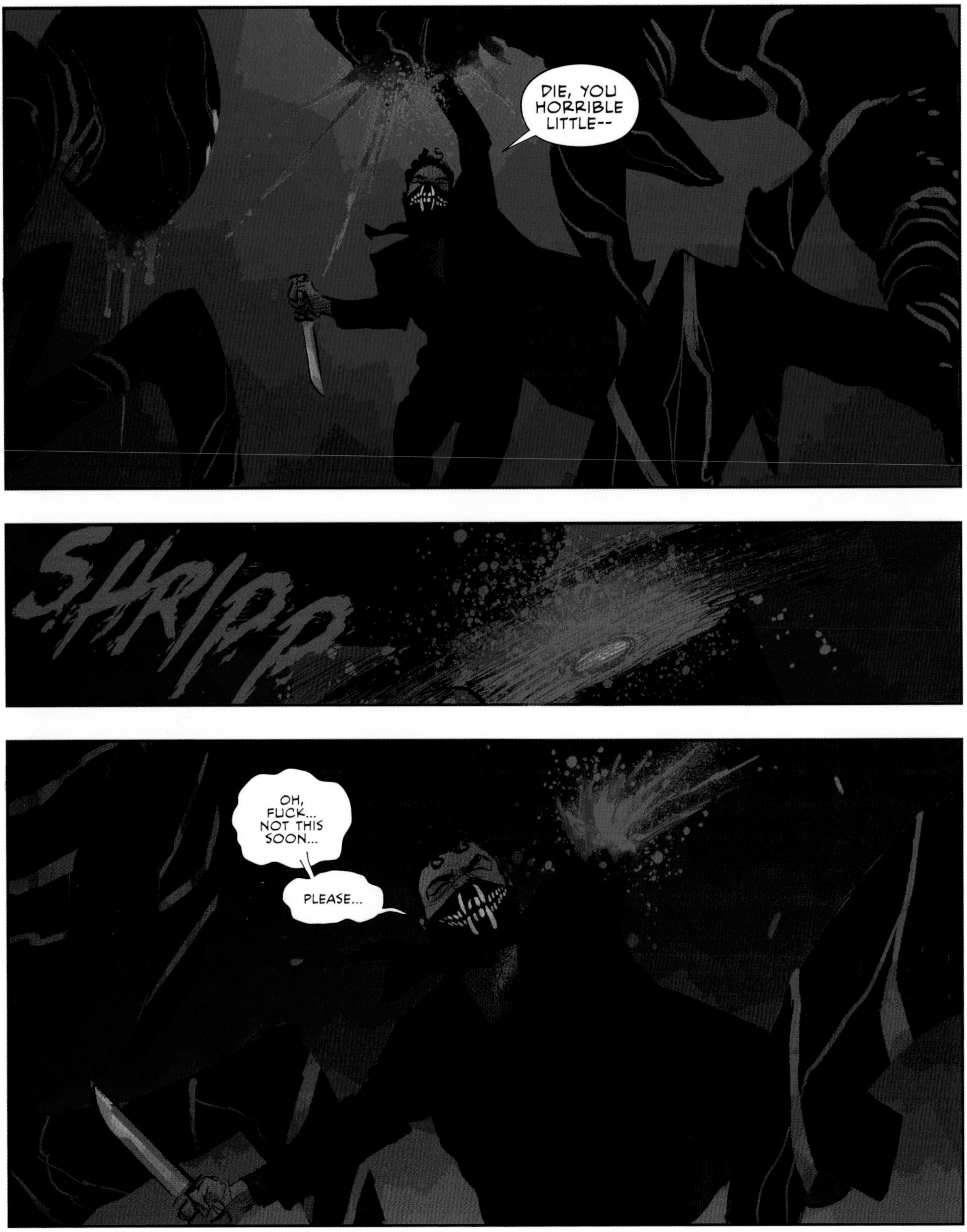
DIE, YOU HORRIBLE LITTLE--
SHRIPP
OH, FUCK... NOT THIS SOON...
PLEASE...

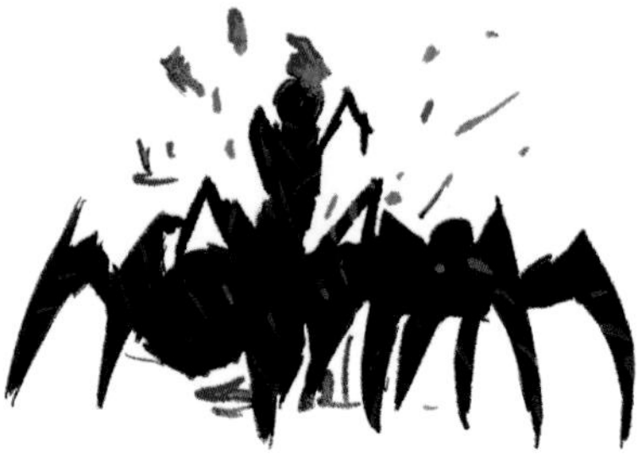

CHAPTER ELEVEN

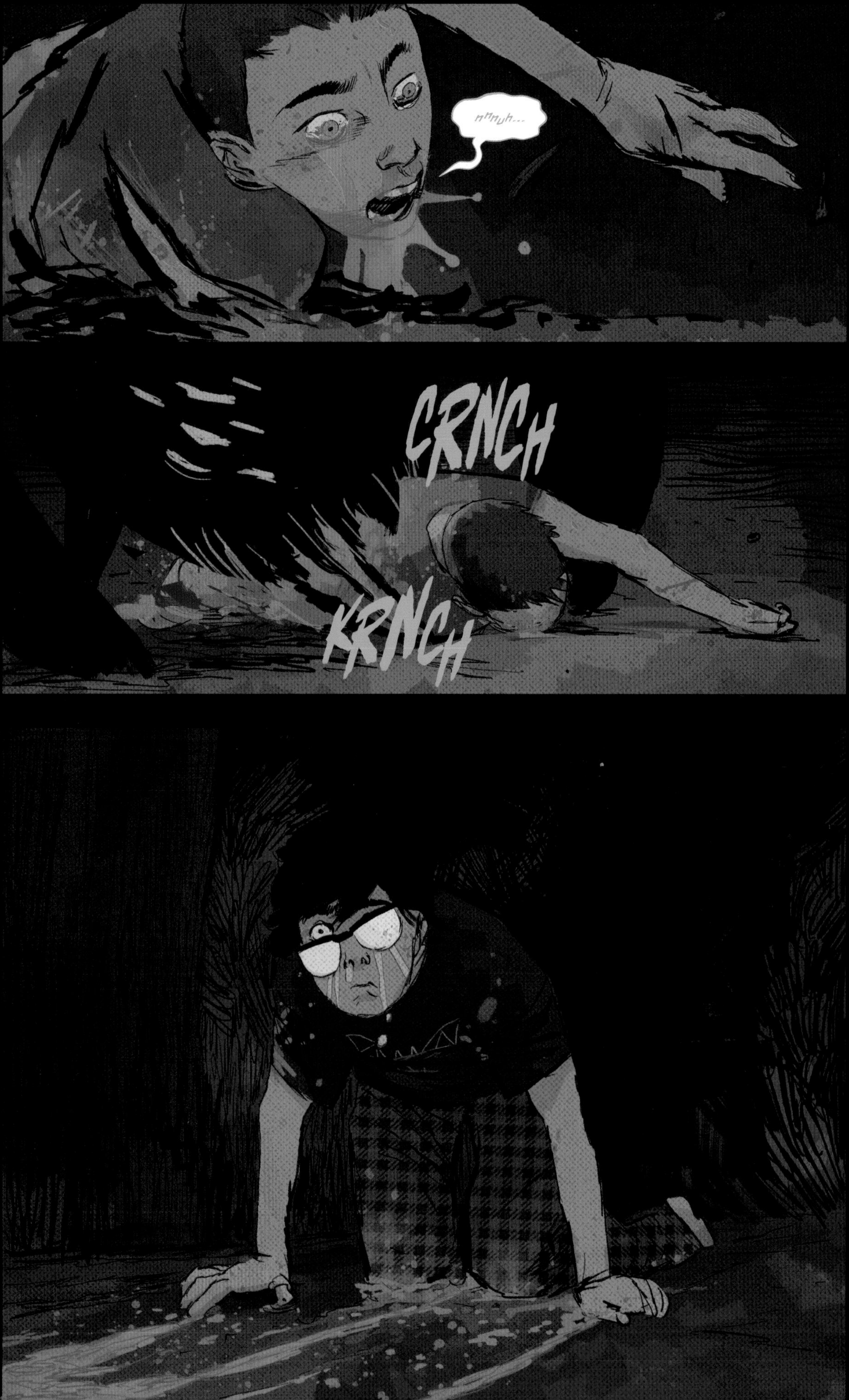
MMMUH...
CRNCH
KRNCH

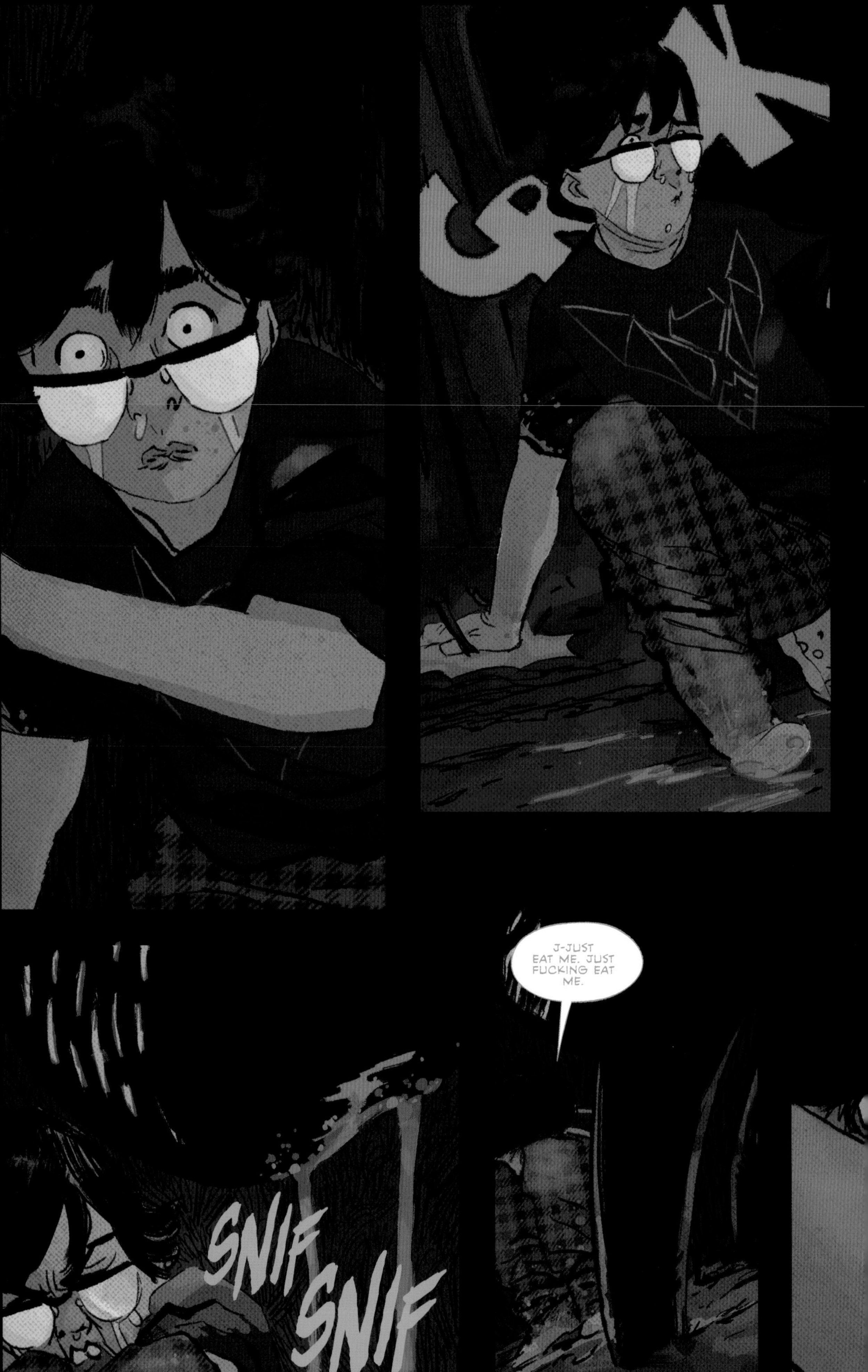
J-JUST EAT ME. JUST FUCKING EAT ME.
SNIF SNIF

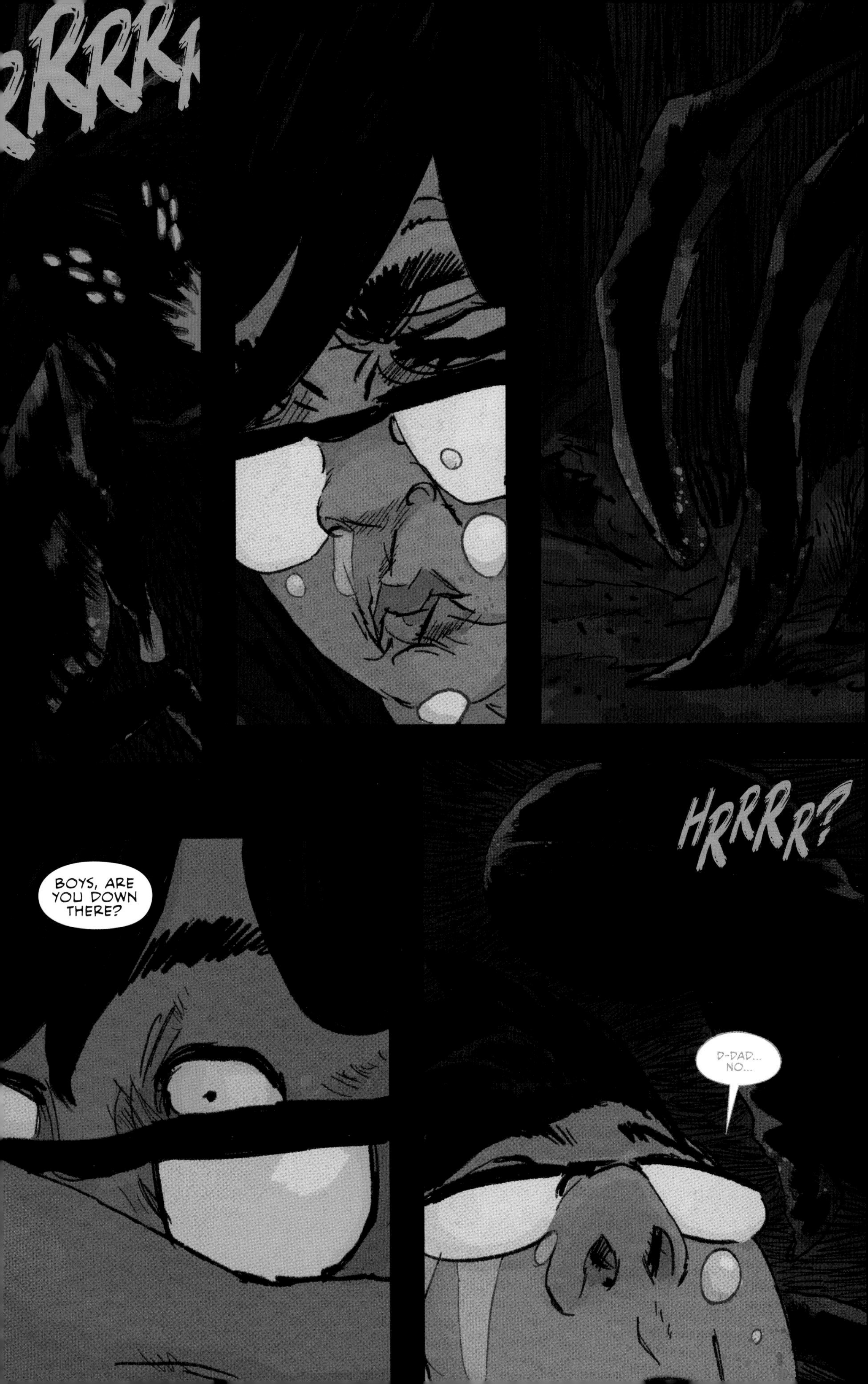
RRRR
BOYS, ARE YOU DOWN THERE?
HRRRR?
D-DAD... NO...

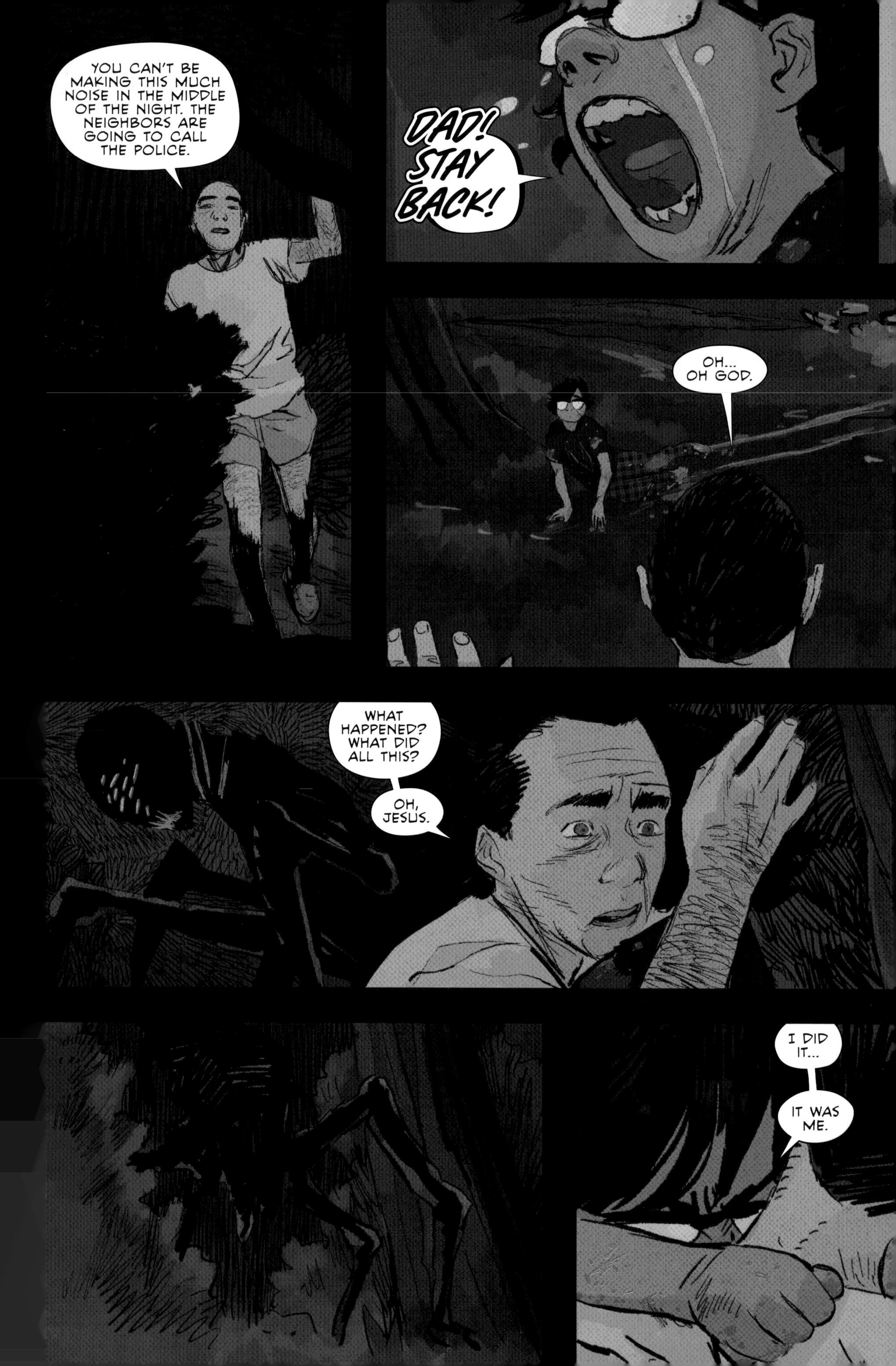
YOU CAN'T BE MAKING THIS MUCH NOISE IN THE MIDDLE OF THE NIGHT. THE NEIGHBORS ARE GOING TO CALL THE POLICE.
DAD! STAY BACK!
OH... OH GOD.
WHAT HAPPENED? WHAT DID ALL THIS?
OH, JESUS.
I DID IT...
IT WAS ME.

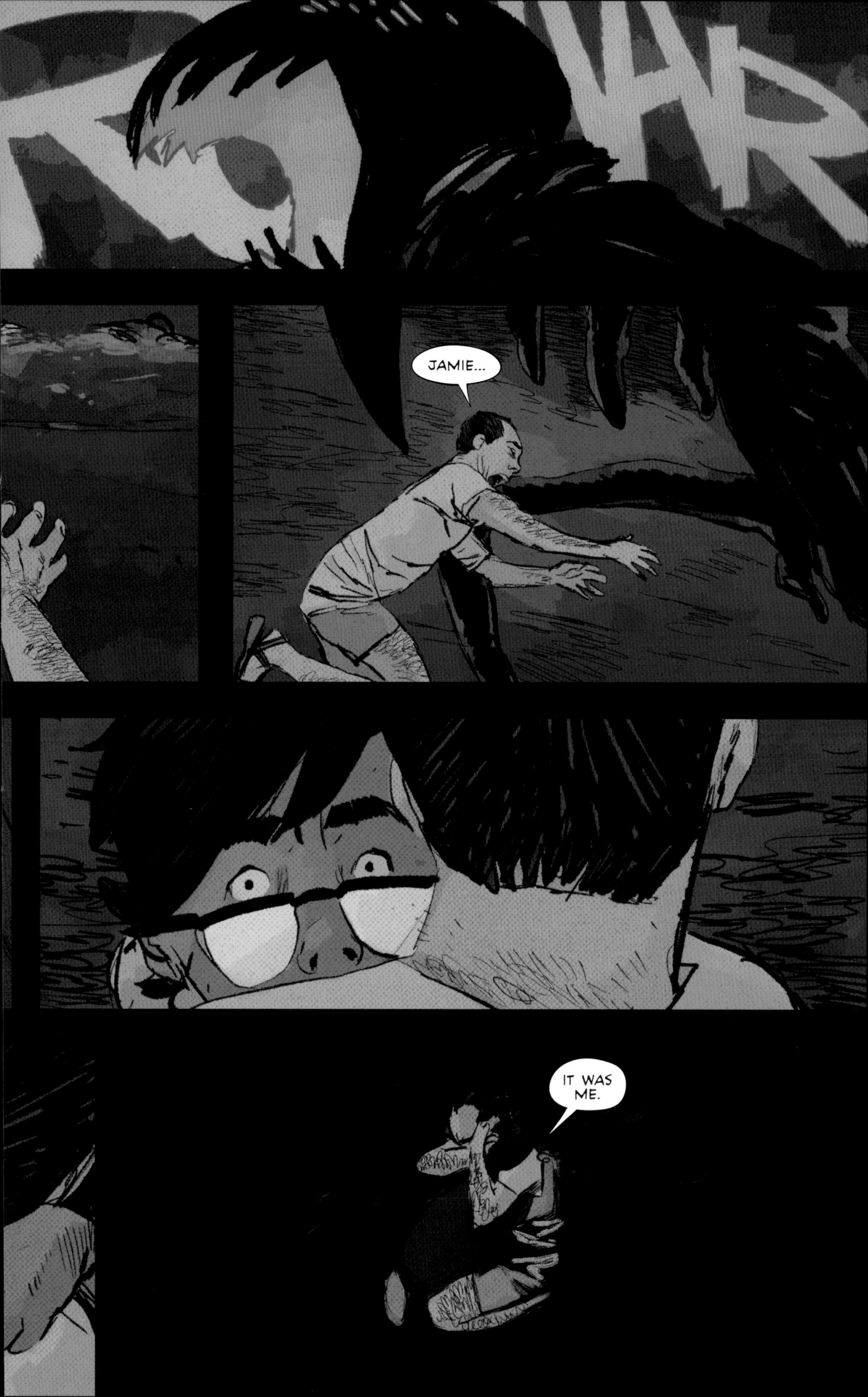
JAMIE...
IT WAS ME.

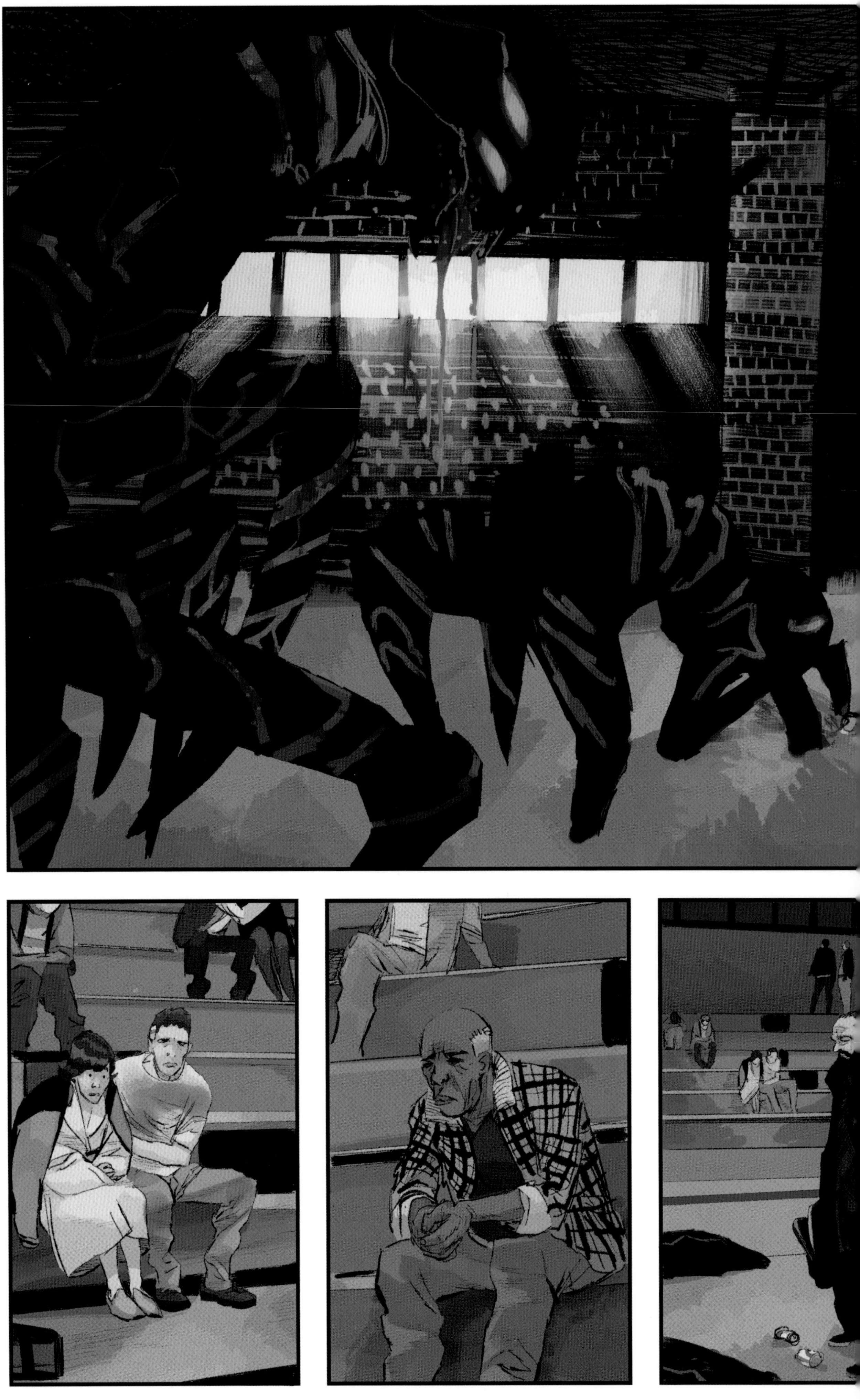

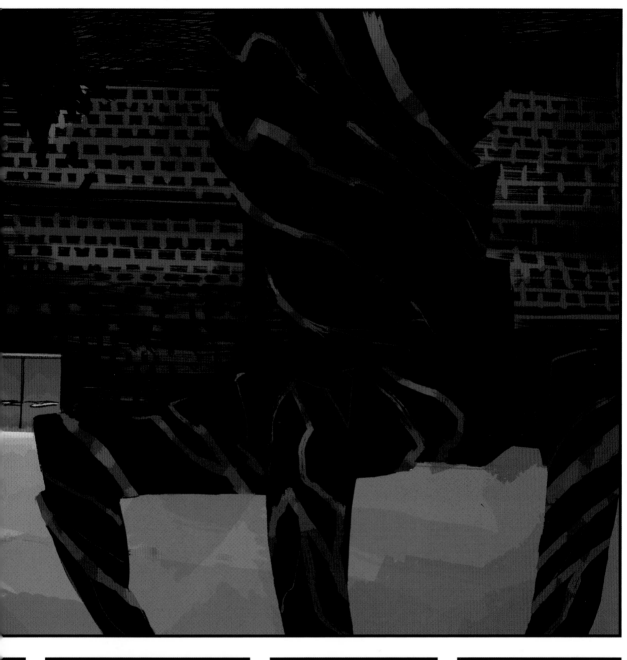

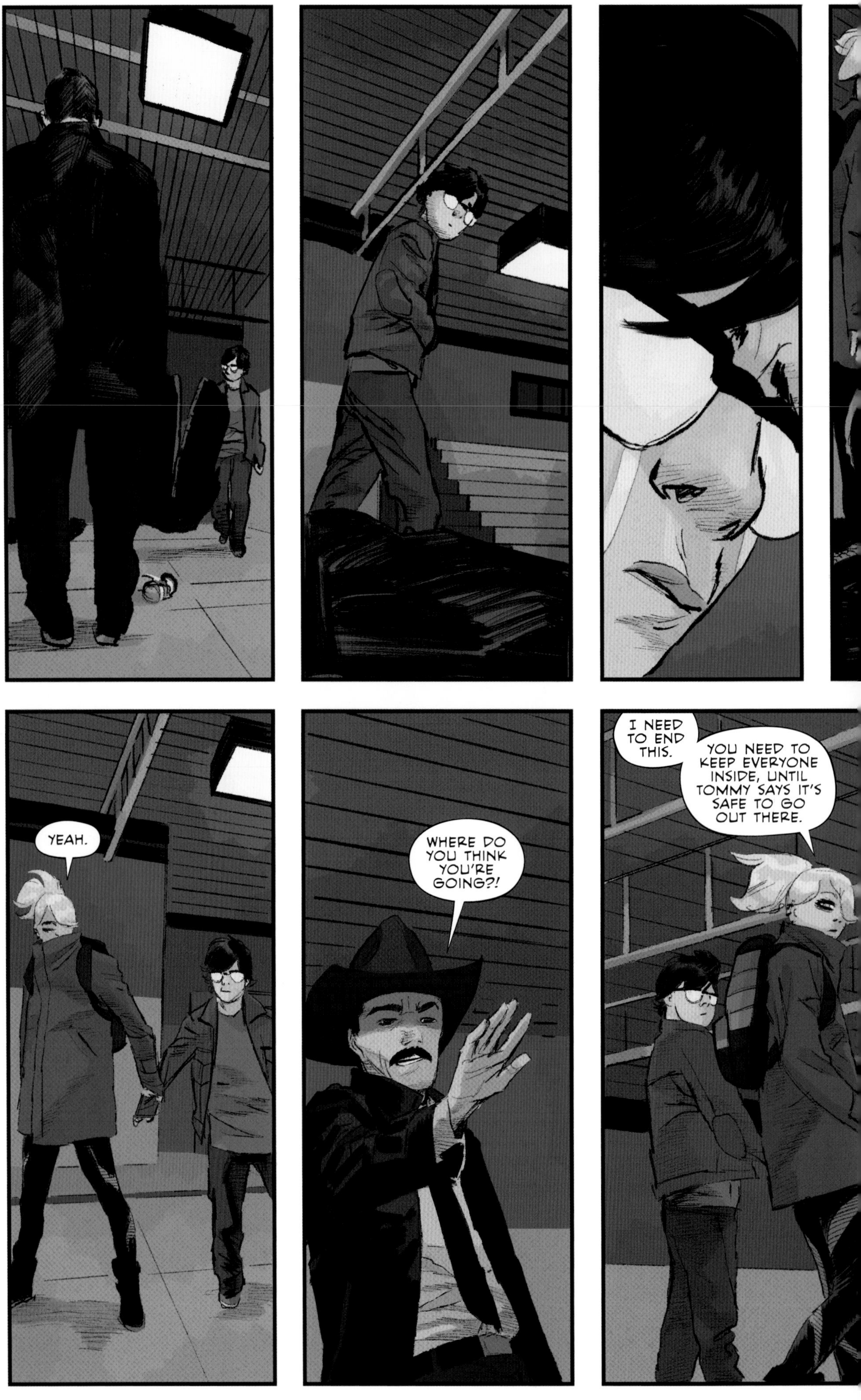
YEAH.
WHERE DO YOU THINK YOU'RE GOING?!
I NEED TO END THIS.
YOU NEED TO KEEP EVERYONE INSIDE, UNTIL TOMMY SAYS IT'S SAFE TO GO OUT THERE.

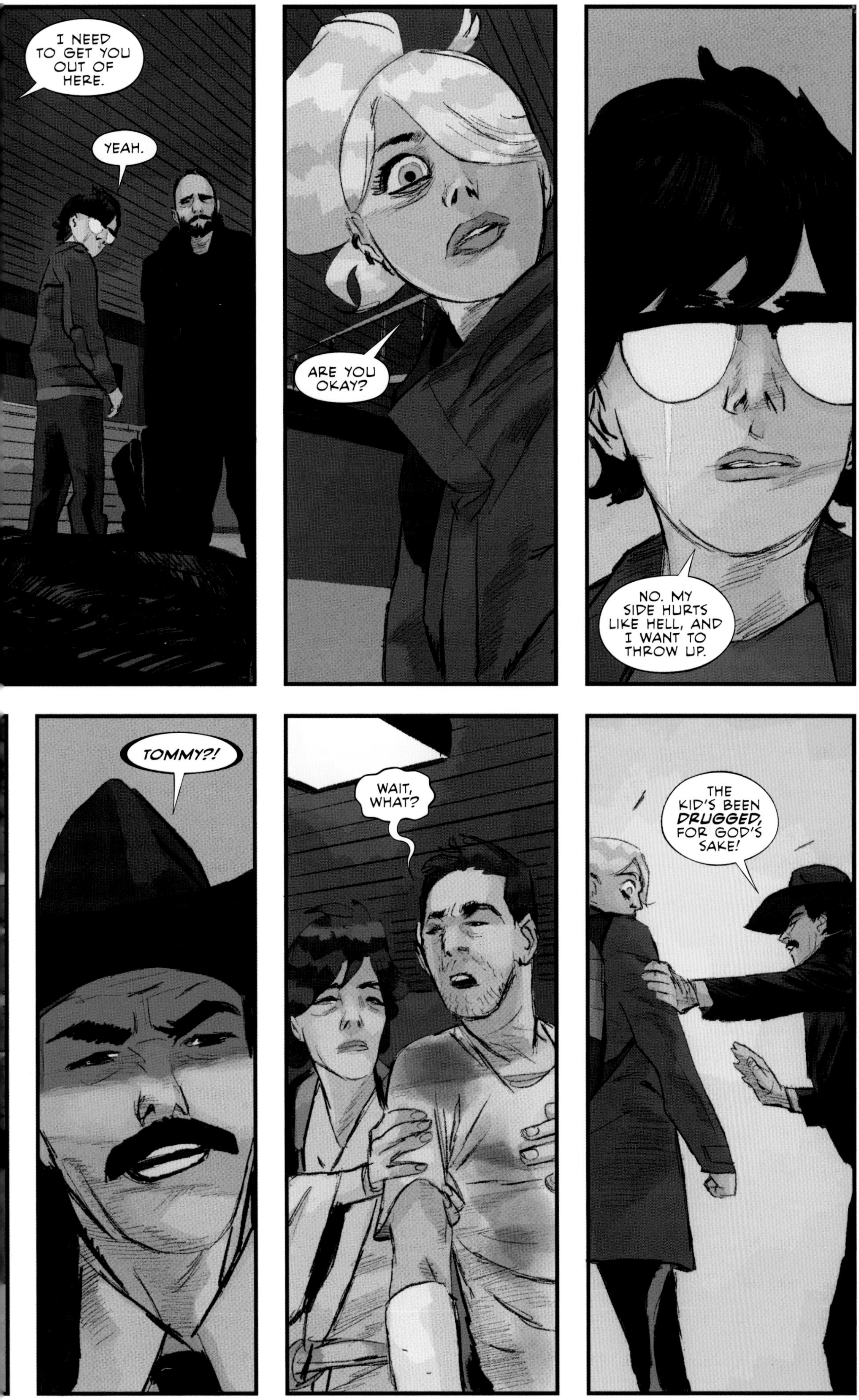
I NEED TO GET YOU OUT OF HERE.
YEAH.
ARE YOU OKAY?
NO. MY SIDE HURTS LIKE HELL, AND I WANT TO THROW UP.
TOMMY?!
WAIT, WHAT?
THE KID'S BEEN DRUGGED, FOR GOD'S SAKE!

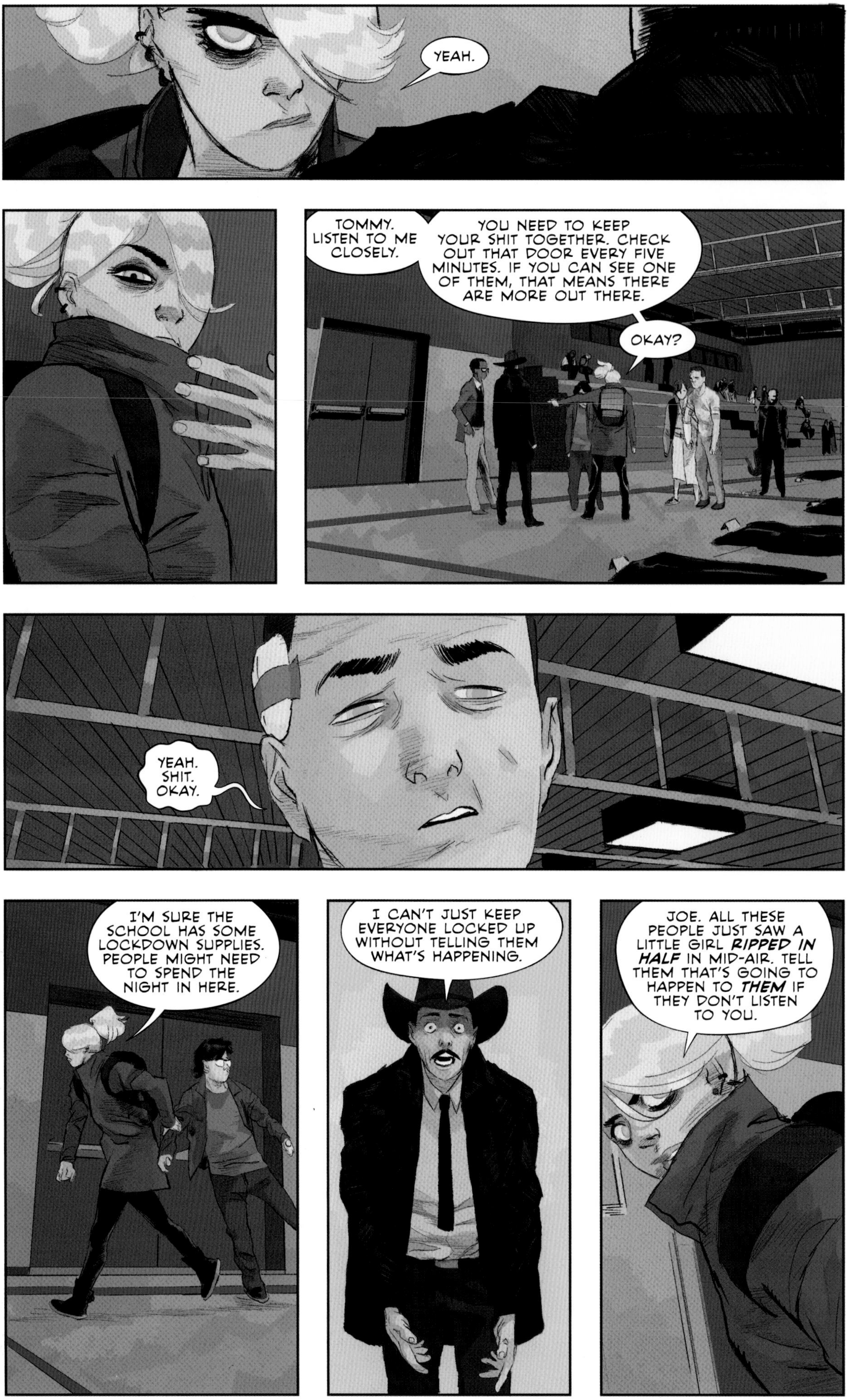
YEAH.
TOMMY. LISTEN TO ME CLOSELY.
YOU NEED TO KEEP YOUR SHIT TOGETHER. CHECK OUT THAT DOOR EVERY FIVE MINUTES. IF YOU CAN SEE ONE OF THEM, THAT MEANS THERE ARE MORE OUT THERE.
OKAY?
YEAH. SHIT. OKAY.
I'M SURE THE SCHOOL HAS SOME LOCKDOWN SUPPLIES. PEOPLE MIGHT NEED TO SPEND THE NIGHT IN HERE.
I CAN'T JUST KEEP EVERYONE LOCKED UP WITHOUT TELLING THEM WHAT'S HAPPENING.
JOE. ALL THESE PEOPLE JUST SAW A LITTLE GIRL RIPPED IN HALF IN MID-AIR. TELL THEM THAT'S GOING TO HAPPEN TO THEM IF THEY DON'T LISTEN TO YOU.

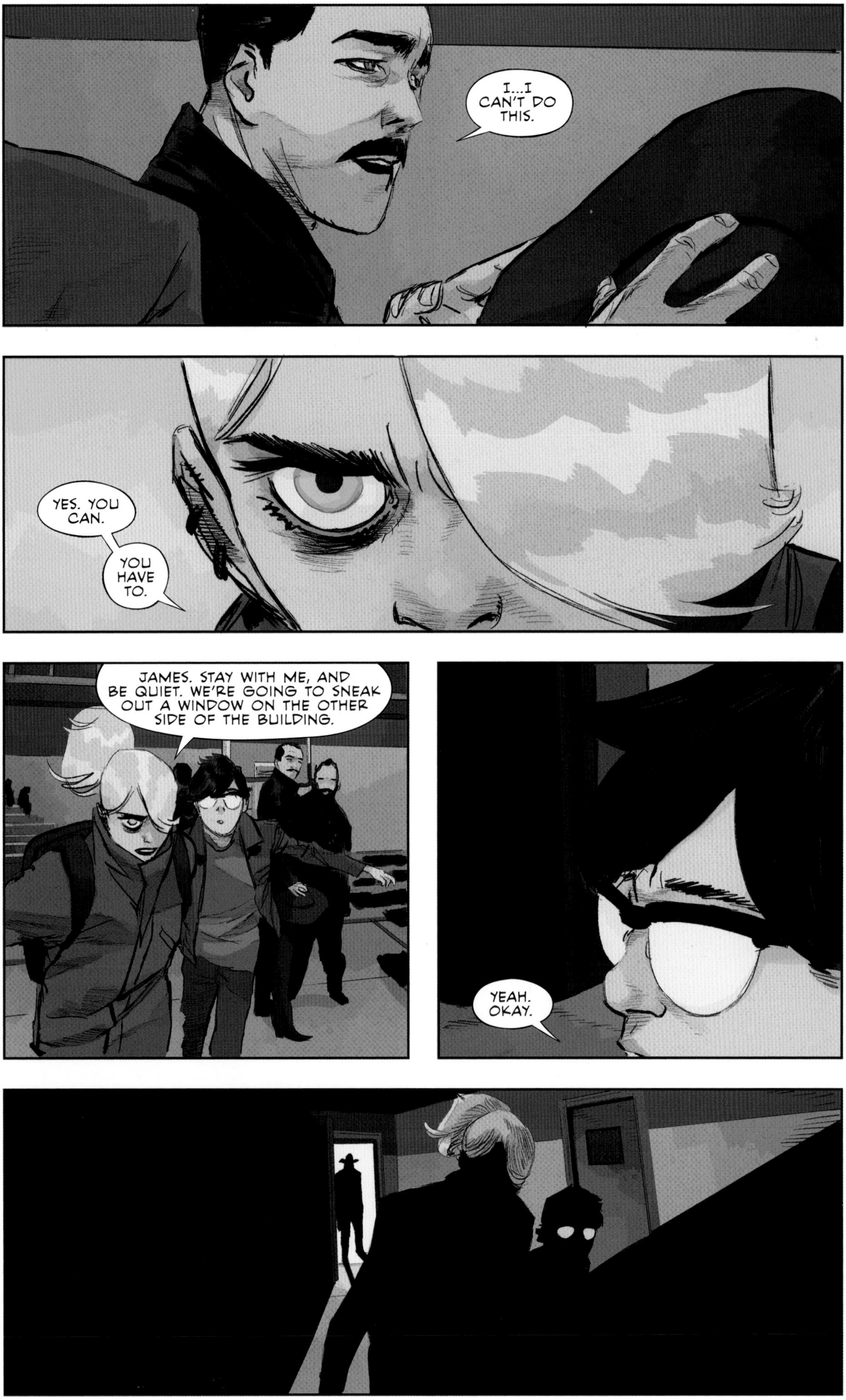
I...I CAN'T DO THIS.
YES. YOU CAN.
YOU HAVE TO.
JAMES. STAY WITH ME, AND BE QUIET. WE'RE GOING TO SNEAK OUT A WINDOW ON THE OTHER SIDE OF THE BUILDING.
YEAH. OKAY.

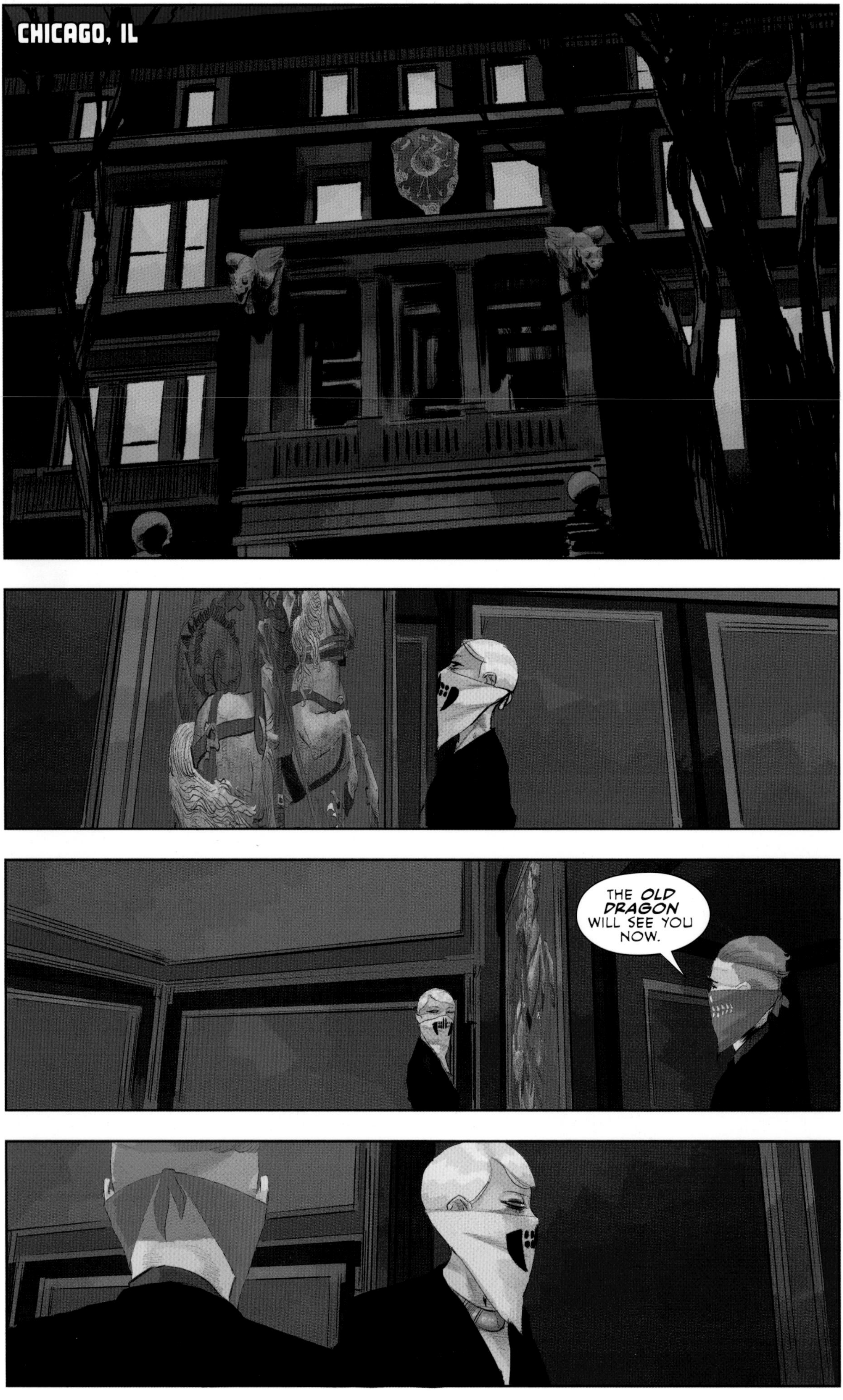
CHICAGO, IL
THE OLD DRAGON WILL SEE YOU NOW.

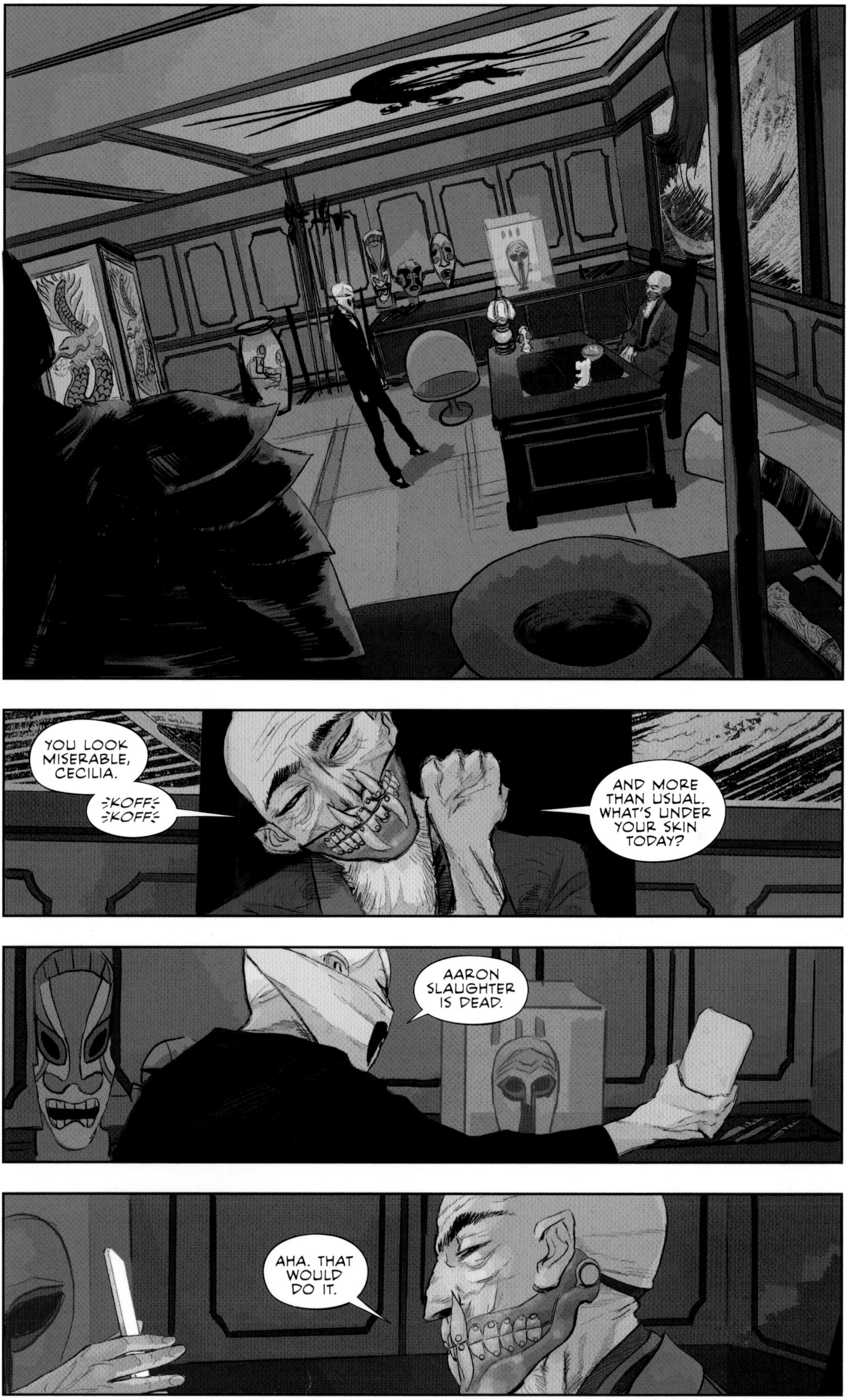
YOU LOOK MISERABLE, CECILIA.
KOFF KOFF
AND MORE THAN USUAL. WHAT'S UNDER YOUR SKIN TODAY?
AARON SLAUGHTER IS DEAD.
AHA. THAT WOULD DO IT.

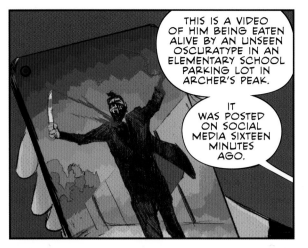

THIS IS A VIDEO OF HIM BEING EATEN ALIVE BY AN UNSEEN OSCURATYPE IN AN ELEMENTARY SCHOOL PARKING LOT IN ARCHER'S PEAK.

IT WAS POSTED ON SOCIAL MEDIA SIXTEEN MINUTES AGO.

IT WAS POSTED SHORTLY AFTER FOOTAGE OF A YOUNG GIRL BEING RIPPED IN HALF MADE ITS WAY ONTO FACEBOOK.

THIS IS ALONGSIDE CHATTER OF BEING TRAPPED IN EITHER A MORGUE OR A SCHOOL GYMNASIUM.

OUR FRIENDS IN SILICON VALLEY HAVE HELPED CONTAIN THE POSTS. BUT I THINK WE NEED TO BE MORE AGGRESSIVE.

AGREED. WE'LL NEED FULL CONTAINMENT. BLACKOUT. NO INTERNET. NO CELLULAR CONNECTION.

ALREADY UNDERWAY.

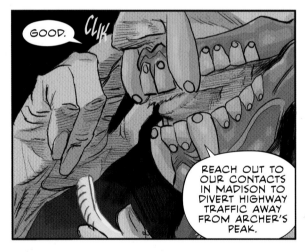

GOOD. CLIK

REACH OUT TO OUR CONTACTS IN MADISON TO DIVERT HIGHWAY TRAFFIC AWAY FROM ARCHER'S PEAK.

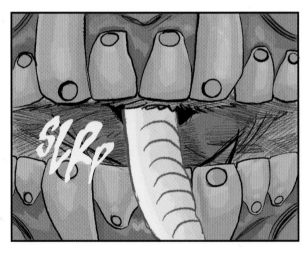

SLRP

YOU TAKE POINT. BRING A FULL TEAM.

TLAC

YES SIR.

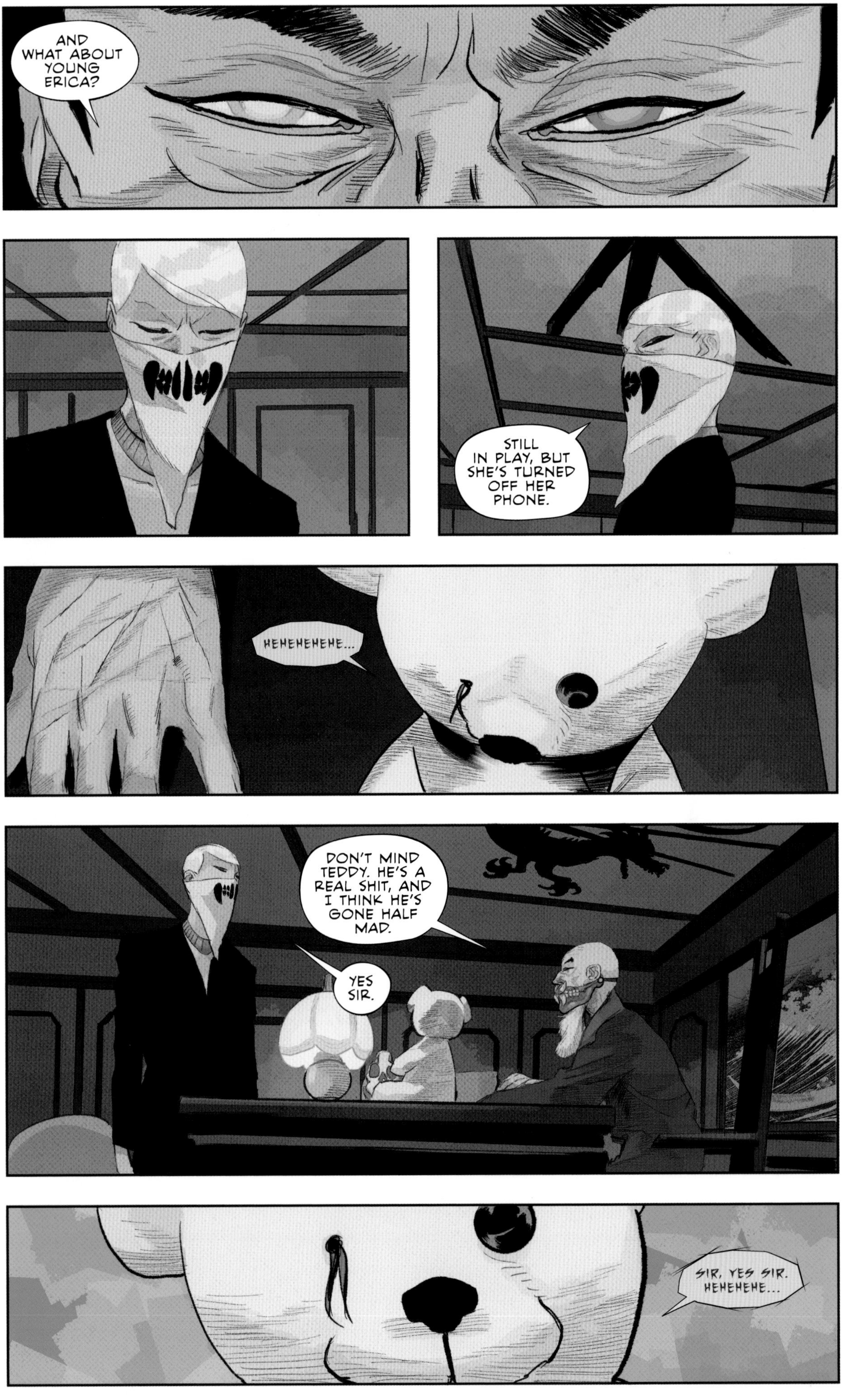
AND WHAT ABOUT YOUNG ERICA?
STILL IN PLAY, BUT SHE'S TURNED OFF HER PHONE.
HEHEHEHEHE...
DON'T MIND TEDDY. HE'S A REAL SHIT, AND I THINK HE'S GONE HALF MAD.
YES SIR.
SIR, YES SIR. HEHEHEHE...

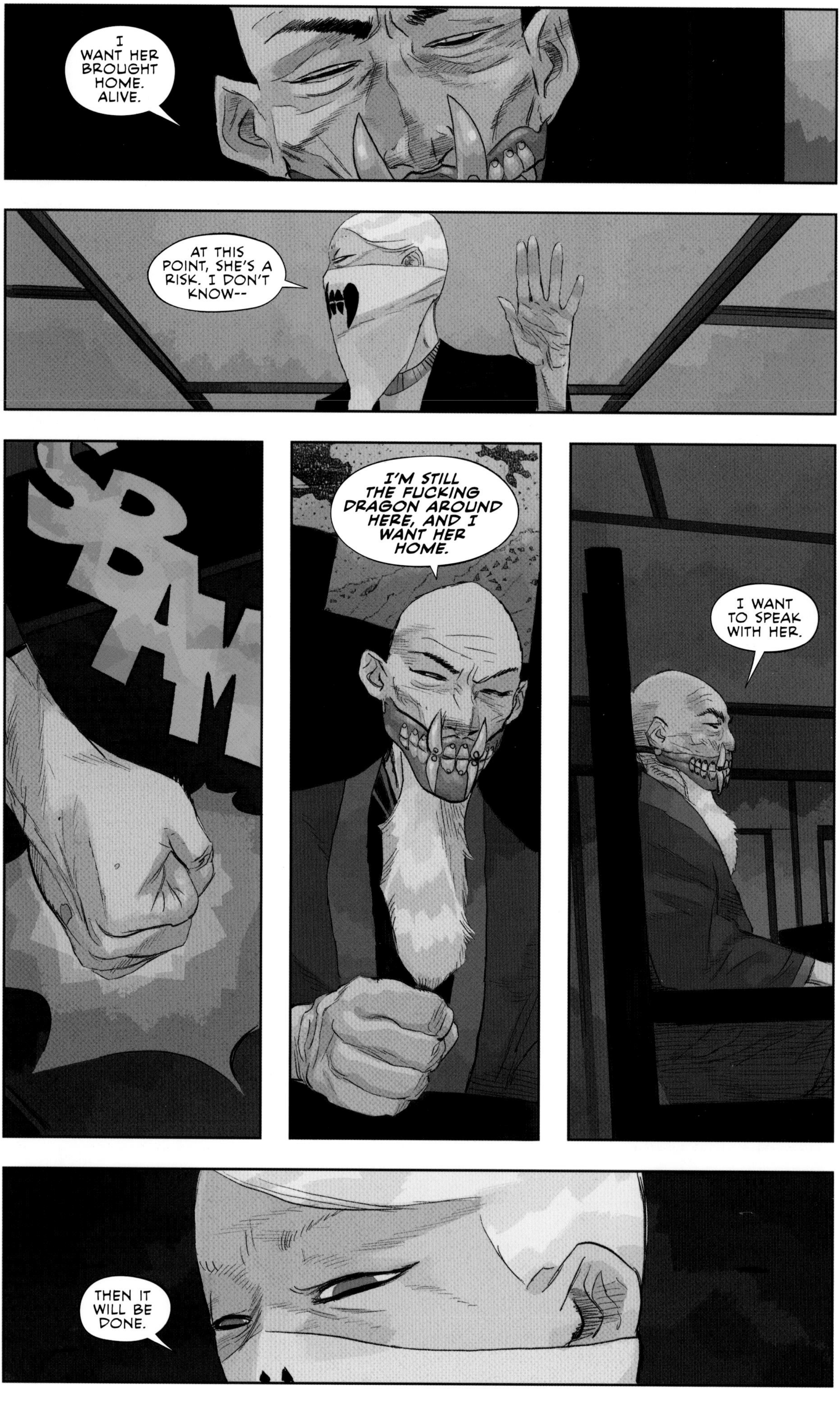
I WANT HER BROUGHT HOME. ALIVE.
AT THIS POINT, SHE'S A RISK. I DON'T KNOW--
SBAM
I'M STILL THE FUCKING DRAGON AROUND HERE, AND I WANT HER HOME.
I WANT TO SPEAK WITH HER.
THEN IT WILL BE DONE.

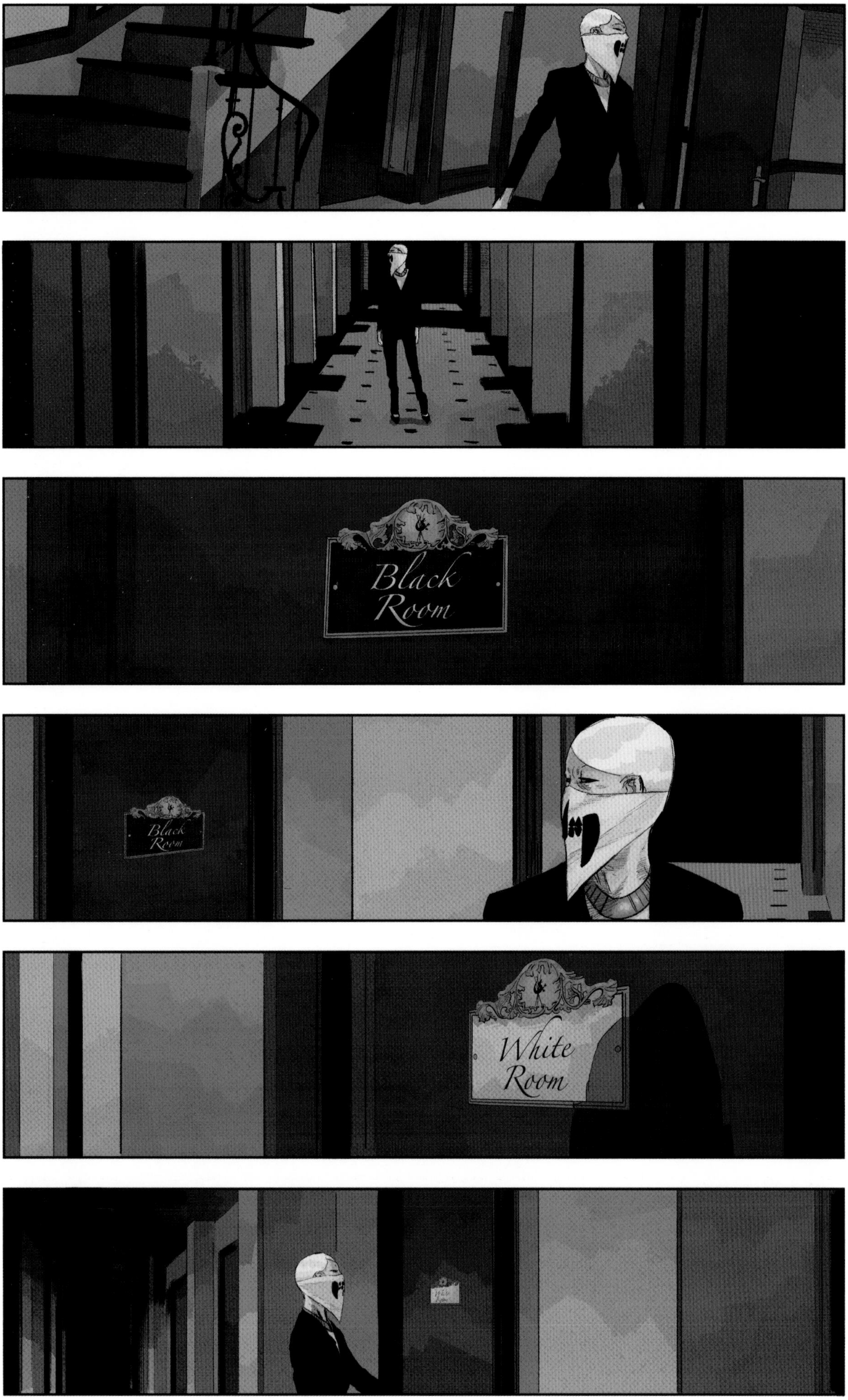
Black Room
Black Room
White Room

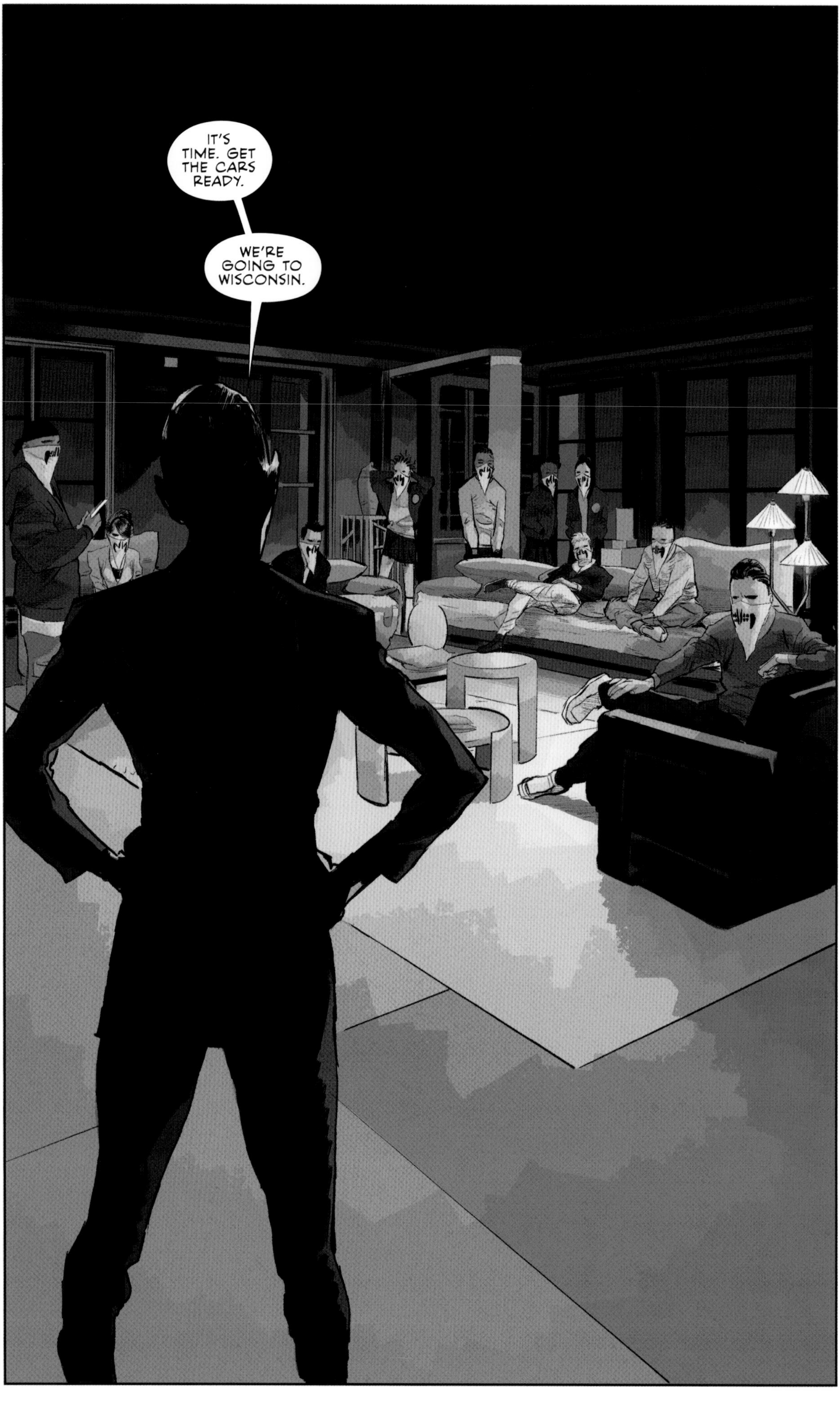
IT'S TIME. GET THE CARS READY.
WE'RE GOING TO WISCONSIN.

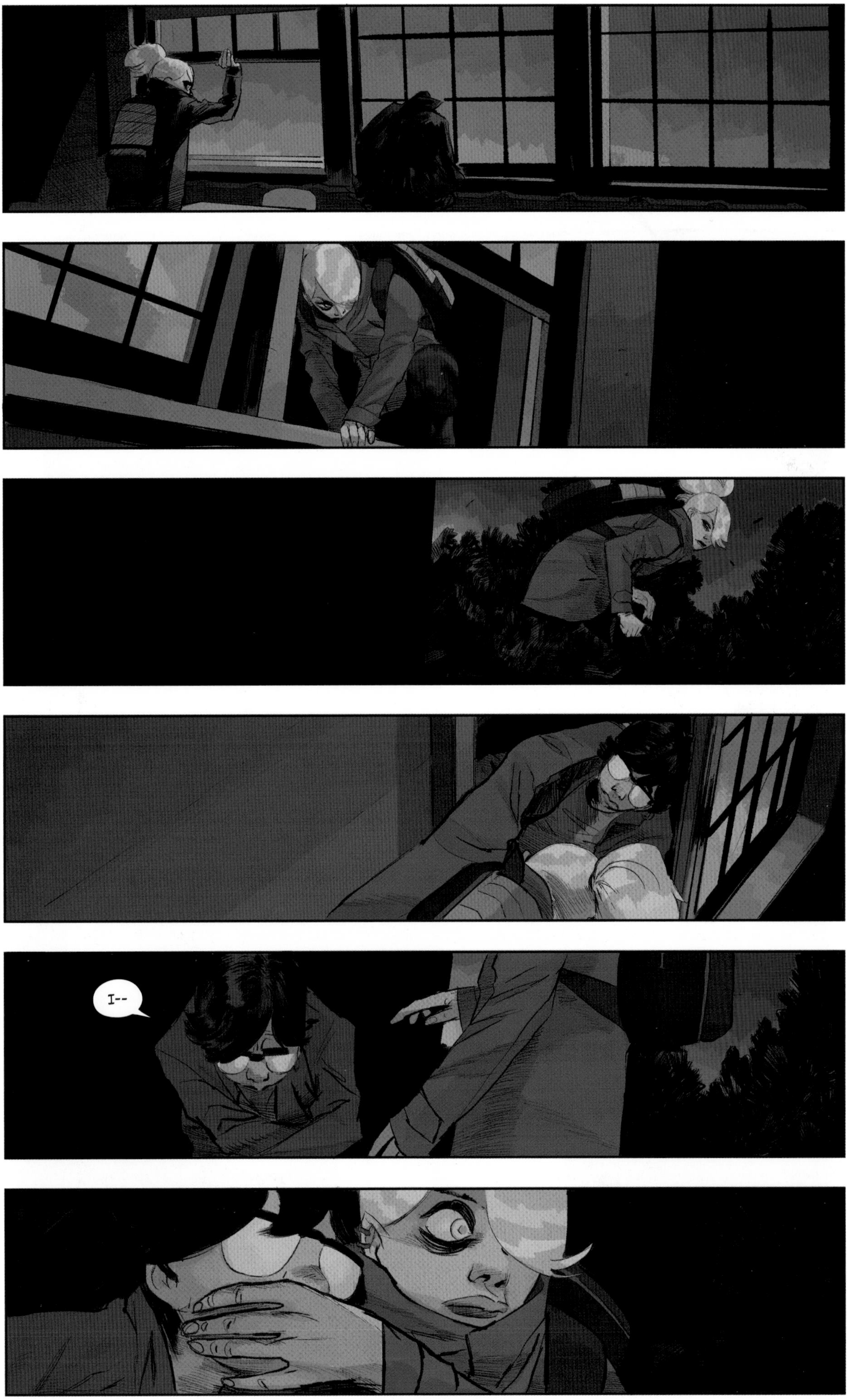
I--

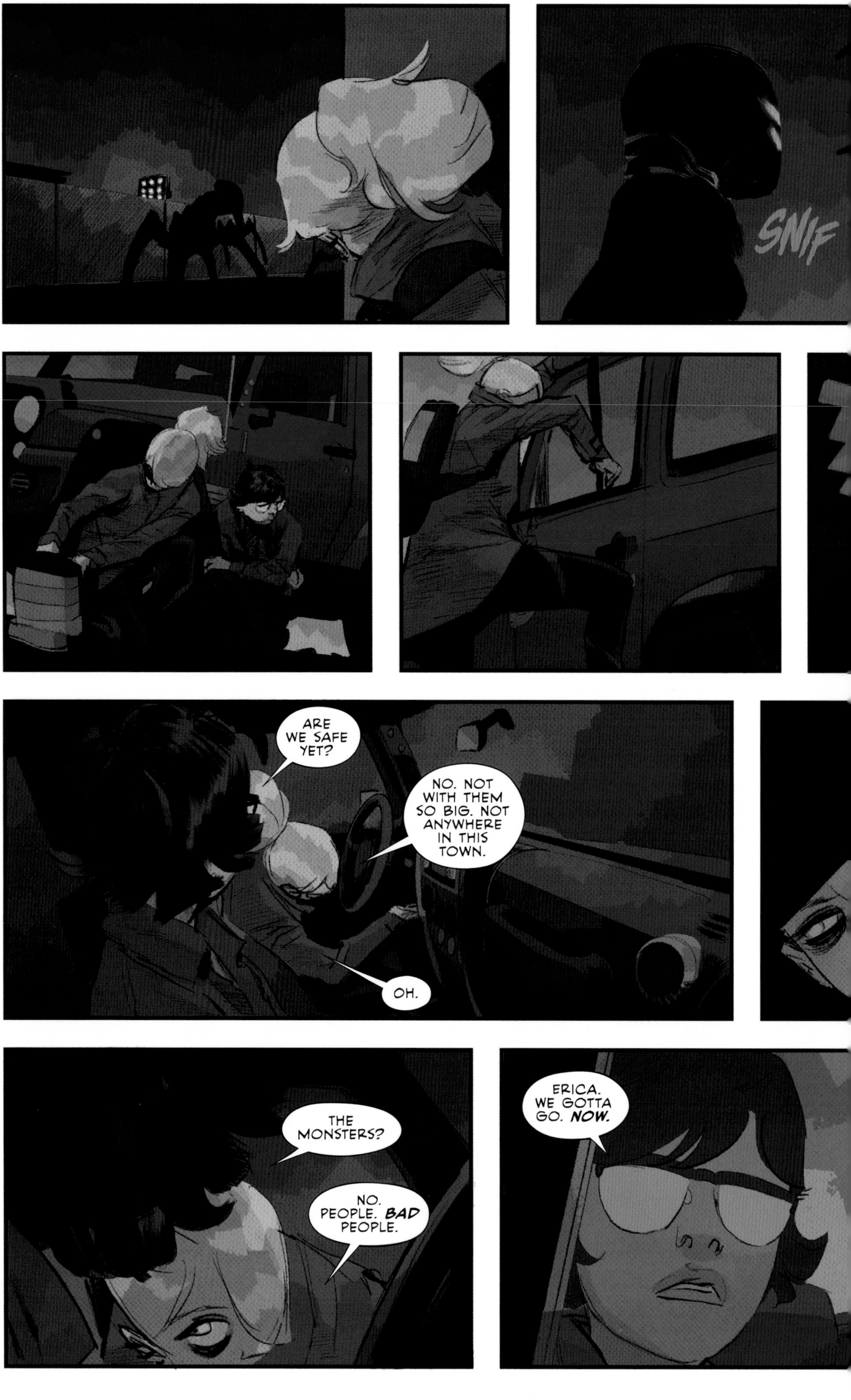
SNIF
ARE WE SAFE YET?
NO. NOT WITH THEM SO BIG. NOT ANYWHERE IN THIS TOWN.
OH.
THE MONSTERS?
NO. PEOPLE. **BAD** PEOPLE.
ERICA. WE GOTTA GO. **NOW.**

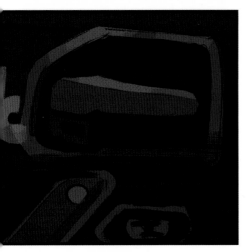

IF WE FIND BIAN, I CAN PERFORM THE RITUAL THAT WILL LET ME KILL THEM. BUT WE'RE GOING TO HAVE TO ACT QUICKLY...

DO YOU HAVE A CELL PHONE?

YEAH...BUT THERE'S NO SERVICE. THAT'S WEIRD. THERE'S USUALLY REALLY GOOD SERVICE AROUND HERE.

OKAY. THEY'RE MOVING FASTER THAN I THOUGHT.

I KNOW, IT'LL JUST TAKE A SECOND.

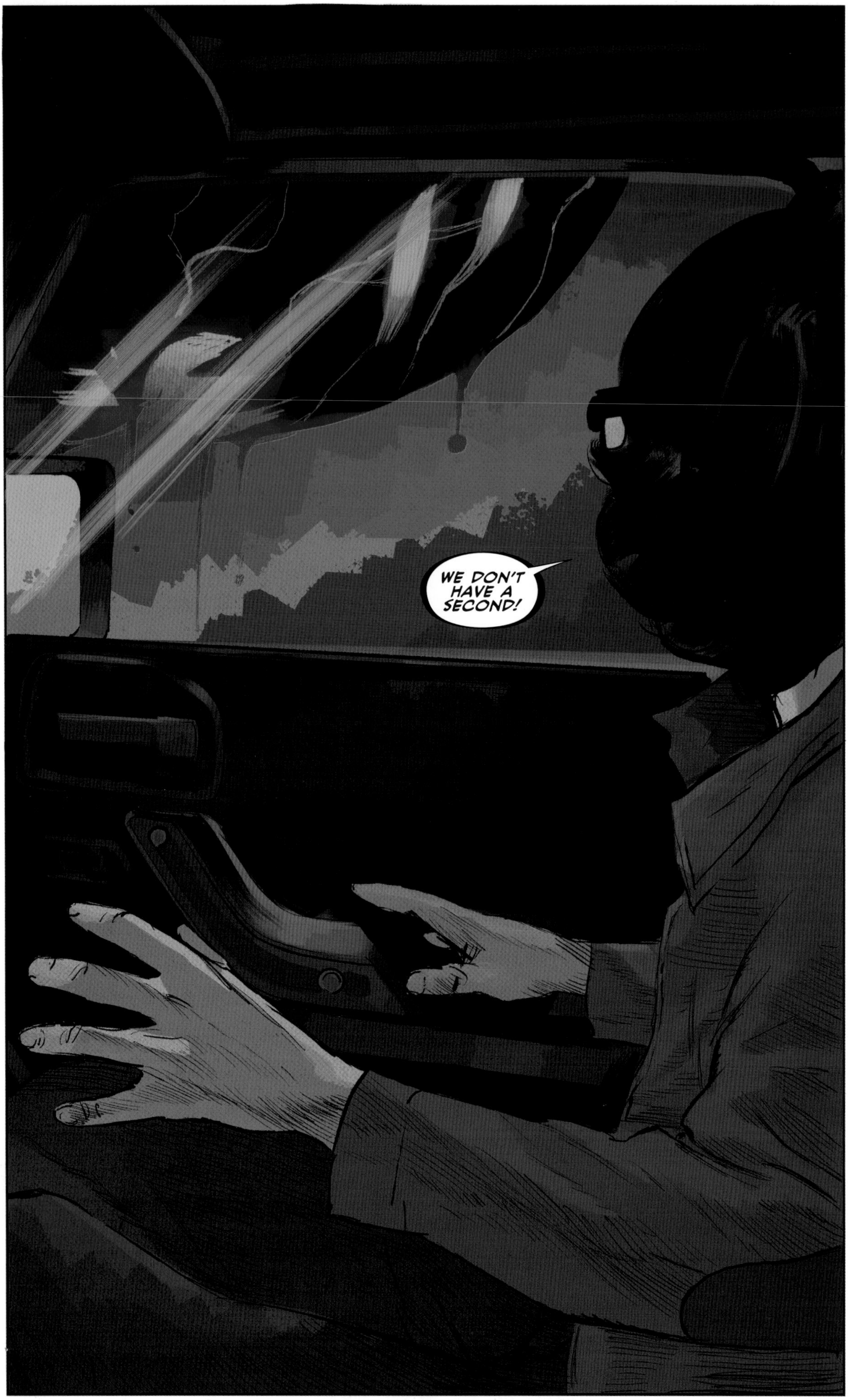
WE DON'T HAVE A SECOND!

CHAPTER TWELVE

HELP...
I NEED
HELP!

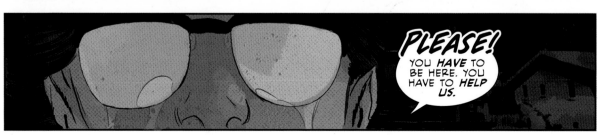

PLEASE!
YOU HAVE TO
BE HERE. YOU
HAVE TO HELP
US.

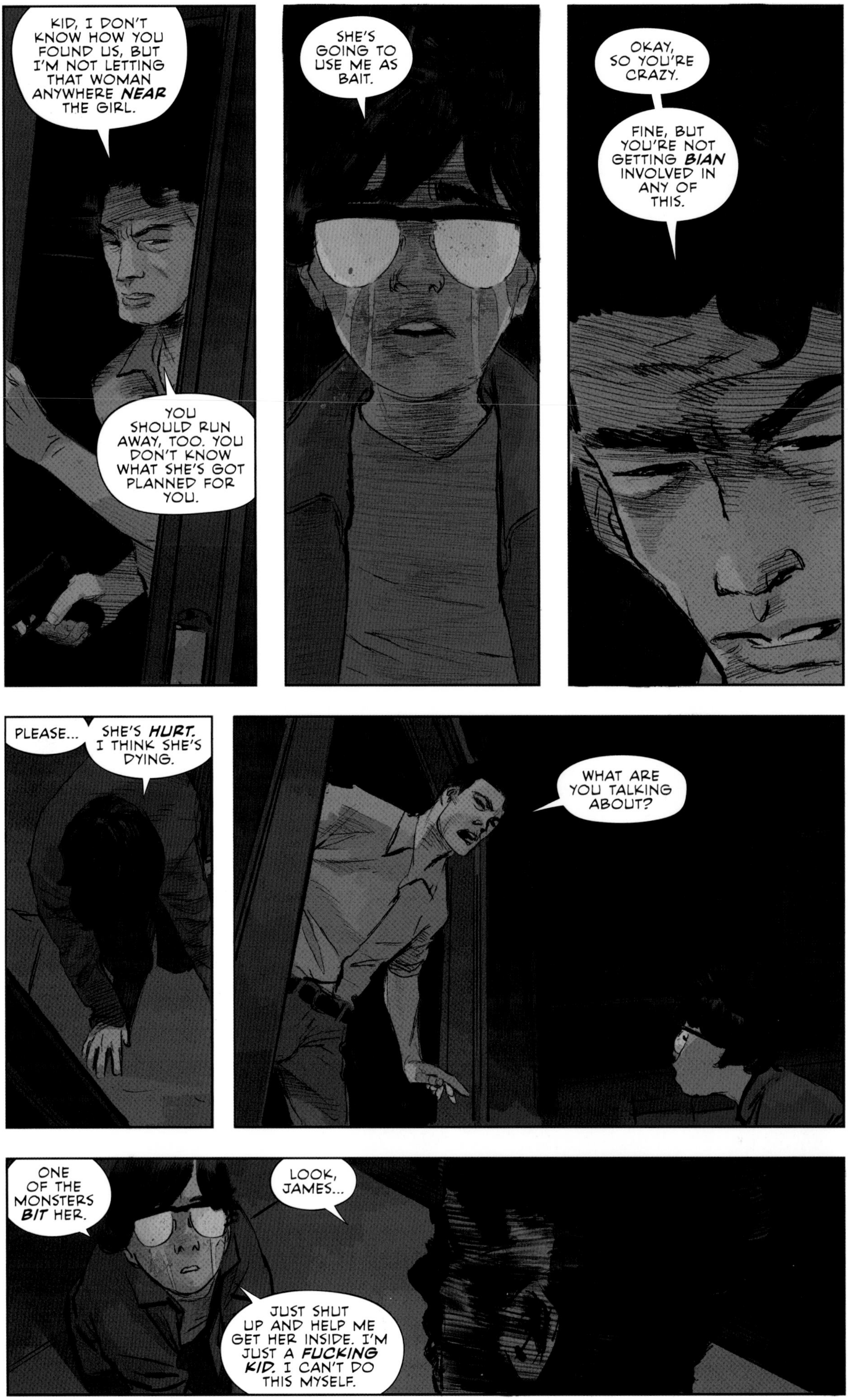
KID, I DON'T KNOW HOW YOU FOUND US, BUT I'M NOT LETTING THAT WOMAN ANYWHERE NEAR THE GIRL.
YOU SHOULD RUN AWAY, TOO. YOU DON'T KNOW WHAT SHE'S GOT PLANNED FOR YOU.
SHE'S GOING TO USE ME AS BAIT.
OKAY, SO YOU'RE CRAZY.
FINE, BUT YOU'RE NOT GETTING BIAN INVOLVED IN ANY OF THIS.
PLEASE...
SHE'S HURT. I THINK SHE'S DYING.
WHAT ARE YOU TALKING ABOUT?
ONE OF THE MONSTERS BIT HER.
LOOK, JAMES...
JUST SHUT UP AND HELP ME GET HER INSIDE. I'M JUST A FUCKING KID. I CAN'T DO THIS MYSELF.

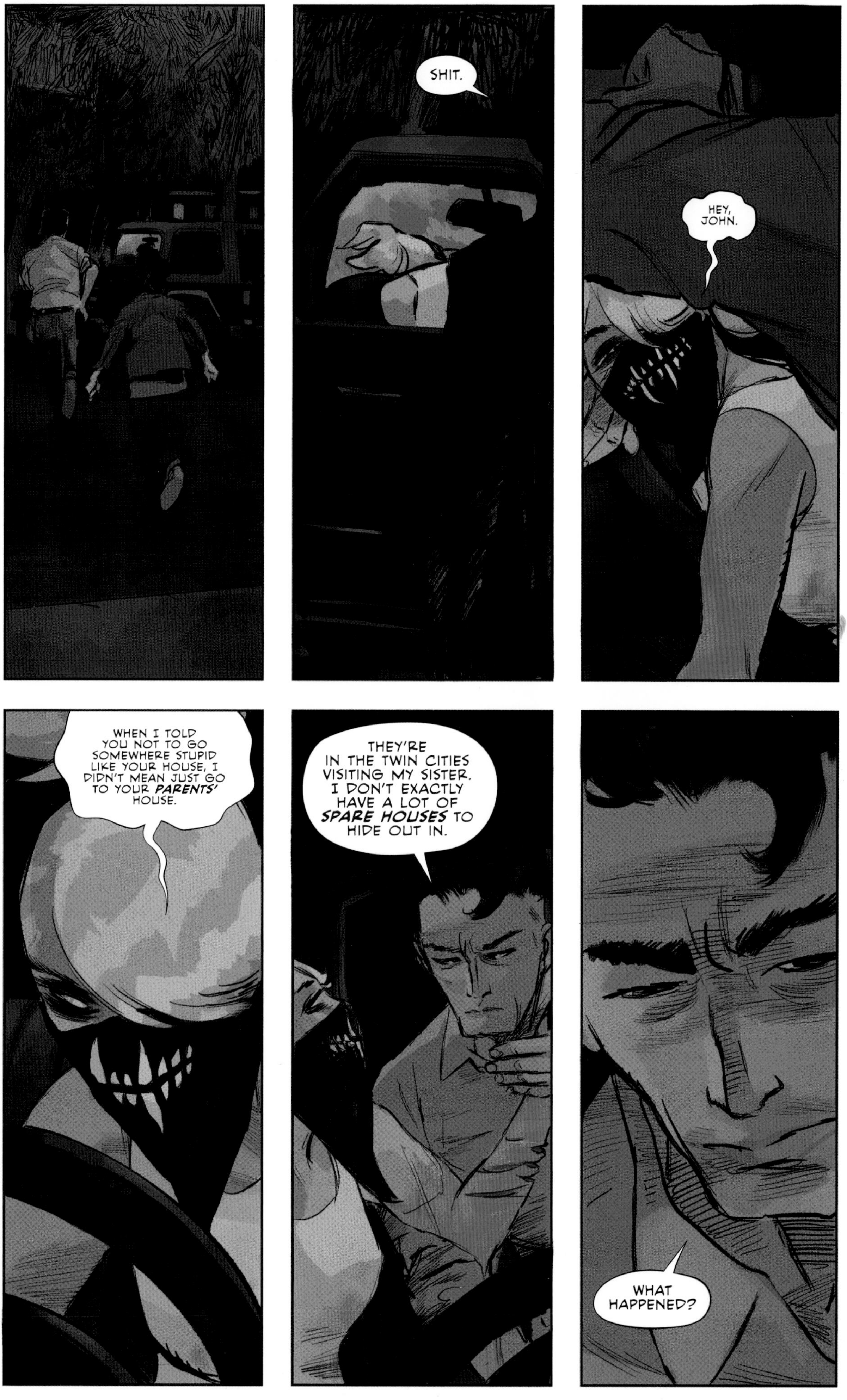
SHIT.
HEY, JOHN.
WHEN I TOLD YOU NOT TO GO SOMEWHERE STUPID LIKE YOUR HOUSE, I DIDN'T MEAN JUST GO TO YOUR *PARENTS'* HOUSE.
THEY'RE IN THE TWIN CITIES VISITING MY SISTER. I DON'T EXACTLY HAVE A LOT OF *SPARE HOUSES* TO HIDE OUT IN.
WHAT HAPPENED?

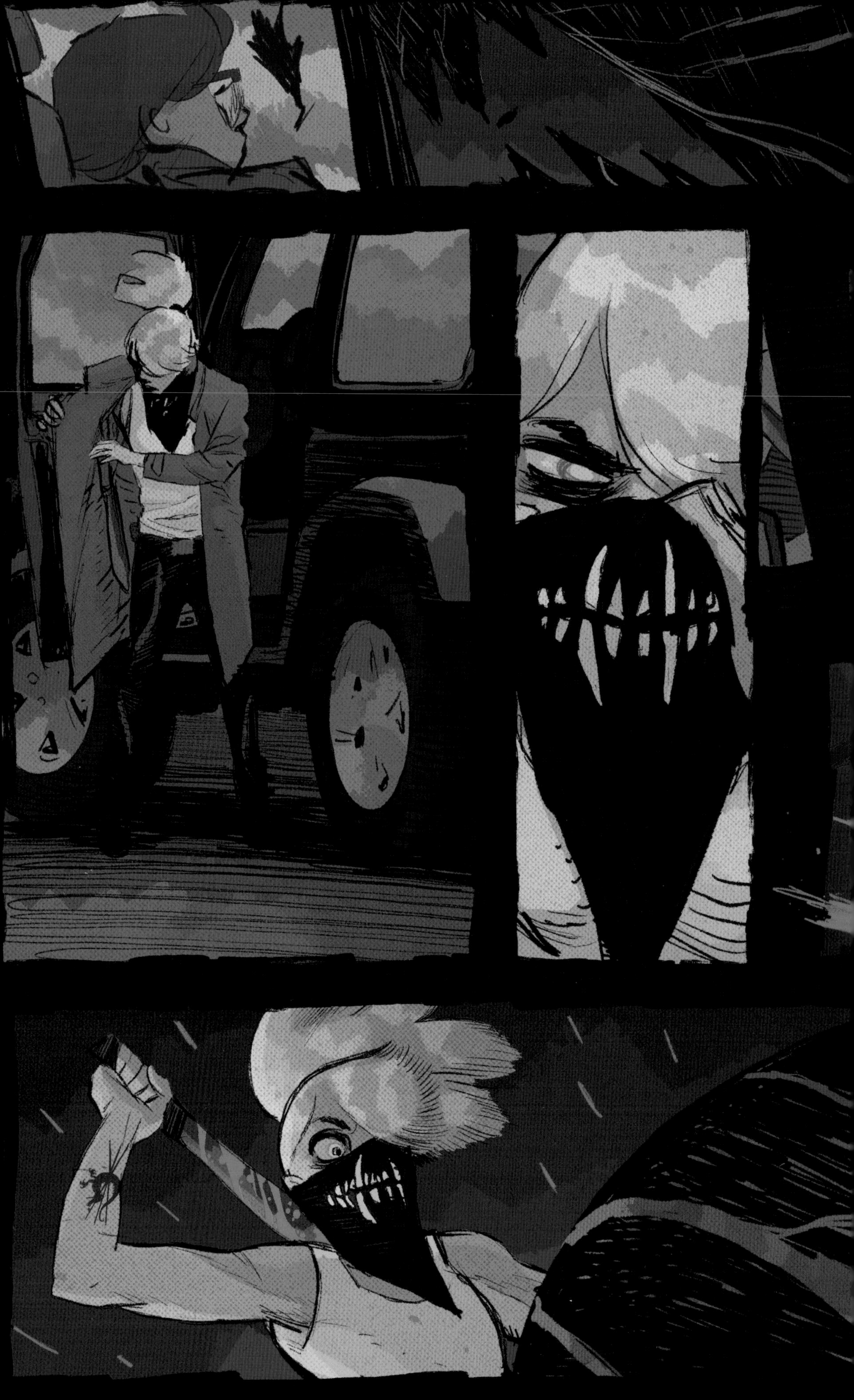

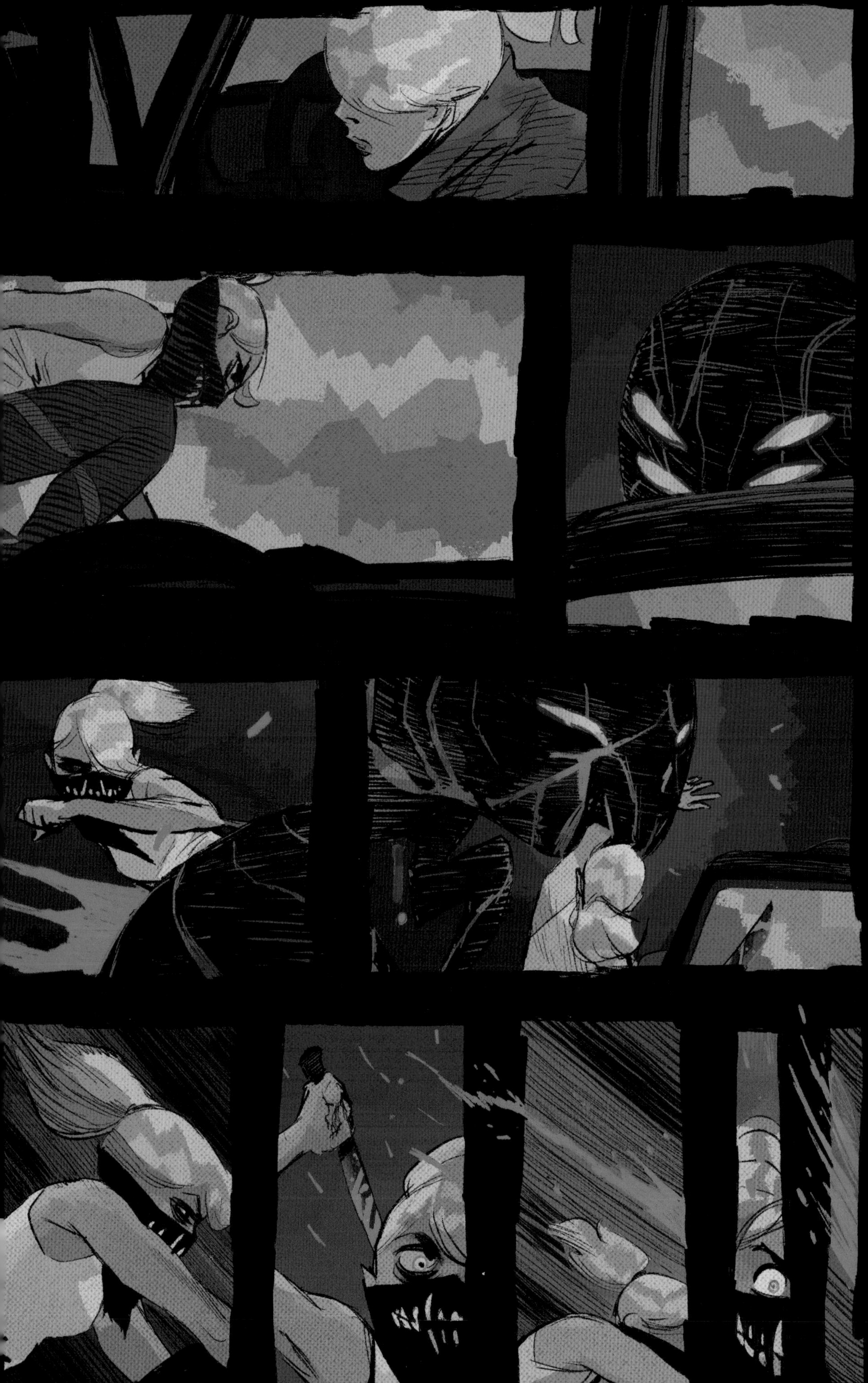

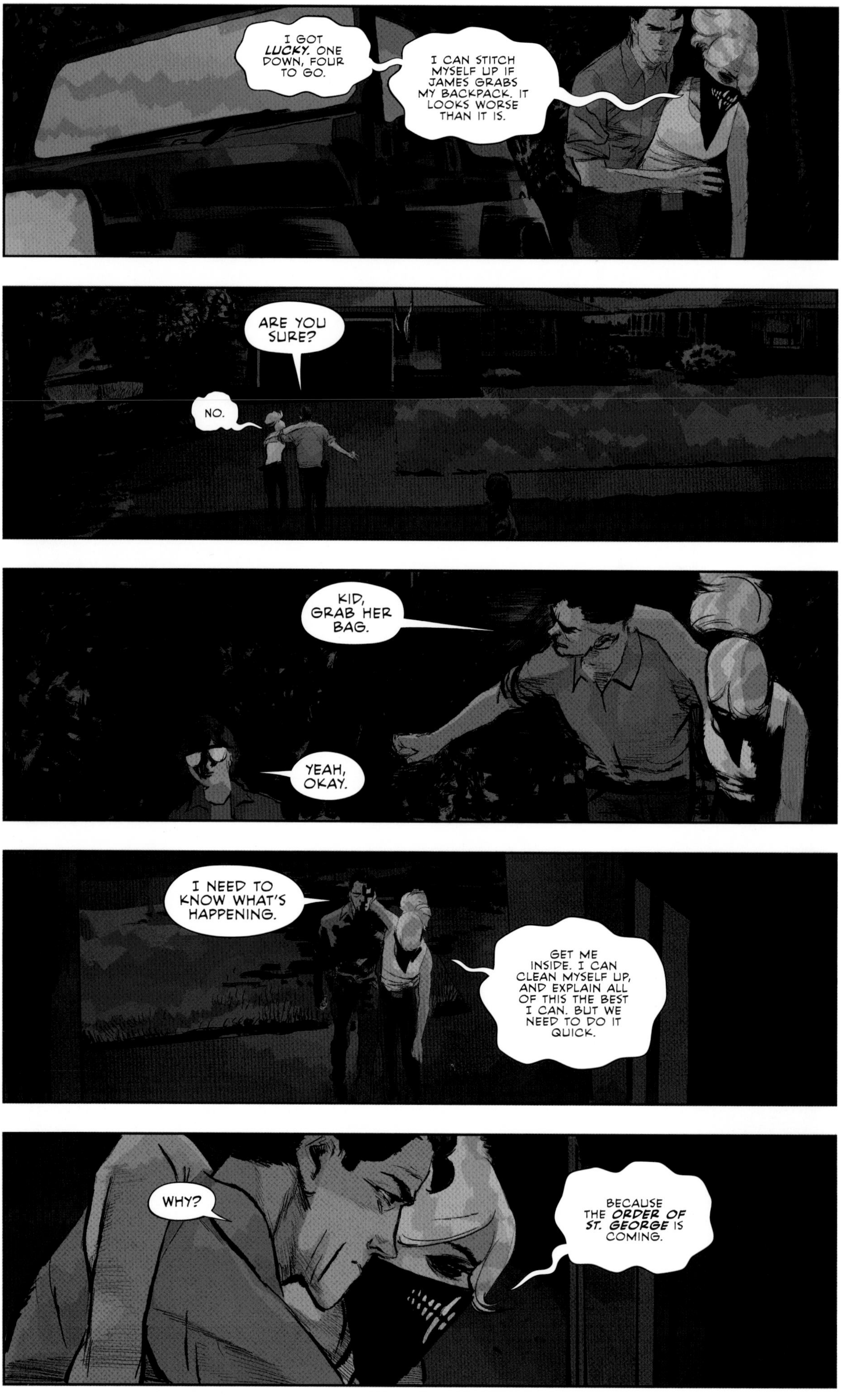
I GOT LUCKY. ONE DOWN, FOUR TO GO.
I CAN STITCH MYSELF UP IF JAMES GRABS MY BACKPACK. IT LOOKS WORSE THAN IT IS.
ARE YOU SURE?
NO.
KID, GRAB HER BAG.
YEAH, OKAY.
I NEED TO KNOW WHAT'S HAPPENING.
GET ME INSIDE. I CAN CLEAN MYSELF UP, AND EXPLAIN ALL OF THIS THE BEST I CAN. BUT WE NEED TO DO IT QUICK.
WHY?
BECAUSE THE ORDER OF ST. GEORGE IS COMING.

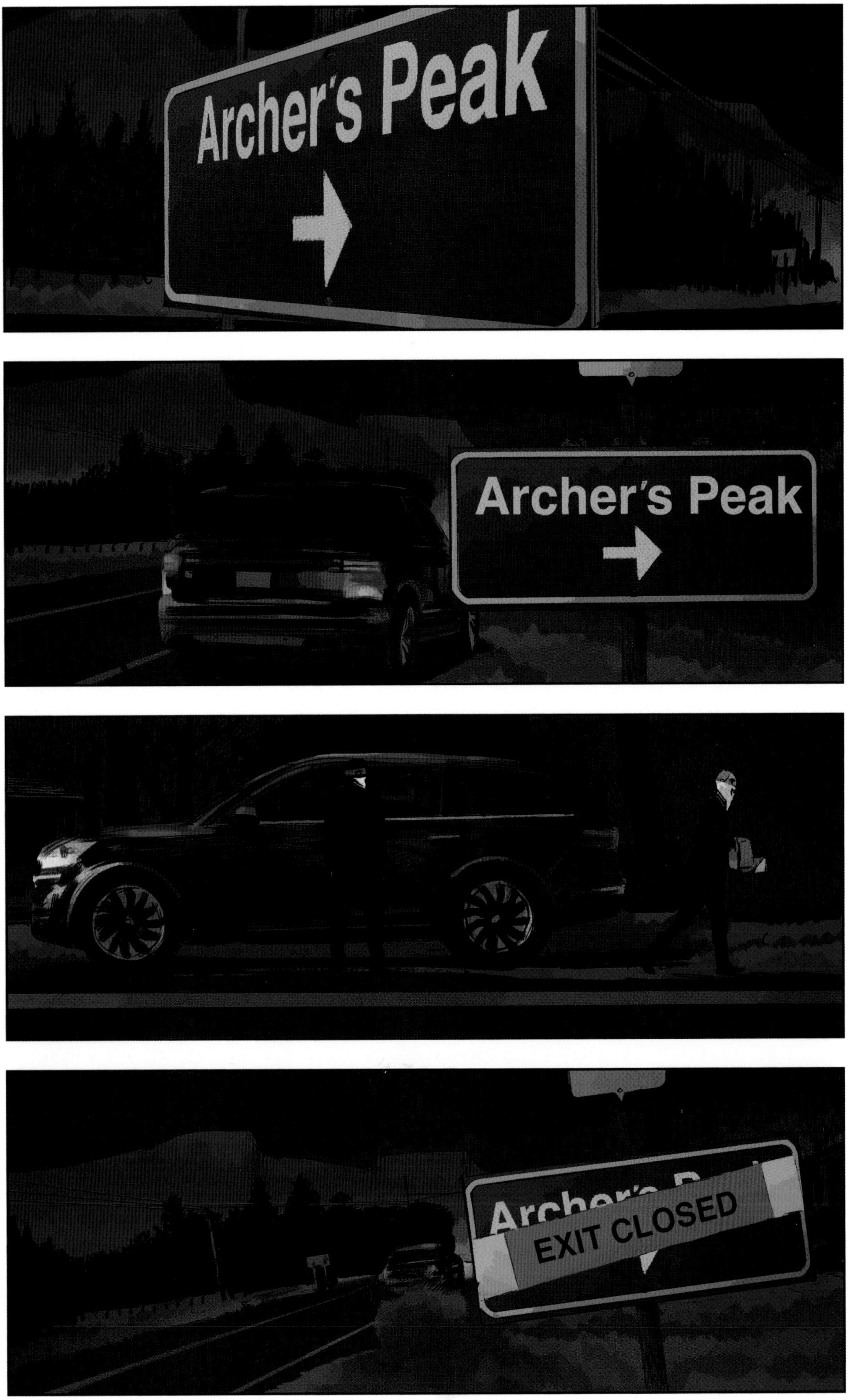
Archer's Peak
Archer's Peak
EXIT CLOSED

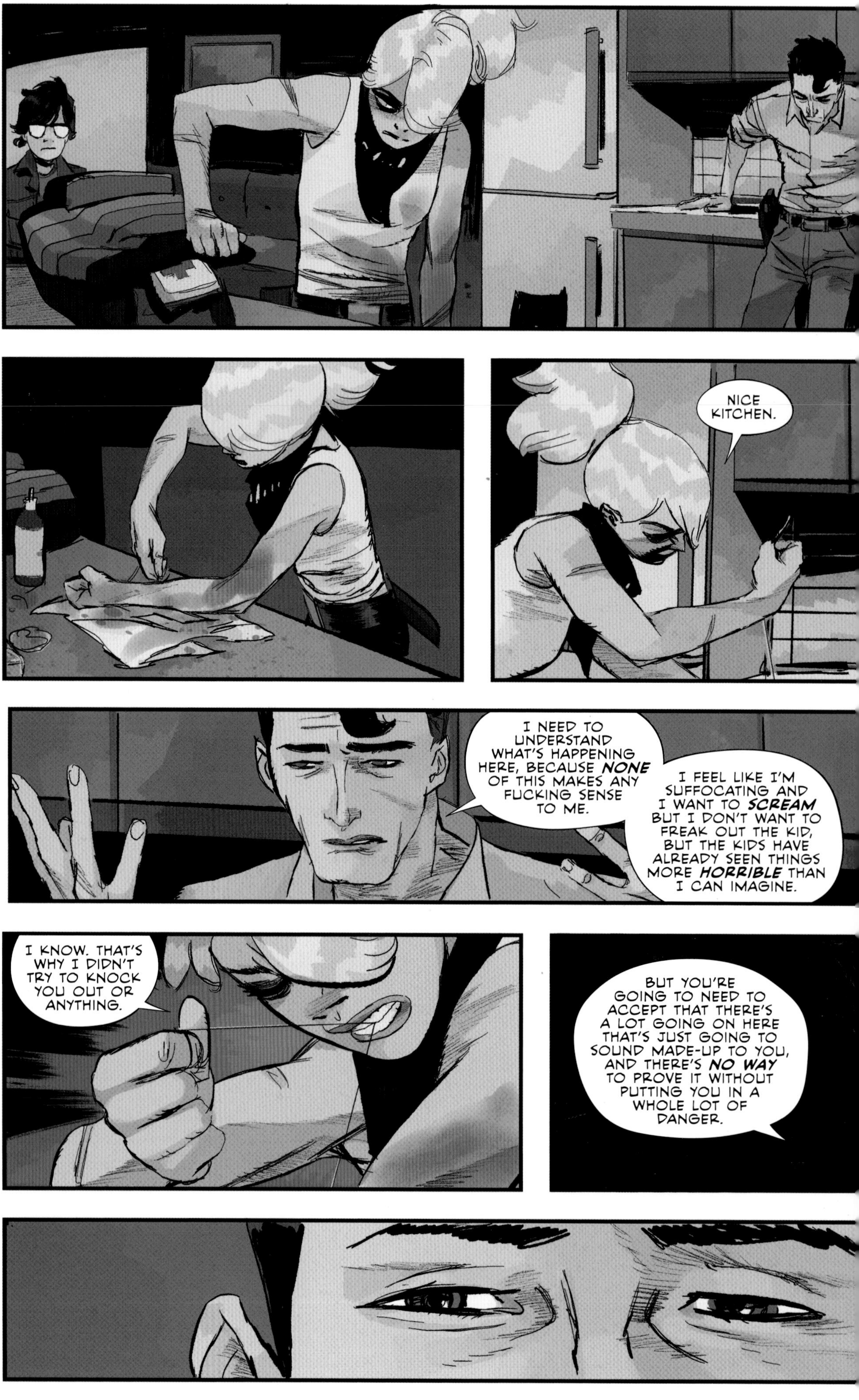
NICE KITCHEN.
I NEED TO UNDERSTAND WHAT'S HAPPENING HERE, BECAUSE NONE OF THIS MAKES ANY FUCKING SENSE TO ME.
I FEEL LIKE I'M SUFFOCATING AND I WANT TO SCREAM BUT I DON'T WANT TO FREAK OUT THE KID, BUT THE KIDS HAVE ALREADY SEEN THINGS MORE HORRIBLE THAN I CAN IMAGINE.
I KNOW. THAT'S WHY I DIDN'T TRY TO KNOCK YOU OUT OR ANYTHING.
BUT YOU'RE GOING TO NEED TO ACCEPT THAT THERE'S A LOT GOING ON HERE THAT'S JUST GOING TO SOUND MADE-UP TO YOU, AND THERE'S NO WAY TO PROVE IT WITHOUT PUTTING YOU IN A WHOLE LOT OF DANGER.

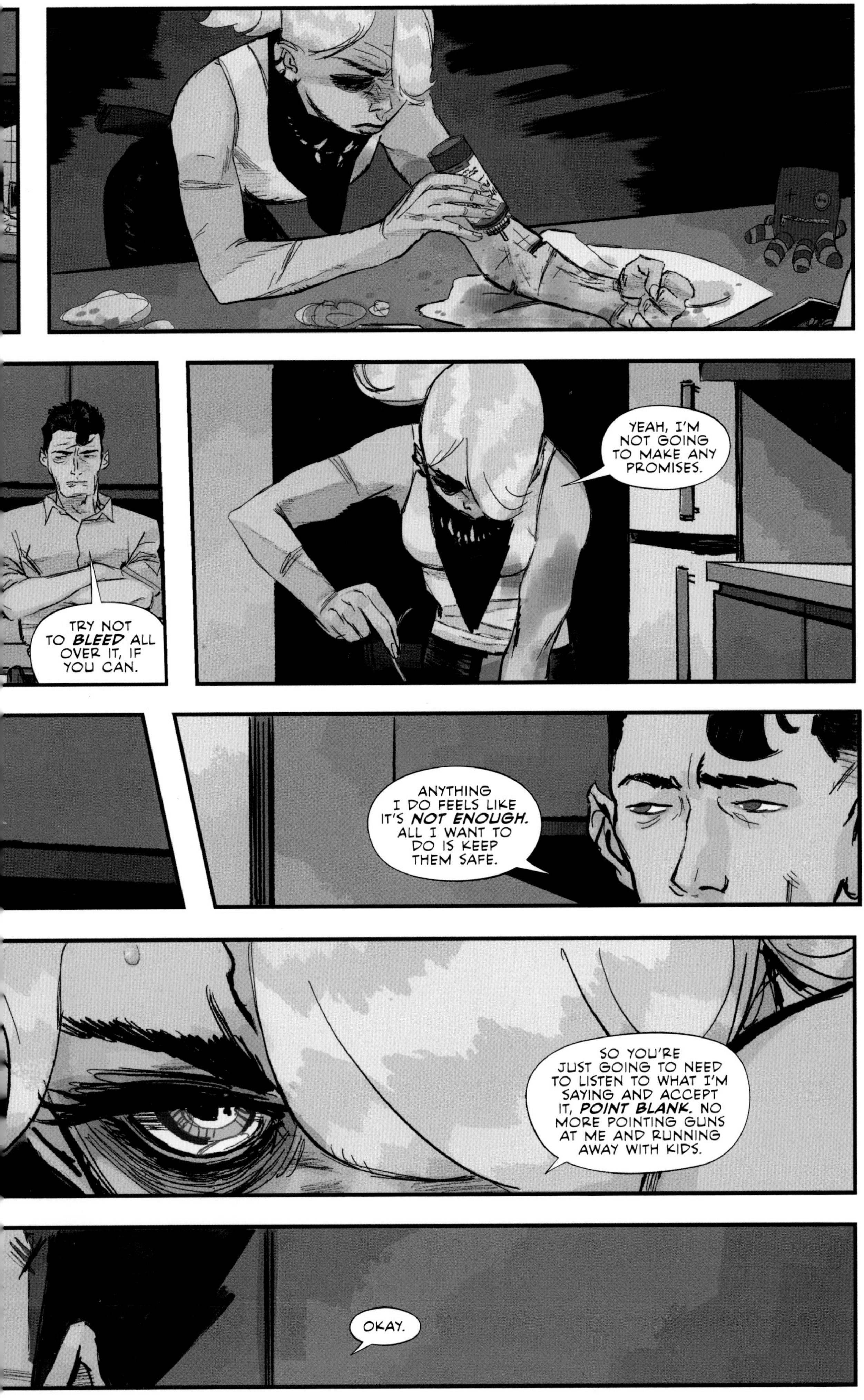
YEAH, I'M NOT GOING TO MAKE ANY PROMISES.
TRY NOT TO **BLEED** ALL OVER IT, IF YOU CAN.
ANYTHING I DO FEELS LIKE IT'S **NOT ENOUGH.** ALL I WANT TO DO IS KEEP THEM SAFE.
SO YOU'RE JUST GOING TO NEED TO LISTEN TO WHAT I'M SAYING AND ACCEPT IT, **POINT BLANK.** NO MORE POINTING GUNS AT ME AND RUNNING AWAY WITH KIDS.
OKAY.

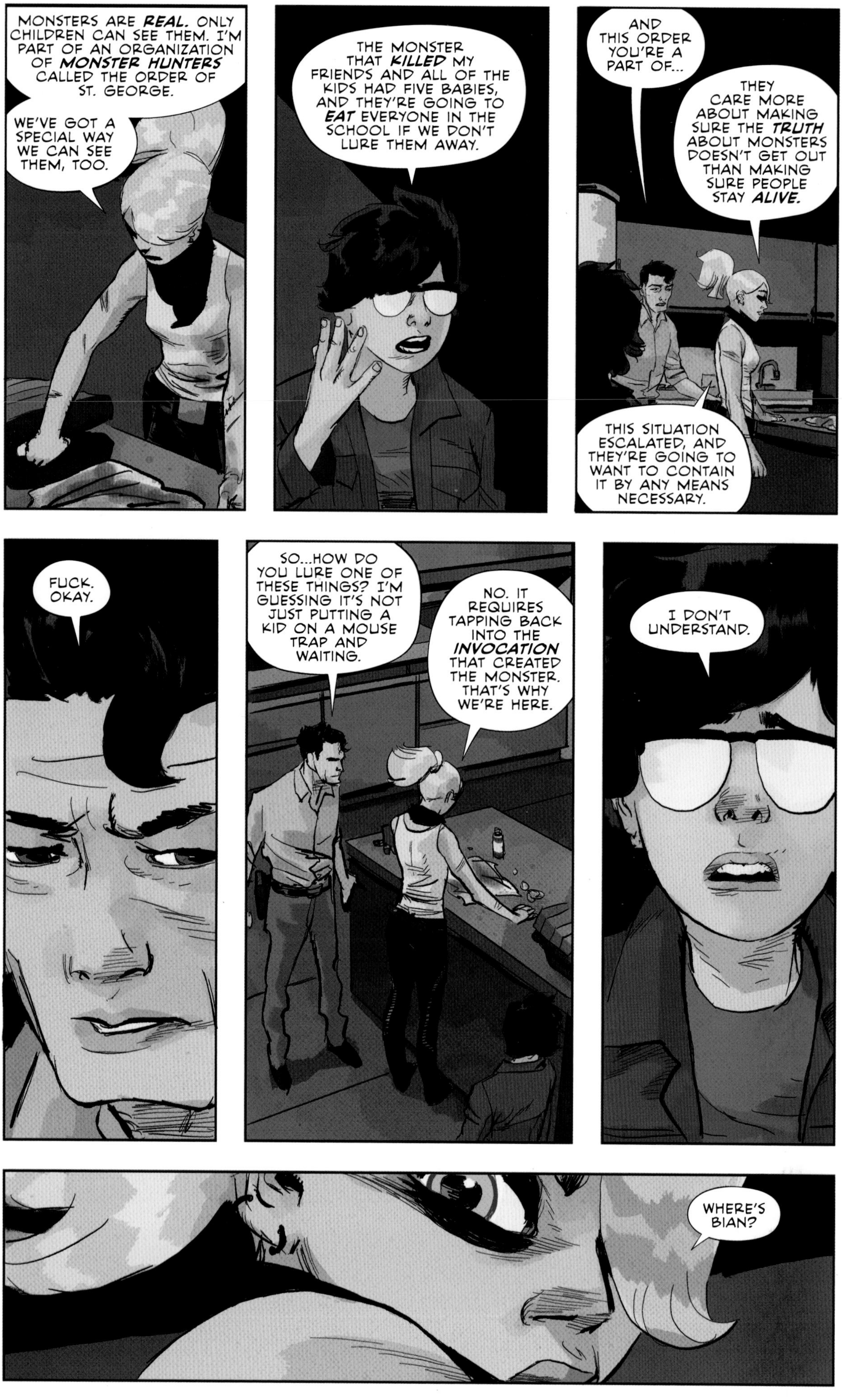
MONSTERS ARE *REAL.* ONLY CHILDREN CAN SEE THEM. I'M PART OF AN ORGANIZATION OF *MONSTER HUNTERS* CALLED THE ORDER OF ST. GEORGE.
WE'VE GOT A SPECIAL WAY WE CAN SEE THEM, TOO.
THE MONSTER THAT *KILLED* MY FRIENDS AND ALL OF THE KIDS HAD FIVE BABIES, AND THEY'RE GOING TO *EAT* EVERYONE IN THE SCHOOL IF WE DON'T LURE THEM AWAY.
AND THIS ORDER YOU'RE A PART OF...
THEY CARE MORE ABOUT MAKING SURE THE *TRUTH* ABOUT MONSTERS DOESN'T GET OUT THAN MAKING SURE PEOPLE STAY *ALIVE.*
THIS SITUATION ESCALATED, AND THEY'RE GOING TO WANT TO CONTAIN IT BY ANY MEANS NECESSARY.
FUCK. OKAY.
SO...HOW DO YOU LURE ONE OF THESE THINGS? I'M GUESSING IT'S NOT JUST PUTTING A KID ON A MOUSE TRAP AND WAITING.
NO. IT REQUIRES TAPPING BACK INTO THE *INVOCATION* THAT CREATED THE MONSTER. THAT'S WHY WE'RE HERE.
I DON'T UNDERSTAND.
WHERE'S BIAN?

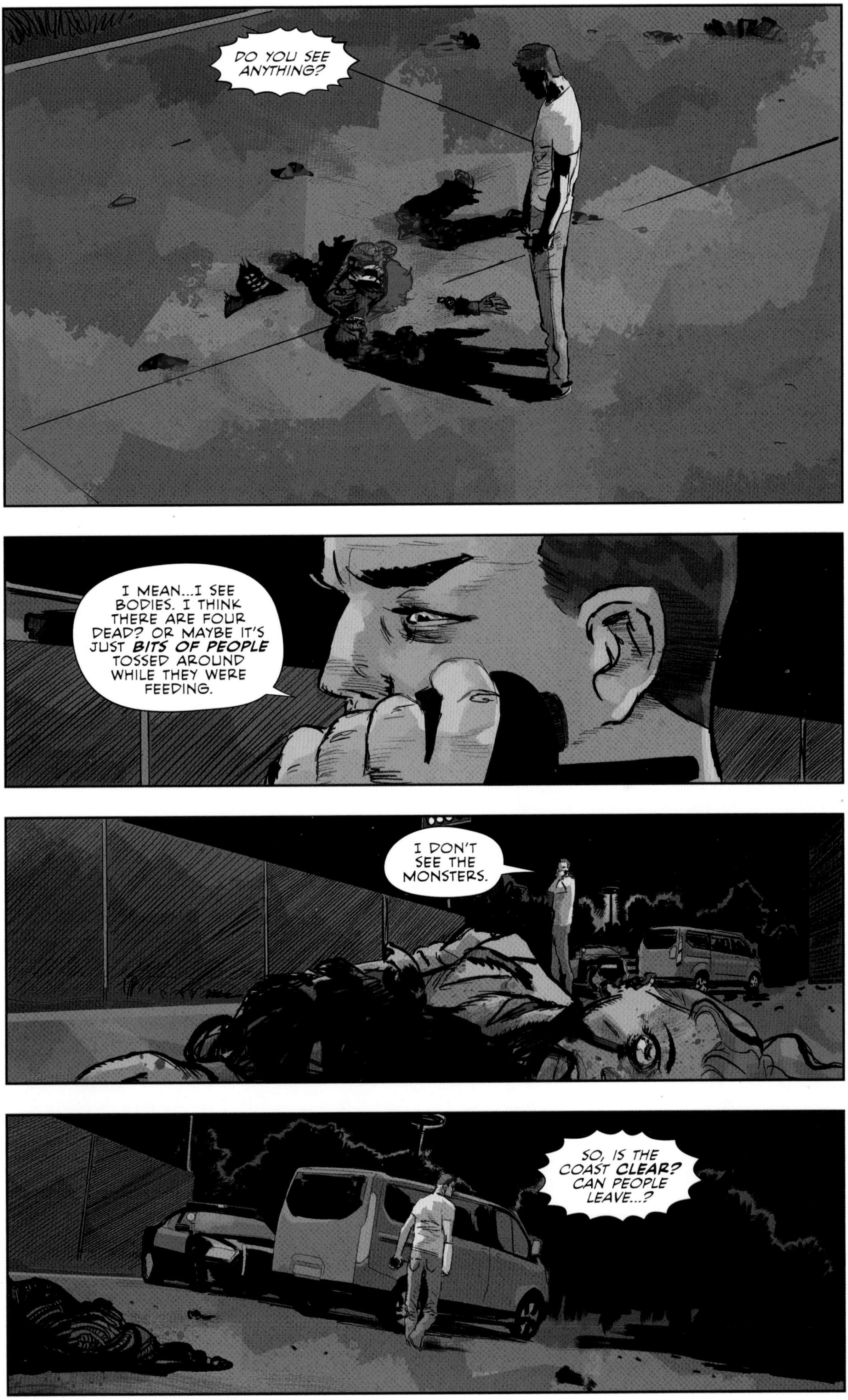
DO YOU SEE ANYTHING?
I MEAN...I SEE BODIES. I THINK THERE ARE FOUR DEAD? OR MAYBE IT'S JUST **BITS OF PEOPLE** TOSSED AROUND WHILE THEY WERE FEEDING.
I DON'T SEE THE MONSTERS.
SO, IS THE COAST **CLEAR?** CAN PEOPLE LEAVE...?

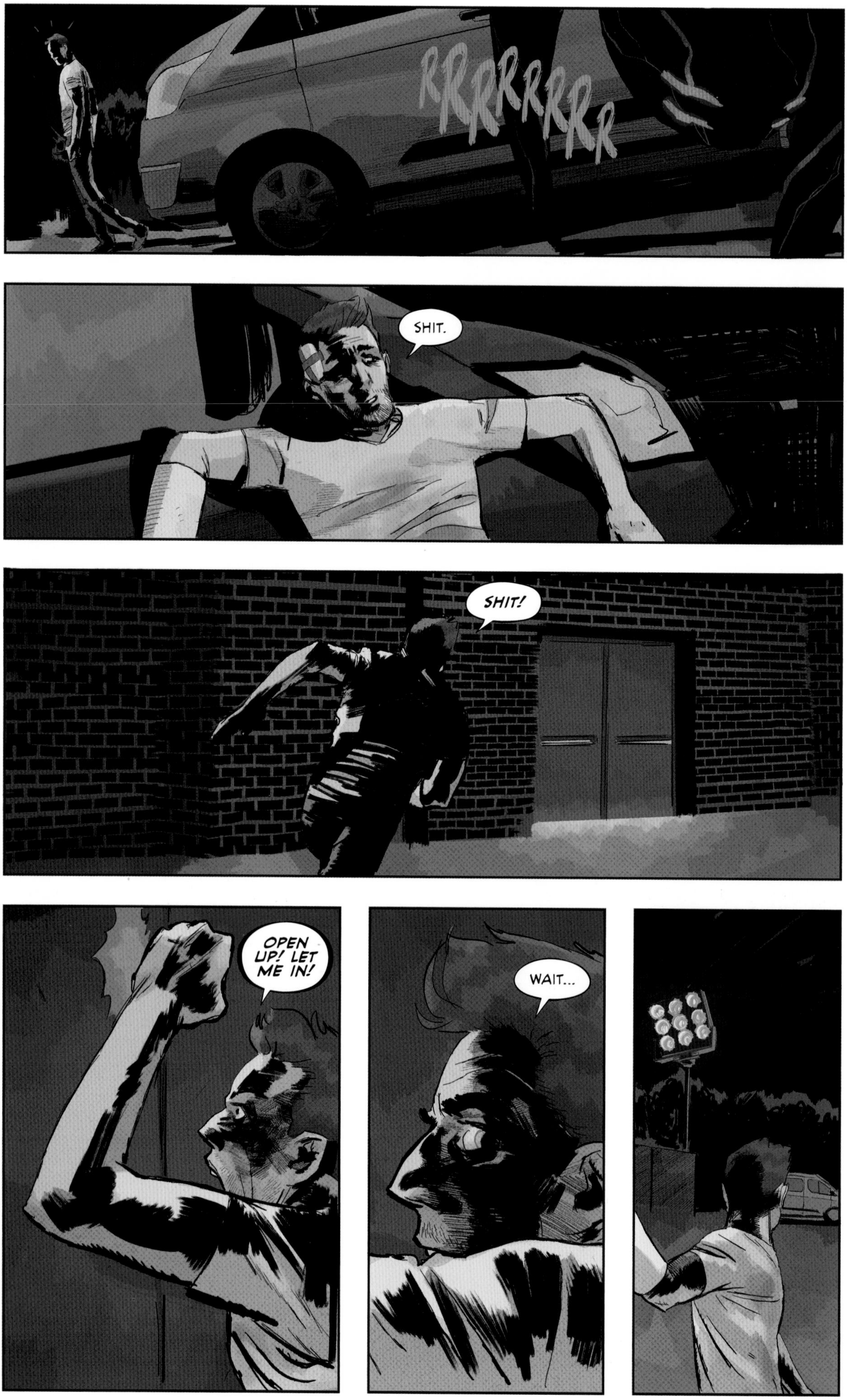
RRRRRRRRR
SHIT.
SHIT!
OPEN UP! LET ME IN!
WAIT...

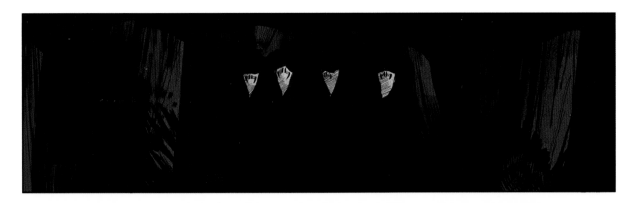

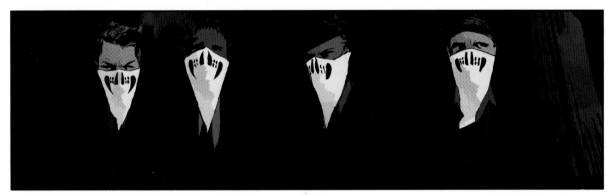

WHAT THE...

GET IN HERE!

WHAT THE HELL HAPPENED OUT THERE?

ONE OF THEM SNUCK UP ON ME. I DROPPED THE WALKIE-TALKIE...

OKAY, SO WE'RE STUCK IN HERE.

THAT'S NOT THE ONLY THING I SAW OUT THERE, SHERIFF...

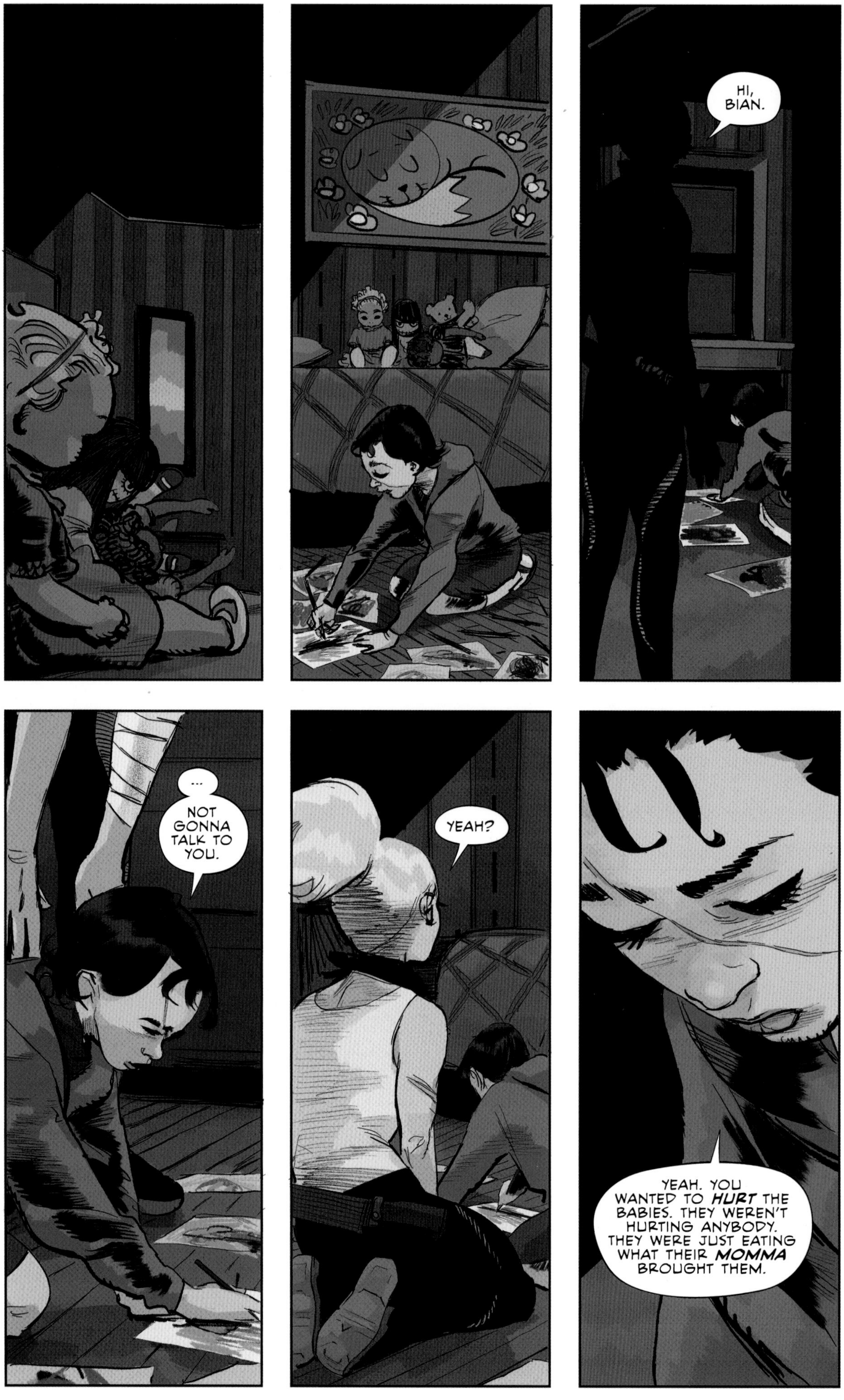
HI, BIAN.
...
NOT GONNA TALK TO YOU.
YEAH?
YEAH. YOU WANTED TO **HURT** THE BABIES. THEY WEREN'T HURTING ANYBODY. THEY WERE JUST EATING WHAT THEIR **MOMMA** BROUGHT THEM.

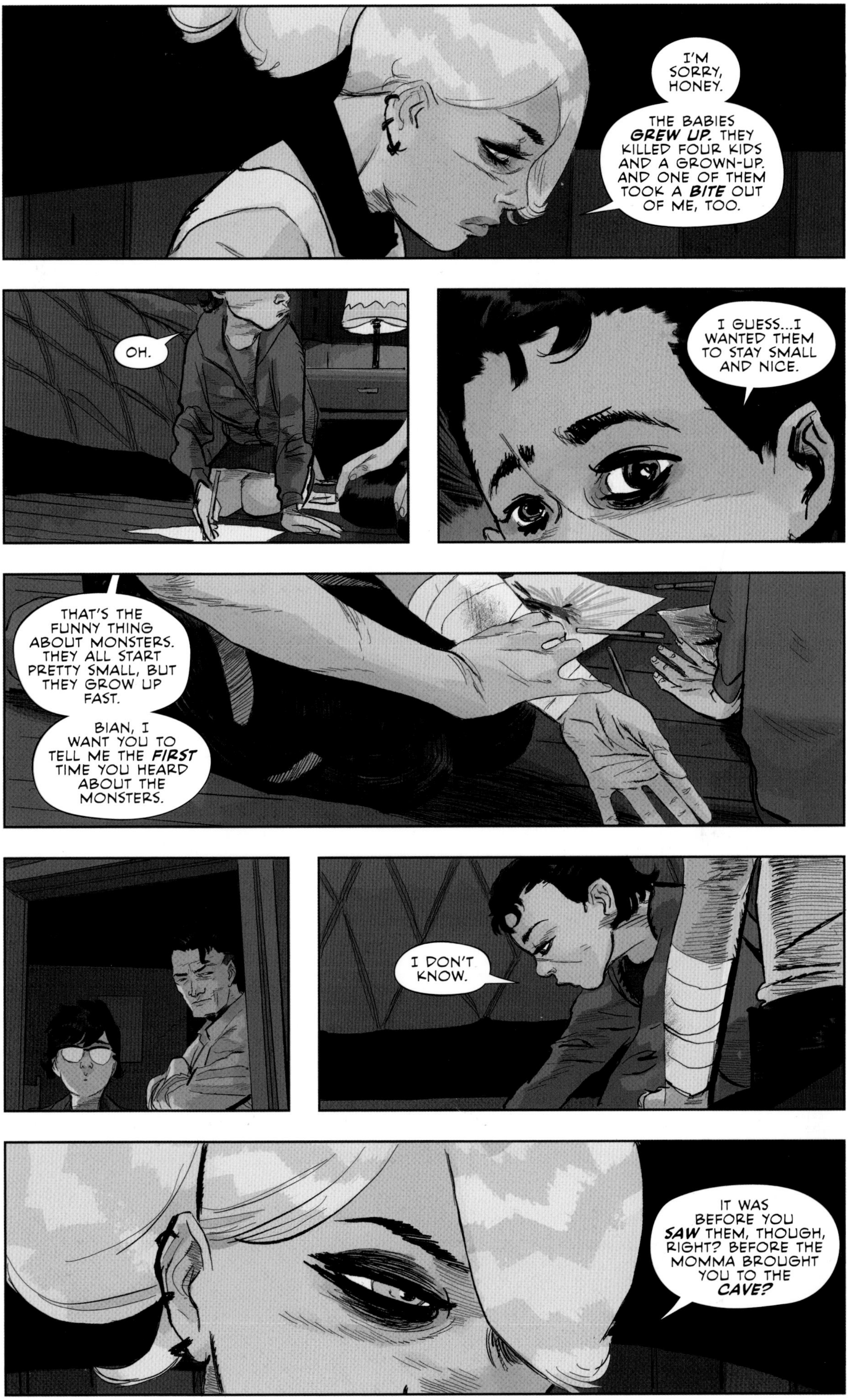
I'M SORRY, HONEY.
THE BABIES GREW UP. THEY KILLED FOUR KIDS AND A GROWN-UP. AND ONE OF THEM TOOK A BITE OUT OF ME, TOO.
OH.
I GUESS...I WANTED THEM TO STAY SMALL AND NICE.
THAT'S THE FUNNY THING ABOUT MONSTERS. THEY ALL START PRETTY SMALL, BUT THEY GROW UP FAST.
BIAN, I WANT YOU TO TELL ME THE FIRST TIME YOU HEARD ABOUT THE MONSTERS.
I DON'T KNOW.
IT WAS BEFORE YOU SAW THEM, THOUGH, RIGHT? BEFORE THE MOMMA BROUGHT YOU TO THE CAVE?

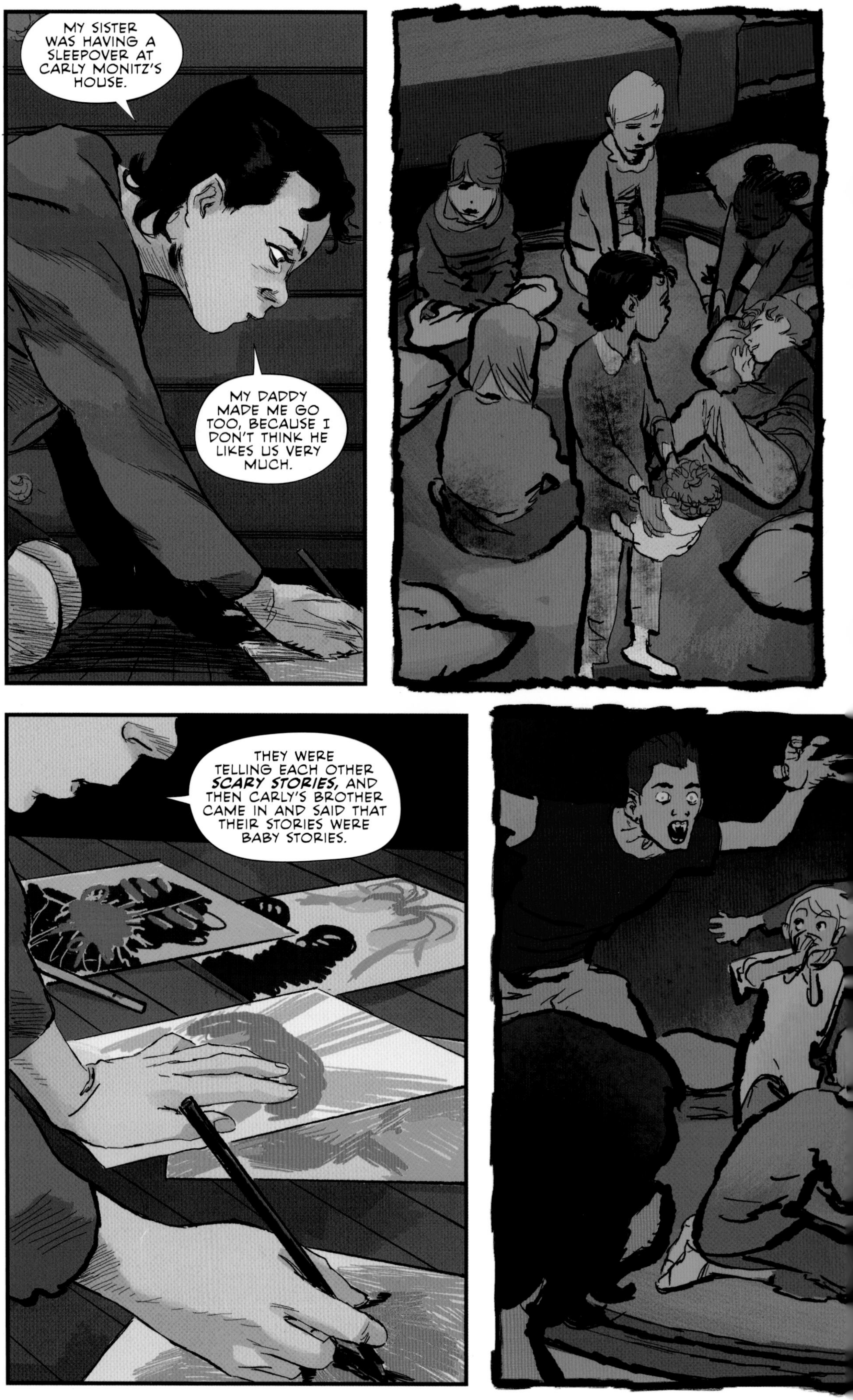
MY SISTER WAS HAVING A SLEEPOVER AT CARLY MONITZ'S HOUSE.
MY DADDY MADE ME GO TOO, BECAUSE I DON'T THINK HE LIKES US VERY MUCH.
THEY WERE TELLING EACH OTHER *SCARY STORIES,* AND THEN CARLY'S BROTHER CAME IN AND SAID THAT THEIR STORIES WERE BABY STORIES.

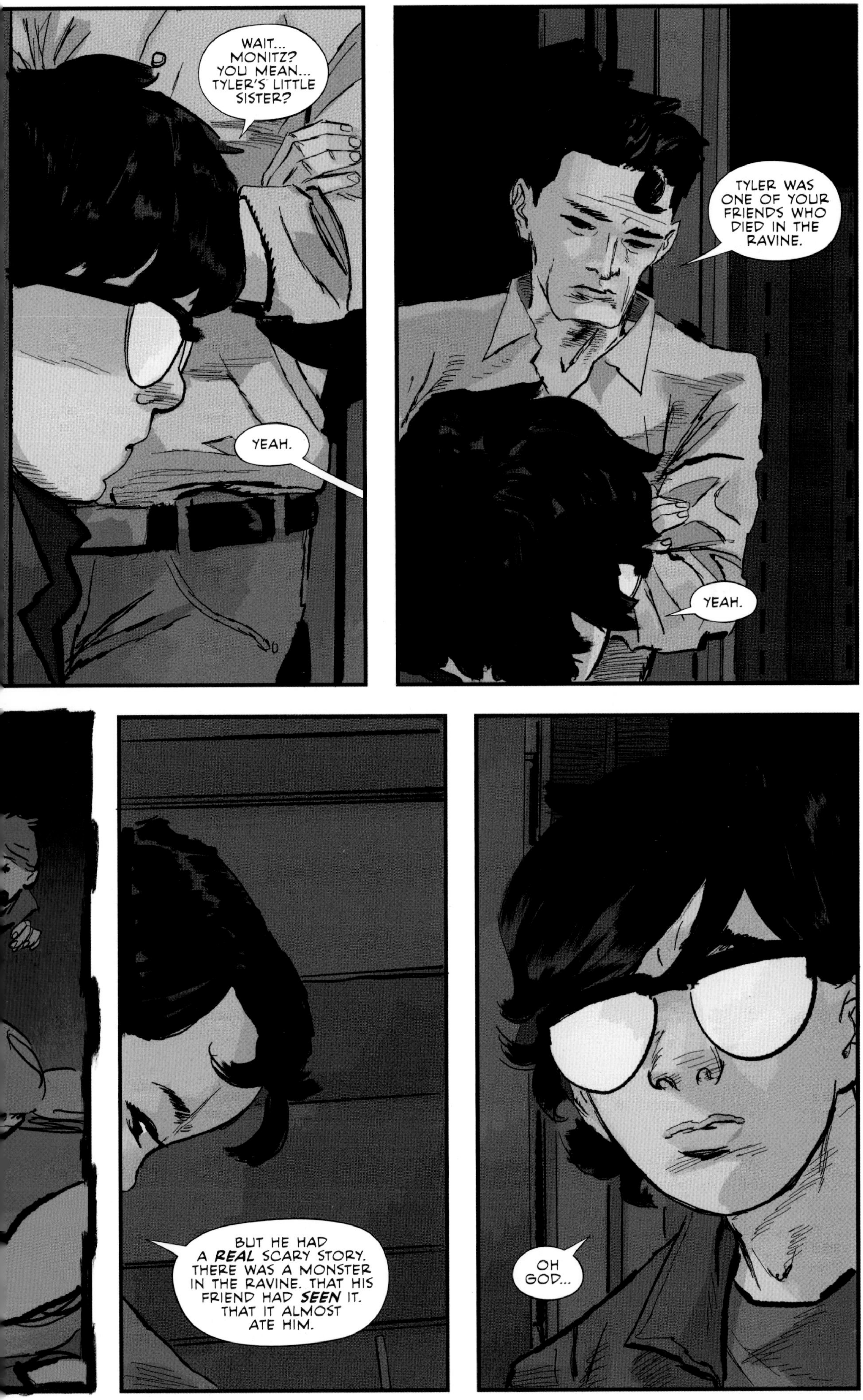
WAIT... MONITZ? YOU MEAN... TYLER'S LITTLE SISTER?
YEAH.
TYLER WAS ONE OF YOUR FRIENDS WHO DIED IN THE RAVINE.
YEAH.
BUT HE HAD A REAL SCARY STORY. THERE WAS A MONSTER IN THE RAVINE. THAT HIS FRIEND HAD SEEN IT. THAT IT ALMOST ATE HIM.
OH GOD...

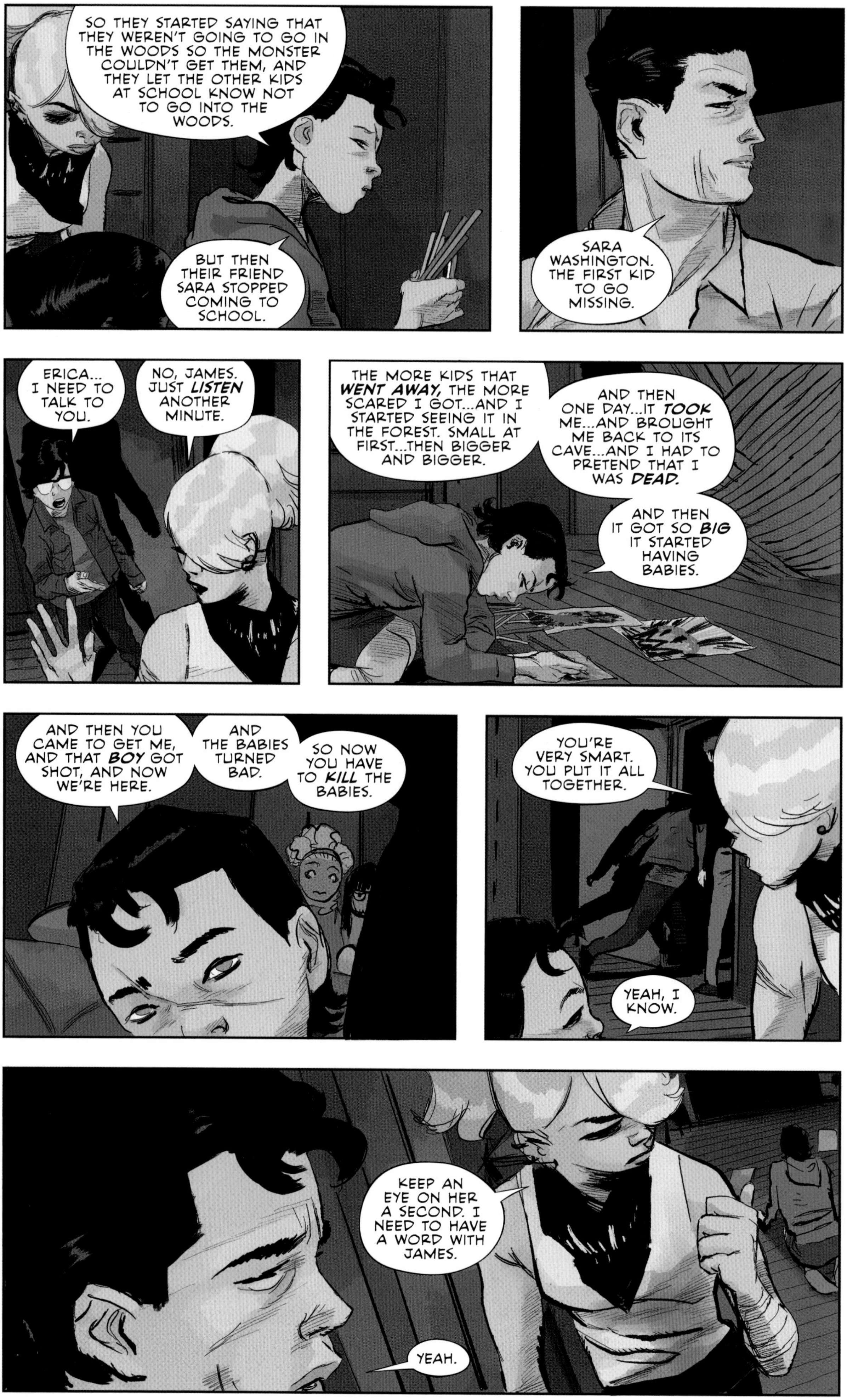
SO THEY STARTED SAYING THAT THEY WEREN'T GOING TO GO IN THE WOODS SO THE MONSTER COULDN'T GET THEM, AND THEY LET THE OTHER KIDS AT SCHOOL KNOW NOT TO GO INTO THE WOODS.
BUT THEN THEIR FRIEND SARA STOPPED COMING TO SCHOOL.
SARA WASHINGTON. THE FIRST KID TO GO MISSING.
ERICA... I NEED TO TALK TO YOU.
NO, JAMES. JUST LISTEN ANOTHER MINUTE.
THE MORE KIDS THAT WENT AWAY, THE MORE SCARED I GOT...AND I STARTED SEEING IT IN THE FOREST. SMALL AT FIRST...THEN BIGGER AND BIGGER.
AND THEN ONE DAY...IT TOOK ME...AND BROUGHT ME BACK TO ITS CAVE...AND I HAD TO PRETEND THAT I WAS DEAD.
AND THEN IT GOT SO BIG IT STARTED HAVING BABIES.
AND THEN YOU CAME TO GET ME, AND THAT BOY GOT SHOT, AND NOW WE'RE HERE.
AND THE BABIES TURNED BAD.
SO NOW YOU HAVE TO KILL THE BABIES.
YOU'RE VERY SMART. YOU PUT IT ALL TOGETHER.
YEAH, I KNOW.
KEEP AN EYE ON HER A SECOND. I NEED TO HAVE A WORD WITH JAMES.
YEAH.

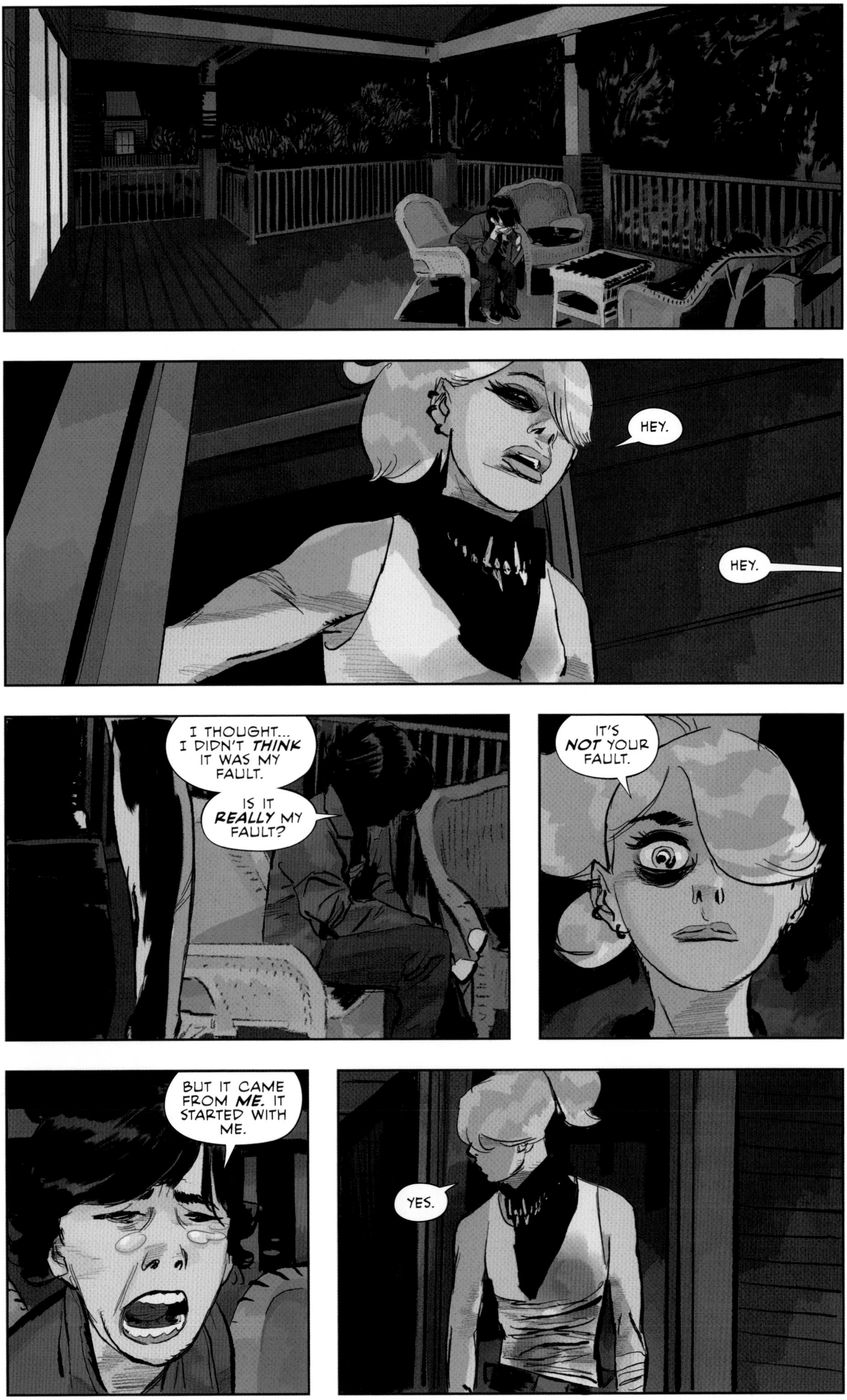
HEY.
HEY.
I THOUGHT... I DIDN'T THINK IT WAS MY FAULT.
IS IT REALLY MY FAULT?
IT'S NOT YOUR FAULT.
BUT IT CAME FROM ME. IT STARTED WITH ME.
YES.

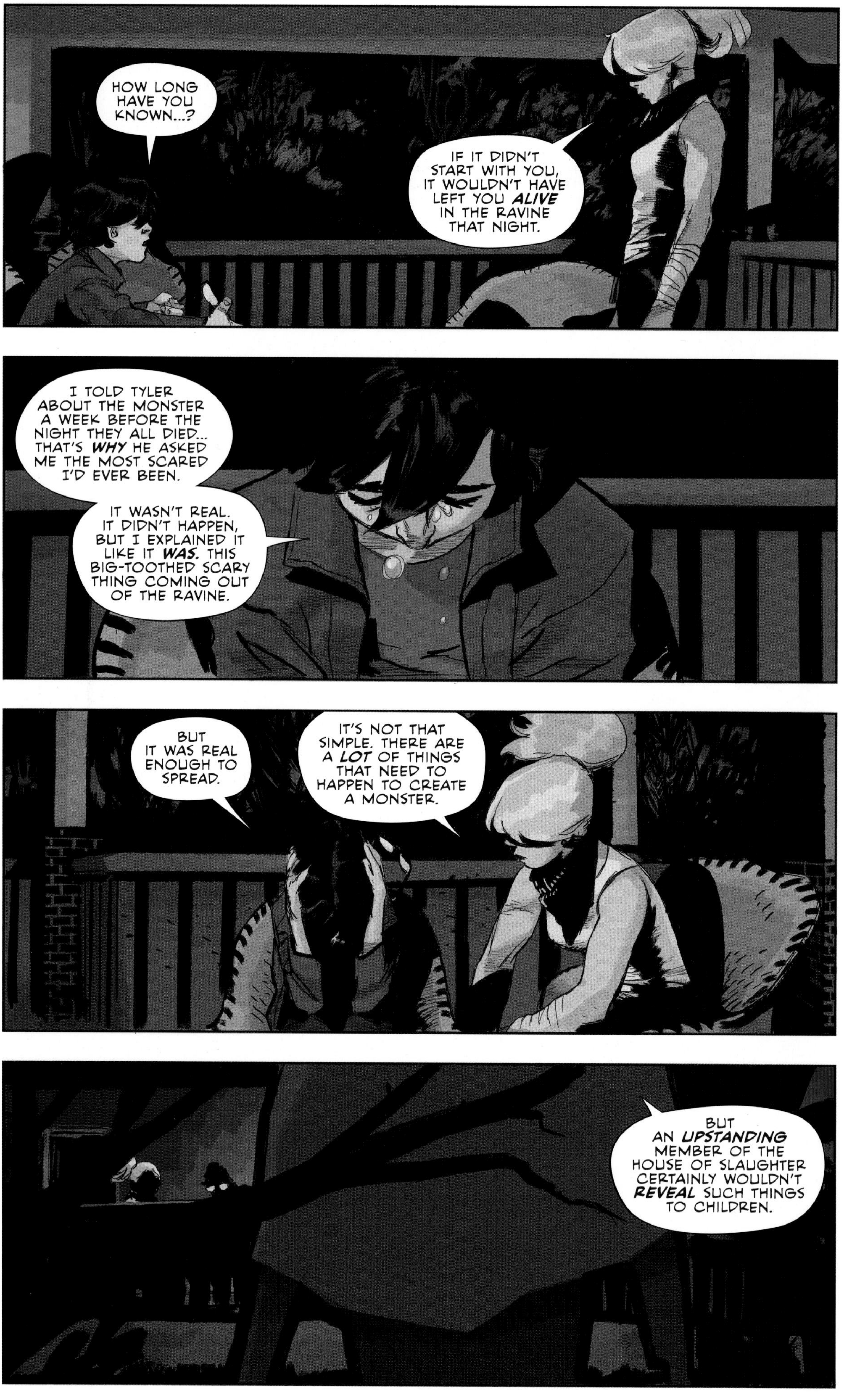
HOW LONG HAVE YOU KNOWN...?
IF IT DIDN'T START WITH YOU, IT WOULDN'T HAVE LEFT YOU ALIVE IN THE RAVINE THAT NIGHT.
I TOLD TYLER ABOUT THE MONSTER A WEEK BEFORE THE NIGHT THEY ALL DIED... THAT'S WHY HE ASKED ME THE MOST SCARED I'D EVER BEEN.
IT WASN'T REAL. IT DIDN'T HAPPEN, BUT I EXPLAINED IT LIKE IT WAS. THIS BIG-TOOTHED SCARY THING COMING OUT OF THE RAVINE.
BUT IT WAS REAL ENOUGH TO SPREAD.
IT'S NOT THAT SIMPLE. THERE ARE A LOT OF THINGS THAT NEED TO HAPPEN TO CREATE A MONSTER.
BUT AN UPSTANDING MEMBER OF THE HOUSE OF SLAUGHTER CERTAINLY WOULDN'T REVEAL SUCH THINGS TO CHILDREN.

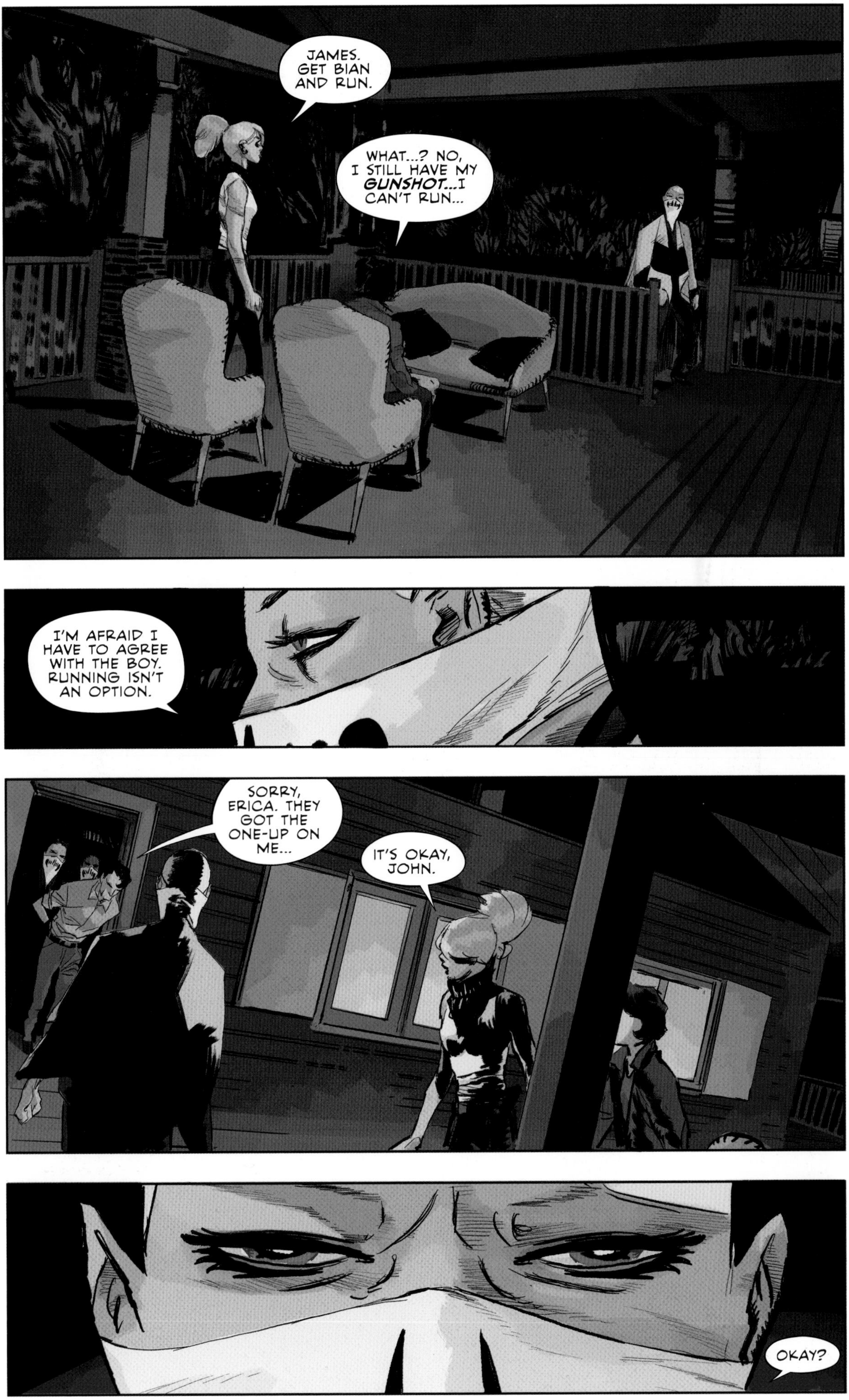
JAMES. GET BIAN AND RUN.
WHAT...? NO, I STILL HAVE MY *GUNSHOT*...I CAN'T RUN...
I'M AFRAID I HAVE TO AGREE WITH THE BOY. RUNNING ISN'T AN OPTION.
SORRY, ERICA. THEY GOT THE ONE-UP ON ME...
IT'S OKAY, JOHN.
OKAY?

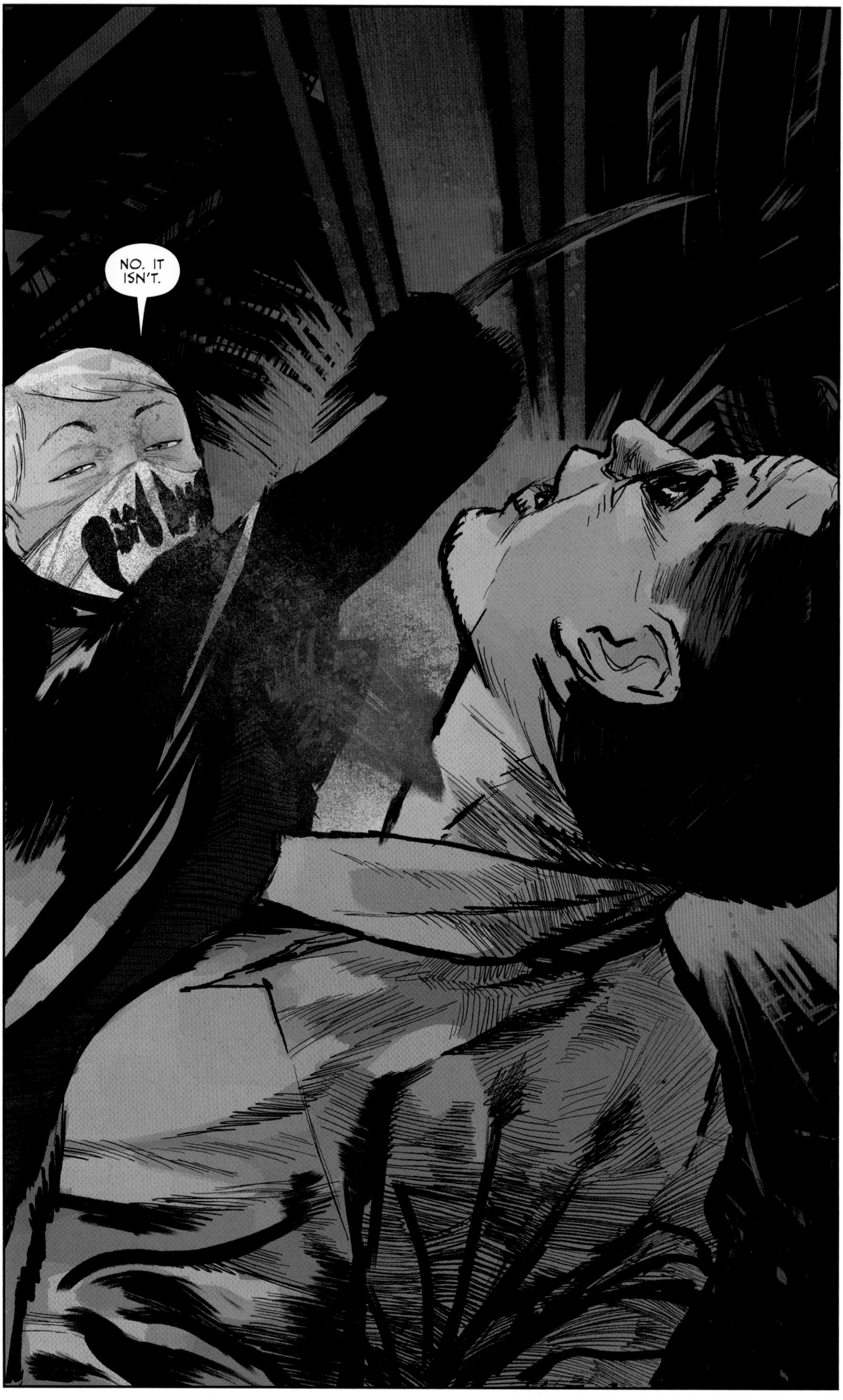
NO. IT ISN'T.

CHAPTER THIRTEEN

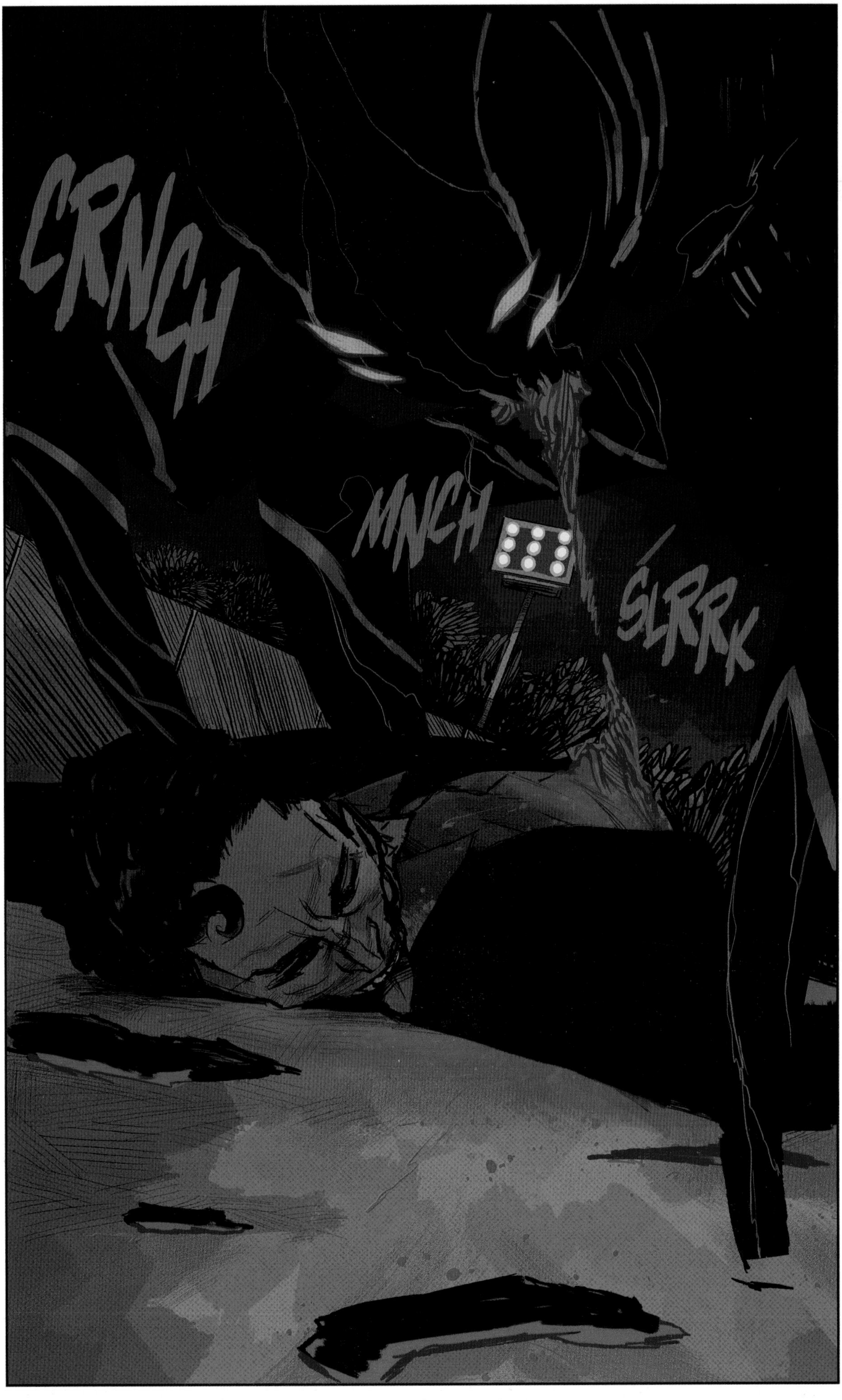
CRNCH
MNCH
SLRRK

THAT'S RIGHT. JUST KEEP LOOKING AT ME.

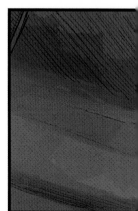

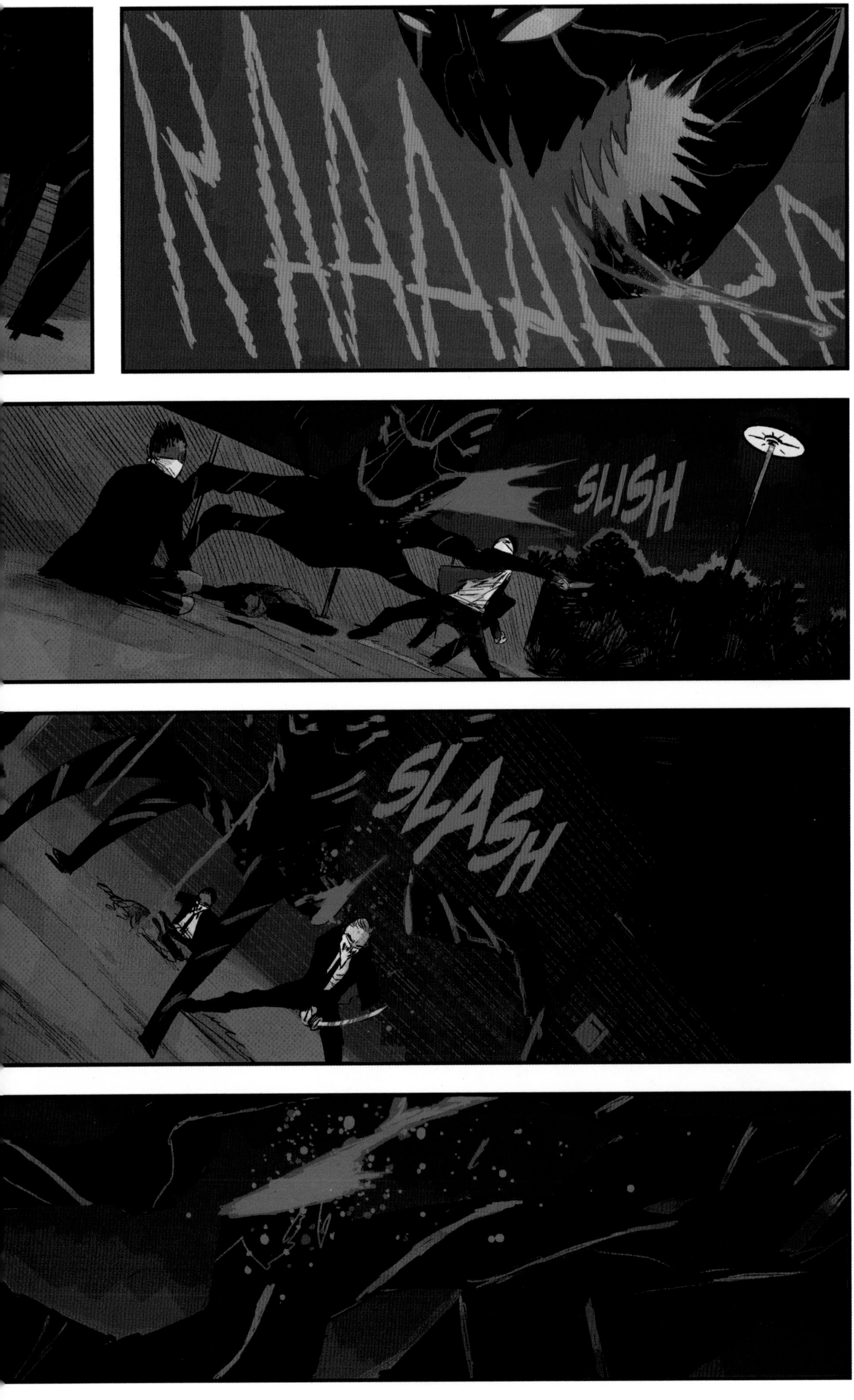
SLISH
SLASH

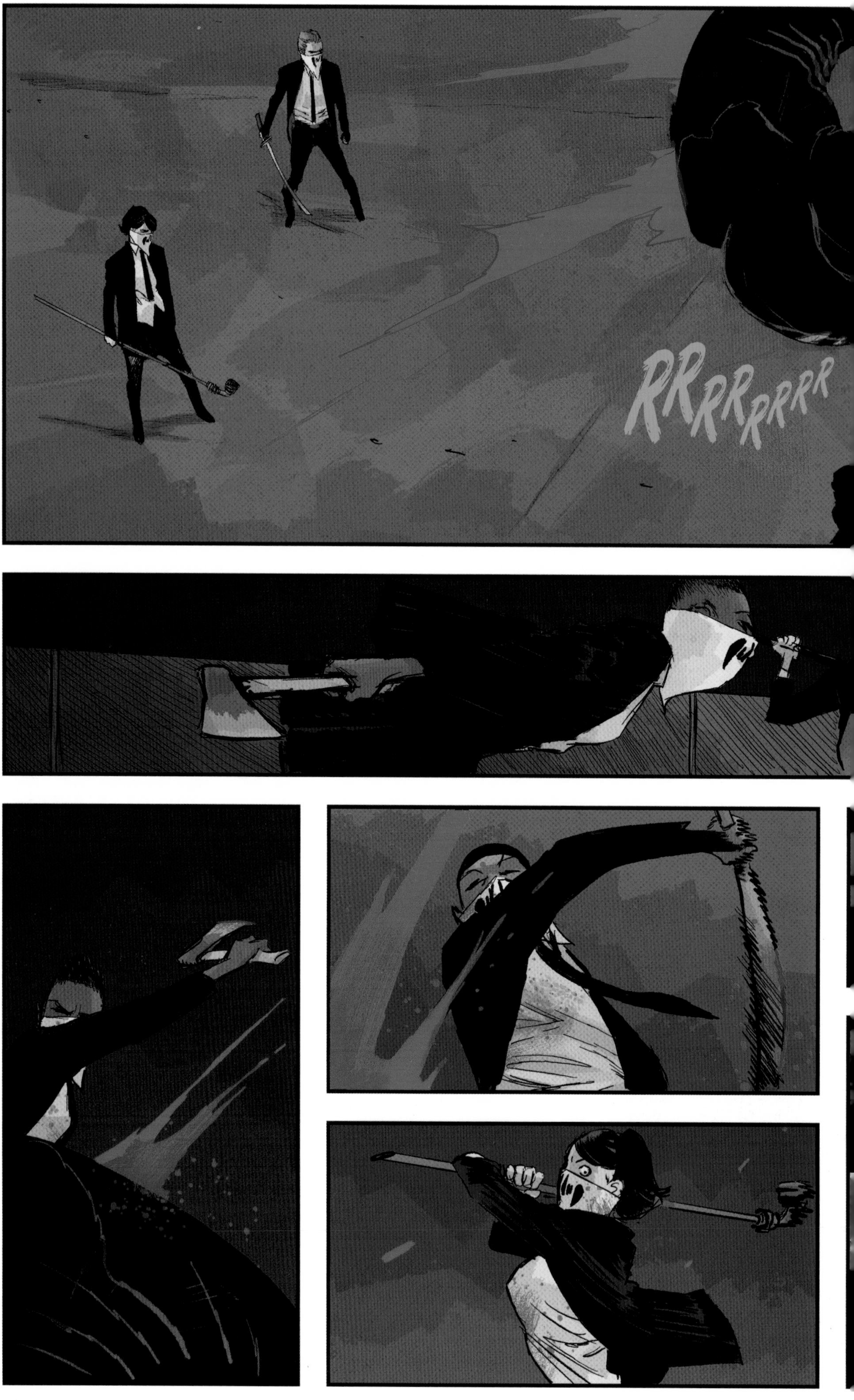
RRRRRRRR

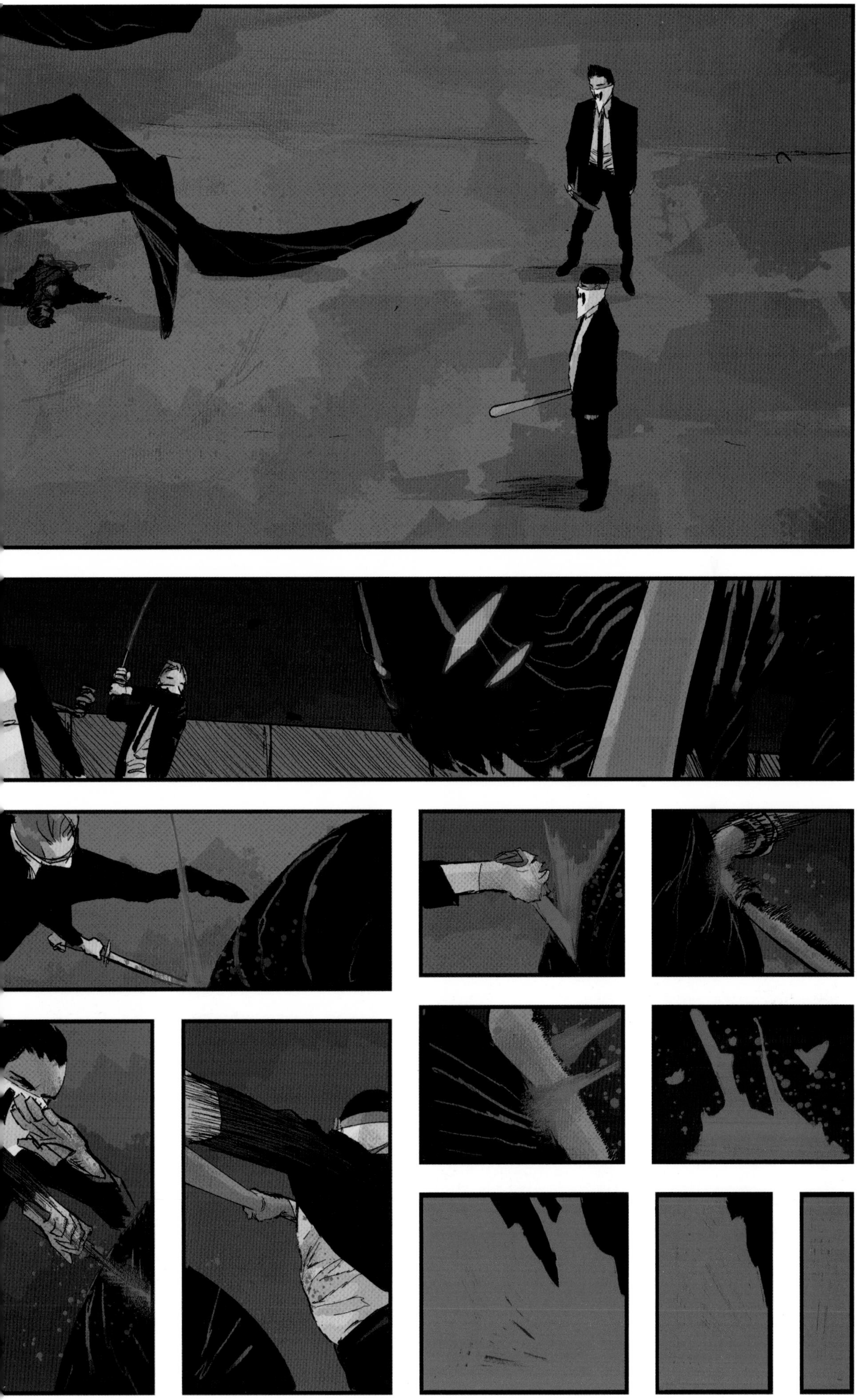

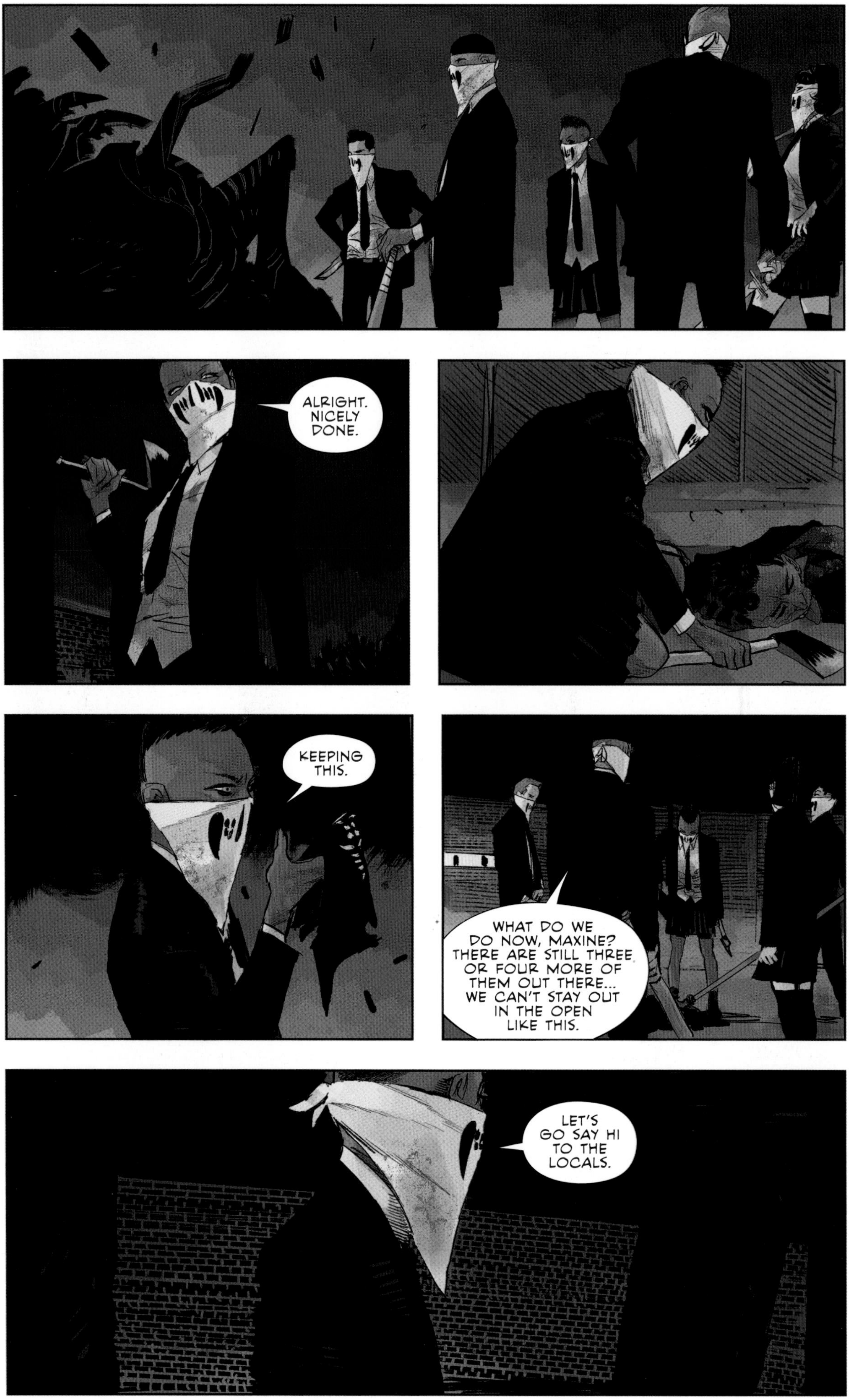
ALRIGHT. NICELY DONE.
KEEPING THIS.
WHAT DO WE DO NOW, MAXINE? THERE ARE STILL THREE OR FOUR MORE OF THEM OUT THERE... WE CAN'T STAY OUT IN THE OPEN LIKE THIS.
LET'S GO SAY HI TO THE LOCALS.

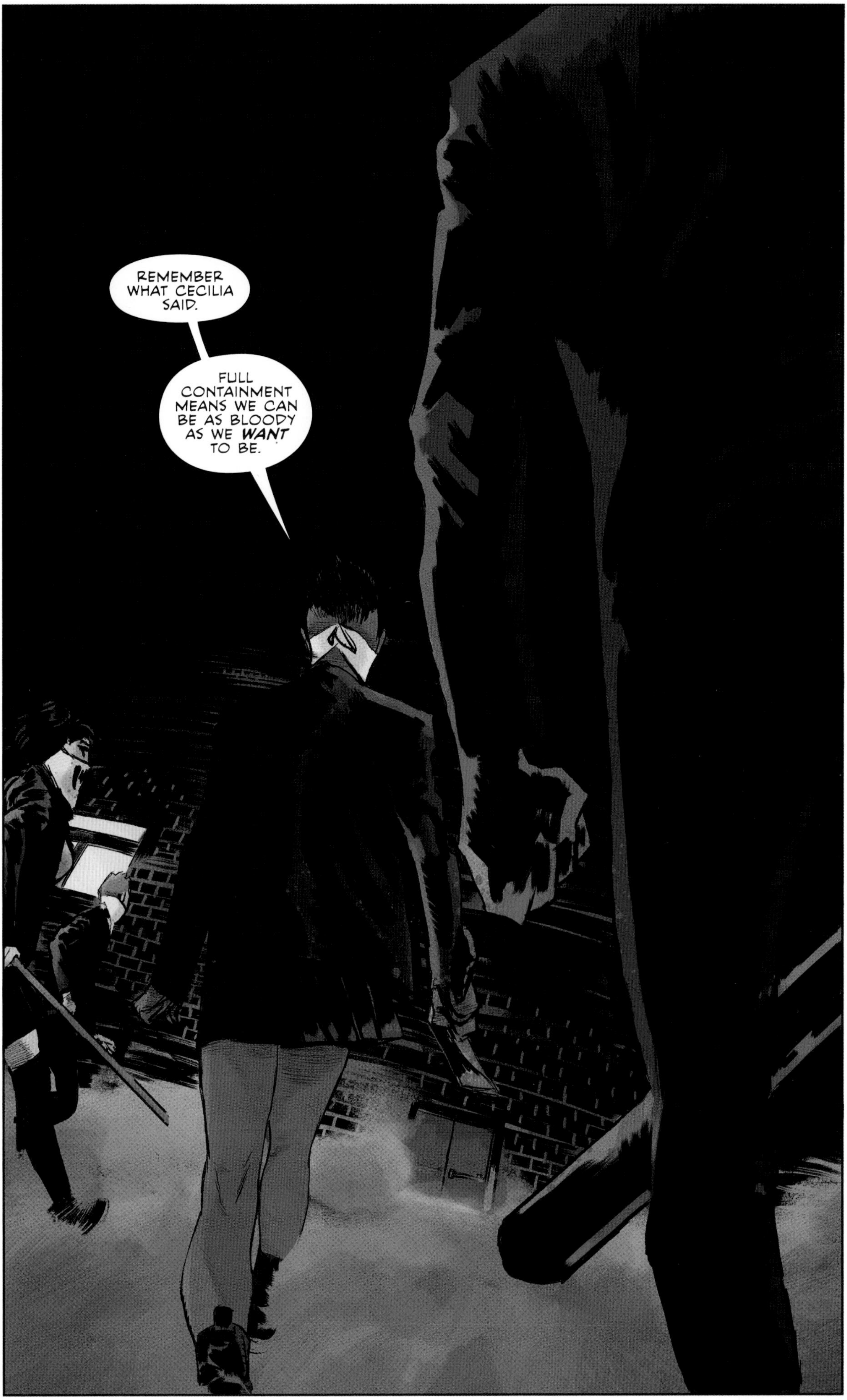
REMEMBER WHAT CECILIA SAID.
FULL CONTAINMENT MEANS WE CAN BE AS BLOODY AS WE *WANT* TO BE.

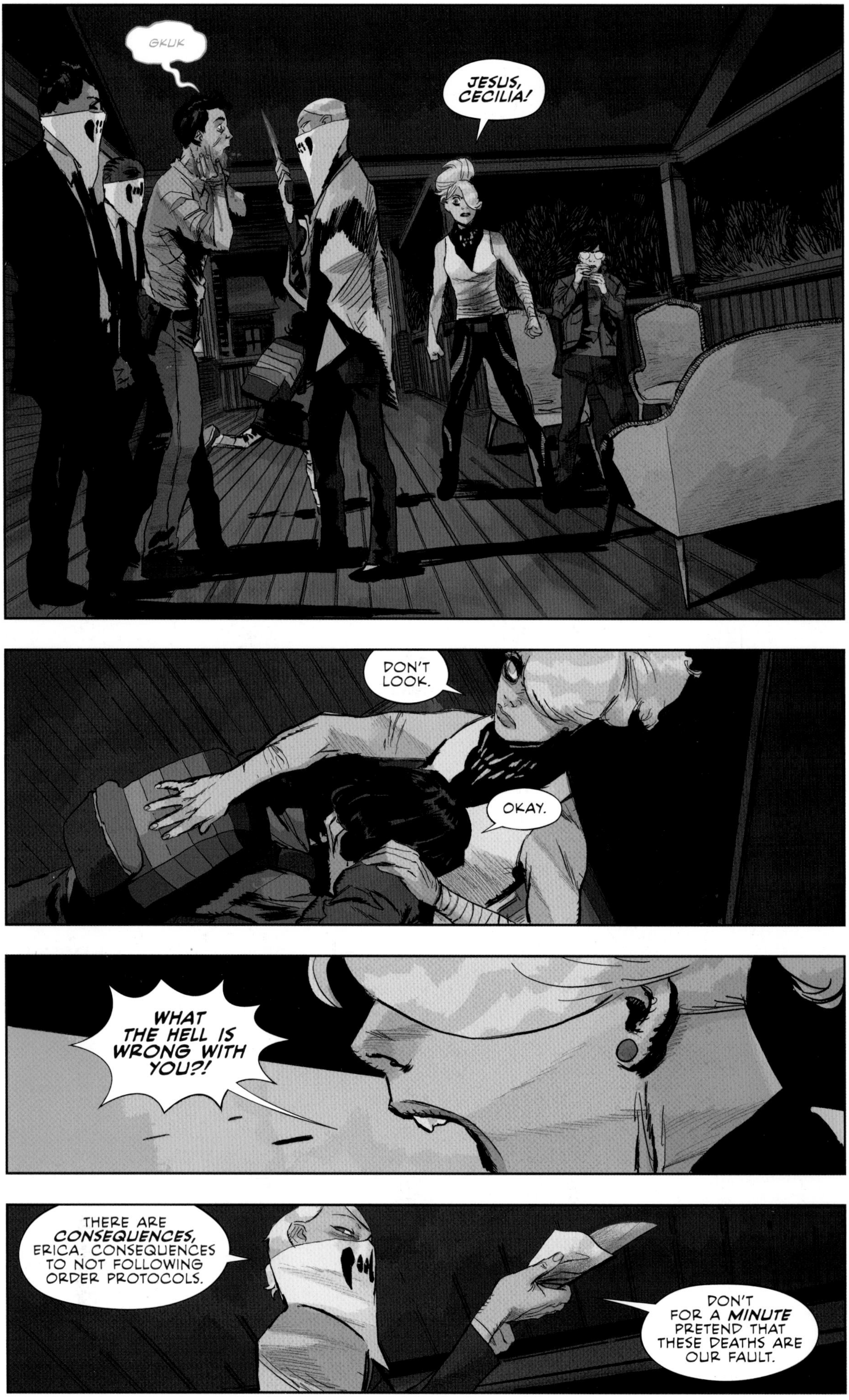
GKUK
JESUS, CECILIA!
DON'T LOOK.
OKAY.
WHAT THE HELL IS WRONG WITH YOU?!
THERE ARE CONSEQUENCES, ERICA. CONSEQUENCES TO NOT FOLLOWING ORDER PROTOCOLS.
DON'T FOR A MINUTE PRETEND THAT THESE DEATHS ARE OUR FAULT.

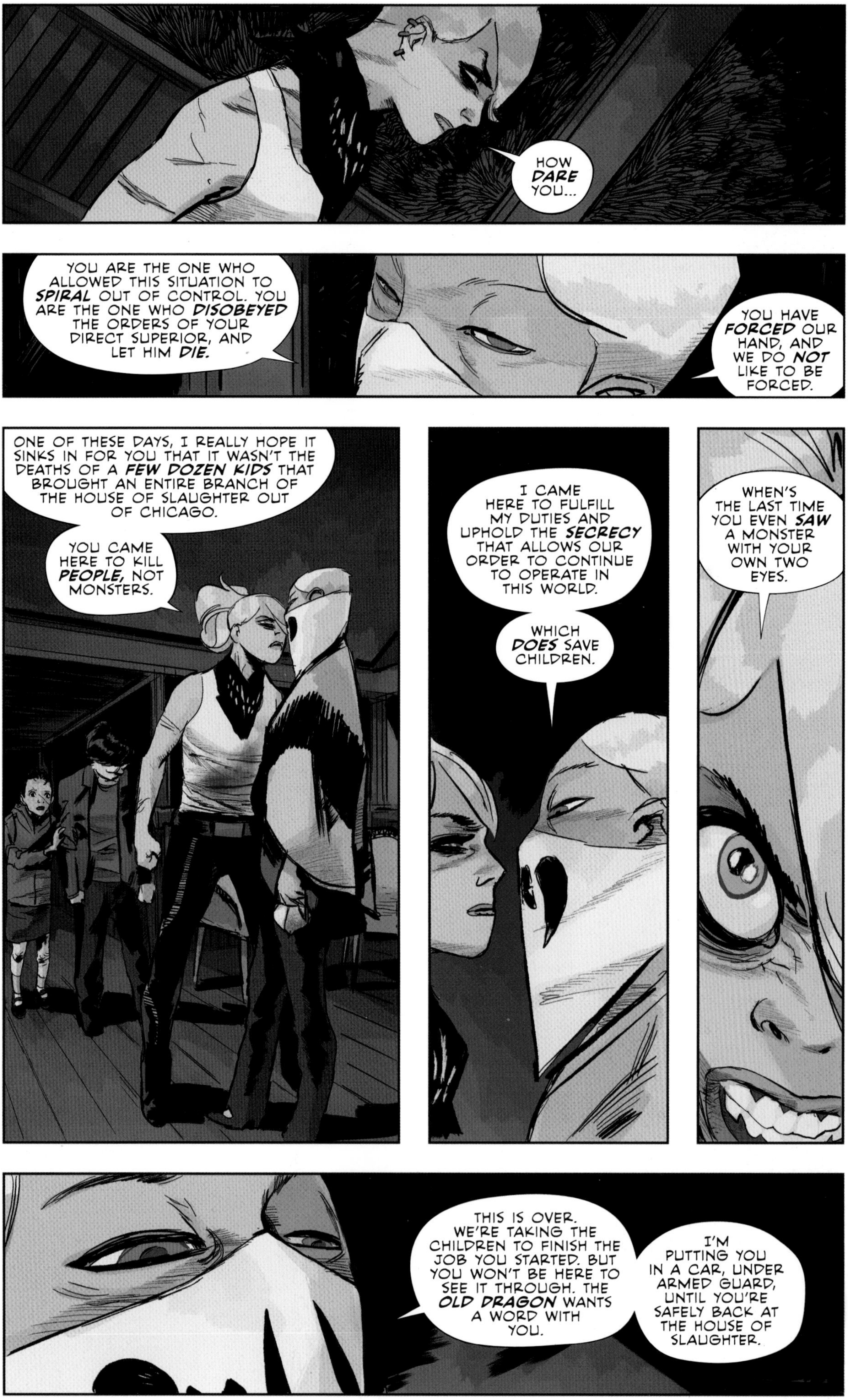
HOW DARE YOU...
YOU ARE THE ONE WHO ALLOWED THIS SITUATION TO SPIRAL OUT OF CONTROL. YOU ARE THE ONE WHO DISOBEYED THE ORDERS OF YOUR DIRECT SUPERIOR, AND LET HIM DIE.
YOU HAVE FORCED OUR HAND, AND WE DO NOT LIKE TO BE FORCED.
ONE OF THESE DAYS, I REALLY HOPE IT SINKS IN FOR YOU THAT IT WASN'T THE DEATHS OF A FEW DOZEN KIDS THAT BROUGHT AN ENTIRE BRANCH OF THE HOUSE OF SLAUGHTER OUT OF CHICAGO.
YOU CAME HERE TO KILL PEOPLE, NOT MONSTERS.
I CAME HERE TO FULFILL MY DUTIES AND UPHOLD THE SECRECY THAT ALLOWS OUR ORDER TO CONTINUE TO OPERATE IN THIS WORLD.
WHICH DOES SAVE CHILDREN.
WHEN'S THE LAST TIME YOU EVEN SAW A MONSTER WITH YOUR OWN TWO EYES.
THIS IS OVER. WE'RE TAKING THE CHILDREN TO FINISH THE JOB YOU STARTED. BUT YOU WON'T BE HERE TO SEE IT THROUGH. THE OLD DRAGON WANTS A WORD WITH YOU.
I'M PUTTING YOU IN A CAR, UNDER ARMED GUARD, UNTIL YOU'RE SAFELY BACK AT THE HOUSE OF SLAUGHTER.

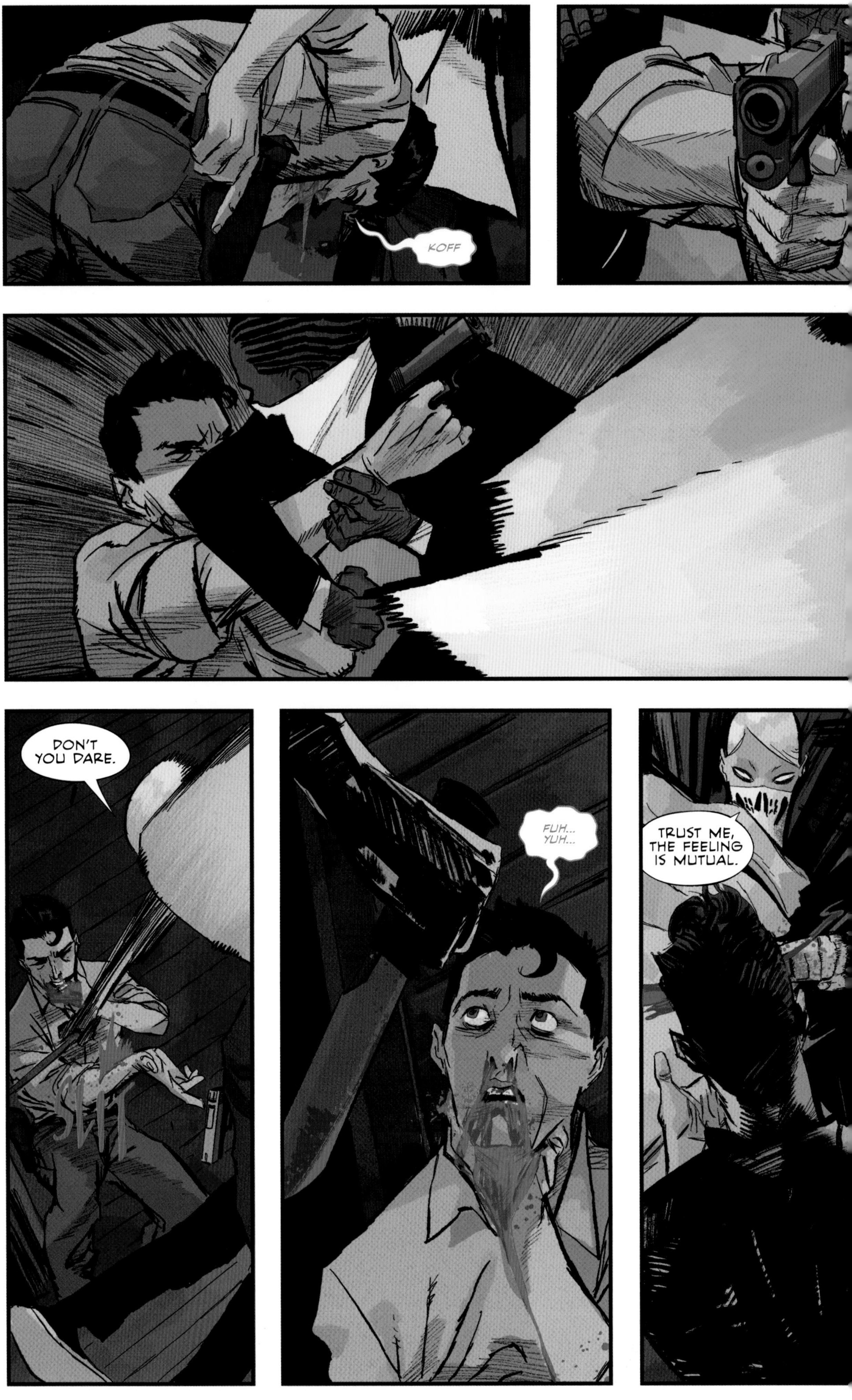
KOFF
DON'T YOU DARE.
FUH... YUH...
TRUST ME, THE FEELING IS MUTUAL.

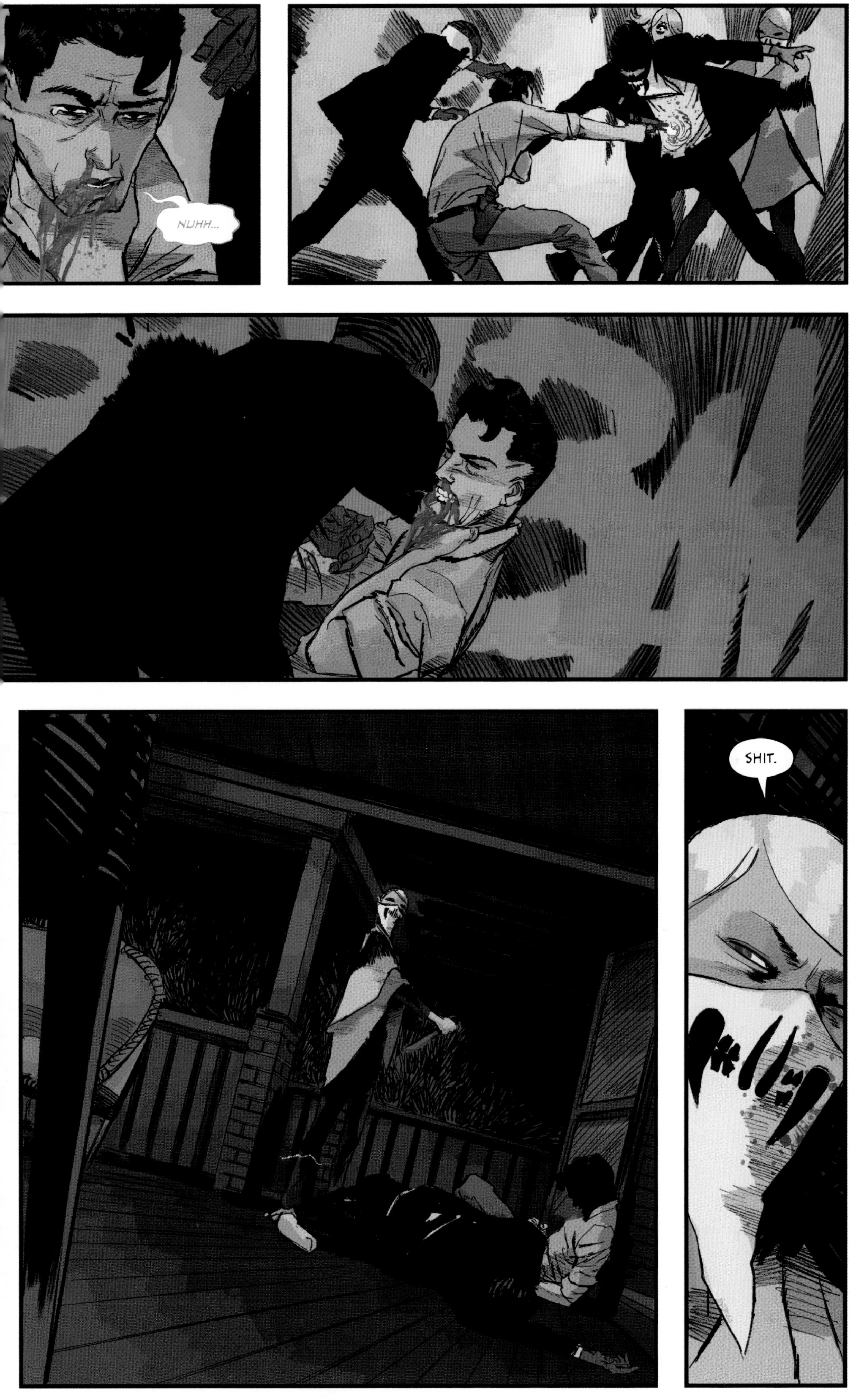
NUHH...
SHIT.

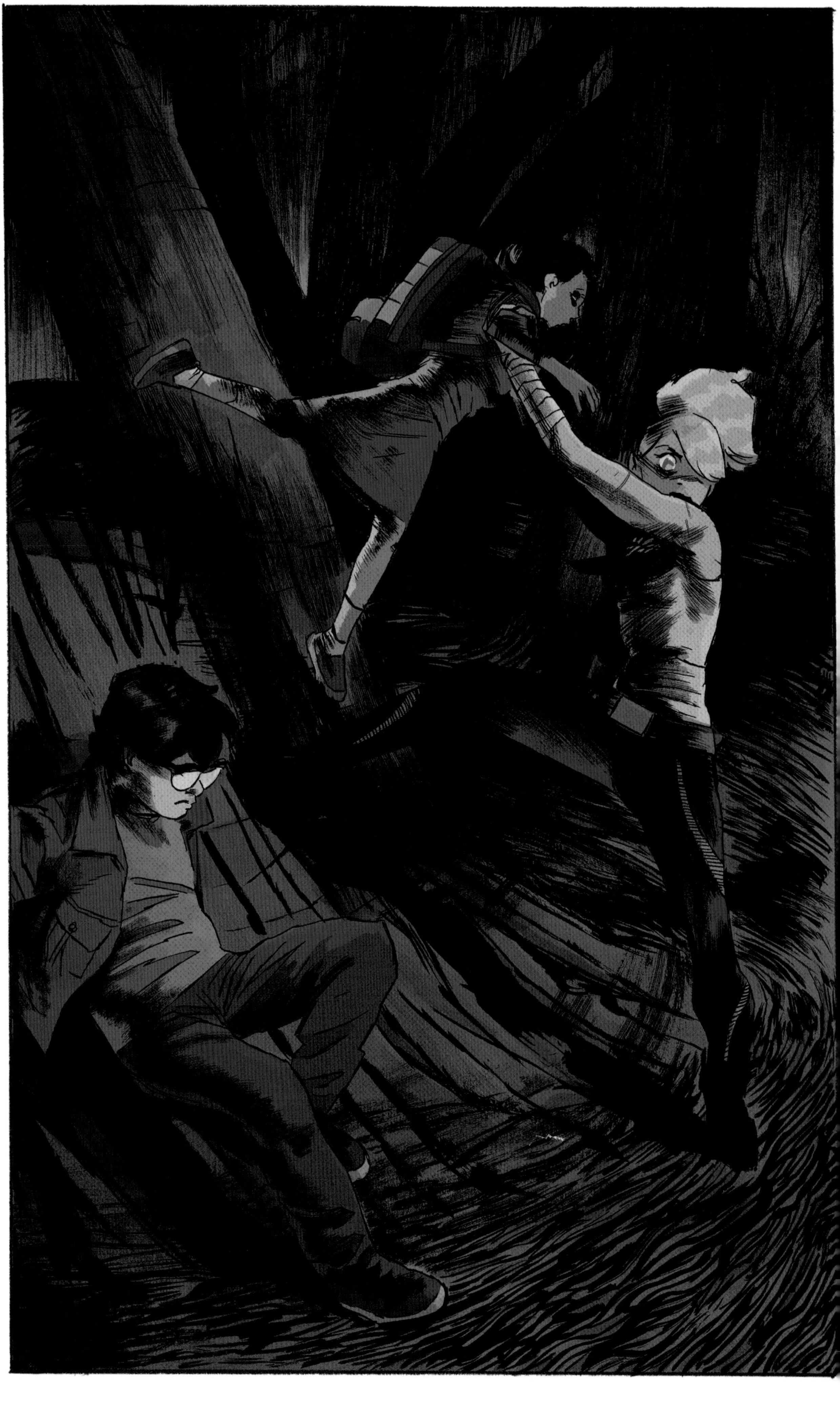

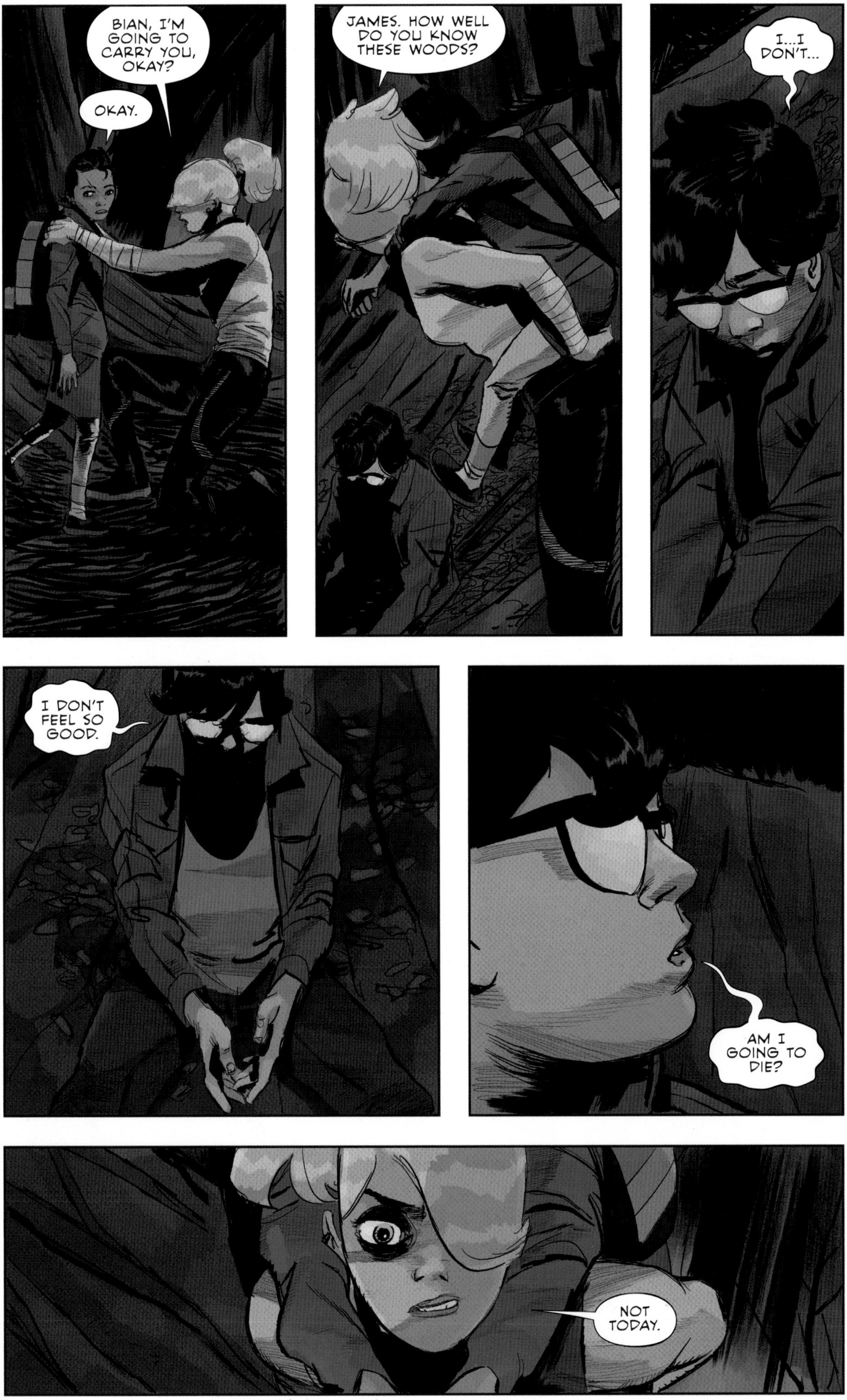
BIAN, I'M GOING TO CARRY YOU, OKAY?
OKAY.
JAMES. HOW WELL DO YOU KNOW THESE WOODS?
I...I DON'T...
I DON'T FEEL SO GOOD.
AM I GOING TO DIE?
NOT TODAY.

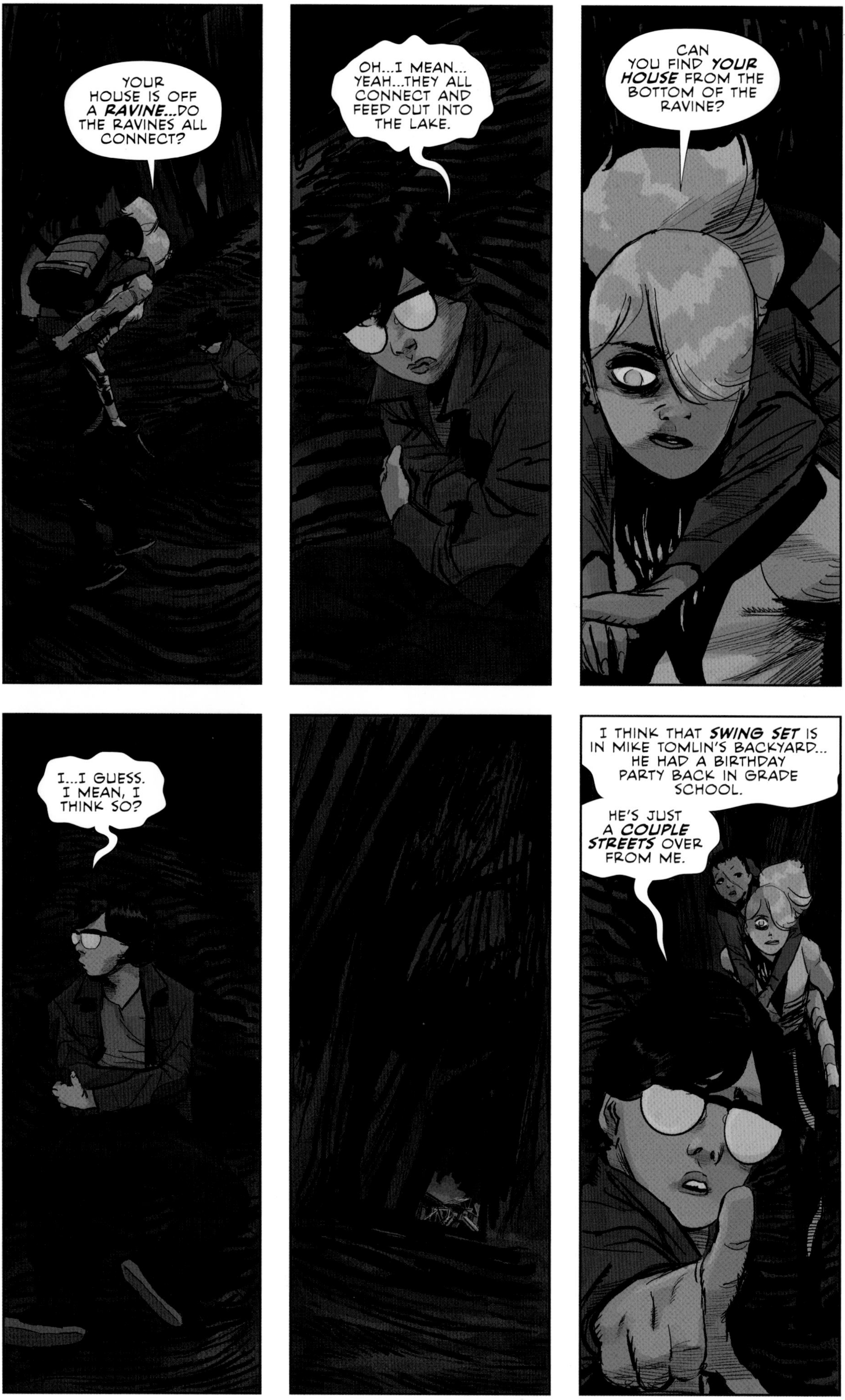
YOUR HOUSE IS OFF A RAVINE...DO THE RAVINES ALL CONNECT?
OH...I MEAN... YEAH...THEY ALL CONNECT AND FEED OUT INTO THE LAKE.
CAN YOU FIND YOUR HOUSE FROM THE BOTTOM OF THE RAVINE?
I...I GUESS. I MEAN, I THINK SO?
I THINK THAT SWING SET IS IN MIKE TOMLIN'S BACKYARD... HE HAD A BIRTHDAY PARTY BACK IN GRADE SCHOOL.
HE'S JUST A COUPLE STREETS OVER FROM ME.

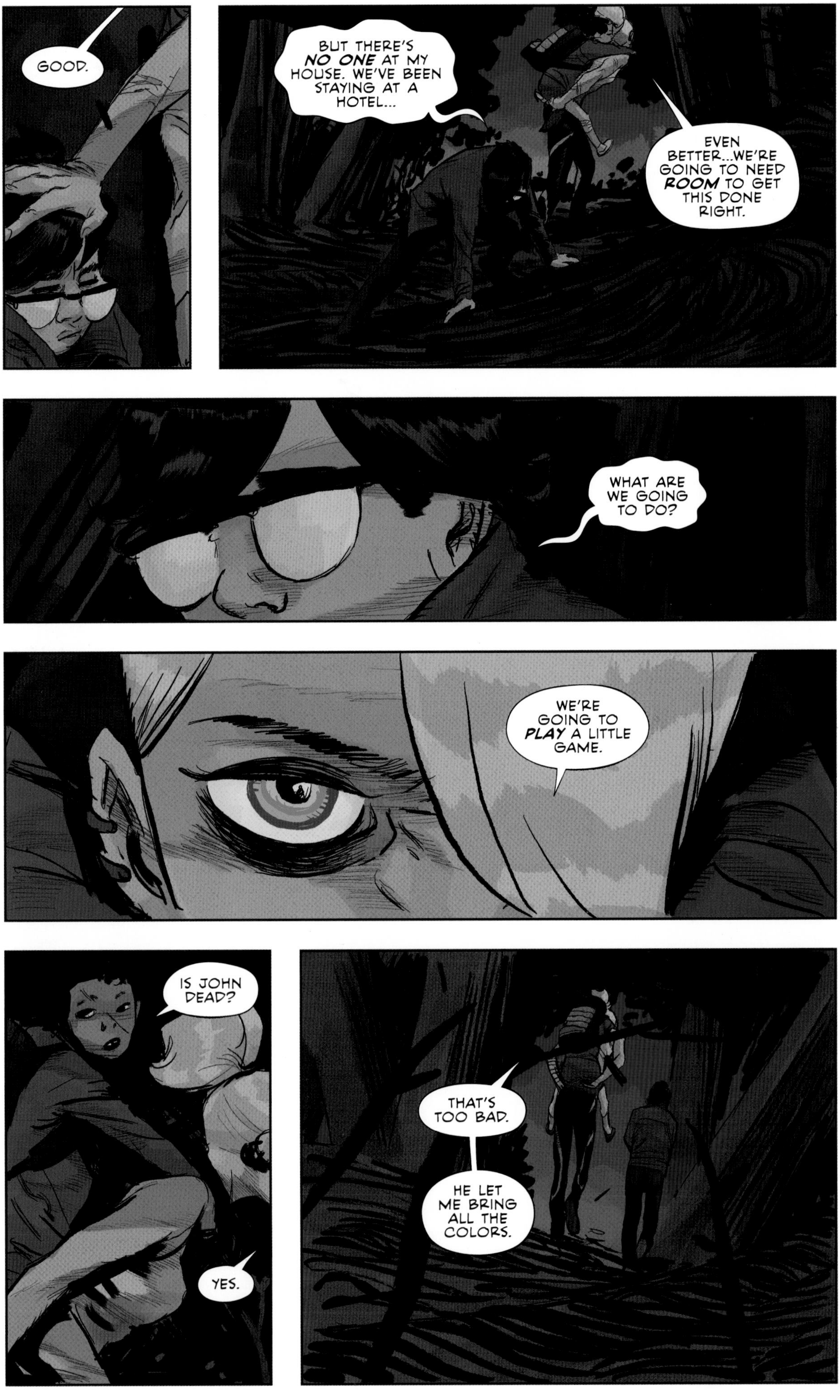
GOOD.
BUT THERE'S NO ONE AT MY HOUSE. WE'VE BEEN STAYING AT A HOTEL...
EVEN BETTER...WE'RE GOING TO NEED ROOM TO GET THIS DONE RIGHT.
WHAT ARE WE GOING TO DO?
WE'RE GOING TO PLAY A LITTLE GAME.
IS JOHN DEAD?
YES.
THAT'S TOO BAD.
HE LET ME BRING ALL THE COLORS.

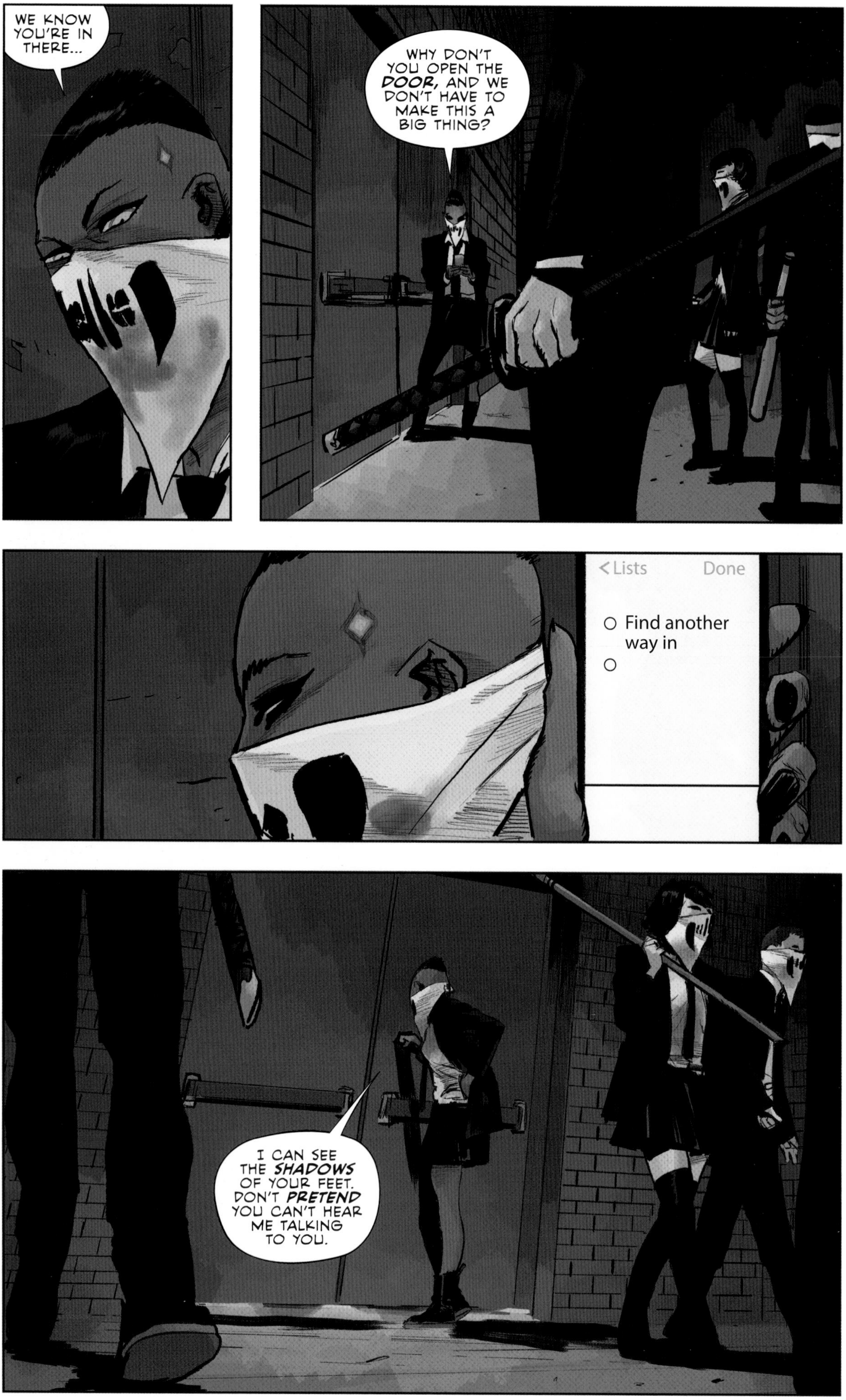
WE KNOW YOU'RE IN THERE...
WHY DON'T YOU OPEN THE DOOR, AND WE DON'T HAVE TO MAKE THIS A BIG THING?
< Lists
Done
Find another way in
I CAN SEE THE SHADOWS OF YOUR FEET. DON'T PRETEND YOU CAN'T HEAR ME TALKING TO YOU.

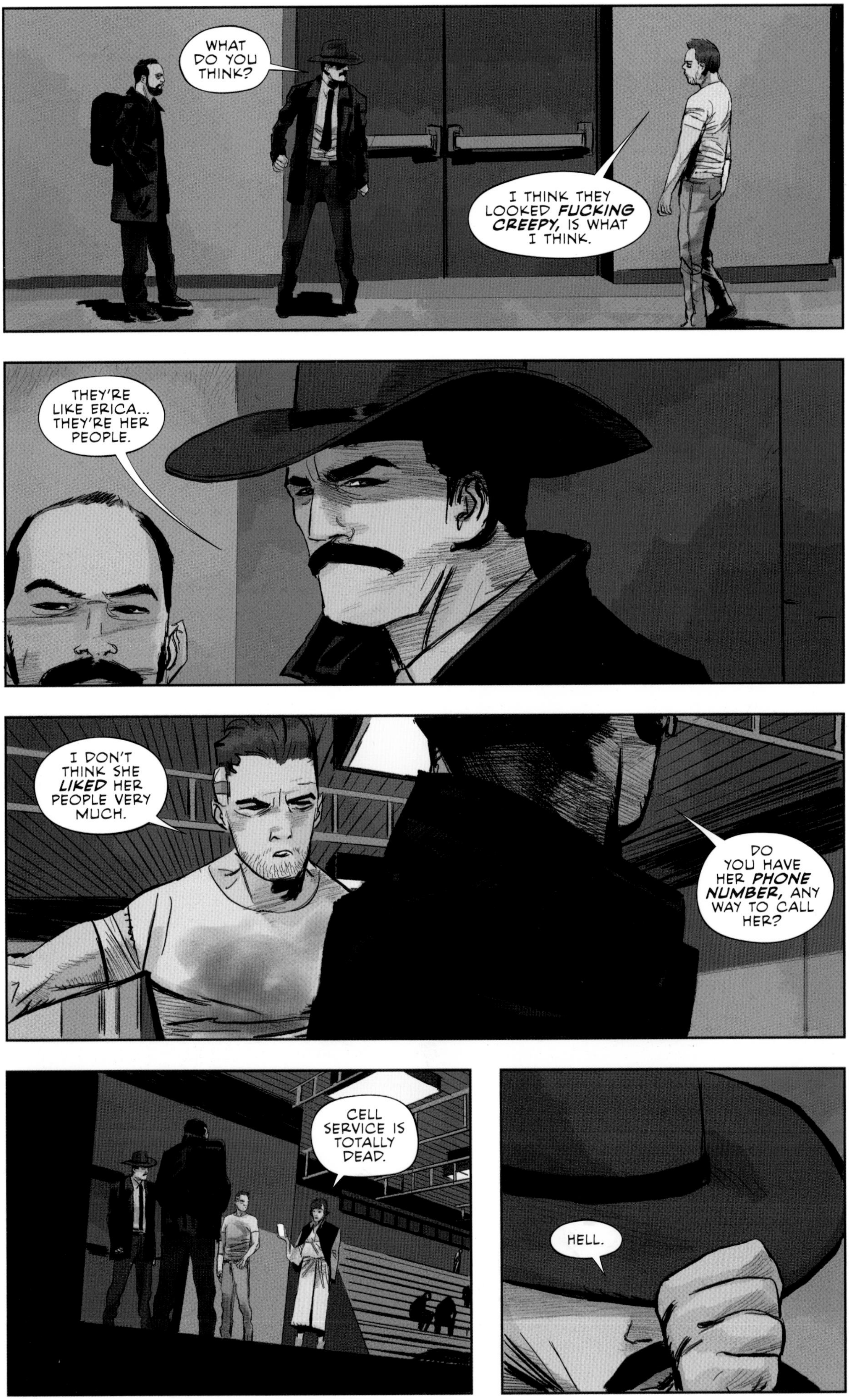
WHAT DO YOU THINK?
I THINK THEY LOOKED **FUCKING CREEPY,** IS WHAT I THINK.
THEY'RE LIKE ERICA... THEY'RE HER PEOPLE.
I DON'T THINK SHE ***LIKED*** HER PEOPLE VERY MUCH.
DO YOU HAVE HER **PHONE NUMBER,** ANY WAY TO CALL HER?
CELL SERVICE IS TOTALLY DEAD.
HELL.

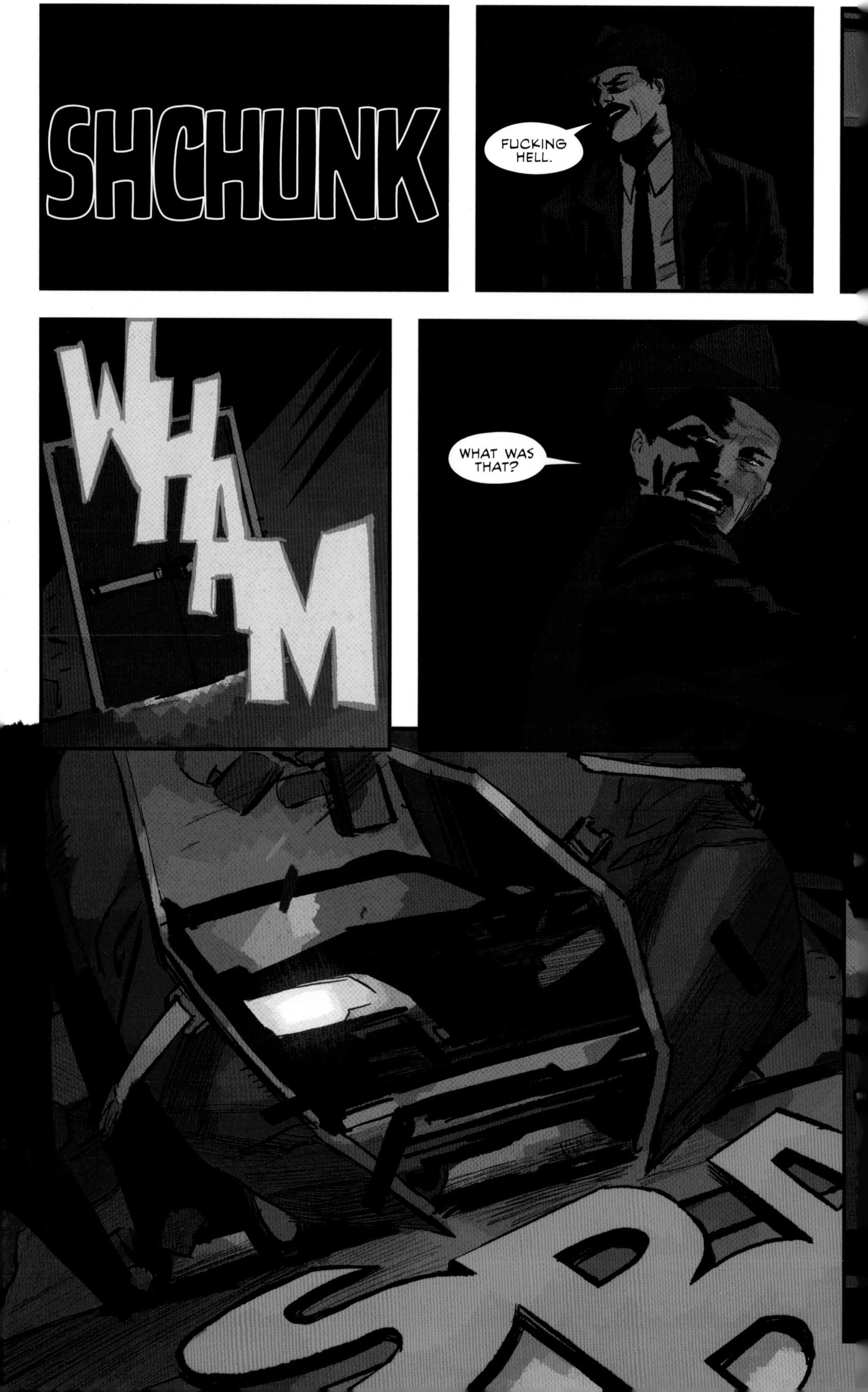
SHCHUNK
FUCKING HELL.
WHAM
WHAT WAS THAT?

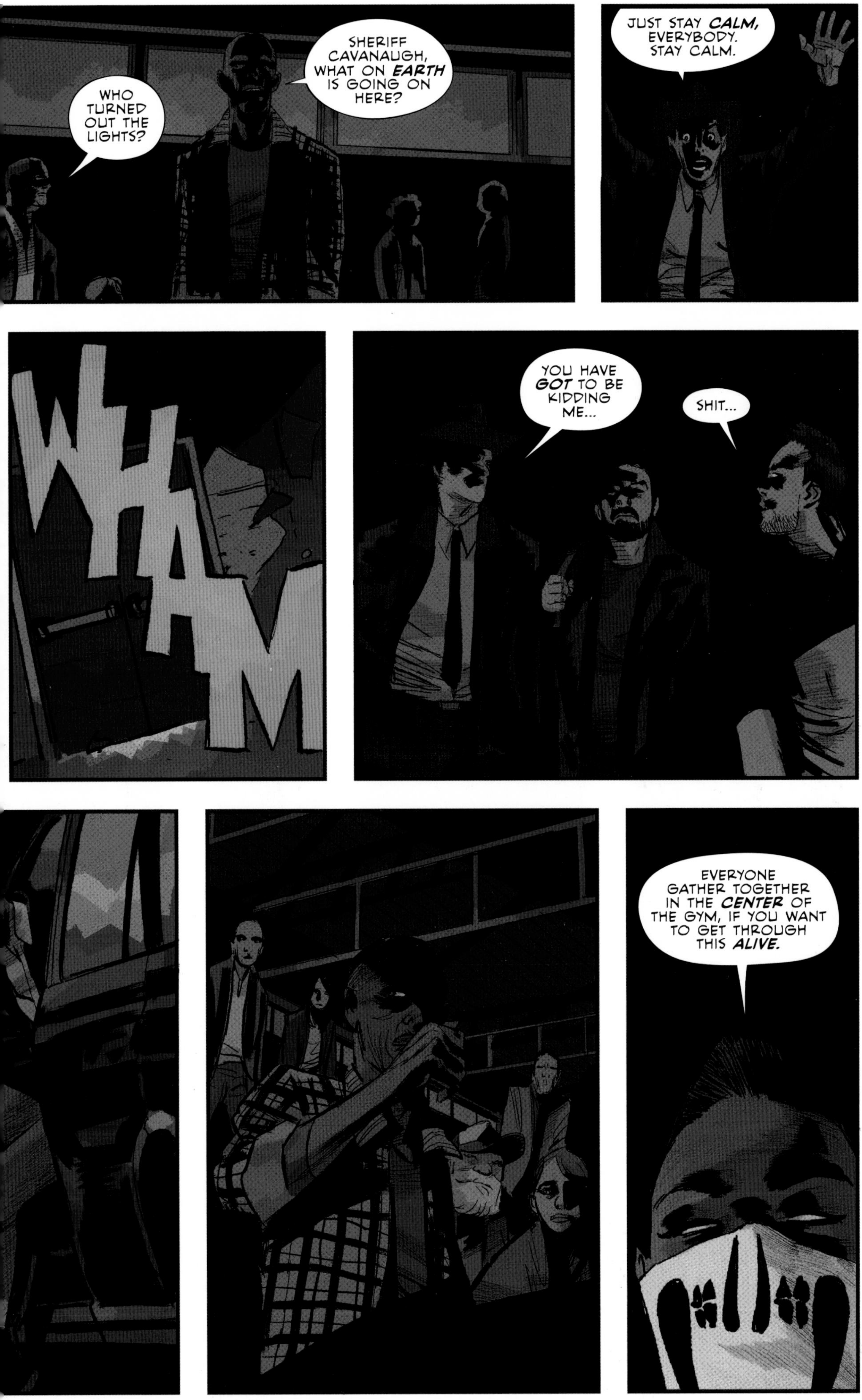
WHO TURNED OUT THE LIGHTS?
SHERIFF CAVANAUGH, WHAT ON EARTH IS GOING ON HERE?
JUST STAY CALM, EVERYBODY. STAY CALM.
WHAM
YOU HAVE GOT TO BE KIDDING ME...
SHIT...
EVERYONE GATHER TOGETHER IN THE CENTER OF THE GYM, IF YOU WANT TO GET THROUGH THIS ALIVE.

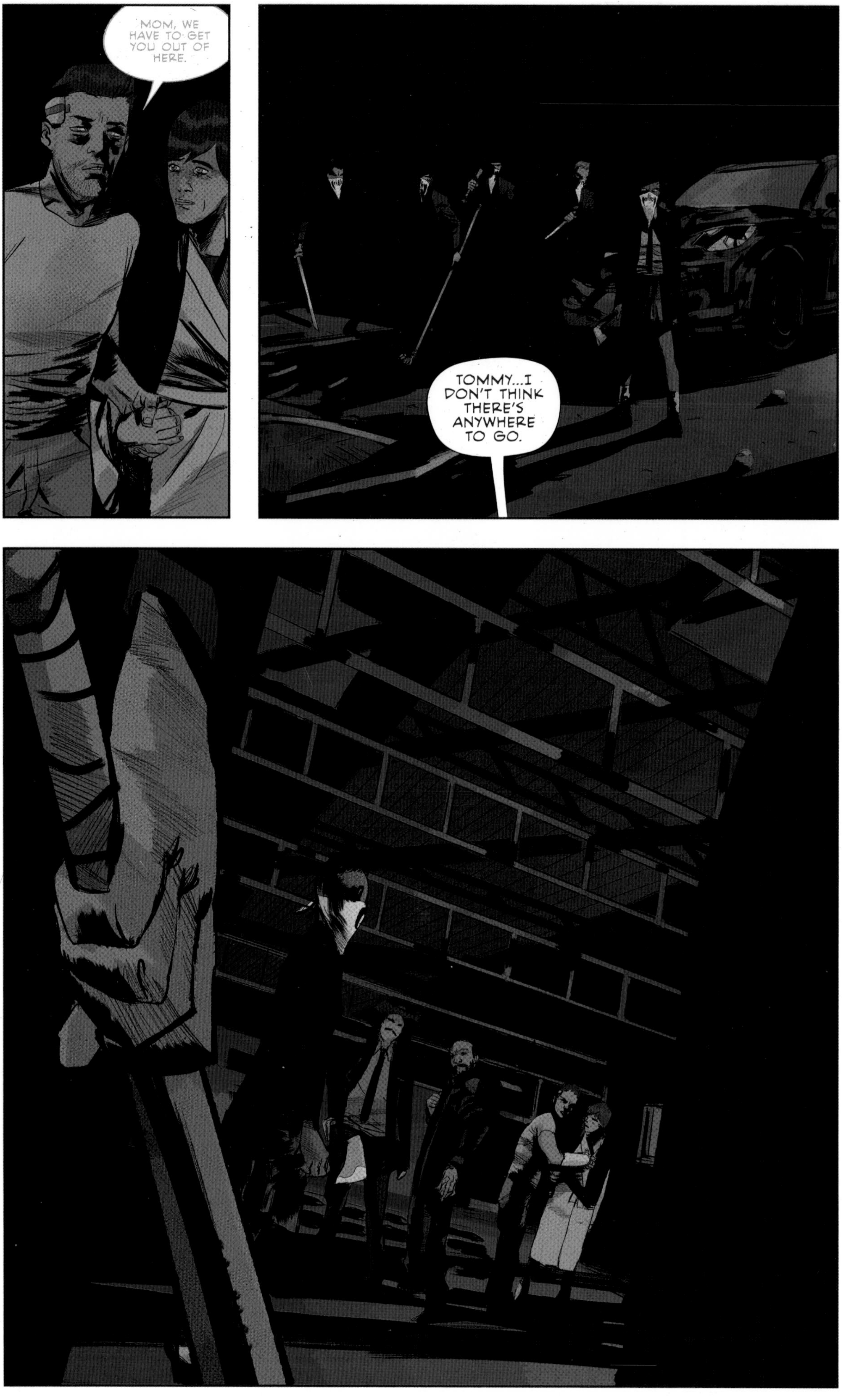
MOM, WE HAVE TO GET YOU OUT OF HERE.
TOMMY...I DON'T THINK THERE'S ANYWHERE TO GO.

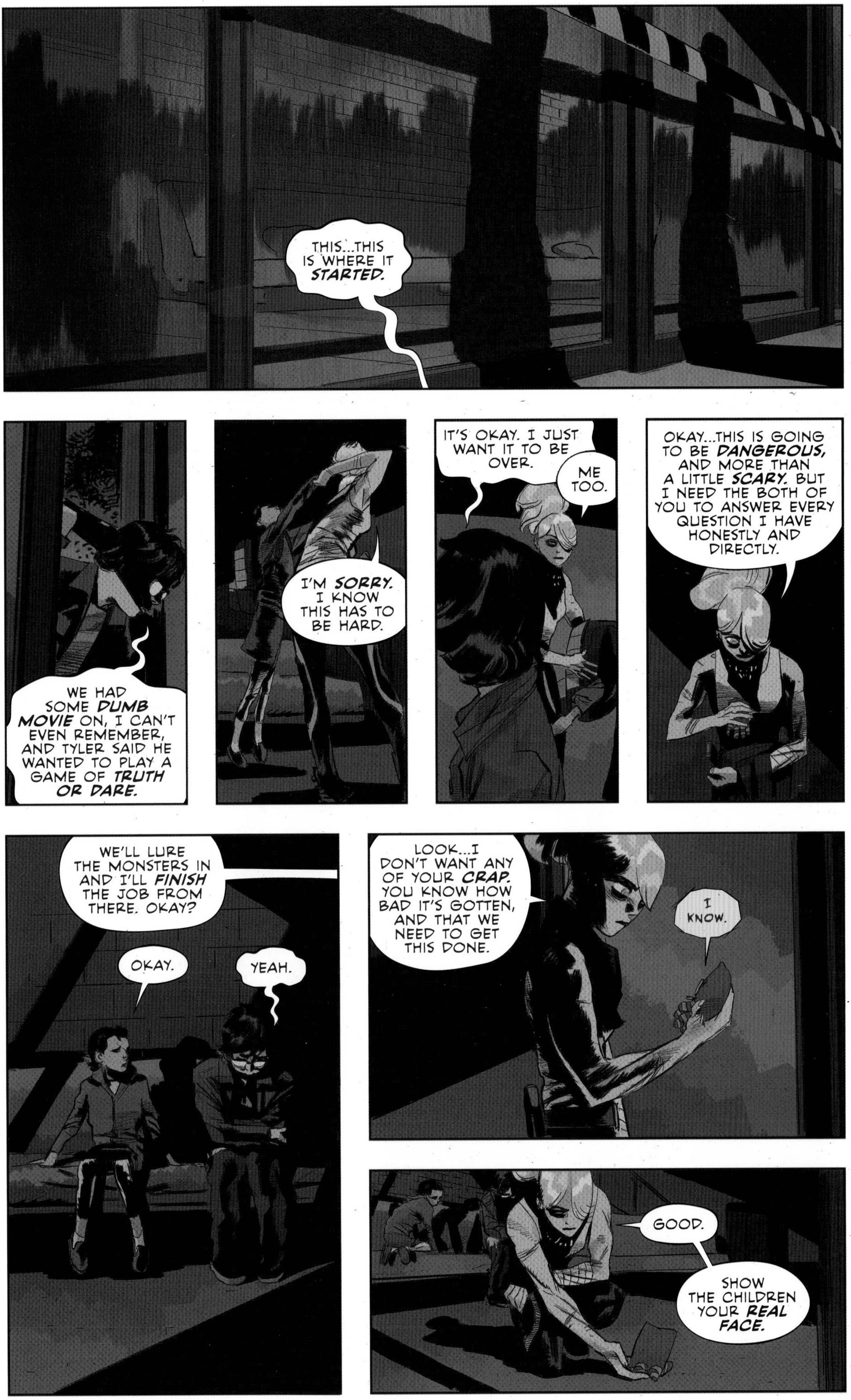

THIS...THIS IS WHERE IT STARTED.
WE HAD SOME DUMB MOVIE ON, I CAN'T EVEN REMEMBER, AND TYLER SAID HE WANTED TO PLAY A GAME OF TRUTH OR DARE.
I'M SORRY. I KNOW THIS HAS TO BE HARD.
IT'S OKAY. I JUST WANT IT TO BE OVER.
ME TOO.
OKAY...THIS IS GOING TO BE DANGEROUS, AND MORE THAN A LITTLE SCARY. BUT I NEED THE BOTH OF YOU TO ANSWER EVERY QUESTION I HAVE HONESTLY AND DIRECTLY.
WE'LL LURE THE MONSTERS IN AND I'LL FINISH THE JOB FROM THERE. OKAY?
OKAY.
YEAH.
LOOK...I DON'T WANT ANY OF YOUR CRAP. YOU KNOW HOW BAD IT'S GOTTEN, AND THAT WE NEED TO GET THIS DONE.
I KNOW.
GOOD.
SHOW THE CHILDREN YOUR REAL FACE.

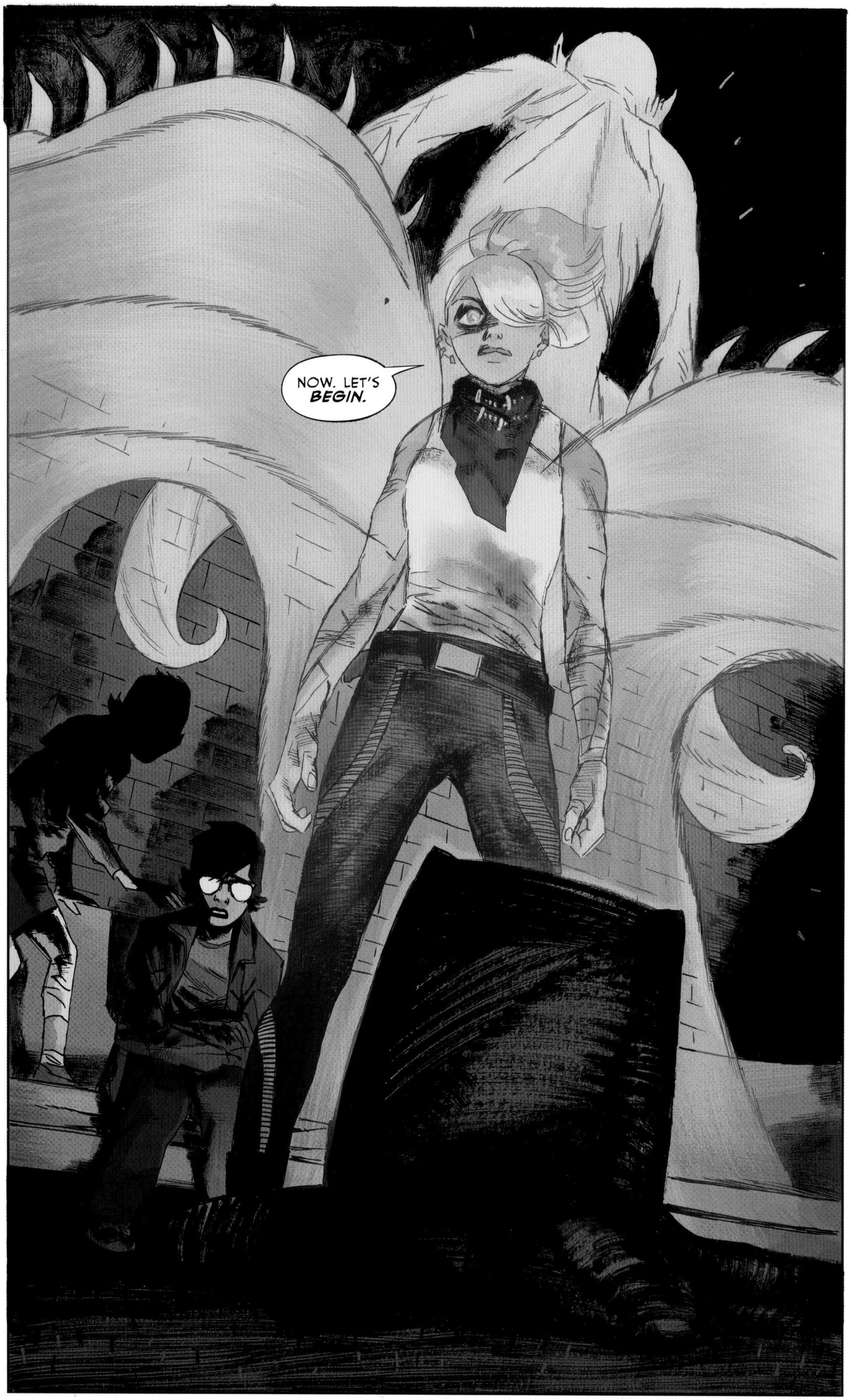
NOW. LET'S *BEGIN.*

CHAPTER FOURTEEN

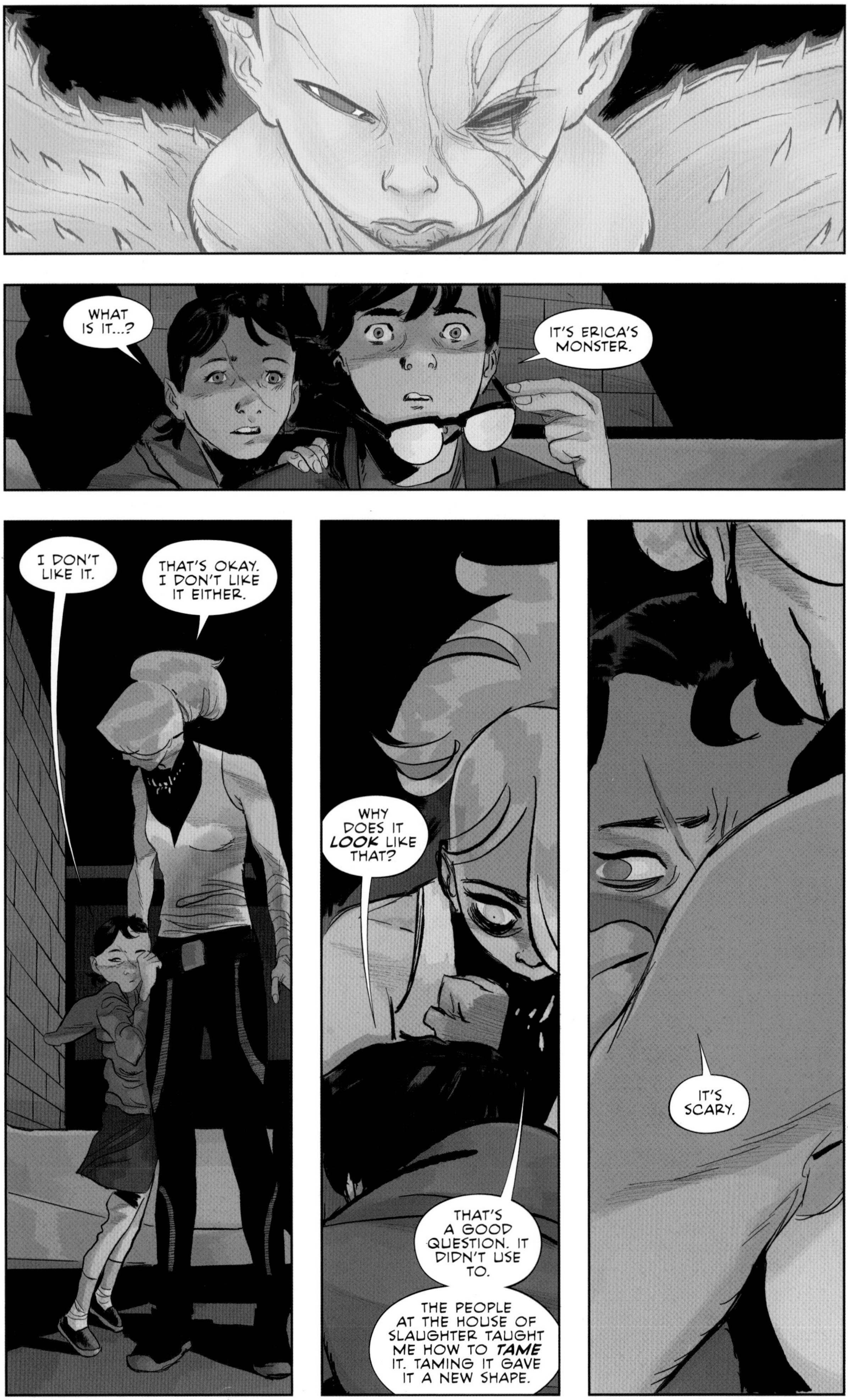
WHAT IS IT...?
IT'S ERICA'S MONSTER.
I DON'T LIKE IT.
THAT'S OKAY. I DON'T LIKE IT EITHER.
WHY DOES IT LOOK LIKE THAT?
THAT'S A GOOD QUESTION. IT DIDN'T USE TO.
THE PEOPLE AT THE HOUSE OF SLAUGHTER TAUGHT ME HOW TO TAME IT. TAMING IT GAVE IT A NEW SHAPE.
IT'S SCARY.

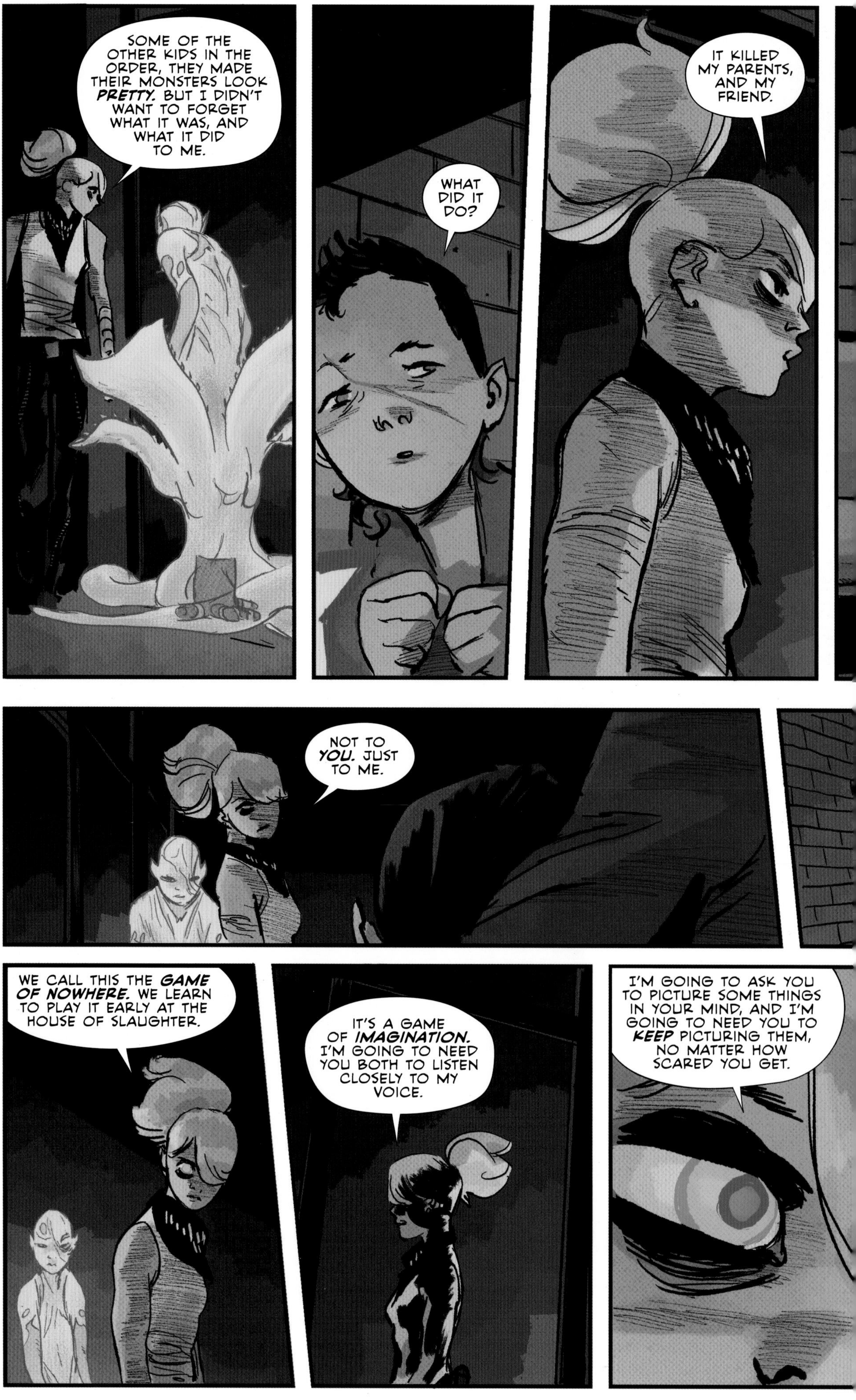
SOME OF THE OTHER KIDS IN THE ORDER, THEY MADE THEIR MONSTERS LOOK *PRETTY.* BUT I DIDN'T WANT TO FORGET WHAT IT WAS, AND WHAT IT DID TO ME.
WHAT DID IT DO?
IT KILLED MY PARENTS, AND MY FRIEND.
NOT TO *YOU.* JUST TO ME.
WE CALL THIS THE *GAME OF NOWHERE.* WE LEARN TO PLAY IT EARLY AT THE HOUSE OF SLAUGHTER.
IT'S A GAME OF *IMAGINATION.* I'M GOING TO NEED YOU BOTH TO LISTEN CLOSELY TO MY VOICE.
I'M GOING TO ASK YOU TO PICTURE SOME THINGS IN YOUR MIND, AND I'M GOING TO NEED YOU TO *KEEP* PICTURING THEM, NO MATTER HOW SCARED YOU GET.

OH.

I'M SORRY.

ME TOO.

IS IT STILL *DANGEROUS?*

YES.

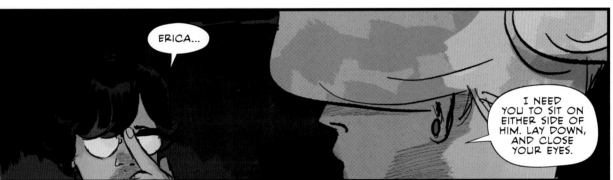

ERICA...

I NEED YOU TO SIT ON EITHER SIDE OF HIM. LAY DOWN, AND CLOSE YOUR EYES.

YEAH. OKAY.

I WANT YOU TO START BY IMAGINING THAT YOU'RE IN A VOID. A BIG, EMPTY WHITE SPACE.

YOU'RE LAYING DOWN IN THAT WHITE LIKE YOU ARE HERE IN THE LIVING ROOM.

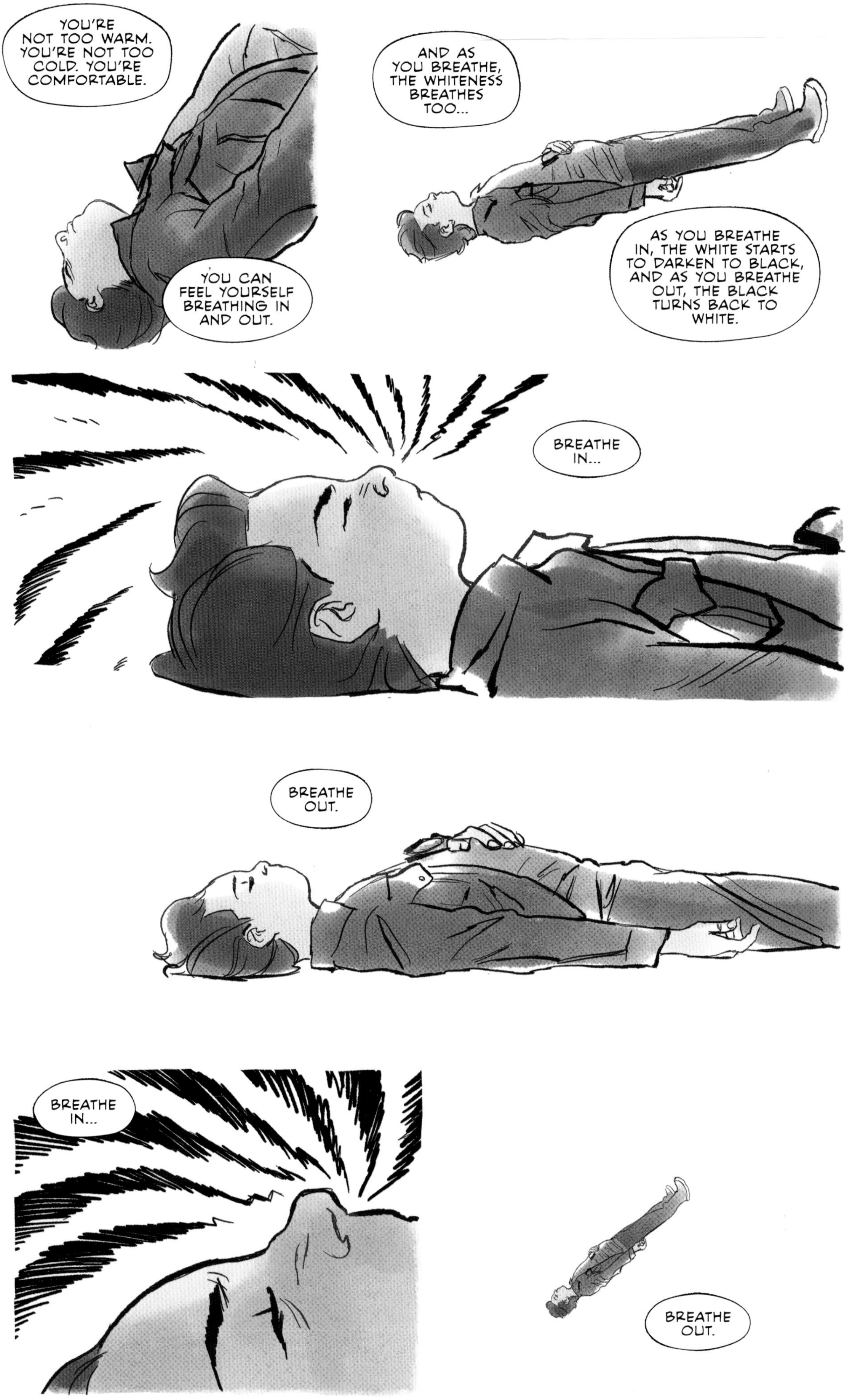
YOU'RE NOT TOO WARM. YOU'RE NOT TOO COLD. YOU'RE COMFORTABLE.
YOU CAN FEEL YOURSELF BREATHING IN AND OUT.
AND AS YOU BREATHE, THE WHITENESS BREATHES TOO...
AS YOU BREATHE IN, THE WHITE STARTS TO DARKEN TO BLACK, AND AS YOU BREATHE OUT, THE BLACK TURNS BACK TO WHITE.
BREATHE IN...
BREATHE OUT.
BREATHE IN...
BREATHE OUT.

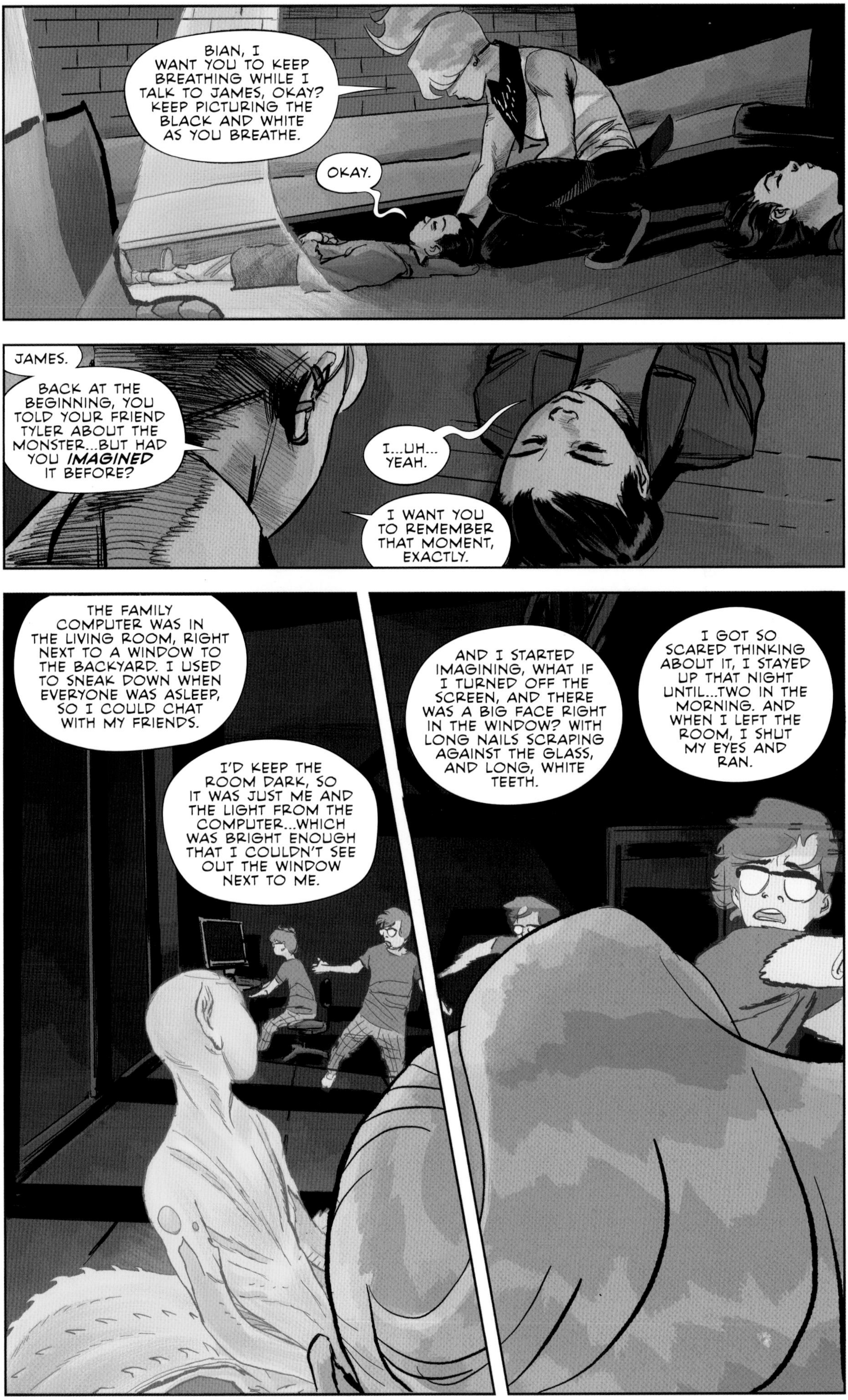
BIAN, I WANT YOU TO KEEP BREATHING WHILE I TALK TO JAMES, OKAY? KEEP PICTURING THE BLACK AND WHITE AS YOU BREATHE.
OKAY.
JAMES.
BACK AT THE BEGINNING, YOU TOLD YOUR FRIEND TYLER ABOUT THE MONSTER...BUT HAD YOU *IMAGINED* IT BEFORE?
I...UH... YEAH.
I WANT YOU TO REMEMBER THAT MOMENT, EXACTLY.
THE FAMILY COMPUTER WAS IN THE LIVING ROOM, RIGHT NEXT TO A WINDOW TO THE BACKYARD. I USED TO SNEAK DOWN WHEN EVERYONE WAS ASLEEP, SO I COULD CHAT WITH MY FRIENDS.
I'D KEEP THE ROOM DARK, SO IT WAS JUST ME AND THE LIGHT FROM THE COMPUTER...WHICH WAS BRIGHT ENOUGH THAT I COULDN'T SEE OUT THE WINDOW NEXT TO ME.
AND I STARTED IMAGINING, WHAT IF I TURNED OFF THE SCREEN, AND THERE WAS A BIG FACE RIGHT IN THE WINDOW? WITH LONG NAILS SCRAPING AGAINST THE GLASS, AND LONG, WHITE TEETH.
I GOT SO SCARED THINKING ABOUT IT, I STAYED UP THAT NIGHT UNTIL...TWO IN THE MORNING. AND WHEN I LEFT THE ROOM, I SHUT MY EYES AND RAN.

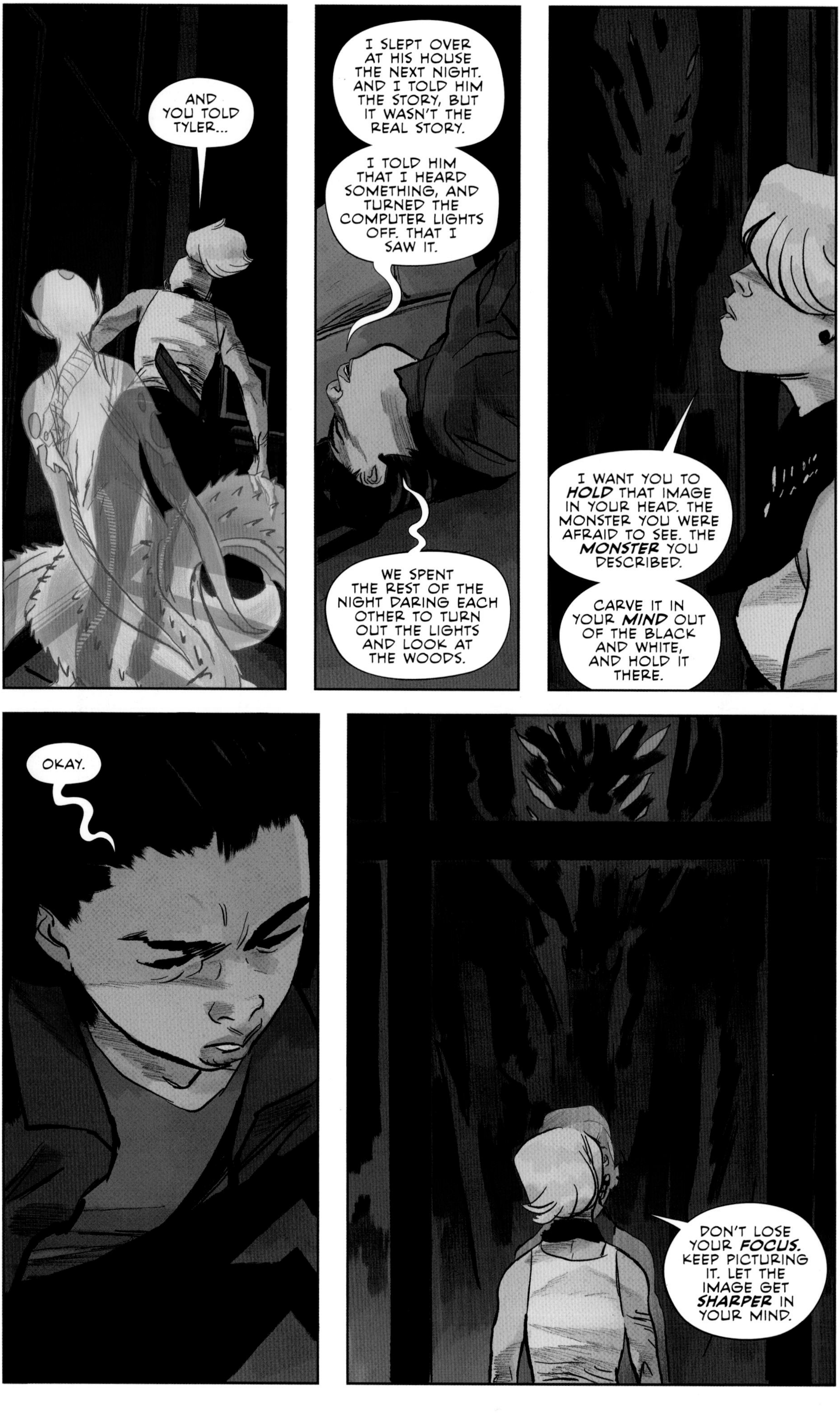
AND YOU TOLD TYLER...
I SLEPT OVER AT HIS HOUSE THE NEXT NIGHT. AND I TOLD HIM THE STORY, BUT IT WASN'T THE REAL STORY.
I TOLD HIM THAT I HEARD SOMETHING, AND TURNED THE COMPUTER LIGHTS OFF. THAT I SAW IT.
WE SPENT THE REST OF THE NIGHT DARING EACH OTHER TO TURN OUT THE LIGHTS AND LOOK AT THE WOODS.
I WANT YOU TO HOLD THAT IMAGE IN YOUR HEAD. THE MONSTER YOU WERE AFRAID TO SEE. THE MONSTER YOU DESCRIBED.
CARVE IT IN YOUR MIND OUT OF THE BLACK AND WHITE, AND HOLD IT THERE.
OKAY.
DON'T LOSE YOUR FOCUS. KEEP PICTURING IT. LET THE IMAGE GET SHARPER IN YOUR MIND.

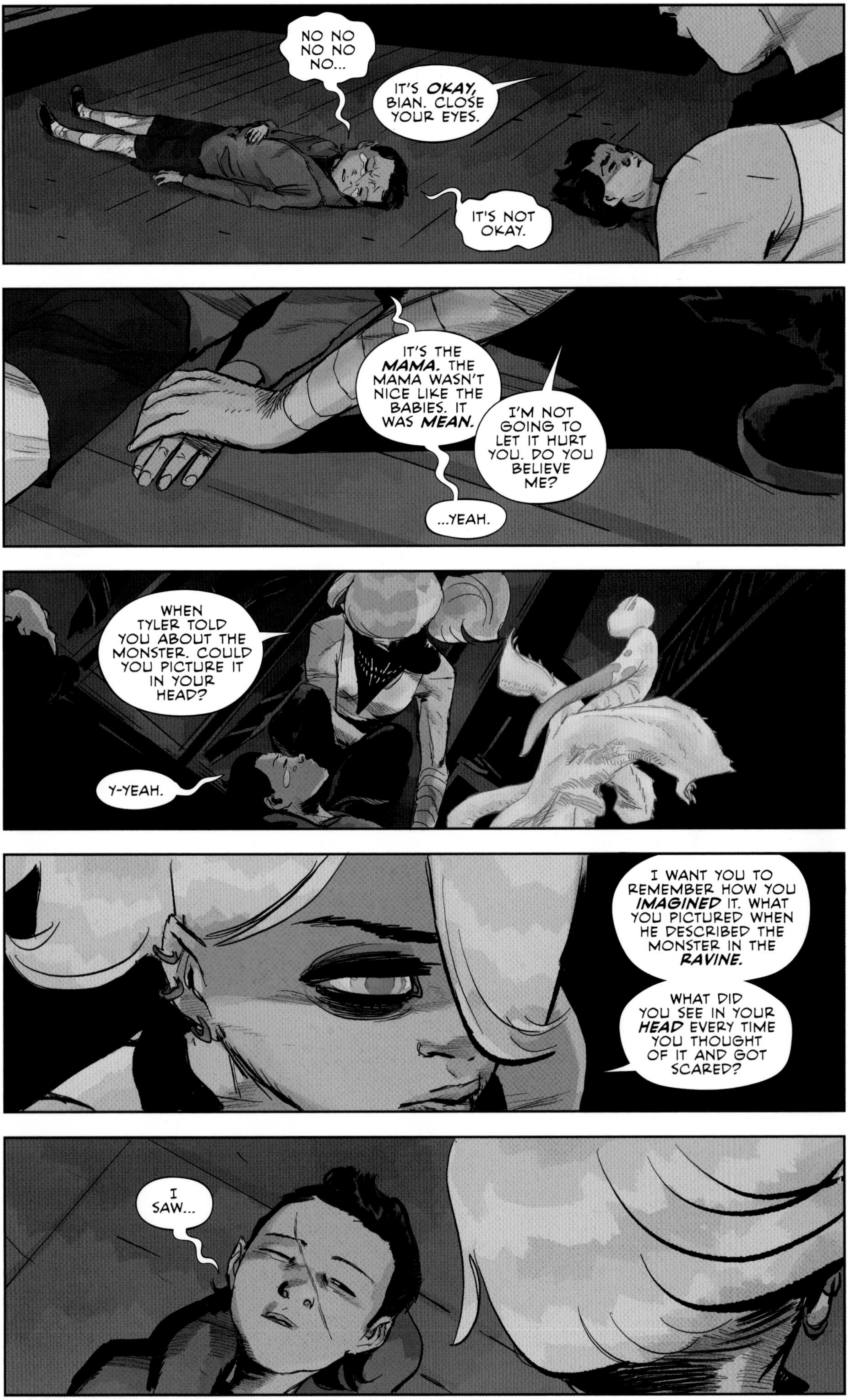
NO NO NO NO NO...
IT'S OKAY, BIAN. CLOSE YOUR EYES.
IT'S NOT OKAY.
IT'S THE MAMA. THE MAMA WASN'T NICE LIKE THE BABIES. IT WAS MEAN.
I'M NOT GOING TO LET IT HURT YOU. DO YOU BELIEVE ME?
...YEAH.
WHEN TYLER TOLD YOU ABOUT THE MONSTER. COULD YOU PICTURE IT IN YOUR HEAD?
Y-YEAH.
I WANT YOU TO REMEMBER HOW YOU IMAGINED IT. WHAT YOU PICTURED WHEN HE DESCRIBED THE MONSTER IN THE RAVINE.
WHAT DID YOU SEE IN YOUR HEAD EVERY TIME YOU THOUGHT OF IT AND GOT SCARED?
I SAW...

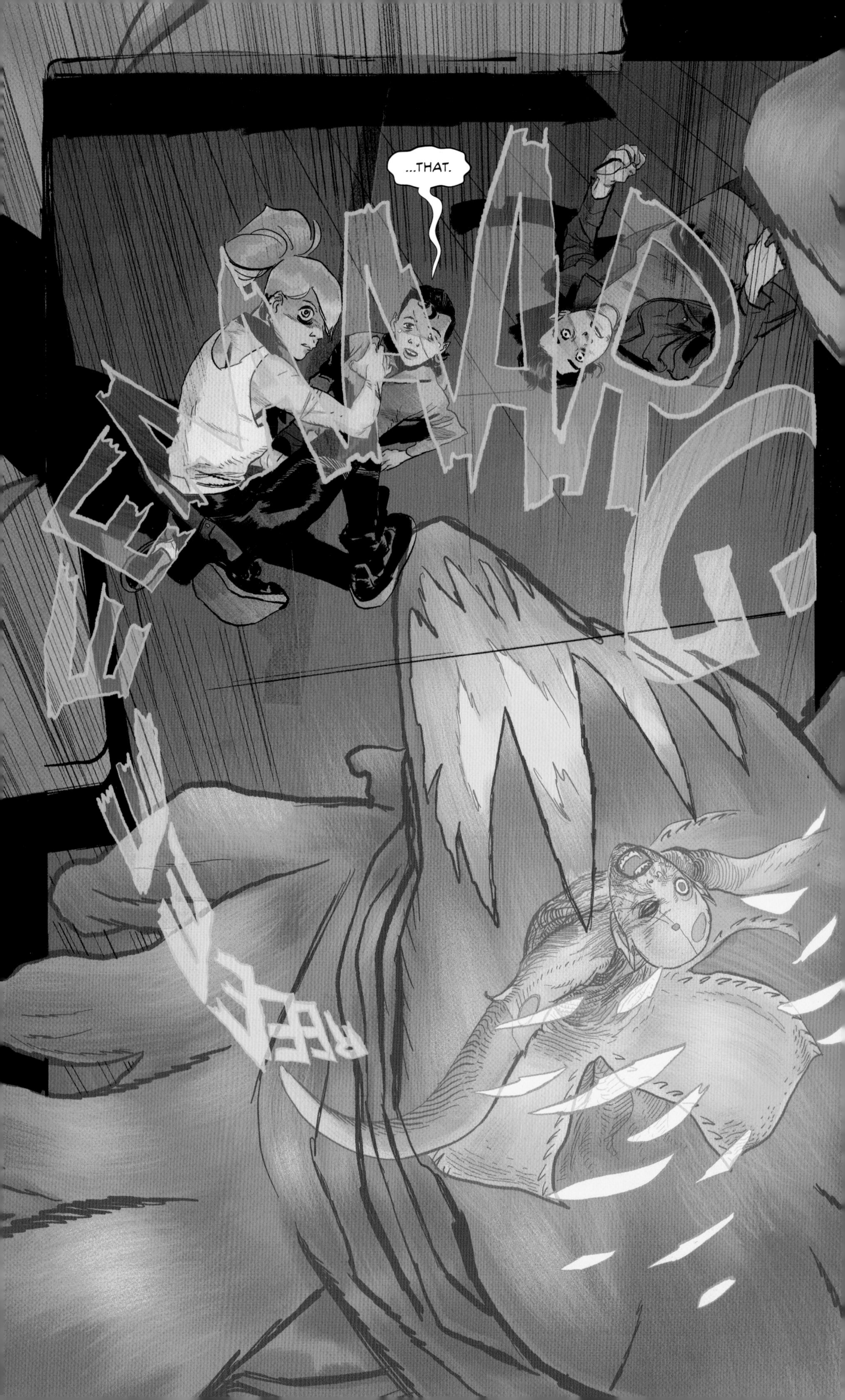
...THAT.

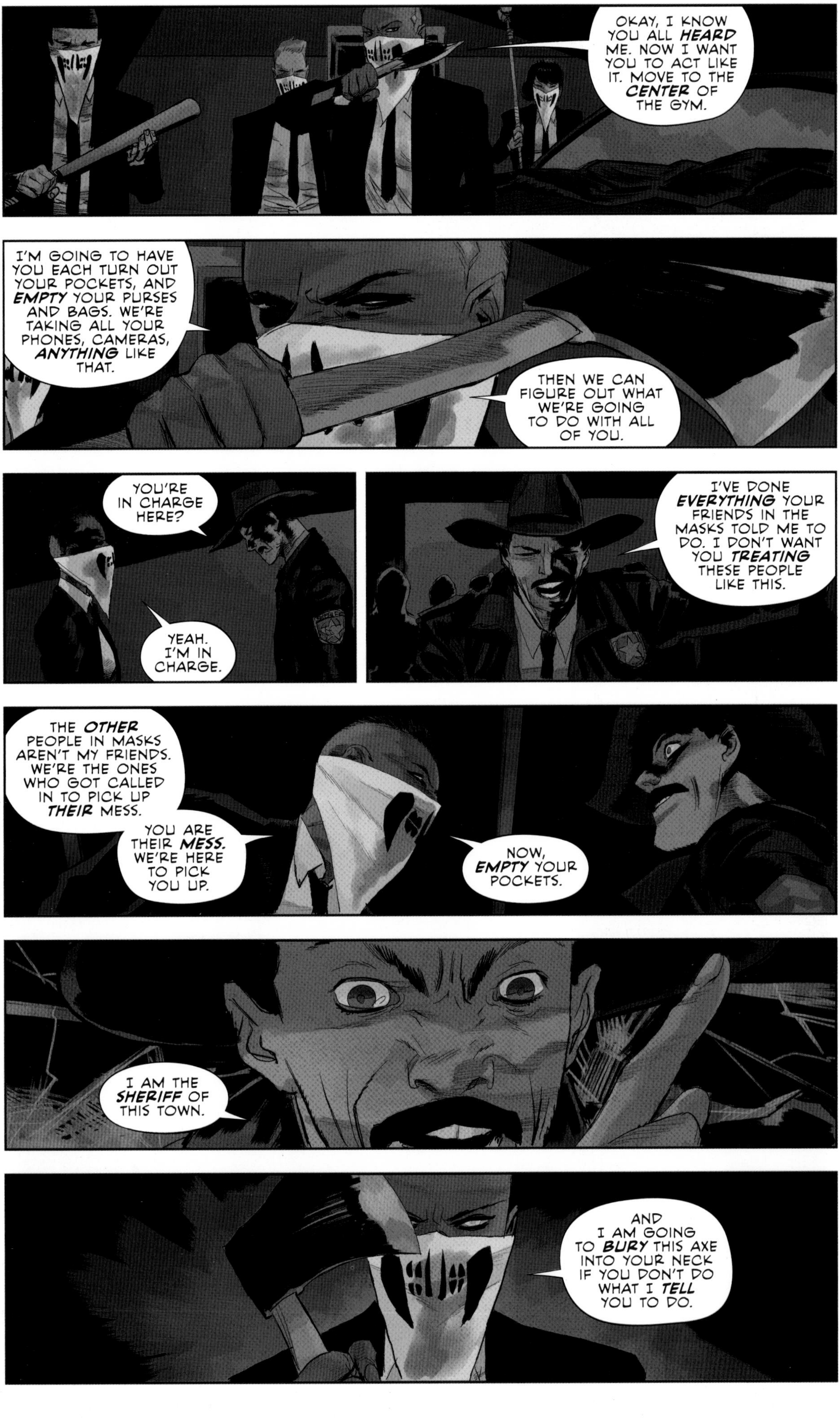
OKAY, I KNOW YOU ALL HEARD ME. NOW I WANT YOU TO ACT LIKE IT. MOVE TO THE CENTER OF THE GYM.
I'M GOING TO HAVE YOU EACH TURN OUT YOUR POCKETS, AND EMPTY YOUR PURSES AND BAGS. WE'RE TAKING ALL YOUR PHONES, CAMERAS, ANYTHING LIKE THAT.
THEN WE CAN FIGURE OUT WHAT WE'RE GOING TO DO WITH ALL OF YOU.
YOU'RE IN CHARGE HERE?
YEAH. I'M IN CHARGE.
I'VE DONE EVERYTHING YOUR FRIENDS IN THE MASKS TOLD ME TO DO. I DON'T WANT YOU TREATING THESE PEOPLE LIKE THIS.
THE OTHER PEOPLE IN MASKS AREN'T MY FRIENDS. WE'RE THE ONES WHO GOT CALLED IN TO PICK UP THEIR MESS.
YOU ARE THEIR MESS. WE'RE HERE TO PICK YOU UP.
NOW, EMPTY YOUR POCKETS.
I AM THE SHERIFF OF THIS TOWN.
AND I AM GOING TO BURY THIS AXE INTO YOUR NECK IF YOU DON'T DO WHAT I TELL YOU TO DO.

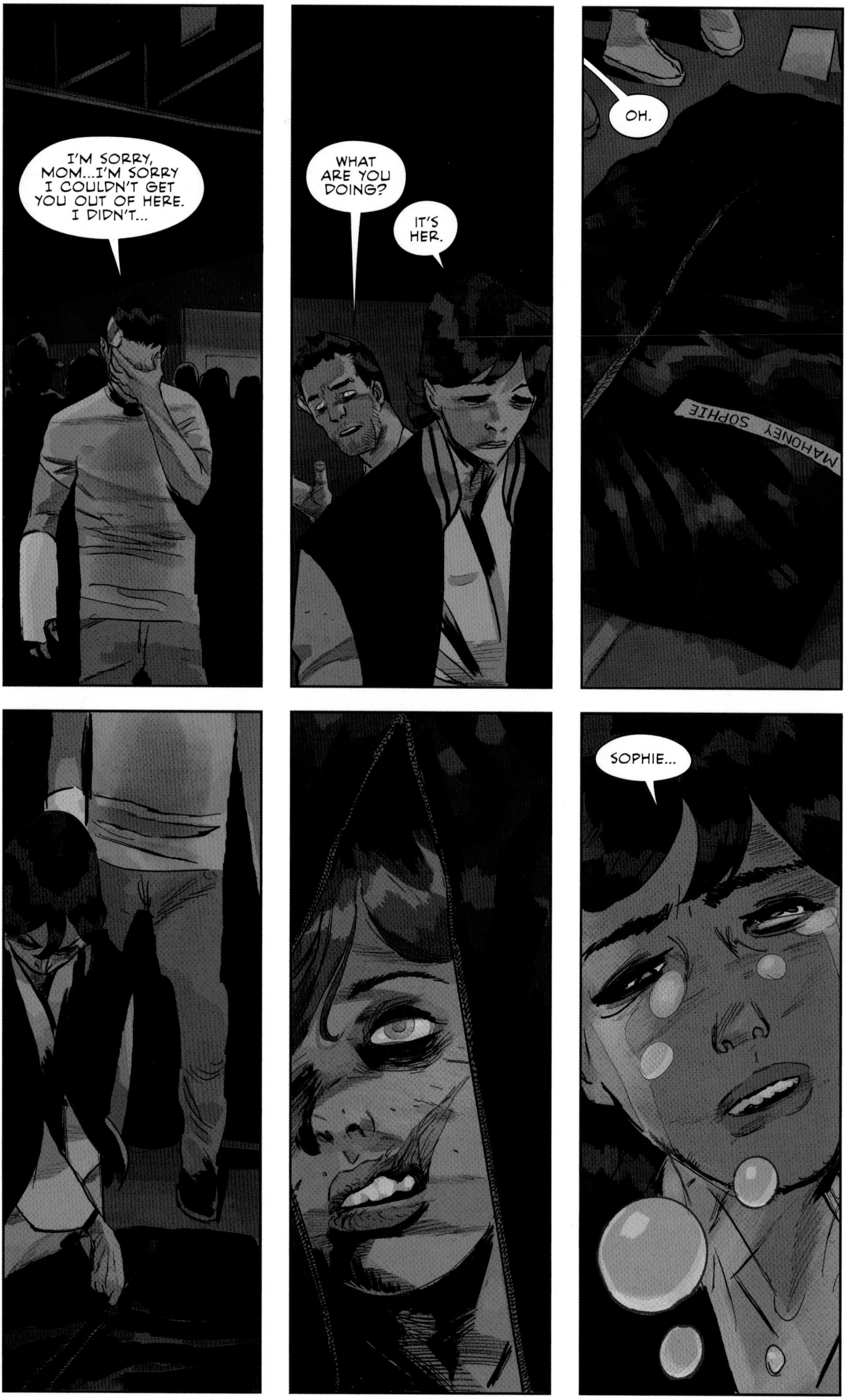
I'M SORRY, MOM...I'M SORRY I COULDN'T GET YOU OUT OF HERE. I DIDN'T...
WHAT ARE YOU DOING?
IT'S HER.
OH.
MAHONEY SOPHIE
SOPHIE...

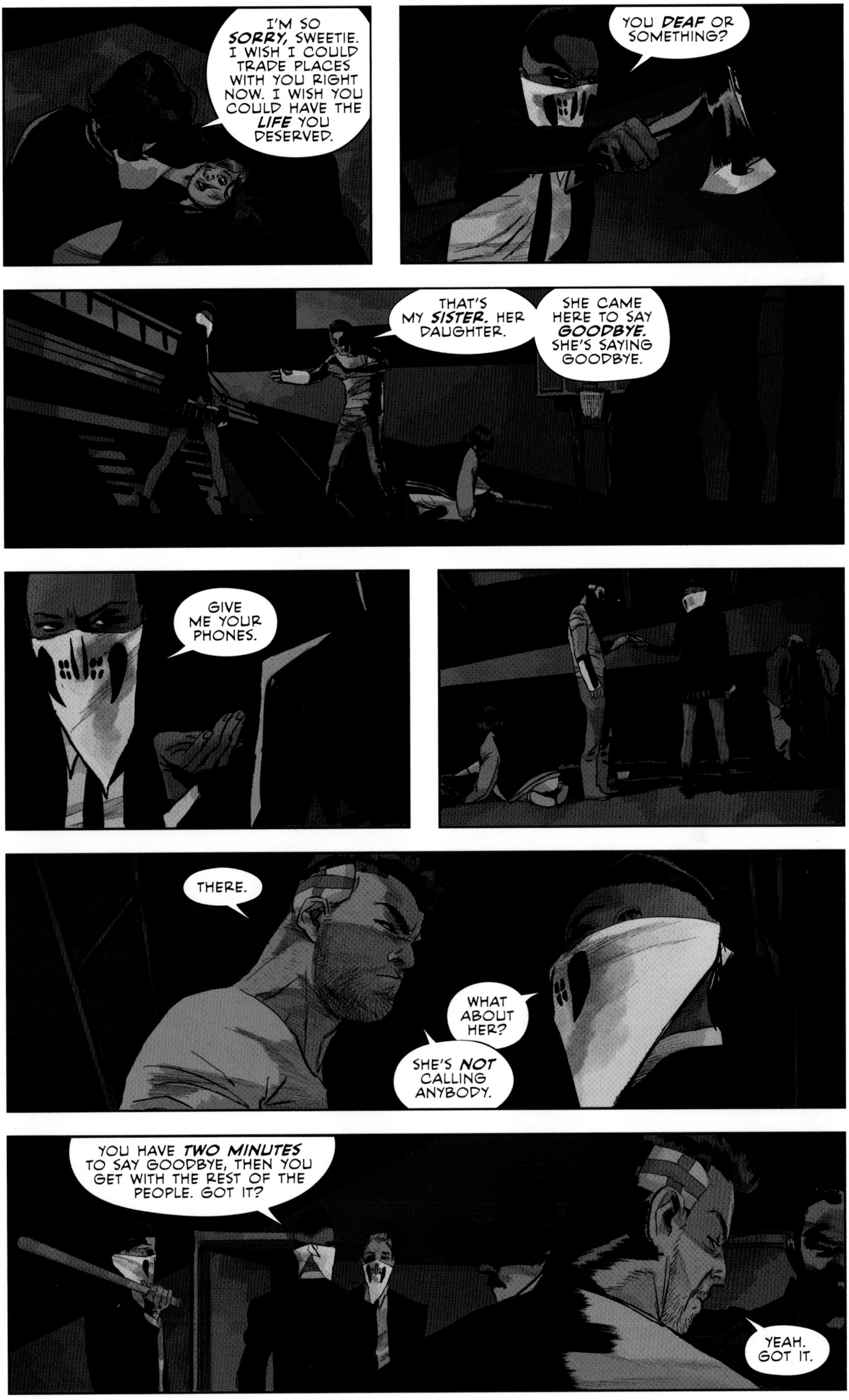
I'M SO SORRY, SWEETIE. I WISH I COULD TRADE PLACES WITH YOU RIGHT NOW. I WISH YOU COULD HAVE THE LIFE YOU DESERVED.
YOU DEAF OR SOMETHING?
THAT'S MY SISTER. HER DAUGHTER.
SHE CAME HERE TO SAY GOODBYE. SHE'S SAYING GOODBYE.
GIVE ME YOUR PHONES.
THERE.
WHAT ABOUT HER?
SHE'S NOT CALLING ANYBODY.
YOU HAVE TWO MINUTES TO SAY GOODBYE, THEN YOU GET WITH THE REST OF THE PEOPLE. GOT IT?
YEAH. GOT IT.

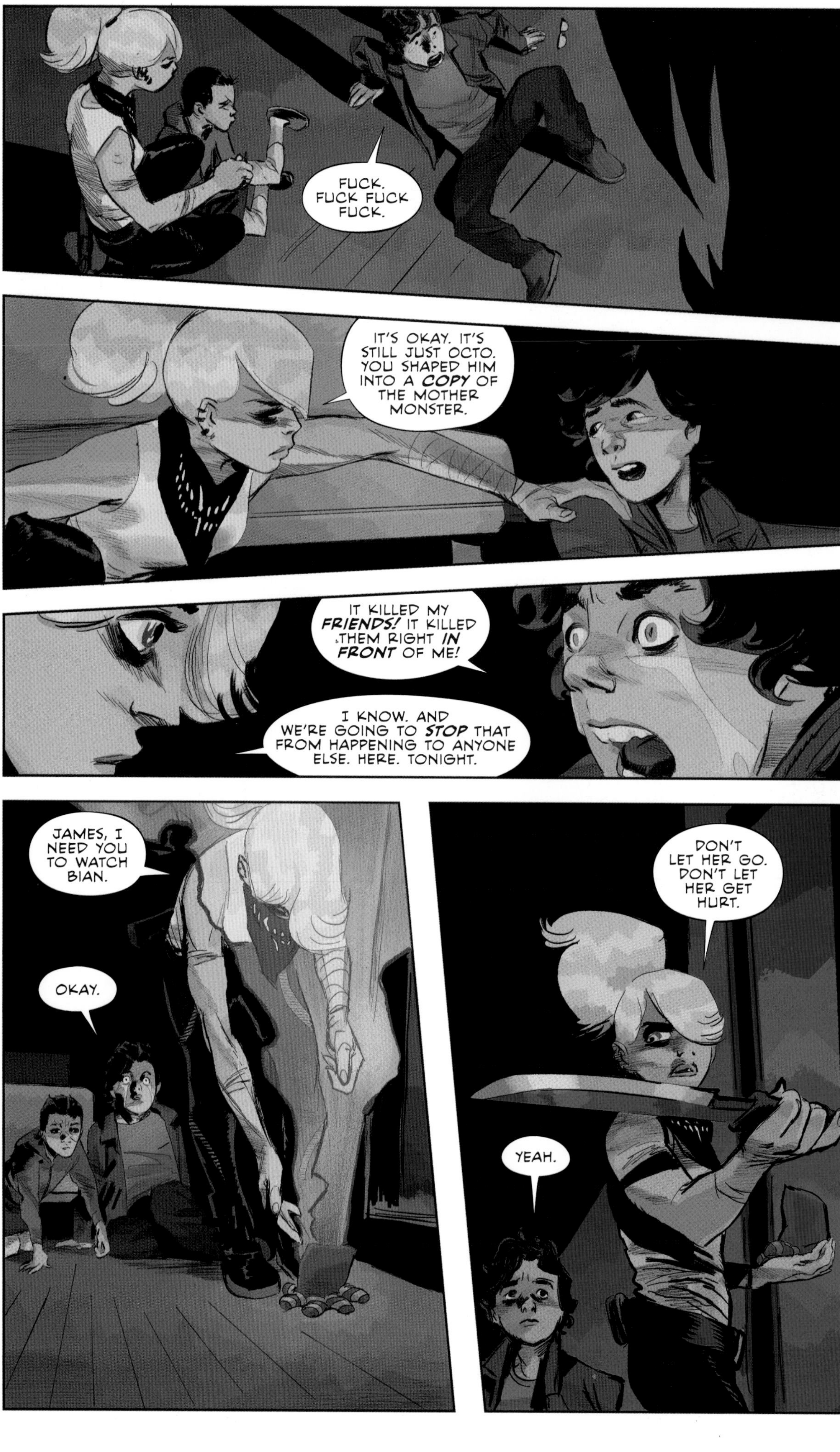
FUCK. FUCK FUCK FUCK.
IT'S OKAY. IT'S STILL JUST OCTO. YOU SHAPED HIM INTO A COPY OF THE MOTHER MONSTER.
IT KILLED MY FRIENDS! IT KILLED THEM RIGHT IN FRONT OF ME!
I KNOW. AND WE'RE GOING TO STOP THAT FROM HAPPENING TO ANYONE ELSE. HERE. TONIGHT.
JAMES, I NEED YOU TO WATCH BIAN.
OKAY.
DON'T LET HER GO. DON'T LET HER GET HURT.
YEAH.

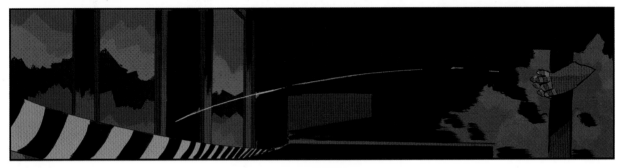

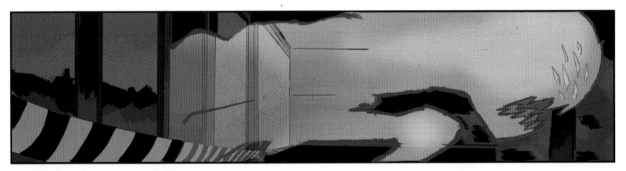

IT'S SO *LOUD.*

IT *HAS* TO BE, OTHERWISE THEY WON'T HEAR THEIR MOTHER *CALLING* FOR THEM.

DON'T WATCH.

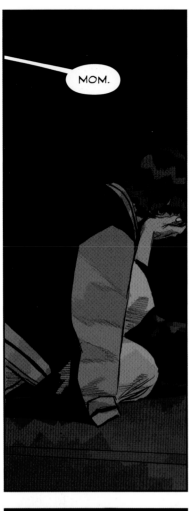

MOM.

COME ON, WE HAVE TO GO.

ARE THEY GOING TO *KILL* US?

I DON'T KNOW.

IF THEY'RE JUST GOING TO KILL US, THEY CAN COME TO ME. I'M *DONE*, TOMMY. I'M JUST DONE.

MOM.

I'M NOT *STRONG* ENOUGH FOR THIS. NOBODY SHOULD HAVE TO BE STRONG ENOUGH FOR THIS.

SHE WAS SO *GOOD*, AND THIS IS ALL THAT'S LEFT OF HER... BONES AND MEAT.

I'M *SORRY* I COULDN'T KEEP HER SAFE, BUT I AM GOING TO SAVE YOU, OKAY? I AM *NOT* GOING TO LET YOU DIE.

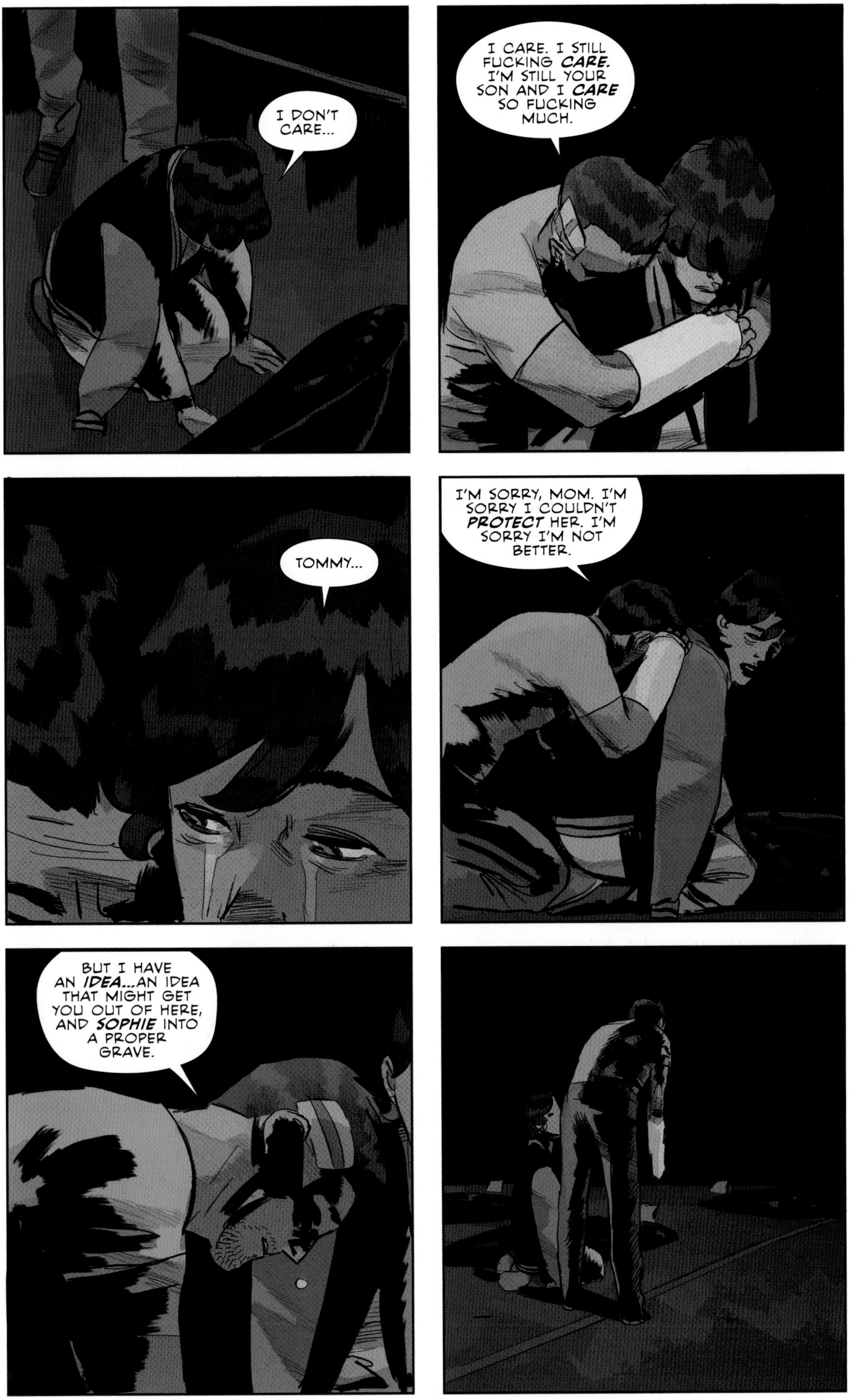
I DON'T CARE...
I CARE. I STILL FUCKING *CARE.* I'M STILL YOUR SON AND I *CARE* SO FUCKING MUCH.
TOMMY...
I'M SORRY, MOM. I'M SORRY I COULDN'T *PROTECT* HER. I'M SORRY I'M NOT BETTER.
BUT I HAVE AN *IDEA...*AN IDEA THAT MIGHT GET YOU OUT OF HERE, AND *SOPHIE* INTO A PROPER GRAVE.

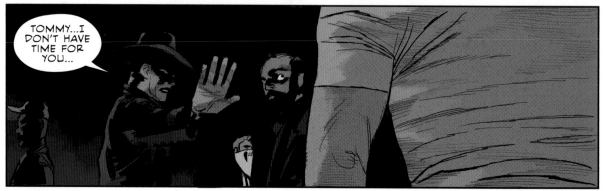

TOMMY...I DON'T HAVE TIME FOR YOU...

THESE PEOPLE...THEY'RE HERE FOR *CLEANUP.* TO MAKE SURE NOBODY SPREADS THE STORY OF A *MONSTER* IN THAT PARKING LOT.

WHAT DO YOU *SUGGEST* WE DO?

GIVE THEM A BETTER STORY.

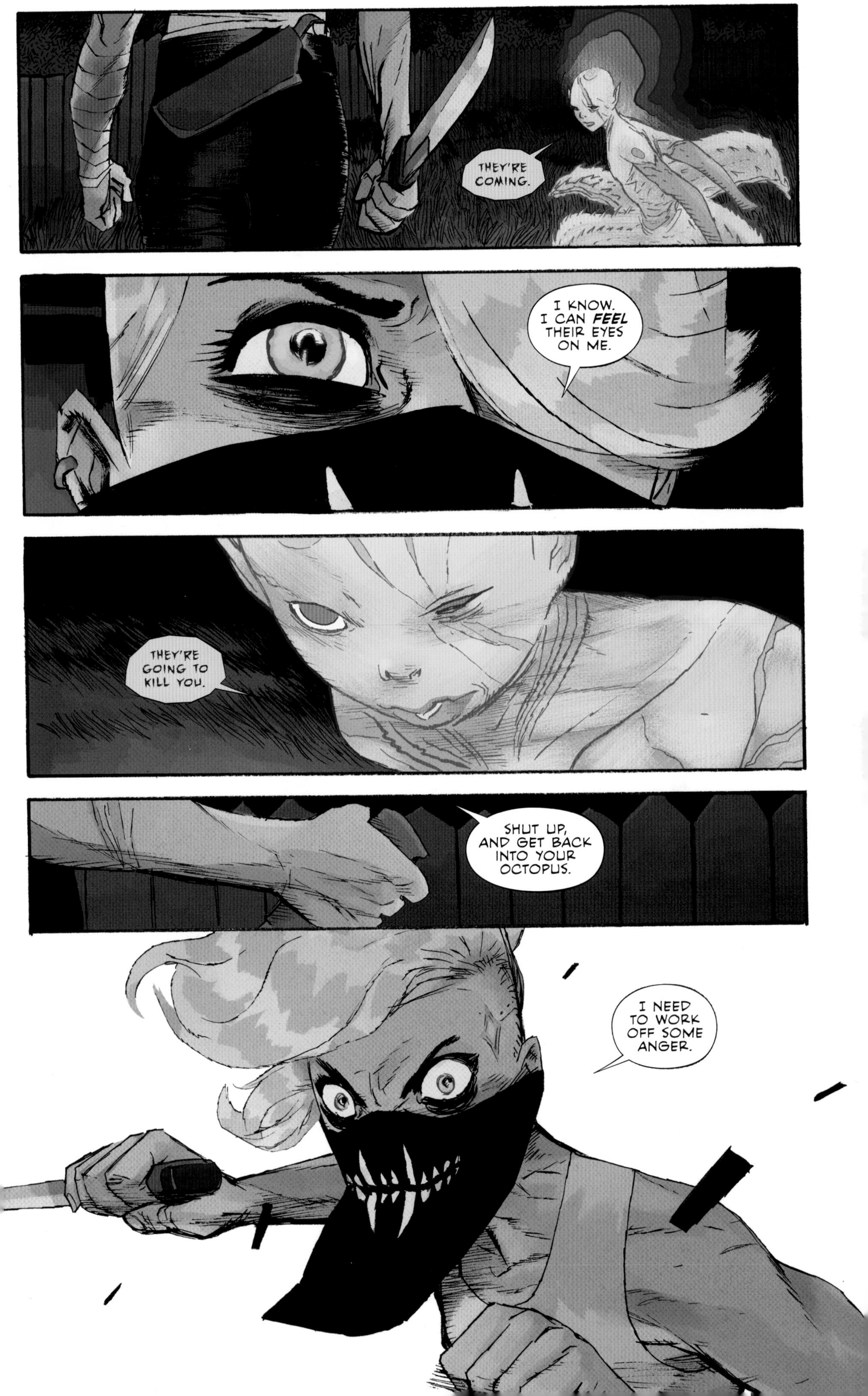
THEY'RE COMING.
I KNOW. I CAN **FEEL** THEIR EYES ON ME.
THEY'RE GOING TO KILL YOU.
SHUT UP, AND GET BACK INTO YOUR OCTOPUS.
I NEED TO WORK OFF SOME ANGER.

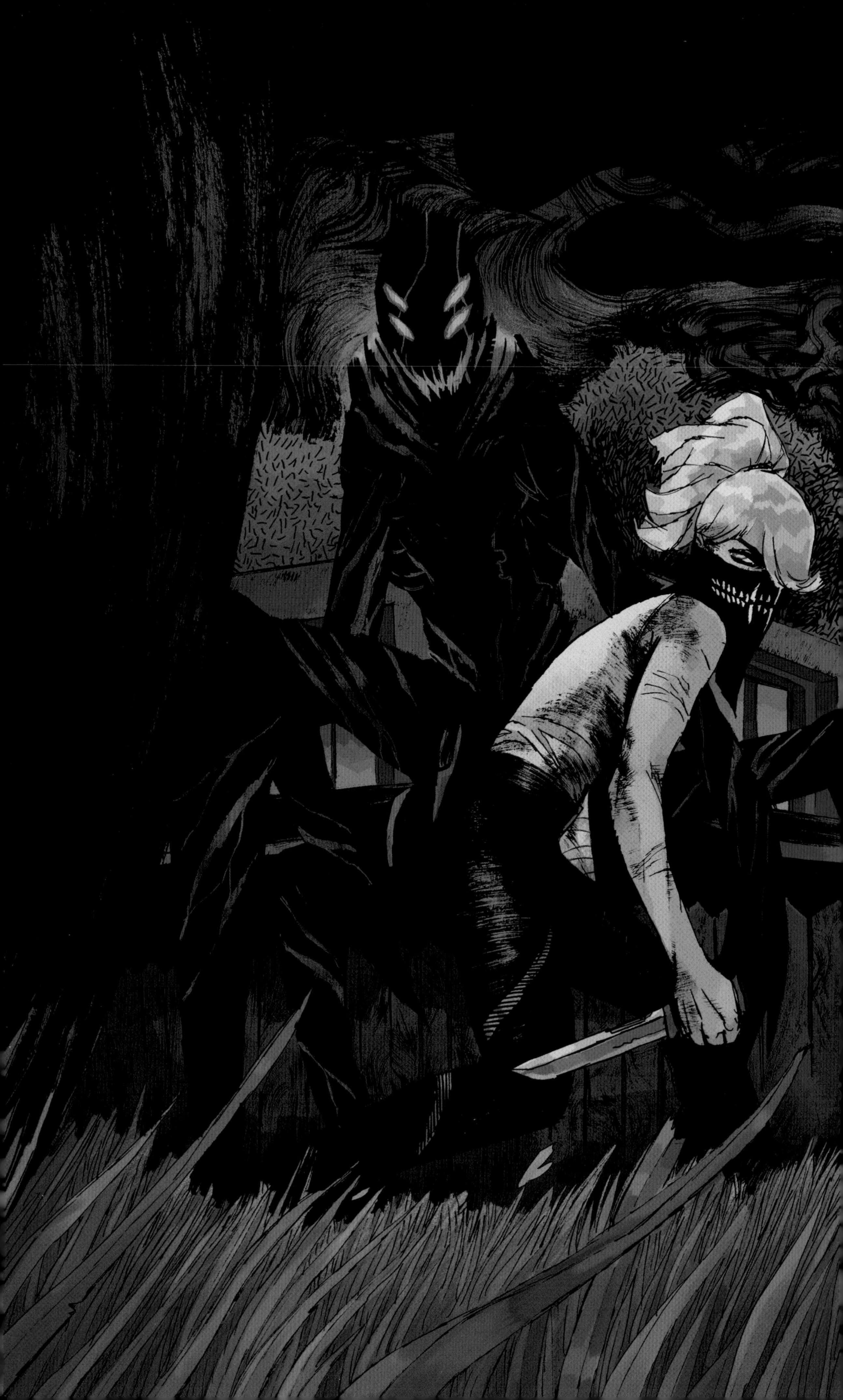

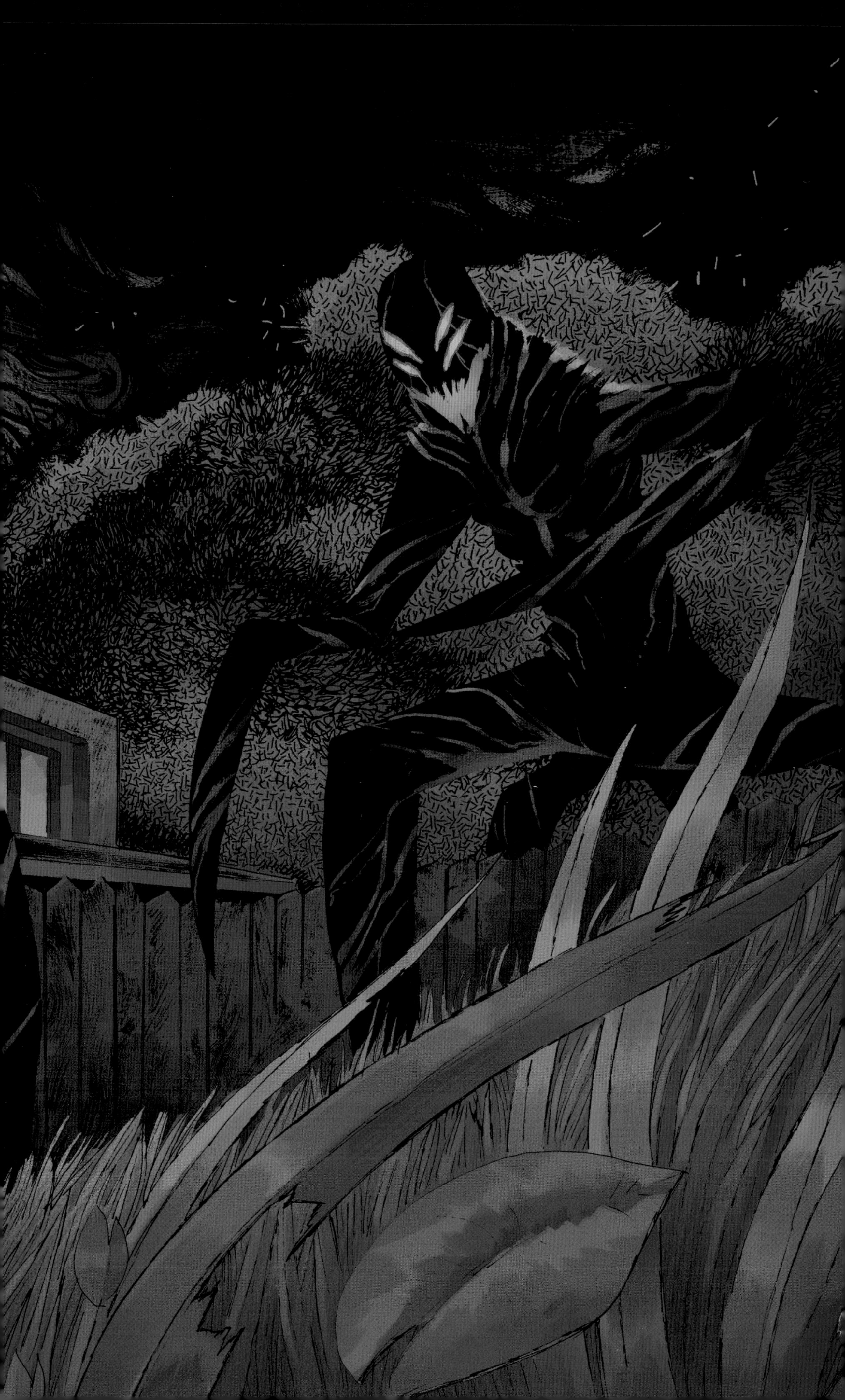

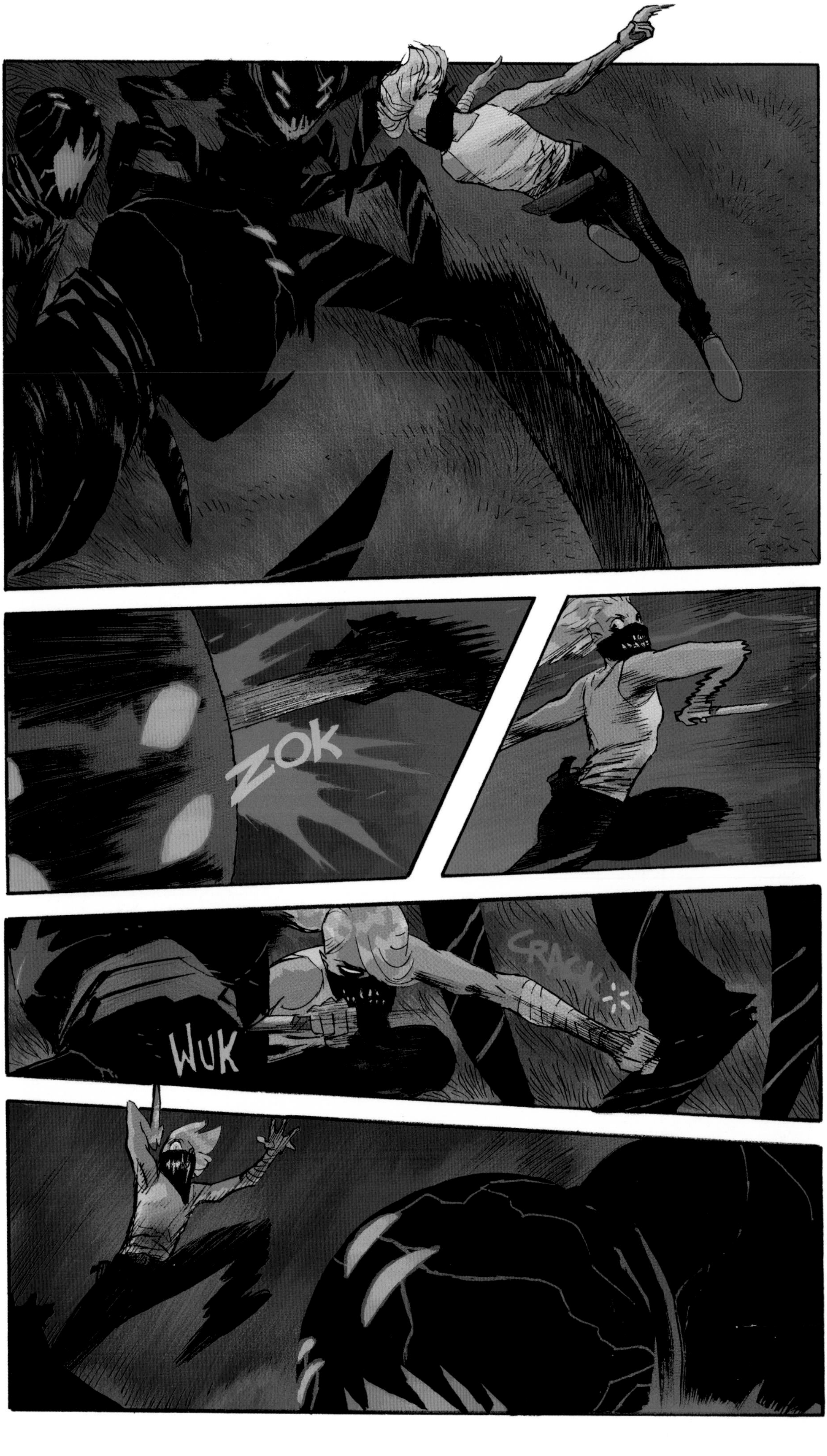
ZOK
WUK

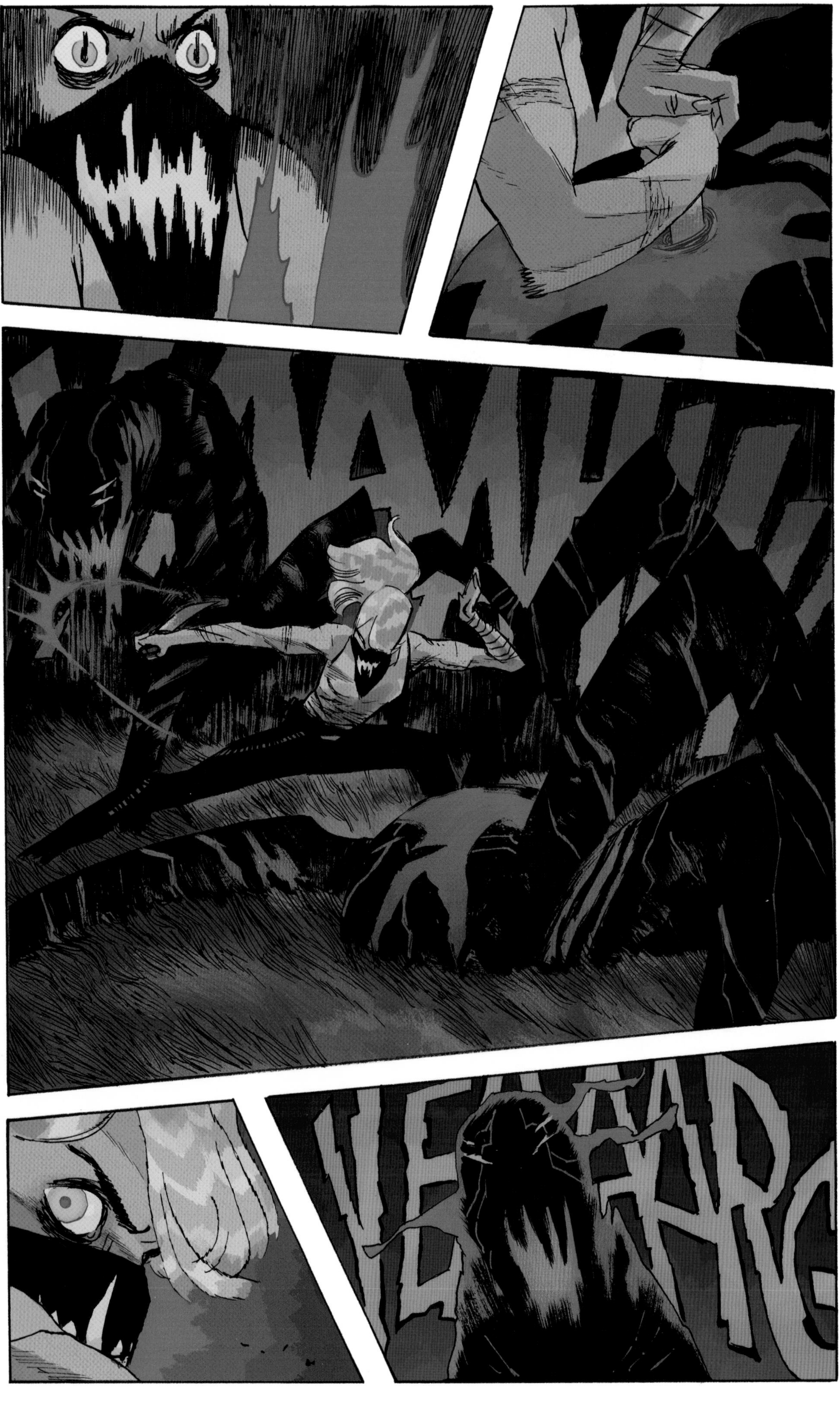

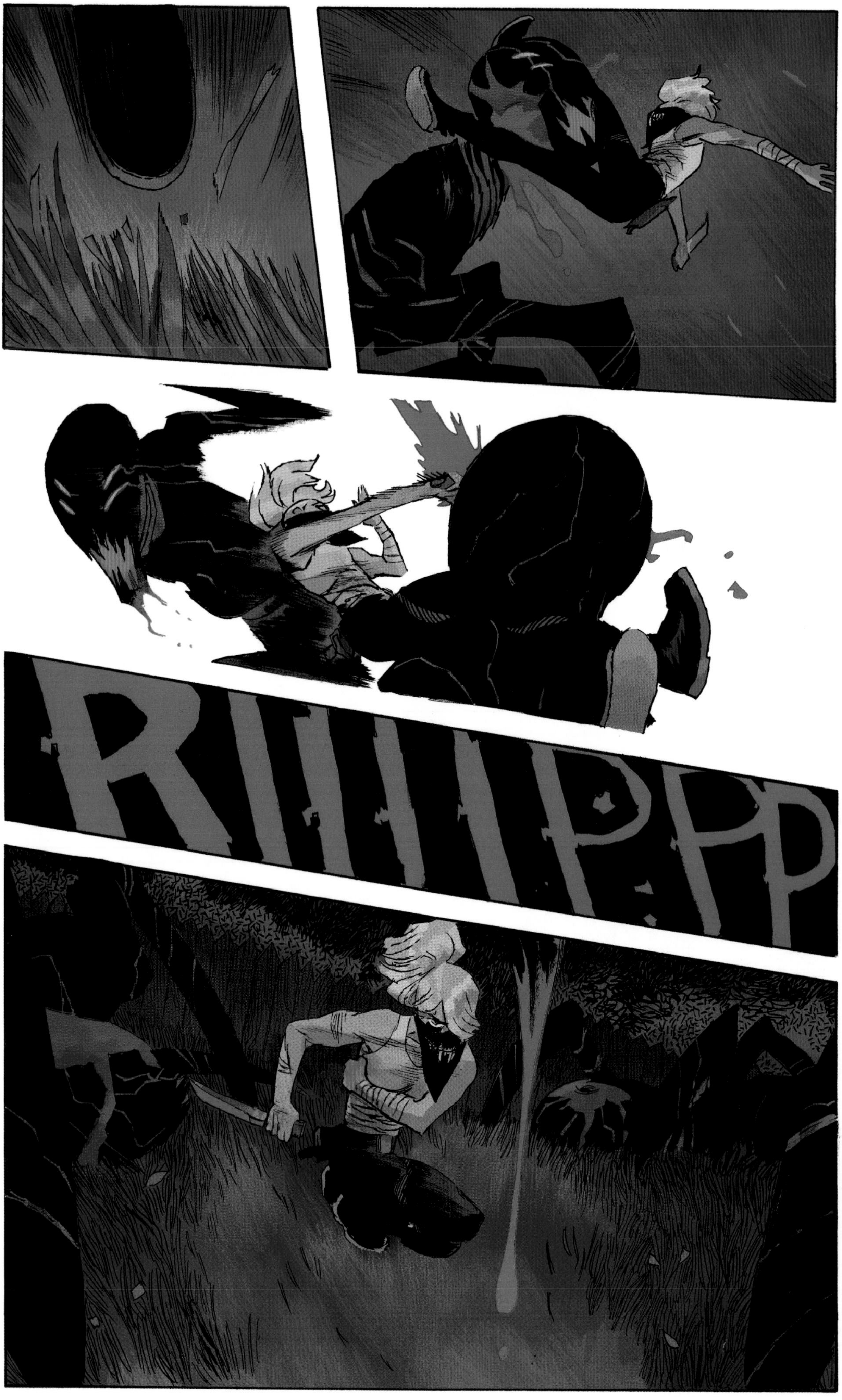
RIIIPPP

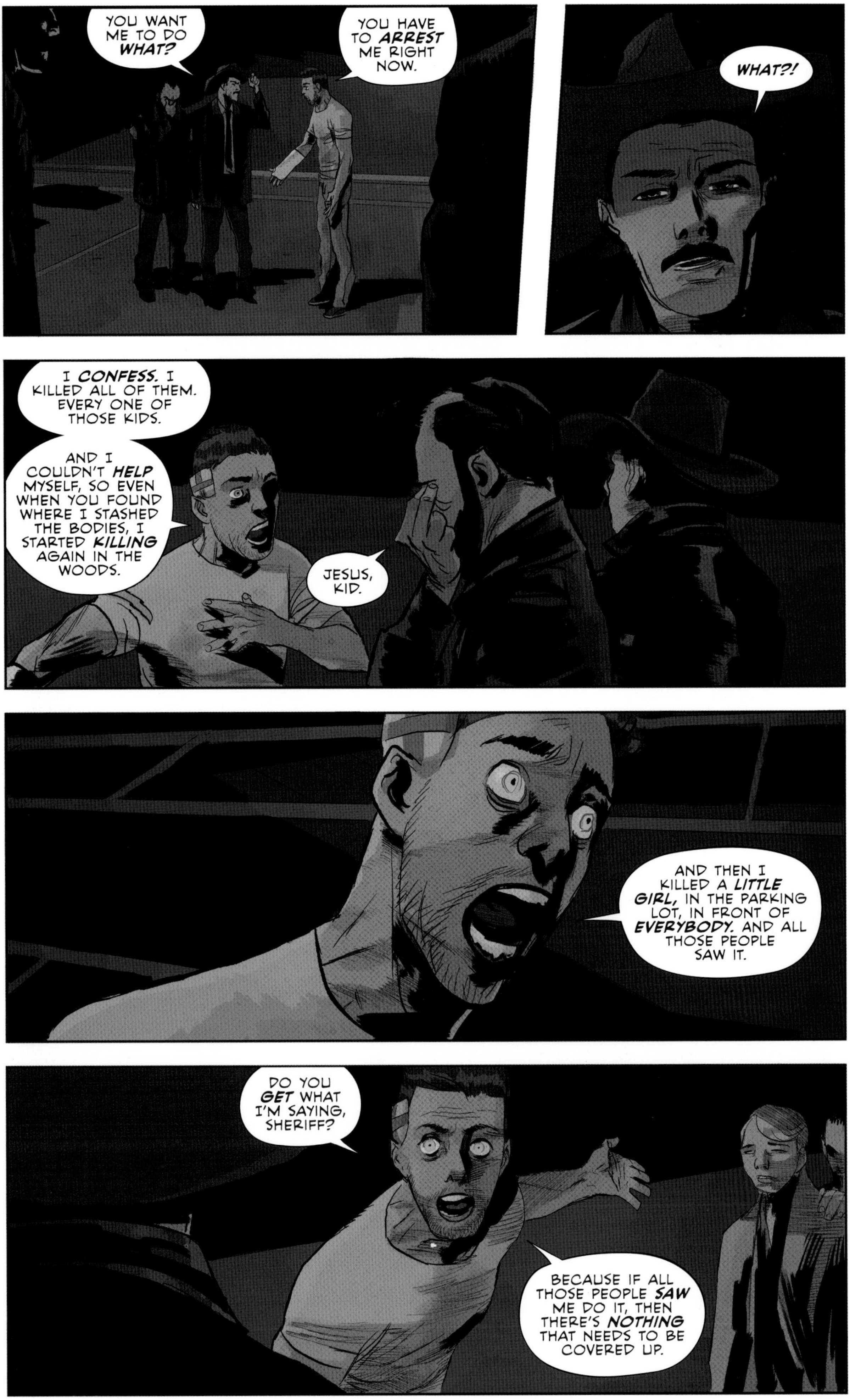
YOU WANT ME TO DO WHAT?
YOU HAVE TO ARREST ME RIGHT NOW.
WHAT?!
I CONFESS. I KILLED ALL OF THEM. EVERY ONE OF THOSE KIDS.
AND I COULDN'T HELP MYSELF, SO EVEN WHEN YOU FOUND WHERE I STASHED THE BODIES, I STARTED KILLING AGAIN IN THE WOODS.
JESUS, KID.
AND THEN I KILLED A LITTLE GIRL, IN THE PARKING LOT, IN FRONT OF EVERYBODY. AND ALL THOSE PEOPLE SAW IT.
DO YOU GET WHAT I'M SAYING, SHERIFF?
BECAUSE IF ALL THOSE PEOPLE SAW ME DO IT, THEN THERE'S NOTHING THAT NEEDS TO BE COVERED UP.

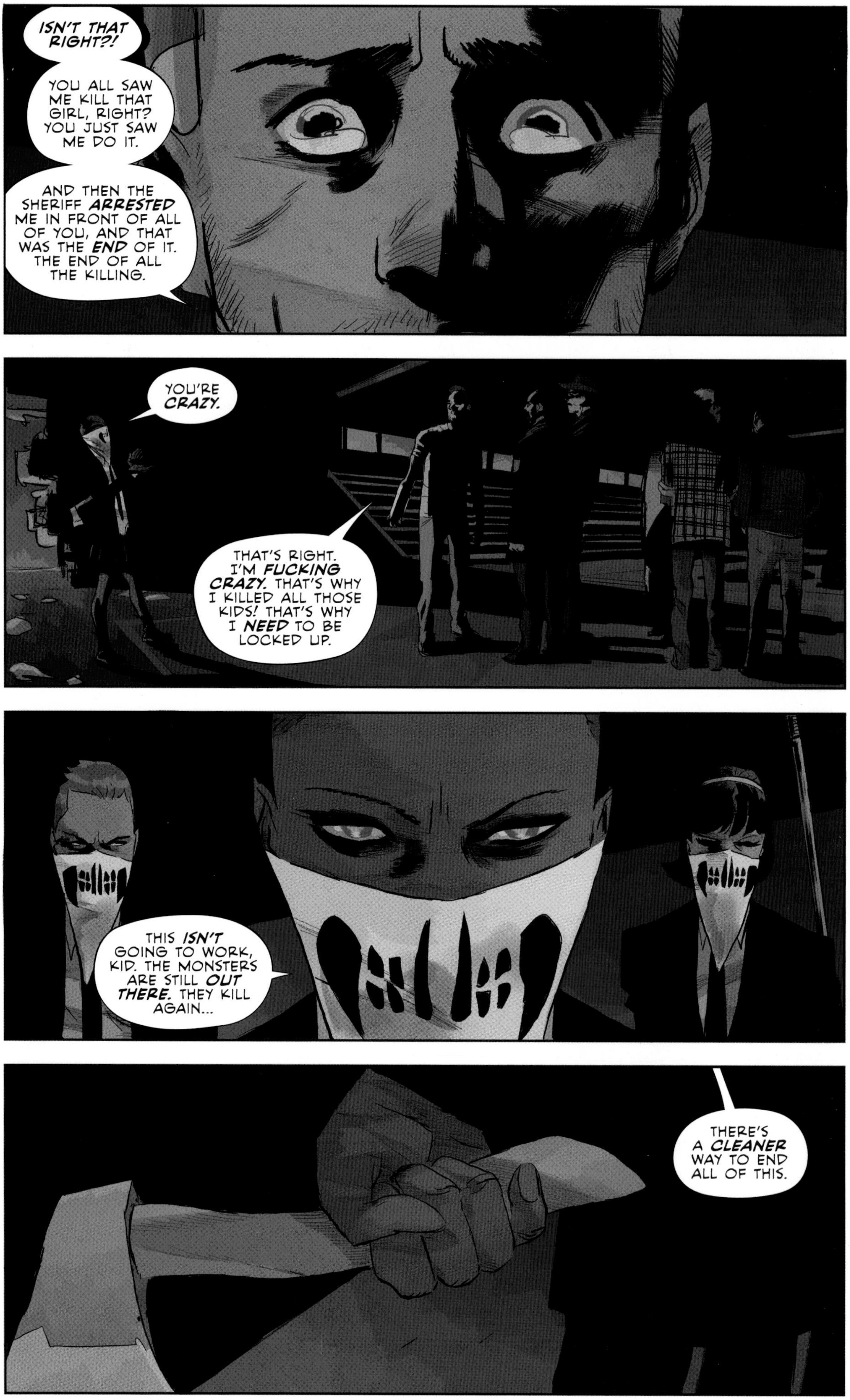
ISN'T THAT RIGHT?!
YOU ALL SAW ME KILL THAT GIRL, RIGHT? YOU JUST SAW ME DO IT.
AND THEN THE SHERIFF ARRESTED ME IN FRONT OF ALL OF YOU, AND THAT WAS THE END OF IT. THE END OF ALL THE KILLING.
YOU'RE CRAZY.
THAT'S RIGHT. I'M FUCKING CRAZY. THAT'S WHY I KILLED ALL THOSE KIDS! THAT'S WHY I NEED TO BE LOCKED UP.
THIS ISN'T GOING TO WORK, KID. THE MONSTERS ARE STILL OUT THERE. THEY KILL AGAIN...
THERE'S A CLEANER WAY TO END ALL OF THIS.

CHAPTER FIFTEEN

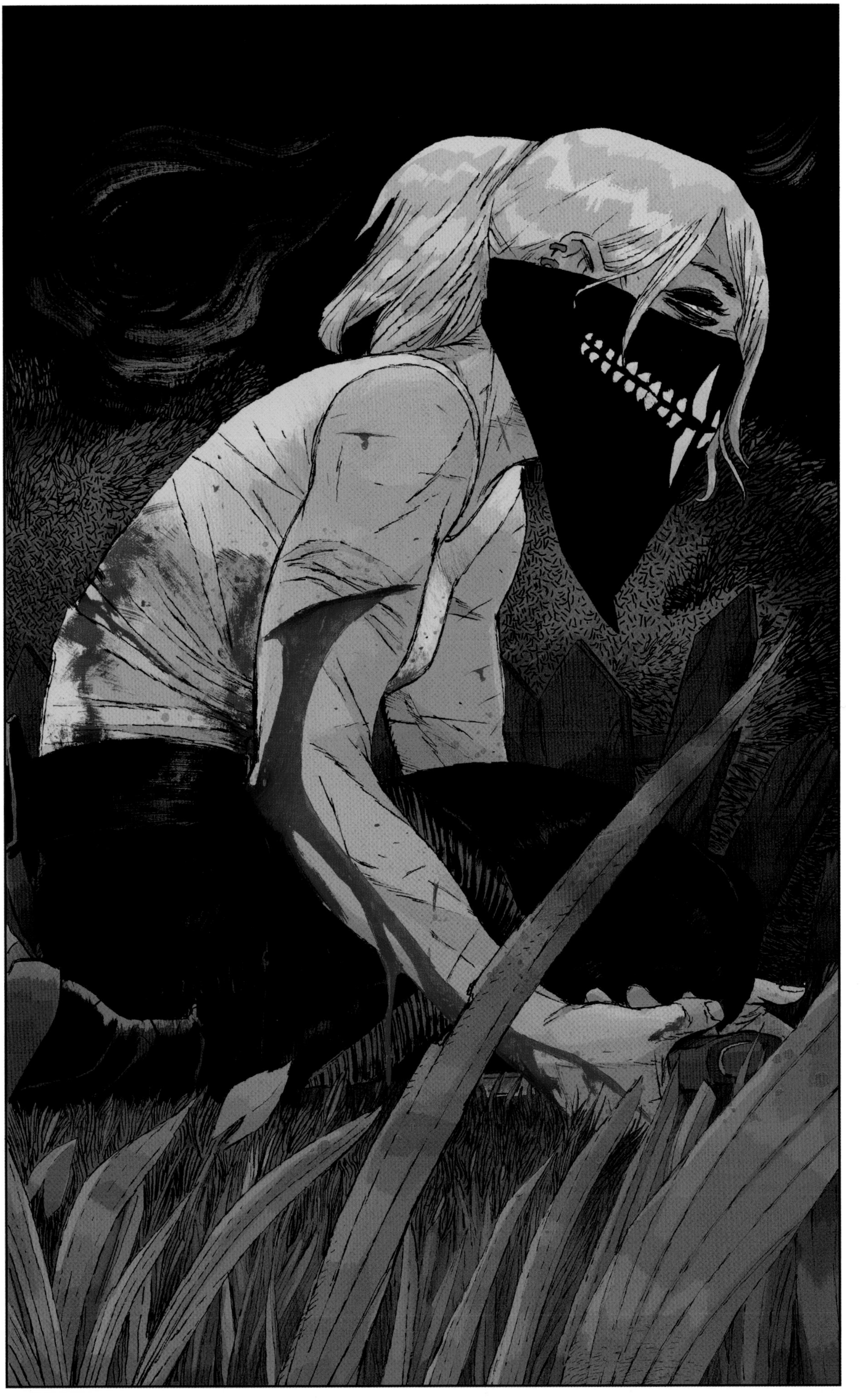

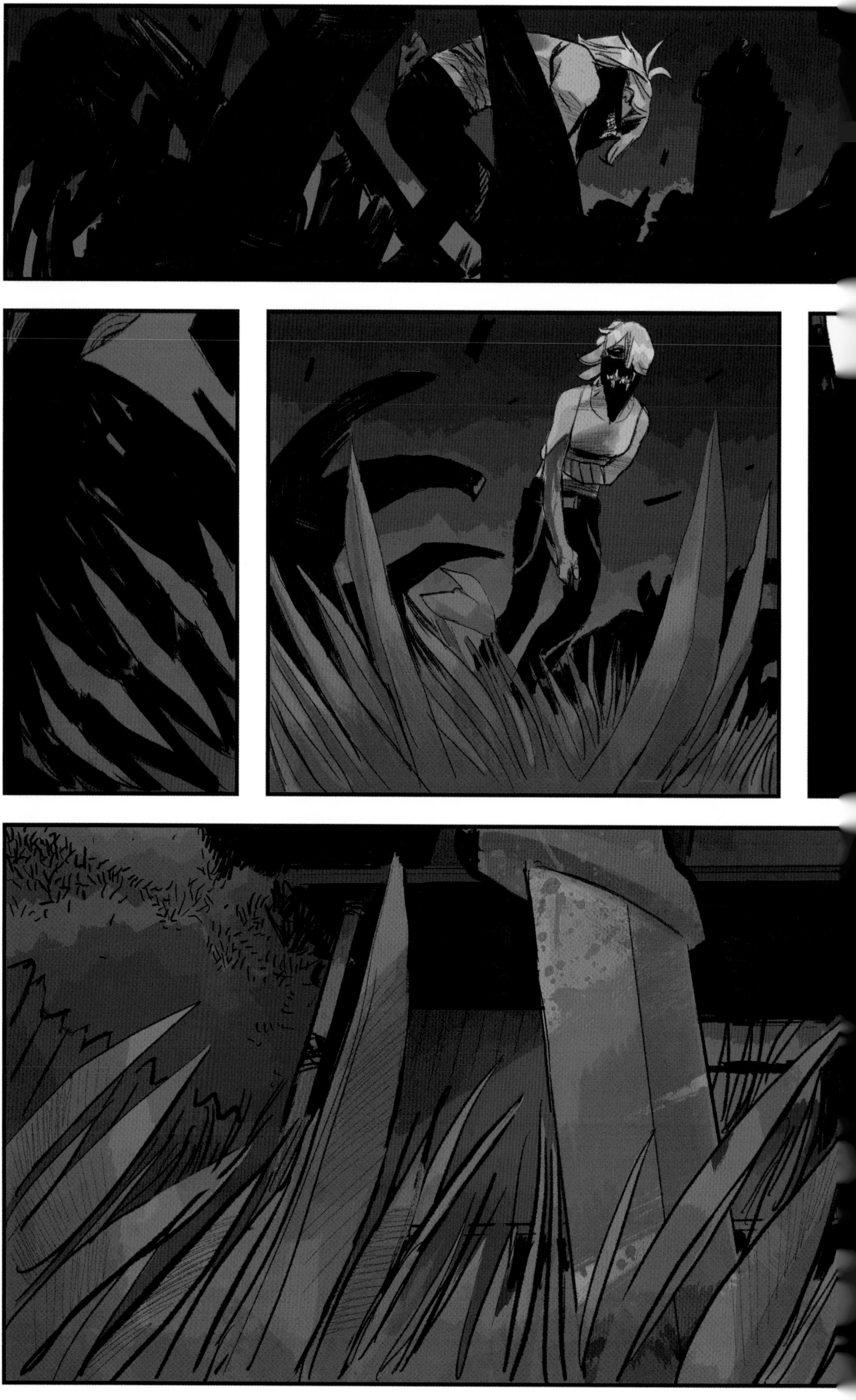

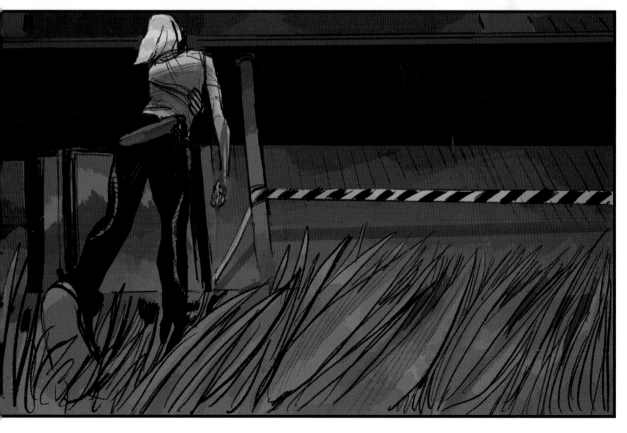

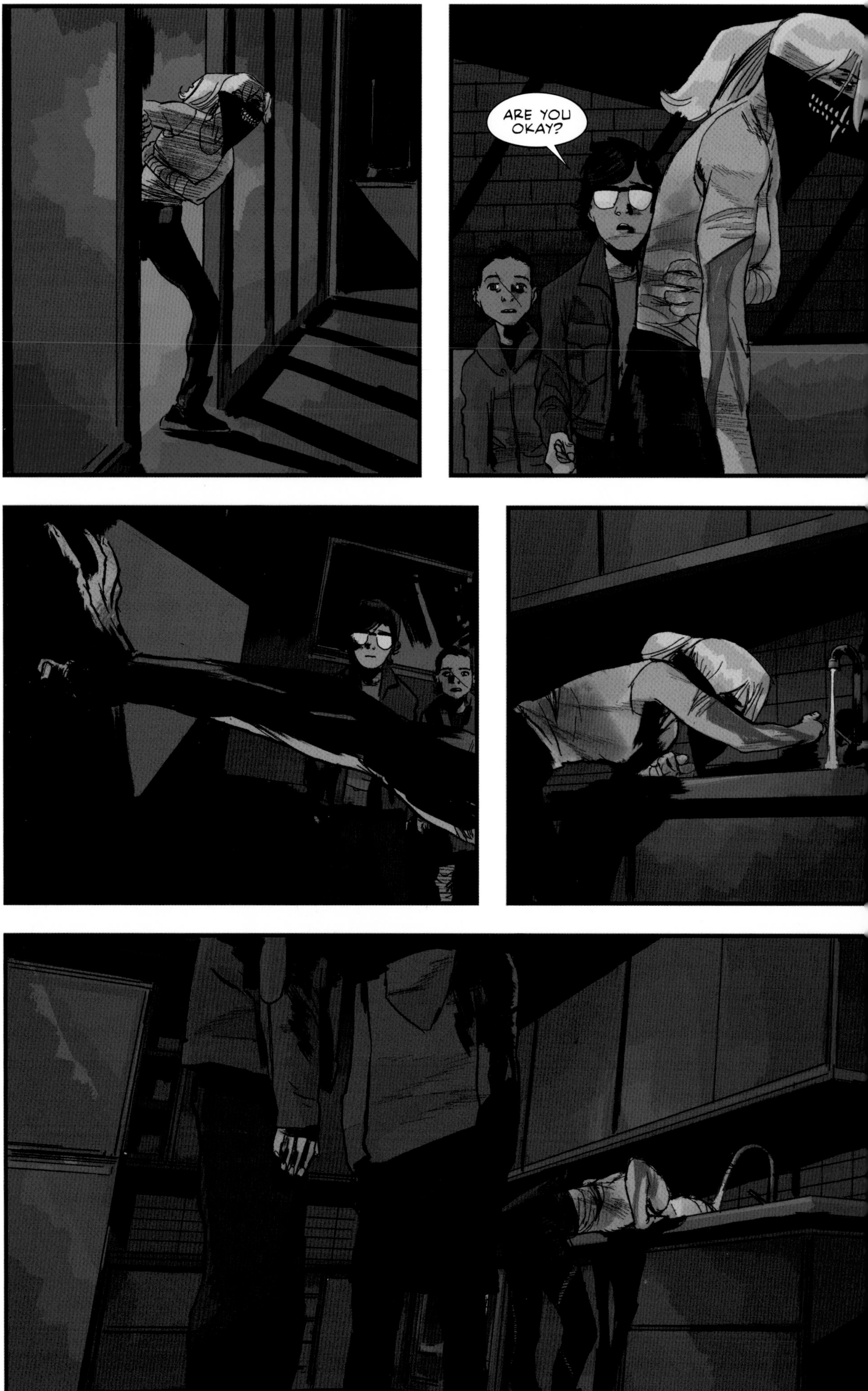
ARE YOU OKAY?

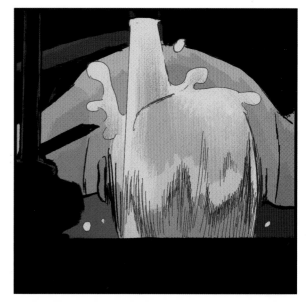

IS...IS IT
OVER?

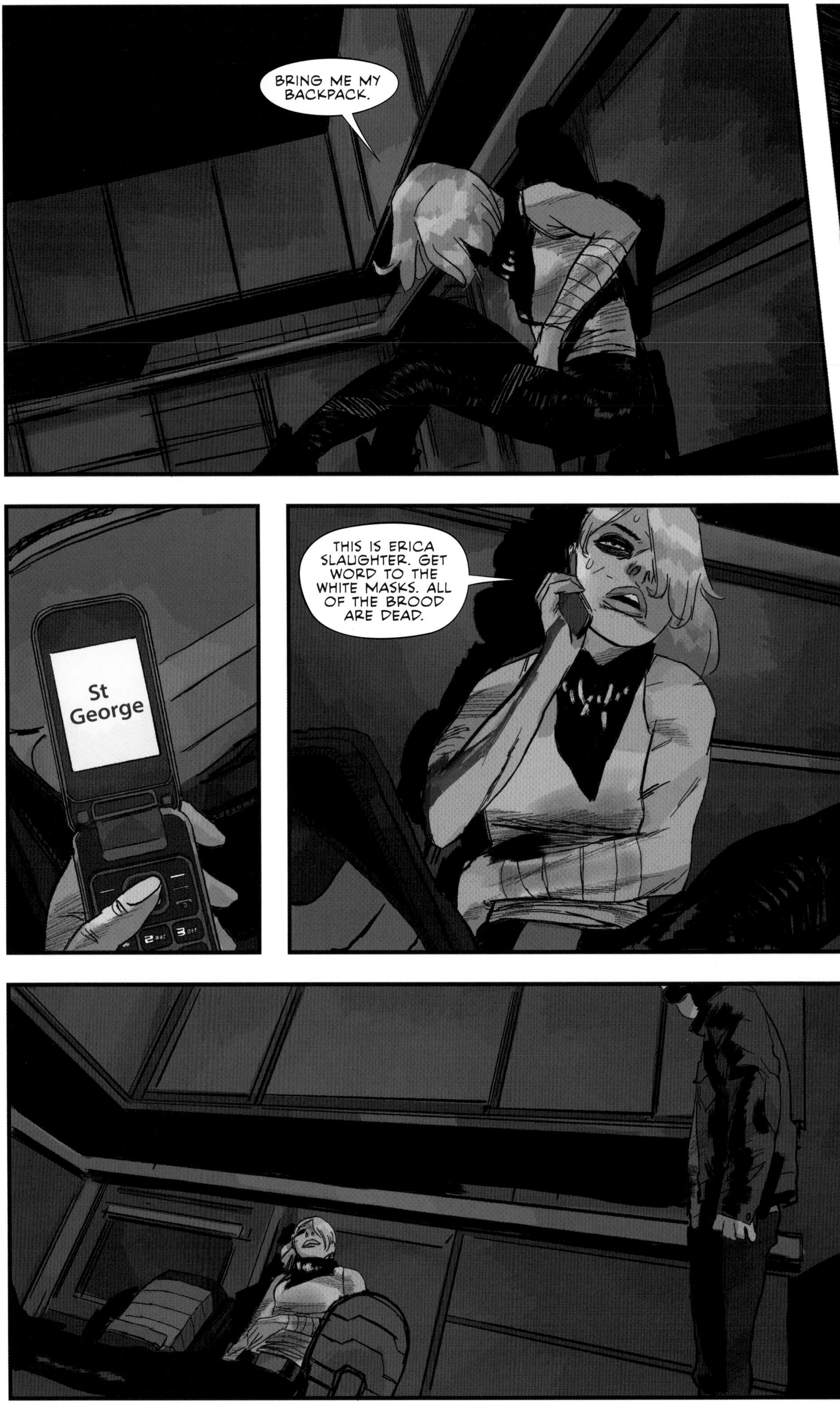
BRING ME MY BACKPACK.
St George
THIS IS ERICA SLAUGHTER. GET WORD TO THE WHITE MASKS. ALL OF THE BROOD ARE DEAD.

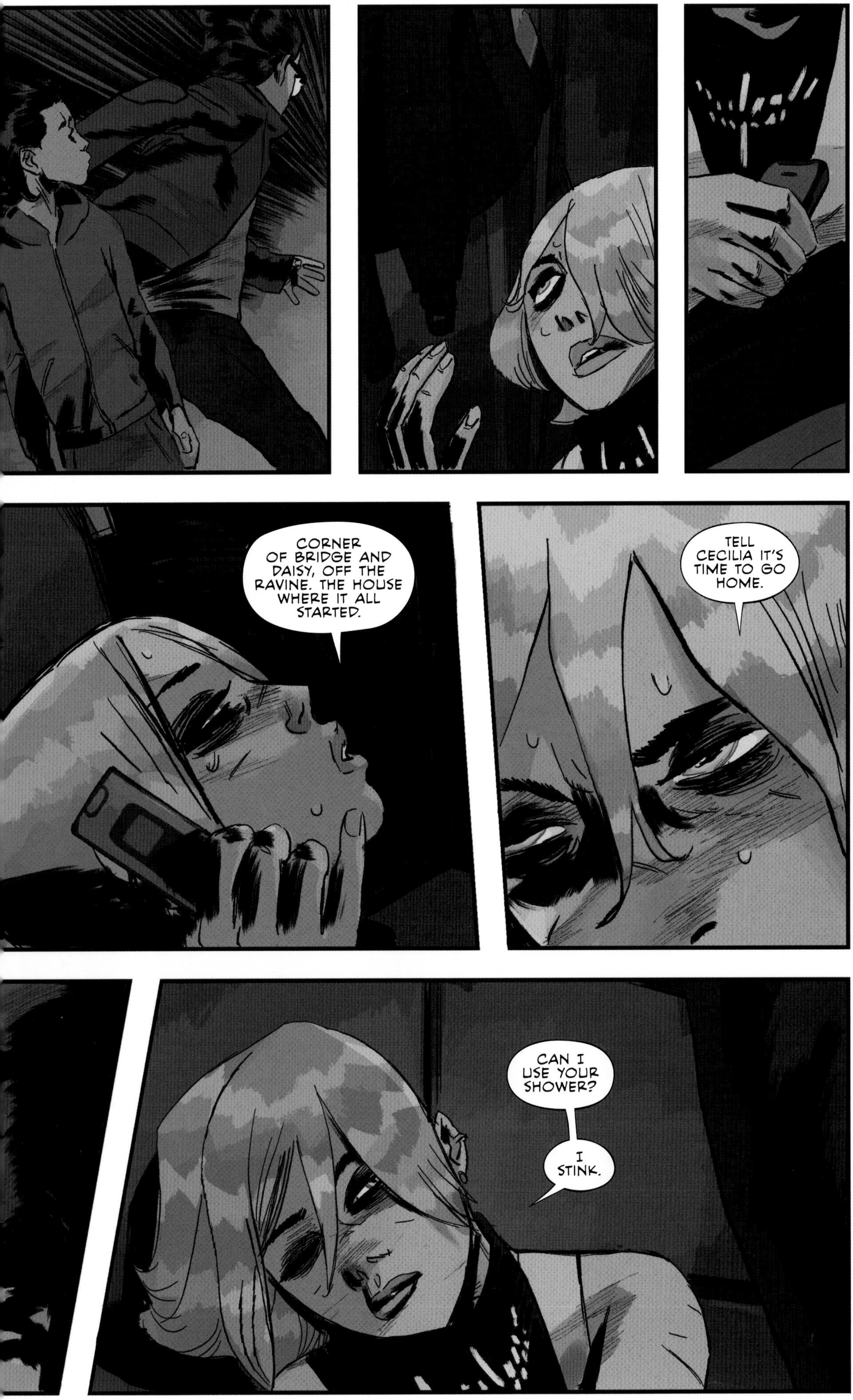
CORNER OF BRIDGE AND DAISY, OFF THE RAVINE. THE HOUSE WHERE IT ALL STARTED.
TELL CECILIA IT'S TIME TO GO HOME.
CAN I USE YOUR SHOWER?
I STINK.

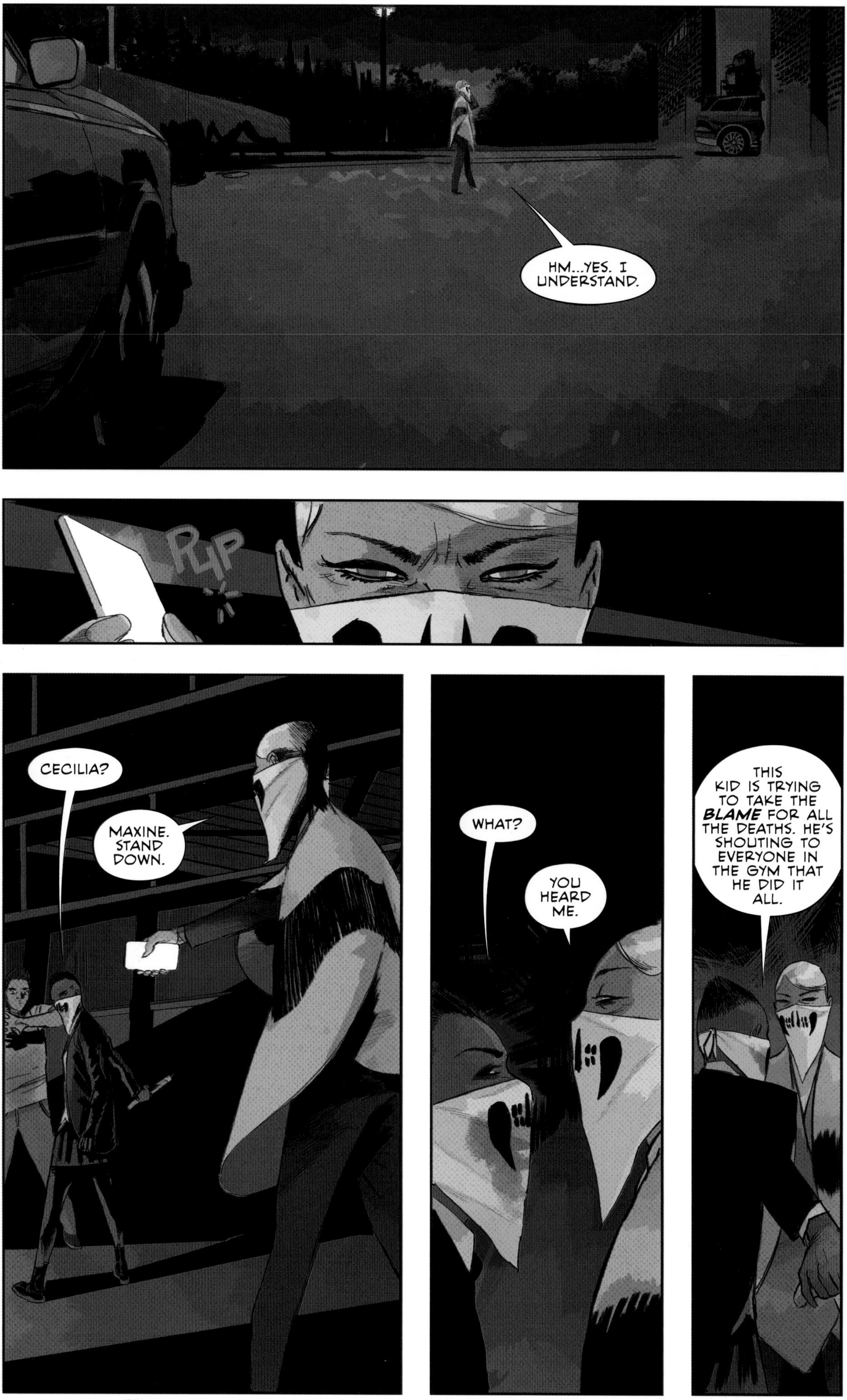
HM...YES. I UNDERSTAND.
RIP
CECILIA?
MAXINE. STAND DOWN.
WHAT?
YOU HEARD ME.
THIS KID IS TRYING TO TAKE THE BLAME FOR ALL THE DEATHS. HE'S SHOUTING TO EVERYONE IN THE GYM THAT HE DID IT ALL.

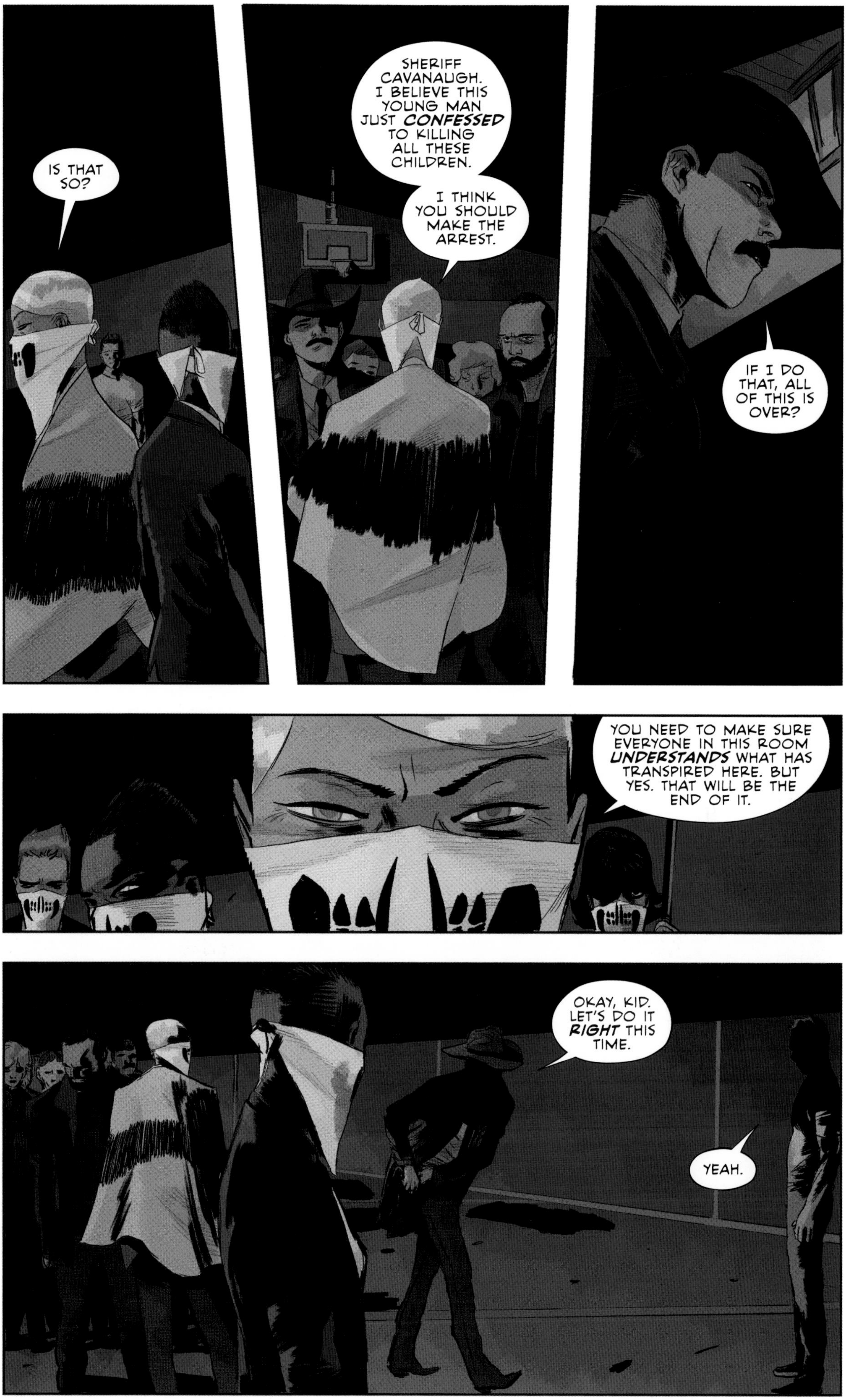
IS THAT SO?
SHERIFF CAVANAUGH. I BELIEVE THIS YOUNG MAN JUST CONFESSED TO KILLING ALL THESE CHILDREN.
I THINK YOU SHOULD MAKE THE ARREST.
IF I DO THAT, ALL OF THIS IS OVER?
YOU NEED TO MAKE SURE EVERYONE IN THIS ROOM UNDERSTANDS WHAT HAS TRANSPIRED HERE. BUT YES. THAT WILL BE THE END OF IT.
OKAY, KID. LET'S DO IT RIGHT THIS TIME.
YEAH.

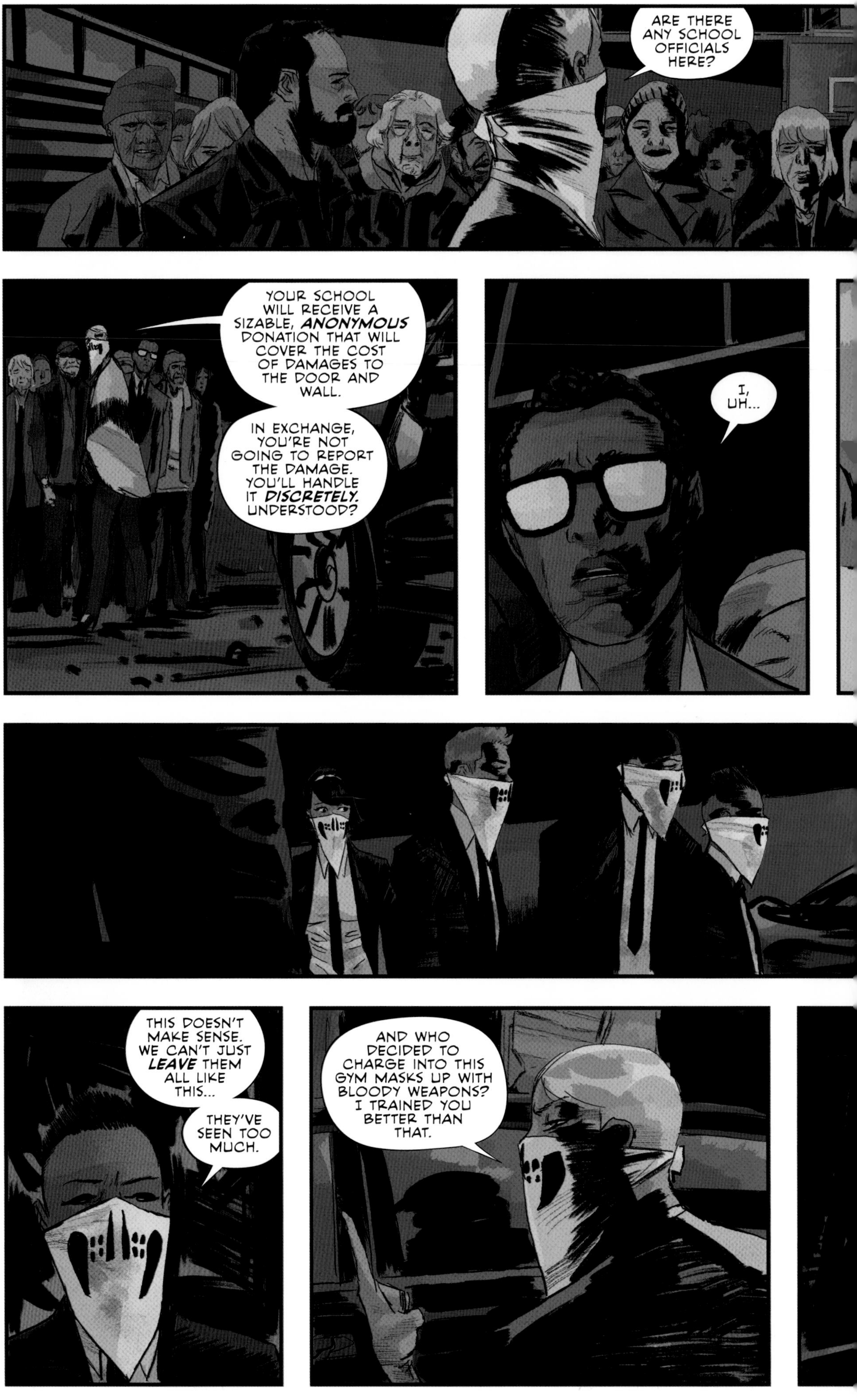
ARE THERE ANY SCHOOL OFFICIALS HERE?
YOUR SCHOOL WILL RECEIVE A SIZABLE, ANONYMOUS DONATION THAT WILL COVER THE COST OF DAMAGES TO THE DOOR AND WALL.
IN EXCHANGE, YOU'RE NOT GOING TO REPORT THE DAMAGE. YOU'LL HANDLE IT DISCRETELY. UNDERSTOOD?
I, UH...
THIS DOESN'T MAKE SENSE. WE CAN'T JUST LEAVE THEM ALL LIKE THIS...
THEY'VE SEEN TOO MUCH.
AND WHO DECIDED TO CHARGE INTO THIS GYM MASKS UP WITH BLOODY WEAPONS? I TRAINED YOU BETTER THAN THAT.

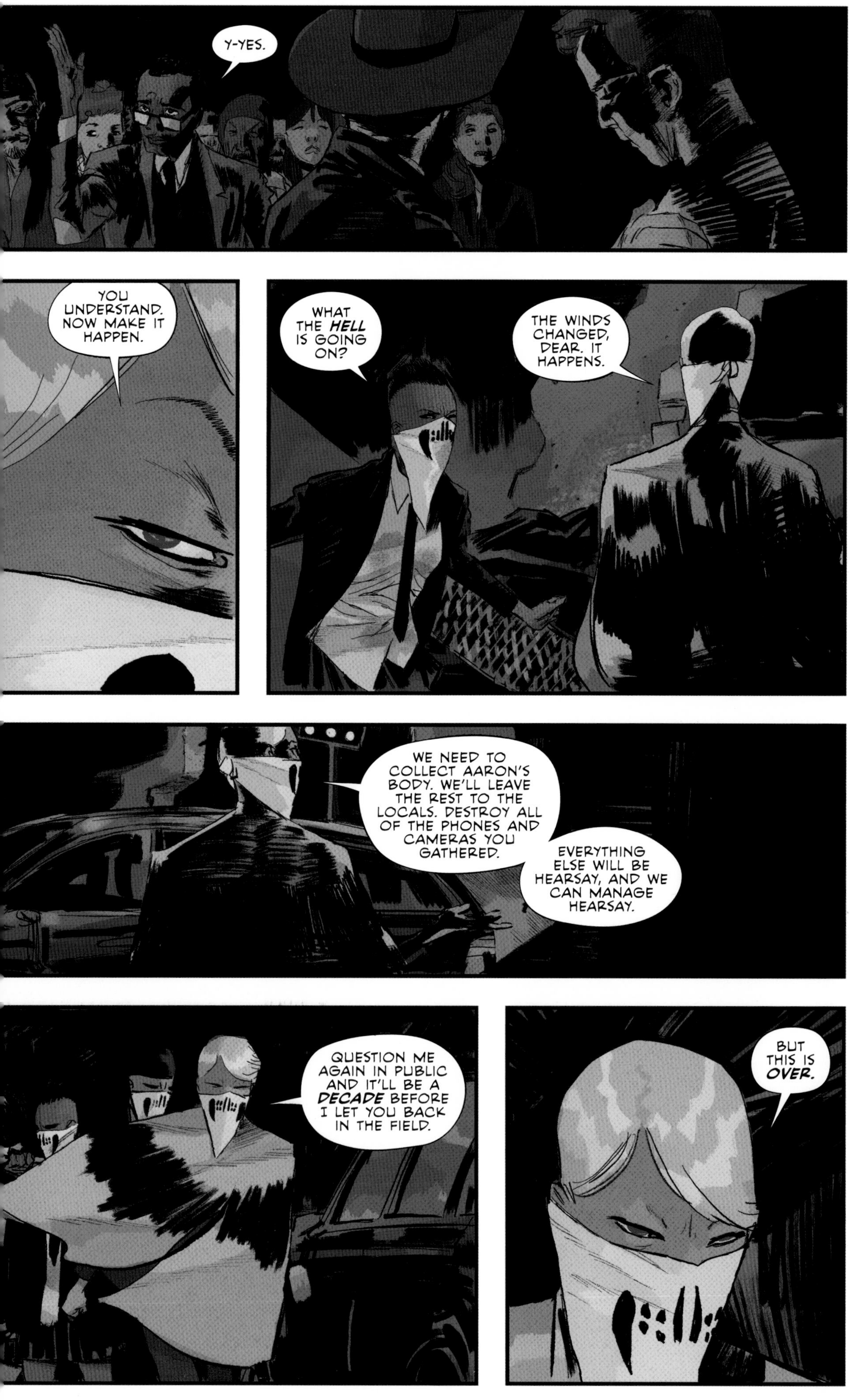
Y-YES.
YOU UNDERSTAND. NOW MAKE IT HAPPEN.
WHAT THE *HELL* IS GOING ON?
THE WINDS CHANGED, DEAR. IT HAPPENS.
WE NEED TO COLLECT AARON'S BODY. WE'LL LEAVE THE REST TO THE LOCALS. DESTROY ALL OF THE PHONES AND CAMERAS YOU GATHERED.
EVERYTHING ELSE WILL BE HEARSAY, AND WE CAN MANAGE HEARSAY.
QUESTION ME AGAIN IN PUBLIC AND IT'LL BE A *DECADE* BEFORE I LET YOU BACK IN THE FIELD.
BUT THIS IS *OVER.*

ONE
WE
L

EK

ATER

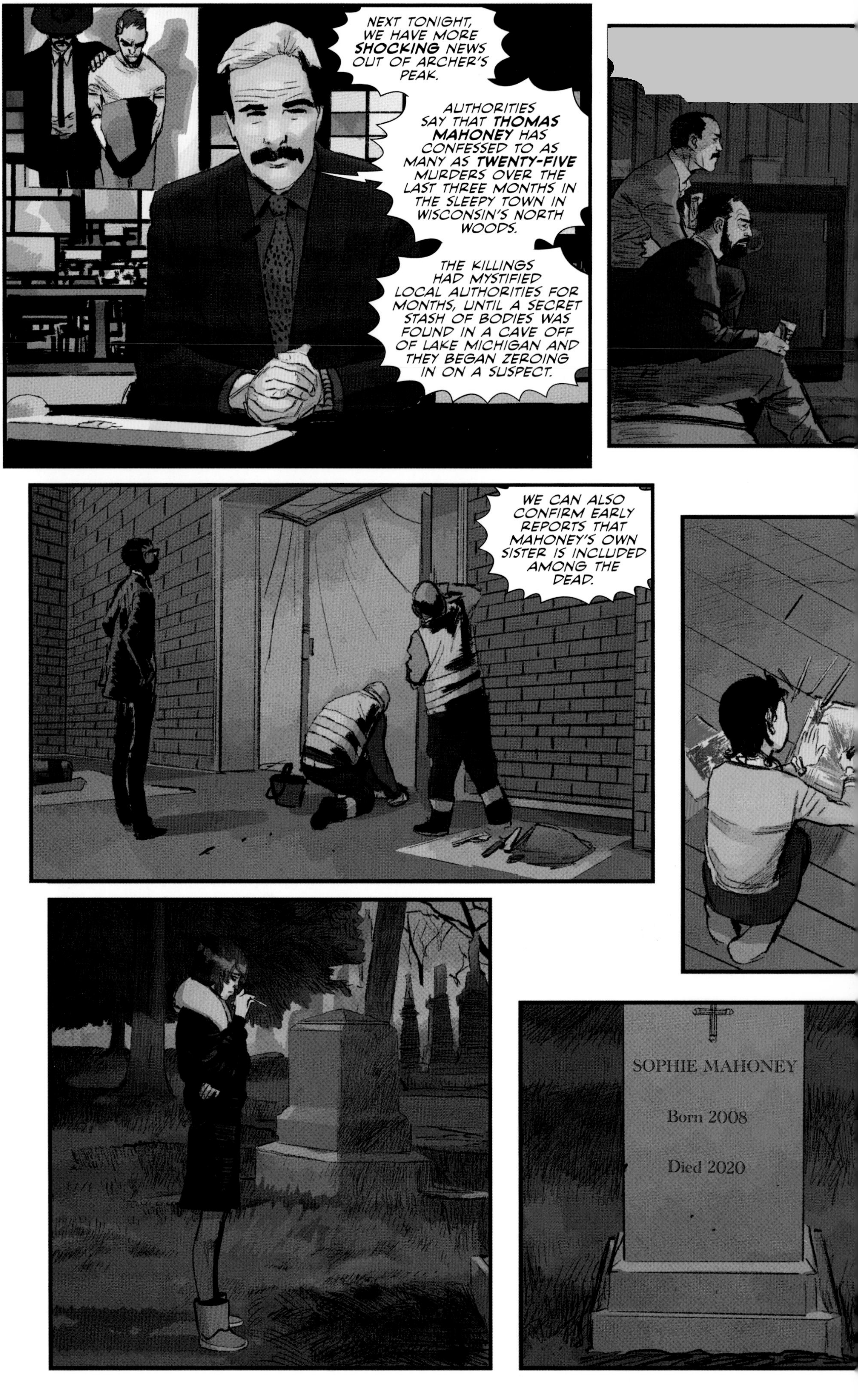
NEXT TONIGHT, WE HAVE MORE SHOCKING NEWS OUT OF ARCHER'S PEAK.
AUTHORITIES SAY THAT THOMAS MAHONEY HAS CONFESSED TO AS MANY AS TWENTY-FIVE MURDERS OVER THE LAST THREE MONTHS IN THE SLEEPY TOWN IN WISCONSIN'S NORTH WOODS.
THE KILLINGS HAD MYSTIFIED LOCAL AUTHORITIES FOR MONTHS, UNTIL A SECRET STASH OF BODIES WAS FOUND IN A CAVE OFF OF LAKE MICHIGAN AND THEY BEGAN ZEROING IN ON A SUSPECT.
WE CAN ALSO CONFIRM EARLY REPORTS THAT MAHONEY'S OWN SISTER IS INCLUDED AMONG THE DEAD.
SOPHIE MAHONEY
Born 2008
Died 2020

...WHO HAD BEEN PROTECTING ONE OF THE ONLY CHILDREN TO ESCAPE HIS MURDER SPREE.

MAHONEY KILLED HIS LAST VICTIM, A SEVEN-YEAR-OLD GIRL, IN FULL VIEW OF A CROWD GATHERED TO PAY THEIR RESPECTS TO HIS VICTIMS.

WE CAN ONLY **IMAGINE** THE RELIEF SWEEPING OVER THIS SMALL TOWN WITH THE MONSTER, A RESTAURANT MANAGER KNOWN TO HIS FRIENDS AS "TOMMY," VANQUISHED, AND THE HORROR HAVING COME TO AN END.

MAHONEY'S ARRAIGNMENT IS SET FOR NEXT WEEK.

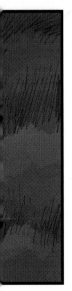

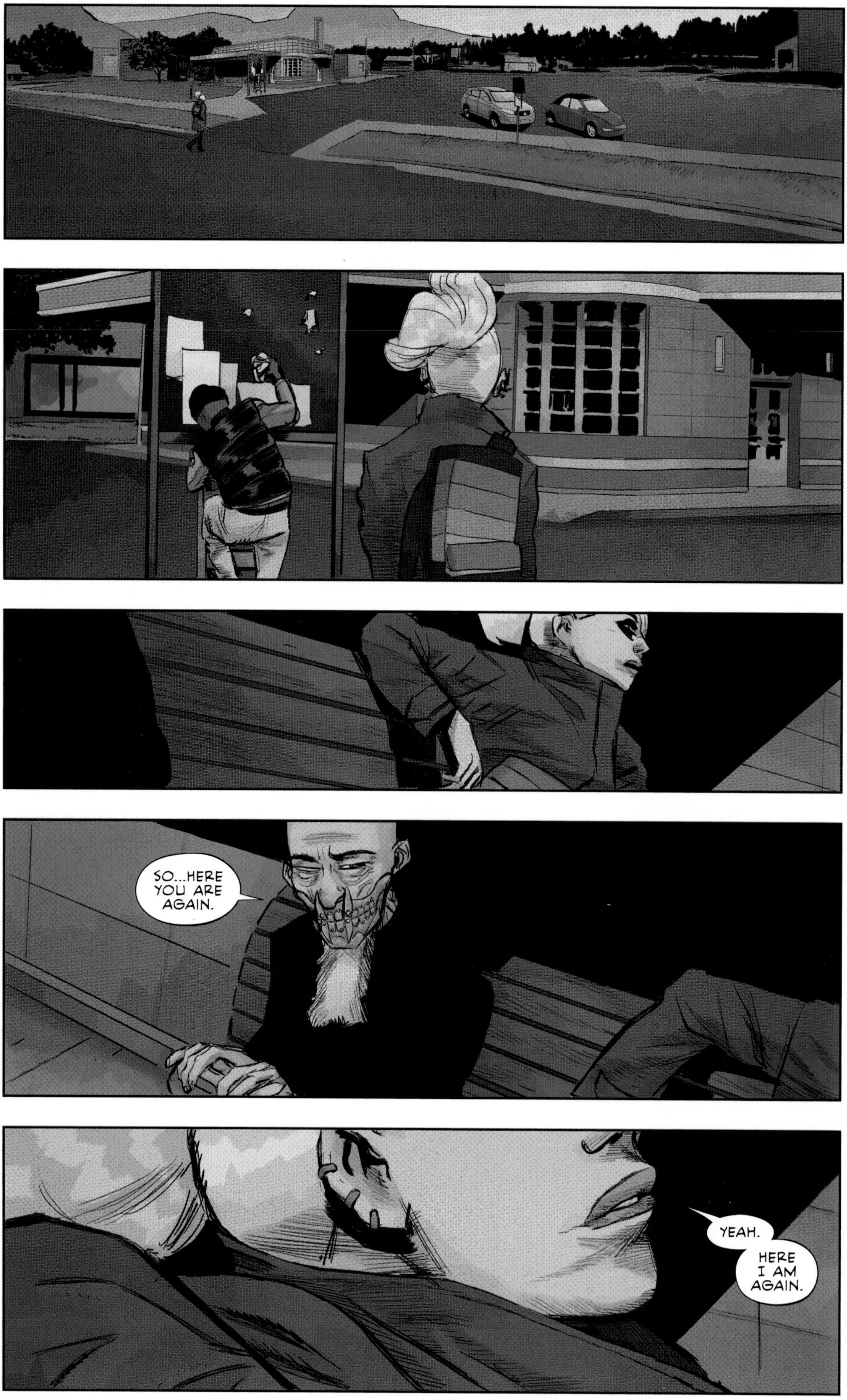
SO...HERE YOU ARE AGAIN.
YEAH.
HERE I AM AGAIN.

ARCHER'S PEAK. IT SEEMS LIKE A NICE LITTLE TOWN.

I'M SURE IT *USED* TO BE. JUST LIKE EVERYWHERE ELSE.

I REMEMBER WHEN YOU WERE JUST A *GIRL.* YOU GOT SO ANGRY WITH US AT THE HOUSE OF SLAUGHTER YOU WALKED HALFWAY ACROSS *CHICAGO* TO TAKE A BUS.

I REMEMBER.

WHERE WERE YOU GOING, DO YOU RECALL?

ORLANDO.

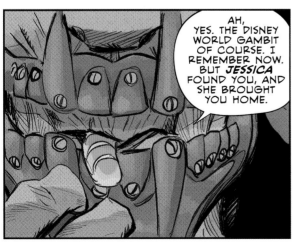

AH, YES. THE DISNEY WORLD GAMBIT OF COURSE. I REMEMBER NOW. BUT *JESSICA* FOUND YOU, AND SHE BROUGHT YOU HOME.

DO YOU REMEMBER WHAT SHE TOLD YOU?

SHE TOLD ME THAT THE ORDER WAS OLD AND IT WAS STODGY AND STUCK IN ITS WAYS, BUT *WITHOUT* IT, CHILDREN WOULD DIE. AND NOBODY WOULD KNOW WHY, OR WHAT WAS KILLING THEM.

SHE TOLD ME TO LEARN *EVERYTHING* I COULD LEARN TO SAVE THOSE CHILDREN.

I MISS HER TERRIBLY.

YOU SENT HER TO HER DEATH.

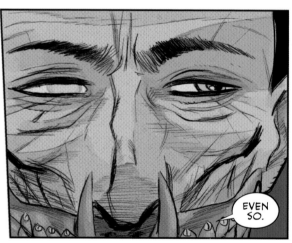

EVEN SO.

YOU'RE *NOT* GOING TO BE ABLE TO CONVINCE ME.

WHAT DO YOU THINK I WANT TO CONVINCE YOU OF, ERICA?

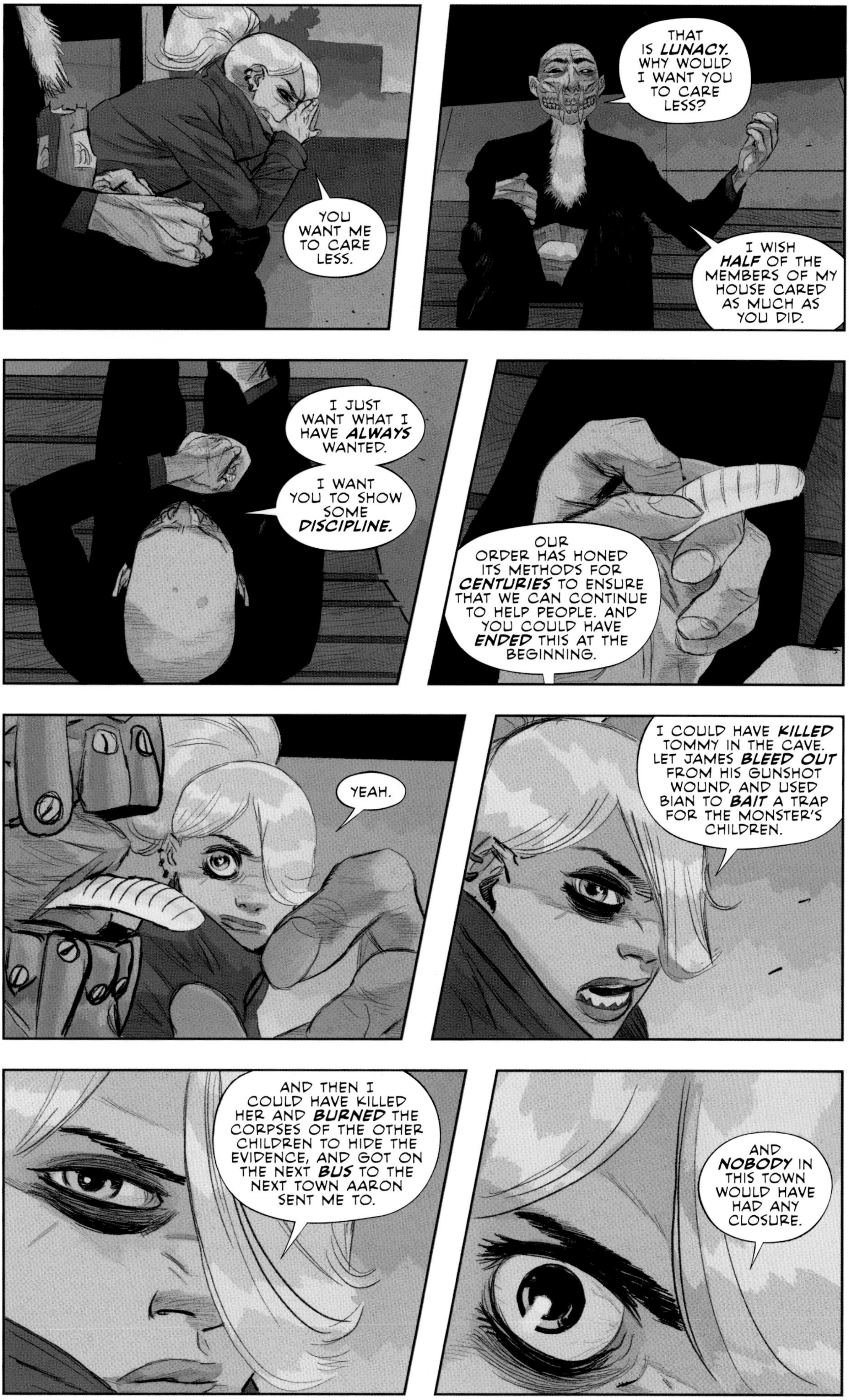
YOU WANT ME TO CARE LESS.
THAT IS LUNACY. WHY WOULD I WANT YOU TO CARE LESS?
I WISH HALF OF THE MEMBERS OF MY HOUSE CARED AS MUCH AS YOU DID.
I JUST WANT WHAT I HAVE ALWAYS WANTED.
I WANT YOU TO SHOW SOME DISCIPLINE.
OUR ORDER HAS HONED ITS METHODS FOR CENTURIES TO ENSURE THAT WE CAN CONTINUE TO HELP PEOPLE. AND YOU COULD HAVE ENDED THIS AT THE BEGINNING.
YEAH.
I COULD HAVE KILLED TOMMY IN THE CAVE. LET JAMES BLEED OUT FROM HIS GUNSHOT WOUND, AND USED BIAN TO BAIT A TRAP FOR THE MONSTER'S CHILDREN.
AND THEN I COULD HAVE KILLED HER AND BURNED THE CORPSES OF THE OTHER CHILDREN TO HIDE THE EVIDENCE, AND GOT ON THE NEXT BUS TO THE NEXT TOWN AARON SENT ME TO.
AND NOBODY IN THIS TOWN WOULD HAVE HAD ANY CLOSURE.

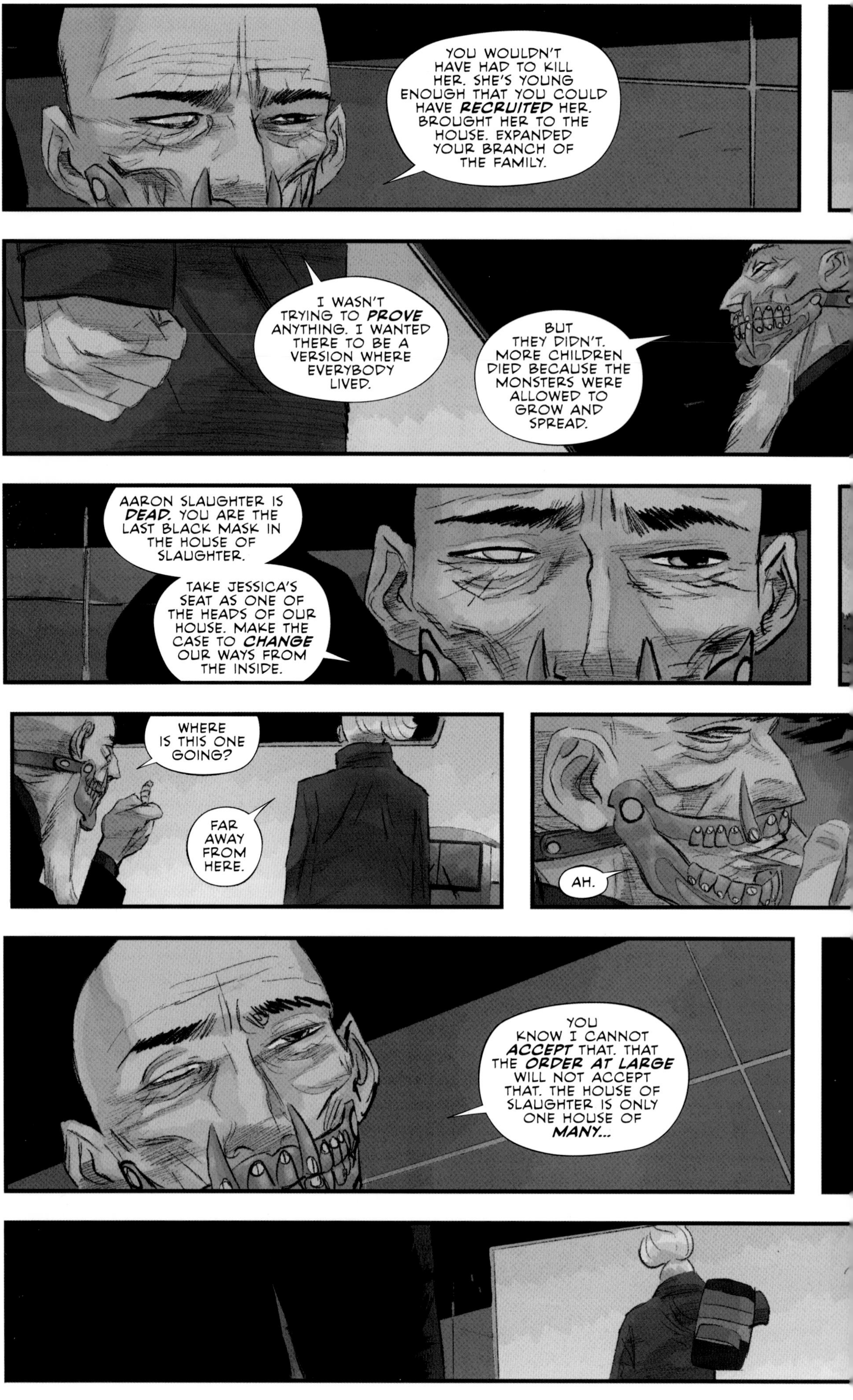
YOU WOULDN'T HAVE HAD TO KILL HER. SHE'S YOUNG ENOUGH THAT YOU COULD HAVE RECRUITED HER. BROUGHT HER TO THE HOUSE. EXPANDED YOUR BRANCH OF THE FAMILY.
I WASN'T TRYING TO PROVE ANYTHING. I WANTED THERE TO BE A VERSION WHERE EVERYBODY LIVED.
BUT THEY DIDN'T. MORE CHILDREN DIED BECAUSE THE MONSTERS WERE ALLOWED TO GROW AND SPREAD.
AARON SLAUGHTER IS DEAD. YOU ARE THE LAST BLACK MASK IN THE HOUSE OF SLAUGHTER.
TAKE JESSICA'S SEAT AS ONE OF THE HEADS OF OUR HOUSE. MAKE THE CASE TO CHANGE OUR WAYS FROM THE INSIDE.
WHERE IS THIS ONE GOING?
FAR AWAY FROM HERE.
AH.
YOU KNOW I CANNOT ACCEPT THAT. THAT THE ORDER AT LARGE WILL NOT ACCEPT THAT. THE HOUSE OF SLAUGHTER IS ONLY ONE HOUSE OF MANY...

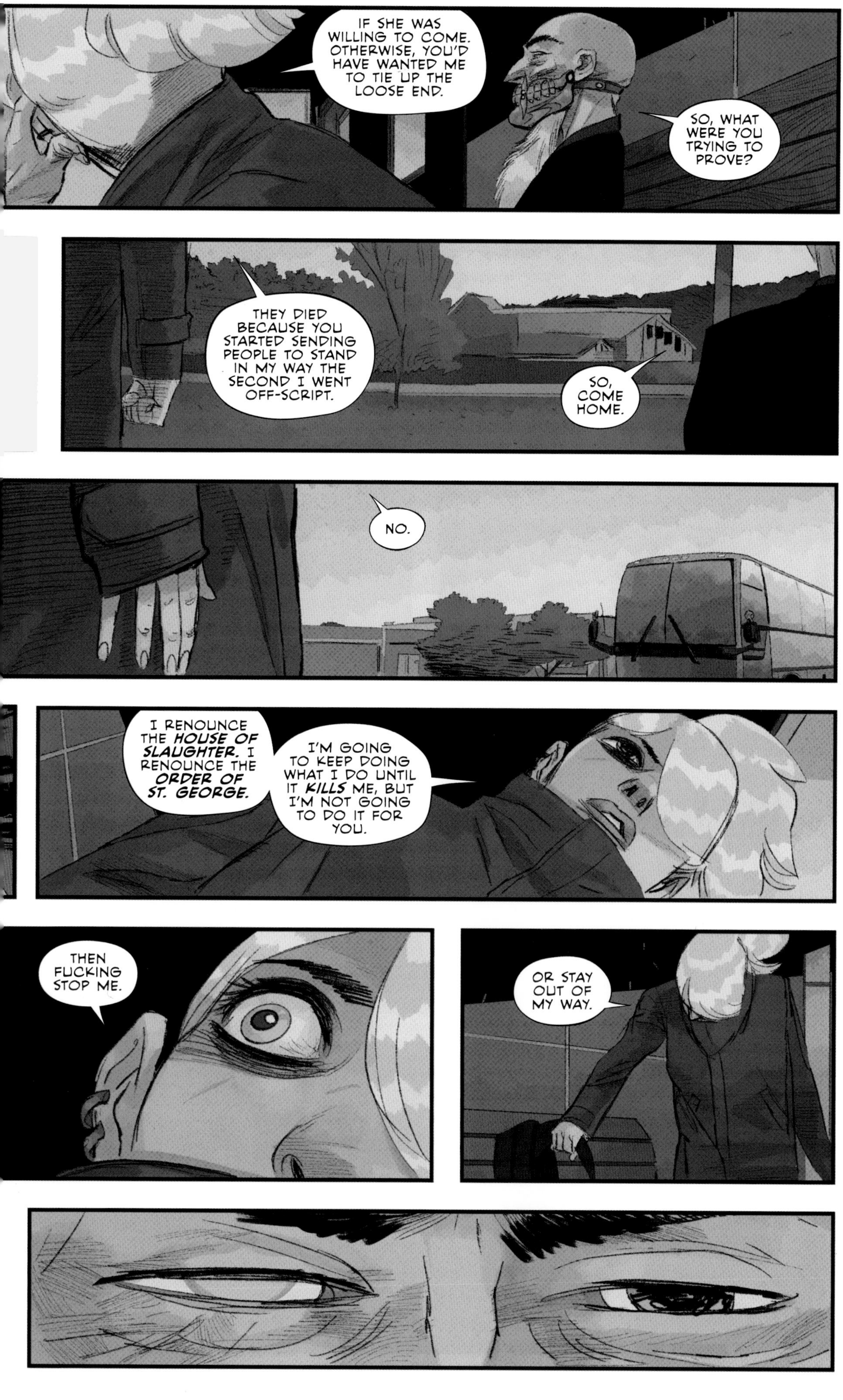
IF SHE WAS WILLING TO COME. OTHERWISE, YOU'D HAVE WANTED ME TO TIE UP THE LOOSE END.
SO, WHAT WERE YOU TRYING TO PROVE?
THEY DIED BECAUSE YOU STARTED SENDING PEOPLE TO STAND IN MY WAY THE SECOND I WENT OFF-SCRIPT.
SO, COME HOME.
NO.
I RENOUNCE THE HOUSE OF SLAUGHTER. I RENOUNCE THE ORDER OF ST. GEORGE.
I'M GOING TO KEEP DOING WHAT I DO UNTIL IT KILLS ME, BUT I'M NOT GOING TO DO IT FOR YOU.
THEN FUCKING STOP ME.
OR STAY OUT OF MY WAY.

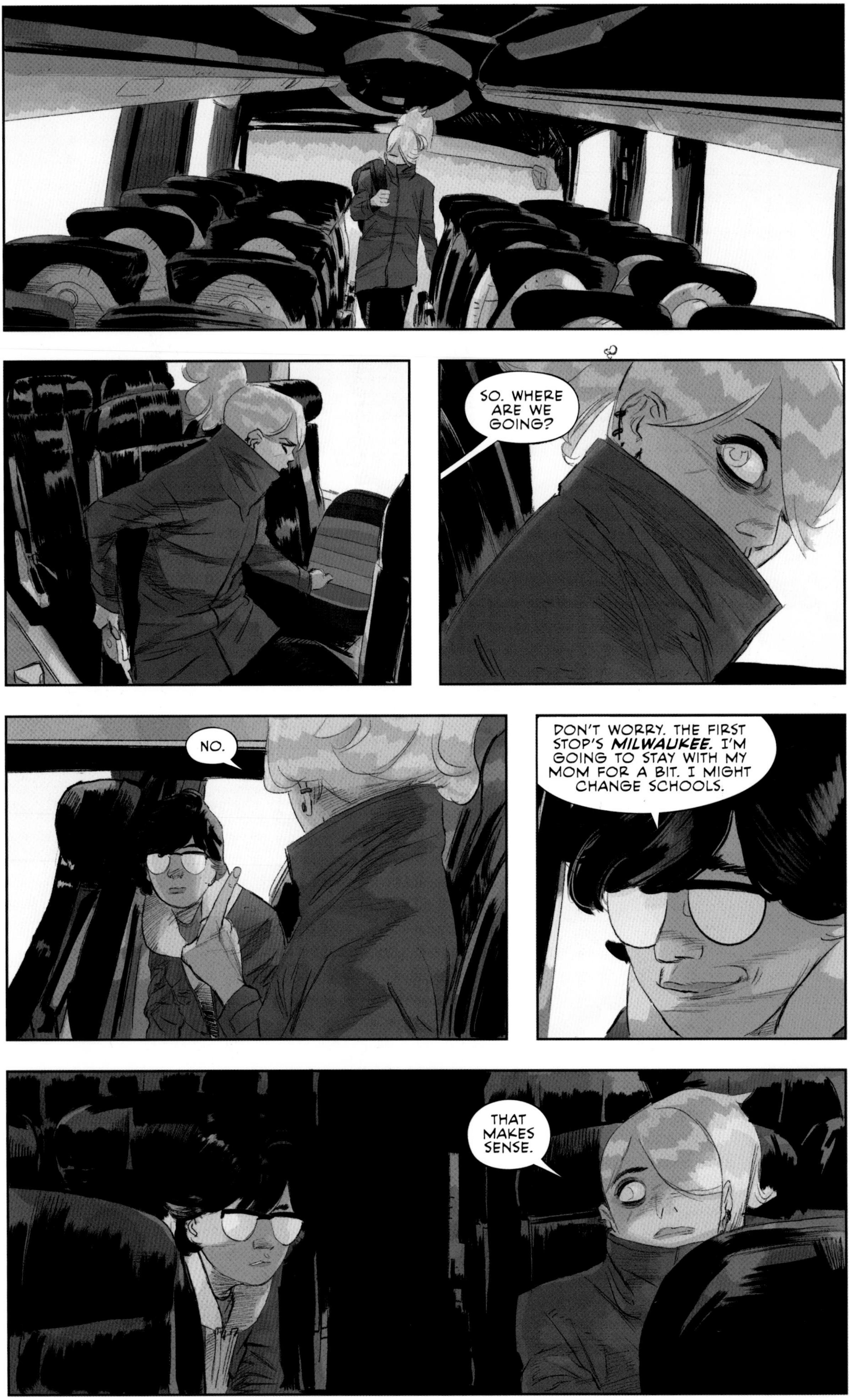
SO. WHERE ARE WE GOING?
NO.
DON'T WORRY. THE FIRST STOP'S MILWAUKEE. I'M GOING TO STAY WITH MY MOM FOR A BIT. I MIGHT CHANGE SCHOOLS.
THAT MAKES SENSE.

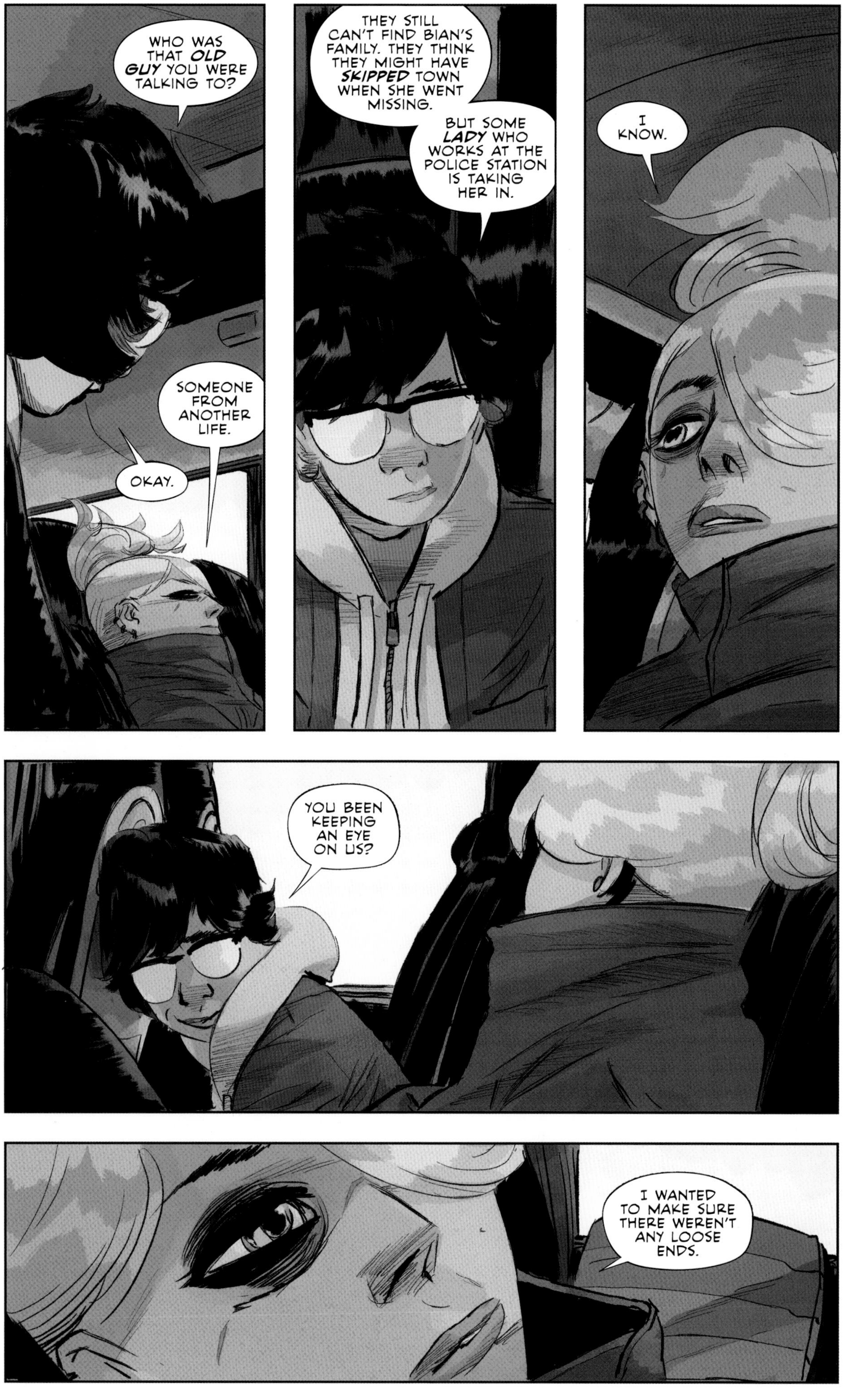

WHO WAS THAT OLD GUY YOU WERE TALKING TO?
SOMEONE FROM ANOTHER LIFE.
OKAY.
THEY STILL CAN'T FIND BIAN'S FAMILY. THEY THINK THEY MIGHT HAVE SKIPPED TOWN WHEN SHE WENT MISSING.
BUT SOME LADY WHO WORKS AT THE POLICE STATION IS TAKING HER IN.
I KNOW.
YOU BEEN KEEPING AN EYE ON US?
I WANTED TO MAKE SURE THERE WEREN'T ANY LOOSE ENDS.

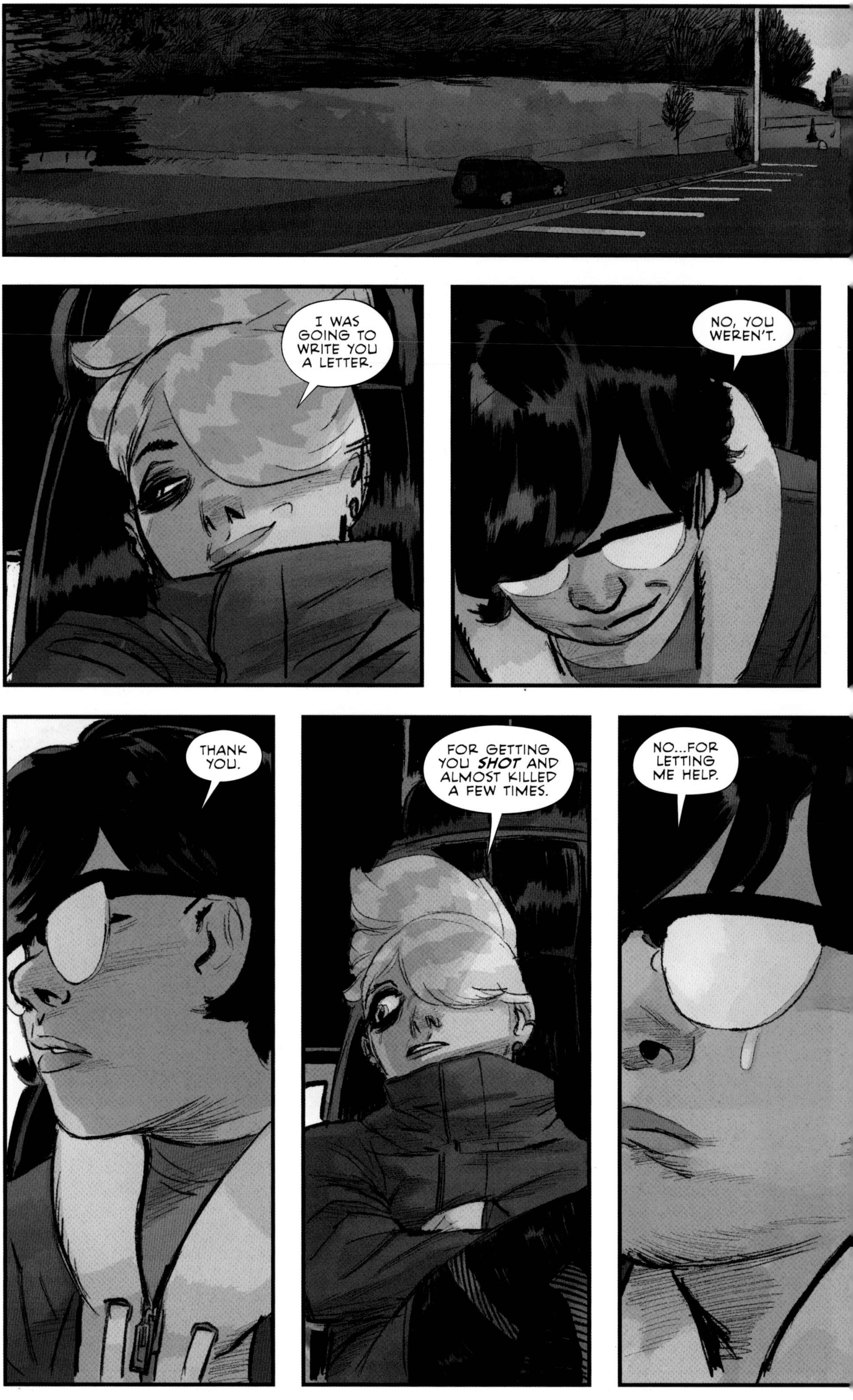
I WAS GOING TO WRITE YOU A LETTER.
NO, YOU WEREN'T.
THANK YOU.
FOR GETTING YOU *SHOT* AND ALMOST KILLED A FEW TIMES.
NO...FOR LETTING ME HELP.

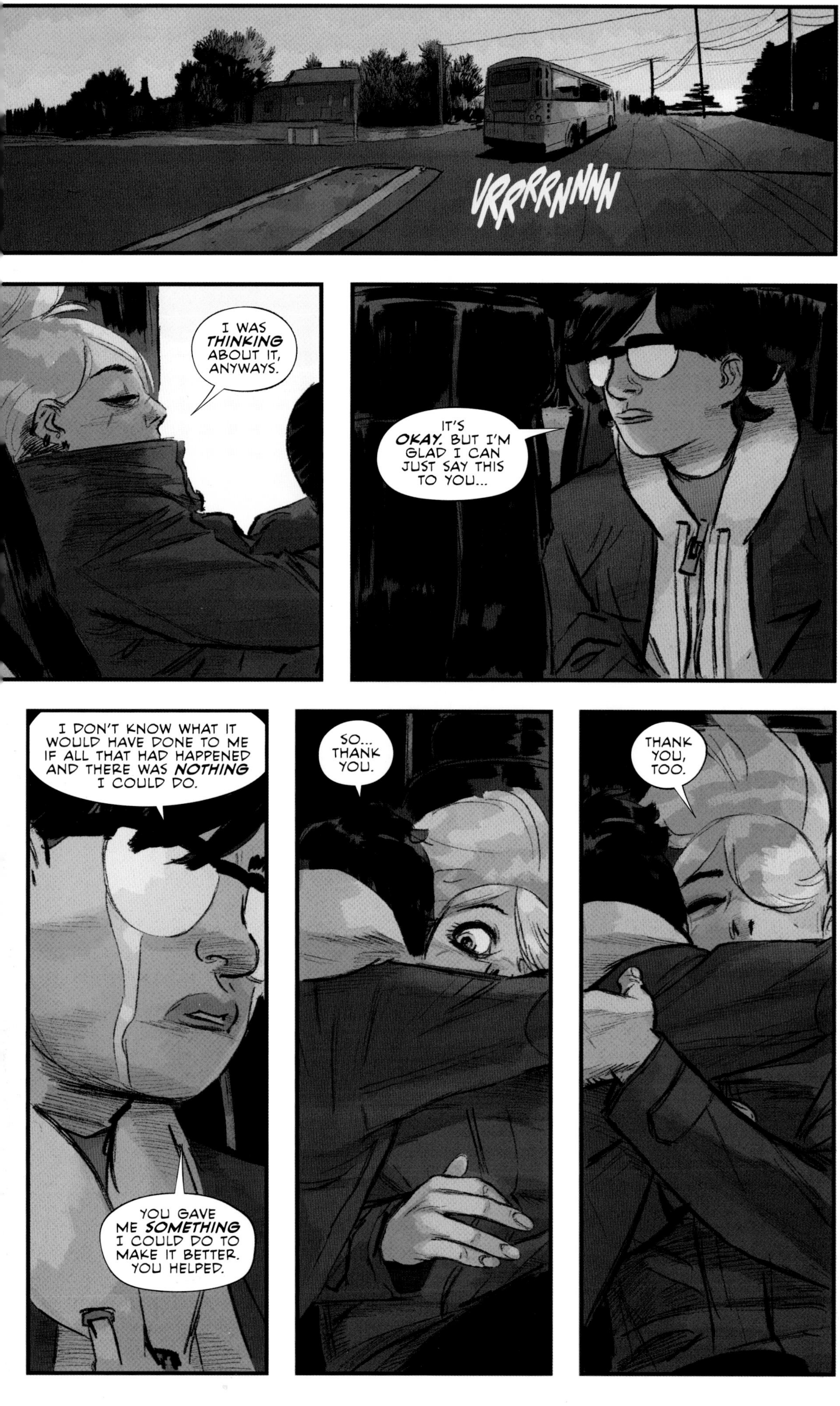
VRRRRNNNN
I WAS THINKING ABOUT IT, ANYWAYS.
IT'S OKAY. BUT I'M GLAD I CAN JUST SAY THIS TO YOU...
I DON'T KNOW WHAT IT WOULD HAVE DONE TO ME IF ALL THAT HAD HAPPENED AND THERE WAS NOTHING I COULD DO.
YOU GAVE ME SOMETHING I COULD DO TO MAKE IT BETTER. YOU HELPED.
SO... THANK YOU.
THANK YOU, TOO.

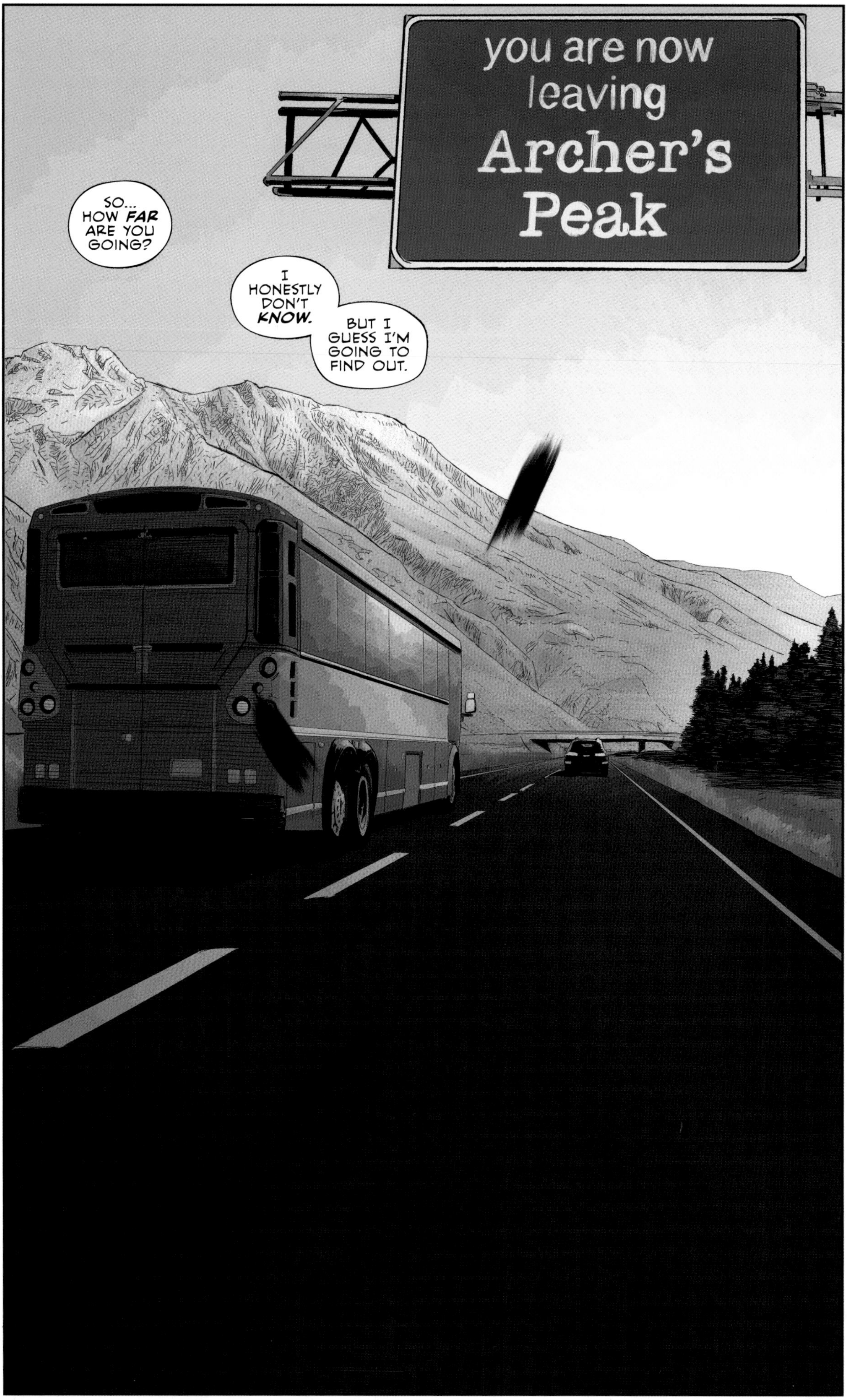
you are now leaving Archer's Peak
SO... HOW FAR ARE YOU GOING?
I HONESTLY DON'T KNOW.
BUT I GUESS I'M GOING TO FIND OUT.

TO BE CONTINUED...

MONSTER HUNTING

Interview by Hassan Otsmane-Elhaou, originally published in PanelxPanel No. 32, March 2020.

Panel x Panel: It seems like **Something is Killing the Children** *wears many inspirations on its sleeve. For all of you, were there any specific things you were channeling heading into working on the series, and what kind of direction did they push you in?*

James Tynion IV [Writer]: I wanted to write something that was the opposite of everything that I was writing for DC Comics. I wanted to do something quiet, understated, and frightening. At the beginning, I saw this as an experimental project. I wanted to write a book that was made up entirely of the sort of interstitial issues you'd get in the middle of a run of a long Vertigo Comics run. The sorts of issues where Morpheus or John Constantine only show up for three pages at the end. A book where every issue has a different main character and has an encounter with this extraordinary, mysterious woman, in different small towns around America.

My pitch to BOOM! was to do it as a five-issue miniseries, where you catch five glimpses of this character (who didn't have a name when I started

writing the one-pager). They were supportive. Then Werther came in with the character design, and I started writing the book... And I realized I was writing a very different comic book than the one I set out to write.

Werther Dell'Edera [Artist]: As a general rule, as far as art is concerned, I let the story lead the way. Obviously there are a lot of things that inspire me, and every one of these things push my art in a different direction. At the moment I'm really fascinated by manga, I read a lot of them and they definitely have effects on my storytelling and drawing. But I find it really difficult to put in more words what happens when I start drawing because usually there's not a lot of planning on my part. Most of the time my processes do not stem from a rational choice, so they aren't really planned. They arise mostly from an inner drive that emerges as I go on with the work. So that's why from time to time I'm drawn closer to a specific style or another.

Miquel Muerto [Colorist]: For this project my mind was closer to modern horror films like *The Witch*, *It*

It also reflects the larger fears of society. And we have a *lot* of fears right now. The sheer noise and trauma of living in this world, day to day, is overwhelming. It's never just one thing we're afraid of, but we're afraid of everything, and for good reason. The old systems feel like they're falling apart, and it feels like everyone all at once remembered that the rules of society are just tenuous agreements that can be ignored outright.

I feel like the world has left us kind of primed for horror. A horror story is a safe way to interact with that fear and give it a face and a name. It helps them put a face to the monsters in their lives, and the desire for that has left people hungry for new horror stories, and I am extremely grateful for the opportunity to deliver some.

Horror and comedy, which are really two sides of the same coin, are trying to elicit reactions from an audience more than they are trying to tell an audience something. They can be blunt instruments, because it's less about the blow the story makes against the person experiencing the story, it's more about the aftermath of that blow. I find it fascinating. It means that you don't have to define things quite as clearly. You are trying to lead someone through an emotional journey, knowing that they might have a wholly different experience to the one you intended. Because you're asking them questions about how they would feel in these situations, and leaving them with the unsettling answers to those questions.

So, the main answer is I wanted to put something honest into the world that reflects the feeling of living in the world today, and horror is the best vehicle for honesty when the world looks like this.

Follows, or *Hereditary*, and how those films use the mundane realism mixed with the invisible horror. On a daily basis, it's natural to be inspired by anything, from video games or other comic books, but for starters, I try to not take anything else but my own previous work, to not repeat myself, to improve.

Deron Bennett (AndWorld Design) [Letterer]: I tried to come into this with a blank slate. I'd recently picked up a couple of jobs that were in the horror genre and when the project was brought to me I wanted to avoid doing something that I was already doing. I try to differentiate my lettering as much as possible and keep it in line with the creative team that I'm working with. To that end, I guess you could say I was inspired by Werther. His art provided my direction.

PxP: James, SIKTC is far from your first foray into horror stories. What is it about the genre that brings you back to it?

Tynion: I think we're living through a raw, frightening moment in history that is best reflected by raw, frightening stories. You can see it happening in film. After a few decades of revisiting and revamping old horror franchises, and old horror tropes, there is an entire generation of young filmmakers desperate to do something new with the genre, and they are being rewarded for trying to tread new ground rather than retread the old. So, the genre feels richer than it has in a while. It's starting to happen in comics, too. From *Gideon Falls*, to *The Plot*, to the entire Hill House line from Black Label… Broadly, it feels like audiences are more willing to check out something outside the box in horror, where they might be more conservative in other genres.

PxP: You mention reality there, and that's really true of this. The more fantastic elements end up quite subdued, for the most part. Erica Slaughter rocks into town and tells the police pretty clearly that she'll take care of the situation without them even knowing what's going on, and she'll head to the next town. The real horror element seems to be the way the town reacts to these killings, and the family connections to missing children making things more complicated and dangerous.

Tynion: After two years of telling stories on a cosmic scale between *Dark Nights: Metal*, *Justice League*, and *Justice League Dark*, I wanted to write the polar opposite kind of story. The way I put it to my editor when I was writing my second issue is that I wanted to be able to not have to fucking explain everything. If a scene takes place in a bar, it takes place in a bar. Same with a gas station, or an Applebee's. You don't need to establish which tier of reality you're a part of, and how these great big cosmic beings are all operating on the same dimension. They got in a car and they went to Applebee's. You don't need an expository paragraph to make that track to a reader. They understand each and every one of the elements.

I hate exposition. I hate it so much that I try to overdo it a bit in my superhero fiction to capture a kind of Claremontian feel, so at least I am evoking something very comic booky that I love when I'm doing it (which has earned me some enemies among comic book critics). But I understand its necessity. You need to explain things to the reader, especially when you're writing a popular character, and you're dealing with complicated continuity and a complicated world where super-scientists, magicians, and aliens all coexist and wear costumes.

But when you write the rules for your own book, you don't have to explain anything you don't want to explain.

Originally, I wanted to do info pages in the story. I wouldn't explain anything about who Erica was or what she was a part of in the actual context of the story. I wouldn't even name her in the first issue (I don't think she's actually fully named until issue three). But you would get pages of the handbook to the Order of St. George, which is the monster hunting order she is a part of. Through that you would get her name, and information on monsters, and information about the House of Slaughter, which is effectively the local diocese of the Order. Knowing that those info pages were going to be in the book made me feel confident in not revealing anything in the scenes, which allowed the scenes to be more emotional than informational. Shockingly, the whole issue felt like it worked better before I had even sat down to *write* the info pages... And then *HoXPoX* came out, and I quickly realized I did not want to be seen as copying something done so well in those books.

PxP: There's a conversation with Erica and the police that does a lot of that exposition, implying a much larger world and more adventures that Erica is part of. Obviously* SIKTC *is moving to an ongoing now, but while working on it as a five-part

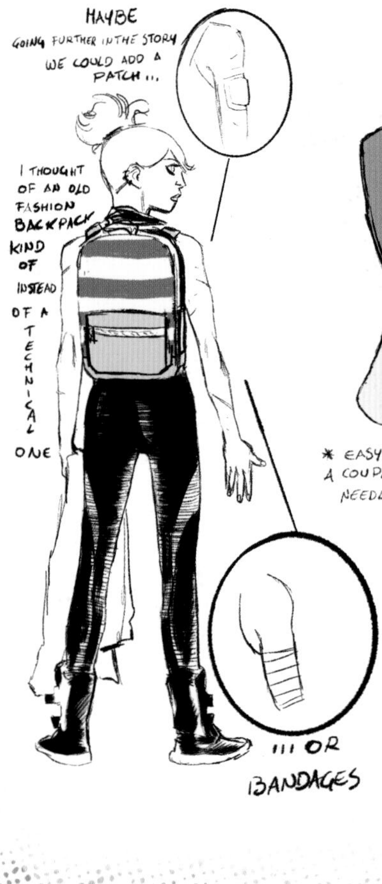
MAYBE
GOING FURTHER IN THE STORY
WE COULD ADD A
PATCH ...
I THOUGHT
OF AN OLD
FASHION
BACKPACK
KIND
OF
INSTEAD
OF A
TECHNICAL
ONE
... OR
BANDAGES

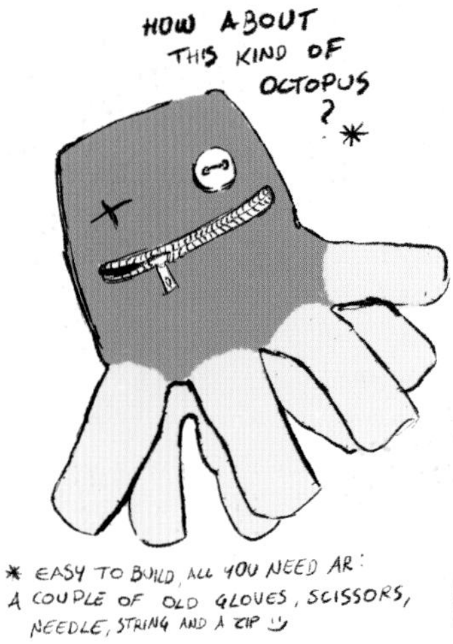
HOW ABOUT
THIS KIND OF
OCTOPUS
? *
* EASY TO BUILD, ALL YOU NEED AR:
A COUPLE OF OLD GLOVES, SCISSORS,
NEEDLE, STRING AND A ZIP :)

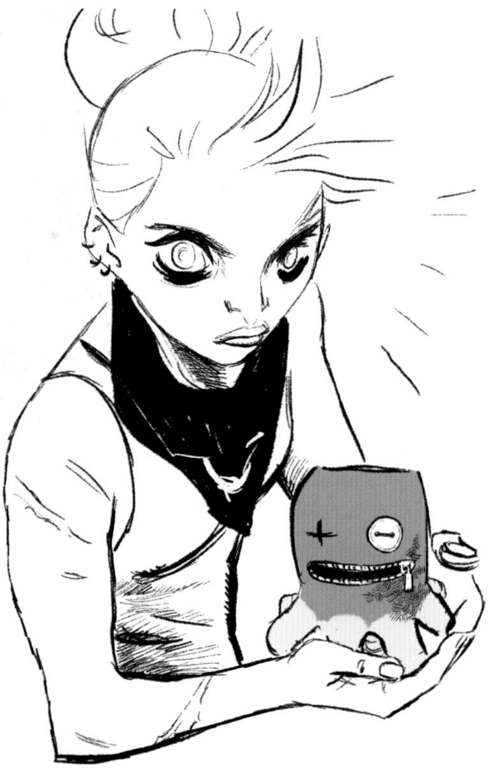

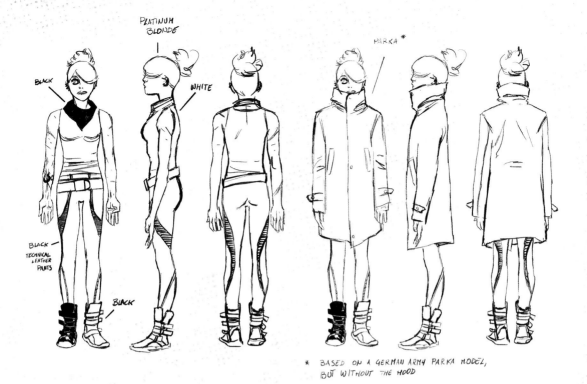

PLATINUM BLONDE

BLACK

WHITE

PARKA *

BLACK TECHNICAL LEATHER PANTS

BLACK

* BASED ON A GERMAN ARMY PARKA MODEL, BUT WITHOUT THE HOOD

series, is there a concern about setting up enough of a larger story in case the series does continue, and still being a satisfying five-part mini?

Tynion: Honestly, no. Not at all. I thought I'd be giving these little hints to a larger world that you would never see, and I would probably never explore. It'd be like having a brief encounter with the Men in Black, who clearly work for some kind of strange authority that you never learn about. I put more thought into defining what was more literally important to the series. What monsters are, and why Erica can see them and interact with them. But once I realized that the series was expanding I knew I needed to sit down and define the mythology underlying the character and her world.

I remember the first time I texted my editor Eric Harburn the phrase "The House of Slaughter." And I remember the first time I extrapolated that they would each have a bandana. They would each have a stuffed animal. From that, I could start picturing some of their rituals, and I started to understand more of their rules and their world. I was already playing a lot with juxtaposition. The idea of Erica being from the mundane world, but trained in the extraordinary world, to come back and fight in the mundane world. So the House of Slaughter feels like a step away from the realism of Archer's Peak, in a way that helps define both worlds. And Erica is trapped in the middle, between them.

PxP: There's a balance with the more fantastical Erica and her House, against the grounded reality of James and the town. Character design and costume are so imperative in establishing it.

What was the design process like between the both of you?

Dell'Edera: Some things were already set when I came in based on James' description. So I worked on characters trying to give back his vibes, adding here and there some details. Or something different. For example, Erica's character is basically as James has described her: blonde, deep shadows under her eyes, a scar, etc. On that description, I've added some details like the bandana. I've also suggested to have her eyes bigger than normal, with one of them always covered by hair, like she would hide it for some reason... (spoiler alert: there is none.)

There are some specific things that we need to visualize before I start drawing, but there are features of the characters that I usually design on the page, because I need to move them on a location for them to act and, before that, I need to read the script to grasp the mood of the scene.

Tynion: I think Werther is wildly understating the importance of that bandana! I just looked over the original email thread from almost exactly one year ago, and it really was a seismic shift. Werther had sent a first draft based on my description of Erica in the original *Something is Killing the Children* pitch document, which reads, "We see a young woman, in her early twenties, in a dirty tank and dirt-stained jeans. She's covered in scars and bruises and has deep, dark shadows under her eyes. She only has a ratty kid's backpack." Another bit described a trepanation scar on her head. Werther's first design had the scar on the center of her forehead, but otherwise took it literally, and even in that design, I'd say she was 60% the character as she currently

a bigger tool available. Do you think this limits the kind of horror you can tell in comics?

Tynion: That's from an old interview! I'm pretty sure I was talking about my never finished horror webcomic, *The Eighth Seal*. But I stand by it. Comics are a bad medium for dramatic shocks. You can build to a page-turn reveal, but you can't really control the speed at which a reader turns the page and experiences it, which can deaden the impact of the reveal.

Dread is something that comics do exceptionally well. Comics are all about pacing, it's a kind of music, and you can take a feeling and extend it and distort it and cut away from it sooner than you expect, or linger in it a bit. But they are also a visual medium, which I think requires a bit more extremity or strangeness when something horrible is on the page. You need a complicated enough image that you force the reader to look at it for more than a split second to absorb the horror of it, and then you use the dialogue coming out of the scene to carry that feeling forward, or turn away from it.

It's all about unnerving the reader. I've been reading the Gou Tanabe Lovecraft adaptations recently and I think he's bringing life to those stories that they've never had in prose, or even on film, entirely because comics are so good at sustaining a feeling of dread.

exists. But after a little feedback he came back with a second design, with the bandana.

And I remember getting chills... I knew we were holding a live wire with the character. A few sketches later, cementing the placement of her scar and her tattoo... And Werther sends an image of Erica fighting a monster with a chainsaw. And I knew this was the character, and that this book was evolving beyond the little pet project I originally saw it as.

PxP: When it comes to monster design, how much collaboration is there? James, did you already have a sense of what the creatures would look like? How much did that change once Werther was on board?

Dell'Edera: As for Erica's character, James here already had a pretty clear idea of what monsters should look like, but again in this case also he has been very open to my visual hints.

Tynion: We're starting with a monster made out of a kind of living shadow, whose form isn't as set as something like a dragon or a werewolf or what have you. So I definitely feel like Werther's made that shadow more of his own... But I think as the series goes on we'll see more types of monsters.

PxP: There's much to talk about in the way horror works within the medium, and I know you've said previously that the jump scare is kind of nullified with the way comics work, so mood is

PxP: How does that help dictate how you establish mood?

Tynion: Dread only works if you can put yourself in the shoes of the person experiencing the dread in the story. I've talked a bit in other interviews about how I used a shortcut that I use on other stories by basically sticking in the names of people I knew and care about before I put them in scary circumstances.

I wanted to feel in the shoes of the main kid, so I named him James and gave him glasses, and effectively made him a version of me in 8th or 9th Grade. Seeing his trauma is, at the start of the story, less important than the reader understanding why the event was traumatic, and the aftermath of that trauma.

So you get that grounding, and then you continue following him through the issue, and by the time you actually see the horrible thing he experienced, by the end of the issue, you feel it harder. I'm all the way under your skin, rather than giving you everything from the get go. It hits deeper. Start with that kind of horror, and then I'd have needed to one-up myself by the end, and that's a different kind of book.

PxP: One of the scariest things for me is the inefficiency of systems. The cops are almost entirely ineffective, there's a coroner who's been hired thanks to nepotism, a headteacher who seems to be just as lost as everyone else. Is this something you feel like you're seeing in the world around us? It really does present a space where it needs someone like Erica just to function.

Tynion: I don't think I'm the only one looking around our world thinking that our institutions are rotting from the inside out. There's a lot of this in everything I write, going back to *The Woods*, and even *Batman*. There's just the basic truth that the center does not hold, and that no system lasts forever. We live in a society that hasn't really functioned properly in twenty years, and there were plenty of people who it didn't even function for then. Your police and teachers and authority figures don't know any better than you. They are just as stressed and in the dark as to why nothing works as you are. They face the same invisible monsters. The idea of learned elders is bullshit. Unless they're working a craft they've kind of perfected through decades of practice, nobody knows anything. We're all kids waiting for the grown-ups to show up, and they never will. We need to be the grown-ups and we need to save ourselves, but we resent that fact.

So while kids see an Erica-type come to town and feel saved, adults see an Erica-type come to town and feel small. And that makes them lash out, because she is evidence that they can't save themselves.

PxP: There's a lot of stacked, full width "widescreen" panels used throughout. Was there discussion on building the visual language of the different sequences?

Dell'Edera: There was not a real discussion here. I've found myself really comfortable with James' script from the very beginning. James gave me a lot of "space" in terms of interpretation of the script and, on my side, I try to fit as much as I can within the script. I love widescreen panels, they fit very well my idea of storytelling.

Tynion: Yeah! That was all Werther, but I think it helps capture the right mood. I know widescreen stacked panels are so tied to the early 00s big action books like *Authority* and *The Ultimates*, but honestly I think it captures a kind of emptiness and quiet in the book that feels perfect for what we're looking to do.

PxP: Werther, as an artist, do you have a sense as to what kind of genre or story you feel your art is most effective? Your scratchy lines and hatching feel so at home with this kind of unsettling horror, for example.

Dell'Edera: I'm not sure if there is a specific genre that my style thrives in. I've worked on very different genres and I found myself comfortable with each of them, so I can't tell you which is the best genre for my style, but I can tell you for sure that if you find my style particularly at home with this kind of story... Well, my mission is accomplished!

PxP: With your characters, it seems like there's a few key elements that get rendered. Erica's hair, for example, is usually just an outline and a couple of lines for her fringe, but her eyes often have many lines set around them, kind of like stage actors and mascara, and for James, the key element is the size of his glasses on his face. Is this what you look for when figuring out the identity of a character?

Dell'Edera: I like to have few elements that describe the character, because the less elements I have to draw and the more I'm able to make the character act. What I love most is when you can feel the gesture in the line, the spontaneity of the drawing. That's why I try to avoid getting too heavy on the gear when imagining a character. You have to understand and recognize the role they play but without it getting in the way of the action and dynamism of the storytelling.

One of the main things that I try to achieve is the uniqueness of the character. Something that distinguishes it and makes it recognizable. I try to find that feature that can single-handedly – or almost single-handedly – describe a character, their personality or at least make them memorable and distinct on the page (and fun to draw, of course).

PxP: I find your gutters really fascinating! They're thick, and I don't think there's many instances of anything breaking beyond them, even in the intense action sequences. It seems to help with image separation, and building panels as individual beats, and you also use them as indicators of times, with a mix of white and black gutters between day and night, which is really aided by their thickness.

Dell'Edera: I find them fascinating too! Initially there is a "graphic" need. When I see them on the pages I find a kind of order (all the more when you see the panels laid out without any content in them). It helps me to make things clear on the page, readable. Sometimes I've used thin gutters, but the end results for me felt always crowded and disharmonic. It definitely helps to set the time on a page and between panels. Also this regularity makes those little variations on the page layout more useful, makes them more effective.

PxP: Miquel, I love the textures in the colors, they really seem to blend to Werther's slightly rougher lines. What is it you look for in story or lineart to push you in the direction of textures, and the appropriate texture? Did you go through many iterations before choosing this particular one?

Muerto: The first proposal was more or less the final one. Although in the beginning, I got a little crazy trying to work with a more pictorial attempt similar to what Jacob Phillips does on *Criminal*. But it didn't work. Without flats, I was pretty lost whenever I needed to do adjustments and all the dirty brush strokes weren't anything more than an imposture from mine. Like trying to have a perfect grunge haircut! Finding the right level of dirtiness was the key to work well with Werther's fine lines. And the texture on top of everything for me is like an essential way to give some charm to the page, especially for digital readers.

PxP: There's quite a bit of green initially, green skies, green jacket... Do you see these colors as having their own imbued emotions? Or do you want to establish color and thematic connections within the comic itself?

Muerto: The theory of color is there, we can't really change that, because the mind is already used to all that our real-life experiences did for us, as well for any other cultural piece of media. Of course, one of the goals as a colorist for me is to create something else, through repetition, or with breaking expectations for what one should feel.

Erica has green eyes, right? Well, then she should see the world... green. With such a silly concept as this one, the first scene was made, when she got off the bus and I imagined the cloudy skies and the greenish tone, a little sticky, ideal for a town that's going through tremendous trauma. Later, almost without me realizing it, I would keep repeating the green tones here and there. When Erica is being interrogated, my head was below an old fluorescent in a dark room without windows. The tension could feel like water, a submarine space where everyone is drowning. Everyone except Erica who is well lighted through the scene.

PxP: Deron, when it comes to designing lettering approaches, what factors do you work towards when getting to a style?

Bennett (AndWorld): I don't get hung up on genre so much. It's important, for sure, but I think the art will dictate what I put on the page more than anything else. For instance in this case, we're doing horror, right? I think Werther and Miquel already bring all of the sensibilities of the genre into the page with their work, so my lettering becomes a product of that as I feed off of them.

One of the things that may go unnoticed in the book is the quality of line on the stroke of the balloons and some effects. If you were to zoom in tightly (or look at the originals) you'll notice that there is a gritty, pencil feel to the outline from a custom brush. It's intentional to draw from Werther's line and texture. A lot of the SFX I was doing were actually modeled from Werther's hand-drawn effects. Some didn't make it to the final print and we opted for digital fonts in the end, but that is the sort of approach that I take. I will use what's given to me so that everything looks cohesive including building from the color palette. I'll often sample some of Miquel's neighboring colors and use them for effects. So really everything trickles down from the art and I take it from there.

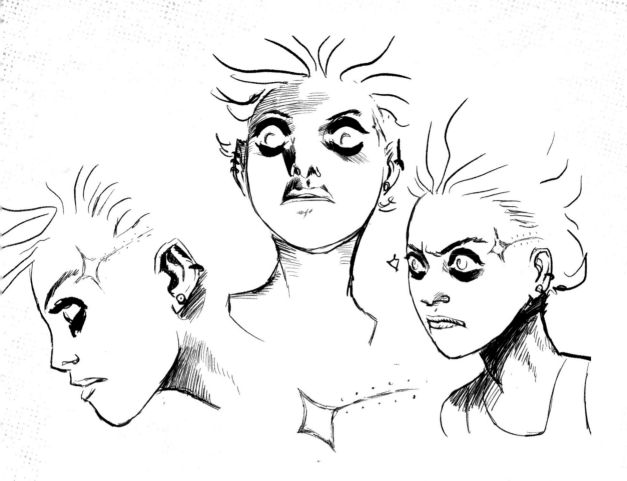

PxP: For all of you, what's been the most creatively challenging part of making SIKTC?

Dell'Edera: To set the story in a place that could be credible. James and Eric Harburn have helped me a lot in staging it.

Muerto: Definitely it was adapting so I could work with a drawing style with such personality, loose lines, and very guided rendering. Finding the right balance.

Bennett (AndWorld): Probably getting the sound effects right. Werther put some really cool hand-drawn effects and I wanted everything else to play off of them. I tried to keep my SFX textured and colored them in similar styles. If I made something that didn't gel with what he had or even that didn't match Miquel's color, it would throw off the illusion.

Tynion: Honestly, it's been the process of letting go. Letting the story drive me rather than me drive the story.

There were two key moments of letting go, which scared me quite a bit. I was writing the first issue, and by the end of the first sequence, the two page title break, I knew that this wasn't going to be a series of one-shots anymore. This was going to be one five issue story. And then there came a moment in Issue #3 when I realized that this was an even *bigger* story. Thankfully the book was successful enough to warrant becoming an ongoing, because

boy-oh-boy, I would have been screwed if Issue #5 had to be the end.

But the process of writing the book is like driving in the fog. It's meant making some mistakes. I'm not at all that type of writer, either. I am usually a "write a twenty page document" kind of writer. People who have worked with me before know how much I like to have worked out before I put a single page to script. It's made the book difficult to talk about, because even though I do have a good sense of where it's all going, I can't say for sure. I feel like it's going to take me a few more places I didn't know it wanted to go.

PxP: And what's been the most rewarding?

Dell'Edera: Erica! Every expression, every time she acts. I really love this character.

Tynion: I second Erica. She's the heart of the series. I knew there was a kind of energy to the raw idea of her as a character, but it wasn't until I saw her on the page for the first time, when Werther turned in the first few designs, and came up with the idea of the bandana, that she came into sharp relief. I feel like she is a character Werther and I discovered, waiting for us, more than we created her. And that's an extraordinary feeling, honestly. I feel like I've stumbled into a model of how I want to create comics for this next era of my career.

Out of some confirmation bias, I also think she's a model for how Western comics in general should move forward. The response to her as a character, from cosplay, to fan-art, to fellow comic artists wanting to come on board and draw variant covers... It feels like it's a lesson that people are hungry for new comic book characters. I think there's a whole generation of fans ready to own their own generation of comic characters, and they don't want them to be superheroes, because that itch gets scratched at the movies or on TV. I think there's been an element missing to the last generation of creator-owned titles. Like a bunch of people writing *Transmetropolitan*, but forgetting to create Spider Jerusalem. Mainstream, mass market comics have always been driven by iconic characters, with iconic visuals.

Muerto: Reaching so many readers, for sure. While you're working you tend to create a certain distance from the work and sometimes you don't even appreciate your part in the final result, so I'm very happy to see every day that somebody is enjoying the series, especially new and young readers.

Bennett (AndWorld): I agree with Miquel. Sometimes you can't see the forest through the trees, but when you take a look at the overall book, I'm really proud of my contribution.

PanelxPanel is the Eisner Award-winning monthly digital magazine celebrating the comics medium. Featuring a range of critics and comics creators in each issue, looking at themes, craft, and why comics are a unique medium for storytelling. Edited by Strip Panel Naked's Hassan Otsmane-Elhaou, it can be found at gumroad.com/panelxpanel

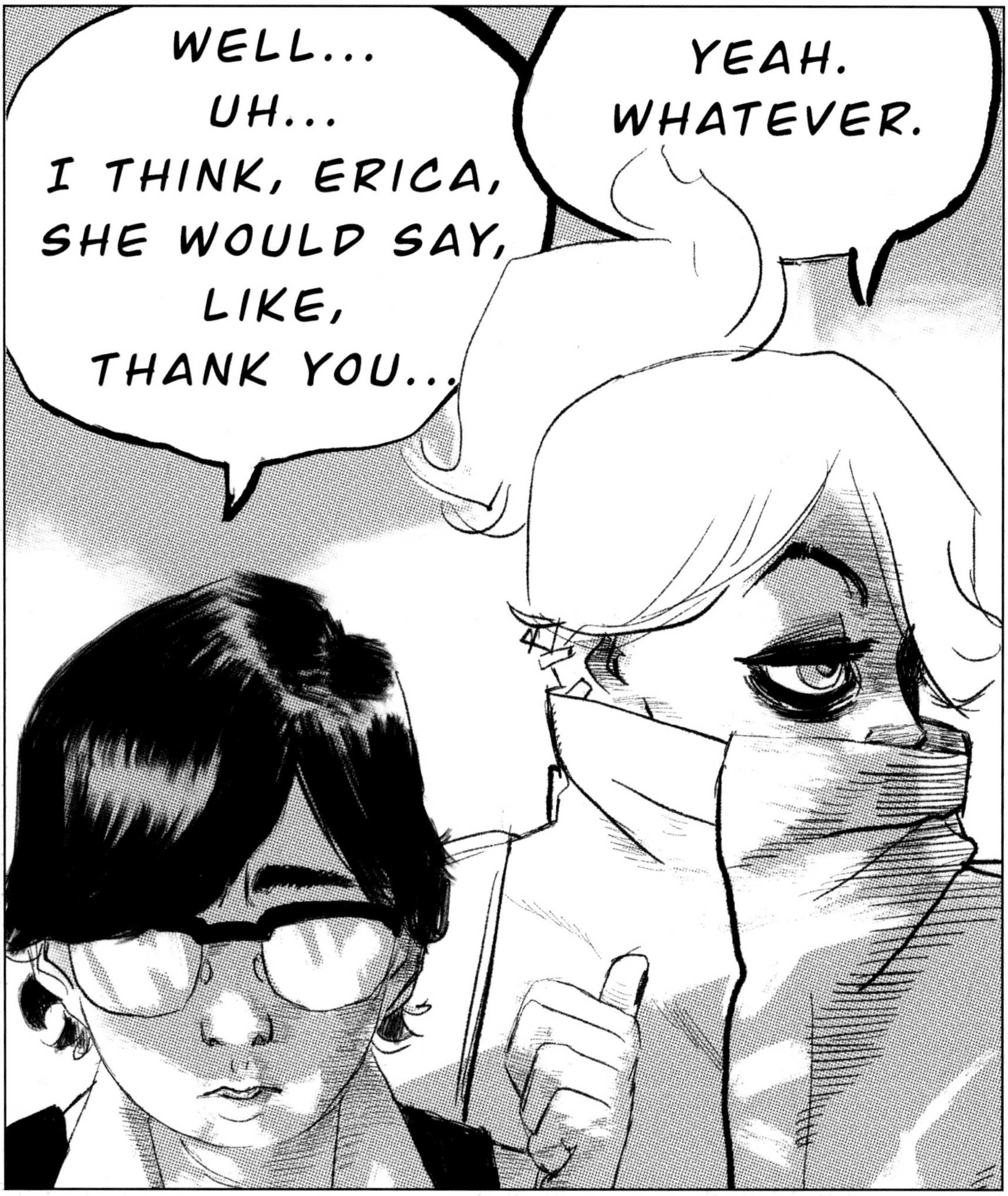
WELL... UH... I THINK, ERICA, SHE WOULD SAY, LIKE, THANK YOU...
YEAH. WHATEVER.

ABOUT THE AUTHORS

 JAMES TYNION IV is a comic book writer, best known as the writer for DC Comics' flagship series, *Batman*. In addition to the 2017 GLAAD Media Award-winning series *The Woods* and *Wynd* with Michael Dialynas, James has also penned the critical successes *Memetic*, *Cognetic*, and *Eugenic* with Eryk Donovan, *The Backstagers* with Rian Sygh, and *Ufology* with Noah J. Yuenkel and Matthew Fox from BOOM! Studios, as well as *The Department of Truth* with Martin Simmonds from Image Comics and *Razorblades* from Tiny Onion Studios. An alumni of Sarah Lawrence College, Tynion now lives and works in New York, NY.

 WERTHER DELL'EDERA is an Italian artist, born in the south of Italy. He has worked for the biggest publishers in both Italy and the U.S., with his works ranging from *Loveless* (DC Vertigo) to the graphic novel *Spider-Man: Family Business* (Marvel). He has also worked for Image, IDW, Dynamite, and Dark Horse. In Italy, he has drawn Sergio Bonelli's *Dylan Dog* and *The Crow: Memento Mori* (a co-production between IDW and Edizioni BD), for which he has won awards for Best Cover Artist, Best Series, and Best Artist.

 Not dead, MIQUEL MUERTO has lived in Barcelona since 1992, where he studied illustration, ran a small press, and worked as a graphic designer until feeling entitled to chase his dream: doing comics! *The Druid's Path* (2016) was his comic book debut as a full artist, a traumatic experience he swore would never happen again. Coloring comics was the first good step he has taken in his career and he has been happily following that path ever since.